Past and Present Publications

The sense of the people

people, the empire, the political subject: all three were contentious issues in the
ilitics and culture of eighteenth-century English cities. This exciting study explores
v these three issues came to occupy central roles in the wide-ranging political cultures
English towns between the Hanoverian Succession and the American war, enabling a
iriety of groups outside the structures of the state to claim a stake in national affairs.
Jrawing on a rich range of sources – from provincial newspapers, prints, and pottery
commemorative sculpture and parliamentary speeches – Wilson argues that the ide-
logies and practices of extra-parliamentary politics in provincial towns and London
ncd ordinary men and women to the implications of state power and imperial ex-
ision. They also defined relations between the state and the citizen in terms of gender,
iss and racial difference. The "sense of the people" thus constructed both a rational,
ertarian political public to which the state was held to be accountable, and exclusionary
nceptions of political subjectivity that would shape notions of national belonging into
next century.

D1612394

Past and Present Publications

General Editor, PAUL SLACK, *Exeter College, Oxford*

Past and Present Publications comprise books similar in character to the articles in the journal *Past and Present*. Whether the volumes in the series are collections of essays – some previously published, others new studies – or monographs, they encompass a wide variety of scholarly and original works primarily concerned with social, economic and cultural changes, and their causes and consequences. They will appeal to both specialists and non-specialists and will endeavor to communicate the results of historical and allied research in the readable and lively form.

For a list of titles in Past and Present Publications, see end of book.

The sense of the people

*Politics, culture and
imperialism in England, 1715–1785*

KATHLEEN WILSON

*State University of New York
at Stony Brook*

CAMBRIDGE
UNIVERSITY PRESS

PUBLISHED BY THE PRESS SYNDICATE OF THE UNIVERSITY OF CAMBRIDGE
The Pitt Building, Trumpington Street, Cambridge CB2 1RP

CAMBRIDGE UNIVERSITY PRESS
The Edinburgh Building, Cambridge CB2 2RU, United Kingdom
40 West 20th Street, New York, NY 10011-4211, USA
10 Stamford Road, Oakleigh, Melbourne 3166, Australia

© Cambridge University Press 1998

This book is in copyright. Subject to statutory exception
and to the provisions of relevant collective licensing agreements,
no reproduction of any part may take place without
the written permission of Cambridge University Press.

First published 1995
First paperback edition 1998

Printed in the United States of America

Library of Congress Cataloging-in-Publication Data is available.

A catalog record for this book is available from the British Library.

ISBN   0-521-34072-1 hardback
ISBN   0-521-63527-6 paperback

Undergraduate Lending Library

*For Alice Wilson
and the memory of M. B. Wilson
and for Nicholas*

Contents

Illustrations

Acknowledgments

This book began life as a Yale University Ph.D. thesis, the writing of which served as a springboard to the ideas and arguments I advance here. Since that period, this manuscript has been dragged back and forth across the Atlantic with me more times than I care to count. I have in the process incurred many debts which it is now my pleasure to acknowledge.

I am most grateful to the following bodies for the financial support necessary to research and write this book: the Henry E. Huntington Library of San Marino, California; the American Council of Learned Societies; and the National Endowment for the Humanities. In addition, the Center for the History of Freedom at Washington University, St. Louis, provided me with a semester's leave during which I was able to pursue my research. A different form of material assistance was provided by the librarians and archivists who helped me at repositories in England and America. I would like in particular to thank the staffs of the Beinecke Library, Yale University; the Huntington Library; the Houghton Library, Harvard University; the Institute of Historical Research, University of London; Newcastle Central Library and especially its director, Mr. Frank Maunders, who allowed me open access to the newspaper collections and local history stacks; the Norwich City Library and the Norwich and Norfolk Record Office; the Northumberland Record Office; the Tyne and Wear Archives; the Avon Reference Library, Bristol; the Worcester City Archives; Liverpool Reference Library and Record Office; Manchester Central Library; the British Library; and the Public Record Office. A special thanks is due Ms. Joan Sussler at the Lewis Walpole Library, Yale University, for her acute and unfailing aid with the prints for this book. Material in Chapters 3 and 4 appeared in different guise in previously published articles: "Empire, Trade and Popular Politics in Mid-Hanoverian Britain: The Case of Admiral Vernon," *Past and Present,* no. 121 (1988), 74–109, and "Inventing Revolution: 1688 and Eighteenth Century Popular Politics," *Journal of British Studies,* 29 (1989), 349–86. I thank the Past and Present Society and the University of Chicago Press for permission to include those materials here.

A great many scholars and friends have contributed to this study with their advice and recommendations. David Underdown, Nick Rogers and Joanna Innes read my dissertation early on and made suggestions and helpful comments. John Styles and Joanna Innes were generous with time and advice on sources. Paul Monod, Michael Walker and Nick Rogers shared research materials with me; David Saunders provided shelter during various trips to Newcastle. Andrew Morgan kindly lent me a computer during a summer in Paris. My colleagues in the History and Literature and Women's Studies concentrations at Harvard University transformed my thinking and my rewriting plan, and the History Department at the State University of New York, Stony Brook, has provided a stimulating and supportive environment in which to finish up. My editor, Frank Smith, deserves accolades for patience and support. Thanks also to Jane Van Tassel, whose careful copy editing saved me from many errors.

Two intellectual debts must be singled out. John Brewer and Linda Colley served as dissertation advisors and remained distinct sources of inspiration and support. John Brewer has been a generous mentor and enthusiastic colleague since my fledgling years; his friendship and his abundant gift for productive historical scholarship have been equally sustaining throughout the writing of this book. Linda Colley's example as a leading woman scholar in a notoriously androcentric field has been as instructive as her astute historical judgments. Obviously, my study would have been written very differently without benefit of their fertile contributions to the field.

All my friends and family have contributed, in ways of which they may or may not be aware, to my work. But for moral support and intellectual camaraderie through this seemingly interminable project, I would like to thank in particular Jan Albers, Darlene Berkovitz, Susan Bortell, Joyce Flynn, Henry Horwitz, Lawrence Klein, Ira Livingston, Iona Man-Cheong, John Miller, John Montano, Jane O'Keefe, Nancy Tomes, Jim Wilson, Kris Wilson and Colleen Zielinski. My greatest debt is to my husband, Nicholas Mirzoeff. He has, of course, been made to suffer through the final stages of manuscript preparation, when he shouldered the wifely burdens of editing and proofreading with manly fortitude (and his typical critical skill). But above all, knowing him has sharpened my wits, enriched my understanding and swelled my heart. This book seems a paltry repayment – but it is dedicated to Nicholas, and my parents, with all my love.

Abbreviations

AA	*Archaeologia Aeliana*
AHR	*American Historical Review*
ARL	Avon Reference Library, Bristol
BL	British Library
Catalogue	F. G. Stephens and M. D. George, eds., *Catalogue of Political and Personal Satires in the British Museum*, 10 vols. (London, British Museum Trustees, repr. 1978)
CJ	*Journals of the House of Commons*
EHR	*English Historical Review*
GPL	Gateshead Public Library
HJ	*Historical Journal*
HL	Henry E. Huntington Library
HMC	Historical Manuscripts Commission
HO	Home Office Papers
JBS	*Journal of British Studies*
JMH	*Journal of Modern History*
LEP	*London Evening Post*
NA	*Norfolk Archaeology*
Namier & Brooke	Sir Lewis Namier and John Brooke, eds., *The History of Parliament: The House of Commons, 1754–1790*, 3 vols. (London, HMSO, 1964)
NCL	Newcastle Central Library
NH	*Northern History*
NNRO	Norfolk and Norwich Record Office
NRCL	Norwich City Library
NRO	Northumberland Record Office
P & P	*Past and Present*
Parl. Hist.	*The Parliamentary History of England*, ed. William Cobbett and J. Wright, 36 vols. (London, 1806–13)

PRO	Public Record Office
SCI	Society for Constitutional Information
Sedgwick	Romney Sedgwick, ed., *The House of Commons, 1715–54*, 2 vols. (London, HMSO, 1971)
SP	State Papers
SSBR	Society of Supporters of the Bill of Rights
TRHS	*Transactions of the Royal Historical Society*
TWA	Tyne and Wear Archives
VCH	*Victoria County History*
WMQ	*William and Mary Quarterly*

I have retained original spelling in all cases save where meaning was impaired. Dates before 1752 are given in Old Style, but the year has been taken to begin on January 1.

The People are independent, because they have nothing to fear, and very little to hope from the Power of the Great; but the Great are rendered dependent upon them; because, without the Assistance or Approbation of the People, they cannot be considerable either in the Senate, or out of it; they cannot either be Ministers themselves, or raise an effectual Opposition to the Ministry of others.

Josiah Tucker, *Instructions to Travellers* (Dublin, 1758)

... there ... [are] a large number of the people without the sphere of the opulent man's influence, namely, that order of men which subsists between the very rich and the very rabble; those men who are possest of too large fortunes to submit to the neighbouring man in power, and yet are too poor to set up for tyranny themselves. In this middle order of mankind are generally to be found all the arts, wisdom, and virtues of society. This order alone is known to be the true preserver of freedom, and may be called the People.

Oliver Goldsmith, *The Vicar of Wakefield* (London, 1766)

... the feelings of the great bulk of the *nation*, are not the same with the feelings of *long parliaments* ... nor will the language of such parliaments to their princes, ever express *the sense of the people*.

John Cartwright, *Take your Choice!* (London, 1776)

Part I

The national context

Introduction: The people, towns and politics in eighteenth-century England

> [Who dares call] the Voice of the People . . . Faction? . . . Is not the Sense of the Inhabitants of London, Edinburgh, York, Bristol, Salisbury, Worcester, Gloucester, and many other principal Towns, besides those of several Counties, to be esteem'd the Sense of the Nation?
>
> *Salisbury Journal*, Feb. 5, 1740

As a statement about the status of urban opinion in the political process, this query was both rhetorical and contentious. The anonymous writer in the *Salisbury Journal* was arguing from the premise that eighteenth-century towns served as the most reliable barometers of the political views, sensibilities and grievances of "the people," and as such constituted the "sense of the nation." Such a claim would become a standard conceit among provincial urban political polemicists over the course of the eighteenth century, just as it had been for the journalists and supporters of the City of London during the political upheavals of the Stuart period. But its status as an ideological construct, designed to impart weight and universality to a particularized political position, should not prevent us from taking it seriously. For the claim to represent the "sense of the people" became an important legitimizing rhetorical strategy in the Hanoverian decades, a crucial part of the wider political contestation under way that had been produced by the emergence of a vibrant, national and predominantly urban extraparliamentary political culture. It is the purpose of this book to examine both the development of that political culture and its ideological content: to contextualize its claims to national and populist significance with reference to the political issues its participants embraced and the social, cultural and ideological environments which gave them meaning. I hope to demonstrate, in the process, the ways in which the vibrant

3

4   *The sense of the people*

extra-institutional political culture of provincial towns and London created an alternative idiom of political discourse that could be used by a
wide range of groups to claim a stake in national affairs.

Such an enterprise may appear to be both brash and impertinent,
given the rich and resourceful scholarship that has characterized the
field of Hanoverian political history for the past two decades. Recent
studies of popular politics, class relations, crime and the law have done
nothing less than revolutionize the ways in which we view and interpret
the expression and exercise of power in eighteenth-century English society, and the means by which authority was transmitted, negotiated
and resisted.[1] The theater of the street and square, the associational life
of the tavern, the productions of press and pulpit, and the symbols and
rituals of the crowd have been, as a consequence, pushed to the center
of the historical stage, throwing up a rich and complex picture of what
politics and authority meant for the majority of eighteenth-century English people. Our notion of the "political" has been correspondingly
liberated from its high-level straitjackets to include a broad range of
social, cultural and symbolic practices that challenged, as well as maintained, the parameters of power.

However, both inevitably and appropriately, the studies of the last
two decades have raised as many questions as they have answered. In
particular, the social provenance, autonomy and ideological significance
of out-of-doors political activity remain matters of vigorous debate.
Edward Thompson has argued that the protest traditions of plebeian
culture offered the only viable opposition to the weak, if overgrown,
patrician power structures of the age; John Brewer has emphasized the
crucial role of the bourgeoisie in both supporting and resisting state
expansionism and strength. For the earlier period, the work of Nicholas
Rogers and Linda Colley has challenged claims about the rapidity and

---

[1] See esp. John Brewer, *Party Ideology and Popular Politics at the Accession of George III* (Cambridge, 1976), "English Radicalism in the Age of George III," in J. G. A. Pocock, ed., *Three British Revolutions* (Princeton, 1980), 323–67, and "The Number 45: A Wilkite Symbol," in Stephen B. Baxter, ed., *England's Rise to Greatness* (Berkeley and Los Angeles, 1983), 349–80; Linda Colley, *In Defiance of Oligarchy: The Tory Party, 1714–1760* (Cambridge, 1982); Douglas Hay, Peter Linebaugh, John G. Rule, E. P. Thompson and Cal Winslow, *Albion's Fatal Tree: Crime and Society in Eighteenth Century England* (New York, 1975); Peter Linebaugh, *The London Hanged: Crime and Civil Society in the Eighteenth Century* (Cambridge, 1992); Nicholas Rogers, *Whigs and Cities: Popular Politics in the Age of Walpole and Pitt* (Oxford, 1989); and E. P. Thompson, "Eighteenth Century English Society: Class Struggle Without Class?" *Social History,* 3 (1978), 123–65, and *Customs in Common: Studies in Traditional Popular Culture* (New York, 1991).

novelty of political change after 1760 while also producing disparate visions of the sources and supports of opposition politics.[2] Equally important, the contributions of the extra-parliamentary nation to the political discourses and practices of the day have not been systematically considered, and by design or default the impact of earlier popular political traditions on the content and composition of radical and loyalist politics in the reign of George III remains almost wholly unexplored.[3]

Above all, perhaps, the paucity of provincial urban political studies remains a serious lacuna in eighteenth-century scholarship. Indeed, in contrast to the Stuart period – and despite ample evidence that the "urban" was fast becoming multi-centered in pre-industrial England – the nature and distinctiveness of political culture in the localities have only just begun to be investigated.[4] The vast majority of studies of Hanoverian political culture have focussed on London, and although the potential importance of provincial politics has been acknowledged, the assessment of its viability has been based upon the metropolitan example and usually a rather uncritical acceptance of the City of London's own rhetorical claims to political singularity and national leadership. Rogers has argued, for example, that the "resilient tradition of civic participation" capable of sustaining a "genuinely popular political culture" was

> specific to the City [of London] ... Many provincial towns lacked this structure of politics, or where it existed in a formal sense there was an absence of political will or civic consciousness to put it into effect. Consequently, provincial politics was extremely susceptible to the management of local elites.[5]

Yet in this period provincial towns were the primary beneficiaries of

---

[2] For the works of these scholars see note 1; see also John Brewer, *The Sinews of Power: War, Money and the English State, 1688–1783* (New York, 1989).

[3] One exception to both of these statements is Paul Monod, *Jacobitism and the English People* (Cambridge, 1989), although he focusses exclusively on Jacobitism.

[4] Earlier and more recent investigations include John Money, *Experience and Identity: Birmingham and the West Midlands* (Montreal, 1977); Thomas Knox, "Popular Politics and Provincial Radicalism," *Albion*, 11 (1979), 224–41; John Bohstedt, *Riots and Community Politics in England and Wales, 1790–1830* (Cambridge, Mass., 1983); Frank O'Gorman, *Voters, Patrons and Parties: The Unreformed Electorate of Hanoverian England, 1734–1832* (Oxford, 1989); and James Bradley, *Religion, Revolution and English Radicalism* (Cambridge, 1990).

[5] "The Urban Opposition to Whig Oligarchy, 1720–60," in M. Jacob and J. Jacob, eds., *The Origins of Anglo-American Radicalism* (New York, 1984), 141–2. Rogers retreats from this position somewhat in his recent work but still insists that London provided the main force in the anti-oligarchic politics of the period: *Whigs and Cities*, 7, 399–403 and passim.

economic and imperial expansion and improvements in communications, building, publishing and internal trade, experiencing the most
dramatic upheavals in population growth and cultural refurbishment
and taking increasingly strident roles in national agendas.[6] Such far-
reaching changes produced broadly based provincial political publics,
engaged by issues emanating from the state and focussed on national
affairs; and it was upon the mobilization of this wider community that
London's claims to national leadership rested. Clearly, the "rise of the
provinces" in negotiating the stability of the Hanoverian state at home
and abroad occurred long before the 1790s, or indeed the 1760s, and
the political interests, grievances and sensibilities of these provincial
urban publics need to be addressed.[7]

   This study demonstrates that the political and cultural vitality of provincial towns was central to the viability of extra-parliamentary politics.
In the following pages, I examine the development of political culture
in urban localities from the accession of George I to the post–American
war period, in both a national context and with special reference to
Newcastle upon Tyne and Norwich. Without ignoring London, I am
concerned to contribute to the recovery of the national dimensions of
urban politics in the eighteenth century, which cannot be extrapolated
from the metropolitan example alone. At the same time, I seek to illuminate three crucial and related aspects of eighteenth-century politics
which have been neglected in most histories: first, the *content* of urban
politics, and particularly the impact of empire and state-building on
political ideologies and the sensibilities of ordinary citizens; second,
the roles of populist and patriotic ideological constructions in shaping,
galvanizing and legitimating extra-parliamentary political culture; and
third, the role of provincial urban culture itself in supporting and furthering extra-parliamentary politics, or, to put it another way, the political significance of the "urban renaissance" of Hanoverian towns.[8]
Through these avenues, I hope to indicate some of the complex ways

[6] Peter Borsay, *The English Urban Renaissance: Culture and Society in the Provincial Town 1660–1770* (Oxford, 1989); P. J. Corfield, *The Impact of English Towns 1700–1800* (Oxford, 1982); Peter Clark, ed., *The Transformation of English Provincial Towns* (London, 1984); Geoff Eley, "Re-Thinking the Political: Social History and Political Culture in Eighteenth and Nineteenth Century Britain," *Archiv für Sozialgeschichte,* 21 (1981), 427–56.
[7] The phrase is John Money's: "Samuel Pipe-Wolferstan and 'The Confessional State,'" *Albion,* 21 (1989), 406–7; cf. J. C. D. Clark, *Revolution and Rebellion: State and Society in England in the Seventeenth and Eighteenth Centuries* (Cambridge, 1986).
[8] The phrase is Borsay's: See his work cited in note 6.

in which political ideas were disseminated, consumed and transformed, and to demonstrate that urban political culture was an instrument of cultural and political struggle that both mirrored new social hierarchies and refashioned the parameters of political debate. In the remainder of this introduction, I wish to do three things: outline the sources and supports of urban political robustness and change in the eighteenth century; describe the conceptual approach and methodology of this study; and place my subject and its treatment in the context of the historiographical debates to which they are addressed.

I

For our purposes, the term "urban" is used to refer to settlements of about 2,500 or more inhabitants, as towns of this size were most likely to be capable of sustaining the resources, structures and personnel of extra-institutional politics. A definition based on population size is somewhat arbitrary, as early-modern urban historians have hastened to point out.[9] In towns of all sizes and legal statuses, politics in a formal sense was always more concentrated and immediate than in rural environs: Not only were they the sites of parliamentary and local elections, but urban communities, as larger settlements with religiously and ethnically diverse populations and greater potential for disorder, required more concerted government, more administration and more vigorous presentations of authority, which engaged residents in a more politicized world. And as the English state grew over the course of the century, so too did the number and diversity of its representatives in provincial towns, giving central government a more salient presence in the localities.[10] However, although all communities could have complex and vital political lives, it was urban settlements with over 2,500 inhabitants – accounting for just under 20 percent of the population in England and Wales at the beginning of our period and just over 30 percent at the end – that were most likely to sustain the infrastructure of extra-parliamentary political culture; they provide the main focus of this study.

[9] For debates over categorizing the urban see Borsay, *English Urban Renaissance,* 4–5; Corfield, *Impact of Towns,* 1–16.

[10] Brewer, *Sinews of Power,* chaps. 3–7; J. V. Beckett, "Land Tax or Excise: The Levying of Taxation in Seventeenth and Eighteenth Century England," *EHR,* 100 (1985), 306; and for the colonies, Gary Nash, *The Urban Crucible: Social Change, Political Consciousness and the American Revolution* (Cambridge, 1979), 26–53.

Even this largely political conceptualization of the urban, however, needs to be further refined. What was "urban" in the eighteenth century should not be perceived as antagonistic or oppositional to the rural, for in many ways town and country complemented each other and shared both resources and population. Provincial towns in large part were service centers for their increasingly capitalized agricultural and industrial hinterlands; seasonal employment and migration meant that many people would spend part of their lives working in urban settings; and most humble country dwellers were as likely to have recourse to the services and markets of provincial towns as the gentry were to take advantage of their recreational and cultural amenities.[11] Further, if "urban" is not to be regarded in this study as the antonym of "rural," neither is it to be taken as a synonym for "modern." For most of the century, urban life, even in London, was clearly a mixture of traditional and dynamic elements; but it was essentially no more transient, anonymous or capricious than life in the hamlets and villages of the countryside in a period of rapid population growth, protracted wars, imperial expansion and growing regional economic specialization and interdependence. In both town and country, people's daily lives were linked together, in varying degrees, by church, parish, neighborhood, tavern, workplace, craft and family, and were influenced by trade cycles, the state of public credit, good and bad harvests, price and wage fluctuations, and war and peace.[12] Similarly, many aspects of eighteenth-century political culture were common to village and countryside as well as to city and town. The smallest country inn not infrequently got the "prints" from the capital and larger provincial towns and could serve as the center of political information and gossip; political propaganda and electioneering were as integral aspects of county as of city political life; and both county and borough electorates were drawn from villages and hamlets as well as cities, with the unrepresented market and industrial towns contributing substantial numbers to both.[13] In other

[11] E. A. Wrigley, "Urban Growth and Agricultural Change: England and the Continent in the Early Modern Period," in R. I. Rotberg and T. K. Rabb, eds., *Population and History: From the Traditional to the Modern World* (Cambridge, 1986), 123–66; Peter Borsay, "Urban Culture in the Age of Defoe," in Clyve Jones, ed., *Britain in the First Age of Party: Essays Presented to Geoffrey Holmes* (London, 1987), 24–40. By midcentury, over half of the English labor force worked in nonagricultural employments; by 1800, over two-thirds did so: Brewer, *Sinews of Power,* 181.

[12] Peter Earle, *The Making of the English Middle Class* (Berkeley and Los Angeles, 1989); Jeremy Boulton, *Neighborhood and Society: A London Suburb in the Seventeenth Century* (Cambridge, 1987).

[13] As Frank O'Gorman has recently made clear in *Voters, Patrons and Parties.*

words, there was a "national" political culture in the eighteenth century shared by country and city alike. This study, for reasons of time,
space and interest, focusses on its manifestations and consequences in
towns, and especially on those larger towns with sufficient resources,
personnel and communications to maintain diversified political opinions.

With this definition in mind, the examination of urban political culture in the Hanoverian decades throws into question many of the most
cherished orthodoxies about the eighteenth-century political system, in
both its electoral and nonelectoral aspects. In the first instance, the
larger provincial towns provided the most solid base of oppositionist
and anti-oligarchic politics throughout the century. Large urban constituencies were the engines of the anti-Walpolean campaigns and the
radical agitations under George III, providing an increasing number of
contests and an increasing proportion of the urban electorate. They thus
exerted counter-currents to the tides of Whig predominance and electoral ossification so evident elsewhere in the nation, and particularly in
the smallest boroughs and counties, where the number of electoral contests fell drastically in the first five decades of the century.[14] Even in
1754–84, a period renowned for its electoral quiet, between half and
two-thirds of the large urban constituencies went to the poll at each
general election – demonstrating a rate of contests comparable to that
exhibited during the "rage of party" earlier in the century. Clearly, the
Septennial Act and Commons committees were not as effective as has
been assumed in stifling the political interest and combativeness of the
voters.

Continuing electoral vitality, however, was only one aspect of the
burgeoning political culture of provincial towns in which all ranks of
citizens participated. Indeed, electoral evidence, excluding as it does
the vast majority of the population, is a wholly inadequate gauge of

[14] If one takes into account the expansion (from 28 in 1701–13 to 35 in 1754–84) and
changes in the hierarchy of boroughs of 1,000 or more electors ranked by size, the
number of contests rose steadily, from 78 in 1701–13 to 94 in 1715–47 to 116 in
1754–84. These boroughs were also two to three times as likely to be contested at a
general election as the smaller boroughs; their voter turnout was the highest, regularly
reaching 90%; and their proportion of the urban electorate grew from 49% in the first
period to 66% in the last. See Donald R. McAdams, "Electioneering Techniques in
Populous Constituencies, 1784–1796," *Studies in Burke and His Time,* 14 (1972), 23–
53; John Phillips, *Electoral Behavior in Unreformed England* (Princeton, 1982), 68–
70. My calculations are based on tables in John Cannon, *Parliamentary Reform 1640–
1832* (Cambridge, 1973), 280–9, Namier and Brooke, i, 515–20, and Sedgwick, i,
117–22.

the extent of popular political involvement.[15] Quite simply, Hanoverian provincial towns proffered a wider array of sources and supports for political activity and consciousness than had their Stuart predecessors. To recognize this is not to have recourse to facile models of "modernization," but to acknowledge the diverse structures, both old and new, of political expression and debate within eighteenth-century English society (which also confound the dichotomous models of "early-modern" and "modern" society wielded by historians of the period). The traditional civic culture of most towns continued to provide many of the sites and contexts for the political involvement and awareness of ordinary citizens. Political and religious ideas and controversies were disseminated in churches and chapels, in lively ward or parish politics, in the taverns and alehouses that were well-integrated aspects of the provincial urban landscape by the early 1700s, and in the street theater and spectacle attendant upon civic and state anniversaries throughout the Hanoverian decades.[16] Moreover, although this period witnessed a decline in the proportion of the wealthiest citizens who took out the freedom of incorporated towns and agreed to take on the burdens of civic office, the lower levels of town and parish government, as well as broad areas of law enforcement and administration, continued to be staffed by middling and plebeian residents – tradesmen, craftsmen and artisans – who correspondingly were integrated into an ever more complex local state and who kept in close contact with local political authorities and issues.[17]

Over the course of the century, traditional civic culture was increasingly supplemented by the effervescense of the urban renewal, or "renaissance," which unfolded, albeit unevenly and sporadically, in many

[15] The idiosyncratic nature of borough franchises and the exclusion of women means that electoral statistics greatly underestimate the numbers engaged by contemporary political culture. Between 1 in 4 and 1 in 6 adult males had the vote over the eighteenth century, but this varied greatly on the local level: See for the first estimate Derek Hirst, *The Representative of the People? Voters and Voting in England Under the Early Stuarts* (Cambridge, 1975), and for the second, Cannon, *Parliamentary Reform*, 30.

[16] For the seventeenth century see Tim Harris, Paul Seward and Mark Goldie, eds., *The Politics of Religion in Restoration England* (Oxford, 1990); Tim Harris, *London Crowds in the Reign of Charles II* (Cambridge, 1987); Gary De Krey, *A Fractured Society: The Politics of London in the First Age of Party* (Oxford, 1985); David Underdown, *Revel, Riot and Rebellion: Popular Politics and Culture in England, 1603–1660* (Oxford, 1985).

[17] Henry Horwitz, "Party in a Civic Context: London from the Exclusion Crisis to the Fall of Walpole," in Jones, ed., *Britain in the First Age of Party*, 173–94; see also Chapter 6.

provincial towns in the first three-quarters of the century, and this had a number of significant repercussions for urban politics. Economic, demographic and imperial expansion, the solidification of a national market, the swelling ranks of the middling sorts, and developments in communications, transportation, building and the press all contributed to the emergence of a distinctive provincial culture that significantly altered the face and texture of urban society. As regional and local economies became more complex and specialized, urban society more intricate and cultural amenities more sophisticated, economic and social relations became organized as much by market forces and competition as by aristocratic and gentry patronage, by cultural aspirations and the pursuit of status as by vertical ties and dependencies. As such, elite clientage, extended to a diminishing proportion of local tradespeople, became less capacious and effective as a means of political control.[18] There was greater cultural and social space, in other words, for townspeople to perceive themselves as independent political subjects. These developments were, paradoxically, reinforced by high political developments within the oligarchic state, as continuing divisions among the parliamentary elites, along with exigencies prompted by war, invasion and rebellion, resulted in appeals to those out-of-doors for support and the introduction of new techniques and arguments designed to mobilize the extra-parliamentary nation.

Secondly, the assemblage of socioeconomic, cultural and political changes that contributed to a provincial urban vitalization also provided many of the structural supports for the wider politicization of ordinary residents. The expansion of the press and the spread of print culture – that is, the spread of both the artifacts of the press and the institutions and types of sociability that subsidized it – were, of course, enormously important in disseminating political values and attitudes, promulgating not only information but also ideologies which proffered particular and often divergent interpretations of the nation, empire and polity. In addition, the cultural refurbishment of provincial towns stimulated the emergence of a proliferation of associational activities – from the building of new cultural arenas like assembly rooms, theaters and hospitals to the formation of a multitude of clubs and societies for self- and public improvement – that had in themselves political implications. Drawing individuals together for cooperative and convivial activities and providing new contexts and settings for political action, the "urban

---

[18] See Chapter 1.

renaissance'' itself could become a source of contestation and conflict in some communities, and could stimulate or embody political divisions. Provincial urban culture thus furnished some of the crucial formal and informal venues for middling and artisanal involvement in civic and political affairs.

Given the inequities of the eighteenth-century electoral system, it is the analysis of this "alternative," partially extra-institutional and variously accessible political culture, first pointed to by Brewer but never examined systematically in provincial towns over the century, that will be the main focus of this study. For it is in this wider political world that the richly expressive diversity of Hanoverian political activity and the cultural, social and ideological dimensions of contemporary notions of political community can begin to be recovered. Accordingly, "political culture" is defined here as the realm encompassing political values and ideologies, the *forms* of their expression – verbal and non-verbal, embodied in both actions and artifacts – and the mechanisms of their dissemination and transformation. It thus includes both formal and informal activities, from street theater, club life and print culture, to instruction and petitioning movements, demonstrations and reforming campaigns – that is, the various modes of political expression and communication in which virtually all classes had a stake.[19] What follows constitutes but one provisional mapping of a rich and robust terrain.

II

Eighteenth-century urban political culture was clearly predicated upon a wide-ranging "media," one that ranged from the press and pulpit to the streets, theaters and taverns of London and provincial towns; it is here that political ideas, ideologies and propaganda found their widest audience. In its very accessibility, contemporary political culture mitigated the harsher aspects of the oligarchy that had been hardening in the formal institutions of the state since the Hanoverian Succession. And by linking individuals in the localities with broader national and even imperial developments, it made more and more individuals aware

[19] The term "popular" is used, like "populist," to describe language or arguments that are supported by, or that champion the rights of, "the people" in political debate and activities. Except where so designated, it is *not* used as a synonym for "plebeian" but is meant to include the middling classes. Hence, my examination of "popular politics" is an investigation of socially inclusive or accessible forms of political activity.

of the impact which state policies and decisions had on their everyday lives and prosperity, and familiarized them with discourses that diagnosed the structure, location and distribution of political power in the state as the source of many social and economic, as well as political, discontents and blessings. Urban political culture thus posed both practical and ideological challenges to the customs and values of patrician society.

The examination of extra-parliamentary politics equally raises conceptual problems for the historian which have to be addressed. Because Hanoverian culture exhibited such a mélange of traditional and transformative elements in both the structural and ideational spheres, the dichotomous models typically used to explain it have become problematic. Elite versus popular, high versus low, patrician versus plebeian and "deferential" versus "autonomous" are some of the oppositions commonly employed to give form and meaning to popular politics in this period. The elite-versus-popular dyad, for example, has permeated a wide range of scholarly work on demotic political activity and protest, as on early-modern culture generally, from the skillful deployment of the Gramscian concept of hegemony by Edward Thompson to the rather more unwieldy commercialization model of cultural change developed by Neil McKendrick and J. H. Plumb.[20] Yet the oppositions contained within these models not only elide or exaggerate the role of the middling classes in the culture and politics of the day, they also, more important, conceal the marked degree to which cultural forms were circulated among and shared by different social groups, despite the often divergent meanings they may have had for each of them. It has been convincingly demonstrated for early-modern France, Holland, Scotland and England that cultural transmission and dissemination depended far less on the emulation of elite culture or the domination of metropolitan cultural forms than on the "appropriation" of various cultural artifacts and activities by different classes in specific contexts. Cultural objects and practices were, in a word, polysemic, and their meanings were contingent upon the social environments in which they were used.[21] Such a multivalent perspective is

[20] Thompson has argued that such a characterization of his work is misleading: *Customs in Common*, 87–96. Neil McKendrick, John Brewer and J. H. Plumb, *The Birth of a Consumer Society* (London, 1982); Peter Burke, *Popular Culture in Early Modern Europe* (London, 1978); Robert Malcolmson, *Popular Recreations and English Society 1750–1850* (Cambridge, 1977).
[21] For the concept of appropriation see Roger Chartier, "Culture as Appropriation: Popular Cultural Uses in Early Modern France," in S. L. Kaplan, ed., *Understanding Popular Culture* (Berlin, 1984), 229–53, and *The Cultural Uses of Print in Early*

particularly valuable in interpreting eighteenth-century political culture, when both extra-parliamentary politics and partisan conflict
depended upon shared, if conflicting, ideologies, values and apprehensions and the access of all social groups to the means of public political communication.

Similarly, the assessment of popular politics solely in terms of conformity to elite party divisions (and thus its "deferential" or "autonomous" nature) has led to a number of conceptual blind alleys which
it is my purpose here to avoid.[22] Implicit in such approaches are the
assumptions that the political choices of ordinary people were the product of *either* autonomous political consciousness *or* elite domination,
that economic clientage blocked the formation of ideological interpretations of political issues (or, alternatively, allowed individuals to see
their "real" economic interests with perfect clarity), and that elite party
identities were capable of both defining and containing political meaning and thus the form and content of individuals' larger political consciousness. They provide, in other words, a view from above and so
cannot recover the mental universes of politics for those outside the
structures of the state. Above all, these models ignore the larger discursive contexts in which "party" identities were produced. The competing constructions of state, nation, empire and patriotism that were
deployed by propagandists and parliamentary orators alike were never
the exclusive preserves of specific parties, but were used by contending
groups in a variety of contexts with very different purposes in mind.
Moreover, the tangible impact which popular political loyalties and
sensibilities had on those above, the ability of middling and lower-class

Modern Europe, trans. Lydia Cochrane (New York, 1984), 6–7; for other examples
of its historical operations see Kevin Sharpe and Peter Lake, eds., *Culture and Politics
in Early Stuart England* (Stanford, 1993); Simon Schama, *The Embarrassment of
Riches* (Berkeley and Los Angeles, 1988); Jonathan Barry, "Popular Culture in Seventeenth Century Bristol," in Barry Reay, ed., *Popular Culture in Seventeenth Century
England* (London, 1985), 56–84; Martin Ingram, "Ridings, Rough Music and the
'Reform of Popular Culture' in Early Modern England," *P & P,* no. 105 (1984);
Nicholas Phillipson, "Scotland," in R. Porter and M. Teich, eds., *The Enlightenment
in National Context* (Cambridge, 1981), 19–40; Margaret Spufford, *Small Books and
Pleasant Histories* (London, 1981).
[22] Hence in psephological analysis "genuine" political involvement is demonstrated by
consistent party voting from election to election, whereas "imposed" political loyalty,
deference or apathy is demonstrated by switching parties or abstaining altogether: See
the analyses in W. A. Speck, *Tory and Whig: The Struggle in the Constituencies*
(London, 1970), and J. C. D. Clark, *English Society, 1688–1832* (Cambridge, 1985),
chap. 1. Cf. Hayden White, "The Fictions of Factual Representation," *Tropics of
Discourse: Essays in Cultural Criticism* (Baltimore, 1978), 121–34.

people to sustain or initiate political action on their own,[23] and the diverse ways in which political ideas entered public consciousness all militate against a straightforward "party" interpretation of extra-parliamentary political culture in the Georgian decades. In the public culture of the period, political articulacy lay in the eye of the beholder, and political consciousness was a many-splendored thing, forged as strikingly through the involvement of individuals in localized contests for power as through participation in national movements that aimed at ousting a minister or reforming the state.

This study proceeds from recognition of the existence of a political culture whose means of communication were widely if not equally accessible, based on public cultural forums, diverse expressive modes and shared, if heterogeneous, values. Questions about the "authenticity" or "autonomy" of political loyalties will be given short shrift in favor of questions about the meanings and significance of politics for ordinary people. To begin to uncover these meanings it is necessary to take seriously the ideological content and contexts of extra-parliamentary politics over the century.[24] In doing so I take cues from three sources: the French philosopher and historian Michel Foucault, whose analysis of discourse as "an event," a site of historical change and cultural formations, has radically altered historical studies; such historians of political thought as J. G. A. Pocock and Richard Ashcraft, who have argued that political ideologies are forms of "self-understanding" that flow through a variety of media and supply the standards that make specific social actions meaningful; and Stuart Hall, whose recognition of the discursiveness of ideology, where meaning lies in "the articulation of [its] elements," has demonstrated its material force and consequences in late-twentieth-century Britain.[25] Given that

[23] A point demonstrated by Gary De Krey in "London Radicalism After the Glorious Revolution," *JMH*, 4 (1985), 591–7.
[24] "Ideology" is deployed in this study to mean the ideas and values which structure political thinking and give shape and content to political consciousness; while appearing unified and coherent, ideologies are always unstable, contested and under construction. See Louis Althusser, "Ideology and Ideological State Apparatuses," *Essays on Ideology* (London, 1971), 1–60.
[25] Michel Foucault, "The Order of Discourse," in Robert Young, ed., *Writing the Text* (London, 1982), 48–78, and *The History of Sexuality*, trans. Robert Hurley, vol. 1 (New York, 1978), 17–34; J. G. A. Pocock, *Virtue, Commerce and History* (Cambridge, 1985), 75–6; Richard Ashcraft, *Revolutionary Politics and Locke's "Two Treatises of Government"* (Princeton, 1986), 5–6; Stuart Hall, *The Hard Road to Renewal: Thatcherism and the Crisis of the Left* (London, 1988), 9–10. "Discourse" is used in this study to denote public and organized ways of speaking about constituted

political ideologies, like political language itself, are by nature ambiguous and dependent upon linguistic and cultural contexts for their meaning (and accordingly changed with the interests, positions and intentions of those who produced and consumed them), both contexts and contents need to be explored. The fragmented and excerpted ways in which political ideologies entered public consciousness (through the newspaper press, sermons, periodical literature, iconography, theater and civic and political rituals, for example), meant that they were frequently consumed in bits and pieces and their central tenets transformed or used in other areas of mental life to interpret or reinvent the individual's relationship to the world.[26] Moreover, although the words and symbols could remain similar over time, their significance and meanings were, at any given moment, multi-dimensional and defined oppositionally, against the meaning given to the words or rhetoric by other groups. It is precisely this contest over language and meaning that is the essence of political conflict and is at the heart of legitimizing – or contesting – political authority.[27]

Such an approach necessitates rejecting a conceptualization of politics as "reflections" of social class or economic interests in favor of one that treats the political as a realm in its own right, a matrix of practices, values and ideologies concerned with power and moral relations within the state and polity, which are both a part of the culture in which they operate and in turn supply values, meanings and expectations that shape that culture, the perceptions of interests and the experience of material realities within it.[28] To do so is not to ignore the

subjects – politics, medicine, science, society – in a specific historical period; in my sense, all discourse is ideological.

[26] See, for example, Iain McCalman, *Radical Underworld: Prophets, Revolutionaries and Pornographers in London, 1795–1840* (Cambridge, 1988); Carolyn Steedman, *Landscape for a Good Woman* (London, 1986), esp. 110–24. Understanding political discourse in this way breaks down the boundaries between public and private that the discourse attempts to erect: See Sara Maza, "Domestic Melodrama as Political Ideology: The Case of the Comte de Sanois," *AHR,* 94 (1989), 1249–64.

[27] See, e.g., my "Inventing Revolution: 1688 and Eighteenth Century Popular Politics," *JBS,* 28 (1989), 349–86; James Epstein, "Understanding the Cap of Liberty: Symbolic Conflict in Early-Nineteenth-Century England," *P & P,* no. 122 (1989), 75–118; Clifford Geertz, "Centers, Kings, and Charisma: Reflections of the Symbolics of Power," in Sean Wilentz, ed., *Rites of Power: Symbolism, Ritual, and Politics Since the Middle Ages* (Philadelphia, 1985), 13–38; Lynn Hunt, *Politics, Culture and Class in the French Revolution* (Berkeley and Los Angeles, 1984); and Edmund Morgan, *Inventing the People: The Rise of Popular Sovereignty in England and America* (New York, 1988).

[28] E. P. Thompson made this case long ago: See *Folklore, Anthropology and Social History* (Brighton, 1979), 18–21, and *The Making of the English Working Class* (New

social dimensions or content of political activities, but rather to reconfigure the relations seen to exist between them in mutually interactive and nonhierarchical ways.[29] Not only were political divisions within social classes marked throughout the century, but presumed socioeconomic groupings were frequently transected by the contending identities that politics constructed, negotiated and mobilized, influencing the formation of social categories themselves. It is these political identities that are the focus of the following analysis.

III

Attending to the ideological content and contexts of politics draws attention to several crucial themes of eighteenth-century political culture which have previously been ignored and which will become clear in the following pages. For now, I wish to elaborate briefly on two of them. The first concerns the role of "the people" in contemporary political discourse. As the title of this book and the opening quotations suggest, "the people," as much as "the nation" constituted an "invented community" in eighteenth-century political argument, one conceived, significantly, as lying outside formal political structures and as having interests dichotomous or potentially dichotomous to those in power.[30] The role of the people in the political process was always contentious, the subject of debates that became more strident as extra-

York, 1963), 9–12; for more recent testaments see Gareth Stedman Jones, *Languages of Class* (Cambridge, 1983), and Joan Scott, *Gender and the Politics of History* (New York, 1989).

[29] Hence my use of the conventional if somewhat anachronistic tripartite social categories of "upper classes" or "elites" (aristocrats, gentry, industrialists, big merchants, financiers and some older professionals), "middling classes" (domestic merchants and wholesalers, "newer" professionals, retailers, victuallers and craftspeople likely to be shopkeepers) and "lesser sorts" or laboring classes (manufacturing and industrial craftspeople and artisans, skilled journeymen and unskilled laborers) as descriptive and relative, rather than definitive, rankings. The difficulties of using these blunt categories are notorious and have been detailed at length by John Phillips, among others: *Electoral Behavior,* 180–5, 205–10. My attributions have been influenced by Phillips as well as by Nicholas Rogers, "Money, Land and Lineage: The Big Bourgeoisie of Hanoverian London," *Social History,* 4 (1979), 437–50; Penelope Corfield, "Class by Name and Number in 18th Century Britain," in Corfield, ed., *Language, History and Class* (Oxford, 1991), 101–30; and R. Campbell, *The London Tradesmen* (London, 1747). For a contending view of the "upper classes" see Lawrence Stone and Jeanne Fawtier Stone, *An Open Elite? England 1540–1880* (Oxford, 1984).

[30] The phrase alludes to Benedict Anderson's oft-quoted designation of the nation as an "imagined community": *Imagined Communities: Reflections on the Origins and Spread of Nationalism* (New York, 1983).

parliamentary political culture became a more important force in Hanoverian life. For many writers and political commentators through the century, "the people" were the citizens – that is, those with sufficient standing and education to engage fully in the political process, and thus were identical with "the public" in Jürgen Habermas's sense: informed and respectable participants in the emergent public sphere who sought to arbitrate both taste and political legitimacy. For others, of course, "the people" were with the "mob," easily inflamed, quick to err and important to control.[31] Yet in contrast to other European countries, such as France, where "the people" were related oppositionally to "the public" in political discourse (as the force of demotic unreason versus the voice of rational, extra-institutional public opinion), in England "the people" subsumed the latter position in the arguments of propagandists and in the self-representations of a variety of contending groups through the 1780s, serving as the shorthand for a tribunal of opinion outside political structures against which state power was assessed, checked and canvassed.[32] At stake in these disputes about the composition and significance of "the people" were not only the meanings and conventions of political language but also the legitimation of constellations of power and authority – that is, access to or control over one of the most compelling "master fictions" of the day that justified the distribution of power in the English state: popular consent.[33]

Historians have been reluctant to confront the meaning or significance of this central issue in Georgian political culture. Those who have examined populist political argument in the period have usually assessed it in relation to the perspectives of parliamentary elites and formal political argument, dismissing or ignoring its extra-institutional and ideologically hybrid expression.[34] Others have insisted that fictions

[31] Jürgen Habermas, *The Structural Transformation of the Public Sphere,* trans. T. Burger and F. Lawrence (Cambridge, Mass., 1991), 51–67.
[32] See Roger Chartier, *The Cultural Origins of the French Revolution,* trans. Lydia Cochrane (Chapel Hill, 1991), 27–35; Mona Ozouf, " 'Public Opinion' at the End of the Old Regime," *JMH,* 60 (1988), suppl. S1–S21.
[33] The term is Geertz's: "Centers, Kings, and Charisma."
[34] Such as J. G. A. Gunn, *Beyond Liberty and Property* (Montreal, 1983); H. T. Dickinson, *Liberty and Property: Political Ideology in Eighteenth Century Britain* (New York, 1977); and J. G. A. Pocock, *The Machiavellian Moment* (Princeton, 1975). This is not to detract from the important contributions of these scholars to our understanding of the period, but merely to point out that there is another universe of political discourse which has barely been explored. For an alternative approach see Shelley Burtt, *Virtue Transformed: Political Argument in England, 1688–1740* (New York, 1992).

of popular sovereignty were never widely disseminated in the eighteenth century, where, they argue, hierarchy was ubiquitous and the duties of deference and obedience were promulgated from every pulpit and court in the land.[35] But hierarchy and notions of consent and popular sovereignty were neither mutually exclusive nor incompatible, and both frequently found a voice in extra-parliamentary political culture (indeed, their conflation in political thought was a European, and not merely English, phenomenon, a hallmark of Continental Enlightenment thought).[36] The most cursory examination of the artifacts of the press in this period – newspapers, pamphlets, prints, magazines, broadsides, squibs and sermons – (sources which historians intent on denying the existence and purchase of alternative idioms of political discourse largely ignore) shows that various strands of populist political argument, from the most mild to the most fractious and radical, were alive and well, a seemingly irrepressible part of the legacy of two revolutions and an exuberant out-of-doors political culture that took national politics – and national history – to heart. Indeed, since it was the (largely mythical) role of the people in the constitution that in most contemporaries' minds distinguished English liberty from Continental absolutism, populist beliefs and discourses were a crucial plank in the construction of national identities and consciousness. Incorporated into both oppositionist and conservative views of the state and polity, and encoded into political practices and activities, ideas about consent and accountability had a much wider purchase among different social and political groups throughout the eighteenth century than has been supposed.

''The people'' were called in to help bolster or justify a variety of political positions and strategies. Because protecting and promoting the interests of the public – the liberties and properties of all English people – was both the heart of the patriotic imperative and the raison d'etre of ruling-class position and authority, those in power were as eager to appear to represent the ''sense of the people'' as those without: Hence

[35] See, e.g., J. C. D. Clark, *English Society,* passim. John Cannon makes a much more convincing case for aristocratic hegemony (although ignoring evidence of middling disaffection and dissidence to do so) in *Aristocratic Century: The Peerage of Eighteenth-Century England* (Cambridge, 1984).
[36] See, e.g., Frederick the Great, ''Essai sur les formes de gouvernement et sur les devoirs des souverains,'' *Oeuvres,* vol. 9 (Berlin, 1848), 207–9; Louis Marin, *The Portrait of the King,* trans. Martha Houle (London, 1988); Margaret Jacob, *The Radical Enlightenment* (London, 1981), 182–214; and Chartier, *Cultural Origins,* 162–68.

first ministers from Stanhope to North were wont to claim the people's sanction for their policies. The phrase was also used to delimit the political nation, "the people" in such cases consisting of those deemed respectable or well-affected enough to be included in its boundaries, and thus excluding as "others" those who were considered at various times not to be fit for membership: the feminine and effeminate (women, the "rabble," homosexuals), Jacobites and republicans, dissenters, Catholics, Scots, Irish, Africans and Jews. Above all, claiming to speak for or represent the opinions of "the people" was used as a rhetorical device by disaffected groups who wished to legitimate their own positions, defining themselves in opposition to those who at different junctures allegedly monopolized political power, corrupted political institutions or obstructed the equal access of all citizens to the political process: Court Whigs, Tories, effete aristocrats, parasitical bourgeoisie, or "Old Corruption," to use Edward Thompson's phrase, by which was meant the entire seemingly ineffable network of patronage and monopolies that kept the state from serving the public interest.[37] In all cases, despite the divergent and often contradictory definitions, "the people" were a continual presence in Hanoverian political discourse in written and symbolic forms: It was their interests that were to be served by this party or that group, by the extension of empire and national aggrandizement and glory, and by the reform or complete restructuring of political institutions. And it was by their consent, however distantly or indirectly given, that both Parliament and new forms of state were legitimated as authentic guardians of the public interest.[38] Discourses about the people thus constructed both a rational, libertarian political public to which the state was held to be accountable, and stridently gendered and variously exclusionary conceptions of political subjectivity that played central roles in consolidating oppositional categories of the domestic and public spheres.[39] The gendered models

---

[37] Thompson, "Class Struggle Without Class?" 141; Jones, "Re-Thinking Chartism," *Languages of Class,* 102, makes the same point. For a differently conceived but complementary examination of populist discourse in the nineteenth century see Patrick Joyce, *Visions of the People: Industrial England and the Question of Class 1848–1914* (Cambridge, 1991).

[38] Brewer, *Sinews,* 221–47.

[39] They were thus instrumental in authorizing binary oppositions of masculine–feminine, public–private, rational–irrational and white–other upon which innovative claims to political subjectivity were based, and which allowed the literary representations of "bourgeois" subjectivity to do their normative work. See Scott, *Gender and the Politics of History,* 28–51; for the changing historical productions of "race" see Henry Louis Gates, Jr., ed., *"Race," Writing and Difference* (Chicago, 1985). Cf. Nancy Arm-

of citizenship, in particular, need analysis, for like those of race, the gender categories produced by and through eighteenth-century political culture were not "natural" but mutable, contested and always under construction.

The populist ideological constructions produced within urban political culture also demonstrated that the "invention of tradition" was not the prerogative of conservative political elites but took place within and through the practices of popular politics.[40] Refashioning "the people" as political actors to fit changing circumstances required the fabrication of continuities and traditions from available cultural materials that imparted credibility to extra-parliamentary forms and tactics as legitimate parts of the political process. Hence even the most innovative aspects of out-of-doors politicking were justified with reference to their alleged continuities with the national, collective and often mythic past. The theory of the Norman Yoke, so masterfully analyzed by Christopher Hill, is only one example of the way in which historical myths could become intertwined in public consciousness with nationalistic anxieties and radical programs.[41] The enduring relevance of seventeenth-century events, for example, to political and religious discourse and conflict throughout the eighteenth bears eloquent witness to the vitality of the struggle for control over the interpretation of English history, for it was the past that gave meaning to the present and held out hope for the future. The Georgian decades constituted a pivotal moment in the debates over contending narratives of English history that could be used to legitimize existing constellations of power or the demands for their radical reformation, represented not least in the production of rival national histories and competing interpretations of their meaning.

These quarrels were also fought out in quotidian domains of custom and culture. The political calendar provides a cogent example of the contestations between the oligarchic state and its representatives and a broader base of citizens who, at least periodically, perceived themselves as political subjects, for it made visible the contradictions of the eighteenth-century political system and the ambivalences of its representa-

strong, *Desire and Domestic Fiction: A Political History of the Novel* (New York, 1987).

[40] For the deployment of this concept to describe the establishment of conservative political traditions see the essays in Eric Hobsbawm and Terence Ranger, eds., *The Invention of Tradition* (Cambridge, 1983), 1–14.

[41] Christopher Hill, "The Norman Yoke," *Puritanism and Revolution* (New York, 1958), 57–8.

tions of legitimacy. A well-integrated part of the official structures of
politics in the Hanoverian decades, publicized in secular and sacred
forums, the calendar was meant to transmit to the public a particularized
interpretation of England's political heritage and the blessings of the
current regime – commemorating, for example, those crucial historical
moments when liberty, moderation and loyalty triumphed over despotism or fanaticism.[42] The political calendar was central to the popular-
ization of the historical and political principles which legitimized
current constellations of power in the state, and it charted the way those
principles changed.

Yet the political calendar could equally be manipulated by other
groups to coax, solicit or express alternative political loyalties. The
official meanings of anniversaries were continually being contested by
dissident or disaffected groups, producing riots, counter-demonstrations
or rival observances that publicized divergent political loyalties. Adherents of the exiled Stuarts, opposition supporters under Walpole, and
Wilkite and pro-American radicals all either staged strategic anniversary celebrations or abstained from official ones, in a public and visible
expression of their political principles. The calendar thus provided a
cultural basis for alternative readings of English history and divergent
views of the legitimacy or effectiveness of state power. As such, it was
a focal point and arena of political struggle for control over the mythic
past, the master fictions of the present and their symbolic representations, a site where contending visions of England's destiny and the
people's political future were conjoined.

If ''the people'' were part of the various visions of the national destiny, so too was the empire. Yet the impact of empire on domestic political sensibilities and consciousness remains a peculiarly neglected
aspect of Georgian political history. Remarkably for a century of protracted imperial wars and colonial revolt, historians long tended to
elide the imperial component in Hanoverian domestic political ideology and culture, or, with a few notable exceptions, noted it only to
dismiss it as part of the ''sub-political'' attitudes or knee-jerk xeno-

---

[42] It consisted of Hanoverian anniversaries (the monarch's birth, accession and coronation days, his consort's birthday and the Prince of Wales's birthday); the dates of war
victories and fasts; and the anniversaries of Charles I's martyrdom, Charles II's restoration and the ''double deliverance'' of the discovery of the Powder Plot and William III's landing at Torbay. For the best description see Brewer, ''The Number 45'';
for seventeenth-century antecedents see David Cressy, *Bonfires and Bells: National
Memory and the Protestant Calendar in Elizabethan and Stuart England* (Berkeley
and Los Angeles, 1989).

phobia of ordinary English people. Literary scholars have been much
more attentive to imperial themes but have tended to ignore politics as
a constitutive arena of imperialist culture that both constructed and
disseminated competing images of the state and nation, Englishness
and otherness, citizenship and exclusion.[43] Yet empire was a crucial
component in fashioning English people's material and imaginative relations with the rest of the world and integral to shaping their own patriotic and nationalist identities.[44] Imperialism – by which I mean the
ideologies, values and practices supporting Britain's push for establishing and consolidating an empire – was historically embedded, an
amalgam of practices, values and attitudes that bore cultural and political meanings and generated tropes of representation specific to the period.[45] Indeed, the examination of English political culture necessitates
attending to the actions of the British state and the constructions and
deployment of "British" (for most of the century used to include the
English, Welsh, Scottish, Anglo-Irish and sometimes white colonial
American populations) as well as English identities (which often contended with the more inclusive "British" designation). That the British empire permeated Georgian English culture at a number of levels,

---

[43] See the citations in Chapter 3. The best available historical views of domestic representations of empire in this period include Bernard Smith, *European Vision and the
South Pacific* (New Haven, 1985); Peter Hulme, *Colonial Encounters: Europe and
the Native Caribbean* (London, 1986); G. S. Rousseau and R. Porter, eds., *Exoticism
and the Enlightenment* (Manchester, 1990); Linda Colley, *Britons: Forging the Nation,
1707–1837* (New Haven, 1992), chap. 3; and Billie Melman, *Women's Orients: English Women and the Middle East* (Ann Arbor, 1992). My differences, as well as
agreements, with these scholars will become clear ahead.

[44] Although patriotism and nationalism were politically protean and could collapse into
each other in eighteenth-century discourse, it is useful to distinguish analytically between them. "Patriotism" denoted love of country, protection of the constitution and
the liberties it guaranteed, and a devotion to the public good, unscathed by personal
interest or private aggrandizement; nationalism, or more accurately the national identity, attempted to invoke commonalities based on the territorial boundaries of the
nation-state, mobilized in pursuit of the collective interest – a fractured and contested
effort in the context of constructing "Great Britain." For the former see my "Empire,
Trade and Popular Politics in Mid-Hanoverian England: The case of Admiral Vernon," *P & P*, no. 121 (1988), 94–5; for the latter see John Tomlinson, *Cultural
Imperialism* (Baltimore, 1991), 82–7. Cf. Colley, *Britons*, passim.

[45] As deployed here, empire subsumes the narrower historical form of colonialism (e.g.,
the West Indies and the North American colonies) as well as the "informal" empire
of trade and arms (India); both, in any case, are contained in the eighteenth-century
English notion of the "Empire of the Sea." For French and Spanish views of empire
in this period see Montesquieu, *Reflections on Universal Monarchy*, in *The Complete
Works of M. de Montesquieu*, 4 vols. (London, 1777), iv; Anthony Pagden, *Spanish
Imperialism and the Political Imagination* (New Haven, 1990); for a current if somewhat problematic definition see Michael Doyle, *Empires* (Ithaca, 1986).

from literature and theater to philanthropy, fashion, gardening and politics, is beyond dispute, but the specificity of eighteenth-century imperial sensibilities still needs to be recovered: the various ways in which the empire was imagined, debated and discussed, and above all the contending meanings which empire held for the various groups involved in or engaged by the mesmerizing spectacle of Britain's global expansion.

The broad social basis within Britain of investment in the imperial project, from the financing of ships and investment in slave cargoes to colonial land speculation, as well as the distribution, consumption and population patterns which spread colonial and British goods and people across regions, oceans and nations, helped ensure that trade and empire were potent political issues throughout the eighteenth century, argued about and debated in a proliferation of printed materials as well as in artifacts, street theater and demonstrations. But interest in the empire was never solely a product of material involvement. Rather, it shaped the national imagination in ways that gave it a particular salience within domestic politics and culture. Although the identities coaxed by the imperial project were far from unitary or invariably unifying, central issues emerged around which national and patriotic discourses contended. Notions of consent and liberty, for example, were central to contemporary conceptualizations of empire, which was frequently imagined to consist of flourishing and prosperous colonies populated with free white British subjects that served as bulwarks of trade, wealth, naval strength and political virtue for the parent state. The health and happiness of the colonies was taken to be a barometer of the effectiveness and legitimacy of domestic political institutions; weak or misgoverned colonies were held up as proof of the corruption or supineness of the nation's ruling councils. Hence, as the national acclaim generated by Vernon and Pitt, the popular violence provoked by the catastrophe of Minorca, and the alienation and outrage produced by the American war demonstrated, empire was an important part of the nationalist sensibilities of eighteenth-century English people, linked to material interests, to strategies of extra-parliamentary organization and resistance, and to patriotism of both the oppositionist and loyalist varieties. At the same time, the militaristic and competitive contexts of imperial acquisition and loss worked to authorize particularized definitions of citizenship that influenced other cultural and ideological initiatives. It has recently been argued that empire was an instrument of national consolidation, unifying the British against the French, the nation's primary "other."[46] Yet the discourses of imperialism produced as many contradictions as unities, championing libertarianism and chauvinism, celebrating the birthrights of white English men while denying those rights to Britons, and vindicating the libertarian reading of English constitutional development while also embedding hierarchies of difference in English political culture. The "others" identified or subdued through the imperial project were internal as well as external, domestic as well as foreign, within as well as without.[47] Understanding the complex nature of imperialist sentiments is crucial to recovering the meanings, dimensions and ideological significance of extra-parliamentary political culture in the period.

IV

This study is divided into two parts. Part I provides an analytical narrative of the structures and content of popular politics in provincial towns and London from the Hanoverian Succession through the years of the American war. Such an overview must, by necessity, be exploratory rather than definitive and episodic rather than comprehensive. Chapter 1 examines the politics of culture within the provincial urban milieu, focussing on the expansion of the press, the rise of associational activities and the emergence of new cultural institutions in the decades between 1720 and 1780 as settings in and through which eighteenth-century English men and women's well-known fascination with politics was nurtured and amplified. Chapters 2 through 5 focus on a number of formative moments in the development of extra-parliamentary political culture: the Hanoverian succession crisis and the opposition to Walpole; the issues surrounding war, invasion and the acquisition of empire; the rise of an independent radical politics and the domestic crisis wrought by the American war. Part II continues to develop these arguments through the more detailed perspective of two case studies, Newcastle upon Tyne and Norwich. The development of extra-parliamentary political culture in the nation was predicated upon the emergence of distinctive provincial urban cultures and publics, and

[46] Colley, *Britons*, 6 and passim.
[47] See Homi Bhabha, "Of Mimicry and Man: The Ambivalence of Colonial Discourse," *October*, 28 (1984), 125–33: Producing colonial subjects who are "almost the same, but not quite," the imperialist discourses of the day made the "national" unnaturalizable and "problematize[d] the signs of racial or cultural priority," thus exhibiting, in my view, the irreconcilable if constantly mystified tensions between empire and nation.

Chapters 6 through 8 illustrate key aspects of the relationship between national and local politics. As prosperous provincial centers with lively political traditions, Newcastle and Norwich were both characterized, albeit in different ways, by broad-based participatory political cultures. A flourishing press, calendar, tavern and street life, as well as charity hospitals, assembly rooms, theaters and libraries, contributed in both cities to the assertive political consciousness of their citizenry. In both towns, too, oligarchy wreaked more havoc than stability for the first thirty years of Hanoverian rule, producing a combative electoral life and ultimately fostering forms of political organization and practice that forced a rethinking of the strategies of politicians at all levels toward the ''sense of the people'' out-of-doors.

This book examines one of the most remarkable developments in eighteenth-century England, the emergence of a lively, predominantly urban extra-parliamentary political culture, engaged by issues emanating from the state and focussed on national affairs. In doing so, it approaches English society from the point of view of some of its most restive, most energetic and, periodically, most critical members. Such a perspective is emphatically a partial one, but it is one which most eighteenth-century contemporaries would recognize. For both the forms and expansion of the state and empire in the first seventy years of Hanoverian rule supported the widespread dissemination of an anti-corruption critique of authority that identified national, social and moral ills with the distribution and exercise of political power. It is here that urban political culture made its most lasting contribution to English culture, for by 1785 its participants had forged an alternative idiom of national politics that could be used to legitimate more expansive definitions of the rights and liberties of ''the people'' and new views of the just relationship between the individual and the state. This provocative and contradictory legacy of the ancien régime would reverberate in popular politics for the next hundred years.

1. *Print, people and culture in the urban renaissance*

[T]he People of *Exeter, Salisbury,* and other large Towns, are resolved to be as great Politicians as the Inhabitants of *London* and *Westminster;* and deal out such News of their own Printing, as is best suited to the Genius of the Market-Place, and the Taste of the Country.

The Freeholder, June 22, 1716

When the People find themselves generally aggrieved, They are apt to manifest their Resentments in satyrical Ballads, Allegories, By-sayings, and ironical Points of Low Wit. They sometimes go farther, and break out into hieroglyphical Expressions of their Anger against the *Person,* whom they conceive to be the Projector of any Injury done, or intended to be done them . . . it behooves a *Politician,* whose Passions are not much stronger than his Reason, not only to READ those Fables and Allegories, under which his Character is exhibited to the World, but to regard them with the greatest Attention, for his own Safety, as well as the publick Good.

The Craftsman, Feb. 10, 1733

In these quotations, Joseph Addison and Henry St. John, Viscount Bolingbroke, offer competing but not incompatible interpretations of the instruments and evidence of popular political consciousness in eighteenth-century England. For Addison, the culture of print and the culture of politics were inextricably linked, and newspapers served as both cause and consequence of the widening political awareness of ordinary people – a trend he decried as perpetuating party strife and disfiguring a civilized polity. Bolingbroke's gloatingly sardonic "warning" to

27

Court Whig politicians, on the other hand, seemed to privilege the traditional symbolic modes of street theater over the artifacts of print culture in expressing "authentic" public opinion. Yet (leaving aside for the moment Bolingbroke's endorsement of a certain *kind* of reading) the irony of attempting to separate the culture of print and that of politics was evident even as it was voiced, for Bolingbroke published his remarks in one of the most widely read weeklies of the day, whose political essays exploited and no doubt supplied many of those "Fables and Allegories" attributed to spontaneous popular expression. Both these texts provide rich examples of eighteenth-century contemporaries' obsession with the socially and geographically heterogeneous compass of the political and its connection with the spread of the culture of print. They also foreground the questions raised by late-twentieth-century scholars trying to interpret the robust extra-parliamentary political culture of the Georgian decades. Whose political culture was it? By what media was it instituted and sustained? For whom did it speak, and why?

This chapter will begin to answer these questions by examining three developments central to provincial urban politics, using Newcastle upon Tyne and Norwich as exemplary, but by no means exclusive, case studies: the expansion of print culture and its complex relationships to other venues of politics and to the state; the proliferation of clubs and societies devoted to self- and public improvement; and the impact of some of the new institutions of the "urban renaissance" on social and political relationships in provincial towns.[1] All three suggest how provincial urban culture gave voice to various contending groups outside formal political institutions while simultaneously creating spaces for participation and engagement by people elided in the self-representations of the male middle classes. For the wide-ranging political culture of towns that had emerged by the middle decades of the century owed far less to aristocratic dominance or the emergence of an "autonomous bourgeois public" than to the struggles within the urban milieu to reconstitute power and authority in ways that refused the hierarchies of the old regime while also containing their own strategies of exclusion and containment. Provincial urban culture thus shaped the notions of the nation, state and subject that circulated through the body politic.

[1] As described by Peter Borsay, *The English Urban Renaissance: Culture and Society in the Provincial Town* (Oxford, 1989).

I. THE POLITICS OF PRINT

Let us begin with a discussion of that preeminent instrument of politicization in the eighteenth century, the press. One need not support the theory of a "printing revolution" in the early-modern period or see a necessary automatic link between print culture and political dissidence to accept that the generation of print in towns throughout the kingdom constituted one of the most striking developments of the period.[2] The culture of print – encompassing both the spread of the artifacts of the press and the institutions and types of sociability that subsidized it – was of enormous importance in disseminating political values and attitudes, promulgating not simply "information" but ideological perspectives which proffered particular and often divergent interpretations of the state, nation and polity.

Most larger provincial towns had three or more printers and booksellers by the 1730s, and thereafter the numbers grew exponentially, with the centers of provincial commercial printing shifting from towns like Cambridge, Exeter, Norwich and Oxford to Bristol, Birmingham, Liverpool, Manchester, Newcastle and Worcester. By the mid 1740s there were 381 printers, booksellers and engravers at work in 174 English towns, rising to 988 and 316 respectively by 1790.[3] These figures

---

[2] Elizabeth Eisenstein, *The Printing Press as an Agent of Change*, 2 vols. (Cambridge, 1979); for critiques of this view see Gary Marker, "Russia and the 'Printing Revolution,' " *Slavic Review,* 41 (1982), 266–83; Keith Thomas, "The Meaning of Literacy in Early Modern England," in G. Bauman, ed., *The Written Word* (Oxford, 1986), 97–131; and, less convincingly, Jeremy Black, *The English Press in the Eighteenth Century* (Philadelphia, 1987). For the political and cultural impact of print culture expansion in England see John Brewer, *Party Ideology and Popular Politics at the Accession of George III* (Cambridge, 1976); John Money, "Taverns, Coffeehouses and Popular Articulacy," *HJ,* 14 (1971), 15–47; John Styles, "Sir John Fielding and the Problem of Criminal Investigation in 18th Century England," *TRHS,* 5th ser., 33 (1983), 127–49; James Raven, *Judging New Wealth: Popular Publishing and Responses to Commerce in England 1750–1800* (Oxford, 1992); and Margaret Spufford, *Small Books and Pleasant Histories* (London, 1981). For comparison see Robert Mandrou, *De la culture populaire aux XVIIᵉ et XVIIIᵉ siècles: La Bibliothèque Bleue de Troyes* (Paris, 1964); Roger Chartier, *The Cultural Uses of Print in Early Modern France,* trans. Lydia Cochrane (Princeton, 1987); and Robert Darnton, *The Literary Underground of the Old Regime* (Cambridge, Mass., 1982).

[3] John Feather, *The Provincial Book Trade in Eighteenth Century England* (Cambridge, 1986), 28–9, which revises dramatically upwards the numbers calculated by Henry Plomer in *Dictionary of the Printers and Booksellers Who Were at Work in England, Scotland and Ireland from 1668 to 1775,* 2 vols. (Oxford, 1922–32). For the localities see C. J. Hunt, *The Book Trade in Northumberland and Durham to 1860* (Newcastle, 1975); Trevor Fawcett, "Eighteenth Century Norfolk Booksellers: A Survey and Register," *Transactions of the Cambridge Bibliographical Society,* 6 (1972–6), 1–18; Jon-

leave out many thousands of individuals engaged in making or distributing printed texts. Postmasters; itinerant traders (whose prosperity and respectability increased as their trading networks became more formalized); commercial and industrial carriers;[4] the proprietors of inns, coffeehouses and alehouses; and the members of circulating libraries and book clubs that proliferated in provincial towns beginning in the 1720s[5] – all played important roles in distributing and circulating printed materials, from newspapers, pamphlets, sermons and novels to ballads, chapbooks and prayer books. Indeed, London's status and growth as a major publishing center depended directly upon the flourishing of the provincial trade. The London tri-weekly newspapers, for example, were produced specifically with the provincial audience in mind (printed on Tuesdays, Thursdays and Saturdays, the days on which the post left the capital), and the success of Edward Cave's ground-breaking *Gentleman's Magazine* stemmed from Cave's exploitation of well-placed provincial printers to create a national market.[6] The rise in urban literacy,[7] as well as the production of printed materials

athan Barry, "The Cultural Life of Bristol 1640 1775" (Oxford University D. Phil., diss. 1985), 352; Manchester Library Committee. *The Manchester Press Before 1801* (Occasional Lists, new ser., 6, 1931).

[4] For distribution see R. M. Wiles, *Freshest Advices: Early Provincial Newspapers in England* (Canton, Ohio, 1965), 115–20; G. A. Cranfield, *The Development of the Provincial Press 1700–1760* (Oxford, 1962), 198–204; Michael Harris, *London Newspapers in the Age of Walpole* (London, 1986), 39–40; Spufford, *Small Books and Pleasant Histories*, 45, 113–23.

[5] Alan Everitt, "The English Urban Inn," in Everitt, ed., *Perspectives in English Urban History* (London, 1973), 91–261; Paul Kaufman, *Libraries and Their Users* (London, 1969); NCL, L027.2, MS Accounts of St. Nicholas Book Club, 1742–6; Brewer, *Party Ideology,* 139–62; Peter Clark, *The English Alehouse: A Social History, 1200–1830* (London, 1983), 228–9. Kaufman counted 268 provincial circulating libraries and 110 book clubs between 1718 and 1800. The number of inns and taverns in larger towns ranged from several hundred, as in the case of Bristol, to 67, as in Liverpool; most had 2 to 5 coffeehouses. John Latimer, *Annals of Bristol in the Eighteenth Century* (Bristol, 1893), 235; *Liverpool Directory* (Liverpool, 1766; repr. and ed. G. T. Shaw and I. Shaw, 1907).

[6] Michael Harris, "The Structure, Ownership and Control of the Press, 1620–1780," in George Boyce, James Curran and Pauline Wingate, eds., *Newspaper History: From the 17th Century to the Present Day* (London, 1978), 87–90; Feather, *Provincial Book Trade,* 19–20.

[7] Literacy rates grew among trades and craftsmen from 60% to 85% in 1700–60, and among women from 30% to 50%: Lawrence Stone, "Literacy and Education in England, 1640–1660," *P & P,* no. 42 (1969), 101–35; R. A. Houston, "The Development of Literacy: Northern England, 1640–1750," *Economic History Review,* 35 (1982), 199–216, and *Literacy and Society in Scotland and England, 1600–1850* (Cambridge, 1984). The figures for women are surely underestimates, since the standard literacy

catering to all levels of a socially and sexually differentiated market, makes it appropriate to locate in the mid eighteenth century the rise of "print capitalism" that made printed artifacts one of the first mass cultural commodities.[8]

Certainly individuals of both sexes and virtually all social ranks, literate and illiterate, urban and rural, had occasion or opportunity to take advantage of the market in information and mechanisms of persuasion created by the spread of commercial printing. Labor disputes between masters and journeymen over wages or training frequently were carried out via handbills and newspaper advertisements, such as in Bristol in 1769, Liverpool in 1756 and Norwich in 1752. In the latter case, several hundred journeymen woolcombers protested their masters' "combining" to hire workers who had not served apprenticeships by removing themselves to a camp on Rackheath three miles outside the city, where they stayed for two and a half months, publishing closely argued manifestoes about their plight in the local newspapers until the masters gave in.[9] Such maneuvers indicate the widespread acceptance of the newspaper press as the proper mediator of the public interest, able to persuade and adjudicate disputes by allowing appeals to "the opinion of the World" (as the Norwich woolcombers would have it). A similar faith was evinced by the moral and religious reform societies of the early eighteenth century, whose zeal for producing and distributing cheap propaganda anticipated if not exceeded that of later societies for radical political reform. Societies for the reformation of manners in London and Bristol printed hundreds of broadsides and pamphlets on the dangers of vice (particularly playhouses) which were distributed by men and women at such middling urban venues as coffee and chocolate houses, inns, taverns and theaters, as well as among "persons of Quality" at church doors. One representative moral missive sent by request to a Mr. Stubs in Greenwich contained "6, [Rev.] Mr. [Arthur] Bedford's Large Bk of the Danger of Plays, 6, Considerations of ye danger of going to Plays, 20, The Letter to a Lady, 6, [Jeremy Collier's] Further Vindication of ye Short View of the Pro-

---

test (the ability to sign one's name) would exclude the many who were taught to read and not write and who were active in transmitting the former skill to children: Thomas "The Meaning of Literacy," 97–9, 102–3.

[8] As Benedict Anderson has argued in *Imagined Communities: Reflections on the Origins and Spread of Nationalism* (London, 1983), 61–2.

[9] Barry, "Cultural Life of Bristol," 79; Edward Baines, *History of Liverpool* (Liverpool, 1852), 423; *Norwich Mercury,* July 25, Aug. 1, 8, Sept. 30, Oct. 7, 1752.

faneness of the Stage, 6, Rev. Mr. Bedford's Sermons, 20, Representations of the Impiety of the Stage, [and] 100, A[rch]b[isho]p
Tillotson's Judgem't on Plays'' – all to prevent a troupe of players
from settling in that suburb.[10] Clearly, belief in the transformative moral
and rhetorical powers of printed texts transected the society, being
shared by religious enthusiasts as well as coffeehouse politicians.

Newcastle upon Tyne provides a neat example of the interaction of
print with the provincial urban culture of the century in both its progressive and traditional modes. A major publishing center throughout
the period, with between ten and fifteen printing, publishing and book-
selling firms operating in most years by the middle decades of the
century, Newcastle's printers produced chapbooks, ballads and histories
for the popular market, and newspapers; literary, political and general
magazines; sermons; political tracts; children's books; and a didactic
literature for self-improvement and entertainment for the commercial
middling and artisanal classes.[11] Of the seven local newspapers started
in the town before 1760, two became especially important, the *Newcastle Courant,* printed by the Tory John White from 1711, and the
Newcastle Journal, begun in 1739 by the Quaker, opposition Whig,
land agent and surveyor as well as printer–publisher Isaac Thompson.
In 1769 these were joined by the *Newcastle Chronicle,* printed and
published by the radical Thomas Slack, by which time the number of
printers in the town had risen sharply.[12] These papers, along with the
news and prints from London and York, were available at many of the
150 or so inns and taverns which flourished in the town by midcentury.
In addition, the town boasted two circulating libraries, established by
Joseph Barber in 1746 and William Charnley in 1757, two coffeehouses, and three subscription newsrooms, and the high rates of literacy
among residents meant that book clubs and debating societies flourished
among the town's artisans and tradespeople.[13] The engraver Thomas

[10] Society for Promoting Christian Knowledge Library, SPCK Minutes, i (1698–1706),
fols. 355–69, Jan. 10 – Feb. 14, 1706; ii–iv, (1706–09), fol. 180, May 26, 1709; SPCK
Abstract Letter Book, vi (1715–16), fol. 4714; ARL, MS B10162, Minutes of the
Society for the Reformation of Manners 1699–1705.
[11] Feather, *Provincial Book Trade,* 29; Hunt, *Northumberland Book Trade,* 105–6.
[12] Richard Welford, "Early Newcastle Typography, 1639–1800," *AA,* 3rd ser., 3 (1907),
127–9; Hunt, *Northumberland Book Trade,* 83; *Newcastle Chronicle,* Nov. 23, 1771.
[13] Richard Welford, *Men of Mark 'Twixt Tyne and Tweed,* 3 vols. (London, 1895), i,
180–1; William Whitehead, *The First Newcastle Directory* (Newcastle, 1778; repr.
1889); Eneas Mackenzie, *A Descriptive and Historical Account of Newcastle upon
Tyne* (Newcastle, 1827), 499; Joan Knott, "Circulating Libraries in Newcastle in the
18th and 19th Centuries," *Library History,* 1 (1969), 230.

Bewick, who owed much of his modest wealth and fame to the national market in books and art, was an active participant in the highly literate artisanal community of Newcastle, attending a variety of the local book clubs and debating and tavern societies, whose camaraderie and adherence to "rational" standards of behavior and decorum impressed him.[14] In conjunction with the town's location, commercial prosperity, national and international trade connections and growing middling sector, the press ensured that Newcastle residents were keenly attuned to and engaged by national political affairs throughout the century. Similar patterns can be discerned in Norwich, Birmingham, Leeds, Bristol, Manchester and York – in most towns, in fact, where historians have investigated the press and its cultural articulations.[15]

The culture of print provided one of the most kinetic aspects of the provincial urban milieu, encouraging the change to a more aspiring, socially complex and politically informed world. It also penetrated more "traditional" forms of culture, becoming deeply implicated in that "commercialization" of popular culture that was so marked a feature of cultural change in this period.[16] Ballad-singing, for example, had been an integral part of Newcastle culture since the sixteenth century and continued into the nineteenth. Bewick recalled that the singing of laments for the Jacobite Earl of Derwentwater, executed in 1715, did much to convince the people of "the cruelty of the Reigning Family."[17] The plethora of ballads published locally helped keep alive this oral tradition, just as the publication of chapbooks increased the life of the stories and fairy tales that Bewick had read to him as a boy. Similarly, local histories, beginning with William Gray's *Chorographia* in 1649 and continuing with the better-known efforts of Bourne and Brand in the next century, chronicled customs and popular eccentricities in ways that preserved them for posterity (while also, perhaps, documenting their decline).[18]

---

[14] Thomas Bewick, *A Memoir,* ed. Iain Bain (Oxford, 1979), 52–3, 91–5, 102–3, 112–13. See also TWA, 1269/32, Bewick Papers, Cash and Ledger Account Books, 1773–4, 1777–8.

[15] Feather, *Provincial Book Trade,* passim; Kathleen Wilson, "The Rejection of Deference: Urban Political Culture in England, 1715–1785" (Yale University Ph.D. diss., 1985), 463–6; John Money, *Experience and Identity: Birmingham and the West Midlands* (Montreal, 1977), 52–79; Raven, *Judging New Wealth,* 112–15; references in note 3.

[16] Clark, *English Alehouse,* 154–5, 230–40; Peter Burke, *Popular Culture in Early Modern Europe* (London, 1978); Robert Malcolmson, *Popular Recreations in English Society, 1700–1850* (Cambridge, 1973).

[17] Bewick, *Memoir,* 8.

[18] See David Vincent, "The Decline of the Oral Tradition in Popular Culture," in Robert

Nor did print displace the visual and the spectacular: A robust street theater remained very much a part of provincial urban life, as of Hanoverian political culture generally. The continued use of the streets to announce and solicit political and social/cultural solidarities must qualify historians' assertions about the *decline* in civic ritual in the eighteenth century, although certainly its provenance and intended functions were changing, becoming more secular in purpose if not personnel, less corporate and more directed to evoking particular political, social and nationalistic meanings.[19] In Newcastle, for example, the observance of the civic and political calendar remained important to elite power and authority, which in conjunction with the public ceremonies attendant upon the *rites de passage* of the local notables could prompt grand parades of power and dignity thirty times a year. Ascension Day gave the magistrates and their wives the opportunity to sail up and down the Tyne with the river jury, throwing figs to the crowds along the banks while guns fired and ships saluted (Plate 1).[20] In Bristol, Liverpool, Norwich, Salisbury and scores of other towns, local elites and middling citizens all took to the streets to announce new political alliances, negotiate status or announce a host of cultural initiatives undertaken for self- and public improvement. Masonic and pseudo-masonic societies, tradesmen's clubs and friendly societies also made clear their contributions to civic robustness and bids to social authority through their processions to church, tavern or meeting, often with music blaring and colors flying.[21] Political anniversaries, both loyalist and dissident, prompted an array of demonstrations and rituals of often quite astounding theatricality and panache, punctuated by effigy-burnings, illuminations and transparencies as well as elaborate parades. And the dramas of elections, local and national, with the canvasses, processions, and

Storch, ed., *Popular Culture and Custom in Nineteenth Century England* (London, 1981), 26–7; William Gray, *Chorographia* (Newcastle, 1649); Henry Bourne, *Antiquities Vulgares* (Newcastle, 1723); John Brand, *History and Antiquities of the Town and Country of Newcastle upon Tyne* (Newcastle, 1789). The interpenetration of print and oral culture and the connections of both to political culture are brilliantly evoked in Bewick's *Memoir:* See, e.g., 15–16.

[19] See, e.g., Peter Borsay, "All the Town's a Stage: Urban Ritual and Ceremony, 1660–1800," in Peter Clark, ed., *The Transformation of English Provincial Towns* (London, 1984), 228–58.

[20] Wilson, "Rejection of Deference," 194–204; Chapter 6. For Ascension Day perambulations elsewhere in the nation see A. G. Wright, *British Calendar Customs,* 3 vols. (Folklore Society, 1936–40), i, 130–1.

[21] *Norwich Gazette,* July 18, 1730; *Newcastle Courant,* Aug. 18, 1725; Dec. 31, 1737; May 29, June 26, 1756; June 27, 1761; *Norfolk Chronicle,* July 28, 1770; *Leeds Mercury,* May 8, 1770; *Salisbury Journal,* March 13, 1771.

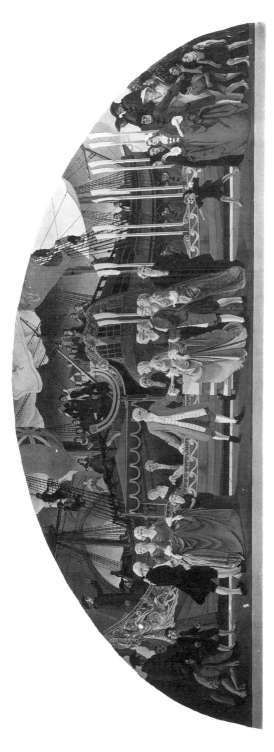

1. J. H. Willis, *Ascension Day on the Tyne*, ca. 1790. From the collection at the Laing Art Gallery, Newcastle upon Tyne. Photograph reproduced with permission from Tyne and Wear Museums.

treating and chairing of successful candidates – activities which frequently involved entire communities, electors and nonelectors, rich and poor, male and female alike – provided implicit recognition of the potential political power of the voters, just as the entire electoral drama played out the myth of popular consent while endowing the English ruling classes with legitimacy.[22] Such spectacle and display were regularly reported and described in newspapers, journals and magazines, thus publicizing their occurrence and authorizing their intended meanings. Print thus played a major role in keeping the visual, the spectacular and the ephemeral at the heart of urban culture, providing a calendar for demonstrations of allegiance to particular political causes, endowing local activities with national significance, and giving form and substance to the political nation.

The culture of print clearly transected a significant proportion of English culture in the eighteenth century, and in the many gaps and gaffes between the production of printed texts and their consumption were "the space[s] where meaning is constructed," as Roger Chartier has noted.[23] Its patterns must contest the oppositions between elite and popular cultures that have become commonplace in the historical literature. What impact did print have on contemporary images of the state and polity? Over half the output of the press was more concerned with spiritual matters than with secular affairs: Religious chapbooks, sermons, homilies and meditations could account for the majority of a single printer's output.[24] Yet, as is evident upon reading through any collection of eighteenth-century sermons, the overlap between the here-and-now and the hereafter was great, and many of the religious tracts and broadsides were concerned as much with *national* as individual salvation and prosperity, with assessing the success of (and individuals' contribution to) England's mission in the world as a Protestant nation, as Linda Colley has recently argued.[25] Moreover, the social contexts of

[22] Frank O'Gorman, *Voters, Patrons and Parties: The Unreformed Electoral System of Hanoverian England, 1734–1832* (Oxford, 1989), 90–100 and passim.
[23] Roger Chartier, "Texts, Printing, Readings," in Lynn Hunt, ed., *The New Cultural History* (Berkeley and Los Angeles, 1989), 161. See also the essays by Peter Lake and Alastair Bellany in Kevin Sharpe and Peter Lake, eds., *Culture and Politics in Early Stuart England* (Stanford, 1993), 257–83, 285–310.
[24] Feather, *Provincial Book Trade*, 38–9; Black, *English Press*, 277–306; see also the reading list of Thomas Turner in his *Diary*, ed. David Vaisey (Oxford, 1985), 347–53; Manchester Library Committee, *Manchester Press*; A. J. Hawkes, *Lancashire Printed Books: A Bibliography* (Wigan, 1925).
[25] Colley, *Britons: Forging a Nation, 1707–1837* (New Haven, 1992), 40–2. My observations are based on my readings in the sermon collections at Beinecke Library, Yale

print culture – centering on the very public arenas of club, coffeehouse, tavern and library – as well as the marked diversification of political ephemera for predominantly urban residents in the decades between 1735 and 1765 to include not only sermons, pamphlets, ballads and broadsides but also handbills, newspapers, tracts and prints, worked to give such publications salience within the arenas of sociability of provincial towns.[26] In these respects, and as contemporary observers were wont to decry, the political press particularly captured the attention of urban residents and facilitated their often vehement engagement with national affairs.

As the Addison quotation at the beginning of this chapter suggests, the newspaper press was of singular importance in structuring the national political imaginary, helping to shape the social, political and national consciousness of middling and artisanal people living in the localities and binding men and women in particular ways to the wider political processes of the state, nation and empire. London, the first center of newspaper publishing, produced by midcentury dozens of daily, tri-weekly, fortnightly and monthly newspapers and journals, both stamped and unstamped, that circulated in the provinces.[27] Provincial newspapers developed more spasmodically but no less significantly: There were 25 in 1735, 35 in 1760 and 50 in 1782; over the century 244 provincial papers were produced in fifty-five different towns.[28] With circulation at 200 to 400 copies per issue in the 1710s and 1,000 to 2,000 in the 1770s, their own regional and national distribution networks, and prices that were as low as the government Stamp Acts and profits allowed, these papers were broadly accessible, the most successful reaching thousands of readers per issue.[29] Given

University; Huntington Library; Dr. Williams's Library; Newcastle Central Library; and Norwich Local History Library.

[26] For the types of political ephemera produced see Brewer, *Party Ideology,* 139–60. My qualification of the timing of this emergence is based upon my own analysis of printed propaganda available in the provinces: See Chapter 3.

[27] Harris, *London Newspapers,* 33–48; Brewer, *Party Ideology,* 142–3.

[28] Harris, "Structure, Ownership and Control of the Press," 88; Wiles, *Freshest Advices,* 22–7, 97–8 and Appendix C, and "Provincial Culture in Early Georgian England," in Paul Fritz and David Williams, eds., *The Triumph of Culture: 18th Century Perspectives* (Toronto, 1972), 50–2. Unlike the London papers, which by 1730 were owned and controlled by large groups of shareholding booksellers, the provincial papers were owned and run by the printers themselves, or by smaller partnerships of two, three or four printer-publishers, so that their viability depended directly upon advertising and readership.

[29] Harris, *London Newspapers,* 65–81; Wiles, *Freshest Advices,* Appendix C. Papers like

the wide dissemination of London newspapers, what accounted for the appeal of the provincial papers? Far from passively replicating news and opinions from the capital, provincial newspapers presented their readers with a particular view of the world that appealed to their interests and aspirations. Indeed, historians' long-standing suspicion of the newspaper press for either its "biases" or its blandness rather miss the point, for any society's historical "reality" is inseparable from the forms of its cultural representations. The " 'lived reality' of national identity," John Tomlinson has noted, "is a reality lived in representations – not in direct communal solidarity."[30] In this respect, by catering to complex social, cultural and political milieus and producing particularized versions of "news" and national life, newspapers offer intriguing evidence for the motivations and sensibilities of the broader political nation.

For example, newspapers in commercial and trading centers such as Newcastle, Norwich, Liverpool, Birmingham and Bristol in the middle decades of the century coaxed and shaped their readers' involvement, both material and ideological, in war, trade and imperial expansion while expressing contemporary conceptualizations of power and market relations at home and abroad.[31] The structure and content of these papers reflected and encouraged a mercantilist world view in which trade and the accumulation of wealth appeared to be the highest national and individual good. The progress of wars in Europe, America, Africa and the East Indies; the comings and goings of merchant ships, often with lengthy lists of the products of their laden bottoms; prices, stocks and bullion values; and advertisements for luxury goods from international and colonial markets – tea, coffee, chocolate and tobacco; calicoes and silks; wines, rum and spirits; fruits and seeds, furs, exotic birds and plants – could together account for one-third of the contents of individual issues of newspapers in the outports.[32] Both the enumeration of

the *York Chronicle* and *Newcastle Courant* sold about 1,000 copies per issue by midcentury.
[30] John Tomlinson, *Cultural Imperialism: A Critical Introduction* (Baltimore, 1991), 83–4.
[31] My analysis is clearly indebted to Anderson's account of the creole colonial press in *Imagined Communities*, 51–63, which in my view is more applicable to the metropole than to the colonies.
[32] These observations are based on examinations of London and provincial newspapers, including *LEP, London Chronicle, Public Advertiser, Farley's Bristol Journal, Cumberland Pacquet, Newcastle Journal, Newcastle Courant, Norwich Gazette, Norwich Mercury, Liverpool General Advertiser* and *Worcester Journal*. See also R. B. Walker, "Advertising in London Newspapers, 1650–1750," *Business History*, 15 (1973), 120–

goods and their seemingly endless variety encapsulated on a small scale the contemporary fascination with the movable products of imperialist accumulation.[33] They also evinced a widespread interest in the processes of colonial acquisition and possession. By the 1740s and 1750s, several provincial papers and most magazines had sections called "American affairs" or "British Plantations" that included not only current news on politics and trade but also the histories and settlement patterns of individual colonies, the competing claims of European powers to them and the "etiquette" of colonization.[34] Such texts did more than literally and figuratively map imperial aspirations and accumulationist desire; they also organized time and space in ways that welded the national and imperial interest, while effacing the crueler aspects of empire, colonialism and "trade" and the subjectivities of the growing numbers of peoples under British rule. Instead, the newspaper and periodical press of this period helped produce a commercial and "patriotic" vision of the British empire and its apparent destiny of spreading profits through the nation while disseminating British goods, rights and liberties across the globe. "Leonard Herd's African Coffeehouse" in Liverpool, which boasted of its "genteel accommodation" and current subscriptions to ten London newspapers (including the *Middlesex Journal,* the *London Evening Post* and the government's *London Gazette*) and *Votes of the House of Commons* in the *Liverpool General Advertiser,* mirrored the conjunction of empire, trade, politics and male sociability that was at the heart of urban print culture.[35]

Other items in the papers integrated the imperial project and Britain's performance and standing abroad with the prosperity and mores of everyday life at home. Local, regional and national politics, Court gossip, the notable *rites de passage* of the local gentry and bourgeoisie, phil-

1, and Harris, *London Newspapers,* 155–78. Thanks to J. Jefferson Looney for his comments on my figures.

[33] Laura Brown, "The Romance of Empire: *Oroonoko* and the Trade in Slaves," in Brown and Felicity Nussbaum, eds., *The New Eighteenth Century* (London, 1987), 51–2.

[34] See, e.g., *Newcastle Journal,* Jan. 27, June 9, 1750; *London Magazine,* 24 (1755), 307–12; *Newcastle General Magazine,* 8 (1755), 7–15, 241–4, 405–9; *Lancashire Magazine,* 1 (1763), 11–12; *Liverpool General Advertiser,* Nov. 17, 24, Dec. 8, 15, 1769; June 15, July 6, 27, Aug. 3, 1770.

[35] *Liverpool General Advertiser,* July 27, 1770; see also the account of the African and American Club in Whitehaven: *Newcastle Chronicle,* June 14, 1766. Such representatives were contested, of course, not least by the growth of abolitionist and anti-imperial propaganda in the 1760s and 1770s, some of which was excerpted in the periodicals. See Chapter 5.

anthropic and economic initiatives and the "quaint" customs or "insensible" behaviors of the common people: Such content endowed readers with the power of possession (*our* colonies, ships, MPs and gentry) and with the sense of entitlement to be on the right side of the vast social and cultural chasms between those who profited from the processes of imperial expansion and those who did not. Along with the endless notices of the meetings of clubs and societies, assemblies, theaters and concerts, and goods, services and land for sale or rent, newspapers chronicled the bids of the urban commercial and middling classes to social authority, mapped consumerist and social aspirations, and laid bare the structures of economic, political and discursive power in the society, of market relations and forms of social, political and sexual commerce at home and abroad. Above all, they made manifest the impact of state actions and politics on daily life and regional and national prosperity and standing, and allowed individuals to participate imaginatively as well as materially in the processes of domestic and imperial government.

Newspapers were thus central instruments in the social production of information: Both representing and verifying local experience, they refracted world events into socially meaningful categories and hierarchies of importance, bestowing order on the disordered and coordinating the imagination of social time and space. They thus helped produce, in Benedict Anderson's felicitous phrase, an "imagined community" of producers, distributors and consumers on both sides of the Atlantic who shared an avid interest in the fate of the empire of goods that linked them together in prosperity and adversity.[36] At the same time, provincial newspapers constructed a view of the provinces as having all of the virtue, culture and civic-mindedness, but none of the vice, of the capital. Provincial urban life was represented in local papers as civilized, intimate and respectable – a marked contrast to the disorder and corruption that reigned in London – and thus helped define the locality and nation both through and against the identity of the capital.

Of course, the ascription of "imagined community" to the world of goods and information constructed by newspapers begs the questions, whose community? and what was it imagined to consist of? Clearly newspapers (or other forms of print) produced not homogeneous cultural identities but a highly mediated "national" belonging that was constructed through and in tandem with other (local, regional, social)

---

[36] *Imagined Communities,* 51–63, 62–3.

identities. Nevertheless, we can discern the social, sexual and racial contours of the national community constructed by the newspaper press. It was imagined to consist of free, flourishing and largely, though not exclusively, white masculine British subjects within the locality, nation and empire; its boundaries were defined and guarded by gender, race, productivity and profits. Hence, despite the participation in the processes of state and imperial expansion by other citizens in the metropolis and provincial towns – women, slave and free Africans, Jews, servants, Catholics, laborers and so on – who worked as victuallers, retailers, craftspeople, carriers and pedlars, supported the state through taxes or otherwise played roles in financing, transporting, distributing, manufacturing or consuming the artifacts of colonial and international commerce, their status as a part of the "publick" appealed to in the newspaper press was usually implicit at best, extrapolated through the claims to status of the male middling sorts or their betters.[37] In this sense, the accessible "universal" identity cultivated by newspapers was in fact a particular one that recapitulated the self-representations of the urban upper and middle classes, and especially their male, white and English members. Further, the metaphor of imagination applies equally to the *political* imaginary, that is, to the representations and ideological significance of the state and its relations with individuals and localities. In this respect, the political content of the provincial papers was crucial, for they familiarized their readers with a political discourse that diagnosed the structure, location or distribution of power in the state as the source of political and social discontents or blessings.

G. A. Cranfield pointed out long ago the marked propensity of provincial printers to capitalize on the predominant hostility to successive Court Whig ministries by reproducing the opposition's point of view (all the while, of course, professing the printers' strict political impartiality).[38] By consistently printing essays and letters from the main op-

---

[37] See my "Empire of Virtue: The Imperial Project and Hanoverian Culture," in Lawrence Stone, ed., *An Imperial Nation at War: Britain, 1688–1783* (London, 1994), 128–57; F. O. Shyllon, *Black People in Britain, 1555–1833* (London, 1977), chaps. 2–5; Todd M. Endelman, *The Jews of Georgian England, 1714–1830* (Philadelphia, 1979), chaps. 1, 5; M. D. George, *London Life in the Eighteenth Century* (London, 1966), chap. 3. For a similar inscribing of subjectivity in travel writing see Mary Louise Pratt, *Imperial Eyes: Travel Writing and Transculturation* (London, 1992). The roles of women, for example, as economic actors and readers were made apparent largely through advertisements.

[38] Cranfield, *Development of the Provincial Press,* 120–40. Newspapers such as *Mist's Weekly Journal, The Craftsman* and the *LEP* were widely plagiarized or excerpted in this manner, as were pamphlets, political-essay papers and weeklies: See Marie Peters,

42   *The sense of the people*

position tracts and pamphlets as well as newspapers, provincial papers
like the *Norwich Gazette, Farley's Bristol Journal,* the *Gloucester
Journal,* the *Salisbury Journal,* the *Newcastle Courant* and the *York
Courant* adopted fairly hostile criteria by which to judge the state and
its leaders that played a large role in shaping attitudes to metropolitan
hegemony, the activities of the oligarchs and the abuses to which, it
was alleged, the constitution was repeatedly subject at their hands.
Equally important, through its representations of the state, the opposition press also constructed the identity of the citizens outside its con-
fines. For example, in the context of Britain's imperial rivalries and of
ministers who seemed disinclined to adopt an aggressively expansionist
foreign policy, the frequent charges of corruption and "effeminacy"
leveled against the state by opposition writers inscribed its reader-
opponents as activist, virtuous, masculine political subjects. It was only
"the people" (a deliberately socially ambiguous designation in the
hands of most opposition journalists), inspired by a "manly, rational
love of liberty," who were capable of serving as guardians of the public
trust. In this way, the oppositionist reading of politics produced definitions of patriotism and political subjectivity that were quite at odds
with those proffered by ministerial advocates.[39]

"Every subject not only has the right, but is in duty bound, to en-
quire into the publick measures pursued," a writer in the *London Magazine* asserted, "because by such enquiry he may discover that some
of the publick measures tend towards overturning the liberties of his
country; and by making such a discovery in time, and acting strenu-
ously . . . he may disappoint their effect."[40] This activist conception of
citizenship proclaimed the *duty* of the subject to ogle, monitor and
canvass the state to ensure the accountability of those in power. It lay
at the heart of oppositionist patriotic imperatives, based on "the original Power of the People," to resist illegitimate power, upon which
scores of writers from Bolingbroke to John Cartwright insisted. Yet

Pitt and Popularity: London Opinion and the Patriot Minister (Oxford, 1982), 20–1;
Brewer, *Party Ideology,* 146–57.
[39] For "effeminacy" and the state see Chapter 3–5; for the longevity of radical conceptions of political subjectivity see my "A Dissident Legacy: The Glorious Revolution
and Eighteenth Century Popular Politics," in J. R. Jones, ed., *Liberty Secured? Britain
Before and After 1688* (Stanford, 1992), 299–326. By "subjectivity" I mean the constructed identity of the autonomous, rational, self-actuated individual, agent of his or
her own actions, as well as the individual placed within authority relations under the
political control of the king or state: a double meaning which is always at play.
[40] *London Magazine,* 7 (1738), 241.

how was such an ideal to be enacted? Between 1720 and 1785 opposition and radical supporters offered a variety of answers to this question that differed according to the issues and agendas at hand, ranging from participating in instruction and petitioning movements, voting for members of Parliament and engaging in political demonstrations or festivals to remonstrating with the throne or setting up alternative conventions to speak the sense of the People. Yet one of the perennial and preeminent ways the "manly, rational love of liberty" could be demonstrated was in the public sphere constructed by the press. Against government supporters' claims that "inquiries into the corruptions and mismanagements of those in the administration, properly and solely belong to . . . Parliament," opposition and radical partisans continually asserted the people's right to monitor the state through the mechanisms of spectatorship provided by a free press. As one pamphleteer argued in 1740, since "the People of Britain in general have an undubitable Right to Canvass publick affairs, to express their sentiments freely, and to declare their sense of any grievances under which they labour,"

treating political subjects freely in print, and thereby submitting them to the view and censure of the Nation in general, is so far from being dangerous that it is really conducive to the Publick Peace. By this means, all Degrees of People, who have leisure and abilities, and a turn to this sort of reading, acquire rational ideas of liberty and submission, of the rights of the church, and of the power of the State, and of their duties as subjects, and of what they may justly claim as *Free men.*[41]

In this argument, literacy becomes the test of citizenship and the instrument of political subjectivity itself, and through print culture both the subject's right to monitor the state and his potential for citizen activism were fulfilled. Clearly, the political press recast politics into spectatorial, critical activities, capable of being exercised privately but more appropriately enacted in the sphere of public society itself. The alehouse, tavern, news room, coffeehouse and club, as well as the counting house, shipyard and shop, made "the people" temporarily visible, but print made it permanent, allowing them to exist through a "steady, solid simultaneity through time," as Anderson has noted.[42] At the same time, through the role of spectator the political subject was

[41] Abel Boyer, *Political State of Great Britain,* 38 vols. (1711–29), xxiii, 166; *The Liveryman, or Plain Thoughts on Public Affairs* (London, 1740), 2, 9. See also *Monitor,* Aug. 9, 1755.
[42] *Imagined Communities,* 52.

delimited in class, gender and racial terms as "independent," rational and masculine – a critical, objective, manly subject, immune to the emoluments of power, whose contrast to the allegedly corrupt, irrational or effeminate aristocratic state could not be more marked.[43] The ideal political subject, like the ideal patriot politician, was not the privatized, isolated individual but the public man willing to renounce all selfish interests in order to promote the public welfare.[44]

Given its ascribed role in attending to "the sense of the people," vindicating their rights and allowing fresh opportunities for their exercise, it is not surprising that the press was mythologized as a unique part of the English political inheritance and liberty. Yet government itself contributed to the tenacity of the opposition press and to the vindication of its liberationist narratives of itself as an organ of the "fourth estate." Since the expiration of pre-publication censorship in 1695, successive ministries exploited their considerable advantages in the attempt to shape the contours and content of "public opinion" expressed in the press. Walpole, for example, resurrected and revivified Robert Harley's complex organization for the production and distribution of government-subsidized propaganda as well as the surveillance of the opposition press. His administration employed writers, printers, publishers and distributors for the four government newspapers and innumerable pamphlets that were dispersed throughout the capital and sent by the tens of thousands through the Post Office every week to provincial towns (where customs and excise officers would oversee their gratis distribution in coffeehouses and taverns). It also hired spies,

[43] Whereas the "feminine" was relegated to the realm of pleasure, eroticism, artifice, sociability and particularity. Not only women but a range of ethnic and racial "others," from Africans to Highland Scots, as well as the English lower classes, were identified in much cultural and political discourse with the symbolic feminine, e.g., as dependent, irrational, sensual or emotional: See Sylvana Tomaselli, "The Enlightenment Debate on Women," *History Workshop Journal,* 20 (1985), 101–24; Vivien Jones, *Women in the Eighteenth Century* (London, 1990), 102–38; Sander Gilman, "Black Bodies, White Bodies," in Henry Louis Gates, Jr., ed., *"Race," Writing and Difference* (Chicago, 1985), 225–35; Richard Popkin, "Medicine, Racism, Anti-Semitism: A Dimension of Enlightenment Thought," in G. S. Rousseau, ed., *The Languages of Psyche: Mind and Body in Enlightenment Thought* (Berkeley and Los Angeles, 1990), 405–42; Londa Schiebinger, "The Anatomy of Difference: Race and Sex in Eighteenth Century Science," *Eighteenth Century Studies,* 23 (1990), 387–405; and Chapters 3–4.

[44] In this respect, the political subject countered the privatized reader–subject usually assumed to be produced by print culture: See Terry Eagleton, *The Rape of Clarissa: Writing, Sexuality and Class Struggle in Samuel Richardson* (Minneapolis, 1982); and Nancy Armstrong, *Desire and Domestic Fiction: A Political History of the Novel* (New York, 1987).

informants, messengers and agents, and enlisted postmasters and excise and customs officers to report on suspicious journalism and survey the press for actual or potential seditious libels. Operating under the political direction of the secretaries of state and the legal oversight of the Treasury solicitor, this array of state employees constituted a formidable surveillance system (costing the government some £50,000) which all journalists and printers had to fear. Although the extent of Walpole's effort was unequaled until the ministry of the younger Pitt, virtually every ministry after him sought to use the power of the state to shape public opinion through the press.[45] This system set up and authorized the spectacle of the government and "the people" monitoring and surveying each other, thus both affirming and regulating the power implicit in such spectating. As Foucault has shown, observation bestows the authority of disinterestedness and power upon those observing.[46] Both the state and its critics claimed a critical authority over each other that rested upon their mutual roles as observer and observed, and legitimized such spectatorship as part of the political process.

Further, the mechanisms of surveillance, like other structures erected to exercise power, both ensured and confirmed resistance to such control and perpetuated the activities they were designed to suppress. For example, the unintended consequences of the government's attempts to control the press included making martyrs out of those prosecuted, increasing the circulation of declared "libels," and precipitating a less than solemn reception for its own propaganda efforts among the seasoned, middling readers in coffeehouses and taverns. Although scarcely an objective observer, the *London Evening Post* reported with glee that the government newspapers were thrown out of most coffeehouses in the capital, and "nay few even of those to whom they were sent down in the Country Ministerially (i.e., *gratia,* Paper and Postage paid) would read them."[47] Secondly, government surveillance also endorsed the *kind* of reading promoted by opposition writers themselves. Bolingbroke's exhortation to the ministry to "*read*" the "Fables and Allegories" of the people, quoted at the beginning of this chapter, is one

[45] Laurence Hanson, *Government and the Press* (repr. Oxford, 1967), 45–110; Harris, *London Newspapers,* 116–45, 134–54; Robert Rea, *The English Press and Politics, 1760–74* (Lincoln, Nebr., 1963), 174–223.

[46] Michel Foucault, *Discipline and Punish: The Birth of the Prison,* trans. Alan Sheridan (New York, 1979), 170–94; for this insight as applied to theater see also Kristina Straub, *Sexual Suspects: Eighteenth Century Players and Sexual Ideology* (Princeton, 1992).

[47] *LEP,* July 5, 1735.

example of the common injunction to double and allegorical reading
that was continually reinforced in the opposition press and street theater
in the first half of the century, a kind of reading that mimicked but also
mocked that performed by the government agents hired to ferret out
potential libels. The political uses of allegory, allusion and innuendo,
of course, were exploited by writers of all political stamps.[48] But the
reconfiguration of opposition rhetoric beginning with the Hanoverian
Succession and the contexts of government authority and resistance
gave these rhetorical strategies particular currency, when the subter-
fuges employed to report on parliamentary proceedings or satirize politics on the stage or in the streets depended upon readers/spectators
performing the double readings. Government surveillance and prosecution in turn aided opposition writers in their efforts to make a range
of historical texts, from those of Shakespeare to the Royal Martyr himself, function as contemporary political critique.[49] By the 1760s, the
shifting relations between parliamentary elites and the wider political
nation and the growing middle-class attachment to "sincerity" were
working to replace allegorical modes of oppositionist discourse with
the more "transparent" discourses of history and constitutional theory
used in reformist and radical propaganda.[50] But in the meantime (and
arguably thereafter), the culture of critique produced by the political
press and its censorship bound government agents, opposition writers
and ordinary readers into one mutually reinforcing system.

The political press had a further role in delimiting, as well as expanding, the political nation, for it simultaneously attempted to contain
or restrict the groups deemed respectable enough to be included within
the boundaries of the political nation and have access to the mouthpiece
of "the people." As I have argued above, while the public created by

---

[48] See, for example, the contending essays in *Craftsman* and *Daily Gazetteer*. For allegory in the graphic propaganda of the day see Herbert Atherton, *Political Prints in
the Age of Hogarth* (Oxford, 1974).

[49] See P. D. G. Thomas, "The Beginning of Parliamentary Reporting in Newspapers,
1768–1774," *EHR*, 74 (1959), 623–36; John Loftis, *The Politics of Drama in Augustan England* (Oxford, 1968), 42–62; L. W. Conolly, *The Censorship of English Drama
1737–1824* (San Marino, Calif., 1976), 54–63; Hanson, *Government and the Press*,
135–6. For a discussion of these questions in the context of French political art see
Nicholas Mirzoeff, "Virtual Antiquity: Late David and the Public Mind," unpublished
paper, Northeast American Society for Eighteenth Century Studies Annual Conference, 1992.

[50] For the concept of sincerity see Gerald Newman, *The Rise of English Nationalism*
(New York, 1987), 127–45, and for the 1790s, Olivia Smith, *The Politics of Language,
1791–1819* (Oxford, 1984).

print was becoming more inclusive, the political public represented by and through the press was being staked out as the preserve of the masculine, commercial and middling classes (in which I include aspiring artisans), who were presented as best able to judge the public interest against competing claims of the luxurious and effeminate aristocratic classes on the one hand and the degenerate "insensible multitude" on the other. What impact did this monopoly of representation have on the other social groups who had a stake in the production or consumption of political print culture?

The gender and social contours of the institutions of print culture are illuminating in this regard, for they were differentiated by their degrees of exclusiveness. Subscription newsrooms were frequently quite expensive – those in Newcastle required a £5. 5*s*. admission fee and a £2. 2*s*. annual subscription – and coffeehouses were usually starkly male-dominated spaces (despite the numerous female proprietors in London and provincial towns), and could also be restricted by occupation or class.[51] Circulating libraries also maintained varying standards of social exclusiveness, although some were fairly open social spaces in which books, pamphlets, newspapers, novels and plays could be read and discussed by men and women, artisans and merchants for as little as threepence a week per book – the cost of a pot of ale, and thus not out of reach of the same mix of persons who were wont to satisfy their appetite for political journalism at alehouses and taverns (which were also socially and sexually mixed for most of the century).[52] And artisan book and debating clubs were common in provincial towns in the second half of the century, giving political and philosophical tracts a much wider reach than they would otherwise have had. The organized aspects of print culture may even have penetrated the mass of the laboring poor.[53]

---

[51] Mackenzie, *Historical Account,* 499; James Boswell, *London Journal,* ed. F. Pottle (New York, 1950), 74–6, 93–4, 104–5, 221–2. César de Saussure noted that the lower classes frequented coffeehouses in London: See *A Foreign View of England in the Reign of George I and George II,* trans. and ed. Madame von Muyden, vol. 2 (London, 1902), 719.

[52] Kaufman, *Libraries and Their Users,* 43–5; Knott, "Circulating Libraries," 230; Welford, *Men of Mark,* i, 180–1; for women patrons of inns and public houses see Clark, *English Alehouse,* 225–6; BL, Add. MS 27,966, Arderon MSS, fols. 241b–243 (1752). Some libraries maintained fees that put them out of reach of all but the gentle and merchant classes, such as those at Liverpool (1758) and Bristol (1728): George Stubbs, *Early Exhibitions of Art in Liverpool* (Liverpool, 1876), 5; Barry, "Cultural Life of Bristol," 97–100.

[53] Bewick, *Memoir,* 95–100; John Feather, "The Ely Pamphlet Club, 1766–76," *Trans-*

Further, despite the emergence of fiction and periodical literature
stressing the domestic arena and motherhood as women's proper
sphere,[54] women were nonetheless active participants in print culture,
not just as consumers but as producers and distributors. Women made
up 30 percent of the patrons at circulating libraries in the country and
accounted for between one-third and one-fifth of the membership in
various book clubs that have left adequate records; as noted above,
they also were patrons of such institutions of print culture as inns and
taverns.[55] Moreover, numbers of women worked in London and provincial towns as writers, printers, engravers, newsagents, stationers and booksellers as well as innkeepers and victuallers. Elizabeth Nutt and Anne
Dodd ran two of the most notorious pamphlet shops in the London area
in the 1720s, supplying subsidiary dealers with oppositionist literature
and appearing frequently in government warrants for libel. Jacobite
lady printers were well known; an example is Elizabeth Adams, who
made a national reputation with her feisty *Chester Courant* and Tory–
Jacobite publications. Sarah Coke printed the *York Courant,* which had
one of the largest circulations of all provincial papers; Elizabeth and
Frances Oliver ran a successful bookshop for four decades in Norwich;
Anna Gomersall of Leeds was one of the many women writers who
contributed to the national market for fiction; and Anne Fisher Slack
of Newcastle wrote the grammars, courtesy books and ladies' memo-
randums published by her husband, the radical printer Thomas Slack.
Her schoolbook *The Pleasing Instructor* was published in association
with London booksellers and was used throughout the country.[56] Hence,

actions of the Cambridge Bibliographical Society, 7, pt. 4 (1980), 457–63; Money,
    Experience and Identity, 111–17.
[54] For this see Kathryn Shevelow, *Women and Print Culture: The Construction of Fem-
    ininity in the Early Periodical* (London, 1989); Lynne Friedli, "Passing Women – A
    Study of Gender Boundaries in the Eighteenth Century," in G. S. Rousseau and Roy
    Porter, eds., *Sexual Underworlds of the Enlightenment* (Chapel Hill, 1988), 234–6.
[55] Kaufman, *Libraries and Their Users,* 223–4; BL, Arderon MSS, fols. 241b–242;
    Clark, *English Alehouse,* 225.
[56] Harris, *London Newspapers,* 38–40; Wiles, *Freshest Advices,* 269–302; Ivy Pinchbeck,
    Women Workers and the Industrial Revolution (repr. London, 1981), 284–5, 295; Paul
    Monod, *Jacobitism and the English People* (Cambridge, 1989), 29–30; Fawcett, "Nor-
    folk Booksellers," 16; Bridget Hill, *Women, Work and Sexual Politics in Eighteenth
    Century England* (London, 1989), 152–3; Raven, *Judging New Wealth,* chap. 6; Hunt,
    Northumberland Book Trade, 83. For other women writers and readers see Mary R.
    Mahl and Helene Koon, eds., *The Female Spectator: English Women Writers Before
    1800* (Bloomington, 1977); Robert Uphaus and Gretchen Foster, eds., *The "Other"
    Eighteenth Century: English Women of Letters, 1660–1800* (East Lansing, Mich.,
    1991); G. J. Barker-Benfield, *The Culture of Sensibility: Sex and Society in Eight-
    eenth-Century Britain* (Chicago, 1992), 161–73; and Moira Ferguson, *Subject to
    Others: British Women Writers and Colonial Slavery, 1670–1834* (London, 1992).

although the modes of differentiation deployed in print culture could replicate those produced discursively within the political press as well as by Enlightenment thinkers who sought to pose gulfs between the public and the private, the domestic and the political, men and women, or "the people" and the rabble, the culture inevitably created spaces for participation and engagement by those outside the privileged halves of these oppositions.[57]

Indeed, in this respect print culture provided a microcosm of the large patterns of inclusion and restriction or containment found in contemporary political culture as a whole, where virtually all classes and both genders were engaged by the issues of the day. Again, craftsmen and artisans, who made up the largest proportion of the electorate, were also prominent in the extra-institutional aspects of politics, where they participated in the aspirations to independence and subject status articulated in the political press.[58]

Women provide another case in point. Despite their legally subjugated status as "dependents" and the often stridently masculinist nature of political discourse, women of all social ranks could be found participating in the increasingly commercialized politics of the day. Sacheverell clearly had a wide female constituency, but after the succession the High Church cause had to compete with Whig loyalism for female support. Upper- and middle-class Whig women formed loyal associations against the Pretender in London and Norwich and sported orange cockades at the theater to counter the Tory and Jacobite women's blue ribbons and white roses. Party loyalties could also influence decisions about the running of the household: Addison told of an acquaintance who dismissed her cook for her support of the suspension of habeas corpus, and there is ample evidence of women influencing their hus-

---

[57] The intermittent invocations of nascent versions of "separate sphere" ideology by periodical writers is better seen as a strategy of containment than as description, whose impact was uneven even when bolstered by the physical separation of work and home in the late eighteenth and the nineteenth century. In fact, such injunctions became most pronounced in periods of intensive political debate and female engagement. For the early eighteenth century see *Spectator,* June 11, 1711ff.; Lawrence Klein, "Gender, Conversation and the Public Spheres," in Judith Still and Michael Worton, eds., *Textuality and Sexuality* (Manchester, 1993); for a trenchant critique of the analytical usefulness of "separate spheres" see Amanda Vickery, "Golden Age to Separate Spheres? A review of the Categories and Chronology of English Women's History," *HJ,* 36 (1993), 383–414.

[58] For the electorate see O'Gorman, *Voters, Patrons and Parties;* for the artisanal component in political culture see Chapters 3–8; for the participation of black Britons in political culture in the 1780s and 1790s see Shyllon, *Blacks in Britain,* 172–8, 230–66; Peter Linebaugh, *The London Hanged: Crime and Civil Society in the Eighteenth Century* (Cambridge, 1992), 415–16.

bands' or fathers' politics.[59] By the 1730s, the development of the market for political artifacts increased the range of things women could buy (and sell) to express their political affiliations. Women of both parties in Newcastle wore appropriately colored cockades and silks to assemblies and balls to signal their political affiliations; female opposition supporters in Norwich, York and Worcester were reported to preside over politically correct tea tables whose cloths commemorated the defeat of the excise bill; and seven years later others in scores of towns sold ballads, garlands or snuff that honored the opposition hero Admiral Vernon. According to George Liddell, the prelude to the Anglo-Spanish War was punctuated by "the women talk[ing] all day long of Conventions, Depredations and *Guarda Costas.*"[60] In the 1750s, women contributed to patriotic associations and philanthropic societies, and in the Wilkite era they were admitted to some of the more progressive debating societies in provincial towns or formed their own.[61] Radical iconography also appealed to those "patriotic ladies" who saw in its female imagery emblems of their own will to stand against corruption in the polity: In Worcester in 1774, Sir Watkin Lewes's female supporters presented Lady Lewes with a large piece of plate depicting the pulchritudinous feminine forms of Britannia, Fortitude and Justice destroying Bribery (here embodied as male), inscribed with the motto "Firm in the glorious enterprize."[62] Women were also participants in riots, demonstrations, chairings and processions and were spectators at the ceremonials of state and nation from anniversary-day celebrations to military reviews, avid attenders at the theater, and, during rebellion and invasion scares, the targets of vigorous propagandizing. Even the

---

[59] For Sacheverell's female support see Anne Clavering's descriptions in *The Correspondence of Sir James Clavering,* ed. H. T. Dickinson (Surtees Society, 178, 1967), 70–5; W. A. Speck and Geoffrey Holmes, eds. *The Divided Society* (New York, 1968), 10–12; and *The Tatler,* ed. Donald Bond, vol. 2 (Oxford, 1987), 378–83; for Whig and Tory women see Joseph Addison, *The Freeholder,* ed. James Leheny (Oxford, 1979), 24n, 52–4, 73–4, 205. As Clavering makes clear, women could appropriate the delegatory view of political authority to authorize their status as political subjects. See also HL, Montagu MSS, 1754–60, which evinces the role of female correspondence networks in exchanging the latest political news and views among women and men.

[60] *Newcastle Chronicle,* April 11, 1766; *Norwich Gazette,* Feb. 9, 1733; Jan. 3, Dec. 19, 1741; Gateshead Public Library, Ellison MSS, A54/11, March 15, 1739, GL to Henry Ellison; see also HL, Montagu MSS, MO 245–6.

[61] *Norwich Gazette,* Nov. 16, 1745; *Printed Annual Reports of the Newcastle and Northumberland Infirmary* (Newcastle, 1753); Money, *Experience and Identity,* 112; Donna Andrew, "Female Debating Societies," unpublished paper, Canadian Historical Association Annual Conference, 1988.

[62] *Aris's Birmingham Gazette,* Aug. 22, 1774.

government itself interpellated women as political subjects by prosecuting them for seditious or treasonable words.[63]

Of course, the social acceptance of women's forays into the political public sphere was variable, mediated by both class and political context. Aristocratic and upper-class women were allowed some influence at Court and behind the scenes, and their participation in *decorous* canvassing (a distinction apparently not understood by the Duchess of Devonshire in 1784) largely accepted; they were also usually indulged in their propensity to crowd into the galleries for House of Lords debates. Lower-class women's political activism, however, was taken as evidence of their degraded natures; attitudes toward middling women's politicking depended upon the agreement between their partisan sympathies and those of their observers.[64] Above all, national political crises or emergencies influenced attitudes toward displays of female patriotism. During the former, intrusions of the feminine in the political sphere could become a focus of intense male anxiety; during the latter, especially in wartime, women's devotion to the state and participation in the ''home front'' was expected, if not lauded.[65]

Clearly, long before the 1790s, in many of the informal and com-

---

[63] O'Gorman, *Voters, Patrons and Parties,* 93–4; Monod, *Jacobitism,* 190–218, 250; E. P. Thompson, *Customs in Common: Studies in Traditional Popular Culture* (New York, 1991), 306–61; *Newcastle Chronicle,* March 19, 1768; *Bonner and Middleton's Bristol Journal,* Jan. 10, 1778; D. Thomas, ed., *Theatre in Europe: Restoration and Georgian England, 1660–1788* (Cambridge, 1989); *Freeholder,* 181–4; [Eliza Haywood], The Female Spectator, 4 vols. (London, 1745–6), i, 140–5; ii, 135–90; *An Address to the Ladies* (London, 1756); Chapters 2–3. Cf. John Bohstedt, ''The Myth of the Feminine Food Riot: Women as Proto-Citizens in English Community Politics, 1790–1810,'' in Harriet Applewhite and Darline Levy, eds., *Women and Politics in the Age of the Democratic Revolution* (Ann Arbor, 1990), 21–59. In a few Anglican vestries and rather more nonconformist ones, women could vote on certain issues: Beatrice Webb and Sidney Webb, *The Parish and the County* (London, 1906), 106–7; Catherine Hall and Leonore Davidoff, *Family Fortunes* (London, 1987), 447–50. ''Interpellation'' is used here in the Althusserian sense, i.e., to call into existence through naming within a field of power relations.

[64] Georgiana Hill, *Women in English Life,* 2 vols. (London, 1846), ii, 28–35; *Georgiana: Extracts from the Correspondence of the Duchess of Devonshire,* ed. Earl of Bessborough (London, 1955), 74–82; for lower- and middle-class women see, e.g., *Freeholder,* 73–4, 182–3 (Jan. 2, April 9, 1716).

[65] See Chapters 3–4. Women's activism in the public sphere during wartime before the 1790s has been better documented for America than for Britain: See Mary Beth Norton, *Liberty's Daughters: The Revolutionary Experience of American Women, 1750–1800* (Boston, 1980); Linda Kerber, *Women of the Republic* (Chapel Hill, 1980); and T. H. Breen, '' 'The Baubles of Britain': The American and Consumer Revolutions of the Eighteenth Century,'' *P & P,* no. 119 (1988), 73–104. For women's roles in the English Civil War see the important forthcoming work of Barbara Donagan, who kindly showed me a draft chapter of her study.

mercialized arenas of contemporary political culture, women could act like political subjects – much to the chagrin of moralists who saw their imaginative or material involvement in affairs of state as symptomatic of moral decline. As such, the politicization of the "fair Sex" was always liable to ridicule. Addison's lampooning of feminine politicking after the Hanoverian Succession was part of a broader effort to channel and stabilize political conflict by delimiting the political sphere as masculine and hence labeling opposition to Whig rule as effeminate and unacceptable. In 1716 he set a pattern when he both urged right-minded women to support the Whigs and satirized their propensity to "*judge for themselves;* look into the State of the Nation with their own Eyes, and be no longer led Blindfold by a Male Legislature."[66] This double bind for women, who were simultaneously urged to promote love of country and constrained by their lack of legal and political status and injunctions to domesticity, were ultimately addressed in the ideas of civic or (in France and America) republican motherhood. But in the meantime it stimulated a great deal of the proto-feminist commentary and journalism of the day. Anne Clavering anticipated Mary Wollstonecraft by eighty-two years when she declared, "I abhor that doctrine [of passive obedience] and am resolve[d] to espouse that of resistance, when 'tis lawfull, but in that I'll be my own judge''; and a number of men and women writers in the decades between the Glorious and French revolutions similarly attempted to adapt patriarchal, libertarian or anti-aristocratic discourse to arguments for enlarging women's educational opportunities and political and legal rights.[67]

Hence, in the realm of politics, as in many other areas of eighteenth-century public culture, women maintained a presence, albeit one circumscribed by ambiguities and contradictions. Just as laboring men with claims to respectability and independence felt entitled to be con-

---

[66] *Freeholder,* 182 (April 9, 1716), and 52–4, 73–4, 205. The hostility of some Whig observers to women's political engagement may have stemmed from the various forms of contract theory that were in wide circulation among political journalists and lawyers of the day. See Carol Pateman, *The Sexual Contract* (Stanford, 1988), 4–6. For women's political activism in the 1790s see Colley, *Britons,* 238–48.

[67] AC to James Clavering, March 23, 1710, in *Clavering Correspondence,* 74–5; Rachel J. Weil, "Sexual Ideology and Political Propaganda in England, 1680–1714" (Ph.D. diss., Princeton University, 1991); Ruth Perry, "Mary Astell and the Feminist Critique of Possessive Individualism," *Eighteenth-Century Studies,* 23 (1990), 444–57; Sophia [pseud.], *Woman No Inferior to Man* (London, 1739); *The Hardships of the English Laws in Relation to Wives* (London, 1735), repr. in Jones, *Women in the Eighteenth Century,* 21–5; *Newcastle Weekly Magazine,* Nov. 20, 1776. For republican motherhood see Kerber, *Women of the Republic,* 265–88; Jane Rendall, *The Origins of Modern Feminism: Women in Britain, France and the United States, 1780–1860* (London, 1984), 33–72.

sidered a part of "the people," women could interpret Enlightenment universalism to include themselves; the injunctions to "manly rationality" could emanate from, and be a source of identity for, writers and readers of both sexes and classes. Moreover, the discourses of politeness and the cult of sensibility could work to legitimize women's participation in print culture and sociability in ways that washed over into politics.[68] On the other hand, women's elision as subjects in political–cultural representations and the complex positions both they and "the rabble" bore within the political public sphere as a whole meant that hostility to their presence could have serious material consequences, not least ensuring their continuing exclusion from formal politics.

In similar fashion, the ideological initiatives of the political press, like print culture as a whole, bore complicated relationships to the "objective" class and gender positions of their consumers. As a mechanism for exercising and contesting power by and upon the various groups involved in its production and consumption, the press did not have mechanistic cause-and-effect influence. On the one hand, print was central to the construction of a "public sphere," cast in the image of the male middling and commercial classes, in which political subjects could act and monitor and canvass the state, and the state could monitor its critics. On the other, print culture, as both constitutive and reflective of that intermediary sphere situated between the structures of the state and those of the family, provided crucial spaces in which women (and other subaltern groups) could enact or imagine their own claims to subjectivity.[69] The political impact of the press lay in its ability to

[68] Catherine Macaulay and Wollstonecraft both urged their female readers to adopt "manliness" (reason, firmness, austerity) as part of their character: *Letters on Education* (London, 1790), Letters 22 and 24; *Vindication of the Rights of Woman* (London, 1792), ed. Miriam Kramnick (New York, 1985), 80–1, 206–7; see also HL, Montagu MSS, MO 1000 [1737]. For women and politeness see Klein, "Gender, Conversation and the Public Sphere;" for the cult of sensibility, see Barker-Benfield, *Culture of Sensibility.* It must be stressed that the "feminine" and the "effeminate" are separate categories in eighteenth-century discourse which, although frequently conflated by political writers, should remain analytically distinct to historians: the first a "natural" category of female characteristics, and hence potentially laudable (within its proper sphere); the second an "unnatural" category of women's characteristics out of place and threatening, undermining or encroaching upon the masculine (and hence reprehensible). Randolph Trumbach has argued that effeminates constituted a third gender that threatened the absolute gulf between male and female: "Sex, Gender, and Sexual Identity in Modern Culture: Male Sodomy and Female Prostitution in Enlightenment London," *Journal of the History of Sexuality,* 2 (1991), 186–203; for France see Lynn Hunt, "The Many Bodies of Marie Antoinette," in Hunt, ed., *Eroticism and the Body Politic* (Baltimore, 1991), 108–30.

[69] See Jürgen Habermas, *The Structural Transformation of the Public Sphere,* trans. Thomas Burber and Frederick Lawrence (Cambridge, Mass., 1989), esp. 51–70.

organize knowledge, shape expectations, mobilize identities and proffer ideals, perspectives and attitudes through which politics could be interpreted. Its expansion in urban environments over the century played a crucial role in attuning ordinary men and women to the issues and implications of state power and expansion, enabling them to formulate and negotiate their sense of England's proper position in the world and their own place in the polity.

II. CLUBS AND SOCIETIES REDUX

Print culture was only one factor in the development of provincial urban culture that mobilized the social bases and cultural arenas of extra-parliamentary politics. The critical advances in population, communications and publishing in this period were supplemented by a new universe of associational activities undertaken by local residents to enhance the urban environment that had in themselves political implications. The efforts to improve public amenities and communications, expand leisure facilities, rebuild churches or found philanthropic institutions, although frequently encouraged or led by traditional elites, were dependent upon the willingness and ability of a wide range of residents to associate themselves and subscribe money and time in order to refashion and regulate their physical and cultural environments.[70] Equally important, the formation of a multitude of clubs and societies dedicated to self- and public improvement and the proliferation of institutions like assembly rooms, theaters and hospitals served to draw individuals together for purposeful convivial or cooperative activity, providing new contexts for political action.

Such patterns of associational life lay at the heart of the "urban renaissance" of provincial towns, a phenomenon which, orchestrated by codes of civility and politeness and galvanized by desire, provided the means and motivation for the urban middle classes and "pseudo-gentry" to negotiate the social and cultural power of ruling elites. Yet the political content and implications of these processes remain matters of debate.[71] How were new forms of social and political authority con-

[70] Peter Borsay, *The English Urban Renaissance: Culture and Society in the Provincial Town 1660–1760* (Oxford, 1989), 60–114; Wilson, "Rejection of Deference," 270–83, 468–76; R. G. Wilson, *Gentlemen Merchants: The Merchant Community of Leeds* (Manchester, 1971), 136–60, 201–15; *VCH Lancashire,* 7 (London, 1912), 34–5; 4 (London, 1911), 181–3; *VCH Yorkshire,* 15 (Oxford, 1969), 245–50.
[71] Peter Borsay, "The English Urban Renaissance: The Development of Provincial Urban Culture, c. 1680–1760," *Social History,* 5 (1977), 581–99. Borsay has suggested

stituted, represented and contested within the spaces and associations of the new public domain? This and the next section will address this question through a discussion of the culture of club life and the politics of philanthropy.

It is necessary first to glance briefly at economic developments in the period in order to make two points of central importance to the argument. The chronicle of England's capitalist expansion in the eighteenth century is well known. Although disagreements over the precise roles of home demand and colonies continue, it is generally agreed that the expansion of England's economic infrastructure was itself predicated upon two interrelated developments: the growth of internal trade, communications and markets that knit the nation together commercially, and the expansion of the larger-scale international markets to which increasing chunks of domestic economic activity were wedded.[72] By 1750, these trends, in conjunction with rising incomes and continuous warfare, had increased the size and prosperity of many provincial towns, from ports, market and county towns to the industrial and manufacturing towns of the East and West Midlands, East Anglia, the West Country and the West Riding of Yorkshire – all of which flourished with the increase in trade and expanding demand for services and cultural facilities.[73] The results were multifold, but I wish to draw attention

that the urban renaissance finally tamed the political divisions that had festered among England's ruling classes since the Civil War: *Urban Renaissance,* 318–19. Geoff Eley has seen the development of a "self-conscious bourgeois public" embodying public opinion in the middle class milieu: "Re-Thinking the Political: Social History and Political Culture in Eighteenth and Nineteenth Century Britain," *Archiv für Sozialgeschichte,* 21 (1981), 438. For questions about the timing, ubiquity and meaning of the urban renaissance see Angus McInnes, "The Emergence of a Leisure Town: Shrewsbury, 1660–1760," *P & P,* no. 120 (1988), 53–87; and Peter Borsay and Angus McInnes, "Debate: The Emergence of a Leisure Town, or an Urban Renaissance?" *P & P,* no. 126 (1988), 189–202.

[72] John Brewer, *The Sinews of Power: War, Money and the English State* (London, 1987), 184–5; D. E. C. Eversley, "The Home Market and Economic Growth in England 1750–80," in E. L. Jones and G. E. Mingay, eds., *Land, Labour and Population in the Industrial Revolution: Essays Presented to J. D. Chambers* (London, 1967), 206–59; Patrick O'Brien, "European Economic Development: The Contribution of the Periphery," *Economic History Review,* 2nd ser., 35 (1982), 1–18; E. A. Wrigley, "Urban Growth and Agricultural Change: England and the Continent in the Early Modern Period," in R. I. Rotberg and T. K. Rabb, eds., *Population History: From the Traditional to the Modern World* (Cambridge, 1986), 123–68.

[73] Borsay, *English Renaissance,* 22–28; Penelope Corfield, *The Impact of English Towns 1700–1800* (Oxford, 1982), 17–98; E. A. Wrigley, "A Simple Model of London's Importance in Changing English Society and Economy 1650–1750," *P & P,* no. 37 (1967), 55–63. For the ports – which usurped London's place as the premier site of the nation's overseas trade after 1700 – see T. S. Willan, *River Navigation in England*

to two: First, a greater proportion of England's domestic and foreign commerce than ever before depended upon empire and colonies; second, the expansion of the tertiary sector of the economy and of the middling sectors of the population owed much to this fact.

Although Europe maintained a larger share of Britain's imports and exports than the colonies into the 1770s (47 and 62 percent respectively), the colonies still constituted Britain's most dynamic markets. Imports from North America increased four times in value, and reexports of colonial goods trebled between 1700 and 1750; by the end of the century, England's combined exports to North America and the West Indies had grown by an astonishing 2,300 percent.[74] The colonial trade visibly changed English economic and cultural as well as political life, both because of the proliferation of luxury goods in shops and households across the country and because the broad social base of investment in overseas and colonial trade gave the empire an immediacy to those in England that supplemented and reinforced its cultural and political significance. As port books, trade directories and advertisements make clear, craftspeople and tradespeople of all descriptions, as well as shopkeepers, farmers, widows and merchants, invested directly or indirectly in the colonial trade in goods and slaves, used its raw materials in manufacturing, and retailed its luxury products from snuff, ivory and tobacco to muslins, silks, sugar and spices.[75] Hence, trade, empire and war underwrote the provincial urban renaissance, and colonies provided many of the crucial raw materials for social emulation and display – facts of some importance in assessing the renaissance's social and political meanings.

1600–1760 (London, 1964), 150–5; Gordon Jackson, *Hull in the Eighteenth Century* (Oxford, 1972); P. G. E. Clemens, "The Rise of Liverpool 1665–1750," *Economic History Review,* 2nd ser., 29 (1976), 211–25; W. E. Minchinton, "Bristol: Metropolis of the West in the Eighteenth Century," *TRHS,* 5th ser., 4 (1954), 71–8; J. E. Williams, "Whitehaven in the Eighteenth Century," *Economic History Review,* 2nd ser., 8 (1956), 396–402. For county towns see Alan Everitt, "Country, County and Town: Patterns of Regional Evolution in England," *TRHS,* 5th ser., 29 (1979), 92–6, and McInnes, "Shrewsbury," 53–87.

[74] Brewer, *Sinews,* 185; Ralph Davies, *The Rise of the Atlantic Economies* (New York, 1973), 231–87; Elizabeth Schumpeter, *English Overseas Trade Statistics* (Oxford, 1960), 18–20, 28; figures from Roderick Floud and D. N. McCloskey, eds., *The Economic History of Britain Since 1700* (Cambridge, 1981), 91–2. See also P. K. O'Brien and S. L. Engerman, "Exports and the Growth of the British Economy from the Glorious Revolution to the Peace of Amiens," in B. Solow and S. L. Engerman, eds., *Slavery and the Rise of the Atlantic System* (Cambridge, 1991), 177–209.

[75] Kathleen Wilson, "Empire, Trade and Popular Politics in Mid-Hanoverian Britain: The Case of Admiral Vernon," *P & P,* no. 121 (1988), 74–109; Nigel Tattersfield, *The Forgotten Trade* (London, 1991); J. H. Plumb, *The Commercialization of Leisure* (Reading, 1977); for directories see Appendix.

Table 1.1. *Commercial, crafts and service occupations listed in Newcastle and Norwich directories, ca. 1780 (percentages)*

	Newcastle (N = 1,396)	Norwich (N = 1,482)
Professional	6.8	18.7[a]
Merchant/manufacturer	15.0	11.2
Retail	46.9	35.9
Crafts	25.7	28.3
Laborers	4.0	3.7
Agricultural	1.5	2.2

Note: Percentages rounded to nearest tenth.
[a]Includes "Esquires and Gentlemen." If excluded, total is 11.4%.
Sources: William Whitehead, *First Newcastle Directory* (Newcastle, 1778; repr. and ed. J. R. Boyle, 1889); *The Norwich Directory; or, Gentlemen's and Tradesmen's Assistant* (Norwich, 1783). For breakdown by occupation see Wilson, "Rejection of Deference," 326, 437.

These developments helped swell the numbers of the middling sort from roughly 20 to 40 percent of all families by the 1760s[76] while also expanding the tertiary and service sectors of urban economies; by 1759 there were 141,700 retailers in England and Wales.[77] The diversification of retail, service and commercial occupations in provincial towns can be suggested by the admittedly selective but useful lists provided by directories.[78] Those for Newcastle and Norwich, for example, document the cities' roles as market and trading centers for their regions as well as for national and international markets; they also show the proliferation of colonial, foreign and domestic goods and services that catered to the needs of the commercial and trading communities as well as the pseudo-gentry (Table 1.1). Appraisers, bankers, brokers, insurance

[76] Peter Mathias, *The Transformation of England* (London, 1979), 186–7, using Joseph Massie's calculations and taking "middling sort" to mean people earning £40–400 per annum (and thus including those traders and craftspeople who paid the poor rate and had a modicum of disposable income). If the income is raised to £50, the figure is lowered to about 20% of all families: See Paul Langford, *A Polite and Commercial People* (Oxford, 1989), 62–3.
[77] Brewer, *Sinews*, 185; see also Ian Mitchell, "The Development of Urban Retailing 1700–1815," in Peter Clark, ed., *The Transformation of Provincial Towns* (London, 1983), 259–83.
[78] Directories possess the distinct advantage over freemen's records and pollbooks of not being sexually restricted. See Jane E. Norton, *Guide to the National and Provincial Directories of England and Wales, Excluding London, Published Before 1856* (London, 1950); P. J. Corfield with Serena Kelly, "Giving Directions to the Town: The Early Town Directories," *Urban History Yearbook* (Leicester, 1984), 22–35.

agents and surveyors joined attorneys in providing essential services to merchants and tradesmen interested in reducing risks and increasing profits, and growing numbers of commercial carriers, land and water, facilitated the transportation of goods and people more quickly over greater distances. Among the established trades and crafts, printers, engravers and booksellers, watchmakers, tailors, milliners, goldsmiths, cabinetmakers and coachmakers, and shops for china, hats, perukes, fabrics, hardware, cheese, glass, haberdashery, musical instruments, tea, wine and cookware flourished, indicating the extent to which surplus wealth was being channeled into luxury items of personal expenditure.[79] And concomitant with the growth of shops there appeared new professions and merchandise that accelerated the refurbishment of each town's cultural life. Music and French teachers, dancing masters, hirable hackney coaches with drivers, furriers, jewelers and milliners, exhibition halls and tearooms in Newcastle; pastry and dancing teachers, drawing masters, organists, punch houses, bowling greens and pleasure gardens in Norwich all helped change the face of each city and the patterns of personal consumption, and provided the aspiring with the means and ends of mobility. As previously noted, both sexes and most ethnicities were involved in these processes; women, for example, worked as confectioners; milliners; tobacconists; perfume, brandy and wine merchants; linendrapers; toy and pastry shopkeepers; clockmakers and coachmakers; and proprietresses of inns, taverns and coffeehouses in Manchester, Liverpool, Norwich and Newcastle (Table 1.2 and Appendix).[80] In the range of their goods and services as well as in their patterns of consumption, men and women linked provincial cultural refurbishment with that of the empire in direct and mediated ways.

Such occupational diversification and specialization could complicate the traditional lines of authority and mobility within the provincial

---

[79] See, e.g., Francis Buckley, "The Watch and Clock Makers of Northumberland and Durham of the 17th and 18th Centuries," *AA*, 3rd ser., 26 (1930), 57–67; Everitt, "Country, County, Town," 99–100.

[80] Given that women made up the majority of the population in most eighteenth-century towns, directories greatly underestimate the female presence in local occupation structures; they worked as servants and street sellers as well as alongside husbands, fathers and unrelated employers in shops and trades. Nevertheless, they reveal the continuing ability of at least some single women (usually widows) to earn a livelihood in urban milieus by the third quarter of the century: See Corfield, *Impact of Towns,* 106; Peter Earle, *The Making of the English Middle Class* (Berkeley and Los Angeles, 1989), 158–76. For restrictions on women's participation see Mary Prior, "Women and the Urban Economy: Oxford, 1500–1800," in Prior, ed., *Women in English Society, 1500–1800* (London, 1985), 93–117.

Table 1.2. *Number of women in provincial directories, ca. 1766–83*

Occupations listed	Newcastle (5.7% of total)	Norwich (14.0%)	Liverpool (5.5%)	Manchester (9.4%)
Professional	2	0	0	2
Merchant/manufacturer	8	5	15	5
Retail	57	69	42	63
Crafts	13	16	5	18
Laborers	0	0	0	0
Agricultural	0	3	0	1
Other[a]	0	114	0	52
Total	80	207	62	141

[a]Recorded as "Widow" or "Miss" with no other occupational designation.
Sources: Whitehead, *Newcastle Directory*; *Norwich Directory*; *Liverpool Directory* (Liverpool, 1766; repr. and ed. G. T. Shaw and I. Shaw, 1907); *The Manchester Directory for the Year 1772* (London, 1772). For occupations see Appendix.

town, not only among and between traditional landed elites and non-landed pseudo-gentry, but between these groups and the "productive" retail and artisanal classes. Among artisans, for example, although masters' punitive power over their journeymen was growing and their relative socioeconomic positions becoming more distant, until the last two decades of the century skilled workers in many trades maintained the ability to stage successful strikes and stoppages to keep up the customary terms of employment or otherwise to attempt to maintain a voice in the processes of commercial capitalism. In conjunction with the growing rates of seasonal and internal migration of labor in urban areas and the decreased economic if not political power of craft guilds, the propensity for "combinations" among workers gave masters less hold over their journeymen and apprentices in many regions than they had previously enjoyed or would do in the future.[81] Secondly, the growth of regional credit and moneylending networks, which drew attorneys, shopkeepers, innholders, cordwainers, weavers and widows, among others, into their webs as suppliers of credit and loans,[82] combined with

[81] C. R. Dobson, *Masters and Men,* chaps. 1 and 4; Robert Malcolmson, "Workers' Combinations in Eighteenth-Century England," in M. Jacob and J. Jacob, eds., *The Origins of Anglo-American Radicalism* (New York, 1984), 149–61. For guilds see Wilson, "Rejection of Deference," 208–10, 298–9; Rogers, *Whigs and Cities,* 358–9.
[82] John Brewer, "Commercialization and Politics," in Neil McKendrick, John Brewer

the increase in local banks (from about a dozen early in the century to 291 in 1799) to link trade, industry and cultural refurbishment to London and international markets; these developments also facilitated middling as well as bourgeois and landed investment and diversification in overseas trade, industry and cultural refurbishment.[83] Urban society was expanding, with the networks of social and economic authority and power becoming more numerous and diffuse than they had been before. The greater density of provincial urban society over the century meant that the urban middling sorts were able to mediate the once unfathomable gulf between rich and poor, creating, as Peter Clark has argued, "a more sectored, multi-linear and diffuse social hierarchy."[84]

In this context, aristocrats and gentlemen neither controlled credit and the money supply nor dominated spending and consumption. As both Borsay and Lorna Weatherill have noted, the growing middling ranks of urban society generated from within their ranks a demand that exceeded that of the upper classes.[85] The upshot was the creation of greater cultural space for middling sorts to act, or envision acting, more independently in political and cultural concerns. Elite or even government clientage could not, on its own, serve as an effective instrument of political control. Indeed, those tradesmen and retailers who found themselves in its grip had all the more reason to chafe at the bit. Particularly in periods of credit contraction, the inequitable workings of the client economy, and especially the distressing proclivity of the great to allow their bills to pile up unpaid at a retailer's or trader's for months

and J. H. Plumb. *The Birth of a Consumer Society* (London, 1982), 204–8; B. L. Anderson, "Provincial Aspects of the Financial Revolution in the Eighteenth Century," *Business History,* 11 (1969), 12–20, "Money and the Structure of Credit in the 18th Century," *Business History,* 12 (1970), 87–98, and "Elizabeth Parkin and Her Investments, 1733–66," *Transactions of the Hunter Archaeological Society,* 10 (1973), 86; Clark, *English Alehouse,* 229–30; Julian Hoppit, *Risk and Failure in English Business, 1700–1800* (Cambridge, 1987), 140–60.

[83] L. S. Pressnell, *Country Banking in the Industrial Revolution* (Oxford, 1956), 10–65, 136, 359; Peter Mathias, "Capital, Credit and Enterprise in the Industrial Revolution," *Journal of European Economic History,* 2 (1973), 125–42; David Cannadine, *Lords and Landlords: Aristocracy and the Towns 1774–1967* (London, 1980); for banking in Newcastle and Norwich see Wilson, "Rejection of Deference," 260–1, 457–60.

[84] An argument also advanced by J. M. Triffit, "Politics and the Urban Community: Parliamentary Boroughs in the Southwest of England, 1710–30" (Oxford University D. Phil. diss., 1985), 15; Peter Clark, introduction, to Clark, ed., *The Transformation of English Provincial Towns 1600–1800* (London, 1984), 30.

[85] Borsay, *Urban Renaissance,* 205–6; Lorna Weatherill, *Consumer Behavior and Material Culture in Britain, 1660–1760* (London, 1988), 192–4. Cf. Thompson, *Customs in Common,* 92–6.

or even years, became the subject of increasingly vocal protest from the middling sorts as early as the 1720s, as some clearly began to view patrician custom as something of a curse, one more unwelcome risk in a social and economic environment beset by them.[86]

This greater autonomy was enacted and expanded, and the anxiety it produced mediated and allayed, in part through the proliferation of clubs and societies formed for self- and public improvement in provincial towns in the decades after 1720. The "clubbing" proclivities among eighteenth-century English people have been imaginatively reconstructed by a number of scholars, who have argued that they lay at the heart of urban sociability and political culture and were the source and support of a variety of independent middling initiatives in local and national life.[87] Unlike print culture as a whole, clubs and societies provided largely homosocial enclaves of conviviality, sociability and social discipline that, among their many manifest and latent functions, endowed their members with greater social and political authority than they could get on their own. Animated by the code of civic patriotism and respectability, voluntary associations were seen by their advocates to benefit the public as well as the private, promoting through social reconstruction both individual character and the public good and forming a dense network for concerted social and political action.[88] The

---

[86] Hence, even in those rather atypical centers where the concentration of Court and gentry patronage was intense, such as Westminster and Bath, clientage produced as much vocal and strident opposition as acquiescence. See, for example, "Cato's Letters," nos. 107–8, *London Journal,* Dec. 15, 22, 1722; *The War Against Spain Declared . . . to Which Is Added a Proposal for Making England the Terror of the Whole World* (London, 1739); *Universal Spectator,* vol. 2 (London, 1756), 145–50; *Newcastle Chronicle,* March 7, 1767; Dec. 22, 1770. For clientage as a political issue in the 1760s see Brewer, "Commercialization and Politics," passim, and for the earlier period see Rogers, *Whigs and Cities,* 168–96. As O'Gorman has noted, even in the dockyard and port towns of Hampshire, where the government's potential for influence was immense, successive Whig ministries were incapable of controlling the electorates: *Voters, Patrons and Parties,* 49–50.

[87] Brewer, "Clubs and Commercialization"; Borsay, *English Urban Renaissance,* 263–83; for the later eighteenth and the early nineteenth century see R. J. Morris, "Voluntary Societies and British Urban Elites, 1780–1850," *HJ,* 26 (1983), 95–118. On the Continent, such associations were much thinner on the ground: See Robert Chartier, *The Cultural Origins of the French Revolution,* trans. Lydia Cochrane (Chapel Hill, 1991), 160–8; Ulrich Im Hof, "German Associations and Politics in the Second Half of the Eighteenth Century," in Eckhart Hellmuth, ed., *The Transformation of Political Culture: England and Germany in the Late Eighteenth Century* (Oxford, 1990), 207–18.

[88] In Norwich there were at least five dozen clubs formed in the period 1715–45 and seventy-eight in 1750–85; in 1749 its 49 box societies for journeymen weavers boasted

shifting social and political contexts of club life thus directly affected
their political significance.

Certainly the clubbing instinct transected provincial urban society,
taking in skilled workers and artisans as well as retailers and the haut
bourgeoisie. The "purse-club habit" was a pronounced feature of journeymen's culture in Newcastle and Norwich by the early eighteenth
century, for example, and friendly societies formed in the 1710s and
1720s endured into the next century.[89] Their numbers expanded with
the growth of trade, allowing "respectable" artisans to participate in
the refurbishment of urban culture in ways that set them off from the
ranks of the unskilled laboring poor. Indeed, prosperity and the ethos
of improvement found expression in an artisan culture which tended to
eschew the polite culture of assemblies, races and concerts, taken to be
the hallmarks of the urban renaissance, for the "rational" pursuits of
book clubs and tavern societies, thus fulfilling the social injunctions to
self- and public improvement while maintaining their own rigid standards of morality, sociability and the public good.[90] Even among skilled
laborers the associational habit had taken root and was used to resist
the structural changes in trade and industry that sought to erode their
independence. The keelmen of Newcastle, for example, well known for
their propensity for "combining" against their employers to keep up
pay and working conditions, built and maintained their own hospital
through voluntary deductions from their wages, staging annual processions in its honor. Many also belonged to a reformation-of-manners
society which prohibited drinking on Sundays and exhorted its members to stay out of jail. Perhaps not surprisingly, the Newcastle magistrates managed to wrest legal control over the charity from the
keelmen in 1723 in order to limit its potential as a strike fund.[91] Other

---

200 members each, or 1 in 5 of the city's adult males. In Newcastle two dozen clubs
and societies can be traced in the first half of the century and four dozen in the second.
By the early nineteenth century, membership in London friendly societies reached
72,829, or 36.6 percent of the adult male population. *British Parliamentary Papers,*
13 (1803–4), 726–8 (thanks to Nick Rogers for this reference).

[89] *Rules and Orders of the Friendly Society of Tailors, Newcastle upon Tyne* (Newcastle,
1825); *Articles, Rules and Regulations of the Tradesmen's Society* (Newcastle, 1820);
Articles, Laws and Rules of the Glassmakers' Friendly Society (Newcastle, 1800);
NNRO, MS 453, History of Norwich.

[90] See, e.g., Bewick, *Memoir,* 101–2 and passim; Jackson, *Hull,* 280–1; Money, *Experience and Identity,* 111–13.

[91] E. R. Turner, "The Keelmen of Newcastle," *AHR,* 21 (1916), 542–5; John Sykes,
Local Records of Northumberland, vol. 1 (Newcastle, 1866), 27; *Journal of John
Wesley,* ed. Nehemiah Curnock, 8 vols., (London, 1910), iii, 14; for the legal battle

friendly societies and convivial clubs among artisans and skilled workers, such as those which proliferated in Norwich in the 1740s, were
more fortunate in maintaining their independence from employers and
magistrates alike, protecting members from the worst aspects of economic hardship while also being careful to contribute to civic charities
– a key aspect of social differentiation within urban milieus and a litmus
test of independence and respectability.[92]

The contribution of such self-help and regulatory associations to the
public and national welfare was clear to contemporaries, who believed
they enabled the fair and disciplined to stave off ruin and promoted
trade and prosperity in the national and local domains.[93] Other kinds
of societies, too, whether devoted to sociability, pleasure or scientific
and medical inquiry and whether under the guises of competitive arch-
ery, annual feasts, philosophical explorations or weekly drinking sessions, were believed to contribute to the public good and civic
patriotism by promoting rationality, knowledge and politeness.[94]
Equally important, however, were the growing numbers of specifically
political clubs that emerged in provincial towns, which multiply shaped
contemporary notions of the nation and the public interest, mirroring
in their leadership, provenance and function the changing social contours and political aspirations of urban society.

Prior to 1740, political societies and associations tended to be thinner
on the ground than they would be thereafter, and to be organized under
the wing of political elites. The clubs formed during the succession
years may not have matched in glamour or literary elan the famous
aristocratic and gentlemen's political clubs of Anne's reign, but they
still managed to serve as important headquarters for political strateg-
izing among party leaders. The Hanover Club, formed in 1712, served
as a base for metropolitan Whig leaders to plan their parliamentary and
extra-parliamentary strategies, from ousting the Tories in office to
stamping out disaffection in the streets. The Duke of Newcastle, a
member, was responsible for encouraging the formation of Loyal So-

with the Corporation see Joyce Ellis, "A Dynamic Society: Social Relations in Newcastle upon Tyne, 1600–1760," in Clark, *Transformation,* 209–12.
[92] See note 22 and *Norwich Mercury,* Aug. 11, 1753.
[93] See, e.g., the pronouncements of the heads of the Societies of Journeymen Weavers
in Norwich, *Norwich Mercury,* Aug. 11, 1753, on their actions against a fraudulent
trader currently in Norwich jail.
[94] Sykes, *Local Records,* i, 222; *Liverpool General Advertiser,* Oct. 12, 1770; NNRO,
MS 122, Transactions of the Society of the United Friars, i, 1785–94; R. Schofield,
The Lunar Society of Birmingham (London, 1963).

cieties, or Mughouses, in London, whose middling and gentlemen members were wont to bash Tory hopes and Tory heads with equal impunity.[95] In provincial towns, too, such as Norwich, Exeter and Bristol, complementary and competing "loyal societies," organized with the sanction or encouragement of local elites, sought to aggrandize their respective parties' causes in street theater and brawls as well as in the occasionally more sedate local and national elections. The Artillery Company of Norwich orchestrated pitched street battles with Tory and Jacobite supporters in various parishes on anniversary days, and the Loyal Society of Worsted Weavers in Norwich, an ostensible friendly society of master weavers, organized journeymen voters for city elections. The Tory Loyal Society of Bristol, founded in 1710 to further philanthropist Edward Colston's brand of High Church Toryism, was implicated in the serious riots that disrupted the city in 1714; it also organized addresses and electoral activities before the arrest of many of its leading members for Jacobitism in 1715–16.[96]

After the succession crisis had passed, more genteel political clubs appeared which sought to consolidate the urban bases of Whig and opposition support. The Whig Constitution Club in Norwich and the Tory Recorder's Club that met at Eubank's in Newcastle were two such clubs, predominantly elite in membership, that combined politics and conviviality in their quarterly meeting and annual feasts, allowing members to negotiate political strategies and alliances. The Sea Serjeants, Cycle Club and Club of 27 in Wales, as well as various masonic lodges in the Midlands and North, were used by Jacobite and High Church Tory gentry to formalize organization and political connections among themselves and their lesser supporters (thus doing in the regional context what party clubs like the Loyal Brotherhood and Cocoa Tree did in the parliamentary). In Bristol the Steadfast Society, founded in 1737 by Tory leaders, coordinated parish electoral societies in their efforts against the Whig Corporation.[97] At a national level, religious,

[95] For the Augustan clubs, such as the Kit Kat, October Club and Cocoa Club, see John Timbs, *Clubs and Club Life in London* (London, 1908); for the Hanover Club see *The Englishman,* ed. Rae Blanchard (Oxford, 1955), Oct. 19, 1715, and Rogers, *Whigs and Cities,* 365–6; for the Loyal Societies see James Fitts, "Newcastle's Mob," *Albion,* 5 (1973), 41–9.
[96] For the Artillery Company, see Chapter 8; *Articles of Agreement ... of the Loyal Society of Worsted Weavers in the City of Norwich* (Norwich, 1726); for the Colston societies see *An Account of the Riots, Tumults, and Other Treasonable Practices Since His Majesty's Accession to the Throne* (London, 1715); Barry, "Cultural Life of Bristol," 176–7.
[97] *Norwich Mercury,* May 9, 23, June 6, 1741; *Newcastle Courant,* April 18, 1747; Philip

philanthropic and commercial associations like the Georgia Society, the Society for Promoting Christian Knowledge, the Sons of Clergy, the Protestant Dissenting Deputies and various merchant societies also created national networks that could be drawn upon for political purposes while educating their memberships in the techniques of petitioning and parliamentary lobbying. The patriot opposition to Walpole in particular owed a great deal to such associations, because they provided crucial, extra-institutional bases through which alliances could form between otherwise disparate groups.[98] At the same time, such societies helped maintain elite leadership of organized politicking and helped construct the vertical identities among the middling and lesser sorts upon which party politics depended.

However, the leadership of and initiative for political clubs began to shift, slowly yet surely, in the 1740s as middling clubs and societies not only became more numerous but began to engage in national political affairs in more spontaneous and autonomous ways. Beginning with the emergence to national prominence of Admiral Edward Vernon, whose capture of Porto Bello in South America in 1740 did so much to galvanize national imperial aspirations and undermine the Walpolean ministry, middling clubs and societies proclaimed their patriotism by supporting trade, liberty and empire against those who would undermine them. The welter of Vernon memorabilia, the plethora of processions and celebrations in his honor staged by tavern and masonic societies, and the outpourings of ballads and drinking songs attesting to his patriotic stature all indirectly indicate the consolidation of a new market for politics in which clubs played an important role.[99] These trends continued even after patriot opposition collapsed in the face of its leaders' apostasy. The outbreak of the '45 brought with it an out-

---

Jenkins, *The Making of a Ruling Class: The Glamorgan Gentry, 1640–1790* (Cambridge, 1983), 156–7, and "Jacobites and Freemasons in Eighteenth Century Wales," *Welsh Historical Review,* 9 (1979), 391–406; Rogers, *Whigs and Cities,* 277–8; for the Loyal Brotherhood and the Cocoa Tree see Linda Colley, *In Defiance of Oligarchy* (Cambridge, 1982), 71–5.

[98] Jenkins, *Ruling Class,* 162; Colley, *Defiance,* pp. 100–1; *An Account of the Society for Promoting Christian Knowledge* (London, 1758); SPCK Archives, Abstract Letter Books, 15 (1729–30), 26 (1732–3); *Newcastle Courant,* Aug. 18, 1725; Diary of John Thomlinson, in J. C. Hodgson, ed., *Six North Country Diaries* (Surtees Society, 118, 1910), 69, 135–44; N. C. Hunt, *Two Early Political Associations* (Oxford, 1961); Dr. Williams's Library, Thompson's List, MS 38.6/2, fols. 2–3; for mercantile associations and lobbying see Alison Gilbert Olson, *Making the Empire Work: London and American Interest Groups, 1690–1790* (Cambridge, 1992).

[99] See Chapter 3.

break of loyal associations (male and female) in the provinces which provided, among other things, a ready market for the staggering quantities of plates, bowls, mugs and punchbowls ultimately produced in honor of the rebellion's suppressor, the Duke of Cumberland.[100] As the decade progressed, societies were founded that undertook local and national cultural and political initiatives for themselves. Confronted with apparently waning national strength and widespread fears of "effeminacy" that were fanned in the 1740s and 1750s by a variety of commentators and events, middle-class men and women formed secular and religious societies which sought to stem the alleged tides of national profligacy, luxury and weakness. The parish-based Religious Societies in the metropolis, the Anti-Gallican Society, the Society for the Encouragement of Arts, Manufacturing and Commerce and the Marine Society – the last three of which maintained provincial and even colonial memberships – are four examples of philanthropic societies with broad middle-class support devoted to making Britain more virtuous and redoubtable, less permeable to French influence and a more formidable counter to French power and aspirations.[101]

The range of contributors to such patriotic initiatives and the extraordinary density and social heterogeneity of urban clubs and associations in this period are nowhere better revealed than in the list of subscribers to the Troop Society, formed by the Marine Society's founder, Jonas Hanway, in 1760 to support the widows and children of British soldiers in North America and Germany. "Gentlemen's" and tradesmen's clubs in Liverpool, Newcastle, Manchester and Sheffield, freemasons in Portsmouth and Wapping, a society of laborers in Knightsbridge Town, Devon, dissenting chapels in Newcastle and Exeter, servants' clubs, friendly societies, a variety of tavern societies, assembly collections in Bath and Lincoln, a "Club of Old Maids" and the "young Ladies at

[100] R. L. Robson, *Catalogue of the Collection of English Pottery in the Department of British and Medieval Antiquities and Ethnography, British Museum* (London, 1905), 138–48, 179; Anthony Ray, *English Delftware Pottery in the Robert Hall Warren Collection* (Oxford, 1968), 112, 125; for volunteer associations see Chapter 3.
[101] For the parish societies see William Dodd, *Unity Recommended . . . Preached Before the Religious Societies in and About London, at Their Annual Meeting* (London, 1759); for the Anti-Gallicans and Marine Society see Chapter 3; for the Society for the Arts see Colley, *Britons*, 88–92. For provincial and imperial memberships see *Norwich Mercury,* April 1, 1758; March 10, Aug. 11, 1759; April 12, 1760; *Rules and Orders of the Society . . . for the Encouragement of Arts, Manufacture and Commerce* (London, 1758); Sykes, *Local Records,* 244–6; Jonas Hanway, *A Letter from a Member of the Marine Society, Shewing the Piety, Generosity and Utility of Their Design* (London, 1757).

Mrs. Hill's Boarding School, Bristol'' were among the groups that expressed, through subscriptions to the charity, their agreement with Hanway on the necessity of not allowing "the wealth and luxury of peace"
to dull the nation's martial spirit.[102] Clearly, the politics of trade and
empire and the issues raised by state expansion worked to galvanize
political consciousness and civic patriotism in new directions, stimulating merchants, traders and shopkeepers, journeymen and servants,
and men and women to initiate political activities on their own or join
national campaigns. The dense social networks created by clubs and
societies in provincial towns by midcentury enabled the London-based
patriotic societies of the 1750s to succeed, linking national and imperial
health, provincial urban culture and prosperity in ways that reflected
and shaped the public-spirited impulses of the citizenry. At the same
time, by their very existence, both local and national associations endorsed a participatory model of citizenship which allowed private individuals to appropriate, define and channel "patriotism" through their
actions in the public sphere.

The middle-class clubs and societies of the Wilkite period, then, were
not new, but they were most disruptive of the patterns of elite leadership or sponsorship evinced by political clubs prior to this time. They
were also more forthcoming in articulating an overtly radicalized vision
of the polity that parliamentary elites would not necessarily sanction.
At least sixteen distinct political clubs supported the causes of radical
politics in Newcastle between 1769 and 1784, with such evocative
names as the Sydney Club, Revolution Society, Capodoseian Society,
Friends to Legal Liberty, Constitutional Club, Philosophical Society,
Friends to Humanity and the Newcastle House of Lords. Whatever their
specific political purpose, all of these clubs met in inns and taverns,
such as Swarley's "Liberty Hall" and Mordue's, and pursued within
fairly unstructured and egalitarian settings their members' devotion to
rational discussion, debate and politics. They mirrored the political sensibilities of their middling and artisanal memberships. Bewick was a
member of one of the many clubs that met at Swarley's in Groat Market, and he considered it "the most Rational Society . . . I ever knew
– the few Rules were only Verbal . . . and the first one was this, that it
was expected that every member should behave with decorum and like
a Gentleman.'' The fourpenny weekly admission fee for members and

---

[102] [Jonas Hanway], *An Account of the Society for the Encouragement of British Troops
in Germany and North America* (London, 1760).

their friends was spent on beer only; and even this modest sum produced excess funds which were disbursed to charities at Christmas and
Easter.[103]

Other clubs observed more formalized and exacting rules of behavior. The Newcastle Philosophical Society, formed in the midst of the
American crisis, regularly debated such provocative questions as
"whether a republic or limited monarchy be the best form of government" and "whether the practice of imprisonment for debt be a dis-
advantage or an advantage" (both were decided in favor of the former).
Yet the Society combined an egalitarian internal structure with an obsession with secrecy and "decorum" (that is, "all the Freedom of
debate that is consistent with a decent attention to established opinions") that could create difficult situations for extremists. The president
and vice-presidents were elected by members every four meetings (thus
attending to the hallowed principle of rotation of power); all questions
and resolutions were decided on by ballot; and no member could speak
twice before everyone had the chance to speak. But drinking was not
permitted, and members could be voted out for refusing to comply with
the Society's rules. Hence, in 1775 they expelled Thomas Spence for
publishing his (previously debated) set of proposals for land reform,
The Real Rights of Man, "in the manner of a halfpenny ballad and
having it hawked about the streets to the manifest dishonour of the
society." The publication of his arguments was contrary to the Society's regulations, and their content – advocating the equal redistribution
of property among the entire English population – clearly did not have
due regard for "established opinions" among the property-respecting
tradesmen in the society, who considered such views "erroneous" and
"levelling."[104]

Debating societies, one of the more distinctive as well as most widespread features of provincial urban sociability in the 1760s and 1770s,
with their low admission fees and relatively open membership, were in
fact frequently the sites for struggles among the middling sort over the
proper balance between decorum and free exchange, the recurrent battle
to prevent liberty from turning into license. In Birmingham, the Free
Debating Society, comprising local artisans, who used the meetings to

[103] Bewick, *Memoir,* 101–2.
[104] *Newcastle Journal,* Nov. 4, 1775; Feb. 15, 1777; *Rules of the Philosophical Society
   of Newcastle upon Tyne* (Newcastle, 1777); Mackenzie, *Historical Account,* 399n;
   Newcastle Chronicle, Nov. 25, 1775.

canvass opinions on such issues as the Middlesex election and the Coercive Acts, soon acquired a reputation for disorderly behavior at meetings which ultimately resulted in the formation of rival societies with higher admission and membership standards.[105] The debating club in Whitehaven met once a week in 1775, but in the context of the divisive war with the colonies may have jettisoned debate in favor of electing a member to read the *Cumberland Pacquet* to the rest of the club each week. Others, like the "Conversation Society" that met at the Angel Inn in Manchester and the society that debated at the Maidenhead in Salisbury, eschewed national politics altogether in favor of the more genteel topics of social philosophy and local affairs.[106]

In general, however, the requirements of ordered and moderate behavior did not preclude vigorous politicking by club members. Meeting in the inns and taverns that mushroomed in provincial towns, clubs and societies like the Revolution Club in Newport, Isle of Wight, which annually commemorated the fifth of November and "the duty and honour of resisting Stuart Tyrants"; the "Patriotic Society" at the Angel in Leeds, formed to commemorate the day of Wilkes's release from King's Bench prison; and the Independent Society in Bristol, devoted to supporting "those measures . . . expressive of Loyalty to the King and . . . the Independency of the People" – all had as their goal a social and political reconstruction capable of reconfiguring the terms of social exchange and political power. As one writer argued, political associations operated from the premise that "government is not an intricate science, but is level to the capacities of those who have *common sense* . . . every person who *feels its consequences* can tell . . . whether it be ill or well-administered."[107] Organized according to the same principles of equality, accountability and exclusivity that were central to demands for political reform, they created environments in which social and political aspirations could be formed, negotiated and lived by. "It is in such societies," a member of the Constitutional Club of Newcastle, Northumberland and Durham wrote to the SSBR in London, "that the persecuted individual finds a certain refuge; and in them, freedom and

[105] *Aris's Birmingham Gazette,* April 25, May 2, July 4, 1774; Money, *Experience and Identity,* 111–13.
[106] *Cumberland Pacquet,* Feb. 2, Apr. 20, 1775; *Manchester Mercury,* Jan. 1, 8, 1771; *Salisbury Journal,* March 13, June 12, 1775. See also Mary Thrale, "London Debating Societies in the 1790s," *HJ,* 32 (1989), 57–86.
[107] *Salisbury Journal,* Nov. 25, 1776; *Leeds Mercury,* April 24, 1770; *Felix Farley's Bristol Journal,* March 11, 1769. Quotation from *Newcastle Journal,* Aug. 25, 1776.

the constitution meet with able and determined advocates.''[108] Against
the urban ethos that politeness and politics, civility and partisanship
were incompatible, radical clubs proffered their own definitions of the
public good and upheld their own stringent standards of decorum that
were just as strongly aimed at reconstructing the terms of social authority and political power. Their success in effecting a transformation
of sensibility was not doubted by their supporters or critics, a fact
demonstrated not least in the imitation of their strategies by parliamentary leaders, who beginning in the 1770s formed political clubs and
political commemorative societies in order to compete with radical associations for extra-parliamentary publicity and support.[109]

Of course, clubs and societies did not promote only dissident kinds
of political sensibilities. The freemasons, dedicated to propagating the
values of charity, brotherhood and the advance of knowledge, provide
perhaps the best illustration of predominantly middle-class societies
which could simultaneously promote social solidarities and nationalistic
consciousness while remaining politically protean (and becoming, by
the third quarter of the century, predominantly provincial).[110] In the
first half of the century, when the numbers of masonic lodges experi-
enced their first spurt of provincial growth, many of the lodges were
resolutely political in their attachments and orientation, their frequently
Tory and Jacobite leadership drawing them into the networks of oppositionist politics. Such was the case in Alnwick, Chester, Bristol,
Bath, Birmingham, Newcastle, Norwich, York and Salisbury.[111] The
affinity with opposition patriotism seemed to continue into the 1760s,
by which time the number of lodges had more than doubled, and lodges
rallied round the cause of Wilkes and Liberty in droves.[112] Yet the type

[108] *Newcastle Journal,* July 4, 1772; see also *Norwich Mercury,* Jan. 2, 1769; *Farley's Bristol Journal,* Nov. 17, 1770.
[109] Such as the Hampshire Club of Winchester, presided over by the Whig Duke of Bolton; the Friends of Cruger and Burke in Bristol, the Gentlemen, Merchants and Tradesmen of the Golden Fleece in Liverpool; and the Friends of Hobart in Norwich: *Salisbury Journal,* Oct. 28, 1776; Nov. 11, 1782; *Farley's Bristol Journal,* Nov. 8, 1775; Nov. 7, 1776; *Liverpool Advertiser,* Oct. 12, 1770; *Norfolk Chronicle,* Sept. 22, 1787.
[110] See Margaret Jacob, *The Radical Enlightenment: Pantheists, Freemasons and Republicans* (London, 1981); and Jenkins, ''Jacobites and Freemasons.''
[111] John Money, ''Freemasonry and the Fabric of Loyalism in Hanoverian England,'' in Hellmuth, ed., *Transformation,* 270, 256–7. See also Jenkins, ''Jacobites and Freemasons,'' 401–2; Monod, *Jacobitism and the English People,* 300–3; John Strachan, *Northumbrian Masonry and the Development of the Craft in England* (London, 1898), 84–5; *Norwich Gazette,* Jan. 7, 1721; Dec. 8, 1739; *Salisbury Journal,* Nov. 18, 1740.
[112] Brewer, ''Clubs and Commercialization,'' 232–3; for numbers see Money, ''Free-

of patriotism supported by freemasonry was compatible with a variety of political positions. Their sensibilities were summed up by one propagandist in his description of a Northumbrian lodge's anniversary revels in 1773, when its members' appropriately pro-imperial and manly (francophobic) tastes were lauded as instances of superior sensibility: No "French *quelque chose* and ragout / Nor foreign wines do here appear, / But London porter, Berwick beer, and Good rum punch I see, / Which our plantations do produce / . . . The Brethren . . . from the bottles draw the corks, / And toast Great George our King . . ."[113] This type of nationalistic bonhomie allowed freemasonry to be taken up with equal fervor by those with conservative as well as reformist political agendas, as John Money has argued.[114] Indeed, the freemasons in many ways embodied the contending impulses in Enlightenment cultural practices, combining respect for hierarchy with a moderate egalitarianism, toleration and a disregard for social rank with social exclusivity, and devotion to rationality with fascination for the irrational, mystical and secretive.[115]

Clubs and societies, then, offered in their internal organization and animating principles a variety of definitions of politics, as well as particularized and sectional definitions of the national interest. They were central to structuring and sustaining extra-parliamentary politics, embodying forms of sociability and engagement capable of shaping their members' social and political relations with each other, with civic culture and with the nation-state itself. Indeed, in the contexts of war and state and imperial expansion, the clubs and societies of provincial towns provided important sites where the public interest was monitored, the "nation" multiply constituted and defined, and the boundaries of citizenship negotiated. Equally important, they supported and shaped the gender identities being formulated elsewhere in the political public sphere, upholding a homosocial, predominantly heterosexual and masculine ethos of conviviality and politics that staked out both physically and ideologically a male domain within the socially mixed and potentially transgressive spaces of urban society. Freemasons were not alone in seeing women and "effeminate" men as potential sources of con-

---

masonry," appendix. There were 12 provincial lodges in 1721, 71 in 1750 and 200 in 1760.

[113] Sykes, *Local Records,* 262; Strachan, *Northumbrian Masonry,* pp. 84–5; see also *Norwich Gazette,* Dec. 8, 1739, and John Smith, *A Sermon Preached . . . On Constituting the St. Alfred Lodge of Free and Accepted Masons* (Norwich, 1770).

[114] Money, "Freemasonry," 259–61.

[115] See Chartier, *Cultural Origins,* 162–8.

tamination that would undermine the rationality and fraternity of their project.[116] Radical club life in the Wilkite period also participated in this preoccupation, when Wilkes's pornographic *Essay on Women,* his own libertine lifestyle (including alleged participation in orgies as a member of the notorious Hell-Fire Club) and his very public stands for the liberty of all male subjects could mobilize a quite explicit sexual, as well as political, libertarianism among his supporters. Wilkes was "free from cock to wig," in the words of a humble (male) admirer.[117] Certainly there were contending masculinities and femininities at play in eighteenth-century society,[118] and homosexuals, women, "men of sentiment" and others whose practices or performances contested the masculinist, aggressive ethos of the political sphere were actors in club life, as in eighteenth-century urban culture more generally, where their presence was required not least for various forms of sexual and social commerce that the new venues of urban culture both promoted and denied.[119] But in the main, by the 1760s and 1770s clubs and societies formed by middling and upper-middle-class men within the provincial urban domain tended to appropriate to their service the particularized versions of masculinity and rationality endorsed by both oppositionist and loyalist patriotism, privileging their members' status as heads of households and citizens while marginalizing both the feminine and the effeminate in the constructions of sociability and politics. Male club

[116] Jacob, *Radical Enlightenment,* 206–8.
[117] Raymond Postgate, *That Devil Wilkes* (London, 1930), 140–5; George Rude, *Wilkes and Liberty* (London, 1963), 85–9; quotation from Richard Sennett, *The Fall of Public Man* (New York, 1977), 103; see also Chapter 4. The voting qualification at the mock election at Garrat was "having enjoyed a woman in the open air within the district": quoted in John Brewer, "Theater and Counter-Theater in Georgian Politics," *Radical History Review,* 22 (1979–80), 8.
[118] See Michael Kimmel, "The Contemporary 'Crisis' of Masculinity in Historical Perspective," in Harry Brod, ed., *The Making of Masculinities: The New Men's Studies* (Boston, 1987), 121–53; Randolph Trumbach, "The Birth of the Queen: Sodomy and the Emergence of Gender Equality in Eighteenth-Century London," in Martin B. Duberman, Martha Vicinus and George Chaucey, Jr., eds., *Hidden from History: Reclaiming the Gay and Lesbian Past* (New York, 1989), 129–40, and "London's Sapphists: From Three Sexes to Four Genders in the Making of Modern Culture," in Julia Epstein and Kristina Straub, eds., *Body Guards: The Cultural Politics of Gender Ambiguity* (London, 1991), 112–41.
[119] Klein, "Gender, Conversation and the Public Sphere"; Trumbach, "Sex, Gender and Sexual Identity," 188–93; Terry Castle, *Masquerade and Civilization* (Stanford, 1986); see also Dena Goodman, "Governing the Republic of Letters: The Politics of Culture in the French Enlightenment," *History of European Ideas,* 13 (1991), 183–99. For women's clubs and societies see, e.g., HL, Montagu MS, MO 247, 1734; Stubbs, *Early Exhibitions of Art in Liverpool,* 51–41. Cf. Catherine Hall, *White, Male and Middle Class* (New York, 1988), 102–4.

life in its social composition and rationale helped delineate the public, political sphere as the masculine counterpart to domesticity and private life (even as it simultaneously displayed the fissures at which such definitions could be contested). It was thus instrumental in constructing the identity of the citizen, the nature of the state and the contours of the political nation in social and gendered terms.

III. INSTITUTIONAL ARTICULATIONS

Our examination of the interaction of cultural politics and political culture in the "urban renaissance" has focussed so far on its informal arenas and contexts. The institutional articulations of provincial urban refurbishment were also crucial in negotiating social and political relationships. Assembly rooms, theaters and hospitals proliferated in provincial towns in the decades after 1730, ostentatious constituents of a new civic culture that sought to document and enact residents' aspirations to civility, refinement and patriotism.[120] Central to this effort was deployment of the contending definitions of citizenship articulated elsewhere in the public sphere, which could have a profound, if variegated, impact on local political relationships. Voluntary hospitals for the care of the sick or maimed poor, which sprouted up in provincial towns in the middle decades of the century, provide a cogent example. Part of a wider series of charitable and reforming initiatives that were galvanized by a convergence of pro-imperial, religious, scientific and moralistic concerns, voluntary hospitals emerged as a distinctive and much-lauded solution to the problems of unemployment, poverty and illness in urban communities while satisfying both the mercantilist imperative to population expansion and the "improving" impulses of the propertied through the surveillance, medical treatment and attempted reform of the poor.[121] In their management, support and representation in the local community, voluntary hospitals also revealed some of the

[120] Admirably documented by Borsay, *Urban Renaissance,* passim and appendices.
[121] See my "Urban Culture and Political Activism in Hanoverian England: The Example of Voluntary Hospitals," in Hellmuth, ed., *Transformation,* 165–4. Between 1720 and 1799, 5 such hospitals were established in the metropolis and 33 in the provinces. For related efforts, from lying-in hospitals and workhouses to prison reform, see Trumbach, "Sex, Gender and Sexual Identity," 194–9; M. G. Jones, *The Charity School Movement: A Study of 18th Century Puritanism in Action* (Cambridge, 1938); M. E. DeLacy, *Prison Reform in England 1700–1850* (Stanford, 1986); Donna Andrew, *Philanthropy and Police: London Charity in the Eighteenth Century* (Princeton, 1989).

social tensions and political divisions that they, and institutions like them, could support as well as accommodate, upholding a variety of definitions of politics while bolstering the claims of middling and artisanal men to subject status.

Most striking about these hospitals' internal structures was their openness (by eighteenth-century standards), which aimed at mobilizing a broad range of community, county and even national support. They combined that ubiquitous method of capital mobilization in the eighteenth century, the subscription, with a participatory structure of government. With few exceptions, the management and administration of provincial hospitals were entirely in the hands of all male subscribers of 2 guineas per annum and benefactors of £20, otherwise known as "governors," each of whom had the right to recommend patients for the hospitals' services and to have one vote each in the management of affairs. As the general Board of Governors, they met quarterly to transact extraordinary business, inspect accounts and elect the weekly house committee which oversaw the daily administration of the hospital.[122] Since duty on the house committee revolved among the governors, all minimum subscribers either became active in hospital administration or hired proxies to do it for them. The principles of accessible management and single voting were thus incorporated into provincial hospital government, at least for its male members. Women, on the other hand, who made up between 10 and 20 percent of annual hospital contributors and up to 25 percent of weekly ones, had to exercise their privileges by proxy, as they did in Anglican and dissenting charity schools.[123]

---

[122] These remarks on hospital government are based upon a sample of 12 provincial and 4 metropolitan hospitals: See my "Urban Culture," 168n. For specific examples, see TWA, 672/168, [Newcastle, Northumberland and Durham] Infirmary Annual Reports, April 1751–3; NNRO, NNH 14/1, Rules and Orders for the Norfolk and Norwich Hospital, 1773; F. F. Waddy, *A History of Northampton General Hospital* (Northampton, 1974), 6. Variations to this plan gave greater power to the largest subscribers: *Rules of the Public Infirmary at Liverpool* (Liverpool, 1749), 4; *Statutes for an Infirmary at Lincoln* (Lincoln, 1745), 7–8.

[123] The figures for women's contributions are based on lists from Newcastle, Norwich, Bath and Liverpool infirmaries and the St. George's and London Infirmary: TWA, 875/1, Printed Annual Reports of the Newcastle Dispensary, 1777; 672/168, Printed Annual Reports of the Infirmary, 1753; *The Nature, Rise and Progress of the General Infirmary at Bath* (Bath, 1754); *Norfolk Chronicle,* March 8, 1771; *Account of the Proceedings of St. George's Hospital, Hyde Park Corner* (London, 1735); *List of Governors and Contributors to the London Infirmary* (London, 1754). Women made up 25% of the weekly contributors to the Bath Hospital, compared with 12% of the

Equally notable, the internal management of these charities incorporated standards that clashed with the practices of patrician society and the structure of the dominant political system. First, the tendency of closed and nonaccountable administration to promote corruption was explicitly acknowledged in hospital regulations. The published rules of the Newcastle, Northumberland and Durham Infirmary stressed that "management is entirely in the Hands of the Governors . . . so that it cannot be perverted or misapplied."[124] Furthermore, there were no rules or requirements that allocated greater power to men of wealth and position, who like all other subscribers of 2 guineas per year had one vote each in the management of affairs. Indeed, the potential for undue influence arising from the elites who usually acted as hospital officers was circumscribed, first, by the use of ballots during contested elections, and second, by the rule, emphasized repeatedly in annual reports, that the books and accounts be available for inspection by *any* subscriber, and an abstract of them printed yearly "for the Satisfaction of the Public."[125] And in a direct challenge to the client economy, which allowed patrons' bills to pile up unattended to for months or even years, persons whose subscriptions were not paid up were prohibited from voting and recommending patients. Even the relations with the local tradesmen who supplied the charities were regulated in hospital by-laws in a way that approximated the commercial ideal of equitable exchange of services, with tradesmen competing for hospital contracts via sealed bids, and hospital committees remitting prompt payment for services rendered.[126] Clearly, the customary operation of clientage was seen as an obstacle to the efficient management of the charity, and it was structured to avoid its disruptive influence.

The pattern of subscriptions, which accounted for one-half to three-quarters of provincial hospitals' annual income, reveals the socially heterogeneous participation in voluntary hospitals. The proportion of town and county elites varied, from 10 percent in the case of the Liverpool Infirmary to 52 percent for Norwich, but the remaining contributors were dominated by merchants, professionals, retailers and

---

annual. For women in charity school management see Hall, *White, Male and Middle Class,* 101–4.

[124] *A Report of the State of the Infirmary* (Newcastle, 1753).

[125] *Rules of the Public Infirmary at Liverpool,* 4–9; *Statutes for an Infirmary at Lincoln,* 11–12, 14; *Report of the State of the Infirmary.*

[126] *Rules of the Public Infirmary at Liverpool,* 10; NNRO, NNH 14/1, Rules for the Norfolk and Norwich Hospital; *Report of the State of the Infirmary.*

artisans.[127] Further, despite what could only be considered the onerous obligations of office, close to 88 percent of the contributors in both Newcastle and Norwich subscribed the 2 guineas per annum that transformed them into "governors" of the charities. This sum could be met in goods and services rather than coin. In Newcastle, the Company of Wallers, Bricklayers and Plasterers contributed 48,000 bricks and twenty dozen bowls of lime for the building; Joseph Barber, bookseller and librarian, gave books to the value of £4. 4*s.* to cure the mental and spiritual, as well as corporeal, maladies of the patients; Dr. John Rotheram donated the proceeds from a course of lectures on experimental philosophy.[128] Other gifts from local tradesmen, craftsmen and artists to provincial hospitals ranged from galley pots, earthenware and linen and wool for bedding to clocks, medicine and communion plates for hospital chapels. Even friendly societies and box clubs subscribed generously to the hospitals in coin and services, thus allowing craftsmen and journeymen to participate directly in civic culture and in the respectability and status it imparted.[129] Just as the participation of aspiring bourgeois in assembly-room culture sprang from a self-conscious attempt to identify themselves with the elite, independent artisans and journeymen could underline their aspirations to respectability and citizenship through the scope of institutionalized charity, which provided a source of independence from the sort of "face-to-face" paternalism that some historians believe they wished to preserve but which their participation in hospitals and friendly societies equally suggests they wanted to escape from.

The contrasts in patterns of participation and attendance provided by the new leisure facilities of provincial towns underscore the significance of institutions like charity hospitals in encompassing a wider civic community. The building of assembly rooms and theaters theoretically mobilized community support as they democratized or "commercialized" elite culture.[130] However, not only were these venues enormously expensive to build, accounting for the largest proportion of the expenditures on culture in this period, but subscriptions for building (which

[127] George McLoughlin, *A Short History of the First Liverpool Infirmary 1749–1824* (London, 1978), 94–7; *Newcastle Courant,* March 9–16, 1751ff.; *Norfolk Chronicle,* March 9, July 13, 1771.

[128] *Newcastle Courant,* April 6–13, 1751; Mackenzie, *Historical Account,* 502–3.

[129] *Newcastle Courant,* March 23–30, April 6–13, 1751; P. M. Horsley, *Eighteenth Century Newcastle* (Newcastle, 1971), 114, 130n; *Report of the State of the Infirmary.*

[130] See, e.g., J. H. Plumb, "The Commercialization of Leisure in Eighteenth Century England," in *Birth of a Consumer Society,* 275–80.

entitled contributors to a say in subsequent management) were allocated in shares ranging from £25 to £200.[131] Subscribers were thus invariably drawn from the wealthiest inhabitants and most important occupations in the community. Not surprisingly, the internal structures of these cultural venues reflected the predominance of wealth and status, privileging class over gender as the primary demarcation of inclusion. Theater Royals, for example, with their formalized interiors and pricier tickets, were designed to emphasize the respectability and "civilizing" status of the stage and the civility of provincial urban culture in a riposte to the more lively and unlicensed theaters that still brought together a volatile cross-section of social classes for the display of emotion and spectacle as well as political and cultural debate.[132] More successful in the goal of social differentiation were assemblies. Their social spaces were strictly regulated according to prescribed rules governing the use of the rooms, the formation of minuets and dances, and the arrival and departure of carriages, all according to social rank and position (while also affording upper-middle-class women a valued status as arbiters of sociability and decorum in conversation and at tea tables).[133] Although relatively modest annual and daily admission fees lowered the social barriers to participation thereafter, such arenas would work to cultivate aspirations and foster a sense of cultural identity with the elite. Indeed, their implicit purpose as well as organization mitigated against such a function: In aiming to create a homogeneous and modestly inclusive elite culture, assembly rooms, concert halls and institutions like them embodied the values and imperatives of polite society, with deference and acquiescence to rank being quite literally built into their structures.

Clearly, voluntary hospitals provided specific opportunities for ordinary citizens to become involved in institutional civic affairs. How

---

[131] See C. W. Chalkin, "Capital Expenditure on Building for Cultural Purposes in Provincial England, 1730–1830," *Business History,* 22 (1980), 51–70; R. J. Broadbent, *Annals of the Liverpool Stage* (Liverpool, 1908), 60; Gateshead Public Library, Cotesworth MSS, *Meeting of the Subscribers for Building New Assembly Rooms in Newcastle, at the Turk's Head, 7 Feb. 1774.*

[132] For the continuing political role of theater see my forthcoming study of the provincial stage, *Staging the Nation: Theater, Culture and Modernity in the English Provinces, 1720–1820.* See also Henry Pedicord, *The Theatrical Public in the Time of Garrick* (New York, 1954), and J. Jefferson Looney, "Cultural Life in the Provinces: Leeds and York, 1720–80," in A. L. Beier, D. Cannadine and J. Rosenheim, eds., *The First Modern Society: Essays in Honour of Lawrence Stone* (Cambridge, 1989), 483–510.

[133] NRO, Blackett (Maften) MSS, ZBL 228, *Rules for Regulating the Assemblies in Newcastle upon Tyne* [Newcastle, 1776]; Klein, "Gender, Conversation and the Public Sphere."

did they affect local social and political relationships? Obviously, participation in civic charity, which had hallowed and centuries-old roots in most urban communities, need not have been a transformative or radicalizing experience. In the competitive social milieus of provincial towns, such participation afforded the aspiring new opportunities to mix and associate with their betters, or permitted the demonstration of managerial skills that could lead to paid posts.[134] Where hospital anniversaries became occasions for prestigious fund-raising events such as music festivals, as in Bristol, Birmingham, Salisbury and Norwich, associational philanthropy could be appropriated as a badge of fashionable, genteel culture, bringing together town and country notables in a dazzling display of the enlightened munificence of wealth and rank which refracted onto even the most modest participants.[135]

However, the impact of hospitals on local relationships was more complex than merely aiding the ambitious. Both the patriotic motives and financial requirements of associational charity necessitated the conscious invention by its proponents of spheres of public activity that were meant both to compensate for the inactivity of the state and to be inviolable to partisan and sectarian antagonisms. As Jonas Hanway argued, on behalf of the Marine Society, the lack of a national policy for helping the poor required that "love of country" among prosperous and respectable citizens be translated into the "social duty" of voluntary philanthropy, thereby creating "societies . . . composed . . . of all parties and complexions, triumphing over all *little passions,* and private *animosities,* actuated by one *common spirit* . . . for the common interest."[136] The institutional expression of such imperatives could have a complicated impact on social and political relationships, certainly promoting a significant degree of cooperation and cohesion between the upper and middle classes, but also underlining and even exacerbating social tensions and political divisions.

Hospitals represented the formation of a rough ideological consensus

---

[134] For example, officers of the Newcastle Infirmary included Sir Walter Blackett, Sir Thomas Clavering, the earls of Tankerville and Northumberland, and the Bishop of Durham; for the Norfolk and Norwich Hospital, the Earl of Buckinghamshire, the Bishop of Norwich, and Sir Edward Astley. For hospital governorships as steps to corporate office see my "Urban Culture and Political Activism," 177.

[135] John Latimer, *Annals of Bristol in the 18th Century,* vol. 1 (Bristol, 1893), 407; Money, *Experience and Identity,* 9–11; *Salisbury Journal,* Sept. 24, 1745; June 2, 1755; Oct. 6, 1760; *Norfolk Chronicle,* July 14, 1787; July 5, 1788.

[136] [Jonas Hanway], *A Letter from a Member of the Marine Society* (London, 1756), 25–6.

between elites and the middle classes with regard to the urban poor, embodying equally, under the banner of patriotic duty, the commitments to order and improve the urban environment and to remodel and regulate the laboring population. Hence the indigent patients in hospital were subjected to an array of strictly enforced moral and behavioral regulations, designed to reward industry and promote habits of mind and practices among them appropriate to their role in a rapidly expanding commercial society.[137] Benefit sermons for the hospitals made explicit this rationale, lauding the superior sensibilities of the benefactors not only as Christians but as employers, willing to save worthy but less fortunate individuals whom accident or chance threatened to rob of their independence and industry. The industrious poor were but "Martyrs to the publick Service," Bishop Secker of Oxford reminded the governors of the London Hospital in 1754; ". . . they are . . . the Servants of you, Merchants and Traders: to whom they are Instruments of earning Wealth and Honours . . . all Persons of Eminence in Trade should be liberal Subscribers" to an institution that could ensure their continued health and productivity.[138]

Further, by allowing contributors to choose, through their recommendations, the "worthiest" recipients of care (invariably defined as not being in receipt of parish relief), they allowed their middling governors to engage in a conspicuous, selective and hence didactic largesse which provided them with a social patronage and authority usually limited to elites. Such status was publicly announced on hospital anniversary days, when contributors would join magistrates, clergy and gentry in parading through town to divine service or dinner, thus underlining the role of middling processioners as benefactors to the indigent.[139] In this way, voluntary hospitals, lying-in hospitals for poor women and the plethora of charitable foundations that were modeled after or sought to improve upon them, such as lunatic hospitals and

[137] These regulations, some of which dealt with intimate details of personal hygiene, also expose the fictive and unstable nature of public–private distinctions. See, e.g., W. B. Howie, "Complaints and Complaint Procedures in the 18th and Early 19th Century Provincial Hospitals," *Medical History,* 25 (1981), 346–8.

[138] Secker, *A Sermon Before the Governors of the London Hospital,* 23–4; see also Robert Lowth, *A Sermon Preached at St. Nicholas Church in Newcastle Before the Governors of the Infirmary* (Newcastle, 1757).

[139] *Newcastle Journal,* June 27, 1752; Aug. 6, 1768; (Newcastle, Northumberland and Durham Infirmary); *Salisbury Journal,* Sept. 26, 1768; Oct. 1, 1770 (Salisbury Infirmary); *Norfolk Chronicle,* Aug. 22, 1772; Aug. 10, 1776 (Norfolk and Norwich Hospital); *Aris's Birmingham Gazette,* Sept. 15, 1777 (Salop. Infirmary); *Leeds Mercury,* Sept. 14, 1784 (Nottingham General Hospital).

dispensaries, provided crucially important institutional mechanisms for setting off the middling sorts and respectable artisans from the laboring poor. Their role in addressing the issues of popular containment and emphasizing the social authority of contributors is aptly summarized by the requirement, stipulated by most hospitals, that discharged patients return their thanks publicly to their recommenders at their places of worship.[140] Hence, although ultimately overtaken by less large-scale forms of associational charity in the 1780s and 1790s,[141] voluntary hospitals provided, for the moment, a potent model of commercial and social relations, in which an accepted social hierarchy distributed roles and status to the middle classes, supported the equitable exchange of services (unobstructed by clientage), and provided for a healthy, industrious and grateful working class.

At the same time, hospitals could also support dissident political sensibilities and intensify political and status divisions under the mask of social unity. Hospital government, with its open account books, equal voting, majority rule and use of ballots for contested elections, embodied the principles of accountability being agitated for in the political realm. They could thus be regarded as providing a model of the possibilities and benefits of a more open politics, in which authority was supervised and regulated by the broader citizenry, and constant public scrutiny kept individuals in power acting in the public interest.

Radical sympathizers in George III's reign clearly saw the analogy. Their hostility to the closed structures of the state increased their support for what they considered to be the public-spirited and moralistic purposes of associational philanthropy, as well as for the social and moral benefits that accrued from their accountable and accessible political structures. Dissident writers in Newcastle used the example of the Infirmary to attack the oligarchic and, from their perspective, self-aggrandizing nature of corporate and parliamentary institutions. As one observer put it in 1774 when arguing for the legitimacy of constituency instructions, "If it be the right of societies to give instructions to those who are appointed to manage their common concerns, it can never be the right of those who are entrusted with their [political] affairs, to act

[140] NNRO, NNH 14/1, Rules for the Norfolk and Norwich Hospital; *Rules to Be Observed by the Patients Who Are Admitted to the Relief of the Dispensary* (Newcastle, 1782). Previously this requirement was limited to charity-school children. For the larger social contexts of popular containment see Borsay, *Urban Renaissance*, 296–300; Thomas Laqueur, *Religion and Respectability: Sunday Schools and Working Class Culture, 1780–1850* (New Haven, 1976).
[141] For which see Andrew, *Philanthropy and Police*, chaps. 4–6.

contrary to their directions.'"[142] Indeed, the paternalist magistrate and
MP Sir Walter Blackett emerged as the arch-villain in the Newcastle
radical press in this period: Not only did his disparagement of constituency instructions affront local dissident political sensibilities, but his
penchant for public and indiscriminate largesse to the poor of the town
ran directly counter to the didactic and selective charity of the kind
epitomized by the Infirmary. His periodic doles to poor freemen were
thus attacked as but a flagrant attempt to bribe electors as he simultaneously robbed them of their cherished rights and privileges.[143] The
link between the new institutions of civic charity and radical political
sensibilities in the town is also supported by the overlap in personnel:
Dr. John Rotheram, physician for the Infirmary, Nathaniel Bayles and
William Smith, surgeons, and Henry Gibson, apothecary to the Infirmary and director of the public lunatic hospital, were also actively
involved in local and national reformist campaigns.[144]

Of course, the closed and intensely oligarchic civic government of
Newcastle did much to make the Infirmary a special example of politically correct administration. In Norwich, the open institutions of civic
government made the Norfolk and Norwich Hospital less a focus of
radical anxiety and hopes. Nevertheless, the management of hospitals
could be held up as a standard by which to judge the local state in
Norwich as in other towns like Warwick, Liverpool and Bristol, where
the effect of excessive partisanship in civic institutions had been clear
for decades.[145] It was not coincidental that in this period, the height of
the urban renaissance, corporations came under attack for their apparent
propensity to spend public monies not on useful projects but on lavish
feasts and luxurious cultural arenas from which the majority of citizens
were excluded.[146] In the context of the nationalistic anxieties and concerns of the middle decades of the century and the obsession with the
accountability of those in power that characterized radical politics in
the period thereafter, participatory civic institutions like the hospitals

[142] *The Freemen's Magazine, or Constitutional Repository* (Newcastle, 1774), 5; the
writer was probably the Reverend James Murray.
[143] *The Contest* (Newcastle, 1774), 19–21; *Freemen's Magazine,* 133–5.
[144] See Chapter 7.
[145] *Norwich Mercury,* March 9, 1771; Nov. 6, 1773; Sept. 14, 1782; *Aris's Birmingham
Gazette,* March 31, 1777; Liverpool Library and Record Office, Holt-Gregson MSS,
942/2, ix, 1730; Rogers, *Whigs and Cities,* 280. For the continued partisanship of
charity in Bristol see Barry, "Cultural Life," 276; *The Bristol Corporation of the
Poor,* ed. E. E. Butcher (Bristol Record Societies Publications, 3, 1932).
[146] *To the Electors of the City of Norwich* (Norwich, 1768); *Freemen's Magazine,* 84–
6; *Contest,* 5–6; *Farley's Bristol Journal,* Sept. 28, 1775.

could underline the oligarchic or self-serving nature of established political structures while allowing private citizens to redefine and appropriate the mantle of patriotism for themselves.

Voluntary hospitals, then, suggest some of the ways in which institutions of the urban renaissance could contribute to political consciousness and activism while underlining the dangers of ascribing broad and monolithic influences to urban culture as a whole. Clearly other arenas and initiatives in the eighteenth-century town provided opportunities for civic participation by ordinary people or fostered appreciation for a more open structure of politics, from the staffing of local government to membership in vestries and nonconformist chapels and commercial lobbies.[147] However, it is problematic to what degree the institutions of provincial urban culture fostered a specifically middle-class consciousness, as some historians have suggested.[148] Hanoverian urban culture embodied the status, material and aspirational divisions within the middling classes and promoted political allegiances that united members of different social groups (such as, in the case of radical politics, intellectuals, professionals, middling retailers and artisans), so that as some of the bourgeoisie became entrenched in the interstices of Old Corruption, others were in the vanguard of an assault on it. Most important, the range of cultural arenas within the provincial town, from the socially stratified world of the assembly room to the more egalitarian and open one of the club, provided alternative structures of power relations that could give form to *political* consciousness. As Thomas Bewick noted, "Were kings ... & their ministers ... to consider themselves as a Royal Society for the promotion of Arts and Sciences and of every thing that can enlighten and ameliorate the condition of their Subjects, they ... then ... would reign in the hearts of the great overwhelming mass of the people, which no conspiracy of Nobles ... could ever upset."[149]

We have come a long way, it seems, from the representational issues

---

[147] For the contours of civic participation in Newcastle and Norwich see Chapter 6. For other accounts of the "participatory situations" of the political and judicial systems see Peter King, "Decision-Makers and Decision-Making in the English Criminal Law, 1750–1800," *HJ*, 27 (1984), 25–58; John Beattie, *Crime and the Courts in England 1660–1800* (Oxford, 1986), 387–9; Lionel Glassey, "Local Government," in Clyve Jones, ed., *Britain in the First Age of Party* (London, 1987), 151–72; Triffit, "Politics and the Urban Community," 50–174, 229–63.

[148] Peter Borsay, "Culture, Status and the English Urban Landscape," *History*, 67 (1982), 12; John Seed, " 'Gentlemen Dissenters': The Social and Political Meanings of Rational Dissent in the 1770s and 1780s," *HJ*, 28 (1985), 322–3.

[149] Bewick, *Memoir*, 93–4.

raised by Addison and Bolingbroke at the beginning of this chapter; but in fact our discussion has addressed the heart of them, revealing patterns of inclusion as well as strategies of containment and marginalization within urban culture that directly affected who could claim to constitute or speak for "the people." Imbricating the national contexts of empire, prosperity and state expansion and the local contexts of urban cultural contestation and refurbishment, print culture, associational life and philanthropic institutions all worked, in different but related ways, multiply to constitute the "national" and provide the sites and means through which ordinary people could view themselves as political subjects despite clientage, oligarchy and class and gender inequalities. Certainly they also promoted visions of the polity that privileged the claims of the white, male commercial and trading classes to political recognition and citizenship. But in the struggles for respectability and independence under way, efforts to mobilize "the people" on behalf of regional and national causes created opportunities for a wider range of groups to enact or imagine their own claims to rights and political status, even if they did so through the claims of the male middling sorts or their betters. In this as in other ways, political culture provided points of contact between different social groups in a period when urban culture sought to promote their separation, creating a restive and contestatory political public. It is to its grievances and concerns that we will now turn.

2. Loyalism abounding to the chief of sinners: The reconfiguration of popular politics, 1714–1735

> What, tho' the *Tories* burst with spleen Sir,
>   And curse the Revolution,
> Yet *George* will disclose, our Popish foes,
>   And settle our Constitution.
>   *A Loyal Song,* 1717[1]

> ... Now all true *British* Worthies,
> With ORMOND are discarded,
> Whilst Treach'rous Knaves, and *German* Slaves
> With Places are rewarded.
>   *A New Ballad,* 1715

> We have two KINGES; the one is true,
>   The other a *Pretender;*
> To him so call'd is that Name due?
>   Or to him called *Defender?* ...
> Is *he* who *Breaks* through *all our Laws,*
>   Or *he* [who] makes no *Transgression;*
> More fit to *Judge* the *People's* Cause,
>   Or, free them from *Oppression?*
>   *The Pretender* [1717][2]

The decades following the Hanoverian Succession witnessed some resounding political upheavals. Despite the successful coup d'état by the Whigs, extensive rioting and a Stuart-backed rebellion threatened the

---

[1] *Mughouse Diversion; or, A Collection of Loyal Prologues and Songs* (London, 1717), 39.
[2] This ballad and the one above are from HL, Collection of English and Jacobite Ballads, 1679–1728, unfoliated.

security of the new dynasty and the consolidation of Whig power, and the purge of Tories in state and local government and Jacobite plotting perpetuated the bitter partisan divisions of Anne's reign, giving popular politics a treasonable edge. After the Jacobite threat appeared to have abated and "stability" was inaugurated with the administration of Sir Robert Walpole, the Whig regime was faced with a new challenge in the form of the rise of a vigorous "patriotic" opposition, both within and without doors, that sought to undermine Whig hegemony. The conflicts of these decades provided the images, rhetoric and social bases for a politics of loyalism and dissidence that would be drawn upon by a wide variety of groups throughout the century. At the same time, they brought about a sea-change in the concerns of the extra-parliamentary nation, revealing both the immediacy which seventeenth-century events still held for eighteenth-century English people and the crucial reconfiguration of ideological politics wrought through the rise of "patriotic" issues and concerns.

I. WHIGS AND LIBERTIES

Given the socially inclusive and virulent nature of political conflict on the eve of the Hanoverian Succession, it would have been extremely unlikely for the "age of party" to die with the last Stuart monarch.[3] And indeed, the religious and dynastic issues of the preceding three decades were far from resolved in 1714. Though historians have been wont to portray the Whig ascendancy as a fait accompli by 1715, Whig power and control was by no means assured. As Linda Colley has shown, the intrigue of the Whig leaders may have disposed the Elector to favor them after his accession, but he was not averse to the Tory party as a whole and had plans for its inclusion within his ministry.[4] And in the broader political nation, Tory power and popularity remained strong even after the rout of Tories from local and national office in 1715. The strength and resilience of grass-roots Toryism was demonstrated in election results,[5] Whig legislative initiatives designed

---

[3] See Geoffrey Holmes, *Politics in the Reign of Anne* (London, 1967); J. H. Plumb, "The Growth of the Electorate in England, 1600–1715," *P & P*, no. 45 (1969), 90–116; and W. A. Speck, *Tory and Whig: The Struggle in the Constituencies* (London, 1970).

[4] Linda Colley, *In Defiance of Oligarchy: The Tory Party, 1714–1760* (Cambridge, 1982), 178–9.

[5] W. A. Speck, "The Electorate in the First Age of Party," in Clyve Jones, ed., *Britain in the First Age of Party, 1680–1750* (London, 1987), 60; Sedgwick, i, 241, 275, 294.

to shore up support in Commons and Lords,[6] and above all the waves of protest, rioting and disaffection which the Whig ascension to power had spawned and which necessitated concerted efforts by the government to bolster Whig support in the nation.

It is the latter development upon which we will first focus. The efforts of the Whig administrations to mobilize and foster loyalty to their regime in the succession crisis is worthy of detailed attention, not least because their exertions in this regard have been discounted as hypocritical adjuncts to their authoritarian, repressive legislation.[7] Yet to ignore Whig politicking and propaganda in the post-succession period is to neglect the very real ideological thrust of Hanoverian Whiggery and its potential and actual bases of support in the nation. Aware of the new regime's instability and of their own position in it, Whig loyalists worked tirelessly to promote their and George I's cause in the nation at large. In this they were continuing their strategies of the last two years of Anne's reign, when party leaders began organizing resources and personnel to capitalize on the new political situation the change in monarch was sure to bring. In the City, the Hanover Society tried to mobilize electoral support in the wards and used sophisticated tactics to improve communications among activists in different parts of the city, and Whig partisans gained leadership of the Honourable Artillery Company, a private militia comprising upper- and middle-class citizens that gave the party a formidable military presence.[8] Extending these efforts, Whig activists produced a barrage of written and visual propaganda that attempted to consolidate their position with the new king and in the nation. Press, pulpit, theater and political calendar were all utilized to lambast the alleged long-standing Tory disaffection to the Protestant succession and allow the Whigs to parade as the only alternative to Catholic absolutism.

The Tories also retained a majority on the London Common Council in 1714, 1715 and 1716, despite the Whig administration's deployment of state patronage in the revenue departments to prevent it: See Henry Horwitz, "Minutes of a Whig Club, 1714–1717," in H. Horwitz, W. A. Speck and W. A. Gray, eds., *London Politics, 1713–1717* (London Record Society Publications, 27, 1981), 9; Nicholas Rogers, *Whigs and Cities: Popular Politics in the Age of Walpole and Pitt* (Oxford, 1989), 27–9.

[6] Such as the Septennial Act (1716) and the peerage bill (1719).

[7] Nicholas Rogers, "Popular Protest in Early Hanoverian London," *P & P,* no. 79 (1978), 74–7.

[8] Gary De Krey, *A Fractured Society: The Politics of London in the First Age of Party 1688–1715* (Oxford, 1985), 262–3; Horwitz, "Minutes of a Whig Club," 16–17; *Flying Post,* Aug. 3–5, 1714; Nicholas Rogers, *Whigs and Cities,* 27–9.

Immediately on the heels of George I's accession, Whig partisans were quick to stage their own didactic pageantry which heralded both their party's claims to national gratitude and their return to the promised land of state employment. The Duke of Marlborough, who the Whigs felt was treated with base ingratitude by the Tory government, was lauded as a hero upon his return to England from his self-imposed exile on the Continent. Passing through Rochester on August 3, the duke and duchess were greeted with "great Expressions of joy from the People," who strewed flowers in their path and decked out their houses with green boughs; once in London, they were greeted by a procession of nobles, gentry, aldermen and grenadiers of the Artillery Company – to the considerable annoyance of Tory crowds, who hissed as Marlborough's retinue passed. To his supporters, however, Marlborough, victor of Blenheim and symbol of national greatness, was a long-neglected hero, and the expressions of popular affection for him intimated only one thing, that "it will soon be as much fashion to give him his just due, as it hath been to vilify and defame him, for doing the greatest things . . . to serve his SOVEREIGN and Country."[9] Thomas Holles, the new Duke of Newcastle, was similarly lauded in print and in spectacle as "the first New Lord call'd to that House in this Reign . . . whose Zeal has been so Conspicuous in the Cause of . . . the Succession in the most Illustrious House of Hanover"; his movements through London were announced with the ringing of bells and the firing of guns.[10]

The establishment of the new dynasty and Whig ascendancy were mutually promoted in other ways. Despite George I's diffidence and disdain of ceremonial, which prompted his late-night entry into London, his coronation a month later was celebrated with the full panoply of state pageantry in the capital, which, if not particularly grand by later-eighteenth-century standards, was still sufficient to impress spectators – and readers, for whom it was recounted in painstaking detail in the provincial and London press – with its splendidness.[11] His accession and coronation prompted sumptuous visual displays in provincial towns that valorized monarchy, hierarchy and popular consent all at once. In

---

[9] *Flying Post,* Aug. 3–5, 5–7, 1714; Harold Williams, ed., *The Correspondence of Jonathan Swift,* vol. 2 (Oxford, 1965), 102–4.
[10] *Flying Post,* Aug. 3–5, 1714.
[11] John Beattie, *The English Court in the Reign of George I* (Cambridge, 1967), 257; for reporting see *Historical Register* (1714), i, 48–62; *Worcester Postman,* Sept. 17–24, 1714; *Flying Post,* Sept. 20–2, 1714; *Newcastle Courant,* Sept. 22–5, 1714.

Gosport, Hampshire, Corporation members bearing red silk flags emblazoned with "God Save King George" led a parade that included the town waits, young men dressed and armed as champions, constables, charity-school children with gold silk flags mounted on large horses, churchwardens and overseers of the poor with white staves, and a hundred additional residents bedecked with orange coronation favors and ribbons, which wove through the streets of the town as cannon fired and fireworks sparkled.[12] Whig-sponsored pageants also occurred in York, Norwich, Colchester and Liverpool; and even in some towns with a strong Tory or Jacobite presence, like Bristol, Newcastle, Worcester, Canterbury, Leicester and Dorchester, celebrations in honor of the new monarch were lavish, if divisive.[13]

Although the loyalism expressed on these occasions was scarcely unalloyed or unchallenged, George I's accession was heralded in some quarters as a deliverance – from a Tory, High Church ascendancy and Jacobite hopes – and in others as an opportunity for a tentative rapprochement with the new dynasty. In both cases, the Whig government and Whig activists in the localities and London tried to capitalize on the relief that initially reverberated through the nation. The press spearheaded this energetic propaganda effort. The journalism of Whig writers like Addison, Steele, Walpole, Thomas Burnet and Arthur Maynwaring had been the despair of Tory leaders before 1714, who had been largely unable to silence them; thereafter it became their scourge, as Whig papers and journalists of every description were promoted and subsidized by the government, and the Tory press severely circumscribed.[14] George Ridpath's *Flying Post,* reemerging triumphant as Whig voicepiece in the new regime, was only one of some thirty-five Whig papers and periodicals that flourished by 1716.[15] In addition, pamphlets, sermons, plays, broadsides, ballads and periodicals were all

[12] *Daily Courant,* Aug. 9, 1714.
[13] ARL, Gough Somerset MS, 14 (I owe this reference to Michael Neil); Abel Boyer, ed., *The Political State of Great Britain,* 38 vols. (1711–29), vii, Aug. 1, 5, 1714; *Flying Post,* Aug. 3–5, 5–7, 1714; *Daily Courant,* Aug. 9, Oct. 26, 27, 1714; *Newcastle Courant,* Sept. 22–5, 1714; Worcester City Archives, Audit Books, A/10/6, 1714–35, Aug.–Nov. 1714–15; *Records of the Borough of Leicester,* ed. G. A. Chinney, 7 vols. (Leicester, Cambridge and London, 1899–1974), v, 71.
[14] Laurence Hanson, *Government and the Press, 1695–1763* (London, 1936), 42–4; P. J. Hyland, "Liberty and Libel: Government and the Press During the Succession Crisis in Britain, 1712–1716," *EHR,* 101 (1986), 863–88.
[15] Hyland, "Liberty and Libel," 870–1; Harris, "The Structure, Ownership and Control of the Press, 1670–1780," in G. Boyce, J. Curran and P. Wingate, eds., *Newspaper History from the Seventeenth Century to the Present Day* (London, 1978), 85–7.

exploited to whip up enthusiasm for the Whig and Hanoverian cause, disseminated throughout the nation via chapmen, hawkers, news agents and booksellers.[16]

For example, between 1714 and 1718, dozens of single-sheet poems and songs and a number of ballad collections were produced honoring George I.[17] Although they ranged in emphasis from the "providential right" of the succession, a favorite theme of Whig bishops under William III, to the paternalism and historic greatness of the Brunswick line, they all had in common the representation of the Hanoverian Succession as Deliverance, Defence (of the Revolution) and the Voice of the People divinely sanctioned: "The Person Whom a People do appoint / Auspicious Heaven do's the same anoint," as a poem put it for the coronation day in 1716.[18] The theme of the popular "appointment" of the new monarch was not only a gesture to assert and mobilize consent; it was also central to the conceptions of political subjectivity that Whig propaganda constructed – a point we will return to.

Other Whig propaganda sought to address Tory fears and counter Jacobite allegations by proclaiming the hereditary and moral as well as political legitimacy of Hanover's claim to the throne. *A Character of His Most Excellent Majesty* GEORGE KING *of Great Britain, etc.*, published in 1715, assured its readers of the family's genealogical descent from James I, as well as of the King's wealth, sagacity, manliness and intimate knowledge of the British constitution.[19] Another fourpenny pamphlet, entitled *The Harmony of the Lutheran Doctrine, with That of the Church of England,* attempted to demolish High Church propaganda by comparing, in adjacent columns, the articles of the Anglican Church and those of the Augsburg Confession in order to prove the superb compatibility of the two variants of Protestantism and George

---

[16] At least 26 provincial newspapers were established between 1714 and 1724, 12 between 1714 and 1718: G. A. Cranfield, *A Handlist of Provincial Newspapers, 1700–1760* (London, 1961).

[17] D. F. Foxon, *English Verse, 1700–1750,* 2 vols. (Cambridge, 1975), i, 245–6; *The Hanover Garland; or, Songs Calculated for His Britannic Majesty's Coronation* (London, 1714).

[18] *Flying Post,* Aug. 3–5, 1714; June 9–11, 1715; *Weekly Journal, or British Gazetteer,* Oct. 27, 1716. See also *Worcester Postman,* Sept. 17, 1714; *A Collection of State Songs* (London, 1716). Some coronation medals portrayed Britannia crowning George I beneath the motto "Proceribus and Populis Consentientibus" – "the Nobles and People Consenting." John Doran, *London in the Jacobite Times,* 2 vols. (London, 1877), i, 21–2.

[19] *A Character . . .* (London, 1715). See also Thomas Davis, *The Indisputable Right of Our Most Illustrious King George to the Throne of His Ancestors* (London, 1716); *Hanover or Rome* (London, 1715).

I's suitability as Defender of the Faith.[20] Sermons thundered their defenses of the Revolution in answer to the Pretender's recent declaration, reminding the audiences of Stuart crimes against local government, Parliament, the church, and subjects' rights and properties.[21] Similar historical memories were evoked on coronation medals and in slip songs and almanacs.[22] In conjunction with paeans to Queen Elizabeth, "who restor'd the Protestant Religion . . . and all the Rights and Liberties of her Subjects," to the Seven Bishops and to Whig martyrs like Lord Russell, and the commemorations of attempted popish atrocities, such as that staged by the Hanover Club on October 23, 1715, to remember the "massacre of 1641," these efforts appropriated the nation's anti-Catholic, anti-absolutist heritage as "Whig" traditions that necessitated the people's support in the present.[23]

Whig industry and inventiveness were not limited to printed and oral propaganda, but extended to other organizational and discursive domains. Just as George I's paternalism was emphasized in verse, his *paternity* and virility, as patriarch of a seemingly endless stream of royal progeny, was emphasized in verses and ballads and through the latter's prominent positions in royal anniversary ceremonials. In London, the Prince and Princess of Wales were literally put on display, dining every day in public at Hampton Court, where people of every rank, "even of the lowest sort and in their common habits," Dudley Ryder noted with surprise, were admitted free of charge. Quite clearly, the prince and princess's affability to their humble audiences was seen as "a means of making the King's cause popular."[24] It seemed to work: In York, Oxford, Casholton, Bridgenorth, Worcester and Chester, even before a recourse to the reversionary interest was contemplated, the Prince of Wales's birthday on October 30 was celebrated as a badge of loyalty to the new dynasty itself. And the prince and princess's own success in procreating was equally celebrated. The birth of Prince Fred-

---

[20] *The Harmony of Lutheran Doctrine* (London, 1715).
[21] [Gilbert Burnet, Bishop of Salisbury], *The Revolution and the Present Establishment Vindicated: In a Memorial Drawn Up by King William's Special Direction* (1715); Benjamin Hoadley, Bishop of Bangor, *The Restoration Made a Blessing to Us, by the Protestant Succession* (London, 1716); Robert Butts, *A Sermon Preach'd at the Cathedral Church of Norwich* (Norwich, 1719).
[22] *Historical Register*, i, 1–48; Bernard Capp, *English Almanacs, 1500–1800* (Ithaca, 1979), 248–51.
[23] *Weekly Journal, or British Gazetteer*, Aug. 11, Nov. 17, 1716; *Englishman*, Oct. 19, 1715.
[24] *Flying Post*, June 9–11, 1715; *The Diary of Dudley Ryder*, ed. William Matthews (London, 1939), 298.

erick was heralded with cannon, fireworks and bells all over the country, and in Westminster on the first of August a loyal society displayed banners emblazoned "The Princess of Wales: Blessed be the *Fertile Princess!*"[25] Through these spectacles and display, legitimate monarchical power – associated with masculinity and virility, virtue and fertility – was recuperated for the nation by both the new monarch and his offspring.

The Loyal Societies, or "Mughouses," proved to be another example of Whig ingenuity. Located at strategic spots throughout the capital and in some provincial towns in order to stage strategic raids on the "Jacks," as their Tory–Jacobite opponents were known, they were pointedly backed by the Duke of Newcastle to serve as "nurseries of loyalty" to George I. Their efforts to promote a "public spirit" among the citizenry included not only ostentatious celebration of Whig and Hanoverian anniversaries and aggressively boisterous songfests but also street fights in which Tory heads were smashed with the blessing of the Whig establishment.[26] More widespread, however, were the loyalist calendrical spectacles staged throughout the nation on political anniversaries, which were designed to seize the initiative for political theater from Tory and Jacobite crowds and malign them for rebellion and arbitrary power. The processions marking the anniversary days of the monarch, the fourth and fifth of November, and the victory over the Jacobite rebels at Preston, organized by local elites and members of various Whig societies, typically brandished oranges and orange ribbons (symbols of William III and the Protestant succession), wooden shoes (Continental despotism), warming pans (casting doubt on the legitimacy of the Stuart claimant to the throne), tartan ("Scotch" Highlanders) and effigies of the pope and Pretender as well as of English Jacobite and Tory leaders like the Earl of Mar, the Duke of Ormonde and Sacheverell in order to ritually humiliate the Tories and identify

---

[25] *Flying Post*, May 29–31, 1715; Boyer, *Political State of Great Britain*, x, Aug. 1, 1715; *Worcester Postman*, Oct. 28 – Nov. 4, 1715; *Weekly Journal, or British Gazetteer*, Nov. 10, 1716; *Records of the Borough of Nottingham*, 7 vols. (Nottingham, 1914–47), vi, 75.

[26] James Fitts, "Newcastle's Mob," *Albion*, 5 (1973), 41–9; John Timbs, *Clubs and Club Life in London* (London, 1872), 38–47; Rogers, "Popular Protest," 78–83. For songfests see *The Mug Vindicated: To Which is Prefix'd, An Account of the Rise, Progress and Constitution of Those Loyal Societies* (London, 1717), and *Mughouse Diversion*. Although many of the members were gentlemen and commercial bourgeoisie, membership was mixed; it included tradesmen, manufacturers, apprentices and domestic servants. See *Newcastle Courant*, July 28–30, 1716; Ryder, *Diary*, 279–80; *Mug Vindicated*, p. ix.

A N
A C C O U N T
O F
𝕿𝖍𝖊 𝖂𝖍𝖔𝖑𝖊 𝕻𝖗𝖔𝖈𝖊𝖋𝖋𝖎𝖔𝖓,

As it was carried thro' the City and Suburbs, &c.

A. B. *Generals* Mar *and* Forſter.   C. *The* Pretender's *Standard.*
D. *A Drum Muffled.*   E. *Six* Scots *Rebels in their* Highland *Dreſs as they*
enter'd London.

2. *An Account of the Whole Procession, As It Was Carried thro' the City and Suburbs*
(1717). Whig political theater during the Succession Crisis. Courtesy of the Trustees of
the British Museum.

them with foreign and domestic subversion, treason and slavery. Such
was the case in Norwich, Newcastle, Gravesend, Chester and York, to
name a few.[27] *An Account of the Whole Procession* (Plate 2) provides

[27] NNRO, MS 217, W. Massey, Acta Norvicensia, 37, 60; *Worcester Journal,* Oct. 28
– Nov. 4, 1715; *Flying Post,* Oct. 27–9, Nov. 6–8, 8–10, 1715; Nov. 13–16, 1716;
St. James's Evening Post, Nov. 12–14, 1716.

a rare visual representation of an eighteenth-century pope-burning demonstration, this one orchestrated by the Loyal Society at the Roebuck
in Cheapside on the return of George I from Hanover on January 19,
1717 (and in the wake of the exposure of the Swedish–Jacobite conspiracy); it included the figures of the pope and Pretender, the leading
Jacobite rebel lords, Mar and Forster, surrounded by Highlanders on
horseback and followed by the devil. That these spectacles worked to
shape popular consciousness in the desired direction was a point of no
dispute to the well-affected. "If the mob for the Government grows
strong and makes a noise and show people will naturally fall in with
it," Dudley Ryder reflected; street theater worked "to encourage the
friends to King George and keep up the spirit of loyalty and the public
spirit among them."[28]

Disaffection and rebellion undoubtedly did the most to mobilize support. Demonstrations and riots over the spring and summer of 1715,
the flight of the Tory leaders Ormonde and Bolingbroke to St. Germain
in the face of their impeachment by the Whig ministry, the outbreak
of the '15 in September and the subsequent Jacobite plots in 1717,
1719 and 1722, were all splendid, well-timed boons to Whig credibility,
skillfully exploited by Whig loyalists to vindicate their allegations
about the Tory predilection for disaffection. The invasion in particular
galvanized active support for the government in many towns, where
residents threw themselves vigorously into putting their towns in a state
of defense. Loyal associations for defense were formed in a number of
towns, including Liverpool, Nottingham, Worksop and Newcastle upon
Tyne; in the latter, residents fortified the town gates with lime and
cannon and raised 700 volunteers for the town guard, with the keelmen
themselves raising 700 more.[29] Elsewhere, as in Bedford, where some
of the townspeople had put the maypole in mourning on George I's
coronation, local elites buried long-standing rivalries sufficiently to
demonstrate unity on the accession day: "*Whig* and *Tory,* if need be,
will unite when a common enemy is in view," one resident reported.[30]

Whig journalists and clergymen decried the disorder in the capital
and provinces, where "*High Church* and *Ormonde* are become the

[28] BM 1607, in *Catalogue,* ii; Ryder, *Diary,* 255, 279.
[29] Edward Baines, *History of Liverpool* (Liverpool, 1852), 398–9; J. A. Picton, *Municipal Archives and Records of Liverpool, 1700–1835* (Liverpool, 1886), 78; *VCH Notting-hamshire,* i (London, 1906), 358–9; Peter Rae, *The History of the Rebellion, Rais'd Against His Majesty King George I,* 2nd ed. (London, 1746), 242–6; John Brand, *History and Antiquities of the Town and County of Newcastle upon Tyne,* 2 vols. (Newcastle, 1789), ii, 511.
[30] *Flying Post,* Aug. 2–4, 1715.

watchwords of the Rebellion.'' The Reverend Charles Lambe conjured up images of the civil strife that would result from the attempt to bring the Stuarts back that stressed the loss of property (commercial and sexual), person and country:

> Have you any notion of a civil war, your Treasury exhausted, your Banks plundered, your Trade decayed, your Companies bankrupt, your Shops rifled, and the various species of Stocks sunk, run down and lost? Have you any idea of Fields flow'd with blood, your streets pav'd with the carcasses of fellow citizens, your Wives and your Daughters torn from your sides, and made a Prey to enrag'd undistinguishing Soldiers?[31]

Joseph Addison, member of the Hanover Club and zealous Whig partisan, played on similar themes in his periodical *The Freeholder* in order to mobilize patriotic emotions in support of the succession. Published between December 23, 1715, and June 29, 1716, in the wake of the suppression of the rebellion, *The Freeholder* provided a running commentary on the ways in which loyalty to Hanover and the Whigs was dictated by love of country, adeptly seizing the ideological opportunities which the rebellion afforded the Whig regime by identifying any form of dissent with treason. "Every *Englishman* will be a good Subject to King *George,* in Proportion as he is a good *Englishman,* and a Lover of their Constitution,'' Addison declared; there could be no legitimate party divisions at a time of national crisis, only a distinction "between *Loyalists* and *Rebels.*''[32] Such distinctions were reinforced by tarring the Tories with the brushes of class and gender as well as party: In supporting a Catholic pretender to the throne, they revealed their attachment to degrading, vain and effeminate ideas, embodied by their lower-class women supporters in the streets, "Oister-women'' and "Cinder-wenches'' who "gather about Bonfires . . . to scream out their Principles.'' Whigs, by contrast, stalwartly resisted the spread of rebellion, even the "ladies'' devoting their persons to propagating loyal principles by wearing orange cockades.[33] *The Freeholder* provided a

---

[31] Ibid., May 29–31, 1715; quotation from Doran, *London in the Jacobite Times,* i, 83.

[32] Joseph Addison, *The Freeholder,* ed. James Leheny (Oxford, 1979), 55, 98, 114; see also 91–6, 153, 159, 246.

[33] Ibid., 264. Such images were a reworking of long-standing Whig slurs against an alleged Stuart effeminacy: See 48, 71–5, 87–90, 135–8, 145–8. Once the crisis had passed, the *Freeholder* returned to more familiar arguments that women engaging in party strife was inappropriate to the beauty and modesty of womanhood: "A Stateswoman is as ridiculous a Creature as a Cott-queen,'' Addison pronounced; "each of

cogent articulation of the principles that animated Whig street theater and rhetoric in the post-succession years and that would be elaborated by Court Whig apologists in ensuing decades, closing down the range of acceptable political positions that truly patriotic subjects could take. Loyal, manly citizens could only be Whig, whereas the rebellious, the effeminate, the unruly were by definition Tory, which here became identical with Jacobite and the "rabble."

Finally, the stage became assiduous in propagating a view of the Whigs and Hanover as bulwarks against Tory treachery and Jacobite restoration during the '15, providing arenas where the political crisis could be displayed, enacted or resolved on stage and off. Audiences sporting orange cockades or white roses reacted to particular plays with boos or cheers according to their political propensities. John Phillips's farce about the '15 and its leader in Scotland, *The Earl of Mar Marr'd*, was performed to enthusiastic crowds in both the capital and provinces, although in some towns, such as Norwich, it also provoked riots. Nevertheless, its popularity was such that Phillips wrote a sequel, *The Pretender's Flight; or, a Mock Coronation,* that was produced in London the following year.[34] Nicholas Rowe's *Tamerlane,* an allegory about William III, also bolstered loyalist reserves in London and Newcastle.[35] Undoubtedly the most celebrated anti-Jacobite theatrical effort was Colley Cibber's adaptation of Molière's *Tartuffe* as *The Nonjuror,* produced at Drury Lane, which lampooned Jacobite–Tory leaders and clergymen alike. One of the latter in the play, the Reverend Dr. Wolf, a nonjuror, is discovered with his account book of expenses "laid-out at several times for the Secret Service of His M——," including two cartloads and six baskets of rue and thyme for Restoration Day; bushels of white roses for June 10; and payments to a juryman "for his extraordinary trouble in acquitting Sir Preston Rebel of his indictment," to one "Abel Perkin, newswriter, for several seasonable paragraphs," and to "John Shoplift and Thomas Highway for endeavoring to put out the enemy's bonfire" on August 1. Cibber thus used farce and the symbols of disaffection to valorize the mythical world of the Whig imagination, in which domestic enemies had infiltrated most aspects of everyday life with their subversive and rebellious designs. The play

---

the Sexes should keep within its particular Bounds, and content themselves to excel within their respective Districts": 205.

[34] *The Earl of Mar Marr'd* (London, 1715); *Norwich Gazette,* Jan. 21, 1716; *The Pretender's Flight; or, A Mock Coronation . . . a Tragi-Comical Farce* (London, 1716).

[35] Ryder, *Diary,* 359; *Newcastle Courant,* Nov. 13, 1725.

provoked a response in the form of Christopher Bullock's farce *The Perjuror,* produced at the Tory theater at Lincoln's Inn Fields in 1717, but Cibber's effort outran his rival's in popularity as performance and text throughout George I's reign, and won for its author the prestigious post of Poet Laureate.[36]

I have described the massive propaganda efforts of the Whig government and its supporters in some detail because they provide the context for understanding the success of the Whigs in many quarters in demonizing all sources of opposition to the new regime as treasonable, subversive and Jacobite. The cultural and political constructions which the Whigs drew on in their propaganda during the succession crisis provided the life force of their conflicts with the Tories in the late Stuart and early Hanoverian periods. As J. G. A. Pocock has pointed out, stereotypes, however inadequate or outmoded, supply materials for the models of itself a society uses for its political thinking, providing an array of political "others" against which national and party identities were defined and valorized.[37] The Hanoverian Whigs accordingly drew upon an iconography and language of anti-Catholicism grounded in late-seventeenth-century experience, when the pope-burnings, street theater and printed propaganda of the Exclusion crisis sought to depict the Catholic monarchy as the propagator of poverty, superstition and tyranny, and Parliament as the bulwark of monarchy, liberty, property and reformed religion.[38] In the face of the threats posed to the security of the state and nation by the invasion of the French-backed Catholic James Edward Stuart and the rising of his English and Scottish supporters, these stereotypes were deployed to construct a "tradition" of Whig libertarianism extending back to a pre-Stuart, Puritan and even Elizabethan past in order to vindicate Whig claims in the present to be the popularly sanctioned and sole guarantees of the Protestant succession and thus of English liberties and religion. Most pertinent, the contexts and contents of Whig ideological initiatives transformed party stereotypes into imperatives of state, necessitating all

[36] Colley Cibber, *The Nonjuror* (London, 1716; 2nd ed., 1718); see also Doran, *London in the Jacobite Times,* i, 292–4. The play also lampooned William Shippen, an outspoken Jacobite in Parliament who attacked standing armies and Hanover as betrayals of British interests.

[37] Pocock, "The History of Political Thought: A Methodological Enquiry," in P. Laslett and W. G. Runciman, eds., *Philosophy, Politics and Society: Second Series* (Oxford, 1962), 199.

[38] See Tim Harris, *London Crowds in the Reign of Charles II* (Cambridge, 1987), 97–115.

loyal citizens to appropriate a "Whig" identity and exert themselves against the dangerous enemies to church, king and constitution that lurked within and threatened from without.

The Whig strategy was, in fact, reasonably effective, having its first and most striking success in George I himself. And contrary to some historians' claims, within the broader political nation the Whig position had an appeal that extended beyond dissenters and placemen.[39] Certainly dissenters were prominent activists in the Hanoverian Whig cause. Long abused by High Churchmen (most recently by Sacheverell) and virulently anti-Catholic, they were most forthcoming in expressing their glee at the winds of political change that swept the country on George I's accession, even when such demonstrations provoked High Church and Tory wrath. In Manchester, for example, dissenting trades-men were indicted for causing a "riot" on the king's birthday in 1715, having on that day "disturbed the King's Anglican subjects by making a triumphant Bonfire", three months later a nonconformist gluemaker was presented for declaring that "the times are on our side – meaning the Dissenters side and against the Churchmen." Not surprisingly, wealthy dissenters became entrenched in the higher levels of Whig government in the decades after the succession.[40] However, it seriously misrepresents the nature, diversity and limitations of the Whig appeal to suggest that dissenters were the Whigs' only (or even necessary) allies. As the street theater and demonstrations suggest and loyal ad-dresses and electoral results demonstrate, there was a fairly broad, so-cially heterogeneous base of support in the nation for the Whigs in the early succession years, one that included not only Whig gentry, big merchants and their middling commercial allies but also lesser trades-men and artisans, in both London and the provinces. Alternatively, some dissenters themselves, if not "slumbering radicals," were less than enchanted with the spirit and substance of the new regime, rightly predicting in 1715 that the Whigs "would serve them [dissenters] no further than their interest led them, and they had not virtue enough to take off the Acts of Conformity and Schism."[41] Nevertheless, that the

[39] E.g., Rogers, "Popular Protest," 75–5, 91–100; Paul Monod, *Jacobitism and the English People* (Cambridge, 1989), 169–70.
[40] PRO, Palatinate of Lancaster Assize Minute Books, PL 28/1, 236, 235. I owe this reference to Paul Monod. For dissenters in government see Nicholas Rogers, *Whigs and Cities,* 135–7.
[41] De Krey, *A Fractured Society,* 168, 170, 177–258 passim, demonstrates that if the Whig party came to encompass the more substantial, and the Tory party the more plebeian, members of the London livery, the former still retained the support of a

sense of crisis wrought by rumors of Jacobite plots, outbreaks of disaffection in the provinces, fears of financial and commercial chaos attendant upon a French invasion, and the profound divisions among the
Tory leadership on the succession question redounded to the Whigs'
advantage was also demonstrated in parliamentary election results. In
the larger urban constituencies where public opinion could withstand
or subvert the forces of influence and patronage, the Whigs returned
majorities in 1715 and 1722.[42] Hence, the Whigs' anti-Catholic message and the historical memories that it evoked had attractions for many
English people who remembered the disasters of James II's reign, as
well as those who looked with horror and disdain upon conflicts and
disorders produced by the High Church furor of Anne's later years.
Clearly, dissenters like Dudley Ryder were not the only ones who had
nightmares about a Stuart – or a Tory – restoration.

However, the consolidation of their power at high and low levels
also occurred through state-sponsored terrorism and physical coercion
geared toward wiping out political dissent that redefined the party's
relation to the extra-parliamentary nation. The exploitation of the Riot
Act of 1715 by Whig magistrates and the free rein given to Whig
loyalists, troops and militiamen to harass and assault – or even kill –
Tory and Jacobite demonstrators in the post-succession years were only
one aspect of the draconian measures employed by successive Whig
administrations to keep order and stamp out disaffection.[43] The rebellion legitimized invasive government measures – such as the suspension
of habeas corpus, the house arrests and seizures of the guns and horses
of Catholics, the use of networks of informants and spies in the capital
and localities (from stockbrokers and doctors to coffeehouse proprie-

---

substantial proportion of voters in the artisan companies (and the latter retained sizable
numbers of voters in the substantial companies) between 1710 and 1722. For the larger
provincial towns see Speck, *Tory and Whig,* 118–20. For dissenting hostility to Stanhope and Walpole's administrations see Ryder, *Diary,* 65, 153, 176–7, and *An Equal
Capacity in the Subjects of Great Britain for Civil Employment the Best Security to
the Government* (London, 1717). Cf. James Bradley, " 'Slumbering Radicalism':
Whigs and Nonconformists in English Politics, 1739–89," *Eighteenth-Century Studies,* 9 (1975), 1–27.

[42] Of the English boroughs with over 1,000 electors, 29 returned Whigs and 22 Tories;
for those with over 500 voters, the figures were 50 and 40 respectively. Speck, "Electorate in the First Age of Party," 60; Sedgwick, i, 79; Colley, *Defiance,* 296.

[43] For the Riot Act – which made gatherings of 12 or more a capital offense if the
members failed to disperse within an hour of a magistrate's final warning – see Rogers,
"Popular Protest," 73–5, 81–3.

tors), the coordination of local committees to administer oaths of allegiance and supremacy, and the rooting out of printers, publishers, preachers, hawkers, chapmen and even ballad-singers who were seen to promote resistance to the new regime – that were elaborated upon and perfected during the Jacobite scares of 1717, 1719 and 1722 and incorporated into the policies of Stanhope's and later Walpole's administration.[44] At the same time, the defeat of the rebellion increased the malicious license allowed Whig crowds and publicists. Mary, Countess Cowper, recorded in her diary the pathetic spectacle of Preston rebels paraded through the streets of London as spectators harassed them with warming-pans, shouts and stones; it was particularly distressing for her to witness, for her elderly kinsman a Clavering of Callaly was among them.[45] The Jacobite trials were subsequently promoted with great showmanship and theater, and Whig actions against Tory and Jacobite demonstrators became increasingly violent and extreme, with armed troops roaming the streets of the capital and assaulting people who dared to wear white roses or ribbons, and local artillery companies performing similar services in provincial towns.[46]

The steady stream of anti-populist measures undertaken in ''the people's'' name was justified, of course, as part of the strenuous defense of the nation against Stuart threats. Yet some of these measures were more credible as acts of state than others. The government's blatant electoral manipulations in urban constituencies were particularly offensive, such as in Coventry, where freemen supporters of the Tory candidates Sir Christopher Hale and Sir Fulwar Skipwith were assaulted and then jailed for shouting party slogans, and the Whig sheriffs rejected over 200 good Tory votes ''openly boasting the Parliament would justify their proceedings.'' In other towns, the petitions that were heard before the bar of the House were invariably decided in favor of the Whig candidates; in the case of Taunton, electoral boundaries were

---

[44] PRO, SP 35/10–11 passim; Hanson, *Government and the Press,* chap. 2; Paul Fritz, *The English Ministers and Jacobitism Between the Rebellions of 1715 and 1745* (Toronto, 1975), 26–7, 51–66, 109–25.

[45] *The Diary of Mary, Countess Cowper,* ed. Spencer Cowper, 2nd ed. (London, 1865), 136; Doran, *London in the Jacobite Times,* 107. As she wrote so touchingly, ''He is above seventy years old . . . A desperate fortune had drawn him from home, in hopes to have repaired it.'' Her account is corroborated by that of the *Flying Post,* Dec. 8–10, 1715.

[46] Boyer, *Political State of Great Britain,* x, 492–3, 582–5; Rogers, ''Popular Protest,'' 80–1; *Flying Post,* Oct. 27–9, 1715; *St. James's Evening Post,* June 2–5, 1716. Of the 1,500 prisoners taken at Preston, 34 were executed.

redrawn to exclude Tory strongholds in future.[47] And the Septennial Act, passed in April 1716, which facilitated the government's concerted campaign to circumscribe popular political participation, deeply alienated urban electorates. As one hostile observer noted, the Act reduced freeborn Englishmen to the status of "Turks and Muscovites," subverting subjects' "constitutional rights" to hold diverse opinions and to have a share in legislative power in order to permit the Whig government to perpetuate itself forever.[48]

The Whigs' ideological initiatives thus worked in tandem with coercive measures to construct a particular view of the subject's political rights. The variant of "Whig libertarianism" put forth in the succession crisis recast the populist principles and rhetoric of earlier Whig campaigns to support an essentially nonresisting version of political subjectivity and liberty.[49] With the Tories politically decimated through their identification with Jacobitism, popular electoral rights circumscribed through the Septennial Act of 1716, and arguments for the subjects' right of resistance rendered treasonable by rebellion, the "liberty" of loyal subjects was shown to consist, at most, in their right to engage in vigilante activities against the disaffected, and at least in the passive enjoyment of that civil and religious liberty provided by a constitution secure from the threat of Catholic absolutism. Establishment Whigs under George I thus endorsed the idea, advocated by Richard Steele in *The Crisis,* that liberty consisted in the people being governed by laws made by their representatives and which they had thus implicitly consented to; the locus of liberty was not in the people but in a Parliament whose sovereignty was absolute and in a ministry which protected Parliament from domestic and foreign threats. The Whig strategy was bound to alienate a variety of groups eager to press on the state their own claims for recognition.

In the meantime, despite the precedents provided by the Whig turn to the "right" in the 1690s and 1708–10, the party's frontal assaults on popular political liberties surprised its supporters more than its opponents. Francis Atterbury's prediction in *English Advice* that the Whigs would repeal the Triennial Act was greeted with astonishment and ridicule by the Whig chronicler Abel Boyer: "How can any rea-

---

[47] Sedgwick, i, 339, 317. In Westminster in 1722, two Jacobites were unseated on petition: 286.

[48] *The Suspension of the Triennial Act the Certain Way to Unite the Nation* ([London], 1716).

[49] A point also made by J. P. Kenyon, *Revolution Principles* (London, 1977).

sonable man conceive that the whigs, whose characteristic is to be strenuous asserters of liberty, should ever be for pulling down those very fences they have themselves cast up to preserve it?''[50] But pull them down they did, and in the process the subjects' right of resistance was relegated by establishment Whigs to the ideological dustbin – where it would be taken up in the decades to come by oppositionist groups of all persuasions who sought to wage their own assaults on the post-Revolution Whig state.

II. JACOBITE DISCONTENTS

The extent and nature of disaffection in the immediate succession years most dramatically illustrates the limitations of the Whig appeal. Quite simply, in the context of a contested succession and the accession to the throne of what to many appeared to be an occasionally conforming nonconformist monarch, anti-Catholicism and an unsubstantiated libertarianism were ineffective in countering the wide-ranging popularity of the Tory party in this period, a popularity based upon its self-appointed role as the preserver of the monarchy and the church against the insidious assaults of the Low Church and dissent. Tory propaganda had long encouraged this identification of the party with church and king while promoting the association of Whiggery with dissent, ''foreigners'' (such as William III) and the ''principles of '41'' which had led to the anarchy and subversion of the mid seventeenth century. ''Down, down, down with them quite,'' a High Church ballad declared in reference to the Whigs; ''Twas they that Caus'd King Charles the First to die.'' In the Tory view, a Whig was inimical to the revered English institutions of monarchy and church: he appeared in Augustan High Church prints as a rebel, half priest and half puritan, who sought to overturn all English institutions in one swift blow.[51] The national endorsement of these tenets in Anne's reign had been demonstrated in the repeated Tory victories at the polls between 1689 and 1713 and in the outpouring of High Church zeal attendant upon Sacheverell's trial in 1710.[52] In the years following George I's accession, the pervasive-

---

[50] Boyer, *Political State of Great Britain,* ix, 25. A few Whig writers did evoke the right of resistance as a liberty worth protecting from Stuart despotism, but they were the exception.

[51] PRO, SP 35/29/62 (1), fol. 227, ''The Loyal Churchman's Health''; *A Trimmer* (1689), BM no. 1231, in *Catalogue,* i, 750; M. D. George, *English Political Caricature to 1792,* 2 vols. (Oxford, 1959), i, 67–70.

[52] See Geoffrey Holmes, *The Trial of Dr. Sacheverell* (London, 1973).

ness of Tory sentiment and the fever pitch of anxieties the succession and change in ministry had produced among the party's supporters were transmuted into a Jacobite idiom as a wave of anti-Hanoverian demonstrations and destructive rioting disrupted the nation. For some, the political consequences of the succession had made it clear that the High Church dream of a united episcopacy and Crown presiding over a unified and moral nation could only be effected by a Stuart restoration.

In contrast to Whig loyalism, Tory and Jacobite protest and loyalties in the post-succession years have been extensively probed by historians. The resulting debates have tended to turn on the "authentic" nature of plebeian Jacobite protest, the pervasiveness of Jacobitism within the Tory party, or, most recently, the status of Jacobitism as the dominant *mentalité* of English people's opposition to the Whig state in the century after the Revolution.[53] The intricacies of these debates notwithstanding, English Jacobitism was clearly an important political and ideological position in George I's reign that would continue to inflect popular politics for some time thereafter; most important for our purposes, Tory-Jacobitism provided the dominant idiom of protest in the extra-parliamentary nation between 1715 and 1722. What alternative constructions of the national political community did it express and disseminate? If, as Paul Monod has argued, Jacobitism was the High Church response to the succession rather than the Revolution,[54] then it needs to be considered in the context of post-succession Whig strategies, part of an ideological tug-of-war between contending conceptions of political legitimacy, the national identity and the nature of English liberty. Tory-Jacobites countered Whig initiatives with an equally wide-ranging campaign of their own, carried out in the streets, pulpits, press and taverns of London and provincial towns, that transgressed the

---

[53] For the contending conceptions of the pervasiveness of Jacobitism within the Tory party see Eveline Cruikshanks, *Political Untouchables: The Tories and the '45* (London, 1979), and her contributions to Sedgwick, i, 62–78; Colley, *Defiance*, chap. 2; and J. C. D. Clark, *English Society, 1688–1832* (Cambridge, 1985), who also argues that Jacobitism provided the dominant mode of opposition under the first two Georges. For Jacobite protest as a "language of political blasphemy" enabling plebeian crowds to antagonize their Whig governors see Nicholas Rogers, "Riots and Popular Jacobitism," in Eveline Cruikshanks, ed., *Ideology and Conspiracy: Aspects of Jacobitism 1689–1759* (Edinburgh, 1982), 76–83. Most convincingly, Paul Monod (who also provides the most complete account of the Jacobite riots and protests over the period) has argued that plebeian and high-level Jacobitism partook of the same discrete world view, the High Church *mentalité* which idealized the unity and uniformity believed to be ensured by the Church of England and the hereditary monarchy and seen to be subverted in the new reign: *Jacobitism,* passim.

[54] *Jacobitism,* 187–8.

boundaries of legitimate protest and thus strategically established the space for opposition politics for the next two decades.

The riots and demonstrations of the immediate post-succession years established the tone and texture of disaffection and adumbrated the content of its critique of Hanoverian Whiggery. Beginning as rumblings in two dozen provincial towns on the accession and coronation days in 1714, they soon spread to London and swelled to a roar in intensity and geographic scope over the winter, spring and summer of 1715, as the dimensions of the Tory rout from government and the nature of the new Whig regime became clear. Over the next five years, anti-Hanoverian or anti-Whig demonstrations had occurred in thirty more towns.[55] The counter-theater staged on these occasions exploited the political calendar to mock the elaborate artifices of loyalty put on by Whig supporters and proffer an alternative system of political meanings. For example, in 1715 Stuart anniversaries, such as Anne's coronation day, Restoration Day and the Pretender's birthday; the birthday of the Tory hero, the Duke of Ormonde; and the new monarch's birthday were all marked by demonstrations of Tory and Jacobite crowds in London. Presbyterian meeting houses were attacked, effigies of Whig heroes such as Cromwell, William III, Marlborough and the Bishop of Bangor were burned to the cries "Down with the Rump, no Hanoverian, no Presbyterian government," and white roses (the badge of loyalty to the Stuarts) were flaunted.[56] These symbolic desecrations were continued during and after the '15, when the battles between the "Mugs" and the "Jacks" continued the theater and counter-theater of loyalism and dissidence, using turnips, horns, effigies and warming-pans as props.[57]

Disaffection in the capital, which fizzled out after 1716, proved easier for the Whig government to quell than in the provinces, where, as Monod has pointed out, nearly every important town was marked by a Jacobite disturbance between 1715 and 1722.[58] Restoration Day in 1715 was marked by riots and demonstrations in a number of towns, such

[55] See *An Account of the Riots, Tumults and Other Treasonable Practices Since His Majesty's Accession to the Throne* (London, 1715), 4–5, 12–13 and passim; PRO, SP 35/74/2–4; Monod, *Jacobitism,* 173–94.
[56] Rae, *History of the Rebellion,* 135–41; *Worcester Postman,* May 27 – June 3, 1715; *Flying Post,* May 29–31, 1715; PRO, SP 35/74/33–4; Rogers, "Popular Protest," 72–4.
[57] Rogers, "Popular Protest," 77–83; Ryder, *Diary,* 138–9; see also *Flying Post,* Nov. 5–8, 17–19, 1715; Nov. 13–16, 1716; *Dank's Newsletter,* June 13, 1716.
[58] Monod, *Jacobitism,* 225–6.

as Manchester, Bristol and Norwich. In Oxford, a Tory mob, consisting
of both townspeople and students and aggravated by the ostentatious
celebrations of the Whig Constitution Club, burned the pulpit and pews
of a Presbyterian meeting-house which it had gutted on May 28 in a
Restoration Day bonfire, crying, "Down with the Roundheads, no Con-
stitutioners, no Hanover, a New Restoration"; later in the day the Baptist and Quaker meeting-houses were pulled down.[59] The summer of
rioting in the Midlands and Lancashire inaugurated on the Pretender's
birthday, June 10, affected forty-two towns and involved several hundred participants and thousands of pounds in damages, mostly to dissenters' meeting-houses and properties.[60] Disaffection thereafter tended
to be less violent and geared to the political calendar. In Worcester,
despite the Corporation's assiduity in staging loyal celebrations on anniversary days, disturbances broke out between troops and local residents on the coronation day in 1715, forcing the mayor to prohibit the
cries "Down with the Roundheads" and "Down with the Jacobites"
within the town's limits.[61] The twenty-ninth of May was kept in Norwich, Newcastle, Bristol and elsewhere for several years with the wearing of sprigs of oak or even the festooning of entire parishes with oak
boughs and flowers – both formerly perceived as symbols of loyalty to
the monarchy but in the new reign a badge of sedition and treason.[62]
The tenth of June was perhaps the main occasion for Jacobite display,
when white roses abounded in towns in the North, Southwest and Midlands as well as in East Anglia; and both George I's birthday and the
first of August could prompt the wearing of rue and thyme – to rue the
day George was born or acceded to the throne and to bid the quick
passing of time until the true king would return.[63] The use of turnips
and horns to symbolize the allegedly cuckolded new monarch – such

[59] PRO, SP 35/4/18; Rae, *History of the Rebellion,* 140–1; *Post-Boy,* June 2–4, 1715;
Flying Post, June 18–21, 1715. See also [Richard Rawlinson], *A Full and Impartial
Account of the Oxford Riots . . . In a Letter from a Member of the University, to His
Friend in London* (London, 1715).

[60] For the summer riots see Dr. Williams's Library, MS 34.4, John Evans, "Account of
the Damages Done in the Riots, 1715"; PRO, SP 35/3/363 (1)–(6); *Flying Post,* June
14–16, 1715. The committee investigating these riots estimated the damage at £5,268.
12s. 7d.: Evans, "Account of the Damages," 2.

[61] Worcester City Archives, Chamberlain Accts., A10/7, 1714–15, 1715–16; *Worcester
Postman,* Oct. 28, 1715.

[62] *Norwich Gazette,* April 28, 1716; June 1, 1717; *St. James's Evening Post,* June 2–5,
1716; Latimer, *Annals of Bristol,* 110.

[63] See PRO, SP 35/16/101, 104, 133 (Leicestershire and Loughborough); SP 35/57/8
(Averly, Essex); SP 35/12/97 (Avington); SP 44/79A, pp. 180–1 (Worcester); *Flying
Post,* June 2–5, 1716 (Norwich); Latimer, *Annals of Bristol,* 110; and Chapter 8.

as at Holesworth, Suffolk, where the magistrates awoke on the first of August 1717 to prepare their accession-day solemnities only to find a pair of bullock's horns with turnips attached hanging on the pillory in the marketplace – served, among other things, to ridicule the Whigs' efforts to portray him as majesty incarnate: The Whig's king, it suggested, was impotent as well as illegitimate, since legitimate power could only be masculine and illegitimate power was demonstrated by emasculation.[64]

Despite Whig propagandists' efforts to identify Tory supporters with the "rabble" (that is, "Black-guard Boys, clean your shoes your Honour, Parish Boys, Wheel-barrow-men, Butchers, Porters, Basketwomen, Ballad-Singers, Bawds, Whores and Thieves"), the social provenance of disaffection, like that of loyalism, was diverse.[65] Disaffected elites organized or sanctioned anti-Whig and anti-Hanoverian demonstrations, perhaps hoping that extensive displays of popular hostility to the new regime would stave off attempts by George I to punish former Tory leaders. The mayor of Nottingham, Alderman Hawkesley, drank "Success to the House of Stuart" on an entertainment he gave for apparently like-minded friends in 1715; he was committed to jail by a fellow magistrate only to be visited by numbers of Jacobite gentlemen from the county. Disaffection also riddled Corporation ranks in Newcastle upon Tyne, Norwich, Taunton, Newcastle under Lyme, Leicester and Lichfield, towns where popular anti-Hanoverianism also loomed large.[66] High Church clergymen were considered by contemporaries to be particularly relentless propagators of anti-Hanoverian doctrine.[67] No doubt influenced by Sacheverell's example, High Flyers were audacious in their denigration of Whig authority, or, more seriously, of the succession, presenting a formidable fifth column against

[64] PRO, SP 44/79a/111 (I owe this reference to Paul Monod); see also SP 35/27/50–7 (Bridgwater, 1721).

[65] *Weekly Journal, or British Gazetteer,* June 2, 1716. As the State Papers and local court records make clear, gentlemen, tradesmen, artisans, laborers and servants participated in riots and anti-Hanoverian demonstrations; see also Monod, *Jacobitism,* 177–8, 188–9.

[66] *V.C.H. Nottinghamshire,* i (London, 1906), 359. Two years later a senior councilman, Mr. William Greaves, was disenfranchised for disloyalty: *Records of Nottingham,* vi, 66; Chapters 7 and 8; PRO, SP 35/74/2; J. H. Y. Briggs, "The Burning of the Meeting House, July 1715: Dissent and Faction in Late Stuart Newcastle," *North Staffordshire Journal of Field Studies,* 14 (1974), 71–3; Sedgwick, i, 276, 319.

[67] See [Daniel Defoe], *A Hymn to the Mob* (London, 1715); *Some Considerations on the Danger of the Church from Her Own Clergy* (London, 1715); *Account of the Riots,* 2; Ryder, *Diary,* 152; Rae, *History of the Rebellion,* 113.

the government before and after 1715. In Northumberland, Jacobite clergymen continued to engage in subterfuge to pray for the Stuarts long after the defeat of the rebellion. The overt Jacobitism of the clergy in Manchester was notorious or celebrated, depending on one's point of view; only one collegiate churchman in Manchester subscribed to the loyalist defense fund to fight the Pretender in 1715.[68] And in Leicester, the High Church Jacobite Samuel Carte, vicar of St. Martin's, clearly presided over a community of clergymen and parishioners who shared his loyalties. During the 1715 parliamentary election, five clergymen led the crowd in an almost deadly assault on the Whig under sheriff at the polls as one allegedly remarked, "If all Elections went like ours, *we would muffle the Gentleman that keeps the two Turks* [George I]." The persistence of local Jacobitism (pro-Stuart demonstrations also occurred in 1722, 1738 and 1744) led to the quartering of troops in the town.[69] The power of the High Flying clergy should not be exaggerated; if churchmen were able to brainwash their flocks, the Whig clergy would have been far more successful than they were. But as local representatives of authority, their articulation of views that were held by a broader cross-section of the population and their willingness to resist Whig hegemony at its inception (which compared favorably with the apparent dull-wittedness of secular Tory leaders in the face of the Whig onslaught) made them both popular heroes and Whig villains. Not surprisingly, Stanhope and Townshend directed great efforts to ridding clerical ranks of the disaffected.[70]

Clearly, neither the provenance nor themes of protest were generated solely from below but were part of partisan cultural identities that circulated through a broad cross-section of society. The counter-theater of disaffection accordingly combined established rituals and symbols of both political and popular culture – oak boughs and white roses, turnips and horns, mock processions and charivaris, chairings and effigy-burnings – to attack the legitimacy of the new monarch and castigate

[68] "The Diary of Rev. John Thomlinson," in *Six Northern Diaries,* ed. John Crawford Hodgson (Surtees Society, 118, 1910), 66, 89; W. E. A. Axon, *The Annals of Manchester* (Manchester, 1886), 84; *The Private Journal and Literary Remains of John Byrom,* ed. Richard Parkinson, pt. 1 (Chetham Society, 32, 1854), 23–9.

[69] Rae, *History of the Rebellion,* 121; *VCH Leicestershire,* iv (London, 1907), 123–6. Even in strongly Whiggish Liverpool, a rector who refused to participate in the thanksgiving for the peaceful accession of Hanover was chaired in celebration by approving citizens: *Flying Post,* Sept. 28–30, 1714.

[70] Chapter 7; Gateshead Public Library, Ellison MSS A36/28, Jan. 25, 1715; "Diary of Thomlinson," 66, 89. In London, the most popular preachers, such as Sacheverell, Atterbury and Welton, were Jacobites.

the Whigs' self-professed identity as the defenders of English liber-ties.[71] In the ideological contestation under way, what was at stake were the readings of national history that gave legitimacy to current con-stellations of power or to the forms and content of resistance to them. Hence, protesters drew in part upon late Stuart and Augustan party stereotypes in order to counter the Whigs' image of themselves as loy-alists and "their" monarch as legitimate. The Whigs were sectarian infidels, the contemporary heirs of the roundheads and regicides of the Civil War, seeking to reintroduce the anarchy and subversion of the 1640s and 1650s. Following this analogy, the Whigs' king was (like Cromwell) a usurper, and resistance to his rule, by solid "revolution principles," was justified. Hence demonstrations as well as poems and ballads refer to George I as having "usurp'd" the throne. As one Nor-wich citizen remarked in reference to George's recent trip to Hanover, *"King G[eor]ge was gone Home for a Certificate."*[72] The cry "Down with the Rump" also evoked seventeenth-century sins as it cast asper-sions on the present, reminding the Whigs, who were parading as the defenders of English liberties, that they were but a self-appointed Par-liament with no basis in popular consent.

Further, the Whigs' historical association with a wider Protestant toleration encouraged their current identification with nonconformity. Since the Restoration, dissenters had peopled the High Church imagi-nation as the primary domestic political other that the nation had to fear, ceaselessly plotting with their republican allies the destruction of church and monarchy. In the post-succession period, the Presbyterians emerged as the most hated variant of dissent, as evinced by High Church crowds' propensity to attack their meeting-houses over others in certain areas.[73] As the most numerous and richest nonconformist denomination in England, comprising between 4 and 8 percent of the population in Northumberland, Dorset, Nottinghamshire, Somerset, Cheshire, Devonshire and Lancashire, sustaining strong electoral influ-ence and, with Quakers, being most visible in local political and eco-nomic structures, the Presbyterians symbolized to their enemies all that was wrong with the post-Revolution settlement, which allowed the in-

[71] See, e.g., E. P. Thompson, *Customs in Common: Studies in Traditional Popular Cul-ture* (New York, 1991), 467–531.
[72] *Weekly Packet,* Oct. 13–20, 1716; see also *Weekly Journal, or Saturday's Post,* June 23–30, 1716.
[73] Michael Watts, *The Dissenters* (Oxford, 1978), 269–70; e.g., the "Loyal Mob of Shrewsbury" singled out the Presbyterians for attack in the summer of 1715: *St. James's Evening Post,* Aug. 2, 1715.

fidel and the intolerant to prosper and subvert from within. Not only
was it believed that Presbyterians were the primary *agents provocateurs*
behind the upheavals of 1641–9 (which Charles I himself suspected),
but in the accession years High Flyers also insisted that Presbyterians
were "worse than papists," "more bloody and cruel in their principles," so that their close alliance with the Whigs and Hanover would
be sure to overturn church and monarchy in one swift blow. "[W]hich
is the greater Slavery, Presbytery or Popery," one Jacobite writer
asked; "which is the greater Slavery, Monarchy or Commonwealth?
. . . to have one King, or seven hundred?" Some clergymen even
claimed that the king and Parliament were all Presbyterians.[74] Sectarian
antagonisms like these remained raw in many provincial towns, Coventry, Maidstone, Manchester, Nottingham, Norwich and Bristol among
them, where a strong dissenting political and economic presence kept
animosities alive. Hence when a mob assailed a local friend to the Whig
ministry in Brecon on June 10, 1718, as "presbiterian," "Grandson to
an old Oliverian Dog, a betrayer of the Church" and "Deputy" of
"Ben Hoadly . . . ye great Devil's Secretary," they were evoking these
past and present conflicts.[75] In a number of ways, High Church Tory
anxieties and historical memories fueled the expressions of disaffection
in the accession years and marked time for a change in measures and
men.

The protest of the period was informed by more than historical and
partisan traditions, however, and by the early summer of 1715 was
attached to an overtly Jacobite critique of Whig and Hanoverian power
that took equally material forms in protest, armed insurrection – and
the press. Indeed, with rebellion broken out in the North, a stringent
Whig crackdown on protesters and rebels under way, a Tory party
demoralized by its divisions and the attrition by death or defection of
the generation of post-Revolution nonjurors, the press took a leading
role in disseminating Jacobite opinion, circulating new agendas, hardening resistance to the new regime and keeping Tory and Stuart hopes

---

[74] For Charles I's suspicions see *An Exact Collection of All Remonstrances, Declarations, Ordinances and Other Passages Between the King's Majesty and His Parliament* (London, 1644) (thanks to Conrad Russell for this reference). For High Flyers'
claims in the accession years see, e.g., *The Rise and Growth of Fanaticism; or, A
View of the Principles, Plots and Pernicious Practices of the Dissenters* (London,
1715); *The Scourge . . . in Vindication of the Church of England,* Feb. 4 – Nov. 25,
1717; quotation from *The Shift Shift'd,* June 30, 1716.

[75] PRO, SP 35/12/75. See, e.g., Judith J. Hurwich, " 'A Fanatick Town': The Political
Influence of Dissenters in Coventry, 1660–1720," *Midland History,* 4 (1977), 15–47.

alive.[76] Lay Jacobite printers, writers and publicists seized the high ground, circulating their propaganda through the fairly anonymous network of alehouses, vestries, printers, markets and nonjuring chapels, and making it notoriously difficult for the Whig authorities to quell all of their operations.[77] Newsagents, mercuries, hawkers, street vendors, chapmen and ballad-singers thus joined the front lines of the anti-Whig offensive, becoming equally the targets of government wrath.[78]

The range and variety of dissident and treasonable literature that was readily available to all citizens was astonishing to contemporaries. Whig loyalists decried the effectiveness of the "seditious pamphlets and traitorous libels dispersed in the streets" of both London and the larger provincial towns in stirring up disaffection.[79] Pro-Stuart verses, doggerel, ballads and slip songs were legion in the aftermath of the succession: One scholar has counted at least ninety treasonable verses produced between 1714 and 1720, and many additional verses and ballads, printed as broadsides, can be discovered in collections of Jacobite ephemera in twentieth-century libraries.[80] Scores of High Church verses with seditious implications were printed on broadsides for distribution; others were copied by hand or just sung in the streets, as their preservation in quantity in the State Papers attests. Equally creative were the "Depositions" about the legitimate birth of James Edward Stuart which allegedly were stuck under doors and dropped about the streets of London. Last dying speeches of convicted rebel lords and rank-and-file alike were also printed as broadsides and enunciated the principles of the true loyalists.[81] Even after the rebellion was defeated, copies of

[76] At least 25 Tory peers, MPs and clergymen were conspirators in the insurrection: Colley, *Defiance,* 29. For nonjurors see William Coxe, *Memoirs of the Life and Administration of Sir Robert Walpole,* 3 vols. (London, 1798), ii, 97–8.
[77] See, e.g., PRO, SP 44/79A/34, 135; Rogers, *Whigs and Cities,* 370–1. Cf. Hyland, "Liberty and Libel"; in my view he overestimates the success of the Whig government's efforts in this regard.
[78] Many of the victims of government prosecution were women. PRO, SP 35/22/166–7; *Evening Post,* July 14, 1715; *Weekly Journal,* May 26 – June 2, 1716; *Weekly Packet,* March 19, 1717; Hyland, "Liberty and Libel," 880, 886. Warrants for arrest can also be found in PRO, SP 44/77/162ff.
[79] NNRO, WKC 7/101/404, Ketton-Cremer MSS, "Some of the Endeavors of the Faction, carried on for destroying the peace of ye Kingdom, since King George's coming to the Crown" [1723]; Doran, *London in the Jacobite Times,* i, 71.
[80] See, e.g., HL, Collection of English and Jacobite Ballads, 1679–1728, and Collection of Jacobite Handbills and Broadsides, 1717–49. For the estimate see Foxon, *English Verse,* ii, 256–7; and Alex B. Grossart, *The Tounley MSS: English Jacobite Ballads, Songs and Satires* (London, 1877).
[81] PRO, SP 35/29/62 (1)–(4), fols. 227–30; 35/21/122b (1); 35/11/85; 35/29/36, fol. 68; 35/49/74 (2)–(3) (I owe the last four references to Paul Monod); *A True Copy of a*

the Pretender's manifesto were still being distributed throughout Bristol, despite authorities' strenuous efforts to stop them.[82]

Pamphlets could also serve the cause and intersect with the popular campaign. Although aimed at a rather higher social bracket than ballads, broadsides and squibs, they were still accessible to a broad range of readers and listeners in the coffeehouses and taverns of the capital and provincial towns and were excerpted, plagiarized or condensed in more ephemeral forms. The Bishop of Rochester, Francis Atterbury, wrote one such anonymous pamphlet, *English Advice to the Freeholders of England,* which was published before the 1715 election and distributed throughout England and Ireland. It provided an exceptionally incisive, vernacular and prescient reading of the probable consequences of a "Whig restoration" that helped shape public conceptions of the new dynasty.[83] Atterbury pulled out all the stops in his attack on the Whigs – monied men and sectarians all, in his view, who had begun poisoning the Elector in Anne's reign with their lies about Tory plans to bring in the Pretender. But he saved his fiercest and most seditious attack for George I himself, painting him as the embodiment and conduit of foreign infiltration and subversion. The king's "first Compliment to his People" was to dismiss the beloved Ormonde from office and rout the Tories from state and local government throughout the three kingdoms, Atterbury declared, thus clearing the way for his plans to undermine the Church of England by extending toleration. What could the English expect? A German and Lutheran by birth and upbringing, the new king was incapable of understanding the English church or the English constitution, and the Prince of Wales and his wife were such devout "Calvinists" (read "Presbyterians") that they had not even taken the Anglican sacrament. The monarch's ill-suitedness to rule was also shown through his black Turkish attendants – an association with Oriental despotism, that antithesis of European civility, that boded ill for his leadership in England. Finally, his cuckoldry and his merciless treatment of his wife's lover, Count Königs-

---

Paper Delivered to the Sheriffs of London, by Richard Gascoigne, Who Was Drawn, Hang'd and Quarter'd at Tyburn, on May 25, 1716 and *The Speech of James, Earl of Derwentwater: Who Was Beheaded on Tower-hill* (both London, 1716).

[82] Latimer, *Annals of Bristol,* 113; *Worcester Journal,* Dec. 13–20, 1717.

[83] (London, 1715), passim. It was still being reprinted in 1716, and the government never discovered the identity of the writer. Townshend ordered magistrates in a number of provincial towns to prosecute distributors of the pamphlet. Hyland, "Liberty and Libel," 886–7; Speck, *Tory and Whig,* 41; for reprinting see *Weekly Journal, or British Gazetteer,* March 9, 1716.

mark, who currently languished in a prison with no prospect of release, indicated what treatment his opponents could expect. If the Whigs remained in power, Atterbury predicted, they would wage war for the benefit of the king's German dominions, levy a general excise and a poll tax, establish an unlimited religious comprehension, augment the standing army, attack and suppress the Tory press, and repeal the Triennial Act to "secure their Usurpation . . . [and] render them as terrible as the Long Parliament in *Forty-One.*" "For my own part, I am not yet *Germanized,*" he concluded; "I can no more Laugh at the Death of Queen *Anne,* than I can Rejoice at the Funeral of *England.*"

Atterbury's nationalist critique of the new monarch had wide currency, influencing or reinforcing the idioms of opposition to the new regime and popular perceptions of the new monarch that were expressed, as we have seen, in protest and verse. They were also common stock in ballads, which identified George I with Turks and infidels, barbarity and tyranny, subterfuge and subversion. *A Prophecy, by Merlin* foretold "When Savage Goths from Rhine Return, / And Crowns aloft on Horns are worn / When a dull Cuckold shall appear, / Usurper, Tyrant, Murderer / With Fool, and Bastard to his Heir . . . / When Turbants shall with Mitres vie, / And Loyal Peers on Scaffolds die . . . ," then "An Exil'd King shall fight her Cause, / Protect the Church, restore the Laws." Another pointed to the savage treatment of his enemies which was also attributed to his "Oriental" barbarity and cruelty.[84] Others more irreverently ridiculed George I's occupation in Hanover as "turnip-hoer," a reference to his alleged origins in poverty and ignorance. And slip songs enthusiastically endorsed the aspersions protesters cast upon his virility. A Westminster spinster was taken up for singing one such song, "Make room for the Cuckoldy King and Send him to Hanover," and called the informant a "presbyterian toad."[85] Cuckolded, foreign, despotic, childish and mean-spirited as well as lacking hereditary title to the throne, George I abrogated all the requirements of "masculine" kingship that had been retailed as a pop-

---

[84] *A Prophecy, by Merlin* (n.p., n.d.); *A Prophetick Congratulatory Hymn to His Sacred Brittannick Majesty King James the III* (London, 1719), both in HL, Collection of English and Jacobite Ballads, unfoliated.

[85] It was a commonplace that when the messengers came to Hanover to announce his succession, George was found in a field hoeing turnips: See *Norwich Gazette,* Oct. 28, 1716; *An Excellent New Ballad* [1716], in HL, Collection of English and Jacobite Ballads; Gravenor Henson, *The Civil, Political and Mechanical History of the Framework Knitter in Europe and America,* vol. 1 (Nottingham, 1831), 130–3. PRO, SP 44/ 79A (I owe this reference to Paul Monod).

ular ideal of monarchy by Queen Elizabeth I herself.[86] True Englishness
demanded his rejection, and the acceptance of the rightful monarch,
James III, who was portrayed as wealthy, virile, charming and English,
the epitome of the kingly qualities needed to preside over a legitimate,
moral and unified polity.[87]

Such themes and arguments focussed attention on the dynastic question and the nature of kingship while painting a dark and ominous
picture of the new monarch as a conduit of foreign subversion. Other
printed missives became more focussed on the consequences of the
succession within the nation at large. Tory newspapers, which had a
larger circulation than their pro-government rivals, were credited with
"keep[ing] up the spirit of Jacobites and ... inflam[ing] the Mob
against the Government and all good Subjects," and were consequently
subject to vigorous government prosecution.[88] Nevertheless, metropolitan papers like the *Post-Boy* and the Jacobite *Weekly Journal, or Saturday's Post* and provincial newspapers such as the *Bristol Postman,
Worcester Postman, Newcastle Courant* and *Norwich Gazette* were all
effective in spreading details about the Whig offensive and the ineffectual nature of the Tory response, which could have a number of
unexpected consequences. Through careful reporting on the full range
of Whig activities – the allegations of disaffection in all parts of the
country, the rounding up of suspects, the use of informants, the mobilization of troops, the persecution of printers, hawkers and singers,
the harassment of ordinary citizens, the attacks on women and children,
and the treatment of convicted rebels – the papers substantiated allegations of government brutality as well as Whig accounts of extensive
subterranean Jacobite plots in London and the localities.[89] Such a representational strategy clearly could work against, as well as for, the
cause of stamping out disaffection, as anti-Whig publicists were well
aware. Tracts such as "A Faithful and Impartial Account of several
thousand Persons ... who (since the Demise of her late Glorious Maj-

---

[86] Louis Montrose, "The Work of Gender in the Discourse of Discovery," *Representations,* 33 (1991), 1–41.
[87] See, e.g., PRO, SP 35/29/62, fol. 288 (1721).
[88] NNRO, Ketton-Cremer MSS, WKC 7/101/404; Hyland, "Liberty and Libel," 886–7.
William Ayscough in Nottingham, Phillip Bishop in Exeter, John White in Newcastle
and Henry Crossgrove in Norwich were among the provincial printers prosecuted.
[89] See, e.g., *Worcester Postman,* Feb. 11, March 11, June 10, Sept. 2, 1715; Dec. 6–13,
13–20, 20–7, 1717; May 16, 1718; *Newcastle Courant,* July 25–8, 1715, Jan. 30 –
Feb. 1, 1716; *Bristol Postman,* Sept. 31, 1715; *Robin's Last Shift,* April 7, 1716;
Weekly Journal, Oct. 20, 1716. Whig papers also provided these details, of course.

esty Queen ANNE of ever blessed Memory) have been persecuted, imprison'd and even butcher'd, in the Most barbarous and inhuman Manner Contrary to all Law, and the known Rights and Privileges of *Englishmen.* With an *Introductory* Essay on the Liberty and Property of the Subject,'' thousands of advertisements for which were distributed throughout the capital in 1716, probably did little to improve Whig public relations.[90]

The extensive reporting on the combative activities of troops and the harassment of citizens throughout the country helped set the stage for a more aggressive discussion of the subject's liberties, which Jacobite newspapers and weeklies took up with relish. *Mist's Weekly Journal,* founded in 1716, and still more the notorious *Shift* papers, beginning the same year, were prominent in this respect. Written by George Flint, a Roman Catholic, and Isaac Dalton, who was also the printer, the papers *Robin's Last Shift, The Shift Shift'd,* and *Shift's Last Shift* were published from February 1716 and February 1717; one was no sooner cut down than another sprouted up (despite the printer and publisher's being frequently in Newgate).[91] Deliberately written to engage "the people," these papers articulated a populist and legitimist Jacobitism that, in the context of Whig repression and judicial terror, held out the promise of deliverance in the form of James III, who would bring liberty and justice to his people. To this end, virtually every issue contained information about "King James," railed against the Revolution, Lockean contract theory (which Flint clearly believed to be the most important ideological prop of the post-Revolution state) and "presbyterian" power and betrayal. They championed instead divine hereditary right and a version of popular libertarianism that upheld the subject's rights against Whig and Hanoverian usurpation and repression.[92] In doing so, Flint moved the discussion of popular liberties forward and resuscitated the notion of the people's right and propensity to resist arbitrary and illegitimate power. For example, attacking that bête noire of the High Church, Benjamin Hoadley, Flint warned him that appealing to the multitude for support, as Whig principles dictated that he should, could be a serious mistake:

---

[90] *Shift Shift'd,* June 23, 1716.

[91] As many as 100 people, from printers to hawkers and mercuries, were arrested in connection with the *Shift* papers: Hyland, "Liberty and Libel," 879.

[92] See, e.g., *Robin's Last Shift,* Feb. 18, 25, March 31, April 7, 1716; *Shift Shift'd,* May 19, June 23, Sept. 8, 1716.

For suppose a free People should think themselves at Liberty to wear
what sort of Cloaths and Ribbons they think fit; and since no Law
forbids, imagine that they may adorn themselves with what Flowers
and Nosegays they fancy, without running any Hazard, much less
losing Liberty, Limits, and even Life itself; And finding themselves
mistaken, shou'd resent the ill Usage as an *Oppression,* and *Invasion
of their Rights?*[93]

Clearly, another revolution might result. Such thinly veiled hints about
the people's propensity to resist tyranny were deliberately affronting to
the Whigs, who had made the right of resistance a "first principle" in
the decade of the Revolution but in the present context had done all
they could to render it treasonable. Yet for observers like Flint, there
seemed little other hope for salvation coming from within. Reviewing
the authoritarian use of the militias in provincial towns and the inactivity of Tory leaders, he exclaimed, "Queen of Nations! Behold thy
Oppressors. S'death! Is there no British Blood left in Britain?"[94]

Flint's strategies first signaled the renewed attention to the liberties
of the subject that had been the stock-in-trade of the so-called "Whiggish Jacobites" of the 1690s and would be followed by Stuart sympathizers Henry Crossgrove of the *Norwich Gazette,* Nathaniel Mist of
Mist's Weekly Journal and Elizabeth Adams of the *Chester Courant* in
the ensuing decades.[95] In the meantime, concern for the fate of the
subject's liberties gave the arguments for hereditary right a populist
thrust. Hence the Pretender's Declaration as well as those of his supporters stressed the hereditary nature of all English rights and liberties
– not only of monarchs, but also of subjects, which were currently
being circumvented and trounced by the Whigs' "foreign" and illegitimate king.[96] A significant degree of popular sympathy for the Pretender no doubt arose from the analogy that seemed to arise between
his plight and theirs: He had been deprived of his birthright by force,
just as they were now being deprived of theirs. As one Kinsey in

[93] *Shift Shift'd,* July 28, 1716.
[94] Ibid., Sept. 8, 1716.
[95] *Norwich Gazette,* March 3, 1716; June 1, 1717; Jan. 25, May 30, 1718; *Mist's Weekly
Journal,* Aug. 24, 1728; for the *Chester Courant* (also known as *Adams's Weekly
Courant)* see R. M. Wiles, *Freshest Advices: Early Provincial Newspapers in England*
(Canton, Ohio, 1965), 399–400, and *Manchester Vindicated* (Chester, 1749). For an
overview of "Whiggish Jacobites'" amalgam of divine right and "country" principles see Monod, *Jacobitism,* 17–33.
[96] Rae, *History of the Rebellion,* 418–70, reprints these declarations along with other
propaganda and statements issued by James's camp.

Loughborough remarked wearing a white rose on the Pretender's birthday, "If the Crown be ye Pretenders right 'tis a pity but he had it."[97]

Although Jacobite propaganda was clearly diversified and wide-
ranging in this period, it nevertheless retained a distinctive ideological
thrust: that the Revolution and the Protestant succession were illegal,
contrary to the laws of God (which clearly sanctioned hereditary succession) and the nation, and thus the cause of the immorality, factious-
ness and divisiveness of the contemporary polity; illegitimate power
bred its inevitable companions.[98] As a Jacobite slip song put it, the true
pretender to the throne could be discerned by reason: He who is made
king "by Choice" and "Convention" instead of birth, who "Breaks
through all our Laws," who would remodel the church according to
the principles of a "Giblet-Comprehension" and who is foreign in
language and sensibility cannot be the legitimate monarch.[99] And without a legitimate and lawful king, there could be neither laws nor liberty.
The indefatigable Reverend Edward Bisse of Somerset was only one
of many Jacobite proponents who tried to convince the people of these
precepts: Bisse was silenced by King's Bench for denigrating the Revolution settlement, only to be convicted later at the Buckingham assizes
for proclaiming, "WE HAVE HAD NO LAWS THESE THIRTY YEARS SINCE
THE TIME OF KING JAMES II NOR SHALL WE HAVE TILL JAMES COMES."[100]

However, faced with a monarch who was not only illegitimate but
extremely unattractive by virtue of his nationality and religion, an authoritarian Whig government which used its power to persecute the true
"loyalists," and ample demonstration of the unpopularity of both, the
right of resistance, even if wielded in the name of nonresistance and
passive obedience, held out the hope of better times to come. Jacobite
journalists thus deployed a version of resistance principles that was
used to taunt the Whigs and justify their own desires and activities.
The pamphlet *Vox Populi, Vox Dei* was perhaps the most notorious
instance of this tactic, borrowing its title from a radical Whig tract of

---

[97] PRO, SP 35/21/111. In this context, Clark's allegations that the Tory party owed its
strength to the "widespread acceptance of deference" and rejection of contractarian
doctrines is extremely unconvincing: J. C. D. Clark, "The Politics of the Excluded:
Tories, Jacobites and Whig Patriots, 1715–1760," *Parliamentary History,* 2 (1983),
209–22.

[98] Paul Monod, " 'For the King to Enjoy His Own Again': Jacobite Political Culture
in England, 1688–1788" (Ph.D. diss., Yale University, 1985), chap. 1. HL, Collection
of English and Jacobite Ballads, 1679–1728.

[99] *The History of Twenty-Nine Years of Rebellion and Usurpation* (London, 1717); *The
Pretender* ([n.p.], 1717), both in HL, Collection of English and Jacobite Ballads.

[100] *Flying Post,* Aug. 2–5, 1715; PRO, SP 35/7/8, 35/12/31.

1709 to argue that by the Whigs' own principles of popular sovereignty James III should be restored. "Sure you ought to fight with more resolution for liberty than your opponents do for dominion," it urged the people; "count your numbers." The authorities responded fiercely to this tract, and one of its printers, John Matthews, was executed. Nevertheless, the Jacobite strategy of using the "Voice of the People" to vex the Whigs and woo the people was embellished and perfected in less seditious form by the Walpolean opposition, becoming an established instrument of oppositionist writers of all stripes for the rest of the century.[101]

Jacobite journalists and protestors thus constructed a critique of Whiggery that, if not providing "the framework for extra-parliamentary radicalism" for the rest of the century, as has been argued, did make important contributions to the latter in content and tactics.[102] Its practical and ideological strategies in resisting Whig power were carried out on a number of levels – in the streets, in the press, from the pulpit, in popular demonstrations and elite political practice – and in ways that established the boundaries of acceptable political dissent by inscribing the limits of the unacceptable. Above all, Jacobitism in this period paradoxically combined a conservative agenda of a unified and monolithic church, a hereditary monarch and a homogeneous polity with the championing of "the people's" liberties and rights against the claims and actions of the state. It thus kept alive a notion of "the people" as a virtuous, libertarian and remedial force in the face of overmighty exertions of state power.

Jacobitism's weakness lay in its desire to alter the Protestant succession, and its successes led to its ultimate defeat. Of course, continuing Tory proscription lent itself to future Jacobite plottings and intrigues, and a covert Jacobite culture of drinking clubs and toasts, tartan fashions and Stuart memorabilia persisted in specific regions throughout England and Wales as well as Scotland.[103] But in the years

---

[101] *Vox Populi, Vox Dei* [London, 1719], passim; for arrests and execution see *Worcester Postman,* June 19–26, 1719; *Norwich Gazette,* July 2, 1720. See also [Mathias Earbery], *An Historical Account of the Advantages That Have Accrued to England, by the Succession in the Illustrious House of Hanover* (London, 1722); and *The Second Part of the Historical Account . . .* (London, 1722), a jeremiad on the rampant corruption and decay within the nation since the Glorious Revolution that strikingly anticipates, or perhaps influenced, the arguments of John Shebbeare in his *Letters to the People of England* (London, 1755–8). For similar complaints thirty years later see *Manchester Vindicated.*

[102] Monod, *Jacobitism,* 346.

[103] Ibid., passim; Philip Jenkins, "Jacobites and Freemasons in Eighteenth Century

following the succession, the Whig government's ability to punish and ostracize the entire Tory party as Jacobite forced the Jacobite idiom underground in England and the empire, where it lingered as a pugnacious strand of political dissent but a dangerous and increasingly untenable dynastic option. In the decade thereafter, the former Stuart sympathizer Viscount Bolingbroke would become a leading voice of an oppositionist initiative that was in certain respects more challenging to the regime than any beleaguered and attenuated Jacobitism could be.

III. EXCISES ARE WOODEN SHOES

> Horse, Foot and Dragoons,
> Battalions, Platoons,
> Excise, Wooden Shoes, and no Jury;
> Then Taxes increasing,
> While Traffick is ceasing,
> Would put all the Land in a Fury.
> *Britannia Excisa: or, Britain*
> *Excised, A New Ballad*
> (London, 1733)

One of the more outstanding changes which had occurred in political culture by the late 1720s was the marked shift from Jacobitism to libertarianism as the idiom of popular protest. The reaction to George II's accession in 1727 demonstrates the magnitude of the change. The observances of this occasion in the localities were marked by their ostentatious, and bipartisan, loyalism. Towns which had been rife with disaffection by 1715–16, such as Bristol, Leicester, Leeds, Nottingham, Norwich, Worcester and York, were particularly lavish in their celebrations in 1727, quickly sweeping away the black crepe which was draped on civic monuments and maypoles to express mourning for George I to replace it with garlands of flowers, green boughs and rushes in honor of his successor; days which began with solemn processions to church ended with bonfires and dancing in the streets.[104] The only

Wales," *Welsh Historical Review,* 9 (1979), 391–406; Bruce Lenman, *The Jacobite Risings in Britain, 1689–1746* (London, 1980). For longevity of Jacobite sentiment in East Anglia see NNRO, Bradfer-Lawrence MSS, Molineux Correspondence, 4/10b fol. 158, Oct. 13, 1770.

[104] *Farley's Bristol Journal,* June 24, Oct. 14, 1727; *Whitehall Evening Post,* Oct. 14, 1727; *Gloucester Journal,* Oct. 17, 1727; *Records of Leicester,* v, 119; *Norwich Mercury,* Oct. 21, Nov. 4, 1727.

cases of disaffection recorded were more anti-ministerial than anti-Hanoverian, displaying, for example, a certain disregard toward recent Whig legislation. Such was the case in several towns and villages in Nottinghamshire, where celebrators on the accession day chose their maypoles from the royal forests of Whitebury and Salcey, a capital offense under the Black Act of 1723. Naturally, the Act was not invoked on this occasion, though the damage caused by the "superlative joy" of the king's subjects was computed at £2,000.[105]

Of course, expressions of Tory jubilation at the accession were based in part on the not unrealistic hope that George II would modify the exclusionary politics of his father; but they were meant to serve as testimonies to Tory acceptance of the succession itself.[106] In this they mirrored the alteration in political apprehensions and preoccupations of the political nation as a whole. Court Whig oligarchic initiatives and garrison politics, the collapse of Convocation, financial scandal, Jacobite plots and the emergence of a coherent, if politically heterogeneous, opposition group in Parliament had all converged to preempt the dynastic issue and focus attention on the nature and structure of the post-Revolution state and the forms and tenor of the power wielded there.

Three of these developments in the later years of George I's reign deserve particular attention as central to the reconfiguration of ideological politics that would be elaborated upon after his son's accession. First, the bursting of the South Sea Bubble in August 1720 was important in shifting attention to the nature and supports of the Whig state. The story of the Bubble crisis has been frequently told; here it is necessary to stress its implications for extra-parliamentary politics.[107] Although far from being merely a Whig disaster, the Bubble nevertheless redounded most heavily against the government, whose members were seen as both accomplices in the scandal and its main apologists.

[105] *Mist's Weekly Journal,* July 1, 1727.
[106] For which see Colley, *Defiance,* chap. 7.
[107] Sunderland, as first lord of the Treasury, had accepted the South Sea Company's bid to take over a large chunk of the national debt; in return, the company expected to reap large profits from the sale of shares and its monopoly over all British–Spanish American trade. Fair and foul means were used to cajole prospective investors into buying South Sea stock (including the company's use of fictitious subscribers), producing a craze of stock-buying, a soaring of share prices and the bust of the late summer. Thousands were ruined – Whig and Tory, merchant, trader and patrician alike; and bankruptcies reached spectacular levels in London and some important provincial towns. See P. G. M. Dickson, *The Financial Revolution in England* (London, 1967), 90–156; John Brewer, *The Sinews of Power: War, Money and the English State, 1688–1783* (London, 1989), 125–6.

A parliamentary inquiry proved incapable of bringing those responsible to justice – the Earl of Stanhope conveniently expired while defending himself in the House of Lords, and Sunderland and Charles Stanhope, secretary of the Treasury, escaped impeachment by tiny margins, sixty-one and three votes respectively – and Robert Walpole's shielding of the "Court" from further investigation amplified public ire (even as it secured his career).[108] This outrage was expressed through a barrage of prints, broadsides, newspapers and pamphlets that lambasted the government and its financial henchmen for having sacrificed the rest of the nation to what was now regarded as an avaricious and self-serving scheme.[109]

The *London Journal* mounted the most wide-ranging attack, where Trenchard and Gordon, writing as Cato, provided a resolutely political critique of the financial crisis that excoriated the Whig state and its financial bulwarks. Stock-jobbers and the rich monopoly companies were grave threats to the nation's commercial and political interests, Cato argued, ruining "legitimate" trade, corroding the principles of fair dealing, promoting fraud, multiplying places dependent on the Court and even justifying standing armies. The structures of high finance and the state were thus seen to be two aspects of the same disturbing phenomenon: the consolidation of arenas of private interests, characterized by privilege, exclusivity and self-aggrandizement, that appropriated power, betrayed the public trust and threatened the constitutional rights and liberties of the people.[110] The diatribes against the "monied interests" sketched out the line of attack on the "corruption" of the Whig state that would be taken with relish by other anti-ministerial commentators in the early 1720s, opposition Whig, Tory and Jacobite alike. The *Freeholder's Journal,* for example, which reputedly sold 8,000 copies per issue after the government had bought

---

[108] Dickson, *Financial Revolution,* 175–6; William Coxe, *Memoirs of the Life and Administration of Sir Robert Walpole,* 3 vols. (London, 1798), ii, 209. The measures taken by the "Screenmaster General," as Walpole was called, provoked mob violence against the company's directors: Doran, *London in the Jacobite Times,* i, 349; Fritz, *English Ministers and Jacobitism,* 102–3.

[109] See, e.g., HL, Collection of Pamphlets, Broadsides and Engravings Relating to the South-Sea Scheme, 1720–30, and *Index Rerum and Vocabulorum, for the Use of the Freeholders of Counties, and Freemen of Corporations* (London, 1722).

[110] *Cato's Letters; or, Essays on Liberty, Civil and Religious,* 4 vols. (London, 1755), i, 15–19, 7–9, 32–3, 42–5 (Nov. 12, 26, Dec. 17, 31, 1720). For the opposition to high finance in political theory see J. G. A. Pocock, "Radical Criticism of the Whig Order," in M. Jacob and J. Jacob, *The Origins of Anglo-American Radicalism* (New York, 1984), 33–57.

off the *London Journal,* propagated these arguments with fervor while also (like the *Journal* before it) calling for a coalition opposition to the Whig regime as essential if the forces of corruption were to be combated.[111] Hence, if its financial consequences for provincial traders were temporally contained, the Bubble still remained embedded in national consciousness as the exemplar of the dangers of stock-jobbing and international speculation and the disasters that could afflict ordinary citizens when the interests of high finance were privileged by the state.[112]

Ultimately, if paradoxically, reinforcing this critique were the Atterbury and Layer plots of 1722 for Jacobite uprisings in the west and east of England. To be sure, the plots, which were intended to capitalize on the discontents produced by the Bubble, were in the short term a boon to the Whig government and the standing of Robert Walpole. He squeezed every ounce of propaganda value out of the conspiracy (which the press and parliamentary accounts had made as colorful as possible by spicing up the sober plans of the Atterbury circle with Norfolk Catholic Layer's scheme to assassinate George I), parading the details of the "wicked Jacobite conspiracy" before a horrified public over the summer with predictable political results.[113] Loyalist addresses to the throne flowed in from towns all over the country; Walpole was able to ingratiate himself with George I, who rewarded him with the Order of the Garter in 1726; and, above all, that central article of Whig political faith since the succession, the identification of Toryism with Jacobitism, was cemented to such a degree that Tory political recovery seemed impossible for the next several years.[114]

Yet the Atterbury plot, if doing little to eradicate Jacobite sympa-

---

[111] *Freeholder's Journal,* Jan. 31, March 23, April 4, 1722. The paper was printed by Nathaniel Mist's partner and Jacobite, Doctor Gaylard; the neo-Harringtonian Tory lawyer Archibald Hutcheson was its leading writer. See also *York Mercury,* Feb. 23, March 28, April 4, 11, 1721; Cranfield, *Development of Provincial Press,* 121–2.

[112] For the long-lasting impact of the Bubble on the concerns of provincial traders see John Brewer, "Clubs and Commercialization," in Neil McKendrick, John Brewer, and J. H. Plumb, *The Birth of a Consumer Society* (London, 1982), 212; Edward Gibbon, *A Memoir* (New York, 1984), 48–9, 52.

[113] E. Cruikshanks, "Lord North, Christopher Layer and the Atterbury Plot, 1720–23," in Cruikshanks and J. Black, eds., *The Jacobite Challenge* (Edinburgh, 1988), 92– 106; *Papers Relating to an Intended Insurrection* [London, 1722]; G. V. Bennett, *The Tory Crisis in Church and State, 1688–1730: The Career of Francis Atterbury, Bishop of Rochester* (Oxford, 1975), 223–57; Fritz, *English Ministers and Jacobitism,* 67–108.

[114] *Political State of Great Britain,* xxiii, 528–30, 542–9; NNRO, Assembly Minute Books, 1714–30, June 11, 1722; Fritz, *English Ministers and Jacobitism,* 105–6; Coxe, *Memoirs of Sir Robert Walpole,* ii, 208–13.

thies, forced a rethinking by the Whigs' opponents of their position and goals, ultimately convincing wavering Tories and committed Jacobites alike of the futility of harping on the dynastic issue in the present political climate.[115] It thus facilitated the move toward a more hybrid opposition, one which could be waged in conjunction with disaffected Whigs and Hanoverian Tories whose alienation from the Whig regime had steadily increased. The 1722 election hinted at the direction of change. Although increasing the Whig majority by thirty-eight, it allowed the Whigs' opponents to propagate the grievances of the past seven years and resulted in the most hotly contested general election of the period, with 154 contests, 35 more than in 1715. Jacobite journalists also began to register the prevailing political winds (while deferring to the desire of the Jacobite Court to ally itself with the parliamentary opposition) by taking up the anti-corruption critique of Whig power. Formerly committed legitimists such as Nathaniel Mist and Doctor Gaylard began borrowing from Cato in discussing the "original contract" and the impact of current corruption on constitutional balance and individual liberties, thus moving discussion on to the nature of the political system that had existed since 1714.[116]

Finally, this shift toward the issue of state power and corruption was aided by developments within the Anglican Church itself. The permanent prorogation of the Convocation of Canterbury by Stanhope's government in 1717, a response to the storm raised by High Church clergymen over the Bishop of Bangor's Erastian views on church government, silenced the principal mouthpiece of the High Flying clergy and staved off a "Church in Danger" crisis when Stanhope repealed the Occasional Conformity and Schism Acts in early 1719.[117] The concentration of episcopal and clerical patronage in Whig hands and Walpole's steadfast refusal to give in to the Protestant dissenters' demands for full citizenship also rendered ineffectual the charges of a Whig assault on the church, for the government could make a persuasive case

---

[115] For attempts at high-level realignments see Colley, *Defiance,* 199–202; for continuing popular sentiment for the good old cause see Rogers, *Whigs and Cities,* chap. 2; Doran, *London in the Jacobite Times,* i, 429–33.

[116] Sedgwick, i, 34, 340; *Norwich Gazette,* March 17, 1722; *Mist's Weekly Journal,* Feb. 3, 1722; May 22, 29, June 12, 19, 1725; *Fog's Weekly Journal* (begun by Mist's associates in the aftermath of the Persian Letter furor), Dec. 25, 1731; March 25, May 6, 1732. For an overview of the shifts in the constitutional position mapped out by Jacobite journalists see Monod, *Jacobitism,* 28–33.

[117] Paul Langford, "Convocation and the Tory Clergy, 1717–61," in E. Cruikshanks and J. Black, eds., *The Jacobite Challenge* (Edinburgh, 1988), 107.

of its standing as a defender of the Anglican status quo.[118] These developments contributed to the dilution of High Church hyperbole if not High Church sentiment among Tory spokespersons. The concern with corruption in high places was also supported by puritan strands of Anglicanism, such as that found in societies for the reformation of manners. Initially formed to combat popery and debauchery, by the 1720s many of their supporters had joined opposition spokespeople to preach against the marked corrosion of public virtue throughout the polity that seemed to be emanating from above.[119]

Hence, although religious strife continued to color political alignments and allegiances intermittently for the rest of the century and plagued Tory relations with dissident Whigs,[120] the most marked feature of oppositionist political discourse in the 1720s was its increasing focus on ministerial corruption and its consequences for national political life, an idiom of opposition that strategically shifted attention away from the issues dividing the opponents of Court Whiggery (among which religion loomed large) and toward those grievances that could promote a tentative unity. By George II's accession and increasingly in the years thereafter, it had become clear that the Hanoverian regime had inaugurated a reign not of "schismaticism" but of single-party rule, overweening executive influence and a growing number of effective mechanisms for interfering in people's private lives and pockets, which were perceived on the popular level as infringements of Englishmen's birthrights. The Riot Act, the Septennial Act, the Black Act, various election Acts which sought to curb popular participation in local and parliamentary elections, and the assault on the opposition press and theater, as well as attempted or actual fiscal measures of the immediate future, such as the salt tax of 1732, the excise bill of 1733 and the Gin Act of 1736 – all stimulated middling and plebeian apprehensions about

---

[118] N. C. Hunt, *Two Early Political Associations* (Oxford, 1961), 77–83, 130–62.

[119] Society for the Propagation of Christian Knowledge Library, SPCK Abstract Letter Book, vi (1715–16), fols. 4714–15; T. C. Curtis and W. A. Speck, "The Societies for the Reformation of Manners: A Case Study in the Theory and Practice of Moral Reform," *Literature and History,* 30 (1976), 45–64; John Disney, *A View of Antient Laws Against Immorality and Profaneness* (Cambridge, 1729); Arthur Bedford, *A Sermon Preach'd to the Societies for Reformation of Manners* (London, 1734). Cf. Shelly Burtt, *Virtue Transformed: Political Argument in England, 1688–1740* (New York, 1992), chap. 3, who stresses the SRMs' use of civil prosecution.

[120] Chapters 7 and 8. See also Jan Albers, "Seeds of Contention: Society, Politics and the Church of England in Lancashire, 1689–1790" (Ph.D. diss., Yale University, 1988); J. C. D. Clark, *English Society, 1688–1832* (Cambridge, 1985) – although Clark defines religious divisions solely in terms of theology.

the intentions of Walpole's domestic policy. At the same time, the expansion of the civil list, growing numbers of placemen in the House of Commons and the maintenance of a standing army composed largely of foreign mercenaries equally alarmed contemporaries, for it seemed to undermine the much-vaunted constitutional balance by giving undue power to the executive. The once pervasive fear that the king would rule without Parliament had thus been transformed into an intense anxiety at the way in which the king and his ministers ruled through it.

In this context, the interests of the parliamentary opposition and the extra-parliamentary nation converged. The coalition of Tories and dissident Whigs in Parliament who faced Robert Walpole after 1725 deliberately played on extra-parliamentary fears and recast the anti-oligarchic critique of the state adumbrated by journalists earlier in the decade through their "patriotic" program for reform. The patriot or country ideology adopted by this opposition, articulated by its leaders like the former Jacobite and now Tory Viscount Bolingbroke and the dissident Whig William Pulteney, and publicized, from 1726, in their mouthpiece, *The Craftsman,* synthesized Tory and Commonwealth Whig ideas in order to argue that Walpole had betrayed the very "revolution principles" that Whigs had long trumpeted as crucial to maintenance of the constitution. Insisting equally upon their loyalty to the reigning monarch and the right and necessity of "the people" to intervene in the face of ministerial corruption, the program of the opposition completed the reconfiguration of ideological politics that had been in progress since 1721, systematizing and legitimating its grievances and remedies through the mantle of "patriotic" principles.

Of course, the patriotic appeal had a broad purchase among different political and interest groups in this period, and could be used with good effect by government and opposition alike, largely because there was essential agreement about its central features.[121] Love of country and the protection of the constitution and the much-vaunted liberties it guaranteed composed the heart of the patriotic imperative; and these tenets necessitated the corollary commitment for the patriotic individual to act always for the public good, unbiased by motives of personal interest or private aggrandizement. Patriotism could thus be used to mask a multitude of partisan or sectional interests.[122] But the opposition proved

---

[121] Quentin Skinner, "The Principles and Practice of Opposition: The Case of Bolingbroke vs. Walpole," in Neil McKendrick, ed., *Historical Perspectives* (Cambridge, 1974), 93–128; Hugh Cunningham, "The Language of Patriotism," *History Workshop Journal,* 12 (1981), 8–33.

[122] Ministerial writers ascribed to Walpole himself a plethora of virtues that included

to be especially successful in appropriating patriotism in its campaign against the government, attaching it to certain populist political principles that gave it an especially powerful resonance in the nation.

In defining Walpolean patronage and policy as the antithesis of patriotic and Revolution principles, opposition ideologues excoriated the full range of ministerial measures, from the Septennial Act and placemen in the House of Commons to local election Acts and excises, as infringements of Englishmen's birthrights and constitutional traditions. At the same time, the "country" party employed arguments and tactics geared to attracting political support, such as the delegatory theory of parliamentary representation, constituency instructions and the three-point program for parliamentary reform.[123] Such rhetoric and strategies were appealing not just to disgruntled Tory backbenchers but also to urban populations whose role in the political process had been sharply curtailed under Court Whig rule, and they facilitated the incorporation of notions of political accountability and trusteeship into a significant portion of patriot ideology. In both discursive and practical strategies, the opposition's patriotic program glossed over religious divisions and denied the existence of dynastic disputes in order to concentrate on the corrupt men and practices that kept true patriots out of power and "the people" from exercising their "constitutional rights."

The excise crisis of 1733 demonstrated the viability of the opposition's strategy. Walpole's proposed bill, with its provisions for increasing the number of excise officers armed with the right of search, stimulated intense anxiety among mercantile groups concerned with their profits, and intense hopes among the parliamentary opposition, who devoted themselves to using the bill as an instrument to bring down the government.[124] Under their joint orchestration, the bill came to be perceived by urban traders of all persuasions as an issue that went

selfless devotion to the national interest: William Arnall, *Opposition No Proof of Patriotism* (London, 1735), 20; Reed Browning, *Political and Constitutional Ideas of the Court Whigs* (Baton Rouge, 1982), 99–101.

[123] For opposition ideology and strategies in this period see my "Inventing Revolution: 1688 and Eighteenth Century Popular Politics," *JBS,* 28 (1989), 349–86; for the Tory contribution see Colley, *Defiance,* 53–174.

[124] Paul Langford, *The Excise Crisis: Society and Politics in the Age of Walpole* (Oxford, 1975); Jacob Price, "The Excise Affair Revisited: The Administrative and Colonial Dimensions of a Parliamentary Crisis," in Stephen B. Baxter, ed., *England's Rise to Greatness, 1600–1763* (Berkeley and Los Angeles, 1983), 257–321. Opposition leaders included Chesterfield in the Lords, Micajah Perry, Sir Abraham Elton, John Barnard and Edward Vernon in the Commons and Pulteney, Wyndham and Bolingbroke directing the out-of-doors campaign.

beyond commerce to the heart of the "liberty and property" of all English subjects. Hence, despite the existence of divisive religious issues,[125] the anti-excise campaign was able to rally the diverse forces of opposition against the administration. It exhibited, in the process, three departures of vital importance for extra-parliamentary politics: the political potency of the communications network within the English mercantile community, the ideological significance of "trade" in urban politics, and the potential of "the people's" interventionist role in the political process, infusing those out-of-doors with a sense of their own weight and importance.

Soon after the bill was proposed, propaganda against it poured from the press, so that the excise became, in the words of one pro-ministerial writer, "the Theme of Coffee-Houses, Taverns, and Gin-shops, the Discourse of Artificers, the Cry of the Streets, the Entertainment of Lacquies, the Prate of Wenches, and the Bugbear of Children." Handbills were dispersed by the thousands in dozens of towns, warning against the excisemen who were going to devour the people's trade and liberties. Ballads were sung in the streets which drew on national prejudices and historical memories to associate the excise with French and foreign subversion.[126] Wooden shoes, teacloths and prints were equally evocative in making people aware of their coming fate. *Excise in Triumph* (Plate 3), for example, depicted "Trade," a sorrowful merchant, languishing over idle goods while Walpole, standing in for "Excise," sits astride a hogshead of tobacco chained to a cowed British lion in wooden shoes and crushes the Magna Carta beneath the hogshead's wheels as a "standing army" brings up the rear.[127]

Instructions from fifty-nine constituencies (twenty from the large urban boroughs) directed their representatives to vote against the bill, and anti-excise demonstrations equally expressed and mobilized public hostility to the measure. At least twenty-one of the fifty-nine instructing towns were reported as having anti-government demonstrations, as

---

[125] Such as the dissenting campaigns for repeal of civil restrictions currently under way: See Hunt, *Two Early Political Associations.*

[126] *A Letter from a Member of Parliament for a Borough in the West, to a Noble Lord in His Neighborhood There, Concerning the Excise Bill* (London, 1733), 10; *French Excise; or, A Compendious Account of Several Excises in France* (London, 1733); *York Courant,* April 3, 1733; *Fog's Weekly Journal,* Nov. 24, 1733. For a detailed account of printed propaganda see Raymond Turner, "The Excise Scheme of 1733," *EHR,* 42 (1927), 38–42.

[127] See also Herbert M. Atherton, *Political Prints in the Age of Hogarth: A Study of the Ideographic Representations of Politics* (Oxford, 1974), 155–7; for wooden shoes and teacloths see Turner, "Excise Scheme," 39.

3. *Excise in Triumph* (1733). Excises as wooden shoes. Courtesy of the Lewis Walpole Library, Yale University.

were five other towns which did not send instructions.[128] The reaction in London alone on April 11, when Walpole barely escaped injury at the hands of the crowd outside Whitehall and his and Queen Caroline's effigies were burned in Fleet Street, Smithfield and Bishopsgate, was immortalized in a popular print and deemed sufficiently serious by the ministry for the Commons to draw up a set of stern resolutions against the tumult, in which some of the opposition leaders concurred.[129] Other

[128] Bedford, Birmingham, Bristol, Coventry, Gloucester, Leicester, Liverpool, London, Maidstone, Newcastle, Nottingham, Norwich, Peterborough, Southampton, Southwark, Warwick, Westminster and York were among the instructing towns; Grantham, Lewes, Portsmouth, Salisbury and Sheffield were among the noninstructing towns which had anti-Walpole demonstrations. Price, "Excise Affair Revisited," 293. *LEP,* April 5, 12, 1733; *St. James's Evening Post,* April 12, 19, 1733; *Craftsman,* April 14, 21, 1733; *Daily Journal,* April 14, 19, 1733; J. F. Quinn, "Yorkshiremen Go to the Polls: County Contests in the Early Eighteenth Century," *Northern History,* 21 (1985), 147.

[129] HMC, *Egmont MSS,* 3 vols. (London, 1879), i, 362; Langford, *Excise Crisis,* 93;

Tory leaders, however, did not seem unduly perturbed. "Publick Blessings naturally produce Publick Rejoicings . . . [such as] that general scene of Festivity, which hath manifested itself thro' all the Parts of the Kingdom," Bolingbroke gloated in *The Craftsman* on news of the bill's withdrawal. "I heartily congratulate them upon their Deliverance, and shall leave the Enemies of Trade and Liberty to humble themselves in Sackcloth and Ashes whilst we are wishing Prosperity to both."[130]

The celebrations in the provinces were less violent, led in most of the larger towns by local merchants who had spent considerable resources agitating against the bill. In Bristol, the Whig Corporation had headed the local agitation against the excise, and the news of the bill's postponement prompted a citywide holiday marked by bell-ringing, displays of colors by merchant ships, public toasts to the "glorious 204" (later to be 205) who had voted against it, and crowds milling about the streets. Other residents chose to express their joy by burning effigies of Walpole and excisemen in an enormous bonfire before the Excise Office and in fashionable Queen's Square.[131] In Liverpool, the Exchange, Town Hall and Merchants' Coffeehouse were illuminated, ships' colors displayed and tradesmen paraded through town wearing cockades of gilded tobacco leaves inscribed "No Excise." "No more Excisemen! No Pensioners," "All True Lovers of Liberty" and "Success to British Colonies with a Dependence on Great Britain" were among the toasts which rang out at taverns in the town. Women in York were reported to hold anti-excise assemblies, teas and card games; and clergymen in several towns commemorated the bill's defeat from the pulpit. A favorite text seemed to be Ezekiel 27: 35–6: "All the Inhabitants of the Isles shall be astonish'd at thee, and their Kings shall be sore afraid . . . The merchants among the people shall hiss at thee. Thou shal't be a Terrour, and never shalt be anymore."[132]

The political victory of the coalition of parliamentary, commercial and popular forces that defeated the bill was savored and built upon throughout the summer and into the next year; anti-excise slogans punc-

LEP, April 5, 1733; *Fog's Weekly Journal,* April 19, 1733; *The London Merchants Triumphant (or Sturdy Beggars Are Brave Fellows), Being a Sketch of the Rejoycings in the City etc.* (London, 1733), BM no. 1927.

[130] April 21, 1733.

[131] Latimer, *Annals of Bristol,* 82–4; *St. James's Evening Post,* April 17, 1733; *Daily Courant,* April 19, 1733; *Craftsman,* April 21, 1733.

[132] *St. James's Evening Post,* April 17, 19, 1733; *LEP,* April 14–17, 17–19, 1733; *York Courant,* April 17, 24, May 8, 1733; *Craftsman,* April 14, 21, 1733.

tuated pre-electoral gatherings and post-election victories alike.[133] The
excise was the central issue of the 1734 election, when in Newcastle,
Coventry, Bristol, Worcester and York, for example, ministerial supporters lost their seats for voting in favor of the bill against constituents'
instructions. The result was that in the large boroughs generally, like
the counties, the "country interest" prevailed (although the ministry
retained a majority overall), and in a handful of constituencies, dissenters alienated by the government's measures and recalcitrance on
repeal broke ranks to vote with the opposition.[134] As the *London Evening Post* gleefully noted, the results showed plainly "that the *Sense
of the People* in general is against the Promoters of the Excise and
other pernicious Projects."[135]

Why did the excise bill rouse such fervent anti-government sentiment
from such a broad range of groups and interests? Both the widespread
concern about the consequences of indirect taxation and state expansion
and the ideological constructions of patriotism that the anti-excise agitation deployed were central. Public hostility to excises and excisemen
had long historical roots, but in the immediate circumstances it was
grounded in the financial initiatives of the Whig state. As John Brewer
has recently shown, the excise department itself exemplified a new and
highly centralized departure in administrative practice that had arisen
since the Hanoverian Succession, shifting the dominant source of state
revenues from land to excises and customs; the former accounted for
55 percent of the government's revenue by 1733.[136] Public relations
were further hampered by the fact that powers of the ubiquitous excise
officers were great. Accused evaders were deprived of the right of trial
by jury and prevented from bringing mitigating circumstances to bear
in court before excise commissioners (or, in the counties, justices of
the peace), so that the conviction rate was high. Above all, excisemen
were hated for their right of search in shops and private houses and
the imposition of heavy fines for noncompliance, which could result in

---

[133] Such as the Shrewsbury races and the Norfolk celebrations on behalf of Sir Edmund
Bacon respectively: *Weekly Worcester Journal,* Oct. 5–12, 1733; Chapter 8.

[134] See, e.g., *Newcastle Courant,* Sept. 15, 1733; Jan. 19, March 16, 1734; J. F. Quinn,
"York Elections in the Age of Walpole," *Northern History,* 22 (1986), 181; Sedgwick, i, 244–5, 339–40, 356; Chapter 7. In county and urban constituencies with over
1,000 voters, the ministry lost 21 seats. Some dissenters broke ranks in Bristol, Liverpool, Coventry, Worcester, London and Kent: Rogers, *Whigs and Cities,* 233, 279–
83; Colley, *Defiance,* 220–1; Langford, *Excise Crisis,* 117–118.

[135] *LEP,* May 2–4, 1734; see also June 6–8, 1734.

[136] Brewer, *Sinews of Power,* 95, 99. By 1783 excises made up 80% of government
revenue. The rest of this paragraph is based on Brewer's discussion.

debtors' prison, bankruptcy and ruin for individual traders, shopkeepers and merchants at all levels.[137] They thus represented the long arm of state power in pungent and acerbic form and were resented by country gentlemen, shopkeepers and merchants alike.

The agitation against the excise bill used patriotic and libertarian language to make the most of an already compelling case against invasive state power. The excise was represented as dangerous to the people of England not only because it was the first step toward a "general excise" (that is, a tax on all commodities) but also because it would precipitate a landslide of executive influence attenuating the subject's liberties. Such a double assault on property and rights was frequently imagined as an army of excise officers who could search a citizen's warehouses, shop and home at will – "even . . . his Wife's *Bedchamber,* visited and rummaged, at all hours of the day or Night."[138] The long-range results of an extension of the excise were held to be even more dismal. Virtually all opposition observers seemed to agree on this scenario: Excises would increase the number of civil officers, who could influence parliamentary elections and thus subvert the freedom and independence of Parliament and "the right of the people to be governed by laws made by their own representatives," a "fundamental principle of our constitution, upon which all our liberties and properties depend."[139] Clearly the anti-excise arguments were deliberate exaggerations, designed to make maximum political capital out of a fairly ordinary and innocuous – and as many observers in the provinces were aware – potentially beneficial measure to end customs fraud and smuggling and relieve colonial tobacco planters. But the language and images of the anti-excise agitation struck a chord with many urban dwellers, whose lives were already touched in unsavory ways by the intrusions of state power.

The anti-excise agitation thus marked the emergence of trade as a "patriotic" political issue, one that placed commerce at the center of

---

[137] Ibid., 113, 99–112. See also Colin Brooks, "Public Finance and Political Stability: The Administration of the Land Tax, 1688–1720," *HJ,* 17 (1974), 282–3.

[138] [William Pulteney], *An Humble Address to the Knights, Citizens, and Burgesses, Elected to Represent the Commons of Great Britain in the Ensuing Parliament* (London, 1734), 30. See also *A Second Review of the Late Excise Scheme* (London, 1734), 26.

[139] Caleb D'Anvers (pseud.), *An Argument Against Excises, in Several Essays, Lately Published in the Craftsman* (London, 1733), 23–5, 65–9, which also quotes Hampden and Locke on the dangers of excises to liberty; *Observations upon the Laws of Excise* (London, 1733).

the national interest and highlighted the monopolizing tendencies of the Walpolean state with regard to both power and property. Newspapers, pamphlets, prints and parliamentary speeches all stressed, often in strident terms, the central importance of merchants and commerce to the national strength, prosperity and public interest. Merchants were "the Heart-Blood of the Body Politic," *The Craftsman* asserted, whose hardships would "diffuse themselves in the same Manner through the whole Mass of the People . . . the fate of the whole Kingdom depends, in great Measure, on the Welfare of the *British Merchants.*"[140] The excise laws were represented as subjecting the most productive portion of the community to the most pernicious and persecuting laws, depriving them of rights guaranteed by Magna Charta and the constitution, with resounding results for the whole community. "The *Merchant,* or *Trader,* being the most useful Member of the Commonwealth, hath a Right, at least, to the common Privileges of his Fellow-Subjects," D'Anvers concluded, "whereas no Person, under the *Laws of Excise,* can be properly called a *Freeman,* or an *Englishman.*"[141]

The prominence of tobacco, wine and general merchants in organizing the stand against Walpolean policy, meeting in coffeehouses and taverns in Liverpool, Whitehaven, Bristol, Newcastle, York, Norwich and London to plan strategy, and forming committees of correspondence to organize anti-excise petitions and letters, confirmed in the public eye the association of trade and commerce with patriotism and the national interest.[142] But so did the activities of all "public-spirited" individuals who associated themselves or demonstrated against the bill. Hence, freemen and Corporation leaders in Leicester, shopkeepers in Farnham and tradesmen in Reading all appeared in the press as activists for the cause of liberty and property against ministerial subversion.[143] This identification was also strengthened by Walpole's dismissal of the merchants who lobbied against the excise bill at the door of the House of Commons as "sturdy beggars" – a judgment which was widely publicized in the opposition press and which in William Pulteney's

---

[140] *Argument Against Excises,* 13, 20; see also *Craftsman,* Sept. 7, 1728; *Egmont MSS,* i, 349–50.
[141] *Argument Against Excises,* 23–4.
[142] Price, "Excise Affair Revisited"; TWA, 988/4, Journal of the Company of Merchant Adventurers, Jan. 24, 1733.
[143] *LEP,* Jan. 4–6, 1733 (Norwich, Leicester, Reading); Jan. 11, 1733 (London grocers); *Newcastle Courant,* Jan. 27, 1733 (Newcastle, Bristol, Liverpool), Oct. 20, 1733 (Farnham). See also *Egmont MSS,* i, 312 (Harwich and Norwich).

view aroused national animus against the bill and the minister.[144] Hence, if extensions of the excise were antithetical to commerce and thus to the public interest, then the merchants and tradesmen who opposed the excise, without view of reward by way of posts or preferments, acted on behalf of commerce, freedom and national prosperity against those who would subvert them all for private gain. As the instructions of the Reading burgesses asserted, quoting Addison's Cato, "Would not every Free Briton think the Promoter of it [the excise] an Enemy to his Country? Would he not justly incur the Censure of the Roman Senate, and deserve to have that Sentence denounc'd against him, *Curse on the Man, who owes his Greatness to his Country's Ruin?*"[145]

The excise debate thus injected opposition patriotism with a commercial ethos that made a straightforward appeal to the economic and political concerns of ordinary people who believed themselves to have a material stake in the "trading interest": "the *Merchants* and *wholsale [sic] Traders*, as well as *Shop-keepers, Innholders, Victuallers, Distillers,* and other *Retailers of imported Commodities*" – designations that tied in the interest of the lowest shopkeeper with the richest overseas merchant.[146] This vertical definition of interest, which paralleled the definitions of political interest and accountability articulated in oppositionist initiatives, did not mobilize all traders into anti-excise activism; shopkeepers in the interior, for example, kept comparatively quiet during the anti-excise agitation, as Jacob Price has shown. Further, the agitation glossed over or denied very real divisions within the English merchant community and especially the division between English merchants and colonial planters, a contest of loyalties in which the interests of the metropole won out.[147] Nevertheless, by integrating the shadowy world of parliamentary lobbying and the glaring lights of extraparliamentary publicity, the excise agitation constructed an effective commercial and libertarian definition of the national interest (and an ideological definition of "trade") that opposed itself to the state, providing a model for other sectional interests to lay claim to political influence in the name of the national, patriotic good. As the London

---

[144] *Egmont MSS,* i, 363; see also Civicus, *The Sturdy Beggars: A New Ballad Opera* (London, 1733).

[145] *Craftsman,* Jan. 20, 1733.

[146] *Argument Against Excises,* 47.

[147] Price, "Excise Affair Revisited," 293, 301–3; Wilson, "Empire, Trade and Popular Politics in Mid-Hanoverian England: The Case of Admiral Vernon," *P & P,* no. 121 (1988), 96–7.

grocers noted in their resolution, their opposition to the excise was
based on their apprehension of its impact "on our Trade as Grocers,
but [also] it will be highly prejudicial to Trade in general, and . . .
dangerous to the Liberties and Properties of the whole Kingdom."[148]

Finally, the populist implications of these redefinitions of the national
interest were reinforced by other aspects of the opposition's out-of-
doors campaign in the early 1730s, which propagated notions of the
people's pivotal role in promoting and protecting the public trust. The
political calendar, press, theater and such pointed instruments of accountability as instructions were all used to celebrate the opposition's
status as champions of the people's liberties and the national interest.
For example, the fifth of November, that traditional holiday for Whig
spectacle and self-congratulation, was appropriated by opposition supporters in several towns in order to champion and redefine those "revolution principles" which the administration continually subverted. The
effigies burned in the traditional bonfires were evocatively dressed in
blue star and garter to mark the "double deliverance, viz., that of the
King from the Gunpowder Plot . . . and that of the Kingdom in general
from the late Excise." The eleventh of April was similarly used by the
opposition to deflate government Whig pretensions. Pointing out in
1734 that the day was not only the anniversary of "our National Deliverance from the late exercrable Excise Plot" but also the anniversary
of William III's coronation, *The Craftsman* suggested that "THIS DAY
. . . be distinguished in the next Almanacks, like the FIFTH of *November,*
on Account of the Double Deliverance from SLAVERY." Popular rejoicings and violence thus marked the anniversary in London, Nottingham and Norwich.[149] Plays like *The Fall of Mortimer,* a meditation on
the catastrophic consequences of illegitimate appropriations of power,
also invited audiences to reflect on the nation's historical struggles
against corruption; their relevance to the present, as well as that of such
satirical *tours de force* as *The Beggar's Opera,* were reiterated by opposition journalists lest it escape audiences' notice.[150]

The appeal to the extra-parliamentary nation deliberately promoted
renewed discussion of the origins and nature of popular political lib-

[148] *LEP,* Jan. 11, 1733; Brewer, *Sinews of Power,* chap. 8.
[149] *Newcastle Courant,* Dec. 1, 1733, April 6, 1734; *Craftsman,* April 20, 1734; *Egmont MSS,* ii, 82; *Records of Nottingham,* 7, 144; *Norwich Gazette,* April 13, 1734; April 12, 1735.
[150] Doran, *London in the Jacobite Times,* ii, 43; Sybil Rosenfeld, *Strolling Players and Drama in the Provinces, 1669–1765* (Cambridge, 1939), 55–6, 228, 286; [Colley Cibber], *An Apology for the Life of Colley Cibber,* 3rd ed. (London, 1750), 428–30.

erties that Britain's "ancient constitution" and 1688 supposedly guaranteed. "*British Liberties* are not the *Grants of Princes,*" the *Newcastle Courant* reminded its readers, appropriately enough, on the anniversary of the Hanoverian Succession, but are "*original Rights,* Conditions of *Original Contracts,* coequal with the Prerogative and coeval with our government.'"[151] The pre-election propaganda of 1733–4 rehashed notions of the sovereignty of the popular will and natural rights, sometimes using Lockean language to stress the degree to which rampant bribery and corruption threatened both. Liberty is the "natural right" of everyone, one writer argued, which is not wholly surrendered when one enters into the "compact" of government, as the Revolution had shown. In such circumstances it was imperative that electors choose representatives who were not willing to bargain away their liberties for the emoluments of office.[152] Opposition supporters and leaders alike also employed extra parliamentary tactics that equally emphasized the canvassing role of the people in day-to-day political processes and the accountability to them of those in power. Prior to the 1734 general election, oaths requiring the candidates to pledge to work for the repeal of the Septennial Act and to renounce bribery were recommended in Newcastle, Bristol and Tewkesbury, and the "country" candidate for Reading reportedly submitted to a "written declaration" not to accept any place or pension under the government and to work for the eradication of standing armies, the restoration of triennial Parliaments, and the prevention of any extension of the excise; these cases were indicative of a wider mood.[153] From here it was a short step to establishing electoral associations to exact pledges from candidates and coordinate extra-parliamentary resistance to Whig oligarchy, and such clubs were established in several provincial towns in the 1730s and 40s, and constituency pledges advocated in the 1740s and 50s.[154]

The revitalization of constituency instructions also galvanized and

[151] *Newcastle Courant,* Aug. 8, 1730, quoting *Craftsman,* Aug. 1, 1730.

[152] *The Freeholder's Political Catechism* (London, 1733).

[153] *Newcastle Courant,* Jan. 19, March 16, 1733; *LEP,* Oct. 18–20, 1733; *Gloucester Journal,* Jan. 8, 1734. See also Linda Colley, "English Radicalism Before Wilkes," *TRHS,* 5th ser., 31 (1981), 7–8, 12–13. Such arguments also animated efforts to challenge oligarchy in town governments, as in Liverpool, Manchester and Norwich: Sedgwick, i, 270–2; Byrom, *Journal,* i, 440–90; Chapter 8.

[154] Such as London, Colchester, Coventry, Birmingham, Bristol and Newcastle: Colley, *Defiance,* 166–7; I. G. Doolittle, "The Half Moon Tavern, Cheapside, and City Politics," *Transactions of the London and Middlesex Archaeological Society,* 27 (1977), 328–32; Rogers, *Whigs and Cities,* 280–2; Chapter 7. For pledges see *LEP,* Sept. 30 – Oct. 2, 1740; *Monitor,* Aug. 16, 1755.

legitimized the people's participation in the political process. The sets of constituency instructions sent during the anti-excise agitation were widely publicized in the press, and if encouraged and sometimes orchestrated by opposition MPs or leading merchants in provincial communities, they still voiced the apprehensions of a wider political community whose concerns were usually vetted and canvassed in taverns and public meetings as well as council sessions and grand jury chambers. In the event, failure to comply with them could lead to electoral defeat, as the excise crisis had proven.[155] Instructions were thus believed to embody the notions of parliamentary accountability that opposition leaders were stressing. Against administration writers who claimed that instructions had no legal basis and could not be binding, opposition adherents argued that such interventions were not only an "inviolable right" of private citizens going back to Edward II and sanctioned by the Revolution, but also imperative, particularly when the people were faced with septennial Parliaments and a minister who claimed, as Walpole did in 1733, that those out-of-doors had no right to meddle in public affairs. MPs were but the "attorneys of the People," they asserted, and must take instructions on matters of national as well as local concern.[156] Instructions and the widespread publicity they garnered were thus celebrated for their resounding success in repelling further advances of ministerial oppression. "The *Spirit of Liberty* is not yet extinct in this Kingdom," exulted *The Craftsman* in the aftermath of the agitation; "the original Power of the People, in their collective Body, is still of some Weight, when vigorously exerted and united."[157]

On a number of fronts, then, the opposition campaign against Walpole in the early years of George II's reign completed a reconfiguration of the terms of political debate from the decade before in ways that allowed the opponents of the Whig regime, with an impressive cross-

---

[155] Wilson, "Inventing Revolution," 368–70; for the representative character of instructions see Rogers, *Whigs and Cities,* 235–50; Colley, *Defiance,* 167–9. For sixteenth- and seventeenth-century precedents see Paul Kelly, "Constituents' Instructions to Members of Parliament in the Eighteenth Century," in Clyve Jones, ed., *Party and Management in Parliament, 1660–1784* (Leicester, 1984), 170–1.

[156] *Craftsman,* March 17, 1733; *The Right of British Subjects, to Petition and Apply to Their Representatives, Asserted and Vindicated* (London, 1733). Some opposition writers even insisted that instructions were binding: *Political State of Great Britain,* 45 (1733), 440–1. For ministerial arguments see *London Journal,* June 22, 1734; *Free Briton,* June 20, 1734; *Daily Gazetteer,* July 6, 1738; *A Letter to William Pulteney Esq.* (London, 1733).

[157] *Craftsman,* April 21, 1733.

section of public support, to set the agenda for future political debates – a task that would have been impossible without the
radicalizing of a sector of elite leadership, an expanding and engaged
provincial political public, and an increasingly effective mobilization
of opinion through press, pulpit and political calendar. Government
propagandists ridiculed "this Boasting of the Sense of the People"
as a mask for "the deluded Multitude [who] have ever been ungrateful to their best Governors," insisting instead that the opposition
were all Jacobites and the genuine political nation composed only of
the landed classes.[158] Such efforts, however, though meeting with
some successes, could not seriously counter the opposition's appeal
in the extra-parliamentary nation. The opposition's deliberate eschewal of resistance theory and, still more, its leaders' ostentatiously
performed Hanoverianism undercut charges of disloyalty. Most important, the constructions of patriotism, libertarianism and the public
good proffered in opposition strategy and argument conceptualized
the state as an arena where illegitimate interests could hold sway, and
thus valorized the people outside the state as the final arbiters of the
legitimacy and effectiveness of power within it. Who "the people"
were, of course, was never clearly defined, which facilitated the appropriation of patriot ideology by nonelectors and others usually considered to be well outside the respectable classes.[159] In general,
opposition writers endorsed a political definition of "the people" as
predominantly male individuals who were able to maintain their independence sufficiently against both ministerial patronage and wages
to act with "public-spiritedness," that is, with disinterestedness and
judgment, for the good of the whole. Such a definition appealed to
a diverse range of interests and aspirations; it also promoted the
widespread if self-appreciative view that in 1733–4 the people had
successfully resisted ministerial oppression. Hence, when at a parish
church in London in 1733 a minister had the audacity to preach

---

[158] An effort designed in part to woo back dissident Whigs and recalcitrant dissenters. *Flying Post,* Aug. 28, 1733; See also *Daily Courant,* March 20, 1734; *Free Briton,* March 28, 1734; *Norwich Mercury,* June 1, 8, 1734; [Daniel Neale], *A Letter from a Dissenter to the Author of the Craftsman* (London, 1733).

[159] Bolingbroke argued that men "of all degrees" should be included in the political nation, for all had a role as "actors, or judges of those that act, or controllers of those that judge"; other writers remained dubious of the ability of the "meaner sort" to resist venality and corruption: *Letters on the Study and Use of History* (1735–6), in *The Works of Lord Bolingbroke,* 5 vols. (London, 1841), ii, 237; for the latter view see *Craftsman,* May 23, July 25, 1741 (Bolingbroke had broken his connection with the paper in 1736).

the unparallell'd Wickedness and Impudence of Tradesmen's meddling into Politics, and particularly of their riotous Procession to
Westminster to petition against the late Excise Scheme ... which he
placed among the Number of deadly Sins, and recommended Passive
obedience and Non-Resistance ... the Audience were so unkind as
to laugh at him so much that he shut up his Book before he had
done, and threatened them with a severe Chastisement.[160]

Indeed, the opposition campaign seemed to prove what patriot spokesmen argued, namely, that when faced with an executive presence that
undermined the independence of the House of Commons, the locus of
liberty was extra-parliamentary – in the sensibilities and virtue of the
people. This would be particularly important after 1735, when the parliamentary coalition's unity was corroding. It was then left to the extra-
parliamentary nation to maintain the momentum of the anti-Walpolean
campaign. Trade, Liberty – and Empire – would constitute the heart of
the new patriotic imperative.

[160] *Newcastle Courant,* Oct. 20, 1733.

3. *Patriotic adventure: Libertarianism, war and empire, 1736–1762*

O! would some god but set her lions free
From warlike peace, and martial pageantry;
Uncag'd, as once in Anna's glorious reign,
They soon would break all Europe's threatened chain,
Tame proud Iberia, shake ye Gallick throne,
Give freedom to the World, and keep her own.
A Skit on Britain (London, 1740)

Britain will never want a Race of Men, who prefer the publick Good before any narrow or selfish Views – who choose Dangers in Defence of their Country before an inglorious safety, an honourable Death before the unmanly pleasures of a useless and effeminate life . . . it is now the Birthright of Englishmen, to carry, not only Good Manners, but the purest Light of the Gospel, where Barbarism and Ignorance totally prevailed.
Richard Brewster, *A Sermon Preach'd on the Thanksgiving Day* (Newcastle, 1759)

Eighteenth-century English imperialism has been unevenly served by historians. Although the expansion of Britain in the Georgian decades has been a central subject of inquiry for generations of scholars, the best-known accounts have tended to eschew ideological and cultural forces in favor of the "great events": battles won and lost, military and naval strategies that succeeded in wrenching colonies and resources from European rivals and indigenous peoples alike, and policies designed to consolidate and build upon a hard-won imperial ascendancy – all with little regard for their impact on or reception among the domestic population.[1] Such an approach is central in understanding the strategic and diplomatic contexts of colonial acquisition and loss in the eighteenth century, but it is of limited usefulness to those who wish to know the meaning and significance of empire at home. How was empire, its acquisition, maintenance and costs, represented, consumed and understood in England by those for whom it existed as much in ideology and imagination as in policy?

For the historian of popular politics, such a question is especially difficult to answer, for despite all the rich and resourceful work that has appeared in recent years on class relations, communications and protest, the meanings and significance of empire in public political consciousness have only begun to be investigated.[2] Although the development of popular nationalisms has been taken on with important results, the evidence of pro-imperial attitudes among a wider public was for a long time dismissed rather than examined, uncritically categorized as instances of chauvinistic excess without any effort to relate them to larger social and political contexts.[3] Literary studies of the relationship between empire and domestic cultural production have elided politics as a constitutive arena of culture that disseminated competing images of the empire and nation, Englishness and otherness, citizenship and exclusion.[4] Even the most recent distinguished assess-

[1] See, e.g., H. H. Dodwell, *The Cambridge History of India,* vol. 5 (Cambridge, 1929); Richard Pares, *War and Trade in the West Indies* (Oxford, 1936); and Kenneth Andrews, *Trade, Plunder and Settlement: Maritime Enterprise and the Genesis of the British Empire, 1480–1630* (Cambridge, 1984).

[2] Ironically, anti-imperialist attitudes have been ably documented: See J. G. A. Pocock, *The Machiavellian Moment: Florentine Political Thought and the Atlantic Republican Tradition* (Princeton, 1975), and *Virtue, Commerce and History* (Cambridge, 1986). The excellent studies by Richard Koebner, *Empire* (Cambridge, 1961); Klaus Knorr, *British Colonial Theories, 1570–1850* (Toronto, 1944); and Peter Marshall, "Empire and Authority in Later Eighteenth Century Britain," *Journal of Imperial and Commonwealth Studies,* 15 (1987), 105–22, focus mainly on official pronouncements about empire.

[3] Exceptions include my "Empire, Trade and Popular Politics in Mid-Hanoverian Britain: The Case of Admiral Vernon," *P & P,* no. 121 (1988), 74–109; Peter Marshall, *"A Free Though Conquering People": Britain and Asia in the Eighteenth Century* (London, 1981); Linda Colley, "Radical Patriotism in Eighteenth-Century England," in Raphael Samuel, ed., *Patriotism: The Making and Unmaking of the British National Identity,* vol. 1 (London, 1989), 169–87; and Nicholas Rogers, *Whigs and Cities: Urban Politics in the Age of Walpole and Pitt* (Oxford, 1989). For popular nationalism see the seminal articles by Linda Colley, "The Apotheosis of George III: Loyalty, Royalty and the British Nation, 1760–1820," *P & P,* no. 102 (1984), 94–129, and "Whose Nation? Class and National Consciousness," *P & P,* no. 113 (1986), 97–117.

[4] See, e.g., Felicity Nussbaum, ed., "The Politics of Difference," special ed. of *Eight-*

ment of British nationalism in the Georgian decades has neglected the multifaceted impact of empire on the public political imagination, for by positioning overseas expansion as an overarching and invariably unifying force that produced latently loyalist "British" allegiances, it underplays the contested, fissured and contending political identities the empire mobilized among those who supported or opposed it at home.[5]

Certainly our lack of knowledge about the imperial component in middling and plebeian consciousness poses a serious obstacle to the recovery of the meanings and dimensions of extra-parliamentary political activity in the Hanoverian decades. In a period when naval victories were likely to spark exuberant and spontaneous (in the sense of self-activated) public celebrations, and national disgrace abroad could provoke outbursts of popular violence, it is clearly inadequate to dismiss such demonstrations as instances of knee-jerk loyalism or, still worse, the rabid "nativism" of the "crowd." For in the 1740s and 1750s, trade and empire, the nature of the national character, and the relationship of all three to Britain's political leadership were potent, and related, issues in and out of Parliament, argued about and examined in coffeehouses and news rooms, dramatic productions and novels, and in a proliferation of printed and graphic propaganda that displayed their marketing to and consumption by those out-of-doors. The influence which empire had on the preoccupations of the expanding and increasingly vociferous political public in these decades needs to be systematically explored.

This and the following two chapters will address some of these questions concerning the impact of imperial acquisition and loss on domestic political culture and ideology. War may be hell, but the wars for empire in the eighteenth century proved remarkably efficient in mobilizing particularized definitions of the national community that articulated, if only ephemerally, the supposedly incommensurable differ-

---

eenth-Century Studies, 23 (1990); Billie Melman, *Women's Orients: British Women and the Middle East, 1707–1907* (Ann Arbor, 1992); Edward Said, *Culture and Imperialism* (New York, 1993). Two notable exceptions are David Shields, *Oracles of Empire: Poetry, Politics and Commerce in British America, 1690–1750* (Chicago, 1990), and Peter Hulme, *Colonial Encounters: Europe and the Native Caribbean, 1492–1797* (London, 1986).

[5] Linda Colley, *Britons: Forging the Nation, 1707–1837* (New Haven, 1992). For examinations of the fractured identities produced by empire see Bernard Bailyn and Philip D. Morgan, eds., *Strangers Within the Realm: Cultural Margins of the First British Empire* (Chapel Hill, 1991), and Nicholas Canny and Anthony Pagden, eds., *Colonial Identity in the Atlantic World, 1500–1800* (Princeton, 1987).

ences separating the English from other nations – or dividing the nation within itself. The present chapter will examine the agitations surrounding war and empire in the middle decades of the century, focussing on the War of Jenkins' Ear, the Jacobite rebellion of 1745 and the crises that opened the Seven Years' War. At these junctures, empire provided a yardstick by which the political public measured the legitimacy and effectiveness of the state's counsels, becoming linked in extraparliamentary political culture with libertarian politics and patriotism of both the oppositionist and loyalist varieties. These junctures also compelled many English people to debate and reflect upon the components of the national identity in ways that embedded normative definitions of citizenship, class and gender in political culture.

I. RULE BRITANNIA: ADMIRAL VERNON AND THE IMPERIAL IMAGINATION

In 1738, a half-decade after the excise crisis, hostility to the Walpole administration had reached a new height, prompted by the ministry's foreign and commercial policies. The slow but steady growth in trade since 1725 had not affected all segments of Britain's overseas merchant community equally,[6] and groups of merchant adventurers in London and the outports were worried about the growing trade imbalance they perceived between Britain and her European rivals, which they readily attributed to the aggrandizing imperial policies of France and Spain. Such fears were not wholly without foundation. France's economic recuperation from the last war and future expansionist intentions had been signaled by its recovery of the island of St. Lucia from the British in 1723, and in the West Indies the French and British battled over not only sugar production but also the highly profitable illegal trade with Spanish America and the British northern colonies.[7] Relations with Spain were equally unsettling. British merchants' lucrative and longstanding contraband trade with the Spanish dominions in South America was scarcely interrupted by the Treaty of Seville in 1729. Spain retaliated by deploying *guardacostas* in Caribbean waters to search

[6] See T. S. Ashton, *Economic Fluctuations in England 1700–1800* (Oxford, 1959), 59–279; Elizabeth Schumpeter, *English Overseas Trade Statistics* (Oxford, 1960), 16–17; Pares, *War and Trade*, 79–81.

[7] Jeremy Black, *British Foreign Policy in the Age of Walpole* (Edinburgh, 1985), 105–6.

British ships and seize contraband goods, which disrupted all commerce, lawful and illicit, in American waters. By 1738, the situation
had reached a crisis point. British West Indian and American merchants
and shipowners from a number of outports, including Bristol, Glasgow,
Lancaster, Liverpool and Edinburgh as well as London, bombarded
Parliament and the Board of Trade with memorials, addresses and petitions against the Spanish depredations, and demanded redress.[8] The
opposition press publicized the merchants' grievances and their demands for tougher measures against Spain, presenting the conflict in
the stark and dramatic terms of a struggle between liberty and slavery,
national honor and disgrace; prints recalled the unfortunate fate of Captain Jenkins or depicted British sailors starving in Spanish prisons; and
rumors were circulated that Spain intended to infiltrate the newly established colony of Georgia.[9] By the summer of 1738, Walpole was
thus faced with a formidable hostile pressure group of Atlantic merchants, both British and colonial, and backed by the parliamentary opposition, demanding a parliamentary review of government measures
and resolutions on the indisputable right of British merchants to freedom of navigation.[10]

The government, however, anxious not to upset diplomatic alliances
on the Continent, negotiated the Convention of El Pardo with Spain in
early 1739. Its announcement in England only inflamed public opinion,
for its weak terms allowed the Spanish to retain the hated right of
search.[11] When Spain used both its grievances against the South Sea
Company and the appearance of British naval forces in the Mediterranean as a pretext for refusing to ratify the treaty, the outcry within
and without Parliament was such as to force Walpole to declare war
on Spain in October 1739. The reaction in the nation was electric:
Wildly joyful celebrations more appropriate to a national victory than

---

[8] Pares, *War and Trade*, 8–58; *CJ*, 23 (1737–41), 53–4, 63, 94–5, 133–4, 247–54, 269–
75; *History and Proceedings of the House of Commons from the Restoration to the
Present Day* (London, 1742), x (1738–42), 96–176 passim, 417–24 passim. The four
dozen petitions and memorials originated from 9 Scottish and 5 English outports over
this year.

[9] *LEP*, Feb. 7–9, March 14–16, March 30 – April 1, July 27–9, 1738; *The English
Cotejo* (n.p., 1738); *Slavery* (London, 1738), BM no. 2355; *The Voice of Liberty; or,
a British Philippic . . . To Which is Prefix'd, a Copper-Plate, Representing the Suffer-
ings of Our Captive Sailors in a Spanish Prison* (London, 1738).

[10] *LEP*, Aug. 17–19, 1738; *CJ*, 23 (1737–41), 133–4.

[11] *CJ*, 23 (1737–41), 247–54, 269–75; *An Exact List of All Those Who Voted for and
Against the Convention in the House of Commons* (London, 1739).

a declaration of war broke out in the localities, and in the larger towns subscriptions were immediately opened to pay for the defense of British merchant ships.[12]

Hostility to the government was soon rearoused and amplified by its seemingly half-hearted prosecution of the war and a succession of British defeats in Atlantic and Mediterranean waters. In this context, Vice-Admiral Edward Vernon emerged as a national hero. In November 1739, he succeeded in defeating the Spanish at Porto Bello, the depot of the Spanish empire and the port from which the *guardacostas* were fitted out. This first British victory of the war was accomplished by a stern critic of the Walpole administration, whose outspokenness against Court Whig domestic and foreign policies vexed government leaders for three decades. In 1729, some months after Admiral Hosier's disastrous attempt to take Porto Bello, Vernon, as opposition MP for Penryn, asserted that the orders given to Hosier "were given by those who understood nothing of the sea" and that he could take Porto Bello with six ships and 300 men. Ten years later, he captured Porto Bello with the requisite six ships, going on to take the fort of San Lorenzo and town of Chagre in March 1740, and to engineer a promising if ultimately unsuccessful attack on Cartagena in 1741.[13] These were Britain's only successes during the war, and they fueled a nationalist ardor at home that was specifically anti-administration. For the next three years, Vernon was the focus of popular politics and the parliamentary campaign against the government, and his highly publicized exploits became a crucial factor in the constellation of forces bringing down Walpole's government.

The news of Vernon's success at Porto Bello reached England in March 1740, when anti-government resentments and demands for a victory over the insulting Spaniards were at their height. Celebrations of this and subsequent victories and of Vernon's birthday occurred in at least fifty-four towns in twenty-five counties in England and Scotland

---

[12] As in Bristol, Newcastle, Norwich, Salisbury and London: *Newcastle Journal,* Nov. 3, 1739; *LEP,* Nov. 3–6, 1739; *The War Against Spain Declar'd . . . to Which Is Added, A Proposal . . . for Making* ENGLAND *the Terror of the Whole World* (London, 1739); Edward Phillips, *Britons Strike Home: A Farce, as It Is Acted at the Theatre-Royal* (London, 1739). For subscriptions see *Salisbury Journal,* Nov. 5, 1739; *Craftsman,* Nov. 24, 1739.

[13] Sedgwick, i, 97–8; HMC, *Egmont MSS,* 3 vols. (London, 1879), iii, 331; *The Vernon Papers* (Navy Record Society Publications, 99, 1958), 4–5. The initial reduction of the fort of San Luis which defended Cartagena led the English public to believe for a short time in May of 1741 that the city had been taken.

(see map).)In Stratford, Essex, for example, an effigy of the Spanish admiral Don Blass was burned in an enormous multi-storied bonfire as crowds around it sang, "Britons strike home." In London, the residents of Fleet Street put on a pageant in his honor in a style not seen for several decades, the main scene of which depicted, against a background view of Porto Bello and men-of-war, a Spaniard on his knees offering Vernon a sword as a flag flies over Vernon's head with the gallant words "Venit, Vidit, Vicit."[14] And in Wymondham, Norfolk, the rejoicing at Vernon's victory at Cartagena evinced the extent of popular pride in the hero:

> Trees [were] planted in the streets like a Grove: A grand procession was made through the whole Town, where in the new rich flag belonging to the Town Society was carried before, and next to it a beautiful flag of divers colours in Wooll by the Combers Company; after which a Person in a grand Manner representing Admiral VER-NON rode on a fine horse, and another in a despicable manner on an Ass representing Don Blass . . . the whole was the general sense and free Act of the People, being in no way promoted by any leading Gentlemen.[15]

The press teemed with information on Vernon and his exploits, beginning with the Porto Bello victory. Prints, poems and ballads appeared at booksellers and print shops and in London and provincial newspapers, glorifying Vernon and his plan of the capture of Porto Bello and Chagres; in the more enterprising papers, maps and prints were provided gratis.[16] On all counts Vernon was exalted in the press as England's sole salvation and the incarnation of British liberty and patriotic virtue, a "True Briton" and "Son of Liberty" who dared to stand up to the Catholic powers of Europe, rivaling Raleigh and Drake

[14] *LEP*, Nov. 13–15, 1740; *Salisbury Journal*, Nov. 18, 1740.
[15] *Norwich Gazette*, May 30, 1741.
[16] *Gentleman's Magazine*, 10 (1740), March, April and Nov.; 11 (1741), May and November and suppl.; *Salisbury Journal, LEP, Newcastle Courant, Norwich Mercury,* March, June and Nov. 1740 and May 1741. Prints: *Catalogue,* iii, 1, nos. 2423, 2464, 2497, 2831, 3969; for verse and ballads, D. F. Foxon, *English Verse 1700–1750,* vol. 2 (Cambridge, 1975), 296. The ballads, tracts and poems produced in Vernon's honor, extant in considerable numbers in the British Library, Huntington Library, Beinecke Library, Houghton Library and local-history libraries in Britain, include *Admiral Vernon's Resolution* [London, 1740]; *A Poem on the Glorious Atchievements of Admiral* VERNON *in the Spanish West-Indies* (London, 1740); *The Spectre; or, Admiral Hosier's Ghost* (Lynn, 1740); and *Vernon's Glory: Containing Fourteen New Songs, Occasion'd by the Taking of Porto Bello and Fort Chagres* (London, 1740). Vernon was also immortalized on canvas by Gainsborough, Vanderbank and Bardwell.

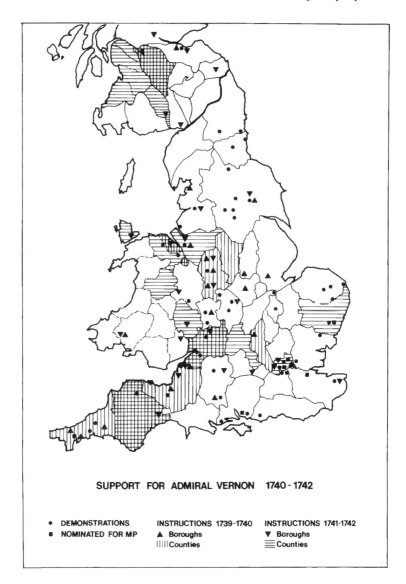

SUPPORT FOR ADMIRAL VERNON   1740 - 1742

- • DEMONSTRATIONS
- ■ NOMINATED FOR MP

INSTRUCTIONS 1739-1740
▲ Boroughs
‖‖‖Counties

INSTRUCTIONS 1741-1742
▼ Boroughs
≡ Counties

as the greatest naval commander the country had ever known. A representative song among the scores written for his birthday in 1740 described him as "the generous hero, and Country's praise . . . Britain's Avenger, and the Scourge of Spain"; another, entitled *The True English-Boys Song, to Vernon's Glory. Occasion'd by the Birthday of That Brave Admiral,* was written specifically "to be sung around the bonfires of London and Westminster" on that auspicious anniversary.[17] Newspapers, prints, ballads and verse not only disseminated information on Vernon's activities and the demonstrations in his honor but also provided a calendar for the expression of allegiance to his patriotic cause.

Although in a number of towns local elites led or paid for anniversary or victory celebrations, most frequently the festivities were planned and financed by the subscriptions of local merchants and tradesmen. This was particularly true on Vernon's birthday. In October 1740, a group of merchants in Liverpool sent a letter to Vernon's wife inquiring about the date of his birthday; when they received an answer – November 12 – they immediately subscribed a guinea each toward an entertainment for that day.[18] In London, whole streets and parishes made "voluntary subscriptions" to provide fireworks for their celebrations; in Southwark, Hackney, Ipswich, Lymington, Durham, Sunderland, Newcastle and Norwich, subscriptions were formed by the middling sorts in early November to buy candles, fireworks, bonfires, liquor and dinners or even hire cannon for birthday observances.[19]

Most of these celebrations took place in the taverns and coffeehouses of provincial towns, centers of news and gossip, which provided a convenient and appropriate setting for Vernon's supporters to express their allegiance to him and his patriotic cause. This was true in the metropolis as well: In both London and Westminster "prodigious numbers of Persons of all Conditions met at different Taverns" to celebrate his birthday in 1741. Publicans boosted their custom as much as possible by publishing advertisements as to the particular celebrations in their establishments, sometimes making available new ballads to sing in Vernon's honor which were printed afterwards in local newspapers.

[17] *Norwich Gazette,* Jan. 3, 1741; *LEP,* Nov. 15, 1740; *The True English-Boys Song* (London, 1741). Drake had died aboard ship off the coast of Porto Bello and was buried in its harbor. *Columbia Lippincott Gazetteer of the World* (New York, 1962), 1506.
[18] *Salisbury Journal,* Oct. 21, 1740.
[19] Ibid., Nov. 4, 1740; *LEP,* Nov. 13–15, 15–18, 1740; *Norwich Gazette,* Nov. 15, 29, 1740; *Newcastle Journal,* Nov. 21, 1740. Owing to confusion over the date, Vernon's birthday was celebrated twice in some towns in 1740; *LEP,* Nov. 4–5, 8–11, 1740.

A few even offered free beer to drink to the patriot hero's health, apparently believing, as did a tavern-keeper in Salisbury, that the great quantities of liquor consumed "never would be employ'd better than in drinking the Health of Him who cannot but be the darling of every free born British soul."[20] Moreover, established tavern societies, such as the Ancient Society of Trammelites in Norwich and the Society of Yorkshiremen in London, met on Vernon's birthday in order to toast "the Heroic asserter of English Liberties." Appropriately, Vernon's head became a favorite public-house sign in the capital and localities for decades.[21]

The dual nature of publican support for Vernon – furthering both profits and the patriot cause – was exhibited in other aspects of his support. Advertisements such as the one which appeared in the *Norwich Gazette* in January 1741 were not at all uncommon: "To be Sold, a parcel of old Havana SNUFF, that comes directly from Admiral VER-NON . . ." In Durham, Messrs. Dove and Booth undoubtedly increased attendance at their "Mathematical Lectures" by promising to exhibit fireworks in honor of Vernon's birthday immediately afterwards.[22] Further, the calendar provided by Vernon's birthday and the anniversaries of his victories created a predictable market for Vernon artifacts, and enterprising manufacturers were quick to exploit it. "It is Admiral Vernon's birthday, and the city shops are full of favours, the streets of marrowbones and cleavers, and the night will be full of mobbing, bonfires and lights!" Horace Walpole wrote in 1741. These "favours" took a variety of forms. For example, at least 102 different medals were struck in Vernon's honor between 1740 and 1743, decorated with his head and legends such as "He took Porto Bello with six ships only" or "The Pride of Spain humbled by Admiral Vernon"; some were made in the form of badges that could be worn on hats, coats and jackets. Remarkably, more medals were struck on behalf of Vernon than for any other figure in the eighteenth century.[23]

---

[20] *LEP,* Nov. 13–15, 15–18, 1740; *Newcastle Journal,* Nov. 14, 1740; *Salisbury Journal,* Nov. 18, 1740.

[21] *Norwich Gazette,* Nov. 15, 1740; Nov. 14, 1741. For Vernon's head as a tavern sign, H. D. J. Schevichaven, *English Inn Signs* (London, 1951), 22, 42–4; for provincial examples see *Newcastle Journal,* Nov. 21, 1741; *Whitehead's Newcastle Directory* (Newcastle, 1778; repr. 1889); BL, Add. MS 27, 966, fol. 232.

[22] *Norwich Gazette,* Jan. 3, 1741; *Newcastle Courant,* Nov. 22, 1740.

[23] *Yale Correspondence of Horace Walpole,* ed. W. S. Lewis, 38 vols. (London and New Haven, 1938–83), xvii, 196; Edward Hawkins, *Medallic Illustrations of the History of Great Britain and Ireland to the Death of George III,* vol. 2 (London, 1885), 530–

Vernon's popularity also precipitated a minor revolution in the pottery industry, stimulating the production of a whole array of relatively inexpensive Astbury, salt-glaze and Delftware pottery which commemorated his glory as it allowed its users to express their allegiance and solidarity. Since the late seventeenth century, monarchs and military figures had been immortalized, if rather crudely, on plates, bowls and platters; and John Brewer has demonstrated the importance of ceramicware in disseminating political loyalties in the Wilkite period.[24] However, it seems to have been precisely the years of Vernon's popularity that prepared the way for later developments. Vernon ceramics clearly constituted the most prolific output of commemorative pieces since the century began, with virtually all the major potteries producing Vernon memorabilia, including Bristol, Brighton, Lambeth, Liverpool, Leeds and Stafford. Vernon's head, opposition mottoes and his flagship, the *Burford,* appeared on such useful items as plates, mugs, teapots, bowls, jugs, inkpots and punchbowls, catering to a middling-to-prosperous market of shopkeepers, tradesmen and merchants (Plate 4). A more limited number of Vernon plates constituted a new departure in ceramicware *design,* like those made by Joseph Flower of Bristol, which displayed in minute and elegant detail the taking of Chagres and the destruction of the fort of San Lorenzo. Such attention to accuracy and realism was a far cry from the crude and often rude portraits that had characterized commemorative pottery prior to this time.[25]

Theater also proved to be a sympathetic medium through which loyalty to Vernon and pride in Protestant England's seemingly inevitable dominion over its ancient Catholic rival was expressed and solicited. A popular play advertised in the provincial press was *The Play of the British Hero; or, Admiral* VERNON's *Conquest over the Spaniards.* As staged in Norwich, the play included "the whole View and Prospect of the Town, Fort and Castles of Porto-Bello, with a beautiful Representation of the Battle, also the Flight of the Spaniards out of the Town

62. Some are on display in the British Museum: Coins and Medals, Case 23, nos. 12–13.

[24] Anthony Ray, *English Delftware Pottery in the Robert Hall Warren Collection* (Oxford, 1968), 6–7, 106–8; John Brewer, "Commercialization and Politics," in Neil McKendrick, John Brewer and J. H. Plumb, *The Birth of a Consumer Society* (London, 1982), 239–52.

[25] Ray, *Delftware,* 125, 130–1; G. Pugh and M. Pugh, *Naval Ceramics* (Newport, 1971), 7–11, pls. 15–20; R. L. Robson, *Catalogue of the Collection of English Pottery in the Department of British and Medieval Antiquities and Ethnography, British Museum* (London, 1905), 182–5.

4. Vernon mug. Staffordshire salt-glazed stoneware, 1740. "He took Porto Bello with
Six Ships Only." Courtesy of the Manchester City Art Galleries.

for Refuge," and was so popular that eager viewers had to be turned
away.[26] The enduring hold that the Porto Bello victory had on the
popular imagination and its symbolic importance in Britain's burgeoning imperial self-image was also shown in the plethora of British "Port
Bellos" that sprang into existence after 1740. Hamlets and suburbs in
Staffordshire, Sussex, Oxfordshire, Durham and Edinburgh and a farm
in London appeared with that name within a decade after 1740, and in
the American colonies, one Lawrence Washington named his Virginia
estate in honorable allusion to the commander under whom he had
served during the Anglo-Spanish war, calling it Mount Vernon.[27]

Support for Vernon also took more conventional political forms.

[26] *Norwich Gazette,* Jan. 3, 10, 1741. The play was also staged in Newcastle: *Newcastle
Journal,* Nov. 21, 1741. Open-air theaters were still presenting pantomimes of the
siege of Porto Bello in 1788: *Public Advertiser,* Nov. 7, 1788.
[27] *Survey Gazetteer of the British Isles* (Edinburgh, 1950), 554; *The London Encyclo-
pedia,* ed. B. Weinreb and C. Hibbert (London, 1983), 616.

Both Court and opposition attempted to exploit Vernon's reputation and acclaim for partisan purposes. Court Whigs in the localities and London were quick to point to Vernon's victory at Porto Bello as proof of the vision and sagacity of ministerial war policy. In Norwich, for example, Whig aldermen presided over public festivities on Vernon anniversaries, and the local Whig fraternity, the Constitution Club, toasted "Walpole and Vernon" as if they were, in fact, unambiguously identified with each other.[28] And in the capital, Vernon was not only courted by the government but was promoted by the Court as a candidate for Parliament in 1741, in an effort to divide and enervate Tory strength in the City.[29] However, the opposition proved to be notably more successful in appropriating Vernon as a partisan political hero. The fortuitous combination of timing and leadership imparted credibility to patriot Whig and Tory claims that Vernon's captures of Porto Bello and Chagres were specifically *opposition* victories, vindicating the patriots' prescriptions for a vigorous and aggressive war policy and a purified body politic. Soon after the outbreak of war, Walpole had been harshly criticized for his administration's refusal to commit maximum military and naval resources to the war. "It is not a little low piratical War, Gentlemen, but a vigorous Prosecution of the War . . . that will . . . maintain and defend our ancient Trade, Commerce and Navigation," complained the constituents of Nottingham in the instructions to their MPs in late 1739; and the government's failure to send out sufficient land forces was blamed for Admiral Haddock's setbacks in the Mediterranean and for Vernon's slow progress in the Spanish West Indies after Porto Bello had been secured.[30] Hence the successes at Porto Bello and Chagres yielded maximum political capital both in and out of doors as an opposition triumph, imparting direction to the coalition opposition's floundering strategy toward the administration.[31]

In the midst of the national furor wrought by the war, Tories and patriot Whigs organized instruction and petitioning movements in the

---

[28] NNRO, Case 18, shelf b, City Chamberlain Accounts, Payments Without Orders, 1740–1, 1741–2; *Norwich Mercury,* May 9, May 23, June 6, 1741.

[29] *Vernon Papers,* 78; Nicholas Rogers, "Resistance to Oligarchy: The City Opposition to Walpole and His Successors," in John Stevenson, ed., *London in the Age of Reform* (Oxford, 1977), 10–11; *Reasons for Electing Sir Edward Bellamy . . . Sir John Barnard . . . Micajah Perry . . . and the Honourable Vice-Admiral Vernon, Members in the Ensuing Parliament for This Metropolis* (London, 1741), a broadside which sought to promote the opposition Whig candidates with Vernon, "Conqueror of Carthagena."

[30] *Great Britain's Memorial* (London, 1740); *The Operations of the War, for the First Twelve Months, Examined and Accounted For* (London, 1740).

[31] Pulteney to Vernon, Aug. 17, 1740, June 16, 1741, *Vernon Papers,* 119–22, 240–1.

150 The sense of the people

constituencies that were greatly aided by the national enthusiasm for the admiral and his richly symbolic cause. Thirty-two constituencies instructed or otherwise addressed their representatives on placemen and other forms of Walpolean corruption between September 1739 and October 1740 (twenty-two of them doing so between June and October); forty-seven in 1741–2.[32] Many of these instructions were reprinted in the opposition newspapers; they stressed the clear connection between present discontents and past political grievances, from the Septennial Act, the attempted excise and the increase in both penal laws and the number of placemen, to the administration's management of the war – all evidences of ministerial corruption that could only be checked by parliamentary reform.[33] Evincing both the close association of pro-Vernon and patriot sentiment and the tight organization of the opposition, twenty of the thirty-one borough constituencies where Vernon commemorations were held either sent instructions in 1739–40 or were located in instructing counties (see map).

Even further, Vernon's popularity and identity as an opposition hero imparted renewed enthusiasm for the anti-Walpolean campaign out-of-doors, leading to political initiatives that often had concrete electoral results. In London, for example, in 1739–41 City voters overwhelmingly rejected Court candidates in several of their former strongholds among the wards.[34] Moreover, the 1741 parliamentary election saw the disintegration of Whig strength in several constituencies. Vernon was nominated as candidate for Parliament in Ipswich, Rochester, Penryn, Portsmouth and Westminster as well as London, boroughs in which government influence was strong. Yet in Ipswich an overwhelming 99 percent polled for Vernon in an election with a 92 percent turnout, vanquishing entrenched Whig interests there.[35] In Rochester and Penryn, too, Vernon succeeded in toppling entrenched Court majorities, and would have done so in Portsmouth had not the Corporation decided

[32] In 1739–40, there were 5 Scottish and 27 English constituencies participating in the instruction movement; in 1741–2, 14 and 33 respectively. Most of the instructions are printed in *Great Britain's Memorial* and *The Second Part of Great Britain's Memorial* (London, 1741); see also *LEP*, July–Oct. 1740.
[33] See, e.g., *Gentleman's Magazine*, 9 (1739), 548 (London), 637–8 (Salisbury), 650 (Nottingham); *An Impartial Enquiry into the Properties of Places and Pensions, as They Affect the Constitution* (London, 1740); [Hugh Hume, Earl of Marchmont], *A Serious Exhortation to the Electors of Great Britain* (London, 1740).
[34] Rogers, "Resistance to Oligarchy," 9–11.
[35] *The Poll for the Members of Parliament for the Borough of Ipswich, Taken May 8, 1741* (Ipswich, 1741); *Supplement to the Poll for Ipswich* (Ipswich, 1741).

to withdraw his candidacy because of his multiple nominations.[36] And in Westminster, where Vernon's nomination and immense support from freemen caught the government completely off guard, the high bailiff used troops to close the polls early in order to prevent Vernon's return, provoking a protracted episode of rioting and violence. Elsewhere in the country, too, such as at Newcastle, Coventry, Norwich, Huntingdon, Peterborough, Liverpool and York, the contrast between Vernon's victories and the government's handling of the war effort was exploited in pre-electoral propaganda. The result was that the opposition bettered its performance in the large boroughs over that of 1734 (a fact much celebrated in the patriot press), and the Court majority was reduced from forty-two to eighteen.[37] Clearly, Vernon's stature as a national hero had complex political repercussions and significance, influencing the strategies of both government and opposition and stimulating grass-roots initiatives that affected the balance of power in Parliament.

How are we to explain the nature and scale of support for Vernon described above, and account for his appeal to such a broad spectrum of interests? The press, demonstrations and artifacts reveal, first, the infrastructure of a "commercialized," accessible and largely urban political culture, national in scope and orientation, and predicated on a vital provincial political public. Demonstrations for Vernon occurred in virtually all corners of England and in parts of Wales and Scotland; in the larger commercial and trading towns, such as Bristol, Liverpool, Glasgow, Edinburgh, Newcastle and Norwich; in manufacturing centers and dockyard towns, such as Birmingham, Leeds and Coventry, Portsmouth and Ipswich; in county towns like York, Denbigh and Worcester; and in tiny villages, such as Harleston, Norfolk, and Beaumaris, Anglesey. The geography of support for Vernon clearly evinces the tentacular reach of the press, provincial and London, and the widespread audience for news in urban centers in the "pre-radical" period of British politics. Equally notable, the exploitation of political sentiments by potters, publicans and manufacturers as well as printers indicates not only the intensification of trends, in evidence since the early

[36] Sedgwick, i, 268, 216, 253.
[37] Nicholas Rogers, "Aristocratic Clientage, Trade and Independency: Popular Politics in Pre-Radical Westminster," *P & P,* no. 61 (1973), 74–5; Wilson, "Rejection of Deference," 237–45; Sedgwick, i, 340, 273–4, 364; J. F. Quinn, "York Elections in the Age of Walpole," *Northern History,* 22 (1986), 182–6; *Norwich Gazette,* Nov. 22, 1740; *LEP,* April 30 – May 3, 1741; *Craftsman,* July 25, 1741; John Owen, *The Rise of the Pelhams* (London, 1957), 6.

seventeenth century, toward the solidification of a national market but also the emergence of a national market for political artifacts.[38]

The press and the market, then, in conjunction with the inns, taverns and streets of the capital and provincial towns, provided the extra-institutional bases for the vigorous national political culture focussed on Admiral Vernon. What is equally clear is that the middling and artisanal classes in the capital and localities provided a substantial portion of the personnel. Certainly, as both the civic processions and effigy-burnings evinced, enthusiasm for the admiral was socially as well as politically inclusive, embracing a heterogeneous range of interests from local elites to the poor.[39] However, merchants, retailers, shop-keepers and traders funded, via subscription, many of the celebratory festivities attendant upon Vernon's successes; published, manufactured, bought and sold the pamphlets, ballads and artifacts in his honor; and offered their taverns for his birthday celebrations. They were of central importance in initiating and sustaining the national fervor for Vernon and the extra-parliamentary politics focussed on him.

The social contours of support for Vernon, however, do little to explain the nature of those aspirations and interests which prompted the often elaborate observances of Vernon anniversaries, which cannot be reduced to the supposedly rampant chauvinism or "sub-political" sensibilities of ordinary English people.[40] Certainly a bellicose chauvinism was at play in the national fervor displayed for Vernon, but it emanated from elite and middling as well as plebeian quarters, acted out in theater productions, tavern celebrations and gentry-sponsored fêtes as well as effigy-burnings. Moreover, chauvinism alone cannot explain either the universal hold which Vernon and his exploits had on the national imagination or their political significance. Rather, Vernon's acclaim must be read against its broader political and ideological contexts, which make clear that the Vernon agitation represented to many of its participants the latest, if most vigorous and widespread, installment of a campaign against Walpolean corruption that had been in progress since 1725, but

---

[38] Joan Thirsk, *Economic Policy and Projects: The Development of a Consumer Society in Early Modern England* (Oxford, 1978); McKendrick et al., *Birth of a Consumer Society.*

[39] For gentry leadership of celebrations, such as in Hexham and Chester, *LEP,* March 25–7, Nov. 4–6, 1740; for self-generated plebeian festivities see *LEP,* Nov. 13–15, 1740; *Salisbury Journal,* Nov. 18, 1740; *Norwich Gazette,* May 30, 1741.

[40] John Stevenson, *Popular Disturbances in England, 1700–1800* (London, 1979), 62. Rogers veers toward such an assessment in his remarks on the invariable "nativism" of the "crowd": *Whigs and Cities,* 377–88.

one which had become inextricably intertwined with expansionist, as well as libertarian, principles.

As we have seen, the opposition championed a delegatory view of parliamentary authority and lambasted the Walpole administration for its anti-libertarian measures in the guise of its "patriotic" program to eradicate executive corruption – the "pollutions of ministerial donatives" which, it argued, currently threatened the constitution and the political process.[41] Its tactics and rhetoric had a strong appeal for urban populations whose role in the political process had been sharply curtailed since the Hanoverian Succession. At the same time, the opposition's deliberate incorporation of commercial and mercantile grievances in its so-called country program and the case against Court Whiggery further enlarged its support out-of-doors. This was demonstrated in the excise crisis of 1733; it was also shown in the sporadic but effective interactions of overseas merchant grievances and opposition tactics since the 1720s, which highlighted the inadequacies of Walpole's foreign policy. Whatever its actual merits in promoting a "balance of power" on the Continent, placating English landowners and protecting the rich monopoly companies that were the financial bulwarks of the post-Revolution state,[42] Walpole's Eurocentric policy was resented by many who felt it served Hanoverian rather than British interests; it was also incompatible with the demands for a bellicose foreign policy geared to colonial expansion that emanated from merchant groups in London and the outports, especially those involved in the West Indian and North American trade, where the monopoly companies held little sway. Although frequently divided on other trade and colonial issues, this mixed constituency of metropolitan and provincial merchants shared a frustration with governmental diplomacy and an increasing apprehension about French and Spanish threats to Britain's empire and commercial preeminence; they also had much to lose by Spanish privateering and much to gain from illicit colonial trade. Not surprisingly, then, they began to publicize their grievances to a wider public. After the fiasco at St. Lucia in 1723 and even more vehemently in the next decade, newspapers and pamphlets argued for the primacy of trade over

[41] *An Impartial Enquiry into the Properties of Places and Pensions,* 9–10.
[42] N. C. Hunt, "The Russia Company and the Government, 1740–42," *Oxford Slavonic Papers,* 7 (1957), 27–65; R. Davis, "English Foreign Trade 1700–74," *Economic History Review,* 2nd ser., 15 (1962), 285–303; Black, *British Foreign Policy,* 36–40; Dame Lucy Sutherland, *The East India Company in Eighteenth Century Politics* (Oxford, 1952), 14–48.

high finance in the national interest, asserting that trade could flourish only with a foreign policy that concentrated not on expensive Continental connections but on England's naval power and colonial supremacy – "the Acquisition of Tracts of Land and Territories to Enlarge Dominion and Power" – which was the blue-water policy advocated by Tories since Anne's reign.[43]

The parliamentary opposition took up the aggrieved merchants' cause in print and in Parliament. Tory and patriot Whig leaders had demanded an inquiry into the loss of St. Lucia, criticized the weakness of the Treaty of Seville, denounced Spanish designs on Gibraltar, Minorca and Georgia, and exposed the French refortification of Dunkirk, thus championing the interests of the disaffected bellicose merchant groups who wanted an expansionist foreign policy.[44] The events of 1738–41 renewed this alliance. Opposition writers, in literally dozens of pamphlets and articles, combined the demands of the merchant petitioners from the outports and London with a strident imperialism that trumpeted the centrality of trade and empire in the national interest as well as the maintenance of the balance of power in Europe. "Of all the branches of our Commerce, that to our colonies is the most valuable . . . it is by *that* alone we are enabled to carry out the rest," the "Boy Patriot" George Lyttelton argued in one of the most important pamphlets of 1739. His colleagues, and especially the patriot Whigs, were scarcely less reticent about what they took to be the goals of the war. Lord Carteret himself, commenting on the government's restrained handling of the war effort, confessed to the Swedish minister in an indiscreet and probably inebriate moment, "What is the good of taking ships? We shall take from Spain some countries in America, and we shall keep them in spite of the whole world."[45]

The expansionist aspirations of opposition elites were echoed in the newspaper press, where writers argued in favor of naval wars and de-

[43] *Weekly Journal, or Saturday's Post,* March 9, 1723; *London Journal,* April 13, 27, 1723; *Articles of the Treaty, Signed at Seville: With Remarks on the Said Treaty* (London, 1729); *Champion,* Feb. 17, 1739; Geoffrey Holmes, *British Politics in the Age of Anne* (London, 1967), 169–70.

[44] *Egmont MSS,* i, 77–8; *Articles of the Treaty, Signed at Seville;* [William Pulteney], *A Short View of the State of Affairs . . . with Relation to Great Britain . . . for Four Years Past* (London, 1730); Henry St. John, Viscount Bolingbroke, *The State of Dunkirk, Faithfully Stated and Considered* (London, 1730); Sedgwick, i, 39–40.

[45] [George Lyttelton], *Considerations upon the Present State of Affairs, at Home and Abroad* (London, 1739); Pares, *War and Trade,* 66. See also [Hugh Hume, 3rd Earl Marchmont], *A State of the Rise and Progress of Our Disputes with Spain* (London, 1739).

manded that the government follow a policy of "take and hold" toward
the Spanish empire in America. Cuba was held to be a particularly
valuable prize, some writers arguing that it offered the only real security
to British trade.[46] Artifacts produced in Vernon's honor positively exuded these sentiments. The scores of maps dedicated to him, for example, usually marked off the British empire in America from the
French and Spanish settlements adjacent to it, self-consciously providing a blueprint for further western expansion. Drinking songs published
in provincial newspapers celebrated the British destruction of Spanish
castles, forts and shipping in America as well as colonial acquisition.[47]
And the prints reinforced these themes. *The European Race* gave
graphic testimony to fears that Britain lagged behind in the competition
of the European powers for dominion in Asia, Africa and America; *A
Skit on Britain* (Plate 5) connected the imperial project with the opposition program of parliamentary reform. It shows the British Lion
accompanying Vernon on his maneuvers in the West Indies while back
in England three placemen express devotion to Walpole as he sits on
a map of England and fouls it.[48] On all counts, trade and empire appeared as the central issues in the vociferous support for Vernon and
were linked to the opposition case against the ministry.

Such arguments were not new to the 1740s: They had been popu-
larized through a plethora of essays, pamphlets, articles and speeches
that had argued about commercial and colonial matters since the century began, periodically galvanized by Britain's obsessive rivalry and
protracted wars with Catholic Europe. From the perspective of the pro-
imperialists, the British empire was imagined to consist of flourishing
and commercially viable colonies, populated largely by free (white)
British subjects and supplemented by commercial outposts in "exotic"
climes, which served as bulwarks of trade, prosperity, naval strength
and virtue for the parent state.[49] The imperial project existed to maxi-

[46] *Common Sense,* April 22, 1738; *Champion,* Dec. 29, 1739; Feb. 21, 1740; Pares, *War
and Trade,* 68; Gerald Hertz, *British Imperialism in the Eighteenth Century* (London,
1908), 7–39 passim.

[47] Maps: *Caribbeana* (London, 1740); [Nathaniel Crouch], *The English Empire in America; or, A View of the Dominions of the Crown or England in the West Indies* (London,
1739); *Newcastle Journal,* April 26, 1740; *Gentleman's Magazine,* 10 (1740), suppl.;
Norwich Gazette, March 21, 1741; drinking songs: *Newcastle Journal,* March 22,
1740; *LEP,* Nov. 13–15, 1740.

[48] *The European Race* (London, 1738), BM 2334; *A Skit on Britain* (London, 1740),
BM 2423, both in Lewis Walpole Library, Yale University.

[49] *London Journal,* Nov. 5, 1720; Feb. 3, 1721; Aug. 25, 1722; *Craftsman,* Sept. 7, Dec.
21, 28, 1728; *The War Against Spain Declared;* Koebner, *Empire,* 85–90. The argu-

5. *A Skit on Britain* (1740) (detail). British imperial promise is hampered by executive corruption and betrayal. Courtesy of the Lewis Walpole Library, Yale University.

mize trade and national power, in other words, and colonies were considered crucial to the "empire of the sea" that contemporaries believed Britain had, or should have, dominion over. This vision, predicated upon a mixture of an adulterated mercantilism,[50] nationalistic anxiety and libertarian fervor, was clearly both rose-colored and self-serving, mystifying or obscuring the brutal, exploitive and violent processes of "trade" and colonization (including the immensely profitable trade in slaves) and homogenizing the differences among various forms of British imperial dominance in the New World (and the Old). Nevertheless, it was immensely attractive to domestic publics, who seemed fervently to subscribe to its view of the essentially fair-minded, just and paternalistic nature of the British, as opposed to the French or Spanish, empire, and the former's ability to "tame the fierce and polish the most savage," civilizing the world through commerce and trade.[51] The energetic insertion of this mercantilist imperial vision in opposition politics in the late 1730s and early 1740s increased the latter's resonances among the broader political nation, where numbers of citizens were increasingly convinced that imperial ascendancy and a populist, virtuous polity must go hand-in-hand.

The attractiveness of the opposition's heady brew of expansionist and libertarian principles can be seen in a number of contexts. First, the synthesis of opposition ideology and mercantilist vision in anti-government propaganda was remarkably successful in identifying mercantile demands and expansionist aspirations with the national interest, thus encouraging their support by public-minded citizens. During the

---

ments against colonies, vociferously voiced if not widely held, are admirably summarized by Knorr, *British Colonial Theories,* 102–25.

[50] Envisioning the world as possessed of finite amounts of wealth and resources that were critical to capture if national power was to be maximized, mercantilist thought of the period believed the state's job was to promote national strength and prosperity by maintaining a favorable balance of trade (that is, more exports than imports) and a foreign policy that focussed on promoting Britain's naval power and colonial supremacy. For a recent discussion of mercantilist thinking and its impact on the state see John Brewer, *Sinews of Power: War, Money and the English State, 1688–1783* (London, 1987), 164–78.

[51] Quotation from George Lillo's immensely popular play *The London Merchant* (London, 1731), III.i.11–19, which was performed to enthusiastic London and provincial audiences throughout the period: See my "Empire of Virtue: The Imperial Project and Hanoverian Culture, *c.* 1720–1785," in L. Stone, ed., *An Imperial Nation at War* (London, 1993), 141–3. Favorable comparisons of British with Continental imperialism were well established in the economic and political literature by the early eighteenth century, as was the assumption of native backwardness and English superiority. See Nicholas Canny, "The Ideology of English Colonization: From Ireland to America," *WMQ,* 3rd ser., 30 (1973), 575–98.

agitation over the excise, opposition writers had reiterated mercantilist arguments about the ubiquitous benefits that accrued to the nation from the growth of trade and colonies, in order to emphasize the critical role of merchants in expanding, and thus ensuring the health of, the national economy.[52] It was but a short step to assert that those most committed to the expansion of commerce were pursuing the good of all British citizens, whereas those more diffident about untrammeled imperial expansion were dedicated to its subversion. Indeed, the Spanish war intensified the identification of colonies and colonial merchant prospects with national wealth, safety, power and individual liberty when middling independent overseas merchants, in explicit contrast to those in the monied companies, were represented in parliamentary rhetoric as well as in graphic and literary propaganda as the bulwarks of national virtue and the natural spokesmen for "the people." "This convention, Sir, I think from my soul, is nothing but a stipulation for national ignominy," intoned the young William Pitt in Parliament in 1739. "The complaints of your despairing merchants, *the voice of England,* has condemned it. Be the guilt upon the head of the adviser."[53] Petitions, addresses and letters all reiterated these sentiments, insisting that the situation in the West Indies bore directly on the interests of every individual, and especially on every English person's right to freedom of navigation. Thus, the genuinely aggrieved or merely self-interested merchants from London and the outports who pressed for war and colonial expansion were all identified as possessing the same "patriotic" characteristics as "the people": Independent, virtuous and therefore incorruptible, both were naturally repugnant to the rapacious ministry and the monied companies it protected.[54]

Secondly, the same body of propaganda made a straightforward appeal to the economic concerns of ordinary citizens, particularly those urban groups who had a material stake in the "trading interest." As we have seen, since at least 1733 this interest had been defined in opposition ideology as comprising not only overseas merchants but

[52] See Chapter 2; for colonies see, e.g., *Craftsman,* Dec. 28, 1728.
[53] Quoted in Stanley Ayling, *The Elder Pitt* (New York, 1976), 65.
[54] Herbert Atherton, *Political Prints in the Age of Hogarth* (Oxford, 1974), 170–1; [Benjamin Robbins], *An Address to the Electors, and Other Free Subjects of Britain* (London, 1741); *Egmont MSS,* iii, 16; *An Authentick Account of the Important Transactions of the Last Assembly of the Political Club . . .* (London, 1739); *Considerations on the American Trade, Before and Since the Establishment of the South Sea Company* (London, 1739). Walpole's lampooning of petitioning merchants in the City as "tobacconists and Rag Dyers" intensified this identification: *LEP,* March 8–10, 1739.

wholesale and retail dealers at every level. But it provided, in fact, a fairly accurate representation of the individuals likely to have a stake in foreign trade. English overseas trade had almost trebled since 1650 (with much of it, from 1700 onwards, becoming concentrated in the provincial ports), and the most dynamic sector was the colonial trade – India, Ireland, Africa and particularly the West Indies and America.[55] Growing numbers of ordinary men and women in the localities accordingly invested in overseas ventures, convinced of their profitability in providing markets or commodities. In Bristol, for example, the men and women involved in colonial trade in the first three-quarters of the century, either as direct investors in cargoes or as lenders to merchants or shipowners, included haberdashers, grocers, hoopers, sugar bakers, printers, gunsmiths, apothecaries, tobacconists, yeomen and widows; investors in smaller ports such as Dartmouth, Bridgwater, Weymouth and Plymouth in the Southwest and King's Lynn in East Anglia came from equally diverse backgrounds.[56] William Stout of Lancaster, Ralph Carr of Newcastle and, according to one contemporary account, a good portion of the inhabitants of Liverpool bought shares in ships and cargoes bound to and from the West Indies, Africa and North America, and traders and shopkeepers in dozens of commercial and manufacturing towns were wont to "launch into adventures by sea," as one Manchester observer put it, buying and selling commodities aimed at colonial and foreign markets or distributing imported goods at home.[57]

---

[55] See Chapter 1. Twelve of the 30 leading provincial towns were ports.

[56] W. E. Minchinton, *The Trade of Bristol in the 18th Century* (Bristol Record Society Publications, 20, 1957), 7–8, 36–7, 184–91; Kenneth Morgan, "Shipping Patterns and the Atlantic Trade of Bristol, 1749–1770," *WMQ*, 3rd ser., 46 (1989), 506–38; Nigel Tattersfield, *The Forgotten Trade: Comprising the Log of the "Daniel and Henry" of 1700 and Accounts of the Slave Trade from the Minor Ports of England, 1698–1725* (London, 1991), 15, 195–201; J. M. Triffet, "Politics and the Urban Community: Parliamentary Boroughs in the South-West of England, 1710–30" (Oxford University D. Phil. diss., 1985), 41–50. Small investors from diverse social backgrounds and of both sexes can also be found among the East India Company's stockholders in this period, although they were concentrated in the metropolis and made up only a tiny percentage overall: H. V. Bowen, "Investment and Empire in the Later 18th Century: East India Stockholding, 1756–91," *Economic History Review,* 2nd ser., 42 (1989), 199.

[57] Roger North, *Life of Lord Guildford* (London, 1742), quoted in J. D. Marshall, ed., *The Autobiography of William Stout of Lancaster, 1665–1752* (Manchester, 1967), 15; William Roberts, "Ralph Carr: A Newcastle Merchant and the Colonial Trade," *Business History Review,* 42 (1968), 271–87; *Newcastle Journal,* Nov. 1, 1739; March 22, Nov. 8, 1740; E. Baines, *History of Liverpool* (Liverpool, 1852), 435; T. S. Willan, *An Eighteenth Century Shopkeeper, Abraham Dent of Kirby Stephen* (Manchester, 1970), 29–40.

Thousands of individuals like these throughout England and Scotland were fervently interested in that "empire of goods" which, as historians have recently argued, linked the producers, distributors and consumers of Britain on both sides of the Atlantic and provided the impetus for imperial growth and prosperity in the eighteenth century.[58] They were thus receptive to the arguments that, as part of the "trading interest," they would benefit from an aggressive commercial policy and that the domestic welfare was inseparable from "Success, Prosperity and Glory Abroad."

Against the background of ideological, commercial and imperial issues, then, Vernon's political significance can be seen. Vernon was, first of all, a *naval* hero, and as such represented the kind of war and military policy that the majority of the nation felt Britain should have. Eighteenth-century Britons' hatred of a standing army was grounded in patriotic and libertarian issues, particularly in the belief that land forces were the invariable agents of absolutism; the navy and the militia were seen as the most efficacious and constitutional methods of protecting the interests of a "trading nation." It was these prejudices, which, along with his political affiliations, had dimmed the Duke of Marlborough's glory and popularity even during Anne's reign, preventing him from becoming an unambiguous national hero.[59] Vernon, Vice-Admiral of the Blue, had none of these shortcomings. Instead, he represented the epitome of British spirit, manliness and integrity in a corrupt and mercenary age. Daring to confront Britain's imperial rivals, hostile to the profiteering that riddled the Royal Navy, and disdainful of the emoluments of title – he declined an offer of a knighthood in 1742 – he was also a just and fair commander, mindful of the needs of the sailors aboard his ships, willing to implement reforms to improve morale and to press their rights in Parliament. His humane treatment of the inhabitants of Porto Bello, as well as his speedy restoration of trade relations between British ships and the Spanish West Indian settlements, added to his already considerable popular acclaim.[60]

[58] Bernard Bailyn, *The Peopling of British North America* (New York, 1986), 20–85; T. H. Breen, " 'An Empire of Goods': The Anglicization of Colonial America, 1690–1776," *JBS,* 25 (1986), 467–99; Philip Jenkins, "Tory Industrialism and Town Politics: Swansea in the Eighteenth Century," *HJ,* 28 (1985), 116–19; Angus McInnes, "The Emergence of a Leisure Town: Shrewsbury 1660–1760," *P & P,* no. 120 (1988), 77–80.

[59] Tony Hayter, *The Army and the Crowd in Mid-Georgian England* (London, 1978), 9–46; Holmes, *British Politics in the Age of Anne,* 190–1.

[60] Sedgwick, ii, 497–8; *Egmont MSS,* iii, 271; *Liveryman,* 26–7; *A Poem on the Glorious Achievements of Admiral* VERNON; *Vernon Papers,* 43–4, 86; *Champion,* March 20, 1740.

Vernon was also an *imperial* hero, both in the geographic extent of the admiration for him and in his efforts to preserve and extend empire abroad. The patriotic language used to celebrate his successes deliberately evoked these imperial dimensions of his cause. Vernon was hailed repeatedly as the ultimate "Free-born *Briton*," a term which not only reflected Scottish and American participation in the agitation but also conflated its political and imperial connotations. Hence the celebrations in Edinburgh on the king's birthday in 1740 were marked by a parade of city troops wearing cockades inscribed "British Liberty and No Placemen," and ended with public toasts to "the renown'd Vernon . . . *True Briton* indeed!"[61] And, of course, Vernon's exploits in the Caribbean vindicated the viability of an aggressive blue-water policy in the Americas, signifying its substantial promise for British commerce. "Free Born Briton, truly Brave! / Born to revenge our wrongs, and Glory Save; / To Teach the World Britannia Rules the Main" was how one writer summarized it in late 1740.[62] He thus not only asserted, if symbolically, British commercial ascendancy in the world, he also coaxed consolidation of a British imperial identity, one in which Caledonians and Americans as well as the English could participate. Vernon thus supported and embodied the spectacular, if imaginary, vision of empire as an extensive, homogeneous polity bounded only by rights, liberties and duties and guided by manly and virtuous leaders. Through him, the empire was refracted back to his supporters as the ultimate patriotic project, diffusing wealth among the domestic population, protecting English freedoms (including freedom of trade and navigation in the world) from the threats of foreign powers and rapacious ministries, and extending British birthrights throughout the world.

Finally, Vernon was the hero of a politics based upon an extreme alienation from the ministry and its supporters in Parliament. Despite the "universal voice of the people" in demanding an effective war against Spain, the government had disregarded what was by its own definition its primary function: to protect British interests and property at home and abroad. Hence Vernon symbolized and defined British patriotism in terms antithetical to the corruption and venality of the administration. "We wish that every Member in the ensuing Parliament

---

[61] *Newcastle Courant*, Nov. 8, 1740. American colonists were also likely to describe themselves as having the manners and customs of "Britons," although white planters in Barbados clung tenaciously to the appellation "English": Charles Inglis, *The True Interest of America* (Philidelphia, 1776); Jack Greene, "Changing Identity in the British Caribbean: Barbados as Case Study," in Canny and Pagden, eds., *Colonial Identity*, 213–66.

[62] *Norwich Gazette*, Nov. 15–22, 1740.

might be a VERNON, or animated by like Spirit: We should see our Country flourishing at home, and giving Laws abroad'' was the response of one writer in 1741 on learning that Vernon had been returned in three constituencies.[63] Equally important, his loyalty was unassailable. His fervent Hanoverianism had been proven in an incident in 1705 when, while serving in the West Indies during the War of the Spanish Succession, he observed a merchant ship celebrating the Pretender's birthday, provoking him to bring the captain back to England in chains.[64] Not even the most paranoid or zealous of government supporters could accuse him, as they could Sacheverell, Bolingbroke, Wyndham and Barber, of disloyalty. Vernon thus gave credibility to the opposition as well as to its charges against the government.

Although the patriotism represented by Vernon as the protector of Protestant Britain against Catholic Spain had an appeal that could extend across the political spectrum, it was as an *opposition* hero, one who stimulated a powerful conflation of empire and liberty, that Vernon's primary political importance lay. The marked enthusiasm for Vernon from the commercial and trading classes of provincial towns and London bear witness to his double-faceted role and evince the affinity between the urban middling classes and oppositionist politics that endured through the American war. Endorsement of the tenets of independence and accountable government meant for them, as it did for later radicals, independence from the client economy and a Parliament that protected the commercial interests – the ''liberty and property'' – of its middling constituents. As one writer expressed it in 1739, justifying the extra-parliamentary agitation for war, the current ''decay of trade'' was a result not only of Spanish atrocities committed against English merchantmen but also of excessive indirect taxation, the bogus financial schemes of the City's monied interests, and

> the Badness of Pay of our Nobility and Gentry, who seem rather to think that we Tradesmen are beholden to them for their Custom, tho' they perhaps never intended to pay Us . . . if the Trading Part of this Nation are not to regard the Publick Welfare, and when they see themselves daily injured are not for Redress of those Grievances to apply to the Senate and the Throne, who are –?

From this perspective, the government had not only revealed itself to be ''an implacable enemy to the British colonies'' but had proven also

---

[63] *Newcastle Courant,* May 2, 1741.
[64] An act which cost Vernon £1,000 in damages on prosecution of the owner of the ship. *Egmont MSS,* iii, 77.

that an effective domestic and foreign policy depended upon the "counsels of a considerate and uncorrupted Parliament."[65] Vernon was thus the ultimate British patriot and hero who seemed to hold out the equally attractive prospects of new markets and a new ministry.

Appropriately, it was the government's continued mishandling of the war effort that proved to be its death knell. The failure of the attack on Cuba in late 1741, blamed on the ministry's failure to send sufficient land forces to support Vernon, undermined all confidence in Walpole's war leadership, finally forcing him from power. His fall in February 1742 was greeted with joyous celebrations and mocking funerals all over the country. "If Bonfires, Illuminations, Healths, Wishes of Success to a new M——y, are allowed to be Demonstrations of the Sense of the People," the *Weekly Worcester Journal* observed, "we may affirm there never was a more general Joy than that which appear'd even upon the Rumour of a late resignation."[66] It was one of many occasions in the eighteenth century when the "sense of the people" had direct and material results, despite the structural odds against its doing so.

The social and political taxonomy of support for Vernon and of the formidable opposition to Walpole that it united are thus worth reviewing. On the level of parliamentary politics, it was the patriot Whigs – Lords Carteret and Chesterfield, Pulteney, Sandys, Pitt, Lyttelton; City aldermen Sir John Barnard and Micajah Perry – who emerged as the leading proponents for war and colonial acquisition, publicizing the American merchants' grievances in and out of Parliament and turning them into a cause célèbre. They were aided substantially, of course, by Tory leaders like Lord Bathurst in the Lords and Wyndham and Shippen in the Commons, as well as by other disaffected groups, such as the Trustees of Georgia, who were aggrieved at Walpole's apparent willingness to turn over the fate of the colony to Spanish plenipotentiaries.[67] Support for Vernon outside Parliament came from equally diverse sources. First, there was the phalanx of West Indian and

[65] *The War Against Spain Declared; Craftsman,* March 10, 1739; *Serious Exhoration,* 7.
[66] As Owen recognized long ago: *Rise of the Pelhams,* 2–5. Quotation from *Weekly Worcester Journal,* Feb. 19–26, 1742; for celebrations and funerals see *Craftsman,* Feb. 13, 1742; *Newcastle Courant,* Feb. 13, 1742.
[67] *History of the House of Commons,* x (1742), 96–176; Rogers, "Urban Opposition," 135–6; *Egmont MSS,* iii, 27. The South Sea Company directors voted overwhelmingly for the Convention of El Pardo: *Gentleman's Magazine,* 9 (1739), 304–11; Sedgwick, i, 152.

American merchants from London and the outports, who initiated the mobilization of public opinion in 1738–9 by coordinating, through committees of correspondence, the protests and petitions against Spanish depredations and the Convention of El Pardo.[68] Their goals and aspirations were mirrored in the enthusiastic support of middling merchants, retailers and traders in the capital and localities who indulged in boisterous Vernon celebrations. Transecting these specific socioeconomic groupings were the political constellations supporting Vernon, embracing the adherents of the parliamentary opposition, from the landed gentlemen who tended to back the plans for naval war and the retrenchment of costly subsidies, to middling sorts anxious for more equitable commercial dealings, and humble men and women in the localities who applauded his defeat of a national enemy, his vindication of Britain's honor and his embarrassment of the ministry. As such, Vernon broadened the bases of opposition support, appealing to a wider social arena than any opposition figure between Sacheverell and Wilkes.

The Vernon agitation constituted a significant episode in eighteenth-century popular politics. The activities generated in his name demonstrate irrefutably the importance of provincial urban political culture in creating a national campaign, as well as the readiness of ordinary citizens to initiate and sustain disciplined political action. Equally important, the agitation revealed the importance of imperial expansion in domestic political and demotic political sensibilities. The convergence of grievances against the Walpolean regime both exploited and expanded the political and imperial aspirations of the extra-parliamentary nation, incorporating into the opposition's patriotic rhetoric and programs libertarian themes about the power of the people and the ascent of political power from below, as well as an imperial vision of Britain's national destiny. Hence Walpolean policy was castigated both because it threatened liberty and property at home and because it threatened to circumscribe Britain's position in the world. In this way, the Vernon agitation kindled and focussed a nascent imperialist sensibility that defined British identity through expansion abroad as well as through birthrights, liberties and constitutional traditions. It was scarcely coincidental that it was in 1740, on the heels of Vernon's victory at Porto Bello, that ''God Save the King'' was first sung in Britain, and that

---

[68] For merchant organization see *LEP*, Feb. 4–6, 23–8, 1738; Feb. 1–3, 1739; Walter Minchinton, *Politics and the Port of Bristol in the Eighteenth Century* (Bristol, 1963), 48n.

the same year brought the first publication of Arne's rendering of "Rule Britannia."[69] The Vernon agitation laid the groundwork for popular support for, and ministerial exploitation of, Britain's greatest imperial effort in the century, the Seven Years' War. Significantly, the Boy Patriot Pitt had served his political apprenticeship in the anti-Walpolean opposition of 1738–42.

II. INVASION BLUES

A little over a decade after Vernon's exploits, the mood of the political nation had changed dramatically. The confidence that, given patriotic leadership, Britain could attain national imperial greatness had been replaced with widespread anxiety that the nation's patriotic verve had been sapped, the victim of a creeping effeminate supineness that had corroded martial spirit and courage to the point where British imperial decline and defeat were all but inevitable. What had happened to produce such a sea-change in public apprehensions about Britain's moral fiber and national character?

Domestic and international developments of the intervening years were central to the transformation. The 1740s were a tumultuous and crisis-ridden decade that had produced a cycle of raised expectations and frustrated hopes. Vernon's exploits in the West Indies had fanned dreams of imperial expansion without being able to fulfill them. Hampered by lack of supplies and quarrelling between land and naval leadership, the Caribbean campaign had petered out by late 1741 as Britain was instead drawn into what would prove to be a longer and equally unsatisfying Continental war over the Austrian succession (1741–9). The "patriotic" ministry of Carteret and Pulteney provided a parallel to the Vernon campaigns in producing wildly inflated expectations and bitter disappointments. Despite the issuing of instructions from fifty-four English constituencies between February and August 1742 demanding substantive political change and parliamentary inquiries into the late ministry, the new ministry only managed to pass an attenuated place bill that prohibited junior officials from sitting in the House of Commons, and to establish a Secret Committee to investigate Walpole's administration that, thanks to the stonewalling of Whig politicians, proved incapable of bringing him or his dependents to justice.[70] The

---

[69] Hertz, *British Imperialism*, 42.
[70] Linda Colley, *In Defiance of Oligarchy: The Tory Party, 1714–60* (Cambridge, 1982), 242–3; for instructions see *Weekly Worcester Journal*, Feb. 19–26 (Westminster),

disillusionment and cynicism that resonated throughout the extra-parliamentary nation was articulated in the provincial press.[71]

Equally important, hopes that the new patriot ministry would see "the *British* glory reviv'd, our Trade Flourish, our numerous Standing Forces either utterly disbanded, or advantageously employ'd, and Old *England* again rise the Terror and Arbitress of *Europe*" were also crushed, hostages to the fortunes of the Continental war that Carteret and George II pursued.[72] Indeed, Walpole's fall permitted George II to undertake policies on the Continent that were ostentatiously geared to shoring up his beloved Electorate's interests, resulting in diplomatic quandaries and muddled land campaigns that secretary of state Carteret's foreign-policy skills were just able to salvage.[73] Tories and the remaining patriot Whigs in Parliament, such as George Lyttelton and William Pitt (the latter made his reputation as an orator denouncing the Electorate), attacked the government's pro-Hanoverian foreign policy and voted against the hiring of 16,000 Hanoverian troops as a betrayal of British interests, while observers in the outports expressed resentment at the inattention given to overseas dominions. George II's shoddy treatment of his British troops during the Battle of Dettingen, which he had led under the colors of the Electorate, was the coup de grâce, resulting in an eruption of anti-Hanoverianism that resonated throughout the nation.[74]

The aftermath of Walpoleanism, then, did not prove to be a propitious time for "patriotism" at home or abroad, and public discontents were swelled by the foreign policy of George II and his new ministers. The commencement of formal hostilities with France in early 1744 and

March 5–12 (Coventry), 12–19 (Chester, Marlborough and Oxford); 19–26 (Hereford), April 2–9, 1742 (Monmouth); *Newcastle Courant,* March 6, 1742 (Bristol); *Norwich Gazette,* Feb. 20, March 13, 27, April 17, 1742 (Denbighshire, Bath, York, Edinburgh, Preston); and *Second Part of Great Britain's Memorial.*

[71] G. A. Cranfield, *The Development of the Provincial Newspaper* (Oxford, 1962), 134–40.

[72] Quotation from instructions of Flint boroughs, in *Second Part of Great Britain's Memorial;* see also the instructions from York, Edinburgh, Bath, Preston and Bristol.

[73] For George II's diplomatic machinations in favor of Hanover and Carteret's ameliorative responses see Paul Langford, *A Polite and Commercial People: England, 1727–83* (Oxford, 1989), 189–92; Owen, *Rise of the Pelhams,* chap. 3.

[74] Colley, *Defiance,* 236–47; Rogers, *Whigs and Cities,* 69; *The Newcomers; or, The Characters of John the Carter, Sandy Long-Bib, Daniel Raven and Old Will* (London, 1742); *A List of the Members of Parliament Who Voted for and Against Taking the Hanoverian Troops into British Pay* (London, 1742); *Norwich Gazette,* Sept. 4, 1742, January 8, 1743; *LEP,* Dec. 27–9, 1743; *The H[ano]v[eria]n Confectioner General* (London, 1743), BM 2584.

the establishment of a nominally "broad-bottom" coalition led by Old Corps leader Henry Pelham later that year ameliorated the harshly critical climate somewhat, and the capture of the French colony of Cape Breton by the British on June 17, 1745, served to raise hopes once again for the pursuit of a vigorous blue-water policy. Ironically, the Jacobite invasion later that year did the most to concentrate attention on Britain's international standing and strength, certainly deflecting criticism for the moment from the administration but also glorifying trade and empire as crucial components of the national identity. Landing in Scotland in July 1745 with a handful of men, Prince Charles Edward on his trek south collected an army of sufficient size to force a surrender of Edinburgh in September, and thereafter began his descent on England. The crisis of the '45 produced and legitimized a politics of identity that put paid to Jacobite alternatives but also, ultimately, raised nagging questions about the national character and leadership.

Certainly the invasion of the Young Pretender did much to galvanize the apparatus of extra-parliamentary political culture to loyalist ends. In the first instance, this took the form of the distribution of a plethora of cheap literature aimed at stirring up the historically embedded anti-Catholic prejudices of the English people. Tracts, some reputedly distributed in thousands, revived memories of Bloody Mary and James II, of inquisitorial murders and of Protestant martyrology.[75] Warming-pan ballads were revived, as were the stock allegations about the dangers the Stuarts represented to English religion and liberties.[76] More striking were the vast number of tracts, loyal addresses, plays, prints and ballads that associated the Stuart threat with the annihilation of England's identity as an imperial power and its subjugation to France. The addresses that had poured in to the throne in 1744–5 simultaneously congratulated George II on Britain's capture of Cape Breton and denounced the pretensions of the "popish pretender" as a potential threat to Britain's

---

[75] Tracts distributed in provincial towns included *An Address to the Lower Sort of People; on the Subject of Popery and the Pretender* (London, 1745); *An Address to That Honest Part of the Nation Called the Lower Sort of People on the Subject of Popery and the Pretender* (London, 1745). Foxe's *Book of Martyrs* and Thomas Harris's *Popery and Slavery Display'd* were also sold for sixpence. *Salisbury Journal,* Sept. 28, 1745; *Newcastle Journal,* Oct. 12, 1745; *Norwich Mercury,* Oct. 12, 1745; Nicholas Rogers, "Popular Disaffection During the '45," *London Journal,* 1 (1975), 5–27.

[76] *Salisbury Journal,* Oct. 29, Dec. 24, 1745; *The Chevalier Charlie's Declaration* (London, 1745).

imperial ascendancy.[77] The panic produced in London financial circles – there was a run on the Bank of England in September 1745, and stocks fell as Charles Edward and his 5,500 troops marched south from Edinburgh to Carlisle and Derby between September and December – accordingly led writers like "The Briton" in the *Salisbury Journal* to urge the "money'd men" to act to support the Bank of England and to contribute to new loans for national defense. Another writer unwittingly exposed the tenuousness of British imperial claims when he warned that through the imposition of the Stuart doctrine of hereditary right, Britain would be forced to relinquish Minorca, Gibraltar and Cape Breton to Spain and France.[78] A song performed at Drury Lane Theater drew these strands together in a scenario of the consequences of a Stuart victory which would have caused any stalwart English person nightmares:

> Shall *Friars* and *Monks* recover their *Land*
> And the *Host* pass in Triumph thro' *City* and *Strand?* . . .
> Possesst of your *Rights* they will lead you a *Dance,*
> ENGLAND must then be a *Province* to *France;*
> *French Laws* and *French Customs* and despotick Power
> Vultures will prey, and like VULTURES devour
> *Cape Breton* is conquer'd, *Cape Breton* we'll keep
> Nor suffer our foes to cajole us asleep.[79]

Such propaganda clearly both solicited and amplified nationalist sensibilities that were resolutely anti-French and commercial as well as Protestant and libertarian. Other tracts and prints were sharply anti-Caledonian, in ways that mirrored contemporary justifications of colonialism and reflected historical antagonisms. Provoked no doubt by the predominance of Highland clansmen among Charles Edward's acquired army – the latter's entry into Manchester in Highland dress was extensively reported on in the press – anti-Jacobite propaganda represented the Scots Highlander as the very antithesis of English manners,

---

[77] Address of the Liverpool Corporation to George II, 1745, in J. A. Picton, *Municipal Archives and Records of the City of Liverpool* (Liverpool, 1886), 106.

[78] *Salisbury Journal,* Oct. 1, 29, 1745; *An Antidote Against the Infectious Contagion of Popery and Tyranny* (Edinburgh, 1745); see also *Newcastle Journal,* Nov. 23, 1745, and M. D. George, *English Political Caricature,* 2 vols. (Oxford, 1959), i, 95.

[79] *A Loyal Song, Sung by Mr. Beard at the Theatre Royal, Covent Garden* (London, 1745). Performances of *Henry V* were advertised as including "the glorious Victory of the English against the French at the Battle of Agincourt": G. W. Stone, *The London Stage: A Critical Introduction* (Carbondale, Ill., 1968), xxvii–xxviii.

civilization and commercial finesse, devoid of any social or political refinement and incapable of comprehending superior cultures – "ignoble savages" indeed. An "unpolish'd Race . . . Unconscious of the nameless Charms which grace and soften Civil Life" was how one ode to the Duke of Cumberland would later summarize it.[80] Tracts such as *The Highlander Delineated* which described the clansmen as unkempt and disease-ridden barbarians were supplemented by gruesome prints of Highlanders looting and killing in English towns, all the while being careful to distinguish the loyal Scottish population from the Highlander rebels.[81] Not surprisingly, perhaps, once the rebellion was quelled, "civilizing" the Highlanders became a central concern of the Pelham ministry, through a combination of coercive and commercial measures aimed, in the words of Lord Milton, at "extirpating their barbarity, with their chief marks of distinction, their language and dress, and preventing their idleness, the present source of their poverty, Theft and Rebellion" – a characterization remarkably similar to that used against the native Irish two centuries before.[82] For the moment, such discourse had the effect of narrowing the inclusive patriotism valorized by Vernon and closing down the types of "Scottishness" permitted to be included in the English/British nation.

Propaganda then, by drawing on the French, Scottish and Catholic phobias of the English public, was undoubtedly instrumental in arousing nationalist ardor. It constructed a series of oppositions against which English and, to a more limited degree, British cultural, imperial and political greatness could be defined and valorized, circulating a range of arguments that simultaneously justified British imperial and English national ascendancy. Where the French and Spanish were popish, slavish, exploitive and treacherous, and the Highlanders infidel,

---

[80] *Worcester Journal,* May 16, 1746; see also *London Gazette,* Nov. 30 – Dec. 3, 1745; *St. James's Evening Post,* Nov. 30 – Dec. 3, 1745; "Beppy Byrom's Journal," *The Private Journal and Literary Remains of John Byrom,* ed. Richard Parkinson, 2 vols. (Chetham Society Publications, 32, 34, 40, 44, 1854–7), ii, pt. 2, 387–8n.

[81] George, *English Political Caricature,* i, 95; *The Highlander Delineated; or, the Character, Customs and Manners of the Highlanders* (London, 1745); *The Pretended Prince of Wales's Manifesto and Declaration . . . Dissected, Anatomized and Exposed to Ridicule* (Newcastle, 1745); *The Highland Visitors* (London, 1746), 36. See also the handbill dated Edinburgh, Sept. 7, 1745, *The Thoughts of an Impartial Man upon the Present Situation of Affairs in the City of Edinburgh,* in HL, Collection on the Jacobite Rebellion, 1734–56.

[82] C. S. Terry, *The Albermarle Papers,* 2 vols. (Aberdeen, 1902), ii, 447, quoted in Langford, *Polite and Commercial People,* 217; Canny, "Ideology of English Colonization."

BRINGS SCOT + ENG. CATHOLICS AGAINST

barbaric, brutish and indigent, the English and Lowland Scots who assimilated English culture were Protestant, virtuous, refined, civilized, wealthy and free. Hence a staunch defense of "Englishness" against these foreign threats to the tissue and texture of everyday life was privileged as the supreme patriotic duty.

The impact of such injunctions on behavior and loyalty was varied. Among party elites and opposition supporters in London and the localities, the invasion precipitated acrimonious disputes and dissension, caused less frequently by latent Jacobite sympathies (no Tory gentlemen came out for the Pretender in '45) than by the ostentatious efforts of Whig loyalists to appropriate loyalty solely to their own party. A number of Tories and independent Whig MPs refused to join the county associations to raise men and money for defense, as in Middlesex, Shropshire and Oxfordshire; declined to engage in the loyalist affirmations sponsored by Whig elites, as in Norwich and Nottingham; or tied their support for loyalist measures to the administration efforts to address popular grievances, as in London, rightly perceiving the loyal associations to be preeminently political and extra-constitutional gestures aimed at deflecting opposition to the administration.[83] To be sure, the survival of Jacobitism in High Church enclaves such as Manchester, where the Young Pretender's emissary was able to raise 300 recruits and £2,500 for the cause, could make such Tory reticence suspect. And reports of disaffection in the North and Midlands and the alleged and actual pro-Stuart sympathies of some leading Westminster Tories and the Independent Electors allowed the government and its supporters to emblazon the standard of patriotism for themselves.[84] But the Whigs' credibility as the sole bulwark of Protestantism and liberty was far from compelling, undermined by years of anti-libertarian policies, the strident allegations of opposition patriots, and the issues raised by war, trade and imperial expansion (as well as the party's recent gestures toward rapprochement with the Tories). In this context, the rebellion

[83] Colley, *Defiance,* 39–40; NNRO, Assembly Minute Books, Case 13, shelf d (2), List of Norwich Loyalist Association; *VCH Nottinghamshire,* ii, ed. William Page (London, 1910), 359; Rogers, *Whigs and Cities,* 73–6. Opposition objections to associations were made on the basis of their creation by royal rather than parliamentary warrant, and their use as a substitute for the militia, in both cases circumventing rights of the House of Commons.

[84] *VCH Lancashire,* vi (London, 1911), 180; J. P. Earwaker, ed., *Manchester Constables' Accounts,* 3 vols. (Manchester, 1892), iii, 19–28, 354–5; "Beppy Byrom's Journal," 385–95, 406–8; R. C. Jarvis, *Collected Papers on the Jacobite Risings,* 2 vols. (Manchester, 1971–2), ii, 318–21; Rogers, *Whigs and Cities,* 81–3; [Elizabeth Adams], *Manchester Vindicated* (Chester, 1747).

forced ministerial propagandists and observers to stress the *unity* of the Young Pretender's threat to the nation and the *unity* of the English people's response to it, rallying together for king, religion, liberty, property, empire – an amalgam of the components of the national identity from which the ministry was conspicuously absent.

As the Bishop of Salisbury reminded his flock soon after the rebellion broke out, the citizen's duty was to "your KING, your COUNTRY, your PEOPLE and YOURSELVES" in the present crisis, which entailed the "laying aside all Party . . . [that you] may upon this important occasion . . . be UNITED . . . and act like ENGLISHMEN and like PROTESTANTS."[85] In fact, such unity was on display in most towns in the nation, where partisan divisions were subsumed within or obscured by the expressions of loyalty to king and country that reverberated among all social ranks and political persuasions. Expressions of plebeian disaffection were at a minimum, for example, plebeian crowds instead participating, often with great theatrical flourish, in the lavish pope and Pretender burnings staged on George II's coronation day and birthday, October 11 and 30 respectively, and the fifth of November.[86] Crowds also mimicked and expanded on the official policy of confining Catholics by attacking or otherwise bringing to the attention of authorities the "others" within – "foreigners," Irish, Catholics – whose patriotism was prima facie suspect in the present crisis. Catholic mass-houses were sacked or fired in Liverpool and Newcastle and threatened in Stourbridge and London; in Whitby, Yorkshire, ships' carpenters armed themselves with axes and cleavers to harass the Catholics who were rumored to have made rejoicings on the government's defeat at Prestonpans.[87] Such a transformation in plebeian sensibilities since the Hanoverian Succession was part of the larger change in national preoccupations wrought by opposition patriotism and the bellicose, competitive nationalism mobilized most recently by Vernon and deliberately revitalized in the anti-Jacobite propaganda of 1745–6.

---

[85] *Salisbury Journal,* Sept. 24, 1745; for similar clerical exhortations see Edward Gibson, *A Pastoral Letter to the People of His Diocese* (London, 1745); John Thomas, *Principles and Practice of a Popish Government Destructive of Liberty* (London, 1745).

[86] Such as in York, Newcastle, Poole, Newport and Deptford: *York Courant,* Oct. 15, Nov. 5, 1745; *Newcastle Courant,* Nov. 2, 1745; *Salisbury Journal,* Oct. 22, Nov. 12, 1745; *Gentleman's Magazine,* 15 (1745), 557, 609; *LEP,* Nov. 2–5, 1745.

[87] Rogers, "Popular Disaffection," 20–2; *Gentleman's Magazine,* 16 (1746), 324; *VCH Lancashire,* vi, 28; John Sykes, *Local Records of Northumberland,* vol. 1 (Newcastle, 1866), 180; Rogers, *Whigs and Cities,* 379; *General Evening Post,* Oct. 19–22, 1745; Jarvis, *Collected Papers,* ii, 313–14.

The volunteer associations for defense equally mirrored unanimous sentiments against the rebellion and coaxed allegiance to the state. When the invasion materialized, George II was in Hanover, the British army in Belgium and the militia largely moribund. The volunteer associations were one response to this military unpreparedness that emanated largely from the citizenry. Composed of local gentlemen, merchants, tradesmen, artisans and apprentices alike, the associators marched through the towns to the wild huzzas of their inhabitants on anniversary and victory days. Such was the case in at least fifteen provincial towns – Alnwick, Bristol, Hull, King's Lynn, Leicester, Liverpool, Lymington, Newcastle, Newport, Norwich, Plymouth, Poole, Salisbury, Worcester and York – which joined the twenty-five counties which had likewise associated for the country's defense.[88] In Liverpool, for example, the 700 volunteers formed the Liverpool Blues, armed and uniformed at the expense of the Corporation and inhabitants, and subsequently played a strong role in taking Carlisle from the rebels in early 1746. In Manchester, despite the considerable number of Jacobite sympathizers in the town, the volunteer response was so great that those who could not be armed with guns carried pickaxes, swords and shovels. Even as far south as Salisbury, the volunteer association was a focal point of local nationalistic and patriotic effervescences, and in Norwich some women formed their own association to raise money for the male volunteers.[89] "Such glorious Ardor," one Manchester observer asserted, "animates every true Briton to rise in support of his Majesty King George, on whose Security . . . the Welfare of the Community entirely depends." This was certainly the hoped-for response to the volunteer associations from the loyalists' point of view. Indeed, the associations were lauded in print, pulpit and Parliament and from the stage as the ultimate embodiments of the patriotic spirit. The provincial press was filled with poems, ballads and verses in honor of the volunteer associations, celebrating their martial spirit as the distinguish-

[88] *Norwich Gazette,* Oct. 12, 1745; *Newcastle Journal,* Nov. 9, 1745; *Salisbury Journal,* Nov. 18, 1745; John Latimer, *Annals of Bristol in the Eighteenth Century* (Bristol, 1893), 256; *Records of Nottingham,* vi, 195; *Records of Leicester,* v (1745–6); Worcester City Archives, Guildhall, A10/7 Chamber Order Book, 1736–63, 1745–6; Thomas, Archbishop of Canterbury, *A Sermon Preach'd at the Cathedral Church of York* (London, 1745). Linda Colley has found 57 such associations formed in three-quarters of the English and Welsh counties between September and December 1745: *Britons,* 83.
[89] Baines, *History of Liverpool,* 411–12; W. A. Axon, *Annals of Manchester* (Manchester, 1886), 84; "Beppy Byrom's Journal," 395–410; *Salisbury Journal,* Oct. 15, 1745; *Norwich Gazette,* Nov. 16, 1745.

ing characteristic of *English* nationality.[90] Prints graphically expressed this claim: *Briton's Association Against the Pope's Bulls* shows a friar and Highlanders on one side of the Tweed, coached by the devil and French commanders, plotting invasion while on the other side Britannia and Neptune, symbols of Britain's military and naval might, beam proudly at a loyal association of middling Englishmen, armed and ready to fight, who fearlessly proclaim for "King, Country, Shop and Family."[91] At the same time, under their auspices defense of the king was heralded from many quarters as the supreme patriotic duty. "All true Patriots, all Lovers of Liberty, by Sea and Land, will defend his sacred Majesty in time of Danger," exulted the inhabitants of Alnwick, Northumberland, where virtually all social and authority levels in the town were represented in the celebrations on the king's birthday.[92] In the heady and rather saccharine renditions of nationalist sentiment that poured out in these months, George II served as a cynosure for national sentiment in a way rarely demonstrated by a Hanoverian monarch before the 1790s and certainly not demonstrated prior to this time.

The '45 and its representations thus privileged a politics of identity which celebrated the English nation for its freedom, religion, prosperity and imperial standing as well as for the patriotic and martial spirit of its inhabitants. In doing so, it put paid to alternative conceptions of the nation proffered by Jacobite ideologues. If Jacobites held out the glittering promise of future unity under the "rightful king," English loyalists could point to the extensive evidence of current unanimity, prosperity and national community mobilized by the rebellion, which a French-backed Pretender and bloody civil war would only shatter. For urban observers, attuned to issues of trade and empire, national aggrandizement and loss, the problem with the Young Pretender was not only that he was Catholic but that he was backed by the French, and the French presented the gravest threat to Britain's national and imperial standing and identity; their motivation for supporting a Jaco-

---

[90] *Salisbury Journal,* Nov. 19, 1745; *Worcester Journal,* Feb. 14–26, 1746; *Four Excellent Songs* (n.p., [1745–6], in HL, Collection on the Jacobite Rebellion; see also the Bishop of Worcester's "Speech for Association" reprinted in *Salisbury Journal,* Oct. 15, 1745. For the stage see Stone, *London Stage,* xxviii. Collections from the audiences were taken for the relief fund for soldiers engaged in suppressing the rebellion: Jarvis, *Collected Papers,* ii, 123.

[91] *Catalogue,* iii, 1, no. 2661, *Britons' Association Against the Pope's Bulls* (London, 1745). See also no. 2664, *The Loyal Associators* (London, 1745), inscribed "For King and Country."

[92] *Newcastle Courant,* Oct. 19, Nov. 2, 1745.

bite invasion seemed all too evident.[93] The Scot James Burgh, writing
while the rebels fled Cumberland's army, remembered the potentially
catastrophic fate facing the nation only five months earlier: "Then did
French Tyranny, Popery and Persecution present themselves to your
Eyes . . . Then did you View your Country as already filled with Blood
. . . and the *British* Empire destined for a Province to France."[94]

Britain's imperial rivalry with France thus produced anti-Jacobitism
as a rallying point for the consolidation of a loyalism that had a distinctly imperialist hue. It was also the lens through which the components of the national identity were brought sharply into focus.
Anti-Catholic, anti-Caledonian and anti-French propaganda attempted
to construct a national community that replaced sectarian and partisan
distinctions with ones based on custom, culture and territorial claims.
It provided a fairly effective picture of what was un-English and foreign, and hence unacceptable and subversive, in "others" at home and
abroad that played to a wide spectrum of nationalist interests and sensibilities. Government propaganda was intent on exploiting these
themes while stressing the need for loyalty to and support for the state
as a neutral locus of British national identity, security and prosperity.
In these respects, the invasion certainly presented an "economics of
loyalism" to English citizens, as Linda Colley has recently argued, but
it also did much more. The nationalist fervor fanned by the rebellion
privileged conceptions of the nation that excluded a range of Britons
and valorized a national and imperial identity that asserted England's
political and cultural superiority over all competitors. The loyalist discourses of the moment thus exhibited the exclusive nature of definitions
of "Englishness" that were always at play and in tension with the
broader categories of "Britishness," or, to put it another way, the irreconcilable tensions between nation and empire.[95] The national identity, as Burgh and other observers acknowledged, was never reducible
to economic interests alone, and the imperial identity as comprehended
in the metropole contained within it the assurance of English superiority.

In this context it was appropriate that the national military hero to
emerge from the '45 should be a member of the royal family, George
II's youngest son, William, Duke of Cumberland. Despite his brutal

[93] A point also made by Colley in *Britons,* 85.

[94] *Britain's Remembrancer, or the Danger Not Over* (London, 1746), 5.

[95] See, e.g., Homi Bhabha, "Of Mimicry and Man: The Ambivalence of Colonial Discourse," *October,* 28 (1984), 125–33.

treatment of the rebels, which earned him the nickname of "the Butcher" among his own men, Cumberland's taking of Carlisle in December 1745, his birthday the following April and above all his victory at Culloden were the occasions for wild junketing in towns throughout England, confirming the popularity his father was currently enjoying and stimulating a near-universal acclamation of the Hanoverian dynasty for the first time as "deliverers" themselves.[96] The extent of bourgeois admiration for Cumberland is revealed through the commemorative pottery manufactured in his honor. Plates, bowls, mugs and punchbowls were produced in considerable quantities – indeed, more ceramic pieces were produced in his honor than in Wilkes's – and depicted his head, the date of Culloden (April 16, 1746) and mottoes such as "Duke William for ever," "Confusion to the Pretender" and, more elaborately, "WILLIAM the Princely Youth with Transport see / He chains th'Oppressor sets th'Oppressed free / Hail friend of Albion and Liberty." In perhaps the most incontrovertible evidence of both his popularity and the commercialized nature of the English economy, porcelain mugs decorated with Cumberland's head (as well as some embellished with the visage of the Young Pretender) were manufactured in China for the English market in this period.[97]

Above all, Cumberland's victory over the rebels was lauded in provincial towns as preserving Britain's commercial and imperial supremacy, keeping both out of the hands of the avaricious French. Many of the middling groups who now toasted him in their taverns considered him to be the latest defender not only of English liberty but of English *trade*. In York, "a select company of tradesmen" who met regularly at a local tavern revealed their priorities by toasting "Prosperity to Trade and Commerce" and then "Our Glorious Deliverer, the Duke of CUMBERLAND" on the thanksgiving day.[98] Cumberland's role as the preserver of public credit and economic stability from the chaos of civil war and invasion was strongly emphasized in commemoratory prints.

---

[96] Celebrations and poems: *LEP*, Mar. 22 – Apr. 4, May 1–3, 1746; *Norwich Gazette*, April 1, 19, May 10, 1746; *Newcastle Courant*, April 19, 26, May 3, 10, Oct. 11, 1746; *Salisbury Journal*, April 21, 1746; *Worcester Journal*, May 16, 1746; *Liberty: An Ode, Occasion'd by the Happy Victory Obtain'd by His Royal Highness William, Prince of Cumberland* (Edinburgh, 1746). Prints: *The True Contrast: The Royal British Hero, the Fright'ned Italian Bravo* (London, 1746), BM no. 2790.

[97] Hobson, *Catalogue*, 136 (pl. E61), 148 (pl. E159), 179 (pl. G43); Ray, *Delftware*, 112, 125; for comparisons with Wilkite pottery see Brewer, "Commercialization of Politics," 250–2. For China mugs see British Museum, Room 46, Case 20.

[98] *Newcastle Journal*, April 19, July 26, 1746.

In one, Cumberland was the personification of "Publick Credit," holding under his arm a "Merchant's book of accounts" as, in the background, British men-of-war and merchant ships sail.[99] The gold box bestowed upon Cumberland by the Newcastle company of masters and mariners, Trinity House, succinctly expresses these identifications, linking the defeat of the rebels with the protection of England's navy and overseas commerce. Britannia was depicted resting on the mossy cliffs of Albion; on each side of her were

> *Scallop'd Shells,* to represent the Origin and Source of *Rivers* and *Navigation.* Britannia holds in her Right Hand, a *Spear,* her Left is supported on her *Shield,* holding an Anchor, the Emblem of *Hope* and *Confidence* . . . Behind her, on both sides are displayed *Banners, Colours,* and *martial Instruments;* over which appear . . . the masts and rigging of *Merchant Ships* and *Men of War.*

Beneath this scene were a crown, sword and truncheon, "proper to the younger Son of his Majesty, and to the Deliverer of the nation."[100] Even in towns where the immediacy of the threat to local economic life was not so strong, Cumberland symbolized the will and possibility of the British to maintain and defend their imperial ascendancy and national position against Continental and Jacobite threats to both.

The '45 was the high point of Cumberland's career and popularity. His later campaigns ended in defeat and humiliation; and by 1749 his political maneuvering at St. James's, his enthusiasm for standing armies and his grossly corpulent physique all had made him extremely unpopular, the object of many satirical and scurrilous prints.[101] But during the rebellion and its immediate aftermath, Cumberland was heralded in the patriotic and libertarian language appropriate to his role as England's defender against France and champion of the British imperial interest. He thus embodied the convergence of patriotism and loyalism which was so marked a product of the national effervescences in these years.

Cumberland's career may also serve as an appropriate metaphor for the fate of the loyalism that resounded through the nation in 1745–6. Certainly, as Nicholas Rogers has stressed, the loyalism generated by the '45 compromised or enervated oppositionist politics in the short

---

[99] *Public Credit* (London, 1745), BM no. 2686.

[100] *Newcastle Journal,* July 26, 1746.

[101] For Cumberland's later career see W. A. Speck, *The Butcher: The Duke of Cumberland and the Suppression of the '45* (Oxford, 1981); for prints see *Catalogue,* iii, 2, 627–9.

term and contested its exclusive claims to patriotism. This is shown in the 1747 election, where the comparatively small number of contests in general and in the large boroughs in particular evinced, with some notable exceptions, the effectiveness of Jacobitism in reinscribing party distinctions and mobilizing support for the Old Corps Whigs. The Tories lost twenty-five seats, three of them in the large electorates, and the opposition Whig presence was reduced from thirteen to seven.[102] In towns such as Bristol, Norwich and Coventry, where coalition oppositions had made some progress in the 1730s, the '45 dealt a blow to their hopes from which it would take a decade to recover. And on the level of high politics, the aftermath of the rebellion forced a dissolution of the broad-bottom coalition, returning Pelham as head of a newly reunited Old Corps Whig ministry that the Tories could not effectively challenge for another decade.

But troubled waters lay not far distant for the Whig ship of state. Pelham's financial reforms may have conciliated City opinion, but they did little to heal over the domestic divisions caused by the '45 and the ministry's betrayals of the Tory party in 1746, which were expressed in violence, riot or electoral strife in a number of communities.[103] Further, for all its patriotic hubris, the '45 had raised the specter of French power and British weakness in ways that could not be easily dispelled. Did Britain possess the character and leadership capable of withstanding France's concerted and continuing attempts to debilitate it? James Burgh was not alone in seeing the rebellion as God's punishment for the luxurious and degenerate spirit that had seized the nation. The languidness of British fleets in Europe was a cause for concern for much of the war, not only among civilian observers but for esteemed officers like Admiral Vernon, whose naval strategies had played no small part in foiling French and Stuart hopes in 1745. In a published letter to the Duke of Bedford, Vernon aired his concerns about the self-interest and corruption of the Admiralty officials who had contradicted his orders and otherwise undermined his authority during his recent stint as commander of the Channel fleet, forcing his resignation in December.[104]

---

[102] Rogers, *Whigs and Cities,* 253–8. There were only 12 contests in the largest boroughs – the fewest of the century: Sedgwick, i, passim and 57. Exceptions include Wigan, where Richard Barry, son of the Jacobite Lord Barrymore, was able to defeat two Whig candidates (Colley, *Defiance,* 253).

[103] Such as Manchester (where nonjuring bishop Thomas Deacon's head festered on a pike), Oxford, Staffordshire, Westminster and of course the Highlands: See Paul Monod, *Jacobitism and the English People* (Cambridge, 1989), 195–220.

[104] TWA, 840/171, F. Paxton to George II, Sept. 30, 1745; *Gentleman's Magazine,* 16

The implications of such maneuvers for national prospects were not hard to discern. "Where men are not rewarded for courage, experience, knowledge, disinterestedness; nor punish'd for cowardice, neglect, ignorance and mercenariness," a writer in the *Old English Journal* warned, "we must expect to see poverty, prostitution and timidity, the most abject and selfish qualities, the general characteristics of our age."[105]

The outcome of the war did nothing to allay these fears about the national character and leadership. The Peace of Aix-La-Chapelle of 1748 instituted a return to the status quo for Britain, which meant the mutual restoration of conquests, including the return of Cape Breton to France. Meanwhile, in the colonies, French and British struggles for preeminence continued in contests over boundaries and territory in America and the West Indies and competition for power by the rival East India companies in Asia. Not surprisingly, the peace was protested against by English merchants in strident but by now familiar language as unfavorable to the "Rights, Properties, Commerce" and national honor of Britain, and fed domestic anxieties that the French were corroding Britain's imperial position.[106] If the people were to rally in support of the state for empire, trade and liberty, should not the state make the preservation and enlargement of all three its primary goals?

III. ARISTOCRATIC TREASON AND THE ANTI-HERO

By the early 1750s, imperial anxieties and widespread francophobia had become mutually reinforcing, producing much oral and printed obsessing over the security and viability of Britain's American colonies and the dangers posed to them by the strong French presence in Acadia and the Upper Ohio country. Newcastle's European diplomacy, which sought to contain French power through subsidy agreements with Austria and German states, only exacerbated these fears. Private correspondence, news reports and a quantity of histories, pamphlets, and

---

(1746), 80–3; G. J. Marcus, *The Naval History of England: The Formative Centuries* (Boston and Toronto, 1961), 261–2.

[105] Quoted in *Gentleman's Magazine*, 15 (1745), 253–5; see also *The Levellers* (1703) (London, 1745; Augustan Reprint Society, 248, 1988), a reprint which complained that men had "grown full as effeminate as the Women . . . and esteem themselves more upon the Reputation of being a Beau, than on the substantial qualifications of Honor, Courage, Learning and Judgement."

[106] See *The Pr–t–st of the M–ch–ts of Great Britain, Against the Preliminary Articles for a Peace* (London, 1748).

maps of British holdings in America argued for the need for better management of the colonial defense, particularly after the French defeated American and British troops in confrontations along the Ohio in 1754–5.[107] These demands were bolstered by a chorus of voices both in and out of Parliament stressing the "High Importance of the *British* Possessions and Rights in *America* to the Trade and Well-being of these Kingdoms" and calling for colonial conquest – particularly of Canada – as the most effective means of defense. "America is become the fountain of our riches, for with *America* our greatest trade is carried on," exclaimed an observer in Newcastle; and for this reason "Canada *must be subdued.*"[108]

The clamor for a strong and aggressive policy in America, then, came from diverse quarters. Backed by the sheer wealth of detailed information provided in the daily and periodical press about the French naval and military build-up in the first half of the decade, these well-publicized demands made the fall of Minorca in May 1756 appear doubly catastrophic for the Newcastle administration and the political nation, for it seemed to intimate both the beginning of French imperial supremacy and the inadequacy of the nation's aristocratic leadership. Minorca, situated on the main trade route to Italy and the Levant, was deemed of vital strategic importance for the protection of English commercial interests, and its fall, but two months after war with France was declared, in conjunction with other territorial losses in America and India and the threat of French invasion, precipitated a sense of crisis that reverberated at all social levels. The details of the Minorca crisis and its impact on British diplomatic relations, London opinion and the parliamentary opposition and leadership have been frequently

---

[107] HL, Montagu MSS, MO 505, 1537, 5747, 6733, Nov.–Dec. 1755; *Newcastle General Magazine*, 8 (1755), 10–15, 241–4, 405–9; *London Magazine*, 24 (1755), 307–12, 403–5; *York Courant*, April 1, 8, 22, June 3, 1755; [John Bowles], *A New Map of North America Wherein the British Dominions Are Carefully Laid Down* (London, 1754); *French Encroachments Exposed; or, Britain's Original Right to All That Part of the American Continent Claimed by France Fully Asserted* (London, 1756); *The State of the British and French Colonies in North America, with Respect to Number of People, Forces, Forts, Indians, Trade and Other Advantages* (London, 1755). See also Dan E. Clark, "News and Opinion Concerning America in English Newspapers, 1754–63," *Pacific Historical Review*, 10 (1941), 75–82.

[108] *Proceedings and Debates of the British Parliaments Respecting North America, 1754–83*, ed. R. C. Simmons and P. D. G. Thomas, 5 vols. (New York, 1982), i, 81, 94–5, 195–6, 299–301; *Newcastle General Magazine*, 8 (1755), 15–16. See also *Monitor*, Aug. 16, 1755; *LEP*, June 24–6, 1756; and John Shebbeare, *A Letter to the People of England, on the Present Situation and Conduct of National Affairs* (London, 1755), 19–32 (excerpted in *Gentleman's Magazine*, 25 [1755], 405).

told.[109] Its impact on the wider political nation, however, has yet to be fully explored; there it exacerbated existing apprehensions about the nature, viability and morality of the nation's aristocratic leadership and the British national character.

Admiral John Byng, the unlucky commander of the ill-equipped British squadron sent to defend Minorca, was burned in effigy by outraged crowds across the country soon after news came of the island's conquest. These demonstrations, a number of which preceded the Tory-inspired batch of instructions and addresses from the capital and provinces that assaulted Parliament over the last four months of the year, provide a reliable index of the extreme degree of public alienation from the Newcastle administration. In South Shields, for example, ship-masters dressed a tar barrel as Byng "with a lac'd Coat and Hat [and] fine Wig" and burned it in the marketplace to cries of "Confusion to him, and all such Traitors to their King and Country"; in Newcastle, effigies of Byng, labeled "This is the Villain that would not fight" were burned before large crowds and the ashes scattered in the streets. Local residents were in no doubt as to where the ultimate culpability lay: Demands made at the assizes for the grand juries of Newcastle and Northumberland included the call for an inquiry into the disaster.[110] Elsewhere in the country, too, Byng's effigy was symbolically defiled in a way which indicted ruling councils. At Devizes, when news of Byng's arrival at Portsmouth reached the town on August 5,

> an Effigy most finically dress'd, and emblematically ornamented, to shew the reverse of a Hero, embellish'd with a Wooden sword girt on his right thigh, and a Truncheon in his left Hand plac'd behind, was advanc'd to Haman's Height on a Gibbet, at Four in the Morning . . . and there hung till Seven in the evening, and then cut down and burnt amidst a vast concourse of People, loudly exclaiming against Treachery and Cowardice, the Bane of our Liberties.[111]

Byng himself was met by a threatening crowd of "thousands" armed

---

[109]   Marie Peters, *Pitt and Popularity: London Opinion and the Patriot Minister* (Oxford, 1982), chap. 3; Rogers, *Whigs and Cities*, 93–107.

[110]   *Newcastle Journal*, July 17, 31, 1756; *Worcester Journal*, Aug. 5, 1756; *Newcastle Courant*, July 31, Aug. 28, 1756.

[111]   *Salisbury Journal*, Aug. 16, 1756. The birthday of General Blakeney, the elderly yet courageous officer in charge of Port Mahon who defended it for some time against a French force that greatly outnumbered his own, was chosen as the most appropriate day in some towns for these "executions": *York Courant*, Aug. 3, 27, Sept. 14, 1756; Latimer, *Annals of Bristol*, 322; *Salisbury Journal*, Aug. 9, 16, 1756; *Worcester Journal*, Aug. 5, 12, 1756; *Newcastle Courant*, Sept. 11, 1756.

with clubs and pitchforks as he was taken by Admiralty officials from Portsmouth to London for his court-martial, and a mob attacked his country house in Hertfordshire.[112]

The symbolic executions of Byng as a traitor, far from working invariably to deflect criticism from the government, as has been suggested, were frequently central in focussing attention and criticism on the ministry and the inadequacy of its leadership. Indeed, they inaugurated and punctuated an extra-parliamentary campaign against the government that increased in intensity and diversity as the autumn progressed.[113] Of course, from the first reports of Byng's unsuccessful engagement with the French, the ministry did what it could to turn public opinion against Byng. The official government newspaper, the *London Gazette,* printed creatively edited versions of Byng's dispatches which made it appear that a lack of will and courage on his part, rather than the lack of supplies and properly repaired ships, prevented him from fending off the French. Ministerial journalists backed up this hackneyed version of events in pamphlets, prints and ballads.[114] And the ministry promoted the street justice meted out to Byng's effigies in an effort to heap the responsibility for the loss of Minorca on his shoulders.[115] In fact, Byng seems to have made a reasonable, if conservative, judgment to retreat on the basis of his resources, and as events unfolded and more information became known there was increasing support out-of-doors for opposition supporters' claim that Byng was but a ministerial "cloak" to hide highly defective foreign-policy planning.

The structures of extra-parliamentary political culture were crucial in this effort, given that Parliament was in recess from before the loss of Minorca to the Duke of Newcastle's resignation in November. The press focussed attention on the responsibility of the ministry for Byng's unlucky campaign. "Mr Byng is stigmatized with infamy, and pursued

---

[112] *Worcester Journal,* Aug. 12, 1756; Donald J. Greene, *Political Writings of Samuel Johnson* (Yale Edition of Samuel Johnson's Works, New Haven, 1977), 10, 216. In London, the effigy-burning on Tower Hill prompted a riot among the sailors present: *Worcester Journal,* Sept. 2, 1756.

[113] See, e.g., *Newcastle Courant,* May 29, 1756; Peters, *Pitt and Popularity,* 48–57. Cf. Rogers, *Whigs and Cities,* 384–5.

[114] Greene, *Johnson's Political Writings,* 214–16, 220–51; *A Letter to the Right Honourable William Pitt, Esq., Being an Impartial Vindication of the Conduct of the Ministry* (London, 1756); *Bungiana* (London, 1756); *The Contrast, or Britannia's Distributive Justice* [London, 1756], BM no. 3365.

[115] Such as in Southampton and Whitechapel, where Admiralty officers and clerks of the Victualling Office respectively gave crowds money to prepare and burn Byng's effigy. *Salisbury Journal,* Aug. 2, 1756; Greene, *Johnson's Political Writings,* 238.

with clamors artfully excited to divert the public attention from the crimes and blunders of other men, and . . . while he is thus vehemently pursued for imaginary guilt, the real criminals are hoping to escape justice'' was how Johnson put it in a review of two pro-Byng pamphlets for the *Literary Magazine* of October 1756, and this view had currency in many quarters.[116] John Shebbeare's *Fourth Letter to the People of England,* widely excerpted in the monthlies, also lambasted the loss of Minorca as but the latest in a long string of blundering ministerial policy decisions that had weakened Britain, threatened the colonies and served Hanoverian interests, exculpating Blakeney and Byng alike for any share of the blame.[117] The periodical press was obsessed with Minorca's loss, as were newspapers like the *Monitor,* the *London Evening Post* and the *Daily Gazetteer,* which promoted the view that Byng was an instrument of ministerial malfeasance.[118] Overt hostility to the ministry was duplicated and no doubt amplified by the scores of prints, lampoons and ballads which were disseminated in the last four months of 1756, such as *The Block and Yard Arm: A New Ballad on the Loss of Minorca and the Danger of Our American Rights and Possessions,* and by handbills affixed to walls throughout Southwark and London, which seditiously asserted that the Newcastle administration accepted bribes to further French power and colonial expansion by its war policies.[119]

Finally, over the autumn, a barrage of addresses and constituency instructions poured in to the central government, demanding a national inquiry into the disaster as well as a change in ministry, greater ac-

---

[116] The pamphlets, *A Letter to a Member of Parliament in the Country, from His Friend in London, Relative to the Case of Ad. Byng.* and *An Appeal to the People, Containing the Genuine and Entire Letter of Admiral Byng to the Secr. of the A[dmiralt]y,* were written by Paul Whitehead, former Westminster independent, and John Shebbeare, current Tory polemicist, respectively, and were reviewed by Johnson in the *Literary Magazine,* 6 (Sept. 15 – Oct. 15, 1756), repr. in Greene, ed., *Political Writings,* 299–309.

[117] John Shebbeare, *A Fourth Letter to the People of England* (London, 1756); *Newcastle General Magazine,* 9 (1756), 484–8.

[118] See, e.g., *Gentleman's Magazine,* 26 (1756); *London Magazine,* 25 (1756); *Newcastle General Magazine,* 9 (1756), July–Dec. passim; *LEP,* June 29 – July 1, July 15–17, 17–20, Aug. 24–6, Sept. 21–3, Oct. 28–30, 1756; *Monitor,* July 17, 31, Aug. 21, September 4, 18, Oct. 9, 1756; *Gazetteer,* Oct. 19, 1756.

[119] *The Block and Yard Arm* [London, 1756]; *Wonder upon Wonder, or the Cocoa Tree's Answer* [London, 1756]; *The Wonder of Surrey! or the Genuine Speech of an Old British Oak* (London, 1756); *The Voice of Liberty: An Occasional Essay, in Opposition to Ministerial Oppression* (London, 1756). For prints see *Catalogue,* iii, 2, 992–1030; for handbills, BL, Add. MSS 35, 594, fol. 148; 32,866, fols. 488–9.

countability from the government, the establishment of a militia and parliamentary reform.[120] Thirty-six constituencies, sixteen counties and nineteen boroughs produced forty memorials (addresses and instructions) over the crisis. Smaller in number than those produced in the Vernon agitation of 1740–2, they were nonetheless equally virulent in tone, more bipartisan in provenance and clear in their insistence that the loss of Minorca was the product of a crisis in the national leadership. Although promoted by dissident Whigs like George Townshend, Henry Legge and Sir George Lyttelton and supported by Tory and patriot Whig leaders in the localities, the addresses and instructions were touted by their supporters as embodying the "Voice of the People," and certainly their geographic and political provenance and vigorous publicizing – along with the notable inability of government agents and supporters to quell them – lent credibility to this claim.[121]

Clearly, then, the pervasive outrage and indignation produced by what was widely regarded as a humiliating defeat at the hands of Britain's historic enemy had focussed attention on the inability of the Old Corps to protect the liberties and properties of the nation, both at home and abroad. Although Byng, certainly, was blamed by many for the nation's defeat at the hands of France, so too were his superiors in the ministry who had directed his efforts. As the letter from "Britannicus" stressed in a damaging polemic that appeared in the *London Evening Post* and provincial papers, despite enormous sums of money given by the public to protect the "trade and commerce of the people and Honors of the Crown" the nation had been reduced through ministerial malfeasance to "distressed and perilous circumstances":

> Have not our Colonies been over-run by a barbarous Enemy, for Want of proper Assistance? Is not our Mediterranean Commerce now suppressed by the shameful loss of Minorca? Are not our Rights, Lives, Liberties, now brought into a very precarious Situation by such unconstitutional Measures, as introducing a Foreign Army, and neglecting our own Militia?

The loss of Minorca could not be looked on as an "uncertain Event of War," Britannicus went on, "but as a certain Event of the Treachery, Negligence, or Incapacity of those who were entrusted with Power,

---

[120] For addresses and instructions see *The Voice of the People: A Collection of Addresses to His Majesty and Instructions to Members of Parliament by Their Constituents* (London, 1756); most of these are also reprinted in the London and provincial newspapers for Aug.–Dec. 1756.

[121] *Voice of the People*, xi–xii, 31–2, 20–1.

more than Sufficient to have preserved it."[122] In this climate, Byng
became the inglorious anti-hero of patriotic virtue, spectacularly failing
to live up to its injunctions of service and leadership – opprobrium that
also redounded in the public mind against the ministry. The hostility
to Pitt's attempt to procure a pardon for Byng in the spring of 1757,
usually pointed to as evidence of the "chauvinism" and blood-lust of
the public that played into the Old Corps leaders' hands, can more
plausibly be read as an index of the (nonetheless bloody) continuing
antagonism toward the kind of ministerial and aristocratic mismanagement of the public trust that Byng had come to symbolize.

The Newcastle papers themselves amply demonstrate the high level
of anxiety among members of the ministry at their inability to contain
public malaise. Already traumatized by the combination of failure
abroad and bad harvests at home that precipitated a rash of food riots
over the late summer and early autumn, the administration made concerted efforts to stave off instructions in the localities, suppress opposition propagandists in London and mount a counter-address campaign
of its own – although with singular lack of success. In Norwich, Horace
Walpole was unable to prevent an address from being organized from
the Norfolk grand jury, and Sir William Harbord was forced to sign it
to avoid compromising his son's chances at the upcoming Norwich by-
election. In Bristol, an address organized by local Tories in early September to protest Minorca's loss and the inadequate protection of
commerce and colonies – reported to the Duke of Newcastle to "smell
strong of Shebbearisms" – stimulated the production of two loyal addresses the following week that expressed full confidence in the government and its management of the war. These were effectively
countered, however, by the strident set of instructions from Bristol "Citizens" lambasting the government for its lack of public-
spiritedness – it was not animated, the instructors claimed, "by the
least spark of national honor, or regard for the public welfare" – and
demanding the restoration of triennial Parliaments and the establishment of a militia to ease the crisis.[123]

At the same time, Newcastle's legal counselors were extremely pes-
simistic about the ability of prosecution of printers and publishers to
turn the tide of hostile public opinion. Attorney General John Sharpe,

---

[122] *LEP*, Aug. 24–6, 1756.
[123] For Norwich see BL, Add. MS 32,867, fols. 262–3; for Bristol see *Voice of the
People*, 12–17, xi–xii; for the ministry's efforts see BL, Add. MS 32,867, fols. 101–
3, 127, 131, 197–8; *LEP*, Dec. 4–7, 1756. See also Add. MS 32,997, fols. 20, 25.

commenting to Newcastle on Shebbeare's *Fourth Letter to the People of England,* called it "a bold, daring and unjustifiable attack upon the Government, and those in the Administration . . . a virulent and inflammatory Libel," but thought prosecution would only increase its deleterious impact. "The surprizing and unaccountable Spirit which at this time almost Universally influences the Minds of the People," Sharpe said, meant there was "very little prospect indeed of a London jury convicting" any of the printers of libel. Lord Chancellor Hardwicke concurred. "Your Grace knows how the Spirit of Prosecution has been suffered to run down for many years past, for which one reason assigned has been the Impossibility of getting juries to convict," he wrote to Newcastle, advising instead a counter-propaganda campaign by the government of "short papers, in some of the daily newspapers, in vindication of the measures of the Administration," since "they are more read, and spread more amongst the Common People [than pamphlets]. This would be following the opposition in their own way; whereas now the People meet with that Scandal every day, and no Contradiction or answer to it."[124] The loss of Minorca thus confronted the Old Corps Whigs with irreducible evidence of a harshly critical extraparliamentary political opinion that was beyond its effective management or control. In this, as in other ways, Minorca precipitated the widespread perception of a crisis in the nation's aristocratic leadership, the effects of which were felt throughout the nation.

IV. EMPIRE AND THE EFFEMINATE BODY POLITIC

Yet the significance of the Minorca crisis and, indeed, of the ultimate success of Britain in the Seven Years' War, must be seen in a broader political and cultural context, namely, that constructed by the widespread fears of the emasculation and degeneracy of the British body politic, a corruption that was seen to seep down through the polity from above. The early 1750s had been marked by a deepening sense of national malaise, stimulated by xenophobia (embodied dramatically in the opposition to the bills to naturalize foreign Protestants and Jews), exacerbated by imperial rivalries and tinged by sharpening antiaristocratic sensibilities. Gerald Newman has documented the cultural protest against foreign and especially French "influence" that was so marked an aspect of much literature and propaganda in the late 1740s

[124] BL, Add. MS 32,867, fols. 135–6, 143–8.

and early 1750s, whereby the aristocracy – and the sycophantic nou-
veaux riches who aped them – were seen as the agents of "alien cultural influence and the associated moral disease."[125] These fears and
grievances were aggravated by the perception that the cultural contagion from above had infiltrated political channels. A virulent strand of
anti-aristocratic sentiment had entered mainstream political discourse
by the mid 1750s, mobilized initially, perhaps, by the naturalization
bills,[126] but then amplified by hostility at government neglect in America, the subsidizing of troops on the Continent, the use of foreign mercenaries at home and such self-regarding pieces of legislation as the
game laws, which were presented by their critics as the ultimate in
class legislation, mean-spirited and self-serving in orientation and reflecting the genuine priorities of the nation's aristocratic leadership. The
letter addressed "To the Nobility and Gentry, Associated for the Preservation of the Game" and printed in a number of newspapers and
periodicals aptly indicated the prevailing mood when it praised the
Society for its "most useful, most excellent, and most laudable purpose" before reminding it of another issue, "however trifling it may
appear to you, and how much soever hitherto neglected . . . the preservation of our country."[127]

Equally damaging, the aristocracy's allegedly feckless pursuit of self-
interest was held responsible for the chilling spectacle of the British
nation's inexorable and, some feared, irreversible slide into "effeminacy." According to this theory – the most recent variant of a perspective forged by both anti-Catholic and English civic humanist
discourse that condemned the iniquitous effects of luxury and wealth
in society – the effeteness and selfishness of Britain's ruling classes
had seeped down and corroded the polity, sapping patriotic fervor and
leaving weakness, ineffectuality and supineness in its place. "Effeminacy" denoted a degenerate moral, political and social state that op-

[125] Gerald Newman, *The Rise of English Nationalism* (New York, 1987), 68–84.
[126] The attempted Jewish naturalization bill in 1753 was interpreted as a sign of aristocratic effeminacy, corruption and dishonor: See *The Repository: For the Use of the
Christian Electors of Great-Britain: In Opposition to All Jews, Turks, and Infidels*
(London, 1753); *The Block and Yard Arm, A New Ballad;* and A. M. Hyamson, "The
Jew Bill of 1753," *Transactions of the Jewish Historical Society,* 6 (1908–10), 156–
88. There were 7 synagogues in the capital in 1753.
[127] Shebbeare's *Letters to the People of England,* esp. *Second Letter, Fourth Letter* and
Fifth Letter (London, 1755–7); *Remarks on the Laws Relating to the Game, and the
Association Set on Foot for the Preservation of It* (London, 1753) and *The Association
1756* [London, 1756], BM 3348; *Gentleman's Magazine,* 26 (1756), 384; *Newcastle
General Magazine,* 9 (1756), 434–6.

posed and subverted the vaunted "manly" characteristics – courage, aggression, martial valor, discipline and strength – that constituted patriotic virtue. Its denigration intersected with other efforts to eradicate behaviors and practices (sexual and consumer as well as political) that blurred gender lines or otherwise threatened masculinity and austerity in the political and cultural realms.[128] In the present crisis, effeminacy was chiefly objectionable because it had produced a weak and enervated fighting force that was undermining Britain's position in the world by relinquishing to France her "Empire of the Sea."

The Reverend John Brown of Newcastle, in his *Estimate of the Manners and Principles of the Time,* perhaps most forcefully propounded the theory of effeminacy as the cause of Britain's distress, which he pointedly identified as the "ruling character" of the present age and chief characteristic of the ruling classes; both had underwritten the nations's dismal naval and military performances abroad. Since "the internal strength of a Nation will always depend chiefly on the Manners and Principles of its leading Members," Brown argued, the "luxurious and effeminate Manners in the higher Ranks, together with a general defect of *Principle* . . . operate powerfully, and fatally" in national conduct and affairs, producing a "general Incapacity" in "the national Spirit of Defence" that "seems to have fitted us for a Prey to the Insults and Invasions of our most powerful Enemies." An effeminate nation is "a Nation which *resembles Women,*" Brown concluded, devoid of courage, liberty, principle and endurance, opposed to public-spiritedness and martial valor, and destined for international ignominy and derision.[129]

Brown's analysis was provocative, and, it must be said, was disputed by many of his contemporaries, but it also systematized ideas that were percolating through the heated political and cultural debates of the mid 1750s (and, indeed, of the preceding two decades) over the causes of

---

[128] For which see John Barrell, *The Birth of Pandora: And the Division of Knowledge* (London, 1992), 72–3; Randolph Trumbach, "Sex, Gender and Sexual Identity in Modern Culture: Male Sodomy and Female Prostitution in Enlightenment London," *Journal of the History of Sexuality,* 2 (1991), 186–203; G. J. Barker-Benfield, *The Culture of Sensibility* (Chicago, 1992), chap. 3; J. G. A. Pocock, *Virtue, Commerce and History* (Cambridge, 1985), 102–23; Kristina Staub, *Sexual Suspects: Eighteenth Century Players and Sexual Ideology* (Princeton, 1982), chaps. 3, 7.

[129] John Brown, *An Estimate of the Manners and Principles of the Times,* 2 vols. (London, 1757), i, 66–7, 78–82, 181–2; ii, 40. Burgh had earlier discerned a luxurious slide into "effeminacy" overtaking the polity and threatening the nation's imperial standing, but believed it bubbled up from the trading and lower orders: *Britain's Remembrancer,* 9–15. Brown's version is also more stridently misogynistic.

the perceived emasculation of the national character. A variety of observers, from almanac writers and journalists to playwrights, philanthropists and village shopkeepers decried the nation's corrupted and "effeminate" spirit, which threatened the collapse of distinctions between public and private, men and women, and resulted in displays of national "impotency" abroad and ignominious imperial decline like that evinced in 1754–7.[130] The debates over militia reform, first proposed by Townshend in 1755 and culminating in the Militia Act of 1757, and of course the invectives directed against the use of foreign troops at home and abroad similarly reiterated contemporary perceptions of the indissoluble connections between an activist, arms-bearing citizenry, a patriotic martial spirit, and national strength, power and prosperity.[131]

The instructions that poured into Parliament on the heels of the Minorca crisis expressed similar beliefs and fears, placing responsibility squarely on the nation's leadership. Ipswich constituents' instructions to the esteemed Admiral Vernon blamed the "childish timidity" of the English fleet and the abandonment of the American colonies to the nation's "injudicious leaders, who have fallen victims to their own inexperience and temerity"; those from the grand jury of Chester declaimed against the "ignorance, cowardice, or treachery" by which "our fleets and armies have been rendered of none effect [*sic*]" and challenged their representatives not to remain "tamely degenerate; for, as yet, you would imagine yourselves free."[132] Anti-Byng demonstrators in the localities were not reticent in identifying the Minorca disaster with ineffectual aristocratic counsels; the fact that Byng was himself the son of a peer added further credibility to the connection.[133] The

---

[130] Shebbeare, *Letters to the People of England,* passim, esp. *First Letter, Fourth Letter* and *Fifth Letter; Newcastle General Magazine,* 9 (1756), 484–94; Bernard Capp, *English Almanacs, 1500–1800* (Ithaca, 1979), 253–4, 260–1; [Henry Dell], *Minorca: A Tragedy in Three Acts,* 2nd ed. (London, 1756); *The Fall of Public Spirit: A Dramatic Satire, in Two Acts* (London, 1757); *The Diary of Thomas Turner, 1754–1765,* ed. David Vaisey (Oxford, 1984), 124–5; Edward Gibbon, *A Memoir* (New York, 1990), 123–4.

[131] Shebbeare, *Second Letter to the People of England* (London, 1755), 22–3, and *Fifth Letter to the People of England,* 2nd ed. (1757), 33–5; *Monitor,* Aug. 16, 1755; May 22, 1756; Brown, *Estimate,* i, 87–91; *An Alarm to the People of England* (London, 1757), 26; *Gentleman's Magazine,* 26 (1756), 121–3; Jonas Hanway, *Thoughts on the Duty of a Good Citizen* (London, 1759).

[132] *Voice of the People,* 19, 53–4.

[133] *Newcastle Courant,* Sept. 11, 1756. Byng was a younger son of the acclaimed Admiral George Byng, first Viscount Torrington, hero of the Battle of Cape Passaro in 1718 and later Walpole's first lord of the Admiralty. Interestingly, Byng's brother

care with which effigies of Byng were dressed in the garb of a courtier
– outfitted in "lac'd coat and Fine wig" in South Shields; in his uniform, "with a little of his usual A-la-mode" in Darlington; and "richly
dress'd in a Blue and Gold Coat, Buff Waistcoat, trimmed, etc." in
London – also signified Byng's identification with aristocratic, french-
ified counsels.[134]

Hence the aristocratic state was identified with "French influence"
and corruption at home and with timidity, effeminacy and ignominy
abroad, and because of this it looked as if France would triumph. As
one broadside put it, the English people had been forced to see their
kingdom, "this once glorious Kingdom, become the Scoff of all the
Nations upon Earth." The demands for an inquiry into Minorca were
therefore also demands for an uncorrupted and accountable government
that actively protected and pursued the national – that is to say, the
imperial – interest. As the *Monitor* reminded the Newcastle ministry
after reviewing the crisis in public and imperial affairs, "Remember
that government is not given you for venal ends, nor power delegated
for your convenience and pleasures . . . forget not that you are accountable servants of the public, and that a learned and inquisitive people
are to be judges of your actions."[135]

Equally important, empire – its attainment, acquisition, settlement
and preservation – was now represented as the antidote to aristocratic
"cultural treason" and effeteness, the bulwark and proving ground of
the true national character, of national (and middle class) potency, identity and virtue. As a number of writers noted, it was among the middle
ranks alone that a "spirit of liberty" and national defense still throve,
as was demonstrated in their ready formation of associations for defense
against the Young Pretender in 1745 and more recently by the martial
valor of colonial militias.[136] Prints of the period gave visual form to

was rumored to be homosexual – much to the disgust of some members of the beau
monde: HL, Montagu MSS, MO 260 [1736].
[134] In Darlington, the effigy of Byng wore a sign with the following message: "A curse
on French gold, and great men's promises / I have never done well since I took the
one, / And depended on the other: but / Take heed my countrymen, *I am not alone*":
Newcastle Journal, Sept. 11, 1756; see also ibid., July 24, 1756. The counterpoint
provided by Vernon could not be stronger: A plain-spoken but well-born commander
(Vernon was son of a secretary of state), disdainful of background or place, Vernon
embodied the genius of Britain over foreign contagion and aristocratic effeminacy
alike.
[135] *A Serious Call to the Corporation of London, to Address His Ministry to Remove
from His Councils . . . Weak and Wicked Ministers* (broadside) [1756]; *Monitor,* Oct.
30, 1756.
[136] Brown, *Estimate,* ii, 25–6, 30; *Monitor,* Dec. 13, 19, 1755; Mar. 13, Sept. 11, 1756;

THE ENGLISH LION DISMEMBER'D

Or the Voice of the Public for an enquiry into the loss of Minorca - with Ad. B___g's plea before his Examiners.

6. *The English Lion Dismember'd* (1756). A midcentury view of the sources of national effeminacy: martial disgrace, aristocratic weakness and French influence. Courtesy of the Lewis Walpole Library, Yale University.

these connections. *Forty-Six and Fifty-Six* contrasted the stalwart patriotic associations formed by middling citizens for the nation's defense during the '45 with the mercenary Hessian troops called in to defend the kingdom ten years later. *The English Lion Dismember'd; or, The Voice of the Public for an Enquiry into the Loss of Minorca* (Plate 6) associated imperial decline and national disgrace with courtiers, game laws and foreign troops; the way out is shown through stout-hearted and patriotic middling Englishmen, willing to defend their country's interests.[137]

Significantly, this period witnessed the creation of extra-institutional supports for a formalized anti-gallicanism, largely through associative activities by private citizens which sought to make England less per-

Jan. 8, 1757; *Gentleman's Magazine*, 27 (1757), 509–12; Shebbeare, *A Letter to the People of England*, 46–8, 50–6. As Colley (and eighteenth-century commentators) has noted, the gentry response to the '45 was much more circumscribed than that of their inferiors: *Britons*, 74.

[137] *Forty-Six and Fifty-Six* (London, 1756); *English Lion Dismember'd* (London, 1756), both in Lewis Walpole Library, Yale University (BM nos. 3477 and 3547).

meable to French influence and to promote what their members described as "manly, rational patriotism." The Marine Society, the Anti-Gallican Society and the Society for the Encouragement of Arts, Manufactures and Commerce, all nationally based in goals and membership, took as axiomatic that France was the greatest threat to British power and prosperity and in different ways attempted to resuscitate British strength and ingenuity in commerce, martial arts and sciences so as to reduce French power and prestige. "They [the French] ever behold with envious eyes the bounties which heaven bestows on this nation, and are watchful of opportunities to *Ravish* them from us," Jonas Hanway, founder of the Marine Society, asserted, envisioning Britain as an enticingly endowed maiden helpless in the face of France's lustful aggression. Not surprisingly, given this conceptualization and the national angst, the Marine Society became a cause célèbre for the next three decades, a favorite object of theatrical benefits and male and female largesse: Devoted to training "stout lads of fifteen or sixteen" as seamen and thereby diffusing "an *active, benevolent, a martial,* and *concordant Spirit*" in the nation and across the globe, auxiliary branches were soon formed in ports and towns throughout the country.[138] Similar in goal if not execution, the Anti-Gallican Society, formed in the aftermath of the '45 and comprising largely middling tradesmen and artisans, also sought to stave off national emasculation by keeping out French commodities and promoting British manufactures and designs, as did the more elite Society for the Encouragement of Arts, Manufactures and Commerce, which, founded "to encourage industry, reward ingenuity and discourage idleness, that greatest political vice," bestowed premiums on new industrial and artistic designs.[139] A print dedicated to both the Anti-Gallican Society and the Society for the Encouragement of Arts, *The Imports of Great Britain from France* (Plate 7), interestingly represented current anxieties as a ship full of French traders and commodities unloading at a London dock. They

---

[138] Hanway, *Letter from a Member of the Marine Society, Shewing the Usefulness and Utility of Its Design* (London, 1756), 4, 12; for provincial benefits see Manchester City Library, Playbills Collection, Oct. 30, 1757; Dec. 11, 1759; *Norwich Mercury,* April 1, 1758. Aristocrats, gentry, clergy, merchants, London livery companies and various provincial trading companies all subscribed.

[139] Colley, *Britons,* 88–92; Isaac Hunt, *Some Account of the Laudable Institution of the Society of Anti-Gallicans* (London, 1781); *Norwich Mercury,* July 16, Oct. 8, 1757; *Rules and Orders of the Society, Established at London for the Encouragement of Arts, Manufactures and Commerce* (London, 1758); Chapter 8. Admiral Vernon was a member of the Anti-Gallicans until his death in 1757.

7. *The Imports of Great Britain from France* (1757). An English nightmare of French cultural imperialism. Courtesy of the Pierpont Morgan Library, New York (III.44.157).

included fops, cooks, dancers, priests, milliners, mantua-makers, tailors, tutoresses and valets de chambre; superfluities like "birth-night cloathes," beauty washes, toilet waters and pomades; and French fabrics, wines, brandies, cheeses and gloves – in short, a materialist nightmare of all the things most likely to increase desire and aggrandize vanity, luxury and the corruption of national manners and spirit.[140]

In the context of these nationalistic anxieties and concerns, the anguish at the loss of Minorca and, indeed, the ecstasy and euphoria over the victories of 1758–62 take on their full significance. The Seven Years' War, which turned France out of Canada, stripped it of most of its Indian, West Indian and African possessions, and captured Manila

---

[140] *The Imports of Great Britain from France: Humbly Address'd to the Laudable Associations of Anti-Gallicans, and the Generous Promoters of the British Arts and Manufactories . . .* (n.p., [1757]). See also *England Made Odious, or the French Dressers* [1756], BM no. 3543, which depicts the Duke of Newcastle, dressed as an old fishwife, forcing Britannia to wear a French dress embroidered with a fleur-de-lis, in *Catalogue,* iii, 2, 1101–2.

and Havana (long the objects of British desire) from Spain, was clearly the fulfillment and ultimate expression of the mercantilist–imperialist goals and aspirations articulated for the past three decades. It bolstered the Atlantic economy, especially the colonial trade in sugar, slaves, tobacco and rum, vastly increased exports to and imports from the North American colonies, allowed Britain to capture the China tea trade and the Senegal gum trade, and produced profits for speculators and privateers alike.[141] The war also catapulted Britain to the status of a world power, correspondingly (so it was thought) plummeting France to a new low of despair and defeat. Politically, ideologically and materially, the war thus enhanced the potency of that heady brew of empire, liberty and national aggrandizement that had been avidly consumed by large portions of the political public since the Vernon agitation. The ministry's orchestration of these well-entrenched sensibilities was evinced not least in the pursuit of an aggressive and expansionist policy in the New World and in the public, if not private, emphasis on the primacy of colonial over Continental campaigns.[142] Pitt's grasp of the libertarian and imperial issues seen to be at stake in the conflict enabled his administration to mark the unlikely eighteenth-century convergence of a popular war and a popular ministry. He was thus acclaimed from virtually all quarters as a hero and patriot who "roused the antient spirit of this nation from the pusillanimous state to which it had been reduced," as the London Common Council put it in an address following his resignation in 1761, carrying "its reputation in arms and commerce to a height unknown before, by our trade accompanying our conquests in every Quarter of the Globe."[143]

But the war was of more resounding import than merely in shoring up Pitt's political career and mythology. Indeed, London's panegyric to Pitt hints at the war's profound importance in consolidating nation-

---

[141] Pares, *War and Trade,* 85–125; Davis, "English Foreign Trade," 285–303, and *The Rise of the Atlantic Economies,* 195–210; Jacob Price, "Capital and Credit in the British Chesapeake Trade, 1750–1775," in V. B. Platt and D. C. Skags, eds., *Of Mother Country and Plantations* (Cleveland, 1971), 9–15; Peters, *Pitt and Popularity,* 150–1.

[142] Hostility to the London-dominated East India Company could undercut provincial enthusiasm for British adventures on the subcontinent: See *Newcastle Journal,* Jan. 27, 1750; Baines, *History of Liverpool,* 441–2; and Bowen, "East India Stockholding," 194, 200. For Pitt's strategy (which allowed him to win support for the much less popular military expenditures on the Continent) see BL, Add. MS 32,885, fols. 523–6; *Proceedings and Debates of the British Parliaments,* 265–7; Rogers, *Whigs and Cities,* 109–10.

[143] Quoted in *Gentleman's Magazine,* 31 (1761), 462–3.

alistic and pro-imperial identities in ways that would configure their roles in loyalist and radical politics in the future. First, largely because of the obsessional fears about French power, international influence and domestic cultural contagion articulated in public discourse in the first half of the decade, the war allowed British global expansion to be mystified as an ultimately benevolent as well as patriotic act. The frontispiece to the *London Magazine* for 1758 bestowed mythological form and an anti-conquest narrative on this version of current events: It depicted Time, an old man, turning to the "terrestrial globe" and pointing to Louisbourg, as History, a young woman, leans on his shoulder and records the "Great Events" that have occurred; meanwhile, Britannia, led by Concord, points upwards to a figure of Victory, "intimating that BRITANNIA shall always be successful."[144]

Other poems, verses, ballads and visual representations of the results of the war equally stressed the essentially humanitarian role of the newly extended British empire in saving the world from French tyranny, Spanish cruelty and Amerindian barbarity alike."May these valuable acquisitions, so gloriously obtained, ever continue a part of the *British* empire, as an effectual check to the perfidy and ambition" of France, the City addressers implored George II after recent successes at Louisbourg and Cape Breton; and an "Ode to General Townshend, On his Arrival from QUEBEC," printed in the *Salisbury Journal,* celebrated his bravery and that of other British commanders in "combat[ing] Savages, a hideous Race! / whose scalping arts Man's origin debase," as well as rival Europeans.[145] Just as both the war and its leaders were celebrated for spreading British freedom and commerce rather than death and destruction over the globe, British imperial ascendancy was glorified as salvation for the world. Although some observers questioned the desirability and morality of extending the empire through war and bloodshed,[146] in the main the war had vindicated the

[144] *London Magazine,* 27 (1758), frontispiece; for an analysis of "anti-conquest" in European narratives see Mary Louise Pratt, *Imperial Eye: Travel Writing and Transculturation* (London, 1992).

[145] *Gentleman's Magazine,* 28 (1758), 393; *Salisbury Journal,* Jan. 14, 1760. Although, as in other periods, English writings on the Indians were profoundly ambivalent, during the war allegations of the Indians' "barbarity" or civility depended on their willingness to ally themselves with the French or English respectively, a division consonant with some of the cultural theory of the period. See, e.g., *Gentleman's Magazine,* 30 (1760), 33–6, "Account of the Rise of a New Indian War in America"; *Universal History,* 40 (1763), 371–5; and John Mayhem, *Gallic Perfidy* (Boston, 1763), quoted in Peter Marshall and Glyndwr Williams, *The Great Map of Mankind* (London, 1990), 208–9.

[146] Unintentionally dissonant was the *Ode for the Year 1759,* published in the periodical

pro-imperial vision as one of expansive wealth and liberty for British citizens on both sides of the Atlantic, mystifying, through nationalistic competition, the exploitive relations upon which the empire was based.

Moreover, the victories in America, Africa and India demonstrated and valorized the national character – courageous, aggressive, conquering, manly – in a way that surpassed even the spectacular historic conquests of national mythology. If the loss of Minorca constituted the symbolic emasculation of the British nation, in other words, then the war and its representation at home reconstituted national masculinity, potency and power. The recovery of British patriotism and manliness through the imperial cause was epitomized for those at home by the death of General James Wolfe at the Battle of Quebec, as the expressions of national pride and grief on the occasion indicated. In an anticipation of Benjamin West's famous painting *The Death of General Wolfe,* a tableau of this historic moment which ended a performance at the Manchester Theater in 1763 depicted

> the *General* expiring in the Arms of *Minerva,* while she crowns him with a Laurel; the Figure of *Hope* with a broken Anchor, weeping over him, an Emblem of past Recovery. *Britannia,* the Genius of *England,* seated in *Commerce,* with an *Indian Prince* kneeling at her Feet, resigning up *America:* And *Fame,* triumphing over *Death,* with this Motto: *He never can be lost, Who Saves His Country.*[147]

The war had demonstrated, then, that "Britain will never want a Race of Men ... who choose Dangers in defence of Their Country before an inglorious safety, an honourable Death before the unmanly pleasures of a useless and effeminate life," as the Reverend Brewster proclaimed in his Thanksgiving Day sermon in Newcastle in 1759. Britain's spectacular successes clearly constituted a forceful repudiation of the anxieties of three years before, endorsing the masculinist version of the national character and reifying the imperial effort into both a national duty and an international blessing.

The war for empire had equally complex consequences for the relationship of the current imperial vision to loyalist politics. First, Bri-

---

press, which offered up images of the incineration of French seamen on burning ships and seas "purpled o'er with streams of *Gallic* blood." More straightforwardly anti-war was "Address of a Citizen of the World to All the Belligerent Sovereigns," which pleaded for peace and an end to the mass destruction and killing. For both see *Gentleman's Magazine,* 30 (1760), 38; 31 (1761), 3–6.

[147] *The Death of the Late General Wolfe at the Siege of Quebec,* Manchester Central Library, Playbills, Marsden St. Theater, Aug. 17, 1763. See also *Gentleman's Magazine,* 29 (1759), 495; *Salisbury Journal,* Oct. 22, 29, 1759.

tain's escapades abroad, watched and aided at home in a mood of patriotic fervor, permitted the political valorization of the once suspect army and military complex more generally as defenders of the nation and props of nationalist sentiment. The navy and the militia, of course, had long been hallowed as especial bulwarks of English liberties and freedoms, protecting English people from outside aggressors while never threatening the liberties and properties of the citizenry within (a characterization which had refracted onto the volunteer associations formed during the '45). Hence the press for seamen in the spring of 1756 was carried out in the localities with all the fervor of a religious mission: Donations to the Marine Society flourished, and local gentlemen took on the mantle of patriotic leadership by upping the king's bounties for recruits and even recruiting men themselves.[148] Once invasion was threatened and the machinery of the Militia Act of 1757 creaked into action, the unceasing drills and colorful processions of the city volunteer companies and county militias won the acclaim and admiration of most spectators (despite both gentry disapproval and violent resistance from plebeian men balloted into service, who believed they would be sent overseas).[149] Merchants, tradesmen and artisans in provincial towns were more likely than gentlemen to volunteer, sometimes in advance of the ballot, as in Bristol, where eighty men offered themselves for fifty vacancies in 1758, or in Dartford, where a publican led a dozen of his customers to the enrollment accompanied by drums and French horns playing martial tunes.[150] Although some observers hinted at the potential for popular insurrection that stemmed from arming "the people," the civic duty to armed service clearly resonated among the middle classes in provincial towns, where militiamen were lauded for enacting the "Duty to themselves, their King and Country, and the most likely Means of preserving and securing our Religion, Liberties, and Properties from French Tyranny and Oppression."[151]

However, the exaltation of the military and the militaristic during

---

[148] See *Newcastle Courant*, March 27, April 3, 10, 1756; Chapters 7 and 8.
[149] *Norwich Mercury*, Oct. 28, Nov. 18, 1758; *Newcastle Journal*, April 21, June 30, Oct. 27, 1759; *Newcastle Courant*, June 30, 1759; March 8, 1760. The Act was suspended for a year in 1758 for lack of gentry support: J. R. Western, *The English Militia in the Eighteenth Century* (London, 1965), 303–40. For anti-militia riots, see *Letters of Spencer Cowper, Dean of Durham*, ed. Edward Hughes (Surtees Society, 165, 1956), 189–92; and Western, *English Militia*, 293–8.
[150] *Gloucester Journal*, Sept. 12, 1758; Western, *English Militia*, 255; *Newcastle Journal*, Oct. 27, 1759; *Salisbury Journal*, June 8, 1761.
[151] *Alarm to the People of England* (London, 1757); *Norwich Mercury*, Oct. 22, 1757.

the Seven Years' War extended beyond those traditional foci of patriotic appreciation to include the army itself. The celebrations prompted by the series of British and Allied victories in 1758–60 exuded an admiration for displays of martial might that seemed to enthrall all social classes. Frederick the Great's spectacular victories over the French and Imperial armies in 1758–9 not only saved Pitt's Continental "diversionary" war policy but also made Frederick a hero in Britain and amplified pro-war sentiment. His birthday was celebrated "by all Ranks and Degrees of People" in Norwich, as in other towns, where laborers raised money and women donated cash and food for his troops, and middling sorts gathered in taverns to drink his health and success to British arms. "All England kept his birthday," Horace Walpole reported in 1758; ". . . the people, I believe, think that Prussia is part of *Old England.*" Significantly, Frederick's likeness graced more pieces of commemorative pottery than had William, Duke of Cumberland's, after the '45.[152] The often wild national celebrations on British successes in America, India and Africa equally roused nationalistic passions and a bellicose, masculinist patriotism that expanded the ministry's popularity beyond any previous bounds. The victories at Cape Breton, Louisbourg, Guadaloupe, Plassey, Goree, Quebec and Montreal all flamed the fires of nationalistic fervor at home in rejoicing where martial spectacle took center stage, emblematic of British potency and might. In Salisbury, among the flags, bonfires, illuminations, free-flowing beer and civic pageantry attendant upon the victory at Louisbourg, Lord Ancram's regiment of dragoons and the Somerset militia maintained pride of place, firing volleys in the marketplace while toasts were made to the king, British arms, and "the brave and victorious Admiral Boscawen and General Amherst." In London, the colors taken at Cherbourg and Louisbourg, were paraded by the horse and foot grenadiers from Kensingston Palace to St. Paul's amidst reportedly cheering crowds; and in Newcastle, York, Manchester and Nottingham, dragoons dazzled assembled spectators with their uniforms and technical prowess at the celebrations in honor of Quebec, Montreal and the coronation of George III.[153] These domestic experiences and

---

[152] *London Chronicle,* Dec. 29–31, 1757; *Norwich Mercury,* Jan. 28, 1758; *Salisbury Journal,* Jan. 30, 1758; *Gentleman's Magazine,* 28 (1758), 41; for pottery (and quotation from Walpole) see Robson, *English Pottery,* 188–9, and Brewer, "Clubs and Commercialization." For tavern signs see *Norwich Mercury,* March 24, 1759.

[153] *Salisbury Journal,* Aug. 21, 28, 1758; June 18, Sept. 17, Oct. 22, 1759; June 1, 8, Sept. 22, 1760; *Gentleman's Magazine,* 28 (1758), 392, 448; *Newcastle Journal,* June 23, Sept. 15, Oct. 27, 1759; *York Courant,* Oct. 14, 1760; Earwaker, *Manchester*

representations of the war encouraged English people to view military spectacles as positive enactments of national power, signifying the "patriotic spirit of defense" rather than slavery – a lasting association that radical observers would decry in the next decade. Equally important, such displays marked for participants and spectators alike the inextricable connections between the localities and the state while celebrating the latter as a locus of loyalty and instrument of defense. The successes of the war thus vindicated the processes of state-building, as well as imperial expansion, as patriotic activities, thereby reversing for the moment the association of the "fiscal–military state" with domestic and imperial coercion that it had had for many English observers for the past two decades. In this respect, the Seven Years' War was crucial in consolidating the cultural bases for the development of a populist, conservative patriotism in the future, ones that the '45 had only adumbrated and the American and Napoleonic wars would embellish.

Finally, the war was important in galvanizing broader and more adventurous definitions of citizenship and rights. As with modern war efforts, the Seven Years' War made extraordinary calls upon ordinary people's financial, physical and emotional resources. They had to pay higher taxes; endure shortages, deprivations and invasion scares; bear up under trade and agricultural depressions; fulfill obligations to armed service at home and abroad; and suffer the loss of fathers, husbands and sons – while the war also afforded, and indeed, demanded through state inactivity or inefficiency, greater opportunities for citizen initiatives and participation in the home front. People from a variety of social and ethnic backgrounds and of both sexes thus donated money and time to patriotic societies, charities and hospitals; contributed to bounties for volunteers for the army and navy; provided food, board and clothing for troops; and drilled in militias or otherwise promoted the war effort while demonstrating their capacity for patriotism by energetic activity in the public sphere.[154] Not surprisingly, perhaps, the war period saw the reemergence of sustained discussion of the nature of English – indeed, of British – political rights and liberties for male subjects that began to be articulated through notions of popular sovereignty and resistance theory. A coronation anthem written for George III demonstrates this point succinctly: "God save the Brunswick Race,

---

Constable Accounts, 98, 111, 115–16, 121–2, 127n, 129; *Records of Nottingham,* vi, 274, 277–80; vii, 3–7, 26–7.

[154] The local news sections of provincial and London newspapers are filled with accounts of such activities: See references above and Chapter 1.

/ Born Albion's Isle to grace, / *Fruits of our Choice*'' its chorus ended – a reference to the centrality of popular agency in the dynastic succession that had been shunned in encomiums to the monarch since the succession crisis.[155]

Admittedly, the political grounds for this development had been laid through a conjuncture of forces which together created greater ideological space for the radical critique of Old Corps Whiggery. The apparent unanimity and pervasiveness of the loyalist response to the '45 was perhaps most important, for it had done much to banish the specter of a Jacobite restoration (a task the Seven Years' War completed) and dissociated political dissent from treason. Thereafter, in the 1750s, disillusionment with the nature and constellations of power in the aristocratic state was accompanied by a strident revival of populist rhetoric that insisted upon the "people's" right to oppose and resist their governors. When William Beckford spoke in Parliament to champion "the Middling People of England – the Manufacturer, the Yeoman, the Merchant, the Country Gent[lema]n, they who bear all the heat of the day, and pay all Taxes to supply all the Expenses of Court and Government" he spoke on behalf of numbers of men and women who felt they had a great deal at stake in effective colonial and national defense.[156] That they saw themselves as the vigilant watchdogs of the public good was evident in the aftermath of the Jewish naturalization bill of 1753, when the ministry's withdrawal of the bill was seen as a vindication of the power of the people out-of-doors in staving off the abuses of overmighty ministers and corrupted parliamentarians alike.[157] These views were expanded on in the anti-Newcastle propaganda of 1756–7, when the propensity of the administration to spurn the addresses and instructions presented on the loss of Minorca provoked opposition writers to rehearse for the benefit of recalcitrant MPs the elementary principles of the theory of delegatory representation. The instructions themselves similarly defended the people's "natural rights" against the assaults of bad ministers and Parliaments, a few

---

[155] *Coronation Anthem* (n.p., [1761]). See also Marie Peters, "The 'Monitor' on the Constitution, 1755–1765: New Light on the Ideological Origins of English Radicalism," *EHR*, 86 (1971), 706–27, and my "Inventing Revolution: 1688 and Eighteenth-Century Popular Politics," *JBS*, 28 (1989), 349–86.

[156] BL, Add. MS 38, 334 (Liverpool papers), fol. 29.

[157] See *The Jewish Naturalization Considered, with Respect to the Voice of the People* (n.p., [1753]); *Voice of the People*, vii; *Monitor*, Aug. 9, 1755; G. A. Cranfield, "The *London Evening Post* and the Jew Bill of 1753," *Historical Journal*, 8 (1965), 16–30.

even claiming the right to bear arms to be a "natural right [of] a free people." The arguments for the militia not only fanned gentry fears of an armed people but also led others to question the propriety of ordinary citizens' risking their lives for "imperious lordlings."[158] Most provocative, writers like Shebbeare and the Beckfords in the *Monitor* revived resistance arguments that had been dormant in mainstream discourse for a generation and that played not only on anti-aristocratic prejudice but also residual anti-Hanoverianism in their calls for "the people" to act to stave off irretrievable national decline. Shebbeare's *Letters to the People of England,* published in several editions between 1755 and 1758, were particularly virulent, indicting both the king and the Whig ministries for current corruption and justifying the author's intemperate exhortations for popular resistance to ministerial tyranny with reference to both natural rights and the precedents set by the Revolution and the Civil War – a rhetorical strategy which Wilkite radicals would develop and refine in the next decade.[159]

The 1750s thus saw a wide-ranging discussion of English rights and liberties, claiming broad rights for "the people" out-of-doors that became common currency in extra-parliamentary discourse. These ideas were compatible, as we have seen, with pro-imperial sensibilities that perceived that corruption from above threatened English people's liberties and properties at home and abroad, simultaneously circumscribing popular liberties and England's position in the world. Yet these ideas remained current even during an imperial war when both libertarian and patriotic sentiments were focussed on the government. Pitt, who consolidated the first empire under the clarion call of spreading the "birthrights of Englishmen" throughout the globe, combined moderate reforms at home and imperial acquisition abroad in ways that mobilized libertarian, pro-imperial and militaristic sentiments on behalf of his government.[160] Significantly, this period also saw a lively discussion of the applicability of English political rights to the colonies.

---

[158] *Considerations on the Addresses Lately Presented to His Majesty, on Occasion of the Loss of Minorca* (London, 1756), 2; *Letters from Algernon Sydney,* excerpted in *Gentleman's Magazine,* 26 (1756), 435–6; *Voice of the People,* ii–ix, 26–7, 24; Colley, *Defiance,* 275.

[159] Shebbeare, *Letters to the People of England* (1755–7), esp. *First, Second,* and *Third,* passim; for resistance arguments in *Monitor* see Aug. 23, 1755; July 24, 31, 1756.

[160] E.g., the Militia Act of 1757, a habeas corpus bill of 1758 to extend habeas corpus to cover impressment and noncriminal confinement, and the landed qualifications bill for MPs: See Rogers, *Whigs and Cities,* 114–15; Peters, *Pitt and Popularity,* 115–50.

The *Monitor* stressed that the truly patriotic leader would preserve the "rights and privileges" of the colonists according to "the system of liberty maintained in their mother country" while also contriving a more effectual system to curb and punish "licentious, arbitrary and tyrannical governors." Shebbeare, too, stressed that the preservation of "English rights" in the American provinces had to be a goal of any patriotic program. Such concerns were reiterated in the provincial and periodical press, where, in one case, a writer reviewed Lockean arguments about the property value of labor which were used to support the colonists' claims that English settlers had in certain instances greater liberties than English subjects at home.[161] Political discourse in a decade of war and empire-building was both complex and innovative, providing materials out of which loyalist and radical political agendas under George III would be constructed.

The period of the Seven Years' War thus constituted a moment when libertarian, imperialist and nationalistic discourses intersected, soothing anxieties caused by imperial expansion and smoothing over the disruptive and less savory aspects of conquest with the emollient of patriotic fervor. At this juncture, imperial aspirations enmeshed with the patriotic critique of corruption and a populist, libertarian vision of the polity in such a way that accountable government, a public-spirited citizenry and imperial ascendancy all seemed to go hand-in-hand. Empire and British national power, of course, were issues that played on the interests and aspirations of a wide range of groups and were compatible with both oppositionist and loyalist political positions, as both the '45 and Pitt's ministry had demonstrated. But since the 1730s they had also become closely linked to radical ideologies, to strategies of extra-parliamentary organization and resistance, and to the form and content of popular political consciousness. Integrated in this way with the development of extra-parliamentary political culture, empire entered public political consciousness as a birthright, as much a part of the national identity as the liberties and constitutional traditions for which Britain was celebrated the world over. This outlook, embedded in a variety of artifacts and pursuits, justified British imperial ascendancy as a benefit to the world.

Empire was not an end in itself in this period, however, but was the means through which national potency could be nurtured and consoli-

[161] *Monitor,* Aug. 16, 1755; Shebbeare, *Third Letter,* 60–4; *Gentleman's Magazine,* 26 (1756), 121–3.

dated – the bulwark and emblem of British and particularly English
superiority in culture and arms. The war for empire helped define and
vindicate the nation, whether it was Britain against Spain and France,
or English people against "native" others – Highlanders, Indians, Africans, "savages." Imperial struggles were viewed at home as battles
over the national character, and support and defense of the empire were
privileged as national duties. It was in the context of these nationalistic
struggles that the mercantile imperialist perspective justified both the
right of Britons to trade freely with the world and their domination of
it: They were freer than the French, less barbarous than the Spanish,
more civilized than the savages. Empire was, in contemporary conceptualization, the means to becoming more independent and self-
contained as a nation, rejecting foreign influences and introducing
English virtue wherever the English dared to tread.

Finally, the imperial effort as represented during the war articulated
notions of citizenship through the axes of class, race and gender as well
as nationality. Aristocratic "effeminacy," foreignness and corruption
seeped into the polity through social and cultural patronage and political power, corroding both national manners and political virtue; their
enervating effect was demonstrated in the inability of the "court" to
pursue the national, imperial interest. Hence, empire was represented
in the graphic and literary propaganda of the war as a middle-class
paradise, promoting wealth, strength, independence and virtue, for both
individuals and the nation. The current injunctions to "manliness"
aimed at countering alleged aristocratic, degenerate softness by requiring an assertive, forceful, disciplined and powerful subject to predom-
inate in the public realm, capable of resisting luxury and entitlements
in order to make the nation strong – a political role to be filled by
patriotic merchants, "countrymen" and other manly subjects with the
good of their country at heart.[162] The discourse of effeminacy, as deployed in the political initiatives of the moment, thus privileged the
claims of the white, trading and commercial classes to political status
while excluding a range of "effeminate" others who threatened their
supposedly distinctive goals: Frenchmen, aristocrats, nonwhite colonial
subjects; the foppish, the irrational, the dependent and the timid.[163]

---

[162] E.g., as in *The English Lion Dismember'd*, where English "countrymen" and London
aldermen stand against corrupted gentry and courtiers alike.

[163] Or "not quite/not white men," to extend Bhabha's epigram. These "others" were
not interchangeable but were signified through shifting hierarchies that depended
upon specific contexts for their particular articulation. For the cultural and "scien-

The masculinist model of English virtue that the imperial project of the 1750s valorized, although opposing itself primarily to aristocratic degeneracy, also affected the symbolic position of women in the national imagination and the valuation of their contributions to the public good. Hence – despite the persistence of an iconography that symbolized the British imperial presence through the female figure of Britannia; the growth of a "cult of sensibility" that could authorize certain kinds of feminine activism in the public sphere; and women's often strenuous participation in efforts on the "home front" as well as in the colonial campaigns[164] – colonial conquest was described and glorified as a *manly* occupation, the proving ground for national potency and effectiveness and the vehicle of paternalistic largesse and duty. As the antidote to national effeminacy, the imperial project constituted its version of masculinity partly through the marginalization, subordination or even ridicule of femininity out of its proper bounds. It thus devalued the "feminine" in its constructions of patriotism and the national character – an authorizing process in which women as well as men participated. Women's place may not have been in the home in mid-eighteenth-century England, but the feminine had no place in the political imaginary of the nation-state at this crucial moment in its development. In this respect, the Seven Years' War and its journalistic and historical narratives anticipated later wars in both calling on women's participation in the public sphere and erasing their presence there, as well as in using empire itself to construct gendered definitions of citizenship.[165]

tific" conceptualization of race see Marshall and Williams, *Great Map of Mankind;* Richard Popkin, "Medicine, Race, Anti-Semitism: A Dimension of Enlightenment Culture," in G. S. Rousseau, ed., *The Languages of Psyche* (Berkeley and Los Angeles, 1990), 405–42; Londa Schiebinger, "The Anatomy of Difference: Race and Sex in Eighteenth Century Science," *Eighteenth-Century Studies,* 23 (1990) 387–405.

[164] For the "cult of sensibility" see Barker-Benfield, *Culture of Sensibility,* 215–396; for the colonies see Linda Kerber, *Women of the Republic: Intellect and Ideology in Revolutionary America* (Chapel Hill, 1980), 8n; for the iconography of Britannia and its relationship to women's public valuation see my "Britannia into Battle: Empire and the Effeminate Body Politic," forthcoming. Cf. Colley, *Britons,* 260–81.

[165] See, e.g., [Eliza Haywood], *The Female Spectator,* 4 vols. (London, 1745–6), i, 104–20; HL, Montagu MSS, MO 569, 1179, 2343, 1756–7; [Richard Baldwin], *An Impartial and Succinct History of the Origin and Progress of the Present War,* first published in serial installments in *London Magazine,* 28–9 (1759–60); Colley, *Britons,* 257–8. For the role of empire in constructing exclusive definitions of citizenship in nineteenth-century British India see Mrinalini Sinha, "Manliness: A Victorian Ideal and Colonial Policy in Late Nineteenth Century Bengal" (Ph.D. diss., State University of New York, Stony Brook, 1988).

The homogenizing imperialist vision produced and confirmed for many citizens by the century's most successful imperial war was short-lived, soon to be fractured by the differing perceptions of the significance and purpose of Britain's expanded empire and by the domestic political divisions they mirrored and reproduced. To some members of the public, the end of the war promised to inaugurate a new era of British imperial ascendancy and American expansion that would spread civilization throughout the globe: "Diffusing freedom and science, political order and Christian Knowledge through those extensive regions which are now sunk in superstitious barbarism" was how the Protestant Dissenting Ministers put it in their congratulatory address to George III, "... imparting even to the most uncultivated of our species, the happiness of *Britons*."[166] To the government, however, newly acquired territories meant burdensome and expensive imperial responsibilities, necessitating revenue-raising schemes and restrictions on colonial settlement west of the Ohio. And to the self-styled patriots at home, Pitt's resignation and the Peace of Paris indicated that the old disjunction between the virtuous and imperialistic public and corrupted and self-serving "Court" government had returned – an apprehension which Wilkes and his followers would do much to amplify.[167] Over the next decade, conflicts with the American colonies and apprehensions about the socially and morally corrosive force of empire raised doubts about the viability of the libertarian, imperial dream. But for a brief shining moment, British glory and British imperial ascendancy were wedded in what seemed to be a secure and permanent union. Not surprisingly, then, in the 1780s, the Seven Years' War and its leader would take on mythical stature as icons of a national supremacy seen to be in danger of precipitous collapse. As the cenotaph erected in the Guildhall of London on Chatham's death in 1778 proclaimed, Pitt (whose figure was draped in Roman robes and surrounded by the cap of liberty and the laurels of victory) had presided over a glorious era characterized by

> unity at home – by confidence and reputation abroad – by alliance, wisely chosen and faithfully observed – by colonies united and

---

[166] *Gentleman's Magazine*, 33 (1763), 291. See also *King George: God Save Great George Our King* (London, 1760); *Proceedings of the British Parliament*, 425–6.

[167] For debates on the peace, Pitt's resignation in 1761 and his replacement by Lord Bute see *Gentleman's Magazine*, 29–33 (1759–63); *Monthly Review*, 21–5 (1759–63); and John Brewer, *Party Ideology and Popular Politics at the Accession of George III* (Cambridge, 1976), 102–7. The richest sectors of London's monied and mercantile communities supported the peace: Peters, *Pitt and Popularity*, 164–74.

protected – by decisive victories by sea and land – by conquest
made by arms and generosity in every part of the globe – and by
commerce, for the first time, united with, and made to flourish by
war.[168]

---

[168] See also Pitt's monument in Westminster Abbey, North Transept, central aisle,
erected in 1779–83, which depicts the former minister as ''extending the sway of
Britannia by means of Prudence and Fortitude over Earth and Ocean.''

4. Patriot's apogee: Wilkite radicalism and the cult of resistance, 1763–1774

> By various means we often see,
> Riches misnam'd gentility;
> Since the rich *by law* assum'd the name
> of *keeping coach* and *killing game*
> And not to rob them of their due,
> Both kill, and well-preserve it to . . .
> As if they thought, to judge it further,
> *Man-starving* nought, hare-killing *murther;*
> This . . . as in all states the case is,
> Made some folk fond of trust and places;
> For power's that curst bewitching thing,
> It spoils the man as well as king,
> So should be held in quick rotation
> From prince to peasant through the nation;
> . . . Rulers are but trustees,
> To do themselves and others justice.
>
> *The Corporation: A Fragment,* 1774

The period from George III's accession through the American war has long been designated a watershed in the history of British politics. Credited with inaugurating a host of auspicious developments ranging from class consciousness to the two-party system, these three decades have been scrutinized relentlessly by historians anxious to unravel the logic of constitutional evolution or the origins of some of the more mystifying political formations of the nineteenth century. Most recently, and most fruitfully, they have been heralded as marking crucial departures in popular politics through the emergence of a vigorous and largely bourgeois radical political culture.[1]

---

[1] John Brewer, "Clubs, Commercialization and Politics," in John Brewer, Neil Mc-Kendrick and J. H. Plumb, *The Birth of a Consumer Society* (London, 1982),

Certainly the early decades of George III's reign were distinguished by the vigor and perspicacity of their radical and reformist campaigns. As the "commercialization of politics" proceeded apace, middle-class activists developed increasingly effective techniques of extra-parliamentary mobilization that attempted to accommodate regional concerns and diversity of opinion. Yet the originality of these agitations lay as much in their ideological strategies as in their organization and sociological composition, and especially in the invention and deployment of indigenous "traditions" of English radicalism – innovations which owed far less than historians have supposed to the reentry of newly radicalized Protestant dissenters into the arena of dissident politics,[2] the exposure of English radicals to the arguments of disaffected American colonists,[3] or the emergence of an insurgent and anti-aristocratic bourgeoisie who suddenly recognized the relevance of Locke to their demands for political recognition.[4] Radical politics drew on established political practices and appropriated historical languages of resistance to propagate conceptions of patriotism and political subjectivity that disrupted older practices and habits of mind. In doing so, urban radicalism in George III's reign forced both elite and demotic politicians to rethink their positions and their strategies toward the "sense of the people" out-of-doors.

I. NEW DEPARTURES

Despite continuities in strategies, leadership and ideology, Wilkite writers and journalists were far less reticent than their "country" predecessors in using notions of contract and resistance in order to attack and criticize the state. "POLITICAL WHIGS ought not to be blinded by names and persons," charged the Newcastle radical activist James Mur-

---

197–262, "English Radicalism in the Age of George III," in J. G. A. Pocock, ed., *Three British Revolutions* (Princeton, 1980), 323–67, and *Party Ideology and Popular Politics at the Accession of George III* (Cambridge, 1976), esp. 139–272. See also John Money, *Experience and Identity: Birmingham and the West Midlands* (Montreal, 1977).

[2] R. B. Barlow, *Citizenship and Conscience* (Philadelphia, 1962); Albert Goodwin, *The Friends of Liberty: The English Democratic Movement in the Age of the French Revolution* (Cambridge, Mass., 1979); James Bradley, *Religion, Revolution and English Radicalism* (Cambridge, 1990).

[3] Brewer, "English Radicalism" and *Party Ideology,* chap. 9.

[4] Isaac Kramnick, "Republican Revisionism Revisited," *AHR,* 87 (1982), 629–64, and *Republicanism and Bourgeois Radicalism: Political Ideology in Late Eighteenth-Century England and America* (Ithaca, 1990).

ray in 1774, "but examine MEASURES strictly, and compare them with
those of Charles I and James II, and if they find them tending to the
same end . . . act as the whigs did then."[5] Other polemicists were also
wont to use this version of "revolution principles" in their opposition
to government policy. A writer in Salisbury in 1764 cited Magna
Charta, the Revolution settlement and Locke to prove the right of the
community to take up the "supreme power" when threatened by such
legislative tyranny as the recent cider tax.[6] Even the rhetoric of regicide
had become a commonplace by the late 1760s: *The Fate of Tyrants;
or, the Road from the Palace to the Scaffold* was advertised in conjunction with *Wilkes's Jest Book* as essential reading for the Friends of
Liberty, and the outbreak of hostilities with the American colonists
stimulated the republication of a 1659 tract which justified "king-
killing," dedicated to the "Great Grandsons of Algernon Sidney."[7]
Hyperbolic, perhaps, but indicative of the degree to which some of the
more extreme tenets of seventeenth-century political argument had entered popular political discourse.

The reasons for the widespread revival of contract and resistance
theories in the 1760s and 1770s were complex, located in a nexus of
political, ideological and socioeconomic developments since the middle
decades of the century. As we have seen, the 1740s and 50s had seen
a gradual diminution of overt partisan conflict and a correspondingly
altered domestic political climate, which internal rebellion and war with
France paradoxically reinforced.[8] By 1760, a modicum of consensus
had been reached on issues which had once provoked fractious and
feverish debate, altering the idioms of mainstream politics accordingly.
That the British monarchy was both hereditary and (at least once)
"elective," that England's stand against James II had involved resistance which was justified, however vaguely, by popular consent, and
that English men had political rights that extended beyond obedience
found expression in both loyalist and radical political argument. The

[5] *The Contest* (Newcastle, 1774), 12. For continuities with earlier Tory oppositions see
Linda Colley, *In Defiance of Oligarchy: The Tory Party, 1714–1760* (Cambridge,
1982), 146–76, and "English Radicalism Before Wilkes," *TRHS,* 5th ser., 31 (1981),
1–19. See also J. P. Jenkins, "Jacobites and Freemasonry in Eighteenth Century
Wales," *Welsh Historical Review,* 9 (1979), 193–206.
[6] *Salisbury Journal,* March 12, 1764.
[7] *Felix Farley's Bristol Journal,* July 1, 1769; KILLING No MURDER: *A Discourse Approving It Lawful to Kill a Tyrant According to the Opinion of the Most Celebrated
Authors* (London, 1775).
[8] See Chapter 3.

result was that out-of-doors political debate was freed of some of its former constraints.

This hardier and more open ideological terrain was consolidated by the new configurations of elite politics after George III's accession and their drastically altered relationship with an expanding, and more socioeconomically complex, extra-parliamentary political nation. The "Tory restoration" to the promised land of high political office after 1760 signaled the formal recognition of the reintegration of Whigs and Tories into a united ruling class that had been in progress since the 1750s. The result for high politics was the transmutation of the remnants of old party groupings into aristocratic connections struggling for office; the most striking consequence for the extra-parliamentary world was that dissident politics was deprived of effective elite leadership.[9] With no new proscription at the center, parliamentary elites had little interest in appealing to "the people" out-of-doors for political support, and the majority were prone to snub popular political aspirations and renounce the delegatory view of parliamentary authority that had previously authorized extra-parliamentary interventions. Whereas Tory and patriot Whig MPs had argued that the independence and integrity of representatives were proved by their attentiveness to the "voice of the people" as expressed, for example, in instructions, opposition MPs in George III's reign were wont to turn this argument on its head: The integrity of the representative was severely compromised by constituency instructions, they argued, and the constitutional balance was undermined by popular pressure.[10] In this context, it is not surprising that James Burgh devoted three chapters of his *Political Disquisitions* to repudiating current arguments against instructions, or that his assertion of their historical sanctity had such wide resonances for radicals in the localities and metropolis. As a Bristol freeman declared just before the furor over the Middlesex election, in language as absolute as that used by defiant parliamentarians, representatives must be reminded that they were elected not on account of any "superior abilities" but "upon a Presumption, that you

[9] J. C. D. Clark, *The Dynamics of Change: The Crisis of the 1750s and the English Party System* (Cambridge, 1982); Colley, *Defiance,* chap. 10; Richard Pares, *George III and the Politicians* (Oxford, 1953), 70–80.

[10] Lucy S. Sutherland, "Edmund Burke and the Relations Between Members of Parliament and Their Constituents," *Studies in Burke and His Time,* 10 (1968), 1005–21. Some MPs made reputations for their responsiveness to their constituents – Sir George Savile, Sir Harbord Harbord, Henry Cruger, Sir William Meredith, Sir Watkin Lewes and Sir Cecil Wray among them – but they were exceptional.

would on all Occasions, *do as you were bid* . . . to consider yourselves
as *empty vessels,* ready to receive what we shall think proper to pour
into you, and to remember that it is your Duty to pour it out in the
great Council of the Nation.''[11]

The expansion, in numbers and prosperity, of the "middling" classes
– that is, men and women of movable property with an income between
£40 and £400 per annum – compounded the impact of the volte face
of parliamentary elites and further corroded relations between opposition supporters within and without doors.[12] Since the 1720s, members
of the middling sort had been preoccupied with issues of taxation, in-
debtedness (both public and private) and the growing power of the
state, and these concerns ebbed and flowed according to the tenor and
policy of successive governments. The intransigence and clout of this
sector of the political nation with regard to state expansion and revenue
options were demonstrated in the excise crisis of 1733; they were revealed again in the anti–cider tax agitation of 1763, when "the people"
(in this case merchants and traders aided by local gentry) successfully
forced the ministry to repeal a tax on domestic commodities and so
limited the government's hand in dealing with the problems of the
North American colonies. Not only had their numbers and political
pretensions swelled by this later date, but in the aftermath of a hard-
fought war for empire for which urban commercial and trading classes
felt they had had to pay, in time and money, a disproportionate share,
increasing numbers of them were attracted to proposals that would eradicate the capricious and discretionary aspects of the patrician state and
secure the accountability of men in power – sentiments which were
completely compatible with the virtually universal belief in the superiority of English political institutions over all others.

The urban middling sorts also came to display a greater readiness
to emancipate themselves from elite leadership and a propensity to
market, and consume, politics in innovative and effective ways. The
Society of Supporters of the Bill of Rights or SSBR, formed initially
to pay Wilkes's debts, was only one of the scores of clubs and societies formed in London and provincial towns independent of elite
leadership and control that provided both alternative foci of allegiance
to the parliamentary parties and an ever-widening extra-institutional
context for political action.[13] The expansion of the press was also sig-

[11] James Burgh, *Political Disquisitions,* vol. 1. (London, 1774), 4, chaps. 1–3, 180–204;
Felix Farley's Bristol Journal, March 4, 1769.
[12] See Chapter 1.

nificant. The number of provincial presses grew threefold between 1750 and 1800, and diversification in the types and growth in numbers of publications available, changes in the structures of ownership and an increase in the venues and forms of sociability that subsidized print culture in urban settings had produced a new world of commercial printing within which political writers of all persuasions competed to shape and solicit favorable opinions.[14] Lord Bute, who despite his energetic efforts to bend public opinion in his favor became the object of the most scurrilous press campaign of the century, was only the first of George III's ministers forced to confront the fact that power and money were insufficient to battle the seemingly irrepressible opposition journalists, who had captured the public imagination with their diatribes and celebrations.[15]

Finally, government policy itself played no small part in the political reconfiguration under way. The debacles of 1763 to 1768, which included government attempts to suppress the press; general warrants; extensive rioting over political and economic issues that culminated in the St. George's Field Massacre of May 1768, when an innocent bystander was killed by troops called in to quell a demonstration in favor of "Wilkes and Liberty"; the Middlesex election of the same year, when Parliament unseated the elected member Wilkes in favor of the defeated ministerial candidate, Colonel Lutterell; and the Townshend Acts, aimed at coercing the American colonists – all caused grave concern among extra-parliamentary observers about the intentions of government policy. As dissident journalists were wont to stress, the present moment was a critical one, when the nation was

> overwhelmed with debt; her revenues wasted; her trade declining; the affections of her colonies alienated; the duty of the magistrate transferred to the soldiery . . . [and] the whole administration of justice become odious and suspected [*sic*] to the whole body of people.[16]

---

[13] Chapter 1; Brewer, "English Radicalism in the Age of George III," 334–6; John Money, "Taverns, Clubs and Popular Articulacy," *HJ,* 14 (1971), 15–47.

[14] Michael Harris, "The Structure, Ownership and Control of the Press, 1620–1780," in George Boyce, James Curran and Pauline Wingate, eds., *Newspaper History from the Seventeenth Century to the Present Day* (London, 1978), 87–90; Brewer, *Party Ideology,* 139–60, 221–6; Linda Colley, "Whose Nation? Class and National Consciousness in Britain, 1750–1830," *P & P,* no. 113 (1986), 101; Robert Rea, *The English Press in Politics 1760–74* (Lincoln, Nebr., 1963).

[15] For the daring of the political press by the 1770s see P. D. G. Thomas, "The Beginning of Parliamentary Reporting in Newspapers, 1768–74," *EHR,* 74 (1959), 623–36.

[16] Junius in *Public Advertiser,* Jan. 21, 1769. See also John Almon's pro-reform peri-

A conjunction of formal and informal political changes, then, had done much to shatter the facade of unity and shared concerns over corruption and accountable government that had seemed so marked an aspect of earlier patriotic campaigns; and government policy was producing an acute sense of crisis. In this context, the initiative for dissident politics was seized by the extra-parliamentary nation itself, particularly its middling and professional members, who resented their marginalized place in a political system now seen as dominated by antagonistic interests. When opposition parliamentarians such as the Rockingham Whigs tried to harness extra-parliamentary radicalism to their own agendas, they met with little success (although radicals would design to enlist their support for specific causes, such as the Middlesex petitioning campaign of 1769). The rise of more sophisticated and independent forms of political activity and acute disenchantment with elite political posturings thus combined to consolidate a wide-ranging public for radicalism who, if individual members were not "radicals" themselves, were nevertheless attuned to the idioms, grievances and goals of the radical program. It was this politically aware and articulate public that Wilkite journalism and protest exploited and built upon, using ideas about contract and resistance to appeal to its interests and conceits and expand the social bases of radical support.

II. RESISTANCE, HISTORY AND GENDER

To this end Wilkite journalists revitalized the party labels and rhetoric of the late Stuart period, although in a refurbished, if historiographically neglected, form.[17] Rather than privileging ahistorical natural rights doctrines per se, radical rhetoric combined natural and historical rights arguments to give primacy to the role of resistance in 1688 and conflate it with "the people's" actions in 1649, and the consequences of this innovative construction for political argument have never been ade-

---

odical, *The Political Register,* 1 (1767), 89–90. For details see George Rude in *Wilkes and Liberty* (Oxford, 1962), chaps. 1–5.

[17] From this perspective, the current "Tory" men in government, after having pretended to be animated by "revolution principles" during Pitt's premiership, had returned to their principles of nonresistance and passive obedience, defending the untrammeled prerogative of the Crown against the independence and rights of the people. Hence the only true Whiggism left was that which existed outside Parliament. See *Letter to the Cocoa Tree* (London, 1763); *Political Controversy, or Weekly Magazine,* 2 (Dec. 13, 1762).

quately appreciated. Apologists of the Revolution had long repudiated such a tactic, seeking to stress the dissimilarities between the moderate and defensive actions of 1688 and the extremism and subversion that were believed to have characterized the upheavals of the mid seventeenth century. In contrast, the Wilkite attack on "secret influence" exerted by the king's cabinet stimulated the conscription of both the Civil War and the Revolution into the cause of radical politics, an effort which gave historical (and a more narrowly inclusive English) specificity to resistance arguments, identified past and present threats to the constitution and subjects' liberties, and so constructed a "tradition" of popular resistance to executive tyranny that legitimized extra-parliamentary action in the present.

A key part of this strategy was the maligning of John Stuart, Earl of Bute, through a conjunction of anti-Scottish and anti-Stuart rhetoric designed to keep seventeenth-century animosities and current national divisions linked in the public mind. Indeed, Wilkes's infamous *North Briton* of 1762–3 set a pattern for oppositionist and radical politics for the next two decades in its attack on the supposedly pusillanimous nature of the Peace of Paris, the "Jacobite" sympathies of the first minister, and the nonaccountability of the king's government to the people. Its idioms and concerns were amplified in extra-parliamentary political culture, where Bute was excoriated in street theater and the press as an effeminate "Scotch-Jacobite" with French interests at heart who sought to fill the Court with his rapacious countrymen, control the king and subvert the people's liberties. On the thanksgiving day for the peace, crowds in several localities paraded and hung from scaffolds jackboots, petticoats (emblems of Bute and his supposed paramour, the Princess Dowager) and effigies wrapped in tartan, which were then hung and burned.[18] The prints satirizing or caricaturing Bute, which exceeded in number and virulence those used against any previous minister, also used the jackboot and petticoat as well as the thistle ("Scotch principles") to signify his secret, sexual and "foreign" influence over the English political system. Even after Bute's resignation in 1764, the Wilkite attack on his continuing "secret influence" succeeded in drawing in a range of opinion remarkable for its social and political heter-

---

[18] *North Briton,* Apr. 23, 1763 (no. 45), July 3, 1762ff.; *Times Past, Present and to Come* (BM no. 5765); John Brewer, "The Misfortunes of Lord Bute," *HJ,* 16 (1973), 7; John Latimer, *Annals of Bristol in the Eighteenth Century* (Bristol, 1893), 357–8; *Salisbury Journal,* Apr. 14, 1766.

ogeneity.[19] By identifying the foreign, the feminine and the corrupt as
imminent threats to the polity and insisting upon Scotland as a source
of domestic pollution, Wilkes made explicit the boundaries of Englishness and citizenship, which were rendered to include patriotic English
men wherever they might live (including America) and exclude those
"foreigners" for whom Englishness could, apparently, never be naturalized.[20] He and his supporters' virulent journalism therefore upheld
an amalgam of patriotic qualities that linked the preservation of empire,
liberty and the constitution with the hegemony of English customs and
culture in the polity.

The cult of resistance developed and deployed by Wilkite journalists,
engravers and writers vigorously partook of this conceptual universe,
linking past and present threats to the subject's liberties in polemical
fashion. The deliberate attempt to exploit historical memories of Stuart
political conflict is evident, for example, in the emergence of the radical
celebration of seventeenth-century Whig martyrs, which served to symbolize current divisions in terms of seventeenth-century polarities.
Prints such as *The Times: Plate II* drew historical parallels between
George III's reign and those of Charles I and James II, and Wilkes
appeared in company with Hampden, Sidney and Russell, martyrs all
to the cause of resistance to executive tyranny and the "Scottish" domination of England.[21] In verse and prose, too, Wilkes joined Britannia
and the seventeenth-century Whig heroes as actors in the struggle to
protect the constitution in English history against foreign and Stuart
threats. "Hampden and Sidney (deathless names and dear!) / Attentive
from the skies shall bend to hear . . . / Let not your great forefathers'
ghost complain / That all their blood was shed in vain" was the advice
which "Britannia" gave through one opposition paper when exhorting
the Middlesex freeholders to defend their "native rights." The identification of Wilkes with Sidney was especially prominent. Wilkite radicals in Newcastle formed the "Sydney Club" to elect other reformers

---

[19] *Sic Transit Gloria Mundi* (BM no. 3913); *The Highland Seer, or the Political Vision*
(BM no. 3867); *Sawney Below the Stairs* (BM no. 4048), all in *Catalogue*, iv, 179,
114–5, 298–9; Brewer, "Misfortunes of Lord Bute," 8–17, 27–30. The belief in secret
influence drew in Grenville, Rockingham and Newcastle as well as the Wilkites.

[20] Anti-Wilkite demonstrations occurred in Edinburgh and Glasgow and in some English
towns with a large Scottish population, such as Newcastle. See *Newcastle Chronicle*,
April 9, June 4, 1768; *Liverpool General Advertiser*, Jan. 5, 1770. In addition, 26
Scottish counties and 33 burghs sent addresses in support of the government's position
on the Middlesex election: James Bradley, *Popular Politics and the American Revolution* (Macon, Ga., 1986), 123.

[21] M. D. George, *English Political Caricature*, 2 vols. (Oxford, 1959), i, 143–5.

to Parliament, and Wilkes's supporters in London proposed renaming the Old Bailey, where the patriot hero was incarcerated in 1769, "Sidney Street."[22] And the historical parallels between George III's reign and those of Charles I and James II became almost an obsession in radical arguments. In the address of the City of London in March 1770, Wilkes's expulsion from the House of Commons was declared an illegality "more ruinous in consequences than the levying of ship money by Charles I or the dispensing power exercised by James II," and his imprisonment was heralded as an "intrepid stand against the prerogative of the Court" comparable to Hampden's stand against ship money in 1637.[23]

The revival of the language of seventeenth-century radical Whiggism, denoting England's historical struggles against despotism, marked a sustained effort to reinvent the events of the Civil War and Revolution as part of a legitimate indigenous radical tradition that justified the people's right to resist tyranny in the present. The historical associations of the Stuarts were played on to maximum advantage in order to demonstrate the sympathy of the government for absolutism, the inevitable consequences of Crown influence and the urgency of the need for reform. In the first instance this allowed radicals to indict the king in Court corruption. Junius's voluminous threats to George III to "profit by the fate of the Stuarts" – which could take pride of place on the front page of some provincial newspapers – are but the more famous examples of the often violent rhetoric against the king before the American Revolution.[24] Printed reminders of Charles I's fate appeared in radical journals like William Moore's *Whisperer,* Almon's *Political Register,* and the *Parliamentary Spy;* and the Wilkite *Middlesex Journal,* edited by Cuthbert Shaw and printed by Wilkes's printer Isaac Fell, displayed a steadily escalating hostility to the king from its inception in 1769 which was reproduced in numerous provincial excerpts and plagiarisms. George III's choice to associate himself and his

---

[22] *Middlesex Journal,* Apr. 21, 1770; *An Essay Towards a Catalogue of Patriots, Real and Pretended* (London, 1769); *Newcastle Journal,* June 11, 1774; *Virginia Gazette,* Mar. 30, 1769; *Liverpool Advertiser,* Jan. 5, 1770.

[23] *Middlesex Journal,* Apr. 21, 1770; *Whisperer,* May 25, 1771; *Political Register,* (1767), 211; *Felix Farley's Bristol Journal,* July 15, 1769. Late Stuart tracts on the right of resistance were also reprinted: See Sir John Somers, *The Judgement of Whole Kingdoms and Nations, Concerning the Rights, Power and Prerogative of Kings, and the Rights, Privileges and Properties of the People* (London, 1771).

[24] *Public Advertiser,* Dec. 19, 1769; *Liverpool General Advertiser,* Dec. 29, 1769; June 1, 1770; Feb. 8, 1771; *Salisbury Journal,* April 9, 1770; *Manchester Mercury,* March 26, 1771.

Court with "foreigners" led one writer to wonder who would support him if the people rebelled; he went on to make solicitous suggestions as to needed changes in men and measures in order to prevent the "sword of millions" from being drawn against him.[25] The frontispiece to Almon's *Political Register* in August 1767, *The Duumvirate,* gave visual form to these threats, depicting, under a double portrait of Bute and George III in a serpentine frame, the moment of Charles I's beheading in front of Whitehall. Such visual rhetoric makes Sylas Neville's report of attending a calves'-head feast on January 30 in this period more believable.[26]

Admittedly, these virulent arguments emanated from the "left" of the radical constituency, whose writers were not infrequently rewarded for their pains by government prosecution. And the issues associated with the Wilkite campaign – freedom of election, freedom of the press, trial by jury and the law of libel – also necessitated defense of the "traditional" rights and liberties of English political and legal culture.[27] But even the most moderate proponents of reformist politics in the Wilkite period were likely to emphasize the role of resistance in past political struggles in order to argue for the centrality of popular sovereignty and trusteeship in the British political system. "If revolution principles are justifiable, that is, if the people may take the power out of the hands of a king or government, when they abuse it, it follows that the king and government are in all cases responsible to the people," a Durham observer declared in 1774 (plagiarizing a passage out of Burgh's renowned *Political Disquisitions*), and variants of these principles appeared repeatedly in the political literature of the period.[28] Radical sympathizers in the North agreed with Junius and Wilkes that the king was but the "prime magistrate," and were also vehement in their assertions that by the same principles, magistrates, MPs and judges were "not the servants of the King, but those of the people." The

[25] *Middlesex Journal,* Sept. 10, 1772.
[26] *Diary of Sylas Neville,* ed. Basil Cozens-Hardy (Oxford, 1950), 149; see also *Norfolk Chronicle,* Mar. 30, 1771; Jan. 29, 1780; *The Contest,* 7; *Whisperer,* Aug. 10, 1771.
[27] See my "A Dissident Legacy: Eighteenth Century Popular Politics and the Glorious Revolution," in J. R. Jones, ed., *Liberty Secured? Britain Before and After 1688* (Stanford, 1992), 320–1; for the Wilkite obsession with legal abuses see John Brewer, "Wilkites and the Law," in John Brewer and John Styles, eds., *An Ungovernable People: The English and Their Law in the Seventeenth and Eighteenth Centuries* (London, 1980), 128–71.
[28] *The Freemen's Magazine, or Constitutional Repository,* ii (Newcastle, 1774), 60; Burgh, *Political Disquisitions,* i, 200; see also *Norfolk Chronicle,* Oct. 29, Nov. 11, 1769.

Robin Hood Society of London debated the question what recourse the people had when their representatives proved unworthy of their trust. It was decided that after "every legal method of redress" was tried with no effect, then "the people were to redress themselves in the same manner they did at the Revolution; that all just power being originally derived from the People, they have a right to recall it whenever it is abused." And the Revolution Society of Newport, Isle of Wight, was established in the belief that "every true Englishman cherishes the doctrine of resistance, as his palladium" (so much for liberty of the press!).[29]

This collective reworking of the national political past was anathema to most members of the parliamentary opposition, whose interests it blatantly did not serve, and who frequently supported the ministry's attempts to silence bodacious publicists such as William Moore of *The Whisperer* or the publishers of Junius even before the radicals' break with the parliamentary opposition in 1770.[30] But it clearly struck a chord in other sectors of the political public, where its idioms and conceits were absorbed into daily discourse. The gentleman merchant, future MP and Wilkite Crisp Molineux of King's Lynn, for example, endorsed the panoply of paranoid radical allegations in his correspondence. In 1772 he referred to "the Motley Crew of passive obedient and non-resistant Toad-eating Tories who now Surround the throne and preach up absolute monarchy and hereditary right" and warned that if the ministry continued to deny the people their liberties and laws, the people would be roused to "a civil war . . . in support of their rights, [and] who are to blame [them]?"[31] Indeed, just as Bute was maligned by observers from all parts of the political spectrum for his alleged covert manipulation of the king and government, so the myth of the people's recourse to the revolutionary tradition in English history against recalcitrant monarchs had remarkably wide currency. It was even rumored that Queen Charlotte herself warned George III of the dim precedents his ancestors had set for the fate of kings who lost the respect and love of their people.[32]

[29] *Newcastle Journal,* Jan. 3, 1771; *Middlesex Journal,* Jan. 3, 1769; *A Charge to Englishmen* (London, 1768).
[30] Rea, *Press in Politics,* 169, 177; John Cannon, *Parliamentary Reform, 1640–1832* (Cambridge, 1972), 60–5. For alternative views held by the Chathamites and Rockinghamites see Brewer, *Party Ideology,* 263–4.
[31] NNRO, Bradfer-Lawrence MSS, Molineux Letter Book, fols. 262–3, CM to P. Case, Jan. 1772; fols. 199–200, CM to Peter Franklyn, April 5, 1771.
[32] NNRO, Neville Papers, MC7/349–3, CF to SN, Nov. 22, 1770.

The refurbished rhetoric of radical Whiggism, then, created an ideological weapon that was effective because of its historicism. In a society which believed that history provided the blueprint of what was possible or acceptable in the present, the revived and often violent language of radical libertarianism and the historical memories it evoked constructed an alternative narrative of English history that endowed radical apprehensions and goals with credibility. Although not without its own fissures and contradictions, this radical master narrative, to which provincial as well as metropolitan writers contributed,[33] clearly contested established Court Whig and Tory verities about English constitutional development and celebrated the violent, if mythical, interventions of the people in the political process while also locating "original liberties" in a pre-Norman or otherwise pre-Stuart past.[34] Catharine Macaulay's multi-volume *History of England,* highly acclaimed by Horace Walpole, Chatham and Capel Lofft as well as Mirabeau and Brissot (among others), in many ways formalized the radical reading of the national becoming. Her account of the "tyranny" of the reigns of the Stuarts and the stalwart efforts of the patriots and republicans who strove to resist them provided English radicalism with historical paradigms that, rivaling those provided by Tory writers like Clarendon and Hume, legitimated its frequently innovative strategies and interpretations of current political trends.[35]

[33] See, e.g., Philodemos, *A Letter to the Gentlemen, Clergy, Freeholders, Free Burgesses, and Other Electors of the County of Norfolk, on the Subject of a Remonstrance to the Throne* (Norwich, 1770); *The Contest;* Fabricus Jr., *Considerations on Our National Grievance: In a Letter . . . to . . . Those Worthy Freeholders, Who Signed the Petition for the County of Durham* (Newcastle, 1770); *Liverpool General Advertiser,* Feb. 16, 1770; *Farley's Bristol Journal,* March 18, 1769.

[34] See Christopher Hill, "The Norman Yoke," *Puritanism and Revolution* (London, 1955); H. T. Dickinson, *Liberty and Property: Political Ideology in Eighteenth Century Britain* (London, 1977), p. 198. The most important tract circulating this theme was [Obadiah Hulme], *An Historical Essay on the English Constitution* (London, 1771).

[35] *The History of England from the Accession of James I to That of the Brunswick Line,* 8 vols. (London, 1763–83). Its views were bolstered or duplicated in *The North Briton* as well as in *Political Register,* 2 (1768), 224–5; *Whisperer,* Aug. 10, 1771; *Freemen's Magazine,* i, 1–16; *London Evening Post,* Aug 5–7, 1773; Society for Constitutional Information, *Second Address to the People of England* (London, 1781). Macaulay's dim view of the Revolution of 1688 as a deal struck between warring aristocratic factions and thus the fount of all subsequent corruption became common currency among radicals in the 1760s and 70s, although it faded thereafter. See L. N. Donnelly, "The Celebrated Mrs. Macaulay," *WMQ,* 3rd ser., 6 (1949), 175–205; Lynne Whitey, "Catharine Macaulay and the Uses of History," *JBS,* 16 (1976), 59–83; and for the foreign as well as domestic impact of her *History,* Bridget Hill, *The Republican Virago: The Life and Times of Catharine Macaulay* (London, 1992).

Gender as well as history was used to naturalize the claims for political subjectivity made through resistance arguments, exemplified most cogently in the Wilkite model of "manly patriotism." Circulated through newspapers, pamphlets, plays and street theater as well as the homosocial milieu of radical club life, the model of manly patriotism simultaneously defined and solicited a particular version of masculinity to be put at the call of patriotism that marginalized and opposed non-resisting and hence "effeminate" others. It defined the true patriot as the austere, forceful and independent masculine subject who would resist, often at considerable personal cost, the illegitimate powers that threatened to overtake the polity: men who distinguished themselves, as one monthly called *The Biographical History of Patriots* put it, "by extending the natural rights and civil liberties of mankind, and in opposing the usurpations of tyranny." Past and present heroes who stood firm against the blandishments of tyranny, from Hampden to Crosby and Oliver and the American Samuel Adams, were celebrated for exhibiting this specifically *English* variant of love of country.[36] The addresses to Wilkes, Crosby and Oliver in the Tower during the printer's case in 1771 thanked them for their "virtuous and manly resistance" to the current effort of the House of Commons to "supersede the law of the land and the rights of citizens"; and Wilkite demonstrations and celebrations were frequently described as exhibiting the inextricable qualities of "moderation" and "manliness." Addison's tragedy *Cato* became a favorite radical play of the period, performed at the request of clubs and societies in the taverns of provincial towns, not least because its hero incarnated the imperative of patriotic resistance, giving his life for the cause of liberty against the tyrannical Caesar.[37]

Continuing the efforts of opposition and radical political culture to shape gender categories, the model of manly patriotism also resonated and was complicit with the rakish, heterosexist libertinism with which Wilkite radicalism was associated. Wilkes's own flamboyant sexual life, which his pornographic *Essay on Women* (available in spurious editions in circulating libraries), fondness for liaisons with married

---

[36] *Biographical History of Patriots* (London, 1770), advertised in *Liverpool General Advertiser,* July 6, 1770. This model of masculinity shared some important features with that proffered by civic humanism: J. G. A. Pocock, *Virtue, Commerce and History* (Cambridge, 1985), esp. chap. 6.

[37] *Universal Magazine,* April 1771, extracted in the BL Bell Collection; *Newcastle Journal,* April 28, 1770; for performances of *Cato* see *Farley's Bristol Journal,* Feb. 25, 1769; *Newcastle Chronicle,* April 28, 1770; Houghton Library, Harvard Playbill Collection, Hull Theater Royal, Dec. 5, 12, 1770.

women, and ill treatment of his own wife had made fairly inextricable from his libertarian politics, was a source of admiration as well as distress to some of his contemporaries. William Beckford was also fond of boasting of the numbers of "natural" (i.e., extra-marital) children he fathered; and Robert Morris, lawyer and secretary of the SSBR, successfully defended Lord Baltimore against rape charges, competed with Wilkes in seducing other men's wives and in 1772 ran off with Baltimore's twelve-year-old daughter, marrying her on the Continent in a ceremony that would subsequently be forcibly annulled by the girl's mother. Even Sylas Neville, who endorsed Thomas Hollis and Caleb Fleming's view that Wilkes, "being an enemy to every obliga- tion of religion and morality[,] cannot be a true friend of Liberty," nevertheless engaged in a succession of sexual dalliances with married women and servants that upheld an endorsement of "liberty" and a notion of manliness that had sexual as well as religious and political components.[38]

Such phallic adventuring appropriated the libertinism formerly as- sociated with the aristocracy (and, indeed, with the Stuart Court), but used it to solidify a renewed backlash against sodomy and other ev- idences of supposedly "aristocratical" effeminacy which were lambasted in the radical culture of the day. Aristocratic manners and especially their "extravagant submission" to women had long been held to be a mark of effeminacy, but by the Wilkite period so too were unconventional sexual practices attached to the anti-aristocratic critique. Hence Beckford himself was lampooned for his effeminate voice and practices by adversarial pamphleteers; and Lord George Sackville Ger- main, future secretary of state for the American colonies and com- mander of the British troops at Minden in 1759 (a debacle for which he was court-martialed and dismissed from the army for disobeying orders), was attacked by Wilkes, Charles Churchill, Junius and other writers as a "buggering hero" in ways that twinned his homosexuality with cowardice.[39] Of course, the connection of the libertine version of

---

[38] Rude, *Wilkes and Liberty,* chap. 1; Horace Walpole, *Memoirs of George III,* 4 vols. (London, 1845), iv, 156–7n; J. E. Ross, ed., *Radical Adventurer: The Diaries of Robert Morris, 1772–4* (Bath, 1971), 9–12, 23–6, 34–6; Neville, *Diary,* pp. 39–40, 160–1 and passim (quotation from 15).

[39] Lawrence Stone, *Family, Sex and Marriage in England, 1500–1800* (New York, 1977), 541–2; Randolph Trumbach, "Sodomy Transformed: Aristocratic Libertinage, Public Reputation and the Gender Revolution of the Eighteenth Century," *Journal of Homosexuality,* 19 (1990), 115–16; *A Letter from a Right Honourable Person* (Lon-

masculine virility to radical politics did not go unchallenged. The men who split off from the SSBR to form the Constitutional Society in 1771 cited the banishment of "regularity, decency and order" from the Wilkite camp as a main cause; and some middle-class supporters of radical politics increasingly had recourse to an ideal of conjugal domesticity that proscribed such discrepancies between public and private virtue.[40] Nevertheless, from the radical point of view, political and sexual subjects were one and the same, and manly patriotism embellished a heterosexist version of masculinity that aggressively eschewed "effeminacy" in the political and sexual realms.

Prints of the period dramatically expressed these contiguous if unstable strands in the gendered model of patriotic resistance while also highlighting the newly charged hostility to the feminine in politics, frequently using the aristocratic and Scottish Bute and traditional female icons to emphasize Wilkes's or his supporters' vaunted manly virtue.[41] *Malice and Fortitude* (Plate 8), which served as frontispiece to the *Political Register* for July 1768, shows Wilkes, standing behind

don, 1761), iv–v; *Interesting Letters Selected from the Political and Patriotic Correspondence of Messrs. Wilkes, Horn, Beckford and Junius* (London, 1769), 35–6; Piers Mackesy, *The Coward of Minden: The Affair of Lord George Sackville* (London, 1979), esp. 254–6. Beckford's homosexual practices seem to have been tolerated by his peers, unlike those of the unfortunate Captain Robert James, who was executed for sodomy in 1772, or of William Beckford, Jr., who was tried and exiled to the Continent by his family for the offense in 1784: Stone, *Family, Sex and Marriage,* 541; Namier and Brooke, i, 79; G. S. Rousseau, "The Sorrows of Priapus: Anti-Clericalism, Homosocial Desire and Richard Payne Knight," in G. S. Rousseau and Roy Porter, eds., *Sexual Underworlds of the Enlightenment* (Chapel Hill, 1988), 101–53. For renewed fears of effeminacy among the upper classes and attacks on sodomites and "macaronis" in the 1760s see G. J. Barker-Benfield, *The Culture of Sensibility* (Chicago, 1992), chap. 3; and Randolph Trumbach, "Sex, Gender and Sexual Identity in Modern Culture," *Journal of the History of Sexuality,* 2 (1991), 190–6.

[40] Catherine Hall and Leonore Davidoff, *Family Fortunes: Men and Women of the English Middle Class* (London, 1987), 108–18; Joan Landes, *Women and the Public Sphere in the Age of the French Revolution* (Ithaca, 1988), 42–6. For the increasing condemnation in these decades of all types of sex outside bourgeois marriage see Stone, *Family, Sex and Marriage,* and Randolph Trumbach, *The Rise of the Egalitarian Family* (New York, 1978).

[41] Cf. Maurice Agulhoun, *Marianne into Battle,* trans. Janet Lloyd (Cambridge, 1981), and Marina Warner, *Monuments and Maidens: The Allegory of the Female Form* (London, 1985), who argue that allegory and sexuality were mutually exclusive. Britannia, as Warner points out, does not *necessarily* convey meaning about the empirical position of women, but she *can* do so, for these prints were also part of the banishment of the feminine from politics that was a social as well as symbolic process of the 1760s and 70s. The signification of female forms is addressed in my "Britannia into Battle: Empire and the Effeminate Body Politic," forthcoming.

Malice and Fortitude.

There is no terror in your threats;
For I am arm'd so strong in honesty,
That they pass by me, as the idle wind.
Which I respect not——

Shakespeare.

8. *Malice and Fortitude* (1768). Wilkes withstands the forces of national corruption. Courtesy of the Lewis Walpole Library, Yale University.

the ''Gates of English Liberty'' and leaning on the pillar of Fortitude, about to be crowned with a laurel by a descending Britannia as a malicious crowd, consisting of Bute with sword drawn, the Princess Dowager with a dagger raised at Wilkes's heart, a malevolent Lord Mansfield and a blindfolded George III, advances. Below the print is a passage from Shakespeare's *Julius Caesar:* ''There is no terror in your threats; / For I am arm'd so strong in honesty, / That they pass by me, as the idle wind, / Which I respect not.'' Wilkes is identified with virtue and greatness, Britannia and the new nationalist icon, Shakespeare, both symbolizing the national spirit and superiority in politics, arms and arts against the foreign, feminine and corrupt elements who would betray their country's honor.[42] The naked, defenseless Truth/Britannia provides the perfect counterpart for Wilkes's manly stand against corruption – a visual strategy geared, perhaps, to appeal to a male audience, whose masculine ire would be accordingly aroused against those who threatened her.[43] Patriotic virtue is represented here as predicated in part upon male mastery, in part upon a willingness to resist the (frequently feminized) forces of corruption.

Equally evocative was the two-part radical print, also published in 1768, *The Colonies Reduced* and *Its Companion* (Plate 9), which represents the probable outcome of the quarrels between England and its colonies as a mutilated and destitute Britannia, incapable of defending herself, her ships for sale and dominions severed. Below, this catastrophe is portrayed as the triumph of Britain's foreign and domestic enemies. Louis XV stabs Britannia in the eye and grabs America, and a Dutchman steals English commerce while Bute holds up Britannia's dress to aid Spain in sodomizing her with a sword. (Bute declares, in a parody of naval slogans, ''Now I show you her Weakness you may strike Home.'') The supposed relationship between tyranny and sexual impropriety, a familiar trope of French republican prints, also appeared as a theme in Wilkite graphic propaganda, as in *The Times: Part II,* where the Princess Dowager obscenely fondles Bute while sitting upon a zebra with George III's head.[44] But here the relationship is inflected differently through a homophobic indictment of the foreign and effeminate forces threatening the nation at home in the Court (through Bute: aristocratic, Scottish and sexually other) and abroad (England's

[42] For the resurrection of Shakespeare as a nationalist icon see Michael Dobson, *The Making of the National Poet: Shakespeare, Adaptation and Authorship, 1660–1769* (Oxford, 1992). The speech comes from Brutus's address to Cassius (IV.iii.67). Brutus is an ambiguous patriot in the play, which may account for the omission of attribution in the print.

[43] See Madge Dresser, ''Britannia,'' in Ralph Samuels, ed., *Patriotism: The Making and Unmaking of the British National Identity,* 3 vols. (London, 1989), iii, 35; *Catalogue,* v, 484.

[44] For French examples see the essays by Sara Maza and Lynn Hunt in Hunt, ed., *Eroticism and the Body Politic* (Baltimore, 1990). The association of women at court with illegitimate influence and sexual impropriety in English history goes back to the Stuarts and beyond: See Rachel J. Weil, ''Sexual Ideology and Political Propaganda in England, 1680–1714'' (Ph.D. diss., Princeton University, 1991), 236–40.

9. *The Colonies Reduced* and *Its Companion* (1768). Britannia dismembered and sodomized through the agency of Bute. Courtesy of the Lewis Walpole Library, Yale University.

effeminate and apparently sodomite rivals) while Britannia herself incarnates the manly alternative by attempting to resist her attackers. Such a scenario not only recapitulated the heterosexist ethos of male club life and radical political culture in general; it also was supremely calculated to arouse the virile, manly resistance exhorted of patriots by its representation of so "unnatural" an act. The politics of gender, sexuality and class at work in this print are in tension and even apparent contradiction, yet would constitute for its viewers a coherent narrative of Britain's imminent decline.[45]

The Wilkite cult of resistance, then, like radical contract theory itself, could express an acute hostility toward both the effeminate and the feminine in the body politic that sought to close down the gender identities available for political subjects in order to enlarge and legitimate more expansive notions of citizenship for the male middle classes. In doing so, it explicitly extended the concerns of political anti-effeminacy arguments to focus on homosexual as well as aristocratic and feminine corruptions of the body politic in ways that participated in growing cultural anxieties about stable gender demarcations, unconventional sexualites and "separate spheres." It was not coincidental that the 1760s and 1770s were the first time in three generations when "liberal" English political thinkers felt the need to emphasize the ways in which male political subjectivity rested in part on their property in wives, daughters and children as well as in their property in trades, shops and labor and their contributions to the state through taxes.[46]

This is not to argue that aristocrats, homosexuals or women were prevented from identifying with the premises of Wilkite radicalism or participating in its politics. For example, women's position in contractarian politics was more complex than recent analyses have suggested.[47] The "patriotic Ladies of Worcester" and the "Lady freeholders of Middlesex" were only two instances of women who engaged in radical

[45] The print wants to have it both ways: Bute and the Continental Europeans are effeminates and sodomites who nevertheless overpower the British nation, whereas the gendered Britannia is meant to embody masculine virtue while also rousing masculine indignation and rage at her "unnatural" violation. The Latin label – "Give an obol to Belisarius" – is meant to identify Britannia with that unfortunate Roman general, who was blinded by the emperor Justinian for alleged disloyalty – the classic example of the fickleness of princes.

[46] See Wilkes's speech for reform in *Parl. Hist.,* xviii (1774–7), 1295; and Burgh, *Political Disquisitions,* i, 37–8. See also Susan Okin, *Women in Western Political Thought* (Princeton, 1979), 199–203.

[47] See, e.g., the otherwise powerful analysis by Carol Pateman, *The Sexual Contract* (Stanford, 1988); and Landes, *Women and the Public Sphere,* 43–6.

demonstrations and festivals, sent Wilkes letters and presents, attended Wilkite balls, contributed to subscriptions or were activists in the political public sphere of propaganda and debate.[48] However, Catharine Macaulay illustrated the dangers of women's too-zealous identification with the precepts and prerogatives of manliness when, after marrying a young Scottish surgeon's mate twenty-six years her junior, her public and private life was subjected to ridicule and censure. Not only did her marriage to a much younger man echo the "disreputable" connection of the Princess Dowager with Bute; but by crossing class and age boundaries she had usurped the entitlements of male political and sexual subjectivity, a subversion of gender codes too serious to be dismissed as mere eccentricity.[49] As Macaulay's experience reveals, the status of women as even "auxilliary" political subjects depended in part upon their conformity to a gender-specific model of sexual virtue; as symbolic or biological mothers of citizens, their private lives had to adhere to the exacting and ultimately hypocritical standards of maternity and domesticity. In this role, women would in future be participants in "moral" political campaigns such as the anti-slavery and reformation-of-manners agitations, engage in loyalist efforts on the home front during the Napoleonic wars, join democratic or socialist movements, or even demand their own formal political recognition – all political deployments of their sexual status that collapsed the distinctions between public and private upon which male claims to entitlement rested.[50] Nevertheless, for the moment, radical patriotism and especially the cult of resistance made explicit an intolerance for the feminine and the effeminate that would continue to be deployed strategically in dissident and loyalist politics for the next several dec-

---

[48] Brewer, *Party Ideology,* 170–5; *Middlesex Journal,* Apr. 11, 1769; *Aris's Birmingham Gazette,* Aug. 8, 22, 1774; *Newcastle Chronicle,* March 26, 1768; Chapter 1; Catharine Macaulay, *Observations on a Pamphlet Entitled Thoughts on the Present Discontents* (London, 1770), and *Letters on Educaton* (London, 1790), where she recommends that women adopt the "manly" qualities of austerity, independence and strength of mind. For homosexuals in radical politics see Rousseau, "The Sorrows of Priapus."

[49] The abuse heaped on Macaulay is well summarized in Hill, *Republican Virago,* 114–18.

[50] Claire Midgley, *Women Against Slavery: The British Campaigns, 1780–1870* (London, 1992); Iain McCalman, "Females, Feminism and Free Love in an Early 19th-Century Radical Movement," *Labour History,* 38 (1980), 1–25; Linda Colley, *Britons: Forging the Nation, 1707–1837* (New Haven, 1992), 238–48; Barbara Taylor, *Eve and the New Jerusalem* (London, 1983); [Anna Wheeler and William Thompson], *Appeal of One Half the Human Race . . . Against the Pretensions of the Other Half* (London, 1825).

ades.[51] Radical patriotism would brook neither in its vision of the
reformed and purified body politic, which would be peopled by manly,
rational political subjects inscribed in much of radical argument as exclusively male and heterosexual.

The cult of resistance, then, made a number of innovative ideological
moves that could be deployed to redefine the nature and boundaries of
citizenship itself, challenge elite claims of political exclusivity and reinvent the nature of political liberty in accordance with principles of
"popular," if masculine, sovereignty (while revealing its deliberately
delimiting deployments). Conflating historical and natural rights, or, to
put it another way, the rhetorics of constitutionalism and republicanism,
the cult of resistance, founded on a revolutionary past, aimed not at
revolution itself but at the restructuring of parliamentary institutions to
make them more responsive to "the people's" demands. Its attacks on
an "arbitrary" House of Commons and its insistence on the right of
the people to resist tyrannical governors served to remind not only an
apostate Parliament but also the people of the origins of its power.[52]

The relationship of contract and resistance to the case for parliamentary reform was thus intriguing. Certainly there was no necessary relation between championing English people's right to resist tyranny and
supporting radical reform. The former could be invoked as occasion
demanded from all parts of the political spectrum, particularly to draw
attention to the "sense of the people" out-of-doors or to enlarge support for such moderate "country" positions as place, pension and anti-
bribery bills. In this respect, it is clearly a mistake to see democratic
reform as the "natural" or inevitable culmination of Hanoverian radicalism: The belief that an uncorrupted Parliament *would* attend to the
people's desires could set limits on how far dissidence would go.[53] On
the other hand, radical rhetoric in the period reflected nothing if not
the extreme frustration of a activist political nation whose role in *formal*

---

[51] See, e.g., Anna Clark, "Queen Caroline and the Sexual Politics of Popular Culture in
London," *Representations*, 31 (1990), 47–68.
[52] See, e.g., *Newcastle Journal*, Jan. 3, 1771; *Bristol Gazette and Public Advertiser*, Oct.
5, 1774. This tactic also forced ministerial writers to utilize notions of consent and
popular sovereignty in their own propaganda: See, e.g., *Farley's Bristol Journal*,
March 18, 1769.
[53] Towns such as Liverpool, Salisbury and Hull supported purification rather than alteration of existing political institutions; in the populist traditions of Norwich, resistance
(the right of the people to demand accountability from their governors) tended to be
privileged over proportional representation until the late 1780s: See Chapter 8.

political processes – albeit an extra-parliamentary one – had been sharply curtailed, and this perception led, sometimes inexorably, to more far-reaching demands for change. The reform programs of Wilkite and, later, pro-American radicals accordingly combined the old country panaceas of place and pension bills and more frequent (triennial or annual) Parliaments with a host of newer demands that sought to give those out-of-doors a more formal and permanent political role, one that would ensure parliamentary accountability and the representation of newer socioeconomic interests. Reform proposals of the period included constituency pledges, which bound parliamentary candidates to pursue their electors' programs or principles in Parliament; secret ballots; and a "more equal representation," which usually meant the elimination of rotten boroughs, a redistribution of seats to reflect new centers of population and wealth, and, by the 1780s, the enfranchisement of all who paid taxes.[54] These measures reflected more than the repudiation of the central tenets of the doctrine of virtual representation: They also demonstrated the hard-won knowledge that an extra-parliamentary agitation without substantial official recognition was ineffective. The "voice of the people" needed institutional form if it was to be heard.

III. WILKITES AND THE PEOPLE

The crucial departures that Wilkite radicalism brought in eighteenth-century popular politics were ideological as well as organizational and commercial, employing a historicist and nationalistic version of resistance principles to invent a tradition of radical activism that legitimated demands for political change. But one still feels compelled to ask what these innovations in the end accomplished. Most historians have agreed that in terms of formal political gains, Wilkite radicalism was a failure: The movement had foundered by 1771 on the rocks of disunity and division, and its "test case," the 1774 election, brought "negligible" gains outside the metropolis, where out of the ten metropolitan seats contested by radicals, only seven were won.[55] Such an assessment,

[54] Burgh, *Political Disquisitions,* i, 37–88; *Reflexions on the Representation in Parliament* (London, 1766), 15; John Cartwright, *Take Your Choice!* (London, 1776). For a fuller account of the radical reform platforms see John Cannon, *Parliamentary Reform, 1642–1832* (Cambridge, 1972), 72–97.
[55] Ian Christie, *Wilkes, Wyvill and Reform* (London, 1962), 60–72; Cannon, *Parliamentary Reform,* 61.

Table 4.1. *Petitions for parliamentary reform, 1739–85*[a]

Years	Counties	Boroughs	Total
1739–41	11	22	33
1756	16	19	35
1769	18	12	30
1779/80	26	11	37
1782/3	12	23	35
1785	2	10	12

[a]England and Wales only. Excludes petitions over the American war which mention parliamentary reform.
Source: John Cannon, *Parliamentary Reform 1642–1832* (Cambridge, 1972), 63, 77, 88, 92; Chapter 3.

however, is anachronistic, not least because it imagines the Hanoverian political system as but an embryonic version of an idealized twentieth-century liberal democracy – that is, a neutral arena in which interest groups competed on an equal basis for political influence – rather than an oligarchic, aristocratic state structured to keep all truly ''competing'' interests marginalized from the avenues of power. From the latter point of view, radicalism between the Seven Years' and American wars was remarkably successful; from the point of view of eighteenth-century standards of extra-parliamentary activism and achievement, moderately so. Twelve boroughs and eighteen counties participated in the petitioning movement initiated and partially organized by the SSBR to protest the Middlesex election and to demand the dissolution of Parliament, a number which, given its lukewarm support from the parliamentary opposition (whose members could not hide their disdain for popular appeals in general and for City radicals in particular), compares respectably with earlier and later campaigns (Table 4.1). Moreover, the conventional accounts of the 1774 election have tended to underplay radical performance. Radical sympathies precipitated opposition victories in Bristol, Bedford, Coventry, Rochester, Dover and Middlesex; produced heated contests, usually for the first time in two decades or more, in Newcastle, Cambridge, Portsmouth and Warwickshire; and engineered impressive disruptions of vested interests in those constituencies where the radicals lost, such as at Worcester and Surrey. Elsewhere, the anti-venality, independence idiom of dissidence worked to orchestrate the smooth return of sitting members or stave off a contest, as in Liverpool, Norwich, Ipswich and Devizes.[56] At the same time, the radical platform codified by the SSBR helped institute a wider use of electoral oaths for candidates in provincial towns and energized grass-roots politicking by enlisting parish clubs and guilds as well as clubs and trade societies in the cause, as in Cambridge, Norwich, Bristol, Worcester and Newcastle.[57] Equally important, radical polemics against malfeasant political institutions at all levels and the Wilkite obsession with legal remedies encouraged disadvantaged freemen to take on magistrates for tampering with civic admissions or otherwise foreclosing opportunities for ordinary men's political participation.[58]

In the event, however, the relationship between Wilkite discursive initiatives and popular political change was more complicated than a review of electoral results or petitioning efforts can disclose. In attacking the institutions of oligarchy and not just the men who controlled them (as anti-Walpoleanists had done and Rockinghamites continued to do), Wilkite radicals transcended an important ideological limitation of their predecessors. Their arguments could be particularly effective in supporting habits of mind and practices that were at odds with the hegemonic ideological structures bolstering patrician power. For example, post-1760 radicalism amplified the anti-aristocratic rhetoric inherited from the 1750s in its critique of the political establishment to generate a straightforward attack on that class whose political power accrued solely from birth. Radical writers in the localities and metropolis continually condemned the overmighty powers of the aristocracy and its monopoly on land, rotten boroughs and sinecures that seemed to make the state but a "system of outdoor relief" for the nobility and its minions, and the conflation of social, legal and political privilege that the political system instituted and upheld – a line of attack that quite easily expanded into a critique of hierarchy itself.[59] Further, the patriotic ethos at the heart of Wilkite radicalism demanded that the

---

[56] Namier and Brooke, i, 76–80, 314–15, 317–18, 380–1, 383–4, 400–2, 425–7; Chapters 7 and 8; *Cumberland Pacquet,* Oct. 20, 27, 1774; *Salisbury Journal,* Oct. 10, 1774.

[57] Namier and Brooke, i, 219, 288–9; Peter Marshall, *Bristol and the American War of Independence* (Bristol, 1977), 19; Money, *Experience and Identity,* 105–6; Chapter 7.

[58] Money, *Experience and Identity,* 106; Kathleen Wilson, "The Rejection of Deference: Urban Political Culture in England, 1715–1785" (Ph.D. diss., Yale University, 1985), 336–8.

[59] W. D. Rubenstein, "The End of 'Old Corruption' in Britain, 1780–1860," *P & P,* no. 101 (1983), 71; Macaulay, *Observations; Political Register,* 2 (1768), 224–5; James Murray, *New Sermons to Asses* (London, 1771), and *Sermons to Ministers of State* (Newcastle, 1780); Joseph Towers, *Observations on Public Liberty, Patriotism, Ministerial Despotism, and National Grievances* (London, 1769).

"grandees," like all others in the state, be judged on the basis of public performance, on their success or failure in serving and adhering to the terms of the public trust. "There is a hobby horse in the world," a Norwich writer declared, "called Nobility by Right of birth; but this nobility, that consists in sound, is an empty and chimerical grandeur ... a nobleman who has no other merit than his rank gives him, has no Merit at all, and is just so much more despicable than a Commoner." This meritocratic ethos salvaged those patricians who distinguished themselves by their public spirit and actions, certainly, but it just as clearly condemned the culture of patrician entitlement. Hence, the opposition lords who protested various ministerial measures from the Middlesex election decision to the coercive policy against the Americans were toasted and celebrated at radical fêtes in London and provincial towns just as robustly as their allegedly rapacious brethren were reviled and lampooned. Like the king, aristocrats were trustees of "the people" and had to act for the good of the whole – a patriotic political imperative that allowed radicals to turn the "language of class" against their rulers.[60]

Secondly, the varied nature of Wilkite political activity and the extra-institutional contexts of its occurrence enriched the definitions of political subjectivity that had been current in opposition political culture since the Walpolean period – defining the political subject as one who monitored the state, protested bad laws, engaged in petitioning or instruction movements, debated policy in pubs and clubs, and participated in political demonstrations and festival – by marketing them to the lower as well as the middling classes. In addition to Wilkes's own widely publicized declarations that the liberty of "all the middling and inferior class of people" was at stake in his tribulations, Wilkite journalists stressed the capacity of the "meanest mechanic" to comprehend the issues at stake in the radical campaign, and accordingly attempted to create and stabilize an accessible language of politics capable of engaging plebeian grass-roots support. Not only was Wilkite propaganda tailored to meet all levels of its socially differentiated audience, but its producers combined the traditions of popular preaching and dog-

---

[60] *Norfolk Gazette,* June 2, 1764; *Liverpool General Advertiser,* Feb. 16, Oct. 12, 1770. See also *The Patricians, or a Candid Examination into the Merits of the Principal Speakers of the House of Lords* (London, 1773), which condemns an effeminate and greedy aristocracy by comparing it with the model of public performance provided by the virtuous Chatham – by birth a commoner whose political practices were taken to vindicate his patriotism. Cf. Colley, "Whose Nation?" 117.

gerel with the "transparent" discourses of history and constitutional
mythology in the effort to present clear enunciations of grievances and
point-by-point programs for reform that would be as clear to the artisan
and mechanic as to the professional man.[61] Admittedly, methods and
goals were not always compatible. The publication of such hallowed
but unhelpful documents as the Bill of Rights in newspapers and magazines so that *"every man* may see what are the principles of English
liberty, and judge how far the modern statutes of the legislature are
agreeable with those constitutional laws" was one such well-
intentioned attempt to enlighten "the people" by addressing them as
political subjects.[62] Probably more successful was the distinctly nondeferential political vernacular that Wilkite language and rhetoric
circulated. In Newcastle, Norwich, Bristol, Worcester, Salisbury, Sheffield, Leeds and elsewhere, radical demonstrations and debate articulated the irreverent and often virulent disdain toward ruling elites on
behalf of the "independent" members of the community that the radical diagnosis of political ills promoted.[63] In Durham, a town not renowned for radical extremism (although the county joined in the 1769
petitioning effort), the celebrations on Wilkes's release from King's
Bench prison in April 1770, carried out in defiance of their official
prohibition, expressed for its participants the requisite disregard for the
confluence of aristocratic, corporate and episcopal power which had
long dominated the politics and representation of the town. Not only
was an effigy of the MP Sir Thomas Clavering, emblazoned with the
words "The Man who was not ashamed to betray his Constituents,"
paraded through the town mounted backwards on a jackass, but the
mayor was derided as an "imbecile . . . and insignificant magistrate"
and "heartily laughed at and ridiculed in all sensible companies for his
Vanity and officiousness, in imagining it [*sic*] could stop the people,
by his silly authority, from publickly shewing their sentiments in favor
of *Liberty.*" Similarly, in Pontefract, where the householders' right to

<hr>

[61] Brewer, *Party Ideology,* 152–6; P. M. Ashraf, *The Life and Times of Thomas Spence*
    (Newcastle, 1983), 18–28; for language see Gerald Newman, *The Rise of English
    Nationalism* (New York, 1987), 127–45, and (for the 1790s) Olivia Smith, *The Politics
    of Language 1791–1819* (Oxford, 1984), 35–67. For examples see any issue of radical
    publications of the day, such as the *Middlesex Journal, The Freemen's Magazine* and
    Almon's *Political Register.*

[62] *Norfolk Chronicle,* Dec. 16, Aug. 5, 1769; *Salisbury Journal,* July 25, 1763; *Middlesex
    Journal,* April 11, 1769; April 26, 1770.

[63] See, e.g., *Farley's Bristol Journal,* March 11, 1769; *Worcester Journal,* Oct. 12, 1769;
    Norfolk Chronicle, Sept. 2, Nov. 25, 1769; *Newcastle Chronicle,* April 21, 1770;
    Salisbury Journal, April 23, 30, 1770.

vote had been steadily abrogated by the politics of oligarchy, the "sham Mayor" was lampooned by local Wilkites, and the town's representative, Viscount Galway, was called "Lord Poney" and compared to a "patagonian pig merchant."[64] And in Bradford, Yorkshire, an intricate tableau constructed as centerpiece to the celebrations on Wilkes's release equally captured the dominant sensibility toward the "Court":

> A large bonfire was erected by the riverside, facing a little Gothic building on the bridge . . . in the middle of the bonfire a gibbet was fixed, with several emblematic figures hung upon it, one with an inscription on its back – *No wooden shoes, Spital Jack,* nor *ten pence a day,* – on a second – *Dick Rugby, Chief of the Bloomsbury gang,* on a third, the figure of a Fox, with an inscription curiously laid on between his *brush* and *neck, unaccounted millions* – a fourth a Jack Boot, with a plaid spur and straps. The bridge was finely illuminated, and the little Gothic building, from . . . the arrangement of candles, made a pretty appearance; on the side towards the bonfire was printed in capitals – THE SCUM OF THE EARTH LET COURTIERS DESPISE / BUT THE SCUM TO THE TOP FOR EVER WILL RISE.

Above the building the cap of liberty, gilded with gold, was fixed upon a long pole.[65] Here the effigies of Lord Barrington (secretary at war and closely identified with recent colonial and domestic troubles over "standing armies"), the Duke of Bedford (whose faction was known for venal office-seeking), Lord Holland (who as paymaster-general in 1757–65 amassed a huge fortune) and Lord Bute (the incarnation of secret and foreign influence) personalized the various illegitimate forces that overwhelmed the political process and prevented it from serving the public interest. The building and the gilded cap of liberty signified the "Gothic liberties" of the subject, which had been steadily undermined by "court" influence for several centuries, according to radical historical mythology; and the slogan emblazoned across the side of the building (which reiterated Stephen Fox's curt dismissal of Wilkes's supporters) served as a dark, brilliant parody of elite disparagements of popular political aspirations and a threat about their ultimate consummation. Such a scenario demonstrated the facility with which "traditional" idioms of protest and their literary supplements expressed complex political themes (here, "resistance," accountability and the

---

[64] *Middlesex Journal,* April 24–6, 1770 (Clavering had voted for the burning of the Remonstrance of London); *Leeds Mercury,* Oct. 9, 1769 (Galway was elected only by official rejection of the householders' votes).

[65] *General Evening Post,* April 26–8, 1770.

political antagonism of the humble toward the great); at the same time, the representations of such demonstrations in the press endowed them with the status of local enactments of the national drama, namely, "the people's" patriotic resistance to "illegitimate" power, in which all social levels could participate.

Wilkite language and practice, then, incorporated traditional forms of political expression in a political vernacular capable of expressing social and political antagonisms. Above all, the rhetoric of resistance constructed a political community – "the people" – whose members were distinguished by their *political* positions and practices: by "independence" (that is, the refusal to be contained by political or economic clientage), public-spiritedness (the willingness to monitor and cashier the state and its rulers) and resistance (the ability to oppose the operations of "illegitimate" power in the polity). Thus it could sustain a heterogeneous constituency that encompassed some country gentlemen and laborers,[66] dissenters and Anglicans,[67] affluent professionals, middling traders, and artisans. The language of patriotic resistance was well suited to enmesh with the fluid social and political identities of George III's reign, when the older sections of the middle classes had not yet aligned themselves with the government, and newer interests who were unprecedently disdainful of the political habits and culture of entitlement maintained by the upper classes, as well as "respectable" artisans of the type who would overtake radicalism in the 1790s, were able to participate in the "bourgeois" aspirations to respectability, decency and order that radical ideals demanded.[68]

However, the ideological strategies of Wilkite radicalism could foreclose the potential of its heterogeneous appeal, containing and channeling its supporters' aspirations and activism and offering members of

---

[66] For which see Cannon, *Parliamentary Reform,* 54; Rude, *Wilkes and Liberty,* 90–104.

[67] Cf. Clark, *English Society,* and James Bradley, *Religion, Revolution and English Radicalism* (Cambridge, 1990), chaps. 4 and 5. Both argue for an exclusive or causal link between religious "heterodoxy" and radical politics. However, dissenters were as divided over radical politics as they were over toleration itself. Their distinctive contribution to radical ideology in this period was a virulent anti-clericalism that saw the established church and its representatives as but pillars in the edifice of Old Corruption: Barlow, *Citizenship and Conscience,* 182–4; Money, *Experience and Identity,* 190–1; independent divine Caleb Fleming's fulminations in NNRO, Neville Papers, MC7/349–5, CF to SN, March 6, 1772.

[68] See John Phillips, *Electoral Politics in Unreformed England* (Princeton, 1982); Frank O'Gorman, *Voters, Patrons and Parties* (Oxford, 1989), and Bradley, *Religion, Revolution and English Radicalism* for craftsmen and artisans' avid and sometimes majority participation in radical politics; Chapters 7 and 8. For their participation in the civic culture of respectability see Chapter 1.

the loosely defined middling classes the most potentially liberatory politics. Women and "effeminate" aristocrats were not the only ones whom the Wilkite injunctions to manly patriotism and public-spiritedness attempted to keep at bay. In the context of the rioting and destruction to property that Wilkite crowds could occasion, the celebration of the virtues of the middling sort in radical literature, the constant invocations to "independence," peace, decency and good order that served as both refrain and defense in sympathetic accounts of radical demonstrations, and the idiom of "manly patriotism" itself all performed the ideological work of, among other things, setting off the "respectable" middling radicals from the mass of urban workers and endowing the former with an authority and weight forever out of reach of the latter. Efforts to distinguish "the people" from the "mob" in Wilkite politicking, and still more the debates over structural political reform, resulted in the explicit closing of ranks on the basis of property and "independence" as well as gender against those who were to remain unenfranchised; literacy alone was no longer conceived of as sufficient for political subjectivity. Hence, although radical ideologues deployed expansive definitions of who composed "the people," and though the laboring poor were clearly conceived to be part of that desirable designation in that their need for fair wages and prices, and sometimes their right as taxpayers to vote, were argued for against the claims of those in power, most reformers – indeed, even such unrepentant democrats as John Cartwright – thought that safeguards had to be erected in a reformed polity to prevent contamination from below as well as above.[69] Dependent, disorderly (irrational) and – unlike the aristocracy – having precious little to lose for their country, the laboring classes' capacity for manly patriotism and respectability was highly suspect. Radicals' repudiation of crowd politics in the later 1770s and 1780s only made this implicit view manifest, opening the space for loyalist politics to mobilize the "mob" for its own ends.[70]

[69] The radical redefinition of "independence" as a matter of choice rather than property could liberate the tradesman but condemned laborers or persons in receipt of alms to exclusion from the political nation: See Brewer, "English Radicalism," 342–3. Price and Priestley were explicit in their desire to limit political rights to those educated or well-off enough to handle them; Cartwright, Burgh and Wilkes upheld the right of the laboring poor as taxpayers to vote, but expected only men of property to hold political office; and Thomas Hollis believed the lower classes should not even be taught to read or write. See my "A Dissident Legacy," 310–11; Dickinson, *Liberty and Property,* chap. 6; Neville, *Diary,* 14. James Murray's journalism is one exception.

[70] Of course, crowd politics was never the sole possession of the lower classes, but a

Wilkite radicalism, then, constructed a language of rights and liberties and a model of political activism – that of resistance – that could be used to express and embody political subjectivity and entitlement on the part of many different groups. At the same time, it offered the male middling sorts – those men with means and aspirations toward "independency" – the greatest opportunities for self-realization. The richness of the Wilkite agitation for supporting a variety of extraparliamentary political initiatives thus lay in the contradictions and ambivalences of its discourses: It deliberately undermined *British* identities and valorized xenophobic nationalism while refurbishing a nationalistic version of resistance theory for widespread appropriation; expanded the bases of popular politics to include women and the lower classes yet adopted ideological strategies and "bourgeois" and masculinist definitions of rights that simultaneously sought to contain and hierarchize that participation; and celebrated the portentous events of 1649 and 1688 to legitimize alterations in the form and substance of the post-Revolution state. In doing so it invented a tradition of English radicalism that influenced the idioms and practices of official and extra-parliamentary politics for the next half-century.[71] More immediately, its constructions of nation and citizenship would play a central role in the debates over the American war.

central part of comtemporaries' strategies of political marginalization was *representing* it as if it were.

[71] As is clear from the analysis of James Epstein (although Epstein himself does not acknowledge it): See "The Constitutional Idiom: Radical Reasoning, Rhetoric and Action in Early Nineteenth Century England," *Journal of Social History,* 23 (1990), 553–74.

5. The crisis: Radicalism, loyalism and the American war, 1774–1785

Our empire is split asunder! – The ties which united us are dissolved in brother's blood – and we can never again be the same people! . . . Are we so destitute of all public spirit, that the authors of our calamity sleep fearless of our justice?

Norfolk Chronicle, Sept. 7, 1776

Writing in 1834, William Cobbett remembered the period of the American war as one of extraordinary divisiveness, even in the sleepy rural Surrey community in which he lived as a boy. In the autumn of 1776 his father took him to a hop fair at Weyhill, where

a great company of hop-merchants and farmers were just sitting down to supper as the post arrived, bringing in the extraordinary Gazette which announced the victory [over the colonists at Long Island]. A hop-factor from London took the paper, placed his chair upon the table, and began to read in an audible voice. He was opposed, a dispute ensued, and my father retired taking me by the hand, to another apartment where we supped with about a dozen others of the same sentiments. Here Washington's health and success to the Americans were repeatedly toasted.[1]

Clearly, the war had wrought a degree of partisanship that disrupted customary patterns of sociability and commerce. Yet the war's profound impact on domestic political culture and the intensity of the rifts in the nation that it produced have only recently received serious attention.[2] The colonial conflict crystallized in England competing ideas

---

[1] *Autobiography of William Cobbett,* ed. William Reitzel (London, 1947), 13.
[2] Among those who have contributed to this rethinking are John Brewer, "English Radicalism in the Age of George III," in J. G. A. Pocock, ed., *Three British Revolutions* (Princeton, 1980), 323–67; John Money, *Experience and Identity: Birmingham and the West Midlands* (Montreal, 1977); Peter Marshall, *Bristol and the American War of*

about the nature of authority and liberty, the meaning of patriotism and the role of the people in the political process that galvanized the case for parliamentary reform. It also provoked a crisis in imperialism that forced most English people to rethink the benefits and dangers of empire, the possibilities of a libertarian or virtuous imperial polity and the nature of its links to the "nation." The years from 1775 to 1785 thus reveal the salience of radical constructions of power in the midst of international conflict while highlighting the contradictions within oppositionist patriotism that forced its reconfiguration.

I. PATRIOTS' DILEMMA: THE WAR FOR AMERICA

A look at the extent and nature of the divisions provoked by the war and the distinctive forms they took is indispensable to the following discussion. The rival petitions and addresses sent by twelve English counties and forty-seven boroughs and towns in 1775–6 embodied the hostilities in crystalline fashion.[3] James Bradley has counted close to 45,000 signatures on these demonstrations of local opinion, and although the loyal addresses to the king supporting coercion outnumbered

---

Independence (Bristol, 1977); John Phillips, *Electoral Behavior in Unreformed England* (Princeton, 1982), and "Popular Politics in Unreformed England," *JMH*, 52 (1980), 599–625; Wilson, "The Rejection of Deference: Urban Political Culture in England, 1715–1785" (Ph.D. diss., Yale University, 1985), chap. 4; John Sainsbury, *Disaffected Patriots: London Supporters of Revolutionary America* (Montreal, 1987); James Bradley, *Popular Politics and the American Revolution* (Macon, Ga., 1986); and Linda Colley, *Britons: Forging the Nation* (New Haven, 1992), 132–46.

[3] "Addresses" is used here to refer to the representations to the King or Parliament supporting coercive measures in America; "petitions," to those pressing for conciliation or an end to the war. The counties and boroughs which sent petitions are as follows:

1766: Birmingham, Bradford (Wilts.), Bristol (2), Chippenham (Wilts.), Coventry, Dudley, Frome, Halifax, Lancaster, Leeds, Leicester, Liverpool, London, Macclesfield, Manchester, Minehead, Newcastle upon Tyne, Nottingham, Sheffield, Stourbridge, Taunton, Witney, Wolverhampton, Worcester.

1775 (Jan.–March): Staffordshire; Birmingham, Bridport, Bristol(2), Dudley, Huddersfield, Leeds, Liverpool, London (2), Manchester, Newcastle under Lyme, Norwich, Nottingham, Whitehaven, Wolverhampton.

1775–6 (July–March): Berkshire, Cumberland, Hampshire, Lancashire, Middlesex, Staffordshire, Westmorland; Abingdon, Bolton, *Bradford (Wilts.), Bridgwater, Bristol, Cambridge, Carlisle, Colchester, Coventry, Halifax, Leeds, London (2), Lymington, Newcastle upon Tyne, Nottingham, Poole, Southampton, Southwark, Taunton, *Trowbridge, Wallingford, *Warminster, *Westbury, Worcester, Yarmouth. (The 4 towns marked by an asterisk sent one petition among them.)

1778: Norfolk; Bristol, London, Newcastle upon Tyne.

1782: Bristol, York.

Table 5.1. *Conciliatory or anti-war petitions, 1766–82*

Issue	Counties	Boroughs	Petitions
Repeal of Stamp Act	0	24	25
Anti-war petitions	8	35	51

Note: Several boroughs and counties sent more than one petition. For petitioning towns and counties, see note 3.
Sources: LEP; Middlesex Journal; Newcastle Chronicle; Farley's Bristol Journal, Leeds Mercury; Cumberland Pacquet; Gentleman's Magazine; Annual Register; Parl. Hist., xvi, 133–6; Bradley, *Popular Politics,* 44, 64–9.

the petitions pressing for peace and reconciliation (Table 5.1), the majority of total signatories favored peaceful concessions rather than coercive measures. In important provincial towns like Bristol, Coventry, Halifax, Leeds, Newcastle upon Tyne, Nottingham, Worcester, Colchester, Taunton, Yarmouth and Southampton, the majority of signers upheld the colonists' rights against the British government's claims.[4] The animosities provoked by these rival efforts to mobilize public opinion were fierce, and the provincial press was filled with the allegations and slurs of contending parties. Passions were so aroused on both sides by the autumn of 1775 in Kendal, Birmingham, York and Salisbury that neither petitions nor addresses could be sent, despite the efforts of organizers on both sides.[5] In Manchester, where merchants had petitioned Parliament against the Coercive Acts in January 1775, the loyal address and raising of £1,280 to support the military effort in America after war was declared stimulated outraged efforts to raise an anti-administration petition, though they never came to fruition. For this, Richard Townley, one of the organizers of the Lancashire conciliatory petition, blamed the obstructionist tactics of the Manchester magistrates, who had called the 4,000 county petitioners for peace ''rebels to King and Country.''[6] Rival groups also fought over the use of civic

---

[4] See, e.g., *Farley's Bristol Journal,* Sept. 30, Oct. 14, 21, 1775; *Leeds Mercury,* Oct. 31, Nov. 7, 1775; *Salisbury Journal,* Nov. 6, 1775. For numbers of signatories and lists of competing petitions and addresses in 1775 see Bradley, *Popular Politics,* 65–9, 137.

[5] *Cumberland Pacquet,* Oct. 5, Nov. 2, 16, 1775; *Salisbury Journal,* Oct. 23, 1775; *Leeds Mercury,* Nov. 7, 1775; *York Courant,* Oct. 31, Nov. 7, 14, 1775; Money, *Experience and Identity,* 199–201. Birmingham sent rival petitions in Jan. 1775: B. D. Bargar, ''Matthew Boulton and the Birmingham Petition of 1775,'' *WMQ,* 3rd ser., 13 (1956), 27–8.

[6] *Manchester Mercury,* Sept. 12, Nov. 2, 14, 1775; Peter Marshall, ''Manchester and

and public venues from which to organize their missives. In Worcester Sir Watkin Lewes and several other leading residents turned Tom's Coffee House into a makeshift town hall in order to draft the petition for conciliation against the Corporation's address; rival merchant groups in Bristol tussled over first use of the Guildhall to formulate their contending petitions (the anti-war contingent, headed by Samuel Brailsford, John Fisher Weare and Richard Champion, won).[7] Obviously, the war from its inception "inflamed the spirit of contest and party" in the localities.[8]

Petitions were just one index of domestic antagonisms in 1775–6. Subscriptions also exhibited (quite intentionally) political divisions over the colonial crisis. Soon after the news of Lexington and Concord reached England in June 1775, John Horne Tooke, acting for the Constitutional Society, advertised in several London newspapers the start of a subscription for the relief of the "widows, orphans and aged parents of our beloved American Fellow Subjects," who, "FAITHFUL to the character of Englishmen, preferring Death to Slavery, were, for that Reason only, inhumanly murdered by the KING'S troops." This tactic resulted in Tooke's prosecution by the government for seditious libel;[9] but it also inspired loyalists in provincial towns like York, Liverpool, Birmingham, Manchester, Newcastle and Bristol to begin the first of several subscription drives to defray the costs of raising troops or supporting their widows and orphans at home.[10] Two years later anti-war activists in the metropolis began a nationwide subscription for the support of American prisoners which by late January had exceeded, with the help of subscribers in Bristol, Nottingham, Birmingham and Newcastle, £4,600.[11] The divisions reproduced in the petitions and subscriptions was also reflected in local and parliamentary elections: Gov-

the American Revolution," *Bulletin of the John Rylands University Library of Manchester,* 62 (1979), 172–3; *Liverpool General Advertiser,* Sept. 22, Nov. 17, 1775. By 1778 Manchester had raised £8,075 and 1,082 men to fight in America: W. E. Axon, *Annals of Manchester* (Manchester, 1886), 105.

[7] *Aris's Birmingham Gazette,* Oct. 30, 1775; *Farley's Bristol Journal,* Sept. 23, 30, 1775.
[8] HW to Sir Thomas Mann, Oct. 10, 1775, *Selected Letters of Horace Walpole,* ed. W. L. Lewis (New Haven, 1973), 202.
[9] Sainsbury, *Disaffected Patriots,* 89–90; *Public Advertiser,* June 9, 1775.
[10] *York Courant,* Nov. 14, 1775; *Liverpool General Advertiser,* Nov. 10, 1775; *Bonner and Middleton's Bristol Journal,* Dec. 23, 1775.
[11] *Farley's Bristol Journal,* Jan. 10, Feb. 14, 1778; *Aris's Birmingham Gazette,* Jan. 19, 1778; *Newcastle Chronicle,* Jan. 17, Feb. 7, 1778; Roger H. E. Wells, *Riot and Political Disaffection in Nottinghamshire in the Age of Revolutions* (Nottingham University Center for Local History Occasional Papers, 2, 1983), 4. For London see Sainsbury, *Disaffected Patriots,* 142.

ernment actions in America were issues in the 1774, 1780 and 1784 parliamentary elections in a number of urban constituencies, including Bristol, Liverpool, York, Newcastle, Norwich and Salisbury, and local politics was also seriously torn by the issues raised by the American crisis for several years.[12]

Clearly, anti-war sentiment circulated in towns and communities throughout the nation where (given the steady incorporation of colonists' grievances into oppositionist celebrations, petitions and propaganda since the Stamp Act) military hostilities against the Americans were easily interpreted as the latest instance of the ''ministerial'' assault on empire and liberty.[13] But once hostilities had broken out in 1775, the London and provincial press propagated competing views of the war with singular fervor.[14] John Robinson, North's secretary to the Treasury, hired authors with such considerable polemical talents as Samuel Johnson, John Shebbeare, James Macpherson, Sir John Dalrymple, William Knox and Israel Mauduit to champion in print government actions and denigrate the principles and behavior of the recalcitrant colonists, and clergymen like Josiah Tucker and John Wesley provided free if not unsolicited missives for the cause.[15] Many of these tracts were distributed gratis by mail throughout the nation.[16] The American Department and secretaries of state, in addition, censored, withheld and otherwise creatively shaped the ''official'' version of events across the Atlantic, as well as the domestic response to them,

---

[12] *Middlesex Journal,* Dec. 23, 1773; *Bristol Gazette and Public Advertiser,* Oct. 27, 1774; *The Bristol Contest* (Bristol, 1781); *A Collection of Papers During the Contest for Representatives in Parliament for the Borough of Liverpool* (Liverpool, 1780); *Salisbury Journal,* June 9, 1780; Chapters 7 and 8.

[13] See P. D. G. Thomas, *British Politics and the Stamp Act Crisis: The First Phase of the American Revolution* (Oxford, 1975); *Letters of Junius,* ed. John Cannon (London, 1978), 29–30, 310–11, 412–13, 432–3; *Farley's Bristol Journal,* March 11, July 22, Oct. 21, 1769; *Liverpool General Advertiser,* June 22, Oct. 12, 1770; *Cumberland Pacquet,* Nov. 27, 1774; John Sainsbury, ''The Pro-Americans of London, 1769–1782,'' *WMQ,* 3rd ser., 35 (1978), 420.

[14] The war stimulated a major advance in press coverage on several fronts: See Michael Crump, *Searching the Eighteenth Century* (London, 1984); Solomon Lutnick, *The American Revolution and the British Press, 1775–1783* (New York, 1967); Thomas R. Adams, *The American Controversy: A Bibliographic Study of the British Pamphlets About American Disputes,* 2 vols. (Providence, 1980); Henry Ippel, ''British Sermons and the American Revolution,'' *Journal of Religious History,* 12 (1982), 197–8.

[15] BL, Add. MS 48,803, William Strahan's Quarto Ledger, 1768–85, iv, passim; Lutnick, *British Press,* 18–20.

[16] As in Birmingham, Bristol, Manchester and Newcastle: Money, *Experience and Identity,* 204; *Farley's Bristol Journal,* Oct. 16, 23, 30, 1775; *Manchester Mercury,* Oct. 24, 1775; *Newcastle Journal,* Oct. 28, 1775.

that were made available for home consumption through the *London Gazette*.[17] The radical and anti-war press retaliated with a campaign of its own which, if not so centrally organized, strove to match that of the government in volume and effectiveness. Familiar with the administration's tricks – Almon's *London Evening Post* ran biographical sketches of the ''mercenary band of *hired* writers, or rather assassins, whom Ministers keep in pay to daily whitewash their proceedings'' – oppositionist writers and printers drew on a decade of experience to produce a sea of anti-war propaganda that washed up on the farthest shores of the kingdom.[18] Copies of anti-war broadsides and tracts were priced to aid mass distribution, marketed as available for 1*s.* 6*d.* to £1. 7*s.* ''per one hundred,'' and the tracts and essays of Arthur Lee, Burke, Richard Brinsley Sheridan, Charles James Fox, Almon and Catharine Macaulay (not to mention Benjamin Franklin and Tom Paine) were excerpted in the newspaper press and monthly magazines.[19] Several new weeklies were founded in the straightforward effort to both promote and profit from English support for the colonists, including Sheridan's oppositionist *Englishman,* the virulently republican *The Crisis* (which circulated in the provinces before it was suppressed by authorities – Plate 10) and the *Newcastle Weekly Magazine*.[20]

[17] Hence the *Gazette* printed the coercive rather than conciliatory petitions: Lutnick, *British Press,* 20–2; Richard Alstyne, ''Europe, the Rockingham Whigs, and the War for American Independence,'' *Huntington Library Quarterly,* 25 (1961), 10–11; Bradley, *Popular Politics,* 108–10. Bradley finds deep significance in the *Gazette*'s suppression of conciliatory petitions, but in fact it was a fairly standard practice of ministries after Walpole to ignore expressions of organized dissidence in their own propaganda. More innovative was loyalists' use of propaganda geared to a popular audience: See, e.g., *Four Excellent New Songs* (Newcastle, 1776), one of which had the memorable refrain ''These wretched jail-birds, pests of our native land / We sent abroad when by law they shou'd been hanged.''

[18] *LEP,* Oct. 14, 1778; see also Sept. 8–10, 1776; *Liverpool General Advertiser,* Nov. 20, 23, 1777. The pro- and anti-war pamphlets were available in the eighteenth century at circulating libraries, book clubs and taverns as well as from booksellers: See Money, *Experience and Identity,* 142–3; Thomas Bewick, *A Memoir,* ed. Iain Bain (Oxford, 1979), 93–7.

[19] Sainsbury, *Disaffected Patriots,* 11–13, 35–9; Colin Bonwick, *English Radicals and the American Revolution* (Chapel Hill, 1977), 87–8; Lutnick, *British Press,* 14–20, 42–6; *Gentlemen's Magazine,* 45–6 (1775–6), passim. Lee's *Appeal to the Justice and Interests of the People of Great Britain* (London, 1775), Price's *Observations on the Nature of Civil Liberty* (London, 1776) and Caleb Evans's *Letter to the Rev. Mr. John Wesley* (Bristol, 1776), as well as lesser-known tracts such as *The Voice of God . . . or Serious Thoughts on the Present Crisis* (London, 1775), were among those to be distributed in this manner; Tom Paine's *Common Sense* was published in weekly installments of the *Newcastle Weekly Magazine* (see note 20).

[20] Lutnik, *British Press,* 15–16; *The Crisis,* nos. 1–91 (Jan. 20, 1775 – Oct. 12, 1776); for provincial distribution see TWA, 840/178, 186, Maude-Ogden MSS. The *Newcastle Weekly Magazine,* published by ''a Society of Gentlemen,'' was printed by T.

10. *The Burning of the CRISIS* (1776). Magistrates burn a copy of the radical republican weekly as one citizen pours the contents of a chamberpot on their heads. Courtesy of the Library of Congress.

What we can see, then, is a propaganda war under way between opposers and supporters of government policy in America. Loyalist prints, papers, sermons and songs echoed the addresses in attacking the opponents of the war as fanatical or disloyal republicans who allied themselves with the rebels in order to subvert legally constituted authority throughout the land – "patrons of sedition," as the Coventry addressers asserted, who encouraged a rebellion "the most unnatural, because excited and fomented by the false representations and encouragement of a desperate domestic faction."[21] Oppositionist voices, both moderate and radical, indicted both the ministry and its supporters in Britain in a "Butean" conspiracy to overthrow legal authority, crush colonial and domestic liberties through judicial subversion and military

Robson and ran weekly from July 31, 1776 to Dec. 27, 1776. It is available at the British Library. See also the *Nottingham Gazette*, which was "run . . . on the principle of the American Revolution": Wells, *Riot and Political Disaffection*, 5.
[21] Published in *Aris's Birmingham Gazette*, Oct. 2, 1775; the content of opposition to the war is analyzed below.

coercion, introduce popery and despotism throughout the empire, pillage the nation's trade and industry, and impoverish the lower orders by conscripting family breadwinners into the cause of "murdering" American citizens. Such bitter political divisions were represented in the street culture of the period, which in this context became a kind of domestic battleground, mirroring the fissures within the nation at large. Royal anniversary days like the king's and queen's birthdays and accession and coronation days served as natural stimulants to loyalist enthusiasm, with military reviews of volunteer regiments and emotive patriotic music imbuing the processions, illuminations and bonfires with appropriate nationalist sentiment.[22] Some of the celebrations for British victories over the colonists were punctuated by the public tarring, feathering and burning of the effigies of American leaders. For example, the colonists' defeats on Long Island and in New York in the autumn of 1776, the first major British successes in the war, were frenetically acknowledged in Bristol, Halifax, Manchester, Liverpool, Leeds and York, and effigies of Washington, Adams, Hancock and Arthur Lee were burned by loyalist crowds. Although in some towns the strength of anti-war sentiment caused the loyalists to be more circumspect in their observances, in others failure to illuminate on these occasions led to smashed windows and sometimes smashed heads, as at the accession-day celebrations in Hull in 1776, the king's birthday celebrations in Nottingham in 1780 and the Bristol celebrations for Rodney's victory at Gibraltar earlier the same year.[23]

The refusal of anti-war sympathizers in many towns to participate in the rites of state loyalty led to charges of unpatriotic and even treasonable conduct. In Bristol, only "part of the Corporation and most of the town" observed the fast in December 1776; and radicals' consistent refusal to observe the king's birthday was held up as incontrovertible proof that local Whigs were "implacable enemies both to King and

---

[22] *Cumberland Pacquet,* June 2, 9, 1778; June 8, Sept. 28, Oct. 26, 1779; *Manchester Mercury,* June 11, 1776; June 8, 1779; June 6, 1780; see also Peter Marshall, "Manchester," 176–8.

[23] *York Courant,* Oct. 22, Nov. 12, 1776; John Latimer, *The Annals of Bristol in the Eighteenth Century* (Bristol, 1893), 392; *Farley's Bristol Journal,* Oct. 12, 1776; *Leeds Mercury,* Oct. 22, Nov. 12, 1776; *Records of the City of Leicester,* ed. G. A. Chimney, 7 vols. (Leicester, 1965), v, 240; *Salisbury Journal,* Feb. 21, March 4, 13, 1780. For riots see *Leeds Mercury,* Nov. 5, 1776; Wells, *Riot and Political Disaffection,* 4; *Farley's Bristol Journal,* March 4, June 17, 1780. In Bristol, men who toasted Washington's success were attacked, and in Nottingham, the news of Cornwallis's final surrender at Yorktown ended in fistfights in the streets and inns.

Constitution.''[24] Radical nonobservance of national anniversaries was, in part, indicative of a growing antipathy to the traditional fanfare of state loyalty and disenchantment with the political calendar as a means of mobilizing popular support. The official political calendar, geared to underline the social and political leadership of elites, was increasingly recognized as an essentially conservative and corrupting force. As early as 1769, radical supporters had decried the use of illuminations at state functions as hurting the radical cause; three years later, the number of spectators ''of all ranks'' who turned out to view the government military review in London, despite recent confrontations between the people and troops there, was considered by one writer to be proof that the English people were ''ripe for Ruin'' and ''fit Subjects for Slavery'':

> Every person will be ready to admit, that the Man who can take a pleasure at gaping at the gallows, on which he must be *hanged,* must be out of his Sense; and yet, the People, who can with pleasure look upon those Military Shackles, which are forged to Enslave them, are certainly as mad.[25]

During the American war, not only radicals but all anti-war adherents, faced with loyalist demonstrations, were forced to choose between participating in, ignoring or heaping disregard and ridicule on the rites of state loyalty. In London, for example, the proclamation of war with America was read at the Royal Exchange ''with all the circumstances of indignity the Lord Maior [Wilkes] could throw on it, the City Man and other officers as usual not being allowed to attend.''[26] Similarly, the anti-war press was filled with lampoons and lambastings against the ''hypocritical'' fast days ordered by a government determined to ''shed the blood of loyal and lawful citizens'' and a church ''fond of blood and desolation.''[27] What observance there was of the calendar by anti-war proponents was dedicated to denouncing government and national political corruption, an activity in which both dissenting and Anglican clergymen participated with avidity. The Baptist minister

[24] *Farley's Bristol Journal,* Dec. 14, 1776; *The Bristol Contest,* 10; *Norfolk Chronicle,* Apr. 7, 1781; *Cumberland Pacquet,* Feb. 23, 1779.

[25] NNRO, Neville MSS, MC7/496, Nov. 11, 1769; *Middlesex Journal,* Sept. 15, 1772. See also Jean Paul Marat, *The Chains of Slavery* (London, 1774); Michel Foucault, *Discipline and Punish,* trans. Alan Bass (New York, 1975); and John Brewer, ''Theatre and Counter-Theatre in Georgian Politics: The Mock Elections at Garret,'' *Radical History Review,* 22 (1979–80), 35–7.

[26] *Journal of Samuel Curwen, American Loyalist,* ed. Andrew Oliver, 2 vols. (Cambridge, 1972), i, 61n. Wilkes was lord mayor in September 1775.

[27] *LEP,* Feb. 15, 1779; *The Fast Day: A Lambeth Eclogue* (London, 1780); [Samuel Parr], *A Discourse on the Late Fast . . .* (London, 1781).

Rees David of Norwich as well as Anglican divines such as Richard
Watson and William Crowe utilized their pulpits to promulgate sympathy for the colonists' position or amplify anger toward the government.[28] Lesser lights did so too: The Presbyterian minister the Reverend
John Carmichael preached before a company of militia in Lancaster on
the king's birthday that a "self-defensive war is Lawful"; and in Norwich Cathedral the Reverend Mr. Peele admonished the incoming
mayor of Norwich, Roger Kerrison, a staunch supporter of the war,
that "the origin, design and object of all good government was the
security and happiness of the people, with which absolute, uncontroul-
able power, from whence there was no appeal, was incompatible."
Certainly the clergy as a group stood firmly on the side of authority
during the war; but there were enough disaffected individuals to articulate the case for the other side, and on national anniversaries they,
too, had a captive audience and eager publicists.[29]

The nation was polarized over the American war as it had been only
infrequently, if ever, before in the century. How can we account for
the strength and virulence of these divisions? Some historians have seen
in the domestic antagonisms of the war years a return to and clarifi-
cation of older party loyalties, symbolized by the return of Tory backbenchers to support of the government. These country gentlemen, many
of whom had voted against the administrations of the 1760s over the
"country" issues of the cider tax, general warrants and the Middlesex
election, consistently displayed a "mindless authoritarianism . . . in the
face of the American challenge," upholding nonresistance to "properly
constituted authority."[30] And certainly the war invoked historical memories that supported a widespread perception of the reemergence of
older partisan loyalties and communities. Contemporaries on *both* sides
now chose to describe current divisions in terms of seventeenth-century
polarities: Tories saw in the colonists' repudiation of British authority
and in domestic opposition to government measures the continuing Pu-

[28] Rees David, *The Hypocritical Fast, with Its Design and Consequences* (Norwich,
1781); Richard Watson, *The Principles of the Revolution Vindicated* (Cambridge,
1776); William Crowe, *A Sermon Preached to the University of Oxford . . . 5
November 1781* (Oxford, 1781), ordered to be reprinted in SCI, *Minutes,* Feb–Aug.
1782.
[29] John Carmichael, *A Self-Defensive War Lawful* (Lancaster, 1775); *Norfolk Chronicle,*
June 20, 1778. Cf. Paul Langford, "The English Clergy and the American Revolution," in E. Hellmuth, ed., *The Transformation of Political Culture in Late Eighteenth
Century Germany and England* (Oxford, 1990), 275–308.
[30] Paul Langford, "Old Whigs, Old Tories and the American Revolution," *Journal of
Imperial and Commonwealth History,* 8 (1979), 106–30, 127, 125.

ritan hostility to Anglican and royal power, and called for the defense of church and king. Hence the American merchant and radical Bristol MP Henry Cruger was maligned by his opponents as a "foreigner" and "regicide" in the propaganda issued during the 1780 and 1781 parliamentary elections, and likened to Cromwell, who had also worked to subvert established government and religion for his own selfish designs.[31] The anti-war proponents, following the Wilkite lead of the previous decade, were equally clear that the colonists were acting on the patriotic Revolution principles of resistance in their stand against illegitimate British measures, exuding a manly patriotism against which the government's recourse to force appeared cowardly and tyrannical. Surely "*true* WHIGS and lovers of their country cannot be *passive* at this critical juncture, and let destruction come on them and their posterity," a Newcastle observer asserted. The Lords' Protest of 1775 similarly insisted that "we cannot look upon our fellow subjects in America in any other light but as *freemen driven to resistance by acts of oppression and violence.*"[32]

However, a "party" interpretation of the domestic impact of colonial crisis, like recourse to the notion of a "Tory resurgence," may obscure more than illumine the depth and extent of the divisions produced by the war.[33] The complexities and sheer novelty of waging a war against the colonies, and the fractious and contradictory demands it placed upon the claims of patriotism and citizenship, ensured that this would be so. First, and most simply, although the pro-war forces were strong for much of the war, both their fortunes and those of their opponents fluctuated with the war's progress and consequences: The ebb and flow

---

[31] *London Gazette,* Oct. 17, Nov. 4, 1775; *Farley's Bristol Journal,* Jan. 17, 24, 31, 1778; Aug. 19, 26, Sept. 2, 1780; Jan. 27, March 3, 1781; *The Bristol Contest,* passim.

[32] *Newcastle Journal,* Oct. 7, 1775; *Parl. Hist.,* xviii (1774–6), 726–7. See also *LEP,* Jan. 6–9, Feb. 6–8, April 2–4, 1776; *Leeds Mercury,* Sept. 26, 1775; *Liverpool General Advertiser,* Nov. 17, 1775.

[33] For the arguments for a "Tory resurgence" in George III's reign see Langford, "Old Whigs, Old Tories"; Paul Lucas, "A Collective Biography of the Students and Barristers of Lincoln's Inn, 1680–1804," *JMH,* 46 (1974), 238–9; Linda Colley, "The Apotheosis of George III: Loyalty, Royalty and the British Nation, 1760–1832," *P & P,* no. 102 (1984), 94–129; J. C. D. Clark, *English Society,* 199–257; James Bradley, "The Anglican Pulpit, the Social Order and the Resurgence of Toryism During the American Revolution," *Albion,* 21 (1989), 361–88. Although there was a revitalization of a recognizably "Tory" party identity and a trend toward the consolidation of both the personnel and institutions of the establishment for church and king in 1775–6, such alignments had less to do with party pedigree (prior Whigs and Tories were part of the latter movement) than with a construction of loyalism that secured the consolidation of the forces of conservatism behind the Crown.

of British military success, economic distress, insurrectionary and invasion scares in 1777–9, the entry of the Bourbon powers into the fray
and the violence of the press gangs all directly impinged upon public
perceptions of the conflict. Equally important, neither parliamentary nor
extra-parliamentary, loyalist nor oppositionist opinion was monolithic
or unified. "Tory," or conservative, opinion within and without doors
was probably most coherent, upholding the sovereignty of Parliament
and the necessity of colonial subordination as the central plank of imperial government, although after Burgoyne's surrender at Saratoga in
1777 even this high road began to sink in the mire of doubt and dis-
piritedness that the entry of France and Spain into the war only partially
alleviated. In the event, many Tory MPs who supported North on
America opposed him on other domestic issues; and conservative anti-
imperialists like Josiah Tucker opposed government attempts to retain
the colonies. The parliamentary opposition fared worse. The Chathamites' outright resistance to the idea of American independence was
a clear impediment to fashioning a coherent anti-ministerial position.
The Rockingham Whigs were hopelessly divided and intermittently de-
pressed until Cornwallis's surrender at Yorktown in 1781, exhausted
from trying to reconcile their traditional "country" opposition to the
growing influence of the Crown, their support of the Declaratory Act,
and the colonists' claim that the king rather than Parliament was sovereign in the colonies. The parliamentary opposition was thus incapable
of leading the anti-war cause in the nation, despite the aid of opposition
members like Burke in penning anti-war petitions or the support for
the radical reading of the crisis by men of standing in the party like
the earls of Abingdon and Effingham and the Duke of Richmond.[34]
Radical sympathizers within and without doors were ironically the most
successful in constructing the political case for opposition to government actions, which could be plausibly portrayed as the result not only
of the pernicious effects of secret influence but also of the corruption
of a Parliament that no longer represented the will of the people. And
though opposition to the war did not necessarily translate into a commitment to radical principles (just as support for it did not mean lack

[34] See Paul Langford, "The Rockingham Whigs and America," in Anne Whiteman, J.
S. Bromley and P. G. M. Dickson, eds., *Statesmen, Scholars and Merchants: Essays
in Eighteenth-Century History* (Oxford, 1973), 135–52; and Alstyne, "Europe, Rockingham Whigs and the War," 3–4, 22–4; for propaganda efforts of Burke, Abingdon
and Richmond see *Correspondence of Edmund Burke,* ed. Thomas Copeland, 10 vols.
(Cambridge, 1958–78), iii, 223–35; *Thoughts on the Letter of Edmund Burke, Esq. to
the Sheriffs of Bristol, on the Affairs of America* (Oxford, 1777).

of sympathy with the colonists' dilemma), it did mean opposition to the ministry, and the radical potential of this position increased as the war dragged on.

The war, then, produced political positions that were contingent and shifting, not automatically amenable to containment by party identities and allegiances. Anti-war writers and activists, many of whom had been influenced by radical arguments about the consequences of corruption in the body politic, played on this fact, insisting that the issues were ones connected not only with the legitimacy of the colonists' or government's claims but also with the contested location and limits of sovereignty in the state and the now fraught relationship between libertarian and imperialist principles. In the stream of petitions protesting government measures that poured in to the throne in 1775–8, for example, three claims stand out: first, that illegitimate government measures were threatening the liberty, prosperity and existence of the British empire; second, that these measures augured an increase in corruption of British political institutions equally dangerous to subjects at home and abroad; and third, that some limits must be made on Parliament's claims to absolute sovereignty. The diagnosis of the crisis offered by 2,700 freeholders in Cumberland touched all three points while demonstrating the continuing influence of the ''secret influence'' theories constructed by Wilkite radicals:

> We believe the Americans have been forced into the present unhappy contest by the new and arbitrary system of government which your Majesty's Ministers have of late years adopted; and by the violation of those rights which they have enjoyed, and exercised to the mutual benefit of every part of the empire, from the commencement of their establishment to the fatal period of one thousand seven hundred and sixty three, which first gave occasion to these disturbances.[35]

The freemen and residents of Newcastle and the electors of Middlesex and Southampton agreed, arguing that the colonists' resistance was based on ''natural'' as well as chartered or prescriptive rights. The inhabitants of Abingdon, Yarmouth and Stafford decried the shedding of the blood of fellow subjects in ''an unnatural and cruel conflict of civil war'' and warned of the inevitability of oppression's spreading from one part of His Majesty's dominions to another.[36] The question

[35] *LEP,* Feb. 1–3, 1776.
[36] Middlesex: PRO, HO/55/13/2; Newcastle: PRO, HO 55/28/19; *LEP,* Nov. 18–21, 1775; *Norwich Mercury,* Dec. 2, 1775; *LEP,* Dec. 12–14, 1775; (all repr. in Bradley, *Popular Politics,* 230–1, 224–5, 220–1, 232–3).

of the limits of parliamentary sovereignty was raised repeatedly. The Wallingford petitioners demanded that Parliament "permanently establish the limits of that subordination which it is no less their desire than their interest and duty to preserve"; the pro-Americans at Nottingham were willing to defend "only the just useful and practicable rights of the English legislature"; and the freeholders of Berkshire could "never be brought to imagine that the true remedy for such disorders consists in an attack on all other rights, and an attempt to drive the people either to unconditional submission or absolute despair."[37]

Moreover, even from these early stages many English observers were aware that the issues stemming from the war were connected with the mercantilist vision of empire itself. Some of the most forceful anti-war arguments were those which emphasized the commercial and imperial, as well as libertarian, reasons for opposing the war. The Common Council of London's "Letter to the Electors of Great Britain," printed in several provincial newspapers, castigated the folly of loyalist writers who argued that government actions would preserve British empire and trade: "Desolated fields, and depopulated provinces, are little likely to contribute to our necessities," the address stated. "To secure our commerce, therefore, can neither be the aim, nor the issue of this war."[38] More moderate writers, aware of how frazzled the imperial relationship was by 1775–6 and convinced war was an ill-conceived way to bring about a rapprochement, opposed government aggression for its impracticality and the mercantilist system itself for its shortsightedness. "It is a war of absurdity and madness," one opponent declared; "we shall sooner pluck the moon from her sphere than conquer such a country"; and another contended that it was folly to believe Britain could forever "tie the hands of the inhabitants of a great continent abounding with raw materials . . . restrain them from using the gifts of nature, and . . . force them to take the products of your own labor."[39] Although virtually all those who opposed the war did so in the hopes of preserving

---

[37] PRO, HO 55/28/21 (repr. in Bradley, *Popular Politics,* 224–7); *Records of the Borough of Nottingham,* vol. 7 (Nottingham, 1947), 137 (Oct. 20, 1775); PRO, HO 55/12/9.

[38] *LEP,* Oct. 3–5, 1775; *Norfolk Chronicle,* Oct. 7, 1775.

[39] *Norfolk Chronicle,* March 7, 1778; *Newcastle Journal,* Dec. 16, 1776. See also the petitions of the Bristol merchants, traders, manufacturers and citizens in *Farley's Bristol Journal,* Oct. 14, 1775; the Westmorland freeholders, printed in *LEP,* Feb. 1–3, 1776; the residents of Nottingham (n. 37); and HL, Pulteney MSS, Box 15, WA to Sir WP, Dec. 20, 1777.

the British empire in North America, these anti-war arguments, simultaneously commercial and libertarian, clearly contradicted certain
tenets of the mercantilist imperial vision that had been articulated
since the early decades of the century. Yet they drew a substantial
number of citizens of all ranks into the anti-war camp, especially from
among middling and artisanal groups for whom empire and colonial
acquisition had always had an appeal and who were, in the present
crisis, hard hit by the economic dislocation of credit and currency
caused by the war.

At the same time, the American crisis undermined long-held beliefs
in the morality, virtue and libertarianism of the imperial project. British commentators had long insisted that Britain's virtue as an imperial
nation lay in not seeking conquest but having conquest thrust upon
it: Colonial acquisition in the Seven Years' War was thus continually
justified, in and out of Parliament, as a *defense* against French aggression.[40] Traditional libertarian doctrine on colonies, as expressed, for
example, by Trenchard and Gordon as "Cato," insisted that force
could have no place in their government: "Liberty and encouragement" alone would allow colonies to flourish, which is why "arbitrary
countries have not been equally successful in planting colonies, with
free ones."[41] The policies of the Pelhams and Chatham had done
nothing to undercut these views; but George III's ministers enacted
measures which seriously confounded them. The Quebec Act, which
provided for the continuation of French civil law, government without
representative bodies and the "free exercise" of Roman Catholicism,
was justified as a requirement of empire by North and his supporters,
and vehemently denounced by his opponents for contradicting what
were believed to be established principles of imperial government.
"No free country can keep another in slavery," Edmund Burke
warned in the House of Commons. "The price they pay for it will be
their own servitude." Chatham and his followers were even more un-
equivocal in their condemnation of the bill, calling it "a most cruel,
oppressive and odious measure, tearing up justice and every good
principle by the roots." And out-of-doors, opposition to the Act's es-

[40] *Proceedings and Debates of the British Parliaments Respecting North America, 1754–83,* ed. R. C. Simmons and P. D. G. Thomas, 5 vols. (New York, 1982), i, 104–9, 265–7; Jonas Hanway, *Thoughts on the Duty of a Good Citizen* (London, 1759), 10.
[41] *Cato's Letters: Essays on Liberty, Civil and Religious, and Other Important Subjects,* 4 vols. (London, 1755), iv, 7–8.

tablishment of "popery and slavery" in the empire was strenuous and violent.[42] Hence, the establishment of "despotic" government in certain colonies, as well as the inefficacy and immorality of forcing submission upon an unwilling population, threatened the loss of a virtuous empire, once "as much renowned for the virtues of justice and humanity as for the splendour of its arms," as the Middlesex electors lamented in 1775 in their address for reconciliation with America.[43]

The wide-ranging opposition to government measures in America, influenced by radical arguments about the nature and appropriate limits of authority in the state and the imperial polity, enlarged in scope as the war dragged on. The entry of France into the fray in March 1778 (and Spain the next year) further transfigured alignments which had been built up since the fighting began. The pressure to support the government in the face of threats from Britain's historic enemy was considerable, and those individuals and groups who had worked to sustain the anti-war campaign became vulnerable to charges of "unpatriotic" conduct. As scholars have frequently noted, in the wake of Americans' declaration of independence, the government could take the high road of championing *British* patriotism against the allied American–French (and ultimately Spanish and Dutch) efforts.[44] But although a tactical advantage for the government, the entry of the European powers did not necessarily shore up the loyalist hand. Indeed, the nationalist appeal, always the government's trump card, was effective in mobilizing support largely from among those groups which had condoned official actions in America from the beginning. The Bourbon entry actually highlighted the inadequacies of the ministry's war policies as a whole and turned the tide of public opinion toward the anti-war camp. This growing opposition to North's policies was evident in 1778–9, when a national furor surrounded the trial of Admiral Augustus Keppel.

---

[42] *Debates in the House of Commons in the Year 1774, on the Bill for Making More Effectual Provision for the Government of Quebec,* ed. J. Wright (London, 1839; repr. 1966), iii–iv, 15–24. For demonstrations against the Act see *LEP,* June 11–14, 1774; *Newcastle Journal,* July 9, 30, 1774; and Jonathan Paul Thomas, "The British Empire and the Press, 1763–74" (Oxford University D.Phil. diss., 1982), 329–68.

[43] PRO, HO 55/13/2 (repr. in Bradley, *Popular Politics,* 230–1).

[44] Most recently Linda Colley, "Radical Patriotism in Eighteenth Century England," in Raphael Samuel, ed., *Patriotism: The Making and Unmaking of the British National Identity,* 3 vols. (London, 1989), i, 177–8, and *Britons,* 143–5.

II. PATRIOTISM REVIVED: ADMIRAL KEPPEL AND
PARLIAMENTARY REFORM

In 1778, a cluster of problems faced North's ministry that illustrated
those which plagued the war effort as a whole. Burgoyne's surrender
at Saratoga in late 1777 not only dispirited observers at home but resulted in his resignation (he was the third of seven senior officers to
resign before the middle of 1779). North's conciliatory proposals of
February, which did not mention repeal of the Declaratory and Quebec
Acts, were expected by English observers to be rejected by the Americans, prompting a new petitioning initiative from several towns for the
dismissal of the ministry. Moreover, the government's recurrent problem in enlisting men to fight in America intensified – and was scarcely
offset by the flurry of subscriptions to bolster British resources and
resolves that was begun by loyalists early in the year (indeed, people
were reported to stay away from urban centers during the war because
of the fear of impressment) – leading to riots and confrontations over
the violence of press gangs in several towns.[45] On the home front, an
economic crisis loomed: A collapsing stock market, scarce commodities, diminished trade, high unemployment and rising taxes had produced strikes, unrest and discontent in many localities. As if to
exacerbate the sense of crisis, American privateers led by John Paul
Jones successfully raided English and Scottish ports on the Irish Sea
for supplies in April, demonstrating to British observers both American
nerve and British vulnerability on the coastlines.[46]

In this context, the predicted French declaration of alliance with
America produced a pervasive foreboding that the existence of the nation was at stake, with unexpected consequences. Certainly it reignited
the smoldering anti-Gallicanism of the English people, mobilizing a
bellicose nationalism in the localities along with the militias and sub-

[45] Piers Mackesy, *The War for America* (London, 1964), 174–210; Van Alstyne, "War
for American Independence," 23; petitions: note 3; loyalist subscriptions: *York Courant,* Jan. 6, Feb. 19, 1778; *Farley's Bristol Journal,* Jan. 24, Feb. 14, 1778; *Liverpool
General Advertiser,* May 29, 1778; Money, *Experience and Identity,* 207; Marshall,
"Manchester and the American Revolution," 178–9; press gangs: Sainsbury, *Disaffected Patriots,* 134–5; Marshall, "Bristol and the American War," 13–15; *Liverpool
General Advertiser,* Aug. 14, 1783; and Edward Baines, *History of Liverpool* (Liverpool, 1852), 467.
[46] P. Deane and W. A. Cole, *British Economic Growth, 1688–1959,* 2d ed. (Cambridge,
1967), 45–9; W. E. Minchinton, *The Trade of Bristol in the Eighteenth Century* (Bristol Record Society Publications, 20, 1957), x–xi; Lutnik, *British Press,* 150–1.

scriptions formed for defense of the coastline. The strength of antagonism toward England's ancient imperial rival supported in some instances a defiantly positive hope for a replay of the Seven Years' War, whereby Britain would defeat France by winning in Europe and the West Indies.[47] But France's entry into the war also provoked parallels with that previous war effort that were less than heartening, and unleashed a storm of invective over ministerial leadership and direction. The government's reticence in formally declaring war on France, and its failure to meet the martial expectations of the British public by aggressively plunging into battle, prompted anti-war opponents to deploy the old charges of cowardice and effeminacy. "We must either tamely surrender our Rights and Privileges to our vanquishing Foes, or bravely repel their Treachery by Force," bellowed a writer in the *York Courant,* noting the lull in military activity in the face of the French threat; the London papers shrieked that the ministers were behaving "like cowards . . . endeavoring to avoid a war with France," something the recently deceased Chatham would never have done.[48] A Norwich observer most colorfully expressed this view: Comparing the flaccid state of the ministry's war effort with the granite spirit of American militias, he concluded: "Our men of rank and fortune have exchanged sexes with the soft and fair. They are fribbles and maccaronies [*sic*], and not soldiers and heroes. A year or two of encampments and rigid discipline, may restore them to virility and heroic hardiness; but alas! the constitution and power of England . . . may in the meantime be extinct."[49] At the same time, the opposition in Parliament was able to rearm itself rhetorically, uniting after Chatham's death in April around Richmond's demand for the unconditional withdrawal of British troops and recognition of American independence. The invasion scares which began in the summer of 1778 and continued through the next summer ironically provided avenues for a different kind of anti-war activism, for they allowed opposition leaders and anti-war advocates to participate with fervor in the "patriotic" effort to raise militias to defend the coastlines.[50]

[47] See *Cumberland Pacquet,* May 5, 12, 19, 1778; *York Courant,* May 19, Sept. 29, 1778; *Farley's Bristol Journal,* June 6, 1778.

[48] *York Courant,* May 19, 1778; *General Evening Advertiser,* June 24, 1778. See also Lutnik, *British Press,* 139–40.

[49] *Norfolk Chronicle,* July 18, 1778; see also Oct. 10, 1778. Effigies of the officers unsuccessful at Camden in October 1780 were hung and burned in Bristol: Marshall, "Bristol," 18–19; *Farley's Bristol Journal,* Oct. 14, 1780.

[50] *Parliamentary Register,* 10 (1778), 320–1; Van Alstyne, "War for American Inde-

In this atmosphere of crisis, frustration and high-level opposition
renewal, Admiral Augustus Keppel agreed to command the Channel
fleet. A former member of Byng's court-martial and a celebrated veteran of the Seven Years' War (when he and his elder brothers, Lord
Albemarle and General William Keppel, had distinguished themselves
by brilliant successes at Belle Isle and Havana), Keppel was MP for
Windsor and a respected member of the Rockingham opposition,
widely known to be hostile to the administration and its policies in
America. He was one of the nine officers of superior rank who refused
to serve against the colonists; he also scorned the management of the
war's naval operations by the first lord of the Admiralty, the Earl of
Sandwich (who was also his personal nemesis). He nevertheless accepted the post offered him by Sandwich to serve against the French,
setting sail with his fleet for Ushant in the summer of 1778.[51]

That the hopes of the extra-parliamentary nation were centered on
Admiral Keppel to end the imperial conflict and vindicate British honor
was evident from the letters and essays that appeared in the press. "The
catastrophe of British independence hangs by a single thread," one
writer gloomily predicted. "All our hopes center in Admiral Keppel. If he does not beat, or is beaten, the empire of Britain is no more
... Admiral Keppel's progress is now the barometer of national
strength."[52] Keppel engaged with a French fleet off the coast of Ushant
in late July in an ultimately indecisive battle that resulted in extensive
damage to both fleets; but Keppel retained possession of the Channel
and so claimed it as a victory, one that proved the English could hold
the French in check. However, when the fleet returned to port at the
end of October, Sir Hugh Palliser, Keppel's senior subordinate officer,
was accused in the press of having ignored his commander-in-chief's
command to wear his ships and reengage after the first battle. Palliser,
a close associate of Sandwich's, from whom he had accepted the si-
necure of lieutenant-general of Marines in 1775, demanded a retraction
of the press report, which Keppel declined to provide, with the result
that the vice-admiral published his version of the action in an October

pendence," 23; *York Courant,* May 19, Nov. 17, 1778; Liverpool Record Office and
Library, *A List of the Prizes Taken from the French* [Liverpool, 1779].
[51] Mackesy, *War for America,* 202–10; Namier and Brooke, iii, 8. Mackesy takes a dim
view of Keppel, whom he categorizes as "deficient in judgement, maritime skill and
presence of mind."
[52] *Norfolk Chronicle,* July 18, 1778; see also *The Reconciliation Between Britannia and
Her Daughter America* (London, 1778) (BM no. 5989.1).

issue of the *Morning Post* and followed this in December 1778 with the demand that Keppel be court-martialed for "misconduct and neglect of duty."[53]

The parliamentary opposition, eager to take advantage of any situation to discredit the government, took up Keppel's cause. Opposition leaders – including Rockingham, Cumberland, Portland and Effingham – flocked to Portsmouth in February 1779 for Keppel's trial, staging processions through the town marked by illuminations, bonfires and bands of music playing such patriotically emotive songs as "Rule Britannia" and "See the Conquering Hero Comes." According to one account, the parliamentary leaders all wore large blue cockades emblazoned with KEPPEL in gold letters – behavior which Lady Pembroke considered "Very Foolish," pointing out that Keppel, as a "sensible man, must have [been] distressed . . . terribly." Keppel, however, probably felt relief. Remembering Byng's trial and his own unsuccessful efforts to obtain Parliament's intervention after the sentence, and well aware of the government's desperation after Saratoga, he had feared that the ministry would attempt to use him as its predecessor had used the ill-fated Byng, and had therefore asked the king for permission to inspect personally the ships to be put under his command. And whatever the judgment of posterity, the nation endorsed his and the opposition's view that the court-martial was a political matter, one which revealed the cowardice of the ministry and the corruption of its war effort. "Admiral Keppel has fill'd the mouth of every Englishman of late . . . and has honours heeping [*sic*] upon him from every quarter except from the government" was how Norwich radical Philip Martineau described the situation in March 1779.[54]

The London and provincial press was filled with the details of his trial, and when the court found the charge to be "malicious and ill-founded" and announced his acquittal, celebrations of his heroism and deliverance broke out throughout the country. In Portsmouth, Keppel was conducted from the court to his house aboard H.M.S. *Britannia,* accompanied by the dukes of Cumberland and Portland and Lords Rockingham and Effingham, while crowds of cheering spectators looked on and the ships in the harbors fired a grand salute. In London, the Corporation of the City bestowed him with its freedom and staged

---

[53] J. H. Broomfield, "The Keppel–Palliser Affair," *Mariner's Mirror,* 47 (1961), 195–205; Mackesy, *War for America,* 239–40; Namier and Brooke, ii, 8–9.
[54] NNRO, Neville MS, MC7/417, Misc. letters and papers, PM to SN, March 30, 1779.

a dinner in his honor, to which he marched attended by the patriotic Marine Society, draped in blue streamers, to considerable popular acclaim. Meanwhile, a crowd burned an effigy of Palliser on Tower Hill and attacked the houses of Palliser, Germain and Sandwich (all leaders whose cowardice, effeminacy and treachery had long been lambasted in the radical press), destroyed a good portion of the contents, and shattered the windows of the residences of Lord North and Captain Hood, the latter having testified on Palliser's behalf. "The defeat of a malicious and ill-founded accusation brought against a character of the most exalted merit, and the detection of the deepest malignity and basest perfidy in the prosecution of it," the *Norfolk Chronicle* observed, "seem to have roused the indignation, and united in opinion all degrees of people however differing in political sentiments."[55]

Demonstrations endorsed this view, in at least seventy-five provincial towns, where mock trials for Palliser, "Judas Rear Admiral of the Blue," were staged and his effigy desecrated in the rituals of popular justice. In Swansea, the local militia fired six rounds as Palliser's effigy was burned; in Woodstock, the effigies of Palliser and Captain Hood were carried backwards in a cart and hung in front of the town hall before being incinerated to "the united acclamation of a vast concourse of people" in the evening. And in Newcastle, the effigy of Palliser (in uniform and holding "an altered logbook") joined those of the ministers who were currently the greatest objects of popular opprobrium, Lords North, Sandwich and Germain, at the "gallows" erected in Bigg Market, where the town hangman consigned them all to flames to the cheers of the assembled crowd.[56] In addition, Keppel received the freedom of dozens of towns and the thanks of the House of Commons for his brave and skillful conduct in the previous summer's battle (see Plate 13). "Scarce greater rejoicings since the release of the Seven Bishops," Samuel Curwen noted in his diary; and the extent of Keppel's popularity captured the commercial imagination of Josiah Wedgwood. In early March, he despaired at not having Keppel's head to reproduce on "pictures, bracelets, ring seals, etc. . . . I am perswaded if we had our

---

[55] *LEP*, Feb. 11–13, 16–18, 1779; *Norfolk Chronicle*, Feb. 20, 1779.

[56] *Salisbury Journal*, Feb. 22, 1779; *Bristol Gazette and Public Advertiser*, Feb. 11, 1779; *LEP*, Feb. 13–15, 16–18, 1779; *Newcastle Chronicle*, Feb. 20, 1779. The number of towns was taken from February 1779 reports in these as well as other papers, i.e., *Cumberland Pacquet, Farley's Bristol Journal, General Evening Post, Gloucester Journal, Leeds Mercury, Liverpool General Advertiser, Norfolk Chronicle, York Courant*, as well as Corporation records and local histories.

wits about us . . . we might have sold £1,000 worth of this gentleman's
head in various ways, and I am perswaded it would still be worthwhile
to dispense with them every way in our power.''[57]

The opportunities for consumerism notwithstanding, the Keppel affair constituted a complex political moment in the vicissitudes of domestic opinion during the war and in the family romance of imperial
relations being worked out. On the one hand, the excessive joy at Keppel's acquittal and the acclaim for his tepid naval leadership and largely
symbolic "victory" were clearly cathartic, a reassurance for the nation
at a critical juncture. Both seemed to provide, less than a year after the
great Chatham's death, a glimmer of the past that held out hope for
the future: the hope that the ruling councils of the nation still had men
of integrity, vision and leadership capable of rousing the people to
national unity and restoring Britain's vaunted naval and imperial supremacy. The slogans of the celebrators in the localities on Keppel's
acquittal expressed this mixture of nostalgia, loss and desire, as in York,
where a fête in Keppel's honor held at a local tavern ended with the
toast "May Great Britain never want a Keppel as an Admiral, a Wolfe
as a General, and a Chatham as a Minister.''[58] Further, as both an
admiral and a "patriot" who refused to wield his power against fellow
American citizens, Keppel not only deflected attention from battles with
the former colonists to those with Britain's ancient Catholic enemies;
he also thereby restored faith in the resilience of the nation's libertarian
traditions, including the navy, which since 1775 had been sullied by
its "ministerial" orientation and actions in America. The court-
martial's verdict in Keppel's favor further reconstituted regard for the
navy as a bulwark of the English and even the British national character
as virtuous, manly and free. Reviewing the Scottish, Irish and English
officers who conducted the court-martial, one observer enthused in a
revealing characterization of his countrymen, "Dependent men have
asserted independency and Scotchmen have become Patriots" standing
forward "in defence of that bravery, skill and virtue" which the British
navy revered; "Scotch, English and Irish – Foreigners and natives, have
acted with one consent . . . They have unanimously agreed in their

---

[57] *Journal of Samuel Curwen,* ii, 52; JW to TB, March 1, 1779, quoted in Neil
McKendrick, "Josiah Wedgwood: An 18th Century Entrepreneur in Salesman-
ship and Marketing Techniques," *Economic History Review,* 2nd ser., 12 (1959–60),
422.
[58] *York Courant,* Feb. 28, 1779; see also *Norfolk Chronicle,* Feb. 20, 1779; *Newcastle
Chronicle,* Feb. 29, 1779.

resistance to villainy.''[59] Such an assessment spoke volumes about the acrimonious nature of the splits within Britain that the war effort could gloss over as well as magnify.

Above all, the celebrations on Keppel's acquittal expressed wide-spread disillusionment with the North administration, signifying the conviction that new men and measures were needed if British liberty and national greatness were to be restored. Noting the show of resentment for the ''weak, odious, and oppressive measures of the ministry,'' the *London Evening Post* predicted hopefully that ''this spirit of the People without doors, will do more towards rectifying the measures of the ministry, and restoring the Constitution of the kingdom, than all the opposition within doors.''[60] America was lost, in the eyes of many English observers – although hopes of some reconciliation continued to be expressed in some quarters until 1782 – and with Britain under attack by her enemies in the Mediterranean and India as well as America, the most to be gained, on this reading, was the swift and decisive defeat of the Bourbon powers and a change of leaders to return the nation to justice. In fact, the surge of anti-administration sentiment out-of-doors marked one of the first convergences of extra-parliamentary political action with that of the opposition in Parliament since the war began. However fortuitous in origin, it provided a boost to the sagging morale and floundering organization of moderates and radicals alike. Palliser went to trial to clear his name, and the parliamentary opposition forced a vote in the House of Commons on a motion of censure on the weakness of Keppel's fleet which was only narrowly defeated.[61] All seemed to augur the long-awaited resignation of the North administration.

North's fall was not to occur for three years. In the short term, his considerable parliamentary skills enabled him to repulse the economic reform initiative of 1779–80, stare down political rebellion in Ireland, and survive the most serious ministerial defeat of the century, Dunning's motion of April 1780 on the need to decrease the influence of the Crown. At the same time, Clinton's victory at Charleston in June allowed the ministry to save face over the practicability of its war policy, and the Gordon Riots earlier in the same month temporarily stalled the anti-war agitation within the channels of institutionalized politics and prevented the opposition from capitalizing on its successes.

[59] *LEP*, Feb. 11–13, 1779.
[60] Feb. 16–18, 1779.
[61] Mackesy, *War for America*, 246–7.

Nevertheless, in the extra-parliamentary nation, the Keppel affair had demonstrated the existence of widespread antipathy to government measures that loyalist representations tried to obscure, and had increased the conviction among anti-war proponents that the ministry was incapable of representing the will of those it purported to govern. On both counts, it contributed to a climate in which parliamentary reform and demands for an end to the war gained a wider hearing out-of-doors. A writer in Whitehaven reflected these sentiments when he listed "the three great ends which are now destroying the country, viz., the loss of American trade, the interest of the national debt, and the salons of placemen," concluding that "the effect of our impolitic quarrel with America is now felt, as well as understood. The merchant, the trader, and the mechanic all universally condemn it."[62] The campaigns for economic and parliamentary reform in 1779–82 were characterized by the more careful organization and closer coordination of radicals and moderates within and without doors, indicated by, for example, the Westminster Committee, which, led by Fox, tied metropolitan opposition to that in Parliament; by the correspondence committees formed in Newcastle, Bristol, Norwich and elsewhere to keep provincial and metropolitan reformers in touch; and by Wyvill's Associations, which, producing thirty-seven petitions for reform from England and Wales in 1779–80 and thirty-four in 1782, most dramatically linked up localities in a national effort to force greater accountability from the state.[63]

Concern with corruption in high places also sparked such innovative organizations as the Society for Constitutional Information (SCI). Formed in April 1780 by a handful of affluent metropolitan and provincial radicals – among them Cartwright, Macaulay, John Jebb, Thomas Day, Granville Sharp, Capel Lofft, George Grieve and Sir Watkin Lewes – it dedicated itself to distributing reform propaganda gratis throughout the nation in order to awaken "the people" to their political rights. Democratic in goals if not membership (which nevertheless extended from Cornwall and Essex to Nottingham and Newcastle upon Tyne), and with its propaganda available in thirty-seven towns and counties in England, Wales and Scotland, it was an intellectually vigorous and radical supplement to the county reform associations that sought, through relentless advocacy of universal manhood suffrage and

---

[62] *Leeds Mercury,* May 25, 1779.
[63] Sainsbury, *Disaffected Patriots,* 150–5; Christopher Wyvill, *Political Papers,* 4 vols. (York, 1795), passim.

annual Parliaments, to move the discussion on reform to the "left."[64] These efforts gave wider circulation to natural rights arguments for universal suffrage in urban environments, where such widely distributed tracts as Cartwright's *Declaration of Those Rights of the Commonalty of Great-Britain Without Which They Cannot Be Free* were used by local dissidents in their battles with recalcitrant magistrates and MPs alike. "They, who have *no* Voice nor Vote in the electing of Representatives, *do not enjoy* Liberty, but are absolutely *enslaved* to those who have votes, and to their Representatives," the *Declaration* asserted, and to this liberty "the poor Man has an equal Right" with the rich one.[65]

Just as the Keppel affair, then, had temporarily revived the hopes and images of patriotic leadership for the nation, so the reform movement, led by a combination of urban radicals and traditional elites and supported by groups of middling freeholders, traders and professionals throughout the nation, restored faith in the resilience of patriotic sensibilities in the polity. At the heart of oppositionist patriotism for the past five decades had been the anti-corruption critique of authority that sought to purify the political process and keep the state responsive to the people, and parliamentary reform in all its guises was conceived of as a way of implementing measures designed to do this by giving greater extra-parliamentary control over its representative institutions.[66] Yet consistent with radical patriotism's inevitable opposition to loyalist

---

[64] PRO, Treasury Solicitor Papers, TS 11/1133, SCI Minutes, 1780 – May 7, 1783, and TS 11/961, Minutes March 14, 1783 – Oct. 7, 1791. See esp. TS 11/1133, fols. 7–10, 143, and 11/961, fol. 1. Membership was 1 guinea a year – out of reach of the middling and artisanal classes that were its intended audience. The tracts of the 1780s, printed in batches of between 1,000 and 15,000 (collected in a two-volume set at Houghton Library, Harvard University), evince the construction of a radical canon that, wildly eclectic but consistently populist, was of lasting influence. For an overview of SCI activities into the 1790s see Eugene C. Black, *The Association* (Cambridge, Mass., 1963), 176–98.

[65] [Cartwright], *Declaration* (London, 1780). At least 14,000 copies of this tract were printed and distributed throughout England in June and July 1780 (TS 11/1133, fols. 14, 19), and it was reprinted as part of Henry Cruger's radical manifesto in 1781: Marshall, *Bristol*, 24–5.

[66] See, e.g., *The Association Meeting at York 30 Dec. 1779* (BM no. 5657), which endowed the Wyvill's Association movement with mythological significance, surrounding the figures of the reformers with the allegorical forms of Britannia, Liberty, Public Virtue and Hope as well as Civil Union, Moderation, Harmony and Election, the latter of whom holds out a sheet inscribed "short Parliaments, Equal Representation, Ballot." At their feet a satyr, representing Corruption, struggles unsuccessfully to reassert ascendancy, and Britannia and America embrace. *Catalogue,* iv, 392.

politics, the proposals and debates over reform irretrievably raised the stakes of structural political change, precipitating a decline in the fortunes of the entire reform cause that Pitt's last motion on its behalf in Parliament in 1785 only confirmed. Why should this have been so?

The answer lay in the complexity of the links between contemporaries' perceptions of the distribution of power in the state and present discontents in the polity, at home and abroad. On the one hand, as Herbert Butterfield argued long ago, the duration and expense of the American conflict caused the "Tory" landed gentry who had formerly supported North to desert him and support the county associations for reform.[67] One could add that the war also undermined gentry authority in the localities, where residents were angered at the precipitous decline in national stature, the political disgrace and the economic hardship which the "ministerial" war had wrought, and were looking for scapegoats. Yet the reform movement itself was undermined by divisions among its supporters over goals and strategies that made it incapable of exploiting these advantages. Wilkite and pro-American radicalism had raised expectations across a broad social spectrum without having any ways, or in some cases any intention, of satisfying them. The SCI exhibited the clash between democratic goals and "bourgeois" strategies and leadership that could hamper effective radical propagandizing. Hence, despite the more vernacular tracts of Cartwright, Jebb and Day, many of the learned treatises on law, rights and history the Society distributed were too rarefied to engage the attention of the humble; and its members' evangelical faith in the ability of texts to transform the political practices as well as the understanding of their audience led them to underplay more mundane but equally crucial forms of grassroots politicking and organization. Admittedly, Society members energetically lobbied MPs to support radical reform; and in 1783 the SCI recommended the establishment of "Parochial Societies" to mobilize petitions and ultimately send deputies to a general meeting in the capital that would meet as an Anti-Parliament. But no concrete measures were taken to promote this goal save the dispatch of especially large packets of SCI tracts to various political clubs in the localities.[68]

Alternatively, Wyvill's Association was organizationally and ideologically capable of appealing to independent country gentlemen and

---

[67] Herbert Butterfield, *George III, Lord North and the People* (London, 1949), 221–80.
[68] PRO, TS 11/1133, fols. 105–38; TS 11/961, fols. 17–18; for parochial societies see SCI, *Constitutional Tracts,* vol. 1 (London, 1783), 85.

freeholders with its moderate "country" reforms of containing the executive influence, abolition of rotten boroughs and increase of county representation, but it was both too radical and too moderate to mobilize wholehearted support from other sectors of the provincial urban public or to satisfy the conflicting array of grievances that the unreformed political system generated. For example, the reform proposals sent out to the localities in a circular letter of November 1782 were peremptorily dismissed by conservative civic elites, who considered the timing inappropriate, the notion of structural reform treasonable and associations themselves "extremely dangerous." "At a time when the almost certainty of loosing [*sic*] the Thirteen Provinces of America, overwhelms with grief every one who wishes well to the country," the mayor of Poole, Benjamin Lister wrote, "I am astonished that you, who ought to think seriously, should patronize and support any Plan of pretended Reformation in the State, a measure which his Majesty told you in his speech, soon after the late Riots in London, was always productive either of ruin to the persons concerned, or of a Revolution in Government."[69] Yet to the middling and artisanal populations impressed by the radical diagnosis of political ills and disaffected by the war, Wyvill's proposals were underwhelming, seemingly incapable of effecting substantive change in the tenor, distribution and exercise of power in the state. The Bridgwater Committee urged the Association to expand its scope of reform, as "we have no less to complain of the extent of the aristocratic Power [in the boroughs] than we have of the increased influence of the Crown"; those in Bridport thought reform must include electoral oaths against bribery; and Newcastle reformers thought that the trading and manufacturing interests of Britain needed to be given a larger share of the representation, rather than the counties, to stem the tide of corruption and make government truly accountable to the public. And of course those metropolitan and provincial radicals committed to the extension of the franchise, redistribution of seats or even to associations of the people to redesign the government considered the proposals of 1782 and 1785 to be sorely inadequate.[70] Wyvill's prop-

---

[69] Wyvill, *Political Papers,* ii, 98–9, 95–6; see also 97, 108–9. Significantly, the "commonalty" of Poole wrote to Wyvill to express support for reform and opposition to the Corporation: 99–100.

[70] Ibid., 114–16, 112–14; *Newcastle Chronicle,* Sept. 28, 1782; Dec. 27, 1783; John Cartwright, *Letter to the Deputies of the Associated and Petitioning Counties, Cities and Towns, on the Means Necessary to a Reformation of Parliament* (London, 1781); John Jebb, *An Address to the Freeholders of Middlesex,* 4th ed. (London, 1782).

agandists, to be fair, attempted to meet these objections, with only limited success.[71] Not only were parliamentary supporters of reform, such as William Pitt, widely known to oppose radical measures, but the retailers and craftspeople in the large urban centers who support-ed radical politics remained distrustful of the county associations' elite leadership, which seemed to duplicate the hierarchies of power and authority which they wished to overcome.[72] Hence, although the 1782 petitioning initiative garnered the largest show of urban support yet (see Table 4.1), important provincial towns like Newcastle, Nor-wich, Bristol, Nottingham and Hull which had supported economic reform in 1780, as well as unrepresented ones like Manchester, now failed to petition in favor of Wyvill's parliamentary reforms, thus un-dermining the credibility of the Association's claims to speak for "the people."

The Gordon Riots of June 1780, when a procession of thousands to Westminster to present a petition to Parliament against its Catholic relief bill of 1778 precipitated a shattering outburst of bigotry and vi-olence in the capital that lasted for six days, may also have contributed to the decline in the reformers' cause, although for rather different reasons than are usually cited. It has become axiomatic amongst his-torians that the riots undermined the radical cause: They sharpened thinly masked divisions within the parliamentary opposition, tore apart alliances among metropolitan radicals, and stimulated and amplified conservative attitudes within the middle classes.[73] Yet the impact of the riots on oppositionist politics as a whole has been exaggerated. Nich-olas Rogers has shown that if the issue of Catholic relief divided met-ropolitan radicals and the riots represented a setback, the radicals also managed to contain the damage. This was also true in provincial towns, where against ministerial supporters' attempts to brush them with the

---

[71] As one tract of 1781 put it, the current "diversity of sentiment" preventing unanimity among reformers had arisen "not from a difference of political principles . . . but solely from considerations of a more prudential nature," namely, that only moderate reform was attainable in the present climate: *The Second Address from the Committee of Association of the County of York,* 2nd ed. (York, 1781), 15–18.

[72] The delegations from the associated counties and boroughs were composed largely of the younger sons of landed families. See Christie, *Wilkes, Wyvill and Reform,* 154–84; Wyvill, *Political Papers,* i, 126–7; for criticisms see Cartwright, *Give US Our Rights!* (London and Chester, 1783); SCI, *Tracts,* i, 136–41. Of the boroughs with electorates of over 1,000, only 5 petitioned.

[73] Ian R. Christie, "The Marquis of Rockingham and Lord North's Offer of a Coalition, June–July 1780," *EHR,* 69 (1964), 388–407; Black, *Association,* 131–73; Sainsbury, *Disaffected Patriots,* 156–8; Money, *Experience and Identity,* 210–11.

stain of disloyalty and rabble-rousing, radicals and reformers blamed
the riots on the ministry's refusal to listen to the "voice of the people"
in the 1779–80 petitions and the prevailing political discontent attendant upon its hateful war with America.[74] Although there were attacks
on Catholic chapels in Bath, Birmingham, Hull, Newcastle and Sheffield and various rumblings in the countryside, the ostentatious mus-
tering of the forces of order in most towns was sufficient to keep
disorder at bay and anxieties at a comparatively low ebb, so that the
street celebrations on news the next week of General Clinton's victory
at Charleston were exuberant and wild, with authorities displaying none
of the dread of the mob that might otherwise have been expected.[75]
Neither did the 1780 parliamentary elections reveal the dimensions of
oppositionist political collapse. Unexpectedly staged by the government
in September partly to take advantage of the conservative reaction to
the riots, there was only one contest fewer in the large urban constituencies than in 1774; and in towns where contests occurred, oppositionist candidates challenged and usually carried the day. Indeed, there
was a significant movement of opinion against the government in *all*
of the open constituencies, including the counties, and a swing to the
opposition of such leading borough-owners as Sir James Lowther and
Sir Lawrence Dundas, as well as lesser ones like Edward Eliot and
Arthur Holdsworth. North's ministry thus returned from the appeal to
the country with a greatly reduced majority.[76]

More important, the riots revealed the limitations of the nativist,
xenophobic themes embedded in libertarian politics in ways that exacerbated the already uneasy relationship between the radical politics
of "the people" and the degenerate license of the "rabble." Catholic
relief, although passed somewhat cynically to enable the government
to recruit Catholics into the army,[77] was bound to be seen by many
people in the current climate as an instance of ministerial despotism
brought home. The historical identification of Catholicism with luxu-

---

[74] Nicholas Rogers, "Crowd and People in the Gordon Riots," in E. Hellmuth, ed., *The Transformation of Political Culture* (Oxford, 1990), 39–55; *Newcastle Courant,* Feb. 5, 1780; *Liverpool General Advertiser,* Feb. 18, 1780; *York Courant,* July 4, 1780.

[75] *Manchester Mercury,* June 20, 1780; *Farley's Bristol Journal,* June 10, 17, 24, 1780; *Leeds Mercury,* June 13, 20, 1780; Money, *Experience and Identity,* 206; *Salisbury Journal,* June 19, 1780; Colin Haydon, "The Gordon Riots in the English Provinces," *Historical Research,* 63 (1990), 354–9.

[76] The government's majority dropped from 47 to 6. See Ian Christie, *The End of North's Ministry 1780–82* (Cambridge, 1960); Namier and Brooke, i, 81–5.

[77] See G. M. Ditchfield, "The Subscription Issue in British Parliamentary Politics, 1772–79," *Parliamentary History,* 7 (1988), 61–2.

rious and corrupting forces, the Quebec Act, the war with the Bourbon powers, and the government's own long-standing and recent sanction of anti-Catholic nationalism as the last resort of national bonding could scarcely prepare the body of people for "enlightened" religious tolerance, no matter how fervently it was held as a principle by leading citizens or how little the current bill actually relieved Catholics of some of their more draconian liabilities. Despite its politically disparate membership, which included arch-conservatives like John Wesley and radical leaders like Crosby and Bull, Protestant Association propaganda deliberately identified its cause – the repeal of the Catholic relief legislation – with the radical agitation against government corruption and the American war, and played on endemic and revitalized anti-Catholic sensibilities.[78] *The English Lion Dismember'd, or the Voice of the Public for an Enquiry into the Public Expenditure* made the connection clear with its depiction of Lord North absconding with public monies as he trampled on the petitions of Middlesex, York and the Protestant Association.[79]

The dangerous attractions of rabid Protestant nationalism, long effective in mobilizing extra-parliamentary political opinion, were highlighted by the social provenance of support for the Protestant Association. In London and Newcastle upon Tyne, the petty bourgeois tradesmen, shopkeepers and parish officials who made up its rank and file had long been a prime constituency of libertarian politics; its leaders were drawn from the advocates of radical politics, and especially dissenters, in both places.[80] Yet for them as for other observers, the riots

---

[78] *The Protestant Packet, or British Monitor*, 2 vols. (Newcastle and London, 1780–1), made use of John Brown's *Estimate of the Manners* (1757) and other anti-luxury, anti-effeminacy tracts; see, e.g., Aug. 4, 1780; Jan. 5, 1781. Caleb Evans, *The Remembrance of Former Days: A Sermon Preached at Broadmead, Bristol, November 5 1778* (Bristol, 1778).

[79] (London, 1780), BM no. 5649. This print reworks the 1756 print of similar title, although here the lion's cut-off limb is labeled "America," and the symbols of virtue are the associators, represented by Fox, Wyvill and Richmond. See also *Association, or Public Virtue Displayed in a Contrasted View* (London, 1780; BM no. 5638) in which "England United" is represented by London, Newcastle, Bristol and Westminster as well as the various counties.

[80] Cf. Rogers, "Crowd and People," 44. For general social provenance see George Rude, *Paris and London in the 18th Century* (London, 1970), 268–92; Joanna Innes, "William Payne of Bell Yard, Carpenter c. 1718–82: The Life and Times of a London Informing Constable," unpublished paper, 71; for the Protestant Association in local context, where its radical connections are irrefutable, see Chapter 7. In London, Bull, Crosby and William Vaughn were members of both the SCI and the Protestant Association, and Joseph Priestley as well as Wesley wrote tracts for the latter.

overstepped the bounds of "resistance," which, as we have seen, was orderly, decent, property-protecting and only potentially revolutionary, and thus disrupted the radical vision of legitimate political activity. Indeed, the post-riot propaganda of the Protestant Association emphasized the social and political distinctions to be drawn between its respectable members and the "mob" that had turned vicious in the capital; the latter's implausible representation in Protestant Association tracts as the tool of "popish emissaries" commissioned to disgrace the petition was nevertheless consistent with radical views of the lower classes as dangerously open to corruption and depravity.[81] Hence, in this sense, the Gordon Riots, in conjunction with other instances of the "mob's" jingoistic support of the government during the American crisis, cemented radical politicians' mistrust of the "bread and circus" style of crowd politics, crystallized beliefs about the threat of plebeian degeneracy, and inaugurated a skepticism towards the nativist themes of traditional libertarian politics that had played central parts in earlier eighteenth-century oppositionist political culture. The "mob" and "the people" had never been so distinct.[82]

In these contexts, the parliamentary politics of 1782–4 ironically may have dealt the gravest blow to the reformers' cause, for it intensified the acrimonious divisions among radicals and suggested to war-weary observers that government could, perhaps, behave accountably to the public and attend to their wishes, thus restoring the dogged belief in the legitimacy of those parliamentary institutions that the Americans had so emphatically rejected. The fall of North and his replacement by the reforming ministries of Rockingham and Shelburne (the former dedicated to making peace with America) initially produced a sense of euphoria in the nation. The new ministries possessed impressive extra-parliamentary support, and the period 1782–3 was marked by unambiguously loyal celebrations at Admiral Rodney's victories over the French in the West Indies and peace-making with the former colonists. Not only had the fact of the new ministry restored to "the people" out-of-doors a sense of their own political weight – the addresses to the throne on the change in ministry thanked George III for having

---

[81] *Protestant Packet,* Aug. 4, 1780; radicals continued to distance themselves from the Gordon Riots "mob" in the next century: See Vicesimus Knox, *The Spirit of Despotism* (London, 1819), 21.

[82] Brewer, "Theatre and Counter-Theatre"; Rogers, "Crowd and People," 51. SCI radicals like Sheridan and Shelburne used the aftermath of the riots to press for police reform in the metropolis to better contain the mob: Black, *Association,* 183–4.

"complied with the wishes of his People" – but its measures for economic reform were believed to strike a blow against Crown influence
and eradicate the worst excesses of patronage and corruption, and its
recognition of the independence of the Irish Parliament seemed to augur
a belated but welcome return to liberal imperial government. The result
was that the seeming near-victory of the motion for reform in Parliament in 1782 was vanquished by a majority (161–141) which turned
out to be deceptively small.[83] After Fox and North joined forces to
bring down the Shelburne ministry over the issue of the peace prelim-
inaries in February 1783, the widespread extra-parliamentary hostility
toward the coalition and its eventual dismissal by the Crown and replacement by minority leader William Pitt resulted in an election in
which both reformers and friends of the prerogative could find common
ground. The rousing endorsement of Pitt, the king's minister and self-
proclaimed reformer, at the polls (a result which owed not a little to
radical activists in the constituencies) served to vindicate the extant
power of the people as a viable force, able to call their governors to
account and act as arbiter in disputes between the branches of the state,
while also resuscitating the reputation of George III.[84] Such perceptions
may have played a role in the diminution of organized support for
reform out-of-doors; ironically, so did Pitt's commercial proposals and
series of commodity taxes, which precipitously lost him support among
the urban middle classes. Some sixty petitions were submitted by manufacturing districts and commercial centers against the new taxes and
trade concessions to Ireland.[85] Pitt's detailed reform proposals of 1785,
on the other hand, mobilized a comparatively tiny number of petitions
and went down to defeat in the House of Commons by seventy-six
votes, thus vanquishing the hopes of reformers for a generation.

[83] Rodney: Marshall, *Bristol,* pp. 22–3; *Farley's Bristol Journal,* May 25, June 7, Nov.
16, 1782; addresses: *Public Advertiser,* May 16, 31, 1782. For the new ministries and
their support see *Annual Register,* 25 (1782), 169–89; Cannon, *Parliamentary Reform,*
78–85, 86–96; I. R. Christie, "Economical Reform and the 'Influence of the Crown,' "
Cambridge Historical Journal, 12 (1956), 144–54.
[84] Paul Kelly, "Radicalism and Public Opinion in the General Election of 1784," *Bulletin of the Institute of Historical Research,* 45 (1972), 73–88; *Leeds Mercury,* Feb.
10, 17, 1784; *Salisbury Journal,* April 26, 1784; *English Review,* 3 (1784), 157–8,
169–70; Colley, "Apotheosis of George III," 106. North himself declared that his
resignation was an instance of "the voice of the people prevail[ing] against the influence of the crown": *Parl. Hist.,* xxiii (1782–3), 826–8.
[85] *Salisbury Journal,* Nov. 1, 1784; June 13, 1785; *Manchester Mercury,* Feb. 15, March
22, 29, 1785; *Farley's Bristol Journal,* July 9, 1785; *New Annual Register* (1785),
151–3.

Hence the heterogeneous coalition of interests, sustained initially by reformist and anti-war politics, fell apart with the collapse of the common enemies capable of uniting them, the North ministry and its war effort. Equally important, the series of reverses in national fortunes wrought by the American war had produced a collective withdrawal from the idea of further changes in the body politic. The remainder of the decade was marked by campaigns for disciplinary, moral and social reforms, such as the reformation of manners, prison reform and anti-slavery, that provided common ground for individuals of disparate political views concerned with corruption in the polity but also, significantly, sought to regulate the behavior of the laboring classes or salvage the "rights of mankind" abroad rather than tamper with the representative structures of the state.[86] As Wyvill himself noted from a later vantage point, in 1785 the nation,

> exasperated by the misconduct of the former Ministers and the palpable corruption of Parliament . . . degraded as a great Political power, and nearly ruined by that Civil War, was eager to enjoy the blessings of Peace, without much adverting to the means of future security.[87]

III. PATRIOTISM UNMASK'D: CITIZENSHIP, EMPIRE AND NATION

The American war was, in the words of one of its historians, "Britain's only clear defeat in the long contest with France which began with the Revolution of 1688 and ended at Waterloo."[88] As such, it was an immensely important episode in domestic politics that magnified the ideological divisions in the nation and transected religious, partisan and socioeconomic groupings. Certainly the war divided traditionally allied groups. Overseas merchants, once the staunch allies of oppositionist politics in general and North American rights in particular, divided over government measures, with a significant, even preponderant, proportion in Liverpool, Bristol, Newcastle, Norwich and Whitehaven as well as London joining government contractors and pensioners in upholding the necessity of government coercion (Table 5.2). Such a show of sup-

---

[86] Joanna Innes, "Politics and Morals: The Reformation of Manners Movement," in Hellmuth, ed., *Transformation,* 57–118; Wilson, "A Dissident Legacy," 301–10; Money, *Experience and Identity,* 191–8. For the disciplinary modes of social reform in late-eighteenth-century Europe see Foucault, *Discipline and Punish,* esp. 135–308.

[87] Wyvill, *A State of the Representation of the People of England* (York, 1792), 5–6.

[88] Mackesy, *War for America,* xiv.

Table 5.2. *Occupational structure of petitioners and addressers*

	Conciliatory	%	Coercive	%
Provincial towns[a]				
Gentlemen/professionals	96	9.0	286	28.0
Merchants	117	11.0	192	19.0
Shopkeepers/retailers	262	24.6	216	21.1
Artisans	554	52.0	314	30.7
Laborers	26	2.4	8	0.8
Others	11	1.0	6	0.6
Total	1,066		1,022	
London				
Professionals	14	3.0	6	1.0
Overseas merchants, financiers, factors, brokers, warehousemen	158	31.0	355	45.0
Single-commodity wholesalers, retailers, craftspeople, packers	334	66.0	421	54.0

[a]Bristol, Newcastle, Liverpool, Colchester, Coventry, Nottingham.
Sources: Provincial towns: Bradley, *English Radicalism,* 374; London: Sainsbury, *Disaffected Patriots,* 194–5.

port for ministerial measures forced radicals to recognize that the mercantile community was no longer the automatic auxiliary of libertarian politics, but was subject to the same narrow self-interest as placemen. "Merchants and genuine patriots are not synonymous terms," one disgusted writer concluded, for their sensibilities had been corroded by their "professional lust of wealth [which] narrows their minds, enslaves their understandings, and throws a callous insensibility over their *public* feelings and affections."[89]

Dissenters, too, were divided by the conflict. An eloquent defense of colonial rights was provided by the leading lights of the dissenting community, and dissenters often took prominent parts in anti-war petitioning and propaganda efforts in such towns as Lancaster, Bristol, Newcastle, Nottingham and Norwich. However, a significant minority of nonconformists in London and the localities sided with the government for the duration of the war, for example Edward Pickard, John Martin, David Ribers, John Clayton and the Protestant Dissenting Deputies.[90] And despite the evident trend for members of the "establish-

[89] *LEP,* Sept. 8–10, 1778 (thanks to Nick Rogers for this reference); Sainsbury, *Disaffected Patriots,* 117–19, 194; Bradley, *English Radicalism,* 374–6.
[90] Bonwick, *English Radicals,* 86; Sainsbury, *Disaffected Patriots,* 196; Chapter 7. The

ment'' to back the administration's policy of coercion, landed and political elites were deeply divided over the crisis, with profound results for local and national politics that quantitative evaluation can obscure. Not only in Parliament but also in provincial towns and the counties, gentlemen, magistrates and MPs displayed their antagonisms in rival activities and support of loyalist and opposition subscriptions, petitions and addresses – divisions not duplicated in the 1790s.

As the evidence from the petitions suggests (Table 5.2), the greatest support for the anti-war agitation came from urban middling and artis-anal classes – men and women who had material and ideological affin-ities with the anti-war cause and who provided the overwhelming majority of urban electoral support for radical politics. Men provided between three-quarters and four-fifths of the signatures to the anti-war petitions from London and provincial towns, and as a group roughly 55 percent supported the colonists' claims, against 45 percent who backed the government. The social contours of support for anti-war politics, and the large proportion of artisans in particular, have led some historians to locate in this period the beginning of the artisanal ''class'' politics that would flower in the 1790s.[91] Certainly the war helped to further the corrosion of vertical identities that earlier radicalisms had galvanized, confirming an analysis of power that could support a spe-cies of ''class'' rhetoric and particularized claims for recognition, albeit ones articulated in the universalist discourses of history and rights. However, the interpretation of the politics of the war in terms of so-cioeconomic divisions (or the tendency to see ''class'' politics as the progressive form of the modern toward which eighteenth-century pol-itics struggled) tends to obfuscate the marked degree to which anti-war politics constructed positions that were extra-economic in character and whose meaning was derived largely from their relationship to the struc-tures of state power rather than productive relations per se. First, the addresses are insufficient indicators of the contours of popular loyalism (since plebeian signatories were not energetically solicited by their or-ganizers), and the lower proportion of artisans signing the addresses reflected elite prejudices that ''public opinion'' was the proper province only of men of weight and property and not of craftspeople and others whom they considered to be part of the ''rabble.''[92] More important,

---

Protestant Dissenting Deputies supported conciliation over coercion by a margin of 19 to 16, though three-quarters of dissenting signers of petitions supported the former: See Bradley, *English Radicalism,* 402.

[91] Bradley, *English Radicalism,* 427–8; Sainsbury, *Disaffected Patriots,* 117–19.

[92] See Chapter 7; Marshall, ''Manchester''; Barger, ''Matthew Boulton and the Bir-

the rifts within the middling social classes were as striking as those between them. Shopkeepers and retailers were almost evenly divided over the war, as were artisans in the City (where their support for rival missives was actively solicited by both sides), and craftspeople were enthusiastic participants in the celebrations and street theater attendant upon the loyalist, as well as the anti-war, campaign.[93] Finally, although there were certainly ample economic reasons for supporting or opposing the war, which disrupted credit and currency throughout the nation, raised taxes on land and commodities, caused slumps in trade and widespread unemployment, and wiped out some local industries geared to the American trade, the divisions in London and the localities bore little relationship to "actual" economic conditions or the ability to fare well or ill by the conflict's prosecution. Rather, they were part of the polarized ideological climate the war had produced, in which contending interpretations of the state, the people and the empire vied for the public's hearts and minds.

The war had consolidated and probably expanded the audience for radical diagnoses of the body politic's ills, largely through the horror and vicissitudes of the military effort, and did not so much link local and national discontents and grievances, which had been perceived to be of a piece since at least the succession period, as confirm what radicals had long alleged, that the venality of government had grown at all levels to a dangerous and irretrievable degree, leading it to pursue policies that were contrary to the true interests of the nation. Significantly, the complexity of political positions produced by the war did not prevent radical sympathizers from seeing them in terms of stark dichotomies: the dependent versus the independent part of the nation, the productive versus the unproductive classes, or the "advocates for a system of corruption and . . . taxes – and those who were advocates for the liberties of mankind," as Thomas Bewick pithily put it.[94] These oppositions consolidated an interpretation of the fiscal–military state as the site and creature of "Old Corruption," where Crown and executive

mingham Petition," 22; *Farley's Bristol Journal,* Oct. 14, 21, 1775. The low proportion of artisan addressers is also strikingly inconsistent with their proportion of the urban electorate as a whole (and their support for "tory" electoral politics): See O'Gorman, *Voters, Patrons and Parties,* chap. 6; and Phillips, *Electoral Behavior,* 290–8.

[93] Sainsbury, *Disaffected Patriots,* 115–17, 196. Of the tradesmen and craftsmen signing the address, 75% had contracts with the government; 24% of the middle-class addressers were so connected (p. 116).

[94] Bewick, *Memoir,* 93–4.

influence circulated through irreducible networks of sinecures, reversions and monopolies, and excessive taxes were levied on the nation to promote selfish and anti-populist designs. Radical observers repeatedly pointed out the connections the war had built up among "tory" government, placemen and contractors, a portion of the aristocracy, the clergy, the older sections of the bourgeoisie, episcopal offices and such rapacious imperial structures as the East India Company, which pillaged defenseless native peoples for the aggrandizement of private interests.[95] Thomas Day similarly beheld

> on one side, the rights of Nature, the interests of Mankind, a rising Empire formed upon the noblest principles of equity and reason, and destined to prove a common refuge from European Tyranny . . . on the other, but the low, illiberal aims of selfishness, avarice, and cruelty, that would, if possible, counteract the designs of Providence itself, engross its blessings, or convert them into curses for all the rest of the species . . . such were the aims of the British Ministry.[96]

To be sure, this rhetoric expressed social as well as political animosities that the war itself had heightened. Anti-war proponents in Bristol, Newcastle and Norwich appropriated a type of "class" rhetoric to attack the "conspiracy of Nobles" believed to be steering the state into disastrous policies that were contrary to the public interest; radical dissenters like the Reverend James Murray and the Reverend George Walker championed the rights of the poor in the face of the plunder and extortion of the rich and the latter's deliberate deceit as to the causes and aims of the war. Other radical organizers interpellated as citizens "those who subsist by honest Industry" against those who were parasitically entrenched within the system of corruption. But in all cases, the problems in church and state were conceptualized as political in origin: Monopolizing power bred greed, exploitation and immiseration of the majority.[97] Hence radical reformers' identification of

---

[95] SCI, *First Address to the People of England* (London, 1780); *Leeds Mercury,* March 28, 1780; John Cartwright, *Take Your Choice!* (London, 1776); W. Rubenstein, "The End of Old Corruption in England," *P & P,* no. 101 (1983), 55–8. In fact, modern political sociology supports these perceptions: See Bradley, *English Radicalism,* 367–70.

[96] *The Second Address to the Public from the Society for Constitutional Information* (London, 1782), 26.

[97] Chapters 7 and 8; *Farley's Bristol Journal,* Feb. 14, 1778; *Address to the People of Great Britain of All Denominations* (1782); James Murray, *Sermons to Ministers of State* (Newcastle, 1780), and *The Finishing Stroke to Mr. Wesley's Calm Address* (Newcastle, 1777); George Walker, *The Duty of a Soldier* (London, 1779), quoted in

the corrupted legislature as a whole and especially the parliamentary
majority "procured by bribery and corruption, by Court influence, contracts, places and pensions" as the nemesis of the people's liberties
had strong resonances. "The feelings of the great bulk of the nation,
are not the same with the feelings of *long parliaments,*" Cartwright
proclaimed, "nor will the language of such parliaments to their princes,
ever express *the sense of the people.*"[98] The politics of identity produced by the war thus defined the people and the patriot with reference
to the tentacular conglomerate of state power, distinguishing both by
their relationships to and positions within and without its structures. Its
critique of the state went beyond earlier "country" criticisms of executive influence both by insisting that the government could not be
reformed from within and emphasizing its nonpartisan and socially heterogeneous dimensions. As Burgh had argued, "in our time, the opposition is between a corrupt Court joined by *an innumerable multitude
of all ranks and stations* bought with public money, and the independent part of the nation."[99]

Such arguments were bound up with the rethinking of empire, and
particularly the relationship between the principles and practices of
mercantilist imperialism and its unlikely marriage with libertarian politics. Political and imperial developments in the years since the Peace
of Paris had produced a growing unease at the enormity of British
possessions, their racial and religious diversity and the increasingly
authoritarian techniques used to govern them. In the 1760s and early
1770s, for example, playwrights, political journalists and parliamentarians alike began to condemn the Asian Indian empire's polluting impact, now designated as a conduit of "luxury, effeminacy and
profligacy" to those at home. The East India Company and its conquests on the subcontinent were a particular source of concern, especially when the parliamentary inquiry leading to the Regulating Act of
1773 made public Robert Clive's misadventures in Bengal and the extent of the huge fortune he had amassed.[100] The West Indian planters

Bradley, *English Radicalism,* 177; Crowe, *A Sermon Preached Before the University
of Oxford* (London, 1782), 3–4; *York Courant,* Oct. 2, 1775.
[98] *Take Your Choice!* xvi; *LEP,* April 2–4, 1776; NNRO, MC7/417, Neville MSS, JW
to SN, June 8, 1777.
[99] *Political Disquisitions,* i, quoted in Thompson, "Eighteenth Century Society: Class
Struggle Without Class?" *Social History,* 3 (1978), 141–2; my emphasis.
[100] *Parl. Hist.,* xvii (1771–4), 857–8 and passim; Samuel Foote, *The Nabob* (London,
1772); *Public Advertiser,* March 14, 1774; July 10, 1769; March 26, 1771; *Lanca-*

also began to be castigated as potent sources of parliamentary corruption and mismanagement who, "being bred the tyrants of their slavish
blacks, may endeavour to reduce the whites to the same condition by
an aristocracy."[101]

Other incidents equally underscored the disturbing implications of
an empire of conquest. British attempts in the late 1760s to expatriate
or exterminate the Caribs on the island of St. Vincent in order to appropriate their lands produced a particularly gruesome and bloody war
on the island that forced English observers to confront, and decry, the
realities of conquest and question the long-vaunted moral superiority
of British imperialism over its European competitors. "The honor of
the British nation is at stake," Alderman Barlow Trecothick exclaimed
in a parliamentary debate on the propriety of the ministry's sending
troops to quell the Caribs' resistance; "a scene of iniquity and cruelty
is transacting . . . on the defenceless natives . . . against [whom] you are
exercising the barbarities of the Spaniards against the Mexicans."[102]
The Pacific explorations of Captain James Cook and his crews in the
same period, widely publicized and celebrated at home, also increased,
for the moment, domestic sympathy for indigenous peoples and mobilized sentiment against the use of force and conquest in the "civilizing" process. Not surprisingly, the anti-slavery movement had its roots
in this period, when colonial examples, the plight of black slaves in
England, and the Somerset case of 1772, which declared illegal the
forcible removal of slaves from England, necessitated that even supporters of colonists' rights acknowledge the brutal ways in which these
rights were denied to other Britons throughout the empire and the growing importance of slavery in the British and American economies.[103]

shire Magazine, 1 (1763), 60–2; 2 (1764), 515–16; Philip Lawson and Jim Phillips,
" 'Our Execrable Banditti': Perceptions of Nabobs in Mid-Eighteenth Century Brit-
ain," *Albion,* 16 (1984), 225–41; H. V. Bowen, *Revenue and Reform: The Indian
Problem in British Politics* (Cambridge, 1991).

[101] *Daily Gazetteer,* Nov. 2, 1767, quoted in Seymour Drescher, *Capitalism and Anti-
slavery* (London, 1986), 178–9.

[102] *Parl. Hist.* xvii (1771–4), 567–73, 722–43; *Scots Magazine,* 34 (1772), 588; Peter
Hulme, *Colonial Encounters: Europeans and the Caribbean* (London, 1986),
chap. 6.

[103] [John Hawkesworth], *An Accout of the Voyages . . . Successively Performed by Com-
modore Byron, Capt. Wallis, Capt. Carteret and Captain Cook,* 3 vols. (London,
1773); [James Cook], *A Voyage to the Southern Hemisphere,* 3 vols. (London, 1778);
Bernard Smith, *European Vision and the South Pacific* (New Haven, 1985); James
Walvin, ed., *Slavery and British Society* (Baton Rouge, 1982), 2–20; F. O. Shyllon,
Black Slaves in Britain (London, 1974), chap. 4.

The American war brought these ambivalences about empire to a head and enhanced the audience for the arguments of the anti-imperialists (always an articulate minority) that empire itself was the primary source of national luxury and corruption. Josiah Tucker, for example, turned the conspiracy theory of the radicals on its head, arguing that the American colonies had become dangerous to Great Britain, because they threatened the domestic polity with the contagion of dissenting and republican principles; they were also unnecessary, he claimed, because the mainland colonies had become more the competitors than the supports of British manufacture and commerce.[104] Even those sympathetic to the American cause perceived that the empire could be a corrupting force. Richard Price provided a scathing indictment of the empire in India as a theater of English despotism. There, Price warned,

> Englishmen, actuated by the love of plunder and the spirit of conquest, have depopulated whole kingdoms, and ruined millions of innocent people by the most infamous oppression and rapacity. – The justice of the nation has slept over these enormities. Will the justice of Heaven sleep? Are we not now execrated on both sides of the globe?[105]

The wave of anti-Americanism that broke out after the fighting had commenced also made some observers despair at the mindlessly authoritarian attitudes which empire had produced among some English subjects, who clearly saw their brethren across the Atlantic as possessions. And both the war and the reaction to it at home led some people to attack the acquisitive, machismo model of patriotism that the imperial project had crystallized. A lecturer at a philosophical society in Newcastle thus claimed that "in every point of view, the laws of war, and the laws of thieving are exactly alike," both valorizing conquest, self-interest and force; and another local writer suggested that the safety and glory of the state might best be found in its adoption of "feminine" values, as the alleged "weakness of women hath not ushered in such a flood of calamities, as these fatal virtues of men."[106] Clearly, empire

[104] Tucker, *Four Tracts and Two Sermons on Political and Commercial Subjects* (Gloucester, 1774), 128–30, *A Letter to Edmund Burke, Esq.* (Gloucester, 1775), 18–20, 43, and *An Humble Address and Ernest Appeal to Those Respectable Personages in Great Britain and Ireland* (London, 1776), passim, repr. in *Gentlemen's Magazine,* 66 (1776), 78–9. For Tucker's anti-imperialism see John Pocock, *Virtue, Commerce and History* (Cambridge, 1983), 37–50, 157–92.
[105] *Observations on the Nature of Civil Liberty* (London, 1776), 58.
[106] *Newcastle Weekly Magazine,* July 31, Oct. 16, 1776.

benefited some English citizens more than others, and could warp as well as nourish libertarian and public-spirited sensibilities.

Hence, the American war tarnished the once-glittering vision of a free and virtuous empire, founded in consent and nurtured in liberty and trade, and forced a dissolution of the union between radical politics and mercantile imperialism, for it made the mercantilist system and the ideology which supported it equally suspect.[107] It was not just the British government's coercion of Protestant English people living in America and the renunciation of their rights, religion and properties that served as the rallying-point for the radical and anti-war cause. It was also the loss of empire and, even further, the blinkered authoritarian vision which considered it both possible and practical to control the trade, commerce, resources and political identity of immense and distant colonial possessions, by arms as well as by law.[108] "What could be more flattering to an Englishman, in the utmost pride of his heart . . . than to see his country the seat of such an empire, the mistress of such a world," a Norfolk observer lamented in 1778, "[and] how are all our well-founded expectations destroyed! Where are we now to seek our glorious dependencies?"[109] Anti-war activists were forced to face the essential incompatibility of mercantilist imperialism with the increasingly expansive and participatory views of English men's birthrights, and with the new notions of the just relationship between the male individual and the state that were articulated in the extraparliamentary politics of the day. For those who had supported the government during the war, the American debacle provided chilling evidence of the results of too conciliatory and permissive an imperial policy; colonial government in the future would proceed upon more authoritarian, disciplinary and "rationalized" principles.[110] The celebration of military conquest in India and pride in Britain's professionalism and benevolence in the India empire in the next decade helped constitute this new ethos that strove to eradicate the lingering doubts felt by British rulers and citizens alike about empire's dangers or ethics.

---

[107] Adam Smith's exposé of mercantilism and balance-of-trade theory has to be seen in this context: *The Wealth of Nations . . .* (London, 1776), bk. 4.

[108] See, e.g., *Norfolk Chronicle,* Sept. 6, 1776; Jan. 24, 1778; *Newcastle Journal,* Dec. 16, 1775; and Peter Marshall, "Empire and Authority in Later Eighteenth Century Britain," *Journal of Imperial and Commonwealth Studies,* 15 (1987), 115.

[109] *Norfolk Chronicle,* Jan. 17, 1778.

[110] Christopher Bayly, *Indian Society and the Making of the British Empire* (Cambridge, 1988), 79–120; Peter Marshall, *'A Free Though Conquering People': Britain and Asia in the Eighteenth Century* (London, 1981), 18–20.

Such reconceptualizations of empire had important consequences for radical, loyalist and sexual politics, for they profoundly affected the competing notions of patriotism and citizenship that were made widely available for consumption among the broader political publics of the late eighteenth century. First, as we have seen, virtually all anti-war proponents defended the colonists with reference to the model of manly patriotism constructed during the Wilkite campaign that asserted both the right and necessity of English people's resistance to illegal authority no matter where they lived – a definition of Englishness and patriotism that the American colonists had themselves initially deployed. Americans had long been lauded by English observers as exhibiting the moral fiber, martial spirit and patriotic toughness eradicated from corrupt European civilization.[111] During the war, they accordingly were perceived to take these qualities to new heights: Eager to defend the "true and complete" principles of England's own revolution nearly a century earlier and stalwart in their formation of spirited militias to do so, they exhibited a variant of manly patriotism that was all too infrequently seen at home. The colonists were "fighting like men – like ENGLISH- MEN, for law and liberty supposed to be violated," according to observers in the Midlands, and their willingness to "give up every worldly interest, and . . . endure the worst extremities" to protect their rights elicited admiration and sympathy from a range of English commentators, who saw it as a touchstone of the national identity.[112] Radical writers in England used this activist model of political subjectivity as well as natural rights doctrines to endow the mass of "the people" with the authority of the public voice (despite simultaneous ambivalence toward "crowd" politics). "To the bulk of any nation, destined to *labour* and not to *study,* to *act* and not to *speculate,*" an SCI address pronounced, undiminished exercise of its "election rights" is essential to the preservation of liberty. But until those rights were enacted, "the people," including the "poor labourer or mechanic," must act as citizens and heads of households to scrutinize their governors and demand accountability and public trust. "It is both the interest and duty of *all men,*" the Reverend William Crowe reiterated, "to be active in examining the conduct of their Magistrates . . . You are never so well

---

[111] E.g., Wilkes was wont to compare the Americans' "manliness of sentiment" with the "luxurious effects of a debauched, vitiated and enervated taste" of Europeans: J. E. Ross, ed., *Radical Adventurer: The Diaries of Robert Morris* (Bath, 1971), 9.

[112] *Annual Register,* 20 (1775), 141; *London Magazine,* 43 (1774), 384; *Aris's Birmingham Gazette,* Oct. 2, 1775.

employed, either for yourselves or your families, as when you are inquiring into your constitutional rights, and examining, *without sedition,*
the conduct of Magistrates and Ministers.''[113] The state and the nation,
like the state and the people, were distinct. Opposition to government
aggression at home and abroad thus both enacted and valorized the
activist model of citizenship that, whatever position one took on democratic reform, insisted upon the right and duty – indeed, the patriotic
imperative – of white, male political subjects to resist illegitimate power
and call their governors to account, to *act like* citizens in the political
public sphere and assert their "natural equality" to survey and scrutinize the state. It thus remained an influential model of political subjectivity for the next century, used in various guises by democratic
reformers, working-class radicals and feminists alike.

Against this model of resistance, government supporters offered their
own very different models of patriotism and political subjectivity. It
has been argued that the government's trump card during the American
war was its ability to appropriate the language of Protestant nationalism
from the radicals on behalf of its war effort.[114] I suggest instead that
the government and its supporters' greater success lay in borrowing
populist rhetoric and tactics from their radical opponents to popularize
an alternative culture of patriotism that could compete with the more
dissident varieties for the next several decades. Lord North's insistence
that the American war was "the war of the people," a case study in
the responsiveness of political institutions to the popular pulse, was
indicative of this important ideological strategy, as were the ostentatious celebrations of royal anniversaries and military victories: Both
deliberately aimed at consolidating the identity and rationale of a loyalist political culture, animated by fierce protectiveness toward church
and king and fueled by popular consent and desire. Indeed, loyalists
insisted throughout the conflict that their constructions of the state and
public good were for the people, of the people and by the people, and
that the opponents of government policy were merely "self-interested

[113] *An Address to the Public, from the Society for Constitutional Information* (London,
1780), 2; Crowe, *A Sermon Preached Before the University of Oxford,* 3. Crowe went
on to stress that "ministers and members of Parliament are as much your servants,
as you are the servant of him, who pays you for your wages . . . Had your Representatives acted as faithful servants, you would not have lost America and your West
India islands."
[114] Colley, "Radical Patriotism," 169–87. Colley sees the war as leaving radicals no
patriotic position to take; Sainsbury argues that it produced an opposition between
patriotism and loyalism (*Disaffected Patriots,* 130–2); I cavil at both suggestions.

incendiaries of the war.''[115] They were most unified from the beginning
in adhering to a view of the state as united above sectional interests
and supreme within the polity, the ultimate adjudicator and judge
against which there could be no appeal. On this view, American "resistance" was rebellion against legally constituted authority, and the
government was acting for the preservation of "the people" by defending the rights and sovereignty of the state against those on both
sides of the Atlantic who wished to subvert them. Yet in practice the
populist dimensions of the loyalists' position were strictly contained.
"The people's" role as citizens was not to petition or canvass, survey
or judge, which should properly be left to men of weight and property,
but rather to support – with their lives if necessary – "the inherent
Rights of the Mother Country," that is, the firm and indivisible authority wielded in the people's name from above, without which English liberty was impossible.[116] Asserting the inextricability of state and
nation, they thus defined an essentially passive political subjectivity as
the heart of the patriotic imperative – the willingness to support unques-
tioningly established structures of the state against all challenges to
them – and propagated this notion of citizenship across the broadest
social spectrum with heretofore unparalleled vigor.

To make their case, supporters of the government were able to appropriate the fear of the effeminate and the feminine in the political
realm for their own purposes, as an anti-radical, anti-American print
entitled *The Parricide: A Sketch of Modern Patriotism* (Plate 11) makes
clear.[117] Wilkes directs the attack of a bellicose, dagger-bearing America on a naked and defenseless Britannia while Fox, Alderman Hayley
(Wilkes's brother-in-law) and other radicals look on. One muzzles the
British lion; another holds Britannia's hands, preparing her for her con-
summate violation; and off to the left a brown-skinned, serpent-haired
savage of revolution celebrates at the scene before her. The threatening

---

[115] *Parl. Hist.,* xxiii (1782–3), 826; Horace Walpole, *Letters,* quoted in Sainsbury, *Dis-
    affected Patriots,* 130–1; *Farley's Bristol Journal,* Oct. 14, 1775.
[116] See, e.g., *Bonner and Middleton's Bristol Journal,* March 21, 1779; for nonresistance
    in the Tory world view see J. C. D. Clark, *English Society 1688–1832* (Cambridge,
    1985), 121–88. For more developed rationales of this kind of conservative populism
    using the metaphors of oppositionist patriotism, see the propaganda of Reeves' As-
    sociations for the Preserving Liberty and Property Against Republicans and Levellers,
    such as *Ten Minutes Caution from a Plain Man to His Fellow Citizens* and *A Word
    in Season to the Traders and Manufacturers of Great Britain* (both London, 1792).
[117] It accompanied the April 1776 issue of the *Westminster Magazine* and signaled its
    change to a pro-ministerialist view. See *Catalogue,* v, no. 5334; and Madge Dresser,
    "Britannia," in Samuels, ed., *Patriotism,* iii, 34–6.

11. *The Parricide* (1776). The feminized and effeminizing principles of rebellion threaten to undo the polity. Courtesy of the Lewis Walpole Library, Yale University.

female figures representing illegitimate power and influence (here equated with the American colonies) or disorder and rebellion (the dagger/penis-wielding America is particularly overdetermined), the excessively feminine and helpless stance of Britannia, the essentially passive role of the men, and the title itself testify to some of the ways women's bodies were used in the visual culture of politics to project masculine categories and ideals (and masculine ideals of the feminine), while simultaneously underlining the inappropriate nature of the feminine and the feminized in the political realm. Above all, the print captures the complexities of patriotic imperatives within an imperial polity that were thrown into stark relief by the conflict. From the "Tory" point of view (one with which Court Whigs under Walpole would have agreed), patriotism, and hence political subjectivity itself, must be essentially nonresisting toward legally constituted authority. Support for the rebellious colonists by English subjects thus constituted an act of "unnatural" rebellion itself that allowed the feminizing principles of rebellion and insubordination to contaminate the body politic, ultimately resulting in its undoing. Such images and themes bombarded the public and competed for their hearts and minds with radical models of manly resistance. It was part of a larger move to the "right" that the war wrought on the part of those in authority, one that coincided with a major initiative to exclude the feminine from the public sphere and contain it within the private realm of domesticity.[118]

In these and other ways, then, the American war brought into sharp relief the irreconcilable tensions between empire and nation. Benedict Anderson has argued that the nation was imagined as a "community," because "regardless of the actual inequality and exploitation that may prevail in each, the nation is always conceived as a deep horizontal comradeship."[119] Yet empire, whose progress and processes played integral roles in defining the British nation and English national identity in the eighteenth century, constantly demonstrated the contradictions and fissures produced by such attempted "national" imaginings. If the discourse of nationality sought to construct homogeneities within the territorial boundaries of the nation-state, it also sought to identify and assert *difference* – those differences, for example, however artificial and tenuous, which distinguished the nation from other nations, as well as those which divided the citizens within its own boundaries. Empire confounded and completed this project in interesting and complex ways. As we have seen, the English devotion to empire lay as much in its role as a bulwark and emblem of English superiority and benevolence as in its profitability, yet, especially as constituted in oppositionist patriotism, empire was imagined to create a far-reaching and inclusive *British* polity that preserved the most valued components of the national identity. "Are we not compelled to . . . value what we hold most dear, next to our own salvation," one dismayed observer inveighed in the midst of the American crisis, "as we value our rights as Englishmen, our existence as a nation, and the safety and dignity of the BRITISH EMPIRE?"[120] Carried out as a right of English men and in the name of English liberties, however, empire could not secure those rights for Britons, who in the context of a heterogeneous empire were not all created equal. Women, Catholics, aristocrats and indigenous peoples as well as Frenchmen were "others," although not interchangeable ones, to the fair-minded masculine English subject that the imperial project valorized, and were part of the amalgam which empire's

---

[118] For which see Catherine Hall, *White, Male and Middle Class* (New York, 1988), 101–19.
[119] *Imagined Communities* (New York, 1983), 16.
[120] "To the ENGLISH NATION," *Norfolk Chronicle*, Oct. 10, 1778.

gendered, commercial and aggressive vision of the national identity sought to subordinate, at home and abroad. Within Britain itself, from the perspective of the metropole, the Welsh and, more gradually, the Scots become naturalized as British, the Irish, Jews and Africans perhaps never do; beyond the British isles, the claims of peoples of different races and cultures to British rights and liberties were even more remote and contingent, and Britishness was conferred or denied not only in relation to the numbers of white British settlers in residence but also to the degree of acceptance by colonial peoples of English hegemony and the legitimacy of British rule.

Of course, colonized groups could destabilize the identities of Britishness formulated in the days of imperial glory and subvert their hegemonic deployment. The American colonists appropriated the "rights of Englishmen" to reject Englishness and to continue to deny those rights to indigenous and slave populations, an effort that both "heritage" and race worked to make relatively successful. The beleaguered Caribs were described by the British planters who desired their land as "idle, ignorant and savage people," exalted by their defenders as exhibiting not only the rights but the temperament of English men – "Fighting for liberty, and every English heart must applaud them"; but they themselves feared they would be made slaves by their new British governors, to the apparent shock and dismay of liberal observers in England.[121] The period of the first British empire thus consolidated a national identity, forged in over two centuries of imperial adventures and national and colonial expansion, that could not be readily naturalized, producing colonial subjects who were "savages" or "almost like Englishmen" but could never be English themselves.[122] The various hierarchical visions of the domestic polity were recognizably if irregularly mapped onto the imperial one, and the incompatibility of the rights of English people and those of Britons laid bare – the first must always take priority over the second, and national belonging kept within strict territorial, cultural and, increasingly, racial bounds.

---

[121] *Parl. Hist.,* xvii (1771–4), 570–5, 735–6.
[122] Homi Bhabha, "Of Mimicry and Man: The Ambivalence of Colonial Discourse," *October,* 28 (1984), 125–33. For related racial theories see Richard Popkin, "Medicine, Race, Anti-Semitism: A Dimension of Enlightenment Culture," in G. S. Rousseau, ed., *The Languages of Psyche: Mind and Body in Enlightenment Thought* (Berkeley and Los Angeles, 1990), 405–2; for their links to evangelical thought see Smith, *European Vision,* chap. 3. For contemporary recognition of and complaints about this conceptualization of Englishness see *Gentleman's Magazine,* 25 (1765), 589–90.

The war, then, forced a rethinking of empire's benefits, dangers and
ethics and of the kinds of citizenship that an imperial polity could
support. Some of the more radical members of the formerly pro-
imperial public retreated into anti-imperialist internationalism, like
Richard Price; others found the corruption of empire confirmed in Fox's
India bill and consequently repudiated imperialism altogether as a prop
of Old Corruption, or, like Cartwright, theorized about a new imperial
relationship based on the internal independence and sovereignty of the
colonies and the external regulation of trade by Britain.[123] And still
others – no doubt the majority – transferred imperial confidence and
aspirations eastward, to India, as the foundation of a grander, more
glorious – and more authoritarian – empire. But for all, imperial identities would have to be reformulated on less tarnished bases than those
of a discredited mercantilism and a tenacious, if embattled, libertarianism.

[123] Price, *Discourse on Love of Country* (London, 1789); Cartwright, *American Independence the Interest and Glory of Great Britain* (London, 1774); Granville Sharp,
A Declaration of the People's Natural Right to a Share in the Legislature (London,
1774).

Part II

*The cases of Newcastle upon Tyne
and Norwich*

6. *Changing contexts: Newcastle and Norwich in the eighteenth century*

> When times went well, and Money circling made
> Its ready courses thro' a spritely *Trade* . . .
> 'Twas then I could to jovial *Clubs* repair
> And pass my Evenings pleasurably there;
> With boon companions talk of Mutual Trade . . .
> Sometimes the public news was our debate,
> The Siege of Cities or Commanders Fate . . .
> Sometimes domestic Cases were our Care,
> A *Sheriff's* Election or a future *May'r* [or]
> What clubs are settl'd at each publick Sign . . .
> Till the long-striking Hours encroaching come,
> And send us all, in cheerful Humour home.
> *The Weaver* (Norwich, 1720)[1]

> I did not like London – it appeared to me to be a World of itself
> where every thing in the extreme, might at once be seen – extreme
> riches – extreme poverty – extreme Grandeur and extreme wretch-
> edness – all of which were such as I had not contemplated upon
> before . . . I tired of it and determined to return home.
> Thomas Bewick, 1776[2]

The development of extra-parliamentary political culture in the nation
was predicated upon the emergence of a distinctive urban culture and
public in the localities. The three chapters on Newcastle upon Tyne
and Norwich will address key aspects of the relationship between "local" and "national" politics, demonstrating the roles of provincial ur-

---

[1] NNRO, MS217, W. Massey, Acta Norvicensia, 1720–9.
[2] *A Memoir,* ed. Iain Bain (Oxford, 1979), 75.

ban politics in producing the national, signifying the state and constructing the populist and patriotic identities that circulated through the body politic. Such an investigation hopes, at the very least, to disrupt the presumed equivalences between "metropolitan" and "national" politics so aggressively asserted by eighteenth-century Londoners and rather uncritically adopted by their historians. To do so it is necessary to provide a sense of place. This chapter will look at the distinctive socioeconomic, ethnic, religious and political topographies of Newcastle and Norwich that shaped their contributions to national political life.

I. NORTHERN EXPOSURES

The political and social life of Newcastle has often come back to us in images of feuding magnates divided by coal, cash and political rivalries and a volatile and fractious populace prone to riot and resistance.[3] There is much that is credible in this picture. With a population of approximately 24,000, the city presented extremes of luxury and want, and its coal-owning magistrates lorded over a town in which the middling sorts were circumscribed by trade and franchise restrictions and outnumbered six to one by the laboring poor connected with the coal trade and its attendant industries: shipbuilding, glass, salt, iron, lead and soap.[4] John Wesley thought the town pleasing to the eye but its inhabitants abhorrent to the ear: "So much drunkenness, cursing, and swearing (even from the mouths of little children)," he wrote in his journal, "do I never remember to have seen and heard before." Eighteen years later Elizabeth Montagu gave Novocastrians an even less flattering endorsement, referring to them in metropolitan colonialist language as "a parcel of dirty savages," and describing Newcastle as "the ugliest [town] in Great Britain, but full of wealth and business . . . I cannot say, with

[3] Roger Howell, *Newcastle upon Tyne and the Puritan Revolution* (Oxford, 1967); Edward Hughes, *North Country Life in the Eighteenth Century: The Northeast 1700–1750* (Oxford, 1952); Joyce Ellis, "Urban Conflict and Popular Violence: The Guildhall Riots of 1740 in Newcastle upon Tyne," *International Review of Social History,* 25, pt. 3 (1980), 332–49; P. M. Ashraf, *The Life and Times of Thomas Spence* (Newcastle, 1983).

[4] Joyce Ellis, "A Dynamic Society: Social Relations in Newcastle-upon-Tyne," in Peter Clark, ed., *The Transformation of English Provincial Towns* (London, 1984), 190–227. Probably 15,000–18,000 were involved in the coal trade: J. U. Nef, *The Rise of the British Coal Industry,* 2 vols. (London, 1932), ii, 137.

the Psalmist, that my Cot is fallen in a fair ground; it is some comfort that it is a rich one.''[5]

Indeed, Newcastle was a large and growing city whose continued prosperity was assured by the dependence of London on its chief product, coal. Between 1700 and 1800, Tyneside coal output had increased threefold, and the spin-off industries also thrived. Moreover, Newcastle stood at the site of the easiest and most important crossing of the Tyne that was still within reach of the sea, and the Corporation controlled the navigation and trade of the river in its chartered capacity as Conservator of the Tyne.[6] The city was also an important financial, marketing and distribution center for the Northeast, serving as a clearing-house for the products of the fertile agricultural hinterland and a distributor of the necessities and luxuries of life to its own large population, the vast majority of whom were consumers rather than producers of food and commodities.[7]

Even in the early decades of the century Newcastle maintained facilities for a polished cultural life that were rooted, in part, in its roles as an ancient corporate town and the administrative and service center for Northumberland. Assize and race weeks provided local notables with the opportunity to parade, socialize and entertain, enhanced by the assemblies, concerts, plays and masquerades that occurred in abundance.[8] During the rest of the year, such activities were pursued at local theaters and assembly rooms. Since the Restoration, plays had been performed in the Moot Hall of Castle Garth (where the Northumberland assizes were also held); they also took place in the Great Booth erected in Usher's timber yard near Black-gate, in the Turk's Head Long Room and finally in a new theater erected in Bigg Market in 1748. A new Assembly Room was built in 1736 for the balls and concerts which magistrates were wont to hold during guild and sessions weeks.[9] By

[5] *The Journal of John Wesley,* ed. Nehemiah Curnock, 8 vols. (London, 1910), iii, 13; HL, Montagu MSS, MO4762, ERM to Matthew Robinson, Sept. 26, 1760.
[6] T. S. Ashton and Joseph Sykes, *The Coal Industry in the Eighteenth Century* (Manchester, 1929), 249–51; Hughes, *North Country Life,* 11–12, 69n.
[7] Nef, *British Coal Industry,* ii, 20; Henry Bourne, *The History of Newcastle on Tyne* (Newcastle, 1736), 54; John Brand, *The History and Antiquities of the Town and County of Newcastle upon Tyne,* 2 vols. (London, 1789), ii, 33–7, 41n. The customs revenue from the town was estimated in 1772 at £56,000 per year.
[8] Brand, *Newcastle,* i, 143; John Hodgson Hinde, "Public Amusements in Newcastle," *AA,* new ser., 4 (1860), 229–33.
[9] Hinde, "Public Amusements," 235–8; Sybil Rosenfeld, *Strolling Players: Drama in the English Provinces, 1700–1760* (Cambridge, 1939), 111–13, 163–4.

the 1760s, such activities had expanded, and bowling greens and arch-
ery fields, concerts and balls and public baths all attracted the custom
of the fashionable and aspiring, aided in the following decade by the
building of luxurious new assembly rooms and the Newcastle Theater
Royal.[10] The social calendar was augmented by the meetings of elite
societies such as the Sons of Clergy and the Society of Florists and
Botanists, at whose anniversary dinners town and county notables
feasted together; at the same time, freemasons, political societies, tradesmen's clubs and friendly societies provided occasions for more socially mixed conviviality and display.[11] Finally, Newcastle was a vital
communications center for the Northeast. It was the stopping-off point
between London and Edinburgh; stagecoaches ran fortnightly in the
early decades of the century, increasing to three daily by the 1770s,
and dozens of weekly commercial carriers served the hinterland. In
conjunction with the town's numerous inns, two coffeehouses and
thriving press, Newcastle's communications connected its residents
with the national and international world.[12]

Despite its varied social and economic life, coal dominated the economy and politics on Tyneside. Coal was a notoriously risky business,
requiring enormous amounts of fixed capital and being subject to a
range of geological, meteorological and political vagaries, from shallow
seams, bad weather and interruptions in trade caused by war or labor
disputes to the endless and expensive legal haggling about wayleaves
(permission to pass over a neighboring landowner's ground).[13] Yet because the massive financial commitments could be redeemed by the
impressive fortunes that could result, the coal industry was as much a
source of conflict as prosperity. The Newcastle Corporation maintained
the exclusive right to sell coal on the river through the Hostmen's
Company, by 1700 a body that included coalowners who were also

[10] *Newcastle Courant,* Sept. 7, 1760; July 4, 1761; John Sykes, *Local Records of North-
    umberland,* 2 vols. (London, 1866), i, 230; Brand, *Newcastle,* i, 121–2; Eneas Mac-
    kenzie, *A Descriptive and Historical Account of the Town and County of Newcastle
    upon Tyne,* 2 vols. (Newcastle, 1827), i, 527, 593.
[11] *Newcastle Courant,* Sept. 17, Aug. 18, 1725; John Strachan, *Northumbrian Masonry
    and the Development of the Craft* (London, 1898), 56–7; Chapter 1.
[12] Sykes, *Local Records,* i, 132; *Whitehead's Newcastle Directory* (repr. Newcastle,
    1778); Appendix; John Feather, *The Provincial Book Trade in the Eighteenth Century*
    (Cambridge, 1988), 29; C. J. Hunt, *The Book Trade in Northumberland and Durham
    to 1860* (Newcastle, 1975).
[13] Peter Cromar, "Economic Power and Organization: The Development of the Coal
    Industry on Tyneside, 1700–1828" (Ph.D. diss., Cambridge University, 1976), 4–29,
    175–82.

members of the Merchant Adventurers (and thus the chief traders in all commodities shipped to and from Newcastle) and who were prone to join in "combinations" or cartels with London dealers to keep prices and profits high. The political and economic rivalries in the industry were so intense that they could lead to attempted poisonings among rivals, as well as to protracted assaults upon the privileges of the Newcastle Corporation by "outside" coalowners (like the Cotesworth, Bowes and Montagu–Wortley families), disgruntled laborers and parliamentary committees alike.[14] At such moments the normally divided Corporation elites would unite to maintain their privileges against outside threats. For example, the arch-Whig alderman, coalowner and governor of both the Hostmen's and Merchants' companies, Richard Ridley, was prepared to spend £20,000 on behalf of the Tory Catholic Claverings, an old Hostman family, to ruin his rival William Cotesworth in the latter's claim to a wagon way that adjoined Sir James Clavering's estate. A year later, the Corporation's refusal to grant way-leave over one of their estates to Cotesworth and George Liddell for their newly leased Heaton colliery in 1717 led the enraged Cotesworth to instigate a lawsuit over the legal title to the property in question, soliciting signatures from disenchanted Newcastle freemen for a memorial to the government attacking the Corporation's "oppressions" as the Tyne's conservator, which led to a parliamentary inquiry.[15] By the late 1740s these rivalries had become more genteel, soothed by exogamous agreements between the Corporation and county families to "regulate" the coal trade and by the dampening of party rivalries within the town. The end of the Seven Years' War inaugurated a twelve-year period of steady rise in demand and a leveling of prices that stimulated investment and expansion; and increasing sales, the availability of cheaper and more efficient steam engines, and the establishment of private banks encouraged the entrance of "newcomers" into the industry, breaking the decades-old monopoly of Newcastle Hostmen and the Grand Allies in the coal trade. Backed by bank capital amassed from the landowners, traders, merchants and others who were

[14] Joyce Ellis, "The Poisoning of William Cotesworth, 1725," *History Today,* 16 (1978), 753; William J. Hausman, "Government and Business in Eighteenth-Century England: Anticombination Acts and the Stability of the Newcastle Coal Cartel, 1700–1750," *Research in Economic History* (1982), suppl. 2, 45–70; F. W. Dendy, ed., *Extracts from the Records of the Company of Hostmen* (Surtees Society, 105, 1901), xxxi; GPL, Cotesworth MSS, CJ3/13, Keelmen's Petition [1711].

[15] GPL, Cotesworth MSS, CP1/3/57; Ellis, "Cotesworth," 755; Cromar, "Coal Industry," 63–75.

depositors, men like William Brown and Matthew Bell began to develop the rich coalfields north of the Tyne. Some of the older monopolists, on the other hand, who had their circulating capital tied up in dead rent or worked-out collieries, were hard pressed to respond to the new economic and technological situation. In this way, the coal industry on Tyne and Wearside became, for the first time, a relatively "open" one which could accommodate entrepreneurs.[16] Internecine conflict and subterfuge could still characterize business relations, but, despite the formation in 1771 of the cartel of Tyne and Wear coalowners which sought to limit output and raise prices, no new extra-economic barriers to entrance to the industry were possible, and sales, employment and local wealth increased.

Coal, then, was one major contributor to the fractious power relations within the town; oligarchy was another. The economic power of Newcastle's landowning industrial gentry was matched by the firm grip that some of them had on the institutions of local government. The election of the mayor, sheriff, ten aldermen and twenty-four common councilmen was a hopelessly convoluted affair with progressively diminishing freemen's participation. In the end, the twenty-four "electors" who filled the corporate offices consisted of the current mayor, aldermen and sheriff and twelve freemen delegates from the guilds and by-trades who were hand-picked by the aldermen from the pool of thirty-six proffered by their members (the ten incorporated trade companies, including the Hostmen, had no role in Corporation elections).[17] Since the Merchant Adventurers were made up of three (the mercers, boothmen and drapers) of the town's twelve mysteries, its members dominated town government, and the Corporation was able to perpetuate itself by cooption.[18] The magistrates and councilors of Newcastle thus consti-

---

[16] Cromar, "Coal Industry," 107–12, 119–22; Ashton and Sykes, *Coal Industry,* 250–5. In the same period, lead-mining, glass works, roperies, soapmaking, salt works, dying, brewing, pottery, linen and worsted manufacture, ironworks, and a highly specialized metallurgical industry that made tools, swords, guns and wheels for clocks and watches expanded. Mackenzie, *Historical Account,* i, 716–17; William I. Roberts III, "Ralph Carr: A Newcastle Merchant and the Colonial Trade," *Business History Review,* 42 (1968), 271–87.

[17] Mackenzie, *Historical Account,* ii, 612; Brand, *Newcastle,* ii, 188–90.

[18] Ninety-eight percent of the mayors between 1715 and 1788 were Merchant Adventurers or Hostmen, with over half serving two or more times; the majority of councilmen were also Merchant Adventurers, with only a minimal number representing the craft guilds. See TWA, 598/6–7, Common Council Minutes, 1656–72; C. H. Blair, *The Mayors and Lord Mayors of Newcastle-upon-Tyne, 1216–1940* (*AA,* 4th ser., 18, 1940); M. H. Dodds, ed., *Register of Freemen of Newcastle-upon-Tyne* (Newcastle

tuted a hereditary oligarchy which wielded economic and political clout in formidable fashion as employers and magistrates, controlling the coal, lead, iron, salt, brewing and glass industries, trade, and the food supply, as well as the extensive patronage and revenues of the Corporation derived from rents, dues, tolls and estates.[19] The town's parliamentary representatives also came from their ranks. Richard Ridley and his son Matthew, Sir William Blackett and his nephew and heir Sir Walter Calverly Blackett, William Carr and Nicholas Fenwick, as aldermen, MPs and Merchant Adventurers or Hostmen, dominated the inner rings of town government and negotiated Newcastle's official relations with the state. Although their vigilance in protecting Newcastle's livelihood and privileges from outside threats could give them robust freemen support, their monopolistic political and economic practices were a continual source of irritation and antagonism that led to strikes, riots and ultimately freemen's radical opposition.

The social as well as political structures in Newcastle necessitated the adoption of a governing style by local elites that was both ostentatiously paternalistic and circumspect. Social analyses of seventeenth- and early-eighteenth-century Newcastle have documented the bottom-heavy social pyramid, where some 70 percent of the local population were laborers, 55 to 60 percent of whom were engaged in mineral, navigational and industrial maintenance employments.[20] Because of its capital-intensive nature, the coal industry did not dominate local occupations, but within the large skilled, if quasi-proletarian, population, the most distinctive and turbulent groups were those connected with the coal industry. They included the articulate and demanding keelmen, whose strikes to retain beneficial terms of employment attracted the central government's attention throughout the century; the pitmen, who formed, in the words of their historians, "an hereditary caste almost as exclusive as that of the owners of mineral rights"; the sinkers, heavers, carters, wagonwrights and watermen involved in getting the coal from the pits to the keels on the river, and the large numbers of sailors who manned the transport ships to London.[21]

---

upon Tyne Record Series, 6, 1926). By the second half of the century, the mayor virtually appointed his colleagues on the Common Council.

[19] In 1725 the town's income was some £12,500 a year; by the 1780s it had risen to almost £20,000: TWA, 543/88, City Chamberlain Accts., Receipts, 1725–6, 1786–7.

[20] Howell, *Newcastle,* 12–13; Ellis, "Dynamic Society," 194–200.

[21] E. R. Turner, "The Keelmen of Newcastle," *AHR,* 21 (1916), 542–5; J. L. Hammond and B. Hammond, *The Skilled Labourer* (London, 1920), 24–5; Ashton and Sykes, *Coal Industry,* 155. TWA, 394/7–10, Petitions, etc. Relating to the Keelmen, 1719–

Though all of the numbers involved in the coal industry were bound men, under contract to work for a particular master for a year, their frequent "mutinies" (strikes) exhibited all too clearly the potentially dangerous power of organized labor on Tyneside.

In these circumstances, the maintenance of order depended upon the combination of a highly theatrical presentation of authority and occasional repressive action. Though the magistrates were always ready to make examples of persistent offenders who goaded others into unruliness, their response to labor unrest and riot was selective and moderate. The keelmen's strike of 1719, for example, occasioned by their opposition to a combination of coalowners, fitters and shipmasters to delay shipments to the capital, put a stop to the trade and caused such social unrest that the magistrates called in troops and incarcerated the ringleaders of the strike, with Whitehall's approval. By June, the majority of the keelmen had gone back to work, and a month later the imprisoned culprits were released without prosecution because they were "sensible and repenting of their Crime."[22] After the divisive and damaging food riots of 1740, the magistrates released without prosecution two-thirds of the rioters. One-third were let off with successful indictments; those involved in the destruction of corporate property received harsher treatment, including transportation and death sentences.[23] The mixture of severity and mercy, with a realistic assessment of public sympathy for the culprits, marked the magisterial response to strikes and riots throughout the century.

The Newcastle magistrates were similarly vigilant in taking highly visible and timely actions in periods of harsh weather, bad harvests and dearth. The procession of the magistrates to the marketplace for the assize of bread, seizing underweight loaves, was a regular and conspicuous occurrence. So too was the distribution of coal, bread, meat and money to the poor in periods of bad trade caused by weather or war. Though prompted undoubtedly by genuine concern, these actions were necessary to blunt a potentially dangerous reaction of the populace to dearth.[24] Just as important to the maintenance of authority was the

71. For the finely differentiated occupational structure of the coal industry, see Royden Harrison, ed., *Independent Collier: The Coal Miner as Archetypal Proletarian Reconsidered* (Hassocks, 1978).
[22] TWA, 394/7, Petitions, Correspondence, and Depositions Relating to the Keelmen's Rising, 1718–19.
[23] Ellis, "Urban Conflict and Popular Violence," 346–7.
[24] *Newcastle Courant,* May 1, 1731; Jan. 5, 1733; April 9, 1736; Nov. 3, 1739; Jan. 26,

civic and religious calendar of Newcastle, which provided regular occasions for the demonstration of elite grandeur, paternalism, largesse
and legitimacy. National and local political anniversaries, from the
monarch's birth and accession days and guild days to Corporation election day on Michaelmas Monday; Anglican fast and feast days; the
opening of fairs and erection of new public buildings; the winning of
new collieries; and the weddings, births and funerals in gentry families
– all could prompt purposeful grand ceremonial displays, marked by
processions of the aldermen, Common Council, clergy and minor officers in their robes and regalia.[25] Though decreasing slightly over the
century, as late as the 1770s the requirement that local magistrates keep
up a rigorous ceremonial schedule as well as lavish elite entertainments
was bewailed by new incumbents, who had to pay a good portion of
the costs out of their own pockets.[26]

Both the quantity and quality of elite street theater suggests that it
served distinctive purposes in the large commercial and industrial town.
The celebrations on George II's coronation were more elaborate than
most yearly observances, but they give a sense of the ostentatious demonstration of elite loyalty and munificence that was common to them
all.

> The Day was usher'd in with ringing of Bells, the magistrates in
> their Scarlet Gowns, accompanied by the Common Council, Clergy
> and Gentry, went from the Guild-Hall to Church, with Musick Play-
> ing, and Canons firing; and from thence proceeded to the Mayor's
> House, where a splendid Entertainment was prepar'd for them, and
> after Dinner they repair'd to the Market-Place, where a Fountain was
> erected, which ran Wine, where the Magistrates, Common Council,
> Clergy and Gentry, drank the Healths of the King, Queen, Royal
> Issue, with many other Loyal Healths, in Presence of many thousand
> Spectators; thence they went to Guild-Hall, where the said Healths

Feb. 2, 1740. John Walter and Keith Wrightson, "Dearth and the Social Order in
Early Modern England," *P & P,* no. 71 (1976), 22–42; E. P. Thompson, "The Moral
Economy of the English Crowd," *P & P,* no. 50 (1971), 76–136.

[25] A typical year could include 30 public observances, e.g., January 30; May 29; the
king's accession, coronation and birth days; assizes; Ascension Day; race week; the
Michaelmas election; 4 guild and sessions days; 7 Anglican holidays; 2 visitations of
charity schools; the opening of Lammas and St. Luke's fairs; and 4 gentry commemorations.

[26] TWA, Chamberlain Accounts, 543/88, 1725–6; NRO, Blackett MSS, ABL 228,
Swordbearer's Account; *Reprints of Rare Tracts, Chiefly Illustrative of the Northern
Counties* (Newcastle, 1849), iii, 107–8.

were repeated and with like Ceremony as above, and the Conduit
running with Wine all the time for the Populace, whilst a great Bonfire erected in the Market Place was burning, the Canons firing for
each Health; they afterwards returned to the Mayor's House, where
there was a Ball for the Ladies, and the Evening concluded with
Rejoycings, Bonfires, Illuminations, ringing of Bells, and all other
Demonstrations of Joy.[27]

Remarkably, such displays were rivaled in grandeur by the pomp exhibited on the rites of passage of the local gentry. The ceremonial
rarefaction of the Blacketts provide an example. Not only was Sir William Blackett's marriage to the daughter of the Earl of Jersey in 1725
wildly celebrated in Newcastle and its environs, but the news of the
consummation of the marriage a few days later provoked public rejoicings which lasted for two days. Three years later his funeral stopped
all town business with a spectacular representation of communal
mourning, in which the scholars from a charity school Blackett had
endowed, his tenants and servants (in livery), the Newcastle Corporation, and over 2,000 freemen with mourning gloves and rings participated.[28] On such occasions, the normally contentious elite could appear
unified: At the funeral of Richard Ridley in 1739, the pall-bearers included his economic rivals and political enemies Walter Blackett and
Sir James Clavering.

The highly theatrical and conspicuous demonstrations of authority
were clearly meant to bolster the magistrates' positions as mediators
between the state and city, demonstrate their munificence and power,
and legitimize their position as guardians and rulers of the Newcastle
community, where the large, turbulent and articulate laboring population was capable of shattering peace and order at any time. And in fact,
the most salient feature of the civic and political ceremonial in Newcastle, apart from its abundance, was the absence of active popular
participation, which contrasts sharply with the civic customs of many
other towns in this period. In Norwich and London, for example, popular customs, such as wreath-making, rush-strewing, street dancing,
plays and pageants were integral parts of the official observances of
mayoral and guild days and political anniversary celebrations. Similarly, in York, Preston, Nottingham, Bristol and Coventry, the trade
companies and craft guilds all joined in civic rituals; in the last, the

[27] *Newcastle Courant,* Oct. 14, 1727.
[28] *Newcastle Courant,* Oct. 2, 1725; Oct. 11, 1728; Sykes, *Local Records,* i, 158.

Corporation played the least important part in the grand civic festival known as the Godiva procession, in which the guilds, bands of local musicians, children, women's societies, masonic lodges and journeymen's clubs all took precedence.[29] Of course the people of Newcastle frequently indulged in their own ceremonial effervescences, such as the mock mayor's procession staged by children on Michaelmas Monday, as well as many others which were meticulously documented in this period by local historians such as the Reverend Henry Bourne and the Reverend John Brand. In general, however, ordinary citizens of the town, including the members of the guilds and trade companies, were relegated to the status of observers on public days or, at best, passive recipients of patrician munificence.[30] From this perspective, the chasm between the "two nations" could scarcely be more neatly, or provocatively, embodied.

The theatrical presentations of authority and community constructed a civic polity serrated by hierarchy, paternalism and privilege even as it recognized the entitlements of the laboring population. But this apparently dichotomous social world was complicated by other lines of identity and allegiance which united or divided local residents among themselves or against their elite rulers, namely, the rights to formal citizenship, religion, and party. Newcastle's civic franchise, which enabled freemen to trade in the town and vote in parliamentary elections, was obtainable only through patrimony, apprenticeship or marriage (i.e., widows retained the rights of freedom only) in one of the twelve mysteries, fifteen by-trades and ten companies of the town. It thus created a freemen's body of 2,500, or about 35 to 40 percent of adult male householders, comprising skilled craftsmen, artisans and middling tradesmen who were markedly different from the industrial laboring population (Table 6.1).[31] Not only were the freemen of higher social

[29] [W. Ewing], *Notices and Illustrations of the Costume, Processions, Pageantry, etc. Formerly Displayed by the Corporation of Norwich* (Norwich, 1850), 1–25; Robert Withington, *English Pageantry: An Historical Outline,* 2 vols. (Cambridge, Mass., 1920), ii, 86–96; *VCH Yorkshire,* xv (Oxford, 1969), 238–48; Thomas R. Flintoff, *Preston's Week of Pageantry* (Preston, 1955), 25–31; J. Blackner, *The History of Nottingham* (Nottingham, 1815), 274–5; Jonathan Barry, "The Cultural Life of Bristol" (D. Phil. diss., Oxford University, 1985), 167–71, 303–30; Benjamin Poole, *Coventry: Its History and Antiquities* (London, 1870), 54–66. I thank Mike Walker for sharing with me his valuable research on civic ceremony among the Coventry guilds.
[30] Henry Bourne, *Antiquities Vulgares* (Newcastle, 1736); John Brand, *Observations on the Popular Antiquities of Great Britain,* 2nd ed. (London, 1813); *Reprints of Rare Tracts,* iii, 105.
[31] Ellis, "Dynamic Society," 201, has argued that the proportion was nearer 50%, but

298   *The sense of the people*

Table 6.1. *Occupational structure of
Newcastle and Norwich electorates*

Occupation	%
Newcastle (1774)	
Gentry/professional	2.5
Merchants	10.2
Retailers	24.3
Craftsmen/artisans	55.2
Laborers	7.6
Others[a]	0.2
Norwich (1761–1802)	
Gentry/professional	11.6
Merchants/manufacturers	5.1
Retailers	16.3
Agricultural	3.3
Craftsmen/artisans	60.6
Laborers	1.2
Other[b]	1.9

[a]Includes agricultural.
[b]Includes largely middling occupations. See John Phillips,
Electoral Behavior in Unreformed England (Princeton,
1982), 321–2.
Sources: Newcastle: James Bradley, *Religion, Revolution
and English Radicalism* (Cambridge, 1990), 374; Norwich:
Phillips, 182.

and occupational status, but they were also religiously and ethnically selected by the nationalistic by-laws of some companies, which prohibited apprenticing Scotsmen or, less frequently, Quakers (both restrictions also working to limit sharply the number of dissenters free of the town).[32] In other words, the freedom could never be purchased outright, as a sort of license to trade or work in the city, in the way it could be, for example, in Norwich; so that instead of a freemen body composed of 155 occupations, as in the East Anglian city, Newcastle's freemen population was composed entirely of English-born, predominantly Anglican members of the thirty-seven ancient craft and trade

in my view she underestimates the rate of nonresidency, which was as high as 45% by the 1770s. The freedom could be obtained by gift, but it was so bestowed only rarely on persons of eminence. In most towns, the expenditure of time and money involved in obtaining the freedom mitigated against a 100% compliance rate, and the proportion of freemen to nonfreemen varied enormously. See J. F. Pound, "The Validity of Freemen's Lists: Some Norwich Evidence," *Economic History Review,* 2nd ser., 35 (1981), 48–59.
[32] Mackenzie, *Historical Account,* i, 665–98 passim.

companies, four of which were defunct by the early eighteenth century, and three virtually so.[33]

The magistrates acted to restrict this group further. Although the guilds'economic power to regulate the local labor market eroded over the century, the magistrates still responded to freemen's complaints by sporadically enforcing company trade privileges by the imposition of hefty annual fines on nonfree traders. More effectively, the powerful Merchant Adventurers prior to 1726 claimed (illegally) the exclusive right to sell goods at retail in Newcastle and contrived to keep the members of other companies from trading in shops; thereafter it continued to restrain persons engaged in retail employments from obtaining their freedom in any guild while forcing nonfree grocers and shop-keepers to obtain expensive permits to trade in the town. Hence, although some Newcastle residents retained voting rights in other towns or in the counties of Northumberland and Durham, others – such as the freeholders of the county of Newcastle, middle-class property own-ers who outnumbered property-owning freemen by the end of the cen-tury, as well as newer professional or middling occupations whose members had no personal links to the established companies, and the majority of laborers, skilled and unskilled alike – were excluded from the town's franchise.[34]

Clearly, the freemen constituted a distinctive economic and political class in the town. Though including men of vastly divergent status and expectations, the freemen tended to be literate, well informed, "re-

---

[33] See *The Newcastle Freeman's Pocket Companion* (Newcastle, 1808) for a full account of the nature of Newcastle's freedom. The companies in order of size of the members voting in 1741 were: Hostmen (301); Smiths (214); Mariners (206); Butchers (198); Shipwrights (185); Merchant Adventurers (175); Barber-Surgeons (116); Coopers (104); Cordwainers (104); Joiners (104); House-Carpenters (100); Ropers (75); Tan-ners (70); Weavers (69); Bakers and Brewers (68); Bricklayers (59); Plumbers, Pewterers and Glaziers (58); Masons (57); Tailors (54); Skinners and Glovers (52); Feltmakers and Curriers (42); Slaters (28); Upholsterers, Tinplate Workers and Sta-tioners (26); Sadlers (25); Goldsmiths (18); Fullers and Dyers (17); Paviours (12); Millers (11); Sailmakers (9); Scriveners (6); Cappers and Drapers (2); Spurriers (1): *The Poll at the Election for Members of Parliament at Newcastle upon Tyne* (New-castle, 1741).

[34] NRO, Ridley MSS, ZRI 27/22/2, Merchant Adventurers Papers, list of persons who were selling goods without freedom or license from the Company, 1738, and Merchant Company Papers, 1771; TWA, Calendar of Common Council Books, Dec. 19, 1720; April 13, 1774; TWA, Petitions, etc., 597/1/25 (1733); Dendy, *Records of the Mer-chant Adventurers,* xliii–xlvi. The 1738 list names 93 persons (men and women); 33 free of other companies) whom the Company had decided to prosecute for retailing items from blue to tobacco. Not surprisingly, retailers and victuallers as well as luxury craftsmen are notoriously hard to track down in pollbooks.

spectable" and privileged beneficiaries of the status that accrued from Corporation membership – a contrast to the industrial laborers, whose literacy and independence decreased over the century.[35] The Newcastle freemen's political volubility will be discussed below; for now it is sufficient to note that, in addition to their economic rights, the freemen by charter could meet as a body in the Court of Guild to oversee the admission of new freemen and present their grievances (although this right was ignored or disputed by the magistrates); they and their widows retained grazing and animal rights on the Town Moor and had access to various charity schools or hospitals. It was also from their ranks that the lower echelons of town and parish government were filled, where they served as churchwardens, vestrymen, overseers of the poor and constables (Table 6.2), thus tempering somewhat the fiercely exclusionary nature of local political institutions.[36] The rights and privileges of freedom remained a contentious issue in the larger civic community while also making electoral evidence alone an unreliable guide to the contours of the town's political culture.

As the patterns above suggest, nonconformity, recusancy and ethnicity were also potentially divisive sources of allegiance, identity and organization. Newcastle had one of the largest dissenting communities in the north of England, comprising some 20 percent of the population and a rich array of denominations and sects which was numerically dominated by Scots Presbyterians.[37] Two of their chapels, the Garth's Head Meeting and the Wall Knoll Meeting, were in Sandgate, residence of a large and hard-working if poor Scottish population; another, the Groat Market Meeting, was near the commercial center of the town, in a building big enough to accommodate 700, and others, including two United secession chapels, were scattered about the town. In addition, the Reverend James Murray's High Bridge Meeting (1765–82), though

---

[35] R. A. Houston has estimated the literacy rate of Newcastle's craftsmen and tradesmen at 89%: "The Development of Literacy: Northern England 1640–1750," *Economic History Review,* 35 (1982), 206, 210–12.

[36] In the four parishes of Newcastle, the reputedly "select" vestries in practice included some aldermen and councilors, as well as all the inhabitants willing and able to turn up for the meetings. In a sample of 84 vestrymen from the parishes of St. Nicholas, All Saints' and St. John's in 1765–80, 33 were merchants, 10 professionals, 11 retailers and 30 craftsmen. Churchwardens and overseers were usually merchants, mariners or retailers: See TWA, 1074/85, St. John Vestry Minute Book, 1760–1835; 183/302, St. Nicholas Rate Book, 1768; 183/171–2, All Saints Vestry minutes, 1766–80.

[37] NRO, 860, Bishop Chandler's visitation, 1736. See also Dr. Williams's Library, MS 34.4, Evans List, 89. In Northumberland, dissenters made up 6.5% of the population: Michael Watts, *The Dissenters* (Oxford, 1978), 272–6.

Table 6.2. *Occupational composition of constables in Newcastle and Norwich*

Occupation	1730–4	%	1765–9	%
Newcastle				
Professionals	0	—	0	—
Merchants/manufacturers	3	6.3	0	—
Retailers	8	16.6	2	12.5
Crafts/artisans	37	77.1	14	87.5
Agricultural	0	—	0	—
Laborers	0	—	0	—
Total	48		16	
Norwich				
Professionals	0	—	0	—
Merchants/manufacturers	2	3.9	1	2.7
Retailers	20	28.9	9	24.3
Crafts/artisans	42	60.9	26	70.3
Agricultural	3	4.3	0	—
Laborers	2	3.9	1	2.7
Total	69		37	

Note: Total number of individuals serving in this office over each period were 131 and 33 respectively for Newcastle, 108 and 40 for Norwich.
Sources: TWA, Land Tax Assessment Books, 23/266, 445, 629, 1098, 1291, 107, 288, 4/1, 652, 814, 1118; Ratebooks, 183/4, 302, 395; Quarter Sessions Order Books, 1720–77; NNRO, Case 16, shelf d, Assembly Book of Proceedings, 1707–45, 1745–73; Case 15, shelf d, Ratebooks, 1725–30; NRCL, MS Colman 486, Ratebooks, 1770–4.

not officially Scots Presbyterian, maintained close relations with the sect. English dissenters congregated at two Unitarian meetings, Hanover Square and Pandon Bank; the particular Baptist meeting at Tuthill Stairs; the Quaker Meeting at Pilgrim Street; an Independent meeting at Manor Chare after 1723; and the Congregational meeting at Postern Chapel in the 1780s. Methodists after 1742 met at the large Orphan House on Northumberland Street. The Sandemanians, or Glassites, who congregated at Forster Street from the 1760s – a radical, egalitarian sect that seceded from the Church of Scotland – included a number of English members. Dissenters also maintained, by subscription, burying grounds at Ballast Hills and Percy Street. Finally, two Catholic chapels in Newcastle and one in Gateshead, as well as a large nonjuring conventicle which survived until 1788, added even greater diversity and opportunities for conflict.[38] Owing to company by-laws and restrictions

[38] "Registers of the Ballast Hills Cemetery, Newcastle upon Tyne," in Newcastle upon

in Anglican charity schools, however, dissenters did not have a formidable presence in the town's institutional political life, comprising
at most 5 percent of the electorate, and although including a number
of rich and substantial families, they tended to be of lower socioeconomic status than the Anglican population.[39] Nonetheless, middle-class
and wealthy dissenters could exert political influence: The tradesmen
and merchants among them included about 150 freeholders who could,
in the county, "make as many votes as their own," as Dr. Evans remarked. They provided visible and reliable support for Whig power in
the town.[40]

Finally, party and political divisions continued unabated through
much of the century, dividing elites, freemen and residents in ways that
mirrored but also transected the social, religious and ethnic identities
consolidated in other arenas of town life. This can be demonstrated
most quickly, if impressionistically, in parliamentary elections. The
contests of 1722, 1734, 1741, 1774, 1777 and 1780 were hard fought
and bitter, with consistently high turnouts of about 85 percent among
resident freemen. The political volatility and independence of the freemen were notorious, and they were canvassed, treated and otherwise
cajoled by the candidates and their agents for weeks before a general
election in their group capacities as members of the incorporated companies, which served in these instances as electoral clubs. Letters to the
various company stewards promised that, in return for support, "any
request or further favour . . . shall be immediately granted," and the
stewards obligingly provided lists of their members to facilitate their
treating at local inns.[41] Moreover, the presence as well as the resources

Tyne Record Series, 9 (1929), 170–2; Dr. Williams's Library, Evans List, MS 34.4,
89; MS 38.6, Thompson List, 1772–3, 59, 106; NRO, 860, Bishop Chandler's Visitation, 1736; 960/2, Visitation of 1774; Mackenzie, *Historical Account,* i, 289, 294,
370, 383, 386, 390, 392–3, 396–7, 399, 402, 408, 416; Brand, *History of Newcastle,*
i, 328–40, 359, 411–49; R. Sharp, "One Hundred Years of a Lost Cause: Nonjuring
Principles in Newcastle from the Revolution to the Death of Prince Charles Edward
Stuart," *AA,* 5th ser., 8 (1980), 35–55.

[39] Bradley, *English Radicalism,* 270, 64–5. As the occupational analyses of Bradley,
John Phillips and Michael Watts indicate, Newcastle dissenters had at least two and
a half times as many laborers, one-fifth the merchants and half the number of gentry
and professionals as in Bristol and Norwich. Phillips, *Electoral Behavior,* 303; Watts,
Dissenters, 350.

[40] Dr. Williams's Library, Evans MS, 89; see also Mackenzie, *Historical Account,* i,
380–95.

[41] TWA, 786/16, Records of the Barber Surgeons' Company, William Carr to the Mem-

of the candidate were required for success: In 1732, Walter C. Blackett was advised by his agent that unless he came to Newcastle immediately to present himself to the freemen as a prospective candidate for Parliament in 1734, he stood no chance of being returned.[42] If the guilds' economic power to regulate the local labor market eroded and the gaps between masters and journeymen grew over the century, the guilds still retained the ability to function as ready-made units for the exercise of patronage and clientage by masters and local elites alike; on the other hand, they could easily transform themselves into tetchily independent craft organizations capable of withstanding – and, in the second half of the century, contesting – magisterial power.[43] But the political community of Newcastle was larger and more unruly than the formal one artificially created by the franchise, and it is only through the examination of its extra-institutional contours and supports that its character and vibrancy can begin to be appreciated.

II. EASTERN VIEWS

Eighteenth-century Norvicensians considered their city to be "next to London . . . the most rich and potent city in England."[44] Even after Bristol had overtaken it in population, Norwich's wealth, political standing, social and economic diversity, and sophisticated urban culture seemed to serve as testament to the town's provincial preeminence. The city also sustained strong traditions of religious dissent and popular political participation, possessing one of the broadest franchises and some of the most democratic institutions of local government in the nation. Indeed, if Norwich's pretensions as the "second city" of the land were encouraged by its close business, personal and cultural ties with the capital, they were also swelled by the citizens' sense of the

bers [1727 or 1734]. See also D. J. Rowe, ed., *The Records of the Company of Shipwrights of Newcastle upon Tyne 1622–27,* vol. 1 (Surtees Society, 181, 1970), 117–20. For treating see NRO, Ridley MSS 27/10, List of the Companies . . . at 5*s.* a Head [1774?].

[42] BL, Add. MS 27,420, Joseph Richmond Letter Book, fol. 50, JR to WB, Dec. 3, 1732; fol. 53b, JR to WB, Jan. 19, 1733.

[43] For a general discussion of the demise of craft solidarities see C. R. Dobson, *Masters and Journeymen* (London, 1980), 38–92; John Stevenson, *Popular Disturbances in England, 1700–1870* (London, 1979).

[44] "The Humble Petition of the Mayor, Sheriffs, Citizens and Commonalty of the City of Norwich," quoted in Sidney Webb and Beatrice Webb, *English Local Government,* 2 vols. (Hamden, Conn., 1963), ii, 530.

04 The sense of the people

city's distinctiveness, which combined with singular grace and aplomb its roles of ancient corporate town, county and episcopal seat, and above all center of Britain's cherished worsted industry. The open fields and gardens within walls gave Norwich the appearance of "a city within an orchard," and the stately public buildings, colorful market, beautiful parish churches, imposing cathedral, and European and international connections in trade, religion and culture were a source of pleasure to the city's numerous tourists and residents alike.[45]

The city's rich cultural life reflected this stature. The assizes and parliamentary elections for both the city and the county of Norfolk, as well as the mayoral inauguration in June, were punctuated by concerts, plays, assemblies, races, exhibitions and military reviews, and brought county gentry and local inhabitants into the city in floods, filling to capacity the 176 inns and 450 taverns within the city walls.[46] But throughout the year Norwich provided its citizens with ample diversion. The town had had at least one and sometimes two companies of players since at least 1717, and a variety of plays and concerts were performed in the theaters of the larger inns, such as the White Swan, King's Head and Rampant Horse, and after 1752 in the elegant new Theater Royal; greater social exclusivity was attained at the assemblies held at nearby Chapel Field House.[47] Strong traditions of club life were revealed in the six dozen elite, middling and artisanal clubs and societies that met between 1715 and 1750.[48] The city was also a center of literacy. Numerous printers, booksellers and stationers and two enduring local

5 [J. Thompson], *History and Antiquities of the County of Norfolk,* 10 vols. (Norwich, 1781), x, 338–9; *The Diary of Sylas Neville 1767–1788,* ed. Basil Cozens-Hardy (London, 1950), 125–7; Charles Parkin, *History and Antiquities of the City of Norwich* (Norwich, 1783), 237; R. Beatniffe, *The Norfolk Tour; or, Traveller's Pocket Companion,* 3rd ed. (Norwich, 1777).

6 For details of Norwich's cultural life see Francis Blomefield, *An Essay Towards a Topographical History of the County of Norfolk,* 5 vols. (Fersfield and Norwich, 1741–5), ii and iii passim, and its supplemented edition, 11 vols. (London, 1805–10), iii and iv – hereafter referred to as Blomefield (1) and Blomefield (2). Inns: BL, Add. MS 27,966, fols. 232–3, Arderon Tracts; NNRO, MS 453, History of Norwich, List of Licensed Alehouses, 1753. R. W. Ketton-Cremer, "Assize Week in Norwich," *NA,* 24 (1932), 13–17.

7 *Norwich Gazette,* Feb. 23, 1717; Jan. 7, 1721; Jan. 3, 1741; Thompson, *History of Norfolk,* 338–9; Blomefield (2), iv, 223–4. At least 20 dancing-masters were able to make a living in early-eighteenth-century Norwich: Trevor Fawcett, "Provincial Dancing Masters: A Postscript," *NA,* 25 (1973), 193–8.

8 *Letters of Humphrey Prideaux,* ed. Edward Maude Thompson (Camden Society, 15 1875), 162; *Norwich Gazette,* Jan. 7, 1721; Oct. 3, 1724; Sept. 20, 1729; Sept. 16, 1749; *Norwich Mercury,* May 2, 1734; March 1, 1740; Chapter 1.

newspapers prospered, and inns, taverns and coffeehouses flourished in all corners of the city. Norwich had the first provincial "city" library in England, established in the 1630s, which continued to serve the public, along with a number of parochial libraries, in the eighteenth century; and books and pamphlets were also lent by booksellers and printers William and Margaret Chase for sixpence a week.[49]

Finally, Norwich maintained strong traditions of ethnic and religious diversity. The town's thirty-six parish churches and the cathedral supported a vibrant Anglican culture that was divided along High and Low Church lines. Yet nonconformity flourished, and Protestant dissenters made up 20 percent of the population in the early decades of the eighteenth century.[50] Though dissenters were scattered throughout the city, reported in twenty-three of the twenty-six parishes that responded to visitation inquiries, most were concentrated in the upper reaches of Wymer and the parishes of Northern wards. Denominationally diverse, the congregations also varied in number, but for most of the period there were two Independent, one or two Presbyterian and three Baptist chapels, as well as a Dutch and a French church.[51] There was a substantial wealthy Quaker presence in the town, and, after 1751, there were a growing number of Methodists, though their numbers did not increase dramatically until the early nineteenth century.[52] Catholicism also maintained a foothold in the city, although by the eighteenth century it embraced predominantly a lower social echelon of poor craftsmen and manufacturers living in parishes in or bordering on Mancroft ward; a nonjuring congregation survived after the arrest of its leader in 1716.[53] Catholics and nonjurors were fairly marginalized from

---

[49] Thirty printers, booksellers and stationers worked in the first half of the century and 34 in the second, publishing 6 newspapers before 1750 and 2 thereafter. See Trevor Fawcett, "Eighteenth-Century Norfolk Booksellers: A Survey and Register," *Cambridge Bibliographical Society,* 6 (1972–6), 1–18; David Stoker, "The Establishment of Printing in Norwich: Causes and Effects," *Cambridge Bibliographical Society,* 7, pt. 1 (1977), 94–111; Thomas Kelly, "Norwich, Pioneer of Public Libraries," *NA,* 34 (1969), 215–22.

[50] Penelope J. Corfield, "The Social and Economic History of Norwich, 1650–1850: A Study in Urban Growth" (Ph.D. diss., University of London, 1976), 265. This proportion had decreased to 15% by the early 1800s; see J. Chambers, *A General History of the County of Norfolk,* 2 vols. (Norwich and London, 1829), ii, 1269.

[51] Dr. Williams's Library, MS 34.4, Evans List, 83–5. In the county, dissenters accounted for 4–5% of the population over the century: Watts, *Dissenters,* 272–6, 509.

[52] Dr. Williams's Library, MS 38.6, Thompson List, 106; Chambers, *History of Norfolk,* i, 1251–69.

[53] G. M. Yould, "Two Nonjurors," *NA,* 35 (1973), 364–81; J. Overton, *The Nonjurors* (London, 1902), 467–96.

the institutional politics of the town; dissenters, by contrast, were firmly integrated within the electorate, and the wealthy Presbyterian community, which included families of French and Dutch as well as English origin, within local government.[54] Religion animated or complicated Norwich politics throughout the century, remaining a recurrent point of contention in local struggles over power, rights and visions of the nation.

In keeping with the divergent roles that the city played in the region, its local economy was diversified. As the premier trading and commercial center for East Anglia, poised at the convergence of the Yare and Wensum rivers, Norwich was a distribution point for the agricultural produce of its hinterland and the imports coming through Yarmouth, maintaining strong links to the region and to London by excellent land and water communications. In 1730, it had weekly coach service to forty towns in East Anglia, tri-weekly coach service to the capital, daily river transportation to Yarmouth and six-day-a-week postal service. Further, the unobtrusiveness of its commercial and manufacturing enterprises allowed the town to be a minor center of fashion.[55] Accordingly, the retail and the craft trades throve. William Arderon, the local chronicler, counted 125 trades in Norwich in 1750, including 44 different types of retailers, an assessment corroborated by the freemen's registers. The service trades were even more numerous, accounting for 25 percent of the freemen in this period and providing food and clothing for the local population as it grew from 30,000 in 1700 to 41,000 in 1780.[56]

Nevertheless, the production of worsted cloth – the high-quality Norwich ''stuffs'' – dominated the economy and employment structure of the city for much of the eighteenth century. In its forty different operations it employed between half and three-fifths of the town's pop-

---

[54] As D. S. O'Sullivan has shown, between 1718 and 1740 27 members of the Presbyterian congregation became mayors, sheriffs, councilmen or guardians of the poor, whereas only 9 did so in 1751–85: ''Politics in Norwich, 1705–1805'' (M.Phil. thesis, University of East Anglia, 1975), 214–15, 221–3. See also NNRO, FC 13/1, Octagon Chapel Subscription List of 1753, and FC 18/80, Some Account of the Congregation Commonly Called Presbyterian Assembled at Octagon Chapel (1796).

[55] W. Albert, *The Turnpike Road System of England, 1695–1830* (Cambridge, 1960), 41; P. J. Corfield, *Towns, Trade, Religion and Radicalism: The Norwich Perspective on English History* (Norwich, 1980), 19–21.

[56] BL, Add. MS 27,966, fols. 234b–235b; Percy Millican, ed., *The Freemen of Norwich 1714 to 1752* (Norfolk Record Society, 23, 1952), passim; Corfield, ''Social and Economic History,'' 92–3, 33, 449.

ulation and tens of thousands of people in the countryside and region.[57] Moreover, despite the lamentations of economic historians and eighteenth-century manufacturers, the industry was prosperous and expanding until the 1790s.[58] Indeed, because Norwich stuffs – camblets, bombazines, damasks, brocades and satins – were used for clothing and furnishings and catered to semi-fashionable markets, their quality and price gave them an edge until the later period over the coarser steam-produced Yorkshire cloths. Still, Norwich cloths remained extremely vulnerable to competition from cottons, fustians and other fabrics which caught the fancy of the prosperous and fickle middle classes. As a result, prior to 1740 the industry relied upon government protection of the home market, which consumed between 60 and 75 percent of luxury worsted. Foreign trade increased thereafter, however – Africa, Southern Europe, Russia, the British West Indies and America, India, and China joined Holland, Flanders and the Iberian peninsula as importers of Norwich stuffs – causing the value of the city's exports to double by 1775 and investing it more deeply in government foreign policy. Even the American war did not disrupt the growth trend significantly. Although it cut off Mediterranean and Western colonial markets and precipitated a trade slump in the early 1780s, recovery after the war's end was almost immediate, and foreign demand exceeded the levels established before the outbreak of hostilities.[59]

Unlike the coal industry, the Norwich worsted industry was labor- rather than capital-intensive and thus not susceptible to the oligopolistic production and marketing strategies that were so prevalent in Newcastle. From the seventeenth to the mid eighteenth century, the organization of the industry was diffuse, productive processes being characterized by the "putting out" system, whereby masters hired out wool or yarn to be combed, spun and woven to journeymen who

---

[57] For estimates see Daniel Defoe, *A Tour Through the Whole Island of Great Britain* (London, 1971), 85; Arthur Young, *The Farmer's Tour Through the East of England,* vol. 2 (London, 1771), 79. There were probably 12,000 looms at work by the 1770s, each of which employed about 10 other people, from sorters, combers and spinners to throwers, warpers, dyers, and pressers. J. James, *History of the Worsted Manufacture in England* (London, 1855), 217–18n.

[58] J. K. Edwards, "The Decline of the Norwich Textiles Industry," *Yorkshire Bulletin of Economic and Social Research,* 16 (1964), 31–41; E. P. Schumpeter, *English Overseas Trade Statistics 1697–1808* (Oxford, 1960), 35–40. Cf. M. F. Lloyd-Pritchard, "The Decline of Norwich," *Economic History Review,* 2nd ser., 3 (1951), 371–7.

[59] Corfield, "Social and Economic History," 61, 65, 73–4, 317, 375; Edwards, "Decline of Norwich," 31, 34; Schumpeter, *Overseas Trade Statistics,* 40–2; James, *History of Worsted Manufacture,* 256–7, 268–9.

worked it for a wage in their own homes or in their masters' shops.[60] The wool-staplers and the merchants were the wealthiest agents in the process, with some of the latter making several thousand pounds a year, but many master woolcombers, master weavers and dyers were affluent members of the middle classes in this period. Master weavers, for example, employed anywhere between four and sixteen journeymen and apprentices, and earned between £40 and £400 per annum. The solidity of their position was indicated by their number in relation to the journeymen – about 500, against 8,000, in 1719 – a proportion which stayed the same for most of the century.[61] At the same time, however, a small group of merchant-manufacturing families that included the Gurneys, Iveses, Harveys and Pattesons were involved in both production and distribution of worsted cloth and provided the leadership for industry lobbying through the Norwich Committee of Trade and Manufacture.[62] Their power increased as diminution of the home market and expansion of the export trade wrought some important changes in the structure of the industry (though not in the modes of production). Their ranks swelling to encompass thirty or forty families, including the Martineaus, Taylors, Kerrisons and Days, this entrepreneurial group worked energetically to expand consumption of Norwich stuffs abroad, sending agents and sons to locations throughout Europe, the West Indies and the East to cultivate markets while maintaining at home the productive capacities and resources necessary to accommodate specific orders. In this way they came to control the distribution of Norwich worsted stuffs, the most profitable stage of the productive process, and influenced local worsted output and wages by the unofficial "gentlemen's agreements" that prevented undercutting.[63] Not surprisingly, these wealthy entrepreneurs led and exemplified the trend toward economic diversification that was under way in the second half of the century. Shipping, banking, general overseas trade, insurance and brewing were some of the additional interests through which merchant-manufacturers stimulated and ultimately dominated the financial and commercial life of the city.[64]

---

[60] For pilfering see John Styles, "Industrial Pilfering and the Law in the 18th Century." I am most grateful to Mr. Styles for allowing me to read the typescript of this article.

[61] R. Campbell, *The London Tradesmen* (London, 1747), 260; James, *History of Worsted Manufacture,* 275, 258–60; Corfield, "Social and Economic History," 66–8.

[62] Hammond and Hammond, *Skilled Labourer,* 140–1; Corfield, "Social and Economic History," 309–11, 323–4; *Gentlemen's Magazine,* 6 (1736), 169.

[63] James, *History of Worsted Manufacture,* 258–61; Corfield, "Social and Economic History," 323–6.

[64] E.g., the Quaker Gurney family moved from merchant-manufacturing in Norwich to

Nevertheless, in the worsted industry as a whole, neither capital nor distributive power was concentrated in a single group's hands; smaller masters, venders and producers of Norwich cloths remained numerous and flourished with the expansion of trade alongside the large and wealthy entrepreneurs. Successful economic transactions required a quick turnover in order to get returns on initial outlays; great risks, great investments or access to great amounts of long-term credit were unnecessary.[65] Equally important, all masters, large and small, knew their interests to be the same where the protection of their profits was concerned, and acted together to control the groups of skilled artisans upon whom successful production ultimately depended. "Embezzlement" – or, in the view of the artisans, legitimate appropriation of work materials – was a source of conflict between masters and journeymen throughout the industry. The masters in the various branches of production worked together to procure Acts of Parliament against the embezzlement of wool, yarn and cloth in 1740, 1749 and 1774, and the populace was ready to riot upon the conviction or public whipping of those indicted.[66]

Indeed, below the masters, the journeymen woolcombers and weavers were well-organized, literate and articulate artisans whose independence matched their high levels of skill. They were as prepared to riot against "foreign" imports which undercut their markets (as in 1726) as they were against an inflated grain market (as in 1740 and 1766). The woolcombers' frequent "combinations" and strikes to keep up wage levels and control entry into their trades led employers to press for and receive parliamentary Acts against these combinations. But legislation did little to discourage either their time-tested methods of collective bargaining or their strategies for self-protection, including their organization into literally scores of friendly societies.[67] The weavers

general trading in Irish cloth, financial and insurance markets, and finally banking in 1775, underwriting commercial enterprises in Liverpool and London as well as Norfolk. See J. K. Edwards, "The Gurneys and the Norwich Clothing Trade in the Eighteenth Century," *Journal of the Friends Historical Society,* 50 (1963), 134–52; for banking and economic diversification see L. S. Pressnell, *Country Banking and the Industrial Revolution* (Oxford, 1956), 333–6; Corfield, "Social and Economic History," 398–9, 364.

[65] The credit requirements of even the largest manufacturers rarely exceeded £200: James, *History of Worsted Manufacture,* 260.

[66] Ibid., 252. In 1753, for example, the public whipping of two convicted embezzlers provoked a serious riot in the marketplace: *Norwich Mercury,* Jan. 27, 1753.

[67] Blomefield (2), iv, 437; NNRO, MS RQG 462/38, John Gurney, Account of the Riots, July 9, 1740; NNRO, Norwich City Records, Case 6, shelf h, parcel 2, City Riots,

were an even more distinctive and visible element in the city. Their
industry and independence were well known; they were as prone to
strike over wages as were the woolcombers. More significant for Norwich politics, weavers made up slightly over half the electorate in 1734
while also displaying the same tendency to religious radicalism that
was exhibited by textile workers in the Southwest, the Midlands and
Europe; many in fact were descendants of French Huguenot and Dutch
Walloon immigrants, and probably over 50 percent of them attended
the meeting-house.[68] They were thus a highly politicized group, central
to the success of the Whig initiative in the decades after the succession
and, as the opening quotation suggests, enthusiastic participants in the
political culture of the town and region.

In sum, despite the high degree of diversification in the Norwich
economy, for most of the century general prosperity was dependent
upon the fortunes of a luxury product. In the first half of the century,
and especially prior to 1735, reliance on government protection of the
home market made the worsted community more inward-looking, more
focussed on the politics of protection, than their non-textile-trading contemporaries, who even in this period saw the acquisition of overseas
markets as essential to economic well-being. Hence, if it was fortuitous
that Walpole's rise to power accompanied the recovery of the East
Anglia industry from the serious depression of 1718–20, his ensuing
protection of domestic markets for Norwich stuffs was both pointed
and deliberate.[69] Nevertheless, the growing involvement of the textile
trade in colonial markets and the tenacious belief in the Norwich industry's importance to national prosperity and preeminence made empire and "trade" as important and volatile, if differently inflected,
issues in the textile town as in other commercial centers. Indeed, the
contending conceptions of trade and empire at work in Norwich shaped
the town's internal politics as well as its relationship with the state.

Consistent with the economic structure of the town, the political

---

1766; Hammond and Hammond, *Skilled Labourer,* 196; *Norwich Mercury,* July 25,
1752.

[68] Defoe, *Tour,* 86. For strikes see, e.g., *Norwich Mercury,* Oct. 31, 1767; Penelope
Corfield, "A Provincial Capital in the Late Seventeenth Century: The Case of Norwich," in P. Clark and P. Slack, eds., *Crisis and Order in English Towns, 1500–1700*
(London, 1972), 264–70; Watts, *Dissenters,* 350–4. According to Watts, 50% of the
adult male Presbyterians in Norwich were weavers.

[69] Walpole procured a royal order in 1733 that Court mourning attire was to be made
only of Norwich crapes, and had placed legislative embargoes on the export of wool
and importation of printed cloth, thus saving Norwich from the worst aspects of the
textile depressions of 1718–22: James, *History of Worsted Manufacture,* 221.

structure of Norwich was distinctive, known for its remarkably open and accessible institutions and broad electoral base. The 3,400 freemen of Norwich – close to half the adult male population – were closely representative of the upper 70 percent of the occupational structure of the city and included freeholders of the town and county.[70] The freemen directly elected the sixty councilors and twenty-three aldermen of the four wards and one of the town's two sheriffs (the mayor, aldermen and sheriffs chose the other); they also chose the mayor from among the senior aldermen each May Day.[71] Within the Assembly, as the Corporation was known formally, the councilors were collectively the most powerful, for by the terms of the city charter their majority vote was required to pass all Acts and ordinances, including those initiated from the Mayor's Court (composed of the mayor, aldermen and sheriffs). Even the Guardians of the Poor, incorporated in 1712 for the centralized administration of poor relief via the three workhouses of the town, maintained impressive degrees of freemen's participation; thirty-two were elected annually at Assembly "out of the most honest, discreet and charitable inhabitants of the city" to join the mayor, aldermen, sheriffs, recorder, and steward of the Corporation on the governing board.[72] Clearly, the freemen maintained a large measure of electoral control over town government, and with no formal property requirements for office, men of middling rank could serve as councilors, guardians and even aldermen as well as churchwardens and vestrymen; the lower levels of town and parish government trickled down to include laborers (see Table 6.2).[73]

Of course, in practice, aspirations to high corporate office were contained by its excessive costs. In contrast to Newcastle, Norwich Corporation was not rich. Its income, gleaned from transport and market

---

[70] Millican, *The Freemen of Norwich 1714–52,* passim; see also Pound, "Validity of Freemen's Lists," 48–59. Nonresidency was low: 80% of the freemen lived in the city or its suburbs in this period.

[71] Blomefield (2), iv, 405–7, 436–53; Webb and Webb, *English Local Government,* ii, 532–8. The four wards were Wymer, Mancroft, Conisford and Northern; each was divided into three sub-wards.

[72] Blomefield (2), iv, 432–5; NNRO, City Records, Case 20, shelf d, Guardian of the Poor Minute Books, 1723–31, 1732–4, 1748–61. The efficiency of this body in segregating the poor was noted by visitors: See HMC, *Portland MSS,* vi, 156.

[73] Printers, brewers, master weavers and woolcombers, grocers, general merchants and retailers, some of them councilmen, served as vestrymen and churchwardens: See, e.g., NNRO, PD 26/73 (s), St. Peter's Mancroft Churchwarden and Vestry Minutes, 1707–52, passim. Almost twice as many retailers were willing to serve as constables of the sub-wards than in Newcastle, although in both towns the position was staffed predominantly by craftspeople and tradesmen.

tolls, fines for the freedom and a few other miscellaneous sources, fluctuated between £1,000 and £2,000 per year, although it did have extensive patronage at its disposal, including contracts to tradesmen and victuallers, the charitable incomes of the town's four hospitals, presentments to twelve clerical livings, scholarships to Cambridge colleges, and private bequests and donations.[74] The lure of wielding the social and political patronage so afforded was often offset by the onerous duties of corporate office, which included having to pay out of pocket for many of the feasts and rituals which incumbents were bound to sponsor. Guild Day, or the mayoral inauguration day in June, for example, was the occasion for extensive civic fêting. Vast parades of town functionaries and citizens, beadles and whifflers in Elizabethan costume, waits, standard bearers, Dick Fools, speech boys from the local charity schools, and a large, gorgeously painted Snap Dragon, with movable parts that flapped and snapped to the delight of the throngs of spectators, marched through the town. Among residents, sylvan rites and customs of hospitality predominated that included adorning houses and shops with pictures and tapestries, churches with boughs and streamers, the streets with trees, strewn flowers and triumphal arches and their persons with garlands of flowers and leaves. Plays and dances were performed in the streets, and the bells of dozens of the churches and the cathedral rang with the peals composed by the various ringers' societies in the city.[75] Yet the multi-course dinner that crowned the day for county and town elites was paid for by the new mayor, as were the public treats and dinners on political anniversary days and during assize week; the mercifully infrequent Corporation fêtes in honor of new bishops were paid for by the aldermen; and the sheriffs' feast was provided by the new sheriffs themselves.[76] In these

---

[74] NNRO, City Records, Case 18, shelf b, City Chamberlain's Accounts, 1714–52; shelf c, 1753–90; T. Turner, *List of Norfolk Benefices* (Norwich, 1843).

[75] See [Ewing], *Notices and Illustrations,* 33–6; *Norwich Gazette,* May 7, June 18, 1737; A. G. G. Thurlow, "The Church Bells of Norwich," *NA,* 27 (1945), 241–84; NNRO, Churchwarden accounts: PD 7/37, St. George's Colgate 1714–16; PD 26/73, St. Peter's Mancroft 1707–52; PD 191/23, St. Swithin's 1608–1762.

[76] Browne, *History of Norwich,* 422–4; [Ewing], *Notices and Illustrations;* NNRO, MS 453, History of Norwich; *Norwich Gazette,* June 18, 1726; Ketton-Cremer, "Assize Week in Norwich," 13–17; *Norwich Gazette,* April 7, 1722; May 16, 29, 1724; Oct. 1, 1743. Prior to 1730, the St. George's Company was central in organizing the mayor's feast by forcing private citizens to pay for it, but the unsavory choice between incarceration and impoverishment provoked a group of local citizens, headed by Alderman William Clarke, to force the society's dissolution: NNRO, MS 79b, Mackerell's History of Norwich, v, ii; City Record, Case 17, shelf b, St. George's Company Wastebook, 1689–1725.

circumstances, it is scarcely surprising that large numbers of wealthy citizens declined to serve in any capacity, or that the strapped Corporation occasionally resorted to the strategy of electing affluent dissenters in order to collect the hefty fines for exemption.[77]

Nevertheless, the straightforward conjunction of coal, capital and corporate power that was so evident in Newcastle was not paralleled in Norwich, where the economic and political elites, though overlapping, were not identical. The more diffused wealth and expansive middling sector in Norwich were reflected in Corporation membership, where no one occupation dominated any office and the richest ratepayers frequently exempted themselves from serving.[78] There was a growing nepotism evident within aldermanic ranks from the 1740s onwards: Families like the Helwyses, Harveys, Iveses and Nuthalls seemed to have an almost hereditary claim on civic office, one which intermarriage and patronage strengthened; and oligarchy marked institutionalized politics after 1750, even at the humble rank of constable (see Table 6.2).[79] But the accessibility and electoral accountability of the institutions of civic government meant that the political style of local elites was qualitatively different from the exaggerated paternalistic magistracy of the Blacketts and Ridleys in Newcastle. The Norwich magistrates' need to acknowledge the broad base and integrity of civic institutions helped sustain the vibrant traditions of popular political participation in the city.

That the civic as well as the parliamentary politics of the town was a focus of a range of contending interests and aspirations was ensured by three final features of the local political landscape. First, there were clear-cut social differences between the upper and lower houses of the Assembly: Aldermen were invariably rich and usually members of the large manufacturer, merchant and professional classes; councilmen, on the other hand, tended to be smaller master weavers, retailers and prosperous craftsmen, representing in almost quintessential manner that

---

[77] NNRO, MS 453, History of Norwich, 26; Mayoral Court Books, 1719–76; Case 16, shelf c, Assembly Minute Books, 1683–1714 (see esp. Aug. 20, 1708).

[78] According to ratebook analyses, elites accounted for 4% of the population and the middling classes for about 28%, compared with 7% and 17% respectively for Newcastle: Corfield, "Social and Economic History," 213, 227–65, 268, 646; O'Sullivan, "Politics in Norwich," 9–12. Only a third to half of aldermen between 1725 and 1774 and one of the councilmen were among the richest ratepayers, and the worsted interest accounted for fewer than half of the occupations of councilmen: O'Sullivan, 43–4.

[79] The average number of years that a councilor served rose from about 6 to 13.4: NNRO, Case 16, shelf c, Assembly Minute Books, 1714–90 passim.

group called the "middling sort." These demarcations were only strengthened by Wapolean tamperings with the civic constitution and were always liable to politicization. Transecting the more horizontal identities encouraged by civic institutions, a serious rift existed between the worsted industry and the retail trades that had political as well as economic consequences. Although neither group was politically homogeneous, weavers and others in the wool trade tended to be Whig, and retailers Tory, throughout the first half of the eighteenth century. Finally, these economic and political alignments were perpetuated and complicated by the ward organization of Norwich. Each of the four great wards was diverse in ethnic, social and occupational makeup, but biases were manifest and enduring. Residents involved in the worsted industry, and especially weavers, tended to be concentrated most heavily in Northern ward, the upper sub-wards of Wymer (the same areas where nonconformists were most concentrated) and the parishes bordering the river in Conisford; in many of the sub-wards in Northern and Wymer, weavers made up 50–60 percent of the population, and the majority of these tended to be stridently Whig. Conversely, the great ward of Mancroft and the central sub-wards of Wymer and Conisford had relatively few weavers and the heaviest concentration of retailers, victuallers and clothiers.[80] Mancroft, in particular, was the acknowledged commercial center of Norwich, the location of the renowned marketplace, the richest of the great wards, and, before the 1760s, inflexibly Tory. The ward structure was an important prop of popular politics, literally mapping out the divergent political identities within the town and providing targets for elite and demotic politicians seeking to mobilize public support. As we shall see, politics in Norwich was never a matter of economic interest alone, but of dynamic interactions of identities and interests that worked to bolster contending views of the local, regional and national destiny.

---

[80] For the occupational topography of Norwich in this period see the excellent analysis by Corfield, "Social and Economic History," 222; for voting correlations see Chapter 8.

7. The rejection of deference: Newcastle, 1715–1785

But then let us own that his Claret we prize,
But we still (God be Thank'd) had the use of our Eyes;
That his dinners smelt well, but he should not suppose
That we e'er could endure to be led by the Nose.
Derry Down.
                    The Merry Patriot (Newcastle, 1734)[1]

No more let Bl[ac]k[et]t beg your votes, that great and rich offender,
Nor young Sir M[at]h[e]w gain his end, he's but a mere pretender:
For how can he that place fulfill, who has such bad directors,
It never shall be said, my boys, we'd trust to such protectors.
Huzza for Phipps and Delaval, true patriots of the nation,
Each loyal soul within the town will drink to their preservation.
                    A New Election Song, Sung to the
                    Tune of Wilkes's Preservation (Newcastle, 1774)

The political culture of eighteenth-century Newcastle upon Tyne exhibited a set of seemingly contradictory characteristics. The town's coal and landowning merchant elites maintained an oligarchic stranglehold on the institutions of local government, oligopolistic control of Tyneside industry and commerce, and orotund domination of a civic culture geared to emphasize their grandeur and authority. Yet in apparent opposition to this constellation of power, party divisions, a politically conscious citizenry, a lively press, tavern and club life, and increasingly complex strategies of political organization contested the forms and substance of elite hegemony. This chapter will examine the configurations and meanings of opposition and radical politics in the northern

---

[1] Quoted in *Newcastle Courant*, Jan. 19, 1734.

town, where institutional and extra-institutional practices forged alternative definitions of political community and citizenship that repudiated traditional strategies of popular containment and control.

I. TORIES ASCENDANT IN A WHIG WORLD

Politics in Newcastle in the first four decades of the century was characterized by deep and bitter divisions which affected all aspects of local life. The same elites who so vigorously united to maintain their authority and economic privileges engaged in pitched and protracted battles over control of town government and the parliamentary representation. On the level of high politics, the consequences of party strife have been misrepresented by historians, who have claimed that the general elections of 1722 and 1727 "set the seal to Whig ascendancy" or exhibited the "territorial" nature of local politics.[2] In fact, virtually throughout the period of "Whig supremacy" in central government and Whig dominance in Northumberland, Toryism was ascendant in Newcastle, and party divisions remained linked to issues generated at the center.[3]

Indeed, in part because of the strength of oligarchy in civic government, the battles waged over the parliamentary representation were highly politicized events that kept residents focussed on issues of state and local power. Voting patterns attest to the strength of traditional party divisions. In 1722, when the seats of the Tory members, Sir William Blackett and William Wrightson, were contested by the Whig William Carr, 37 percent of the 2,027 voters plumped for Carr, thus throwing a vote away rather than giving it to either Tory candidate. In 1741, known as the "Great Contest" in Newcastle political lore, the two Tory members, Walter Blackett and Nicholas Fenwick, were opposed by two Whigs, Carr and Matthew Ridley, and the rate of split voting was less than 15 percent in an election with a 95 percent turnout.[4]

[2] Edward Hughes, *North Country Life in the Eighteenth Century* (New York, 1956), 260–70; Nicholas Rogers, *Whigs and Cities: Popular Politics in the Age of Walpole and Pitt* (Oxford, 1989), 226.

[3] See Wilson, "The Rejection of Deference: Urban Political Culture in England, 1715–1785" (Ph.D. diss., Yale University, 1985), 205–10. A Tory majority on the Corporation was maintained throughout the period and increased dramatically after 1727.

[4] *The Poll at the Election of Members to Serve in Parliament for the Town and County of Newcastle upon Tyne ... 1722* (Newcastle, 1722); *The Poll ... for Members of Parliament for ... Newcastle upon Tyne* (Newcastle, 1741). In 1722, Carr's success was based upon the high number of plumpers and split voters (25%).

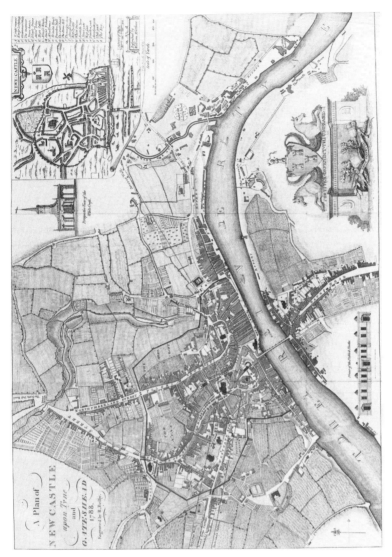

12. Eighteenth-century Newcastle, from John Brand's *History of Newcastle*, vol. 1 (1789). Courtesy of Newcastle Central Library.

The divided political loyalties of Newcastle's elite were rooted in
late Stuart and Augustan animosities. The Restoration had been warmly
welcomed by Newcastle Anglicans, and the clergy eagerly availed
themselves of the Act of Uniformity, persecuting the ''holy saints . . .
bearing double-edged swords . . . to bind kings in chains and lords in
iron bonds'' who had been integrated into local government during the
midcentury upheavals.[5] The strength of dissent, however, was demonstrated again after James II's first Declaration of Indulgence, when the
local magistracy became so religiously diverse that, in the words of
one contemporary, ''the cap, the mace and the sword were one day
carried to the church, another day to the Roman Catholic chapel, and
on a third to the dissenting meeting house.'' High Church sensibilities
and culture responded in kind into the Augustan period, producing not
only such an energetic Tory feminist as Mary Astell but a virulent
parliamentary contest in 1710. A post-election song from that year
made the issues clear: The returned Tory MPs, Sir William Blackett
and William Wrightson, stood for ''the Church, the Queen, for Peace
and the Protestant Succession'' against ''the Whigs and Dissenters . . .
Fanaticks.''[6] Not surprisingly, political animosities had scarcely receded in 1715, when Sir William Blackett, whose progenitors included
two staunchly royalist mayors under Charles II and James II, and Richard Ridley, whose father, Nicholas, replaced the dissenter William
Hutchinson as mayor when the town received Lord Lumley and declared for the Prince of Orange, continued to head the rival parties that
coalesced around the historical and current issues that continued to
plague Newcastle politics.[7]

On the Tory side, the divisions over the succession and the '15, the
ascendant position of Whiggism in the county thereafter and the nu-
merical strength of dissent made party adherents combative and defensive. Indeed, Whig patronage and protection of English and
Scottish dissenters made the latter a particular target of High Churchmen, who were quick to interpret all divisions in the local community
in religious terms. On the anniversary of Charles I's martyrdom in
1724, for example, the Reverend Henry Fetherstonhaugh preached a

[5] Eneas Mackenzie, *A Descriptive Account of the Town and County of Newcastle upon
Tyne,* 2 vols. (Newcastle, 1829), i, 95–6; *Life of Ambrose Barnes* (Newcastle, 1829),
15–18.
[6] *The Whigs Defeated, Being an Excellent New Song from the Newcastle Election* (Newcastle, 1710).
[7] Richard Welford, *Men of Mark 'Twixt Tyne and Tweed,* 3 vols. (London, 1895), i,
306; ii, 317.

furious sermon before the Corporation that lambasted dissenters as the descendants of "the murderers of KING CHARLES . . . full of fanatical Rage . . . as far from being Protestants, as they were from being true Subjects."[8] On the other side, the defiance and resilience of local Toryism, the large numbers of Roman Catholics and nonjurors in the North, and Tory leaders' prominence and popularity in local government made Whiggism strident and aggressive. The most prominent Whigs of the town and surrounding countryside were Richard Ridley, Matthew White, William Carr, the Newcastle Hostmen Sir Henry Liddell and his son, George Liddell, and in Gateshead, William Cotesworth, all of whom reaped large financial gains through the purchase of Jacobite and Catholic estates after the '15.[9] Yet local Whigs were united in little else besides their partisan animosities: White and Ridley were partners in coal, salt and glass industries on Tyneside and later were connected by marriage between their offspring, but both were economic rivals to the Liddells and Cotesworth, whose "Grand Alliance" with nonfree coalowners continually sought to subvert the profits and trade of the Newcastle magnates. Such divisions helped prevent the Whigs from permanently enervating Tory power in the Corporation or encroaching upon their position among the freemen. Hence, the succession failed even to produce a Whig candidate for the 1715 election in Newcastle, and the peaceful contest among three Tories, Blackett, Wrightson and James Clavering, returned the two sitting members in a poll for which little over half the electorate turned out.[10]

Still, the '15 managed to do what even a Crown-backed party could not: namely, topple the Tory ascendancy by providing substantive proof of the Jacobitism of a portion of the party's leadership and rank and file. Most Newcastle Tories were Hanoverians, rallying to the support of George I and the defense of the political and economic status quo on Tyneside under the leadership of the Tory mayor Henry Dalston: raising a militia, mounting and arming tenants, and stationing trained bands on Killingworth Moor outside the town walls. By the time the rebels were defeated at Preston in November, the local acclamations mollified even the suspicious Henry Liddell: "You see a joy thro'out

[8] Henry Fetherstonhaugh, *A Sermon Preached Before the Right Worshipful Mayor, Aldermen, Sheriff, etc. of Newcastle upon Tyne, on 30 January* (Newcastle, [1724]).
[9] Peter Cromar, "Economic Power and Organization: The Development of the Coal Industry on Tyneside, 1700–1828 (Ph.D. diss., Cambridge University, 1976), 73–8; HMC/NRA, *Ridley (Blagdon) MSS,* Introduction by Viscountess Ridley (London, 1965), 2.
[10] Sedgwick, i, 298.

ye City which can't be well paralleled, and ye Court [i.e., the Corporation] show no less satisfaction."[11]

Nevertheless, strong pro-Stuart loyalties clearly existed in Newcastle, as in Northumberland more generally. Cotesworth served as a government agent in the North, and his informers, George and Henry Liddell, suspected that disloyalty existed among a whole range of townspeople, from the clergy to the customs collector, excisemen and keelmen. The nonjuring chapel in Newcastle had been tolerated by Newcastle magistrates since 1689, and clergy throughout the area were covert, if not outright, Jacobites – such as John Thomlinson, curate, and his uncle, the incumbent of Rothbury.[12] Further, the middling classes of Newcastle were not impervious to the politically seductive charms of the exiled dynasty. Richard Swinburn, Thomas Robinson and Robert McMorran, merchants, were alleged to have drunk James III's health at a co-conspirator's house in 1715 and "said he was king of the Realme." Swinburn was later discharged from Common Council upon his election in October 1728 for "neglecting or refusing" to take the oaths of allegiance, even though Robinson and McMorran had compromised their principles sufficiently to vote as Tories in 1722.[13] And plebeian Jacobitism was rife both during the rebellion and for several years after, when several people were taken up in and around Newcastle for drinking the Duke of Ormonde's and the Pretender's health and confusion to the Hanoverians, and Restoration Day and the thanksgiving day for the suppression of the rebellion in 1716 were marked by the wearing of oak boughs and roses and by anti-Whig and anti-Hanoverian taunting.[14]

Upper-level Jacobitism was even more dramatic in its consequences.

[11] John Brand, *The History and Antiquities of the Town and County of Newcastle upon Tyne*, 2 vols. (Newcastle, 1789), ii, 511; TWA, Calendar of Common Council Books, 1699–1718, Oct. 10, 1715; H. Liddell to W. Cotesworth, Oct. 20, 1715, quoted in Hughes, *North Country Life*, 414.
[12] GPL, Ellison MSS, A36/28, HL to WC, Jan. 25, 1715; "Diary of Rev. John Thomlinson," in *Six North Country Diaries*, ed. John Crawford Hodgson (Surtees Society, 118, 1910), 66, 89; D. D. Dixon, "Notes on the Jacobite Movement in Upper Coquetdale, 1715," *AA*, 2nd ser., 16 (1893), 93–112.
[13] PRO, SP 35/8/112 (1), Newcastle, April 12, 1717; TWA, Calendar of Common Council Books, October 1718; 1722 pollbook.
[14] TWA, 540/3, Quarter Sessions Order Books, 1700–19, Oct.–April 1715–16; NRO, Quarter Sessions Orders and Papers, QSB 46, 1717, 60, 66, 82; *St. James's Evening Post*, June 2–5, 1716; *Flying Post*, June 14–16, 1716; *Evening Post*, June 19, 1716; *Worcester Postman*, May 16, 1718. For continued optimism among Stuart supporters as to the Jacobitism of the colliers of Northumberland see Paul Fritz, *The English Ministers and Jacobitism* (Toronto, 1975), Appendix 3, 155.

Not only had Lords Derwentwater and Widdrington and the Northumberland MP Thomas Forster come out for the rebellion, but also several prominent gentry families of Newcastle and the environs were directly implicated in pro-Stuart plots such as the Fenwicks of Bywell and the Claverings of Callaly; suspected of Jacobite sympathies, such as the Catholic Sir James Clavering of Axwell and the two Newcastle MPs, William Wrightson and Sir William Blackett; or had "suspicious" connections with Catholics and Jacobites in the county (such as the Delavals).[15] Blackett was perhaps most famous, or notorious, for his sympathies, which were sufficiently ambiguous to warrant the close attention of both government and Stuart agents. He and Fenwick had allegedly given money to the rebels and had intended to march up to meet them with Sir William Swinburn and Peter Potts, attorney of Newcastle, both of whom were out for the Pretender. Further, before the outbreak of the rebellion Blackett had ordered his colliers and keelmen "to provide themselves with arms and be ready to follow one who was a kind of a Steward or governor" over them; but it was undetermined whether this person was to be in the government's or the Pretender's service. Admittedly, some of the rumors of his collusions were far-fetched, but horses belonging to Sir William were discovered at the home of his steward, Robert Todd of Kenton, a Jacobite "at whose house the Rebells had frequent cabals."[16] Whatever his genuine sensibilities, Blackett was forced to flee from Wallington, his country estate, to elude both rebel and government forces, finally escaping to London to kiss the king's hand before returning to Newcastle in early 1716 to great popular acclaim.[17]

Blackett's influence and popularity among Newcastle residents were such that the rumors of his covert activities and wavering sympathies did not deter, although they did complicate, local regard for him, where he was selected mayor in 1717.[18] Thereafter he seemed to do little to discourage passive disaffection locally. After Stanhope had directed General Wills and his troops, stationed at Newcastle, to raid the nonjuring conventicle in April 1717, arresting its minister and nineteen men in the congregation, the conventicle's members went unpunished during

[15] Sedgwick, ii, 529; John Robinson, *The Delaval Papers* (Newcastle [1891]), 196.

[16] Robert Patten, *History of the Rebellion* (London, 1745), 23–4; Hughes, *North Country Life,* 409; GPL, Cotesworth MSS, CJ 5/4, Letter on Lt. Robert Durham of Wallsend.

[17] *Memorandum Book of Sir Walter Calverly, Bart.* (Surtees Society, 77, 1883), 140–2; *Newcastle Courant* (hereafter *Courant*), Jan. 21–3, 1716.

[18] Blackett's election was not secured until he had produced two letters from the secretary of state testifying to his loyalty: Sedgwick, ii, 465, 559.

Blackett's mayoralty, despite government orders to the contrary.[19] Rumors of continuing or aborted Newcastle and Northumberland risings and the shadowy meetings of Jacobites on the heath at night continued. Even after the reports of a possible Jacobite invasion from Spain in late 1717 had sent the inhabitants of Newcastle into "a pannick fear," George Liddell was able to report to Cotesworth that in Newcastle and Northumberland the rebels "swarme," and were "so Uppish that they bragg that they were in the Rebellion"; other convicted rebels who were to have been transported appeared "publickly and *No Notice taken by the Civil Magistrates.*" Not surprisingly, then, local Jacobitism survived the '15, and Stuart ballads, artifacts and memorabilia continued to be produced and circulated in the Newcastle area until the 1770s.[20]

More immediately, the rebellion and its bloody aftermath, particularly the execution of Derwentwater and the outlawry of Forster, rent the county and city communities to a degree unprecedented since the Civil Wars, which redounded to the Whigs' advantage. The Tory party's lack of favor with the Crown led to party infighting among the Newcastle aldermen, and the Tory MPs' consequent inability to protect Newcastle's interests at Westminster allowed their opponents to engineer their first and only clear parliamentary victory of the period. The force behind the Whig offensive was, of course, Richard Ridley. That Ridley was detested by a vast number of his fellow citizens seems clear. He was posthumously condemned as "revengeful, bitter, ready to oppress; / the City's Torment, and the Poor's Distress," and charges of venality and treachery were also articulated by his contemporaries.[21] Yet he was also respected by the freemen for his tough stands in support of Corporation privileges against the claims of county families, London coal traders and parliamentary committees alike, and his patronage and defense of dissenters and Low Church traders against High Church barbs and exclusions gave him a permanent following in the town. In 1717–24, Ridley's bid for dominance was aided by Tory di-

[19] The conventicle itself lasted until the death of Charles Edward Stuart in 1788: R. Sharp, "One Hundred Years of a Lost Cause: Nonjuring Principles in Newcastle," *AA,* 5th ser., 8 (1980), 38–9.

[20] PRO, SP 35/8/112 (1), (2); W. T. Matthews, ed., *The Diary of Dudley Ryder* (London, 1939), 265; *Worcester Postman,* May 16, 1718; *Six Northern Diaries,* 83; GPL, Cotesworth MSS, CP1/32, GL to WC, April 5, 1718; Welford, *Men of Mark,* i, 179; John Sykes, *Local Records of Northumberland,* 2 vols. (London, 1866), i, 121–2.

[21] [Edward Chicken], *No, This Is the Truth* (Newcastle, 1741); *Six Northern Diaries,* 63; BL, Add. MS 27,420, fols. 50–9.

visions and ineffectuality at Court, as well as a set of lawsuits brought against the Corporation by Grand Allies Cotesworth and Liddell in 1717–24, which enabled him to strengthen his position among the freemen. The Allies' actions had thrown into question both the Corporation's rights to the Walker estate, which housed a hospital for distressed freemen, and the rights of the Hostmen's Company to levy ballast charges on ships coming up the Tyne.[22] Ridley, as governor of the Hostmen's Company, took the opportunity to show his own political clout, seizing the coals of fitters not free of the company, sending articulate and able spokespeople to testify in the Corporation's defense in London, and organizing a strong counter-petition defending the Hostmen's economic practices. Meanwhile, a prominent Tory alderman, Matthew Fetherstonhaugh, outraged local opinion by testifying in London against Ridley with regard to ballast duties.[23] Ridley was thus able to solidify his support locally through his crusade to vindicate Newcastle's "rights and privileges" not only from the attacks of outsiders but from the duplicity of its Tory magistrates. His maneuvers, aided by rumors of Jacobite plots, enabled the Whig William Carr to defeat William Wrightson in the 1722 parliamentary election. Carr succeeded in procuring a royal grant of the title to the disputed Walker estate in late 1723, becoming alderman and mayor in 1724 and something of a local hero.[24] At the same time, the impact of the Allies' lawsuits soon persuaded most of Newcastle's coalowners, with the notable exceptions of Ridley and White, to agree to a "regulation" which controlled coal prices and output on Tyneside until the 1750s.[25]

The Whigs' moment of ascendancy in Newcastle politics was produced by their successful defense of Newcastle privileges against outside threats, demonstrating in cogent fashion the role of "localism" in eighteenth-century parliamentary politics in general and the Newcastle freemen's requirement that their magistrates and MPs protect their interests at Westminster in particular, the failure of which could override

---

[22] Welford, *Men of Mark,* i, 498; TWA, Calendar of Common Council Books, Minutes, April 19, 22, 1719; April 30, 1722.
[23] TWA, 248/2 Hostmen's Company Records, Minutes and Accounts, 1654–1742, orders, Sept. 1722; F. W. Dendy, ed., *Extracts from the Records of the Company of Hostmen,* (Surtees Society, 105, 1901), 186–7; GPL, Cotesworth MSS, CP1/57, 68, 73.
[24] TWA, 589/7, Common Council Act Books, Feb. 7, Oct. 14, 1724; Calendar, April 5, 1725; Welford, *Men of Mark,* i, 496.
[25] Cromar, "Coal Industry," 84–101.

strongly entrenched party loyalties.[26] But like all moments, this one was evanescent. The parliamentary inquiry into the coal trade had focussed attention on the role of the central state in promoting or hampering regional and national prosperity, and these were concerns that the emergent patriot ideology of the parliamentary opposition would systematize. The general election on George II's accession precipitated strenuous canvassing by Blackett and his fellow Tory alderman and current mayor Nicholas Fenwick, and it resulted in Carr's resounding defeat, 1,202 and 1,189 votes to 620.[27] Although Carr and his supporters petitioned the Commons against the return on the ground of bribery, before the House could act on the matter Sir William Blackett died. When the petition came up in committee, no one appeared against it, and Carr was returned on March 26, 1729. George Liddell, as MP for Berwick, described the situation in this way: "Carr had no opposition [appearing against the petition] . . . so that by disqualifying 605 [voters] he had a majority of 23. I think there was scarce anybody believed the witnesses."[28]

Indeed, patriot ideology and the anti-corruption critique of Whig power in central government worked to reposition Toryism within the constellation of local political forces and redefine the party's premises and concerns. Central to this reconfiguration was the integration of Toryism within the dynamic structures of urban culture. The flourishing print culture of Newcastle, evinced in the expansion in the number of booksellers and printers, the proliferation of printed materials that ranged from local histories to John Wesley's abridgment of *Pilgrim's Progress,* and the viability of local newspapers, kept Newcastle residents linked with broader regional, national and international developments. The quality of the town's four newspapers, and especially John White's *Newcastle Courant* and the Quaker and opposition Whig Isaac Thompson's *Newcastle Journal* in 1739, was attested to by their preeminent stature throughout the North, where they served as the primary organs of legal, political and cultural information for Durham, Cumberland and Edinburgh as well as Northumberland.[29] All were fo-

---

[26] Hence many who split their votes in 1722 between a Tory and Carr voted for two Tories in 1741.

[27] TWA, 51/14 (3), Records of the Armourers, Feltmakers and Curriers' Company, election notice from Blackett and Fenwick, June 24, 1727; Sedgwick, i, 298.

[28] Welford, *Men of Mark,* i, 309; quotation from Sedgwick, i, 532.

[29] C. J. Hunt, *The Book Trade in Northumberland and Durham* (Newcastle, 1975), 105–6, 187–8; *Courant,* Jan. 19, 1723; Dec. 18, 1731; Sept. 13, 1735; Jan. 28, 1744. The other papers were William Cuthbert's *Newcastle Gazette, or Tyne Water Journal*

rums for trenchant political discussion and debates on issues of national and local consequence while bolstering popular Toryism in Newcastle by reflecting the opposition's point of view. The *Newcastle Weekly Mercury* regularly reproduced Cato's letters for its readers; and White of the *Courant* was arrested by the government for seditious libel in 1715 and taken into custody again in 1731 for reprinting an especially scurrilous *Craftsman* essay. These brushes with the law, however, did not squelch his predilection for provocative opposition and even Jacobite journalism, and he continued to reprint essays from *Mist's, The Craftsman* and the *London Evening Post.*[30]

These papers were available for reading and discussion in the town's inns and taverns and coffeehouses as well as in circulating libraries and book clubs, which also seemed to have large Tory memberships. The local masons, for example, were dominated by the Fenwicks, long known locally for their pro-Stuart sympathies but now emerging as prime advocates of "patriotic" politics, as well as Walter Calverly Blackett, maternal nephew to Sir William, who held the mortgage on the property where Newcastle's first masonic lodge was built and served as grand master in 1734. St. Nicholas Book Club included several Tory clergymen as members, and politics as well as theology, travel and history were staple fare.[31] Local and visiting theatrical troupes also enlivened political debates with their performances: Rival performances of *The Beggar's Opera* were staged by visiting acting troupes in 1728, and the freemasons commissioned a performance of *The Committee* at Moot Hall Theater which was attended by such a sparkling "appearance of ladies and gentlemen as was never before seen." The popularity of the stage was sufficient to warrant Richard Baker's building a new theater in 1748.[32] Conjoining the oppositionist

(1744–55); Leonard and Thomas Umfreville's *North Country Journal* (1734–9) and Robert Akenhead's *Newcastle Weekly Mercury* (1722–3). For influence see R. M. Wiles, *Freshest Advices: Early Provincial Newspapers in England* (Canton, Ohio, 1965), 451–60; R. C. Jarvis, *Collected Papers on the Jacobite Risings*, 2 vols. (Manchester, 1971–2), i, 6–8.

[30] PRO, SP 44/77/198; Wiles, *Freshest Advices*, 282–3; *Newcastle Weekly Mercury,* Feb. 2, 16, April 13, 27, May 4, 11, 1723; *Courant,* Jan. 10, 27, Feb. 10, 1733.

[31] PRO, SP 44/77/198, 207; Sykes, *Local Records,* i, 142; *Newcastle Weekly Mercury,* Feb. 2, 16, Apr. 13, 27, May 4, 11, 1723; Hunt, *Northumberland Book Trade,* 187; *Memoirs of the Public Life of Sir Walter Blackett* (Newcastle, 1819), viii; John Money, "Freemasons and Loyalism in England," in E. Hellmuth (ed.), *The Transformation of Political Culture* (Oxford, 1989), 256–7; NCL, LO27.2, MS Accounts and List of Members, St. Nicholas Book Club, 1742–6.

[32] Sybil Rosenfeld, *Strolling Players: Drama in the Provinces, 1700–60* (Cambridge, 1938), 112–13.

culture articulated in print, tavern life and theater were the activities and leadership of young Blackett himself, who not only involved himself in the refurbishment of urban culture but also appropriated his uncle's grandiose paternalistic style to make his own mark in the political life of the town. Elected MP in 1734 and alderman and mayor soon thereafter, eschewing the Jacobite links of Sir William and firmly allied with the Tory–patriot opposition in Parliament, Blackett endowed a library and hospitals, liberally gifted charity schools, contributed to subscriptions for local improvements and bestowed alms on the poor with legendary munificence, all the while signifying his actions and local position through the rhetoric of opposition patriotism. Through his canvasses – attended "by above 500 gentlemen, tradesmen, etc., some of whom had weight with almost every freeman" – solicitous attentions to merchant and middling economic interests, and unbridled opposition to the Court, Blackett dominated Newcastle politics for the next three decades.[33]

The newly defined and rearticulated Tory party's clout became evident in 1733–4 when Tories orchestrated the local anti-excise agitation and won the 1734 parliamentary election. Dissenters' ostracism from the town's institutional politics, the virulent High Church sentiment among local Tories and the animosities from the '15 that still rankled among the county and civic leaders made a coalition opposition to Whig ascendancy in central government unlikely, if not impossible on the local level before the advent of the Quaker Isaac Thompson's explicitly opposition Whig journalism in 1739. Nevertheless, it was clear that the High Church hyperbole of earlier campaigns was outmoded for present purposes, when it was crucial to identify Walpolean corruption with the Whig interest in their own midst and to see their efforts as part of a national campaign against corruption at all levels. The bipartisan Merchants Adventurers had instructed the Newcastle MPs to oppose the bill, with enthusiastic support from local traders and retailers, who remembered recent government efforts to "regulate" the coal trade to the detriment of Newcastle's interests and who argued now that the measure was to be part of a larger assault on the liberties and properties of the trading community.[34] The news of Walpole's withdrawal of the bill prompted spontaneous public rejoicings. "Scarce a town in England has shewn greater Demonstrations of Joy upon ye late

[33] *Courant,* Oct. 26, 1734; TWA, Calendar of Common Council Books, Oct. 1734, 1735; Welford, *Men of Mark,* i, 316; *Courant,* Jan. 5, 1733; Jan. 1, 1743.
[34] *Courant,* March 25, Nov. 3, 10, 17, 1733.

Victory than . . . Newcastle," Blackett's agent noted in April, and the celebrations at local taverns were marked by toasts and 204 candles in honor of the 204 "Worthy Patriots" who had voted against the bill.[35] Yet Ridley, who as governor of the merchants' company had sponsored the recent instructions, received little credit for his role in the national drama. Indeed, his colleague William Carr's vote for the measure led to his and Ridley's being snubbed by townspeople, whereas Fenwick was cheered by large crowds assembled to greet him on his return to Newcastle.[36] In conjunction with Ridley's recent machinations in Common Council when he tried to preempt Walter Calverly Blackett's bid for Parliament by pushing his son, Matthew, into an aldermanic seat and mayoral office over the claims of other Corporation members, these developments worked to turn the Whig rhetoric of 1722–4 against former proponents. "People can't help seeing that he studies nothing more than mayking ye Corpn. subservient to his own Interest," Joseph Richmond noted. Ridley thus seemed to embody the same kind of self-serving and anti-populist political sensibilities as Walpole himself.[37]

The Tory candidates in 1734 stressed this identification while emphasizing their own adherence to the libertarian and commercial interests of the Walpolean campaign, such as Fenwick's opposition to the excise and vote to repeal the Septennial Act in March 1734, as well as Blackett's political heritage as nephew of the city's greatest benefactor. The ensuing election evinced the nature and terms of Tory support in the town. Though the recommendations of the *Courant* to administer pledges to all the candidates to oppose standing armies and excise laws and to refuse all places and pensions from the government were not followed, the polling was extended by the requirement, enforced by "the principal Tradesmen," that the oaths against bribery and those of Supremacy and Allegiance be administered to all the voters.[38] Blackett and Fenwick were returned against Carr by resounding majorities, with resulting protracted celebrations by freemen and residents alike, who seemed to view their indiscriminate pre-electoral treats or their votes as a hard-won reward for service to local, "independent" interests.[39]

[35] TWA, 988/4, Journal of the Merchant Adventurers, 1675–1733, Jan. 17, 1733; *Courant,* March 25, July 14, April 21, 1733; BL, Add. MS 27, 420, fol. 60(b), April 21, 1733.
[36] *Courant,* Sept. 15, 1733.
[37] BL, Add. MS 27,240, fol. 59, JR to Sir Walter Calverly, March 24, 1733.
[38] *Courant,* April 6, March 16, 1734; GPL, Ellison MSS, A17/7, Robert Ellison to Henry Ellison, May 1, 1734.
[39] *Courant,* May 11, 1734; "The Merry Patriot," *Newcastle Courant,* Jan. 19, 1734.

The Tories' adoption of the patriotic program allowed them to set the terms of the debate, and the Whigs, unable to proffer an effective alternative idiom, were left vying for a "patriotic" status of their own.

The excise crisis and its repercussions in Newcastle also highlight how the opposition triad of "trade, liberty and commerce" could become priorities in the provincial views of the national interest. Newcastle shared with most other large provincial towns pride in its own energetic and enterprising spirit, its bustling combination of industrial, service and distributive activities which contemporaries called "Trade," and its appreciation of the benefits of commerce and its expansion which included but were not limited to the coal trade. Indeed, despite the Merchant Adventurers' dominance of internal and external trade, ordinary Newcastle residents, from blockmakers to sailmakers and shopkeepers, were becoming increasingly involved in investments in cargoes and ships trading in colonial and overseas markets and even in the Atlantic trade.[40] They thus provided a receptive audience for the opposition's commercialist as well as libertarian propaganda.

The complex of forces animating opposition political culture was further reconfigured in 1738–41, when buoyant support for war with Spain, a damaging food riot and struggles for power in the Corporation culminated in the "Great Contest" of 1741, a parliamentary election that brought 2,400 voters to the polls and focussed political energies for close to nine months. Since the seventeenth century, Newcastle had maintained a firm opposition to wars with the Continental powers, largely because they disrupted trade, fostered the commandeering of crews and collier vessels to serve in the fleet, and dislocated the coal industry. But in 1738–9, local sentiment against the Convention Treaty was strong, so that Blackett and Fenwick, although initially diffident, voted against it in the division of March 8, 1738.[41] The declaration of war by the mayor and aldermen in October 1739 ended with "loud Acclamations, Firing of Guns, etc." and public toasts to the king and "Success to British Arms"; a subscription concert a few weeks later concluded with "Britons Strike Home" and "To Arms," at which the audience stood and cheered.[42] Not surprisingly, then, Newcastle resi-

---

[40] S. P. Ville, "Patterns of Shipping Investment in the Port of Newcastle-upon-Tyne, 1750–1850," *NH*, 25 (1989), 207–10; PRO, Customs Book 84/5, Newcastle, 1738–42; Kathleen Wilson, "Empire, Trade and Popular Politics in Mid-Hanoverian Britain: The Case of Admiral Vernon," *P & P*, no. 121 (1988), 82–3; Chapter 3.

[41] *Gentleman's Magazine*, 9 (1739), 304–10.

[42] *Newcastle Journal* (hereafter *Journal*), Nov. 1, Dec. 1, 22, 1739.

dents participated fully in the national celebrations for Admiral Vernon beginning with his victory at Porto Bello, and artifacts, maps, poems and ballads all expressed the considerable extent of local acclaim for the hero who had so fearlessly extended British liberties and markets abroad. His birthday the following November was specially observed in local taverns by clubs of tradesmen, at least one tavern renaming itself the Admiral Vernon for the festivites.[43]

Meanwhile, Corporation politics had been complicated by rivalries in the coal trade and a food riot in June 1740.[44] Richard Ridley's death in 1739 had left Whig supporters at sea, and his son, Matthew, alienated his fellow magistrates by his withdrawal from the coal cartel a month after his father's death, raising realistic fears among coalowners and laborers alike that a price-cutting war would result. The paralyzing winter weather of 1739–40 aggravated these tensions, for the price of bread and commodities had soared, and in early summer riots broke out across the Northeast, prompting the march of troops south from Berwick to suppress them. But before they had reached Newcastle, a food riot erupted which lasted through the week of June 19 and resulted in one death, the looting of the Town Hall by the rioters, the capture of £1,200 and the destruction of the Corporation's cherished portraits of Charles II and James II.

The Newcastle magistracy's response to the riots reflected its internal divisions. At the first outbreak of disorder, the Tory mayor, Cuthbert Fenwick, had appealed to coalowners to summon their employees to help restore peace. In response, Matthew Ridley appeared in Newcastle early the next morning heading a posse of "sixty men well-mounted and above 300 on foot, well-provided with Good Oaken Cudgels," all with green boughs in their hats. Though they managed to disperse the rioters, stability was by no means assured. The Grand Allies had refused to call up their employees to help Newcastle magistrates, and a ship loaded with foreign grain remained docked at Quayside, exacer-

---

[43] *Journal,* Jan. 12, March 22, April 26, May 3, 1740; *Courant,* March 22, April 21, Nov. 13, 20, 1740; Jan. 10, 1741. For the Admiral Vernon Inn and local performance of the siege of Porto Bello see *Journal,* Nov. 21, 1741.

[44] For the best account of the riot see Joyce Ellis, "Urban Conflict and Popular Violence: The Guildhall Riots of 1740 in Newcastle upon Tyne," *International Review of Social History,* 25, pt. 3 (1980), 332–49. The next three paragraphs are based upon Ellis's account, supplemented by NRO, ZRI 35/12, i, Ridley to Dobson, Nov. 30, 1739; ZRI 27/8 [Matthew Ridley], MS Account of the Riot [1740]; H. T. Dickinson, ed., *The Correspondence of Sir James Clavering* (Surtees Society, 178, 1968), 213; and Sykes, *Local Records* i, 166–7.

bating discontent. It was also known that some merchants in town were
hoarding grain, as the merchants' company had sold small quantities
of oatmeal cheap the day before. Yet after the first wave of rioting
had receded, Mayor Fenwick, disdainful of Ridley's show of self-
importance, refused to sign the orders to retain the militia and departed
for his house in Elswick, leaving the town unguarded. Hence, when the
crowd assembled again on the 26th, Ridley panicked and, rounding up
some young apprentices, provided them with muskets and undertook
the distribution of the shipment of rye. A fight broke out, and some of
the "White Stocking regiment," as they were derisively called, fired
into the crowd and killed one man, wounded others and thus precipitated the crowd's wreaking vengeance on the Town Hall.

As a piece of pre-electoral politicking, the death of the rioter and the
perceived arrogance of Ridley did little to ameliorate the latter's relations with the Tory freemen or his colleagues in the Corporation. The
Common Council voted the freedom of the city to the military officers
who had at last arrived in town to quell the riots (Ridley was conspicuously ignored) and ordered that the "unanimous approbation" of the
Council be given by Mayor Fenwick to Walter Blackett and Nicholas
Fenwick for their consistent opposition to the "Court" and support of
the Spanish war. At the Michaelmas Corporation elections the following week, the Tory recorder, Edward Collingwood, was returned as
mayor, and the Tories had firm control of the town government.[45] The
next nine months witnessed some of the most intensive politicking of
the period as Blackett and Fenwick prepared to face Carr and Ridley
in the general election. The rival birthday celebrations of the leading
Whig and Tory candidates set the tone. Ridley announced his candidature to the town in a public procession on his birthday, November
14, marching through several neighborhoods with his entourage to the
ringing of bells, firing of guns, and bonfires and providing a public
entertainment in the evening on Quayside, where "Success to Admiral
Vernon" was toasted. A month later, Blackett and his supporters observed his birthday with an impressive piece of street theater that demonstrated the unassailable nature of a popularity founded on "country"
opposition and a paternalistic civic policy. A British flag was hoisted
to the highest steeple of St. Nicholas's Church, Blackett distributed his
usual dole of bread, beef and money to every "poor and necessitous"

[45] TWA, Calendar of Common Council Books, Oct. 1740; 589/7 CC Account Books,
Oct. 1740. For the Tory rejoicings on this event see *Courant,* Oct. 11, 1740.

family in the city, and the afternoon was spent in public rejoicing considered to be "entirely proper for so zealous a Patriot for Liberty." Bells were rung, ships on the river saluted with their flags, and the city guns were discharged in the high and low parts of town every hour until ten in the evening. Meanwhile, a grand procession toured the streets with music and singing, ending up at Blackett's house on Pilgrim Street, where citizens toasted their host, the king and Admiral Vernon.[46]

The canvass began in earnest the following April. Ridley's followers painted him as a supporter of the king and constitution, Corporation interest and local prosperity, a studied contrast to Tory candidates whose loyalties and motives were sullied by disaffection and malice. On Blackett's side, voters were warned to be wary of men of "such a Stamp, that his [Vernon's] Virtue would disdain, and his very Soul abhor," and Ridley lambasted as a "Corrupter," venal and vengeful, who sought to destroy the church, oppress the poor and extinguish liberty. His actions during the food riot of 1740 were depicted as a means to "Destroy the Town's Honour by a sham Pretence / of heading Fops to stand in its Defence / [and] pull down its Grandeur for a private end . . ." Blackett was rather bombastically styled "The Patriot," the "Opposer of the Court," "The Father of the Poor," and "The Great Promoter of true liberty . . . who from oppression set you safely free."[47] Nevertheless, he and Fenwick were returned by a majority of just under two to one, in the largest turnout of voters in the century. The widespread celebrations on the election's outcome carried over into the weekend, when Newcastle indulged in "the greatest Rejoicings that ever were known on any occasion" after receiving the news of Vernon's victory at Cartagena.[48]

The partisan dimensions of the contest were indicated by the voting within the companies, where the Tories procured majorities in all but eight.[49] Indeed, Blackett's influence over local politics was so great at this point that at the mayoral elections the following October, he thwarted the election of the former Whig and recent ally Francis Rudston in order to advance his long-time supporter Robert Sorsbie to the

---

[46] *Courant,* Dec. 20, 1740.
[47] Ibid., May 2, 1741; [Chicken], *No, This Is the Truth.* See also *Is This the Truth?* (Newcastle, 1741) and *No – That's a Mistake* (Newcastle, 1741), pro-Ridley verses; *Memoirs of Walter Blackett,* xv.
[48] *Courant,* May 23, 30, 1741; 1741 pollbook (see n. 4).
[49] The Mariners, Scriveners, Upholsterers, Millers, Sadlers, Fullers and Dyers, Shipwrights and Paviours had majorities for the Whigs.

mayoral chair.[50] But the bitterness, rancor and, most of all, the expense of the 1741 election would be regretted later by all involved, and the contest crippled the finances of Fenwick, who had to seek the protection of Holyrood. Walpole's fall the following February was heralded in the local press by mock sermons, satirical poems and accounts of the often spectacular rejoicings elsewhere in the region and nation – "at this happy Event all INDEPENDENT Britons must feel a generous joy," the *Newcastle Journal* reported; ". . . so shall our Country's *Honour* Revive and our Trade flourish, no longer the dupe of *France* and the *Scorn* of Europe" – but was received in Newcastle without any public celebration.[51] Within the next three years, a Jacobite invasion would focus local patriotic sentiment on the monarch.

The emergence of the national anti-Walpolean campaign furthered the development of popular politics in Newcastle. Yet the content and consequences of the vibrant "patriotic" political culture which flourished in the period from 1727 to 1742, though strongly influenced by the national agitation, was distinctive within the constellation of opposition politics. The succession had not resulted in long-lasting Whig hegemony, and when the long arm of official Whig influence was extended to the northern town it was ineffective in combatting entrenched Tory loyalties within the Corporation and ineffectual in helping local Whig leaders to negotiate a competitive position among the freemen. The local political situation thus enabled the Tory elite, who actively participated in and protected extreme oligarchy in the institutions of local government, to encourage popular oppositionist sensibilities against the Whig predominance in the state and the Whig presence in the Corporation, largely because these sentiments supported local Tory hegemony. Of course, the middling freemen were inclined to acquiesce in magisterial power, not least because it was effective in maintaining order among the vast number of quasi-proletarian residents in the town and in protecting the freemen's status and privileges against them and other "outside" threats. Hence, in contrast to Liverpool and Chester, where the freemen used the rhetoric of opposition patriotism to campaign against oligarchy in civic government, the popular opposition in Newcastle never attacked the distribution of power within the town per se, only its Whig manifestations.[52]

At the same time, Newcastle was a thriving commercial center, and

---

[50] GPL, Ellison MSS, A17/27, RE to HE, Oct. 6, 1741; A17/28, RE to HE, Oct. 9, 1741.
[51] Ibid., RE to HE, Jan. 3, 1742; *Courant,* Feb. 13, 1742.
[52] Sedgwick, i, 270–1, 203–4.

the patriot ideology which stressed the primacy of trade and empire over high finance in the national interest clearly struck a responsive chord among its residents. Local participation in the national opposition campaign spawned a clear identification between the political concerns of Newcastle's freemen, which turned upon the choice of representatives and the deflection of challenges to the chartered privileges which ensured local prosperity, and the political concerns of the nation at large, which centered on the overweening and corrupting executive power which was believed to threaten the birthrights, liberties and properties of all English people. Indeed, for many the similarity between local and central corruption could not be more clearly drawn: The perception of venality and duplicity of Whigs like Ridley in town affairs was consistent with the tenor and trend of Whig government at St. Stephen's and St. James's. The local oppositionist political culture thus fostered a sensitivity to national political issues and a preoccupation with executive corruption that would endure. More contested and fragile was the amalgam of sensibilities which drove the anti-Walpolean opposition in Newcastle, combining a "country" critique of Whig government and a demand for the protection of local interests with Anglican hegemony and a traditional regard for the paternalist functions of the ruling class – an amalgam exhibited, not fortuitously, by the "King of Newcastle," Walter Blackett.[53]

The Jacobite invasion of 1745 went some way in temporarily vitiating these party distinctions, for it mobilized loyalist, at the expense of oppositionist, patriotism among the citizenry and helped erase the scars left by indigenous struggles over the dynastic issue. Initially, on the outbreak of the rebellion in August 1745, Newcastle residents were far more concerned about the enemy without, advancing through Scotland to the north of England, than the ones in their own ranks. The *Courant* felt sufficiently secure about the reaction of local inhabitants to publish Charles Edward's manifesto; but the surrender of Edinburgh to the rebels threw Newcastle into a panic. As Wesley noted, there was an exodus of people and personal property out of Newcastle on news of the rebellion – a response which the vicar of St. Nicholas's, the Reverend Dr. John Brown, would later denounce as evidence of the "effeminacy" of the local gentry and leading citizens – and an even greater deluge of inhabitants from northwestern counties as well as

[53] See Linda Colley, *In Defiance of Oligarchy: The Tory Party, 1714–1760* (Cambridge, 1982), 85–117, 146–75.

Northumberland into the city over the next several weeks.[54] Civic leaders, however, proved more stalwart. Mayor Matthew Ridley summoned all the householders of the town to meet him at the Guildhall, where over 3,000 reportedly entered into a loyal association to defend Newcastle against the enemy. By the time the Northumberland militia had reached the town some days later, a second city militia had been raised by Sheriff Aubone Surtees, the town walls had been fortified, and cannon were mounted on the towers, preparations which deflected a party of rebels advancing on Newcastle in October.[55]

What was most pronounced in the city's response to the rebellion was its essential unity. Clergy of all denominations banded together to preach loyal sermons on the dangers of popery, and the local press burst forth with anti-Stuart tracts and essays which drew on the nationalist and patriotic sensibilities of readers.[56] Significantly, local propaganda drew upon anti-French and anti-Catholic prejudices more than on anti-Caledonianism. Indicating in part a wariness of alienating the large number of poor resident Scots involved in the coal trade and more positively acknowledging their loyalty to Hanover and long-entrenched hostility to Catholicism, local appeals to "the people" differentiated the "savage Highlanders" from the more civilized Lowland Scots in the effort to solicit a common British identity among its audience. Of course, anti-Jacobitism always contained the fear of a range of "others" within – the poor and dispossessed as well as Tories, Catholics or Scots – that its aggressive identification of the enemies without could never entirely mask. Hence the author of *Address to the Common People* attempted to make clear the benefits accruing to "freeborn Britons" for any who may have questioned their own "free and flourishing" condition, but fell back on using the ethnocentric noun to do so: If a French-backed pretender ever triumphed, he concluded, British trade and empire would be gone, and "instead of *Three Meals* a Day, the *Englishman's* Birthright, you won't have one a Week, unless you should be so lucky to find a dead Horse."[57] In the event, the keelmen and pitmen, groups which

[54] *Courant,* Aug. 17, 1745; *The Journal of John Wesley,* ed. Nehemiah Curnock, 8 vols. (London, 1910), iii, 211–12; John Brown, *Estimate of the Manners and Principles of the Times,* 2 vols. (London, 1757–8), i, 90–1; Jarvis, *Collected Papers,* i, 219–25.
[55] Wesley, *Journal,* iii, 210; *Journal,* Sept. 21, 1745; Brand, *Newcastle,* ii, 525; TWA, Calendar of Common Council Books, Sept. 11, 1745; Jarvis, *Collected Papers,* i, 202.
[56] Brand, *Newcastle,* ii, 527; Wesley, *Journal,* iii, 210–18; Thomas Turner, *A Sermon Preached at St. Nicholas's Church in Newcastle-upon-Tyne, Dec. 18, 1745* (Newcastle, 1746); *Journal,* Oct. 5, Nov. 23, 1745.
[57] *Courant,* Oct. 19, Nov. 2, 1745; Jan. 4, Feb. 15, 1746; *Newcastle Journal,* Oct. 12,

included many Scots, proffered their own associations for defense of
the town and country against the Pretender, stridently vindicating their
own and, by implication, their Scottish countrymen's capacity for Englishness and national loyalty in the present crisis.

Hence, despite the hardships caused by the stoppage of trade, the
quartering of General Wade's troops and a severe shortage of specie
in the town, loyalty and spirit was the predominant response to the
rebellion, demonstrated in street theater and military performances as
well as printed effusions.[58] There were rumors of disaffection among
groups of pitmen and keelmen, and several men from Newcastle and
more in the county were detained on suspicion of treasonable practices
and seditious words.[59] But in general, popular sentiment was more anti-
Catholic than Jacobite, indicated by the alacrity with which a plebeian
crowd set two mass-houses on fire in order to provide an "illumina-
tion" for the Duke of Cumberland.[60] Indeed, Cumberland's local stature was attested to when he visited Newcastle in July. Fêted by the
corporation with all imaginable pageantry, he was also saluted by the
residents with mock Pretender burnings and a set of elaborately engraved gold boxes containing the freedoms of the town and Trinity
House, the iconography of which iterated current preoccupations with
England's political greatness, imperial destiny and military valor.[61]

The '45 and its aftermath, then, had important political consequences
in Newcastle. First, it fostered the accommodation between the city's
feuding elites grudgingly begun after the last election. Ridley's prompt
and vigilant actions in preparing the town's defense had earned him
the king's personal thanks and a greatly increased popularity among

19, 1745; *An Address to the Common People on the Pretenders' Declaration* (Newcastle, 1745). The Corporation's gold box presented to the Duke of Cumberland in
1746 was engraved with the figure of Britannia trampling on a Highlander, standing
for Rebellion: TWA, 543/100, Chamberlain Accounts, 1745–6.
[58] *Courant,* Oct. 12, Nov. 2, 9, 1745.
[59] PRO, SP 36/83, fols. 45–6, 143–5; SP 36/85, fol. 37 (thanks to Paul Monod for these
references); TWA, 540/5, Quarter Sessions Order Book, 1743–7; *Courant,* Jan. 14,
1746. The suspicions about the keelmen were borne out in 1750 when a group of
them proclaimed Charles Edward "King of England, France and Ireland and Defender
of the Faith"; but this incident occurred in the midst of a keelmen's strike which was
both bitter and refractory. *Courant,* May 5, 1750.
[60] Sykes, *Local Records,* i, 180.
[61] *Journal,* July 26, 1746; *Courant,* July 26, 1746. For a description of the Trinity House
box see Chapter 3. Cumberland's birthday and the anniversary of his victory at Culloden became regularly observed civic holidays in Newcastle through the 1780s: *Courant,* April 19, 26, 1746; April 18, 23, 1748; NRO, Ridley MSS, ZRI 27/10, Account
of the Ceremonies.

his fellow citizens.[62] Moreover, by 1747 he had solved the financial problems created for him by the '45 by at last agreeing to "regulate" with the Grand Allies and other coalowners of Newcastle, thus fostering a more genteel rivalry among the local elite. They could then be found socializing together: The elite Recorders' Club at Eubanks, formed specifically for the annual observance of the victory at Culloden, had both Ridley and Blackett as members.[63] Secondly, the Tory's oppositionist stance in the town became more muted and accommodating. Although the *Newcastle Courant* reminded its readers to take the "oaths of Patriots" against bribery at the general election in 1747, the fierce party rivalries which had plagued the town for the past four decades had been tamed. Blackett could remark that he hoped for no contest at the general election, for "I delight not in party, and have been a witness to, if not an actor in, the absurdity of it." He had his wish: Fenwick withdrew from the election rather than face the exorbitant costs of a contest, and Ridley and Blackett were returned unopposed, as they would be until 1774. Together they were in an economic and political position to dominate town politics for the next two decades.[64]

Nevertheless, if the party conflict of preceding decades acted in part as a salve which soothed freemen's frustration and resentment at elite occlusion in corporate affairs, it also focussed attention on the issues arising from state expansion and power. Party ideologies constructed vertical definitions of interest and patriotism that solicited support from like-minded individuals of all ranks, whether to help oppose executive corruption, promote trade and empire and restore a pure House of Commons, or to maintain the Hanoverian Succession against its insidious challengers, and thus bolstered elite political leadership. But they also familiarized residents with a critique of the state that identified the structure and distribution of political power as the source of many social, economic and political discontents, and the impact would survive the elite electoral compromises and realignments of the 1750s.

---

[62] Mackenzie, *Newcastle,* 259; *Courant,* Sept. 8, 1787. See the nave in St. Nicholas's Church, Newcastle, erected in Ridley's honor, which depicts him in a Roman habit trampling on Rebellion and Sedition.

[63] Cromar, "Coal Industry," 107–12; *Courant,* April 18, 1747; April 23, 1748; Sykes, *Local Records,* i, 190.

[64] *Courant,* June 27, 1747; NRO, Allgood MSS, ZAL/35/5, WB to LA, June 9, 1747 (thanks to Professor W. A. Speck for bringing this reference to my attention). In 1749, Blackett inherited the baronetcy on the death of his father; Ridley came into Sir Matthew White's vast interests in coal, lead, glass and salt through his wife, Sir Matthew's daughter.

II. RADICAL POLITICS AND RADICAL PUBLICITY

In an age when the polite arts,
By general encouragement and emulation,
   Have advanced to a State of perfection,
Unknown in any former period:
The first stone of this edifice
Dedicated to the most elegant recreation
   was laid by [Mayor] William Lowes Esq.
   on the 16th day of May 1774.
      Dedicatory plate for the new Assembly
      Rooms, Newcastle, 1774[65]

In an age, when the tide of corruption,
By R[oya]l encouragement, deluged the land,
When luxury had advanced to A State of Perfection
Unknown in any former period . . .
   When a stagnation of trade
   and the high price of provisions
   Had reduced the poor to the greatest extremity . . .
To their everlasting disgrace, the gentlemen of *Newcastle*
Continue to waste their time, And spend their substance
In celebrating the Rights of *Venus* and the ceremonies of *Bacchus.*
Five thousand Pounds were rais'd by subscription
Through a Vicious emulation to excel in politeness . . .
The pious Sanction of W. L[owe]s Esq.,
Engraved in brass, continues to show the profligacy of this age.
      Freemen's Magazine (Newcastle, 1774)

The electoral compromise reached by Ridley and Blackett in 1747 marked the beginning of two decades of relative political concord in Newcastle. The growing identity of interest among the once fiercely divided elite was demonstrated in cooperative efforts to further local and national projects, from the establishment and management of turnpikes to the manning of collier vessels for the war in 1756.[66] Although Pelham's foreign policy and such Tory–Anglican issues as the Jewish naturalization bill roused anti-administration sentiment,[67] the accession of Pitt to power temporarily suspended the current of persistent oppo-

[65] Brand, *History of Newcastle,* i, 121–2n.
[66] Chapter 1; Sykes, *Local Records,* i, 188, 191, 264; *Courant,* March 13, May 1, 1756.
[67] *Journal,* May 6, Nov. 11, 1749; *Courant,* Feb. 11, April 22, 29, 1749; June 2, 9, 30, Aug. 11, Sept. 15, 29, Oct. 13, 1753. Blackett joined the Prince of Wales's program for moderate constitutional reform in 1747: Sedgwick, ii, 464.

sition to the Court which had characterized Newcastle's popular politics
in the preceding three decades, and support of the imperial war was
enthusiastic and bipartisan. As Newcastle's overseas trade expanded
and involved a larger and more socially varied set of investors, local
traders began to voice their objection to the restrictions placed on international and imperial commerce by the London-based monopoly
companies, which, they felt, served to aggrandize only their "private
interests" at the expense of independent British merchants. As one
observer charged while reviewing the exclusive practices of the East
India, Hudson's Bay, Turkey and African companies,

> for carrying on and extending Commerce all the World over every
> *Individual* has an *equal Right,* and the whole *Community* receives a
> *Benefit* . . . by what Authority can any Man, or Body of Men, in this
> Kingdom be invested with the *Sole Privilege* of trading to particular
> Parts of the World, with powers to exclude all other Subjects [from]
> the common Benefits of Nature and Society?[68]

The contradiction between these sentiments and the fierce support of
Newcastle's own chartered rights and privileges notwithstanding (for it
did not seem to trouble contemporaries), the dichotomy posed between
the government-protected monopoly companies and the independent
merchants of the outports articulated the hostility of provincial traders
to what they felt to be an obstruction to their birthright as Britons, the
"natural right" of trade.[69]

Such concerns ensured that the Newcastle administration's handling
of the French threat in America and Europe would be carefully monitored. Isaac Thompson's *Newcastle General Magazine* contained extensive coverage of international and imperial affairs, especially, from
the early 1750s onwards, the state of colonial defense and French and
ministerial policy in America. Hence allusions to the "bungling" response of the government to the French advance on Minorca appeared
quickly in the local press, and the fall of the island sparked a rash of
anti-Byng demonstrations in Newcastle and environs as well as demands for "national and constitutional Inquests" into the disaster.[70]

---

[68] *Newcastle Journal,* Jan. 27, 1750. In fact, the Royal Africa and Levant Companies'
charters were given up in the early 1750s.
[69] *Journal,* Jan. 27, June 9, 1750. Newcastle traders argued that the monopoly companies' rights allowed French merchants to undersell the British, which in fact was
correct: See James Riley, *The Seven Years War and the Old Regime in France*
(Princeton, 1986), 103–10.
[70] *Courant,* March 27, April 10, May 1, 29, 1756; demonstrations: *Journal,* July 24, 31,

The extent of discontent in the region was reported on by the Bishop of Durham to the Duke of Newcastle, who warned the first minister that ''had the Assizes [in the North] been a week later, so as to have given more time for a Ferment, I cannot say what might have happened.''[71]

Accordingly, after Newcastle's resignation in November 1756, public opinion swung firmly behind William Pitt and stayed there with little ambivalence throughout his ''patriotic'' wars.[72] Local notables contributed generously to the Marine Society – indeed, a ''club of gentlemen'' at the Turk's Head Inn were among the original subscribers to the charity – and offered additional bounties for recruits for the army and navy.[73] More humble citizens' energies were vented in the donation of bread and clothes for Prussian and British troops and in jubilant celebrations that followed the seemingly endless series of British victories beginning in 1758, when relief at the nation's eschewal of effeminate leaders and at the recovery of manliness, patriotism and imperial supremacy was emphatically expressed.[74] Not surprisingly, Pitt's resignation in 1761 was widely lamented in Newcastle, and his successor, Lord Bute, was widely unpopular, with a number of consequences for popular politics.

At the same time, the wars completed the reintegration of elites into a united ruling class and placed them in a flattering position with the freemen. In particular, Blackett and Ridley's self-styled ''independency'' in Parliament gave them a broad base of support in Newcastle.[75] Both Newcastle MPs took the ''popular side'' on many of the issues of the 1760s, voting, for example, with the opposition over Wilkes and

---

1756; *Courant,* July 17, 31, 1756; inquest: *Courant,* Aug. 28, 1756. See also *Newcastle General Magazine,* 9 (1756), 484–5.

[71] BL, Add. MS 32,867, fol. 133, Bishop of Durham to Newcastle, Aug. 28, 1756.

[72] The Corporation participated in the ''rain of gold boxes'' on Pitt and Legge: Paul Langford, ''William Pitt and Public Opinion,'' *EHR,* 88 (1973), 54–80; TWA, Calendar of Common Council Minutes, June 16, 1757.

[73] Jonas Hanway, *A Letter from a Member of the Marine Society, Shewing the Piety, Generosity, and Utility of Their Design,* 3rd ed. (London, 1756), 38; *Journal,* April 21, 1759; *Courant,* March 8, 1760. Lancelot Allgood marched into Newcastle from Hexham ahead of 20 stout recruits, all hailed as exhibiting ''a truly *British Spirit*'': *Courant,* April 10, 1756.

[74] *London Chronicle,* Dec. 29–31, 1757; *Journal,* June 23, Aug. 8, Sept. 15, Oct. 27, 1759; Sykes, *Local Records,* i, 226; Richard Brewster, *A Sermon Preached in the Church of St. Nicholas, in Newcastle-upon-Tyne . . . on the Day Appointed by His Majesty for a General Thanksgiving* (Newcastle, 1759).

[75] Namier and Brooke, iii, 352–3; ii, 95–6.

the Middlesex election. Blackett thus continued through most of the decade with his reputation as the "Great Patriot" intact (despite his vote against the repeal of the Stamp Act in 1766), and Ridley enhanced his reputation by voting against the colonial tax and the Townshend duties in 1769. In this way, the political positions of the magistracy and citizenry appeared to be consistent until the end of the decade, when the latter challenged their representatives' "independency" by initiating political actions themselves.

The chronology of radical politics in Newcastle in the period of the Wilkite agitation and the American war has been extensively examined by historians, and with good reason, for Newcastle activists sustained a remarkably energetic campaign that produced sixteen political clubs, five petitions on parliamentary corruption and reform, a remonstrance to the throne, two sets of parliamentary instructions, two lawsuits against the local magistracy, several different subscriptions, a dozen addresses and innumerable local demonstrations.[76] Most important for our purposes, the culture of dissident politics in Newcastle, simultaneously anti-magisterial and anti-administration for most of the period, coopted popular politics by successfully appropriating the mechanisms of political publicity for dissident ends, propagating enduring definitions of subjectivity and patriotism that contested the politics of deference.

The events of 1769–70 established the battle lines which would remain drawn for the duration of the radical campaign. In early 1769, several Newcastle freemen, led by glazier Thomas White, called a general meeting of burgesses and inhabitants to consider a set of instructions to their representatives. Drawn up by the Committee of Stewards first formed in 1764 to inquire into magisterial abuses of the Town Moor, the instructions provided a comprehensive list of political, legal and commercial grievances that animated the fledgling movement, advocating the adoption of the Wilkite reform program, greater safeguards for the rights of habeas corpus and trial by jury, the redress of American grievances, and protection of subjects' commercial property against the damaging actions of the Court of Exchequer. Although the Stewards

---

[76] See H. T. Dickinson, *Radical Politics in the North-East of England in the Later Eighteenth Century* (Durham, 1979); Thomas R. Knox, "Popular Politics and Provincial Radicalism: Newcastle upon Tyne, 1769–85," *Albion*, 2 (1979), 224–41, and "Wilkism and the Newcastle Election of 1774," *Durham University Journal*, 41 (1979), 23–37; P. M. Ashraf, *The Life and Times of Thomas Spence* (Newcastle, 1983); Wilson, "Rejection of Deference," chap. 6; and James Bradley, *Religion, Revolution and English Radicalism* (Cambridge, 1990), passim.

Committee solicited signatures from all of the aldermen individually, only the mayor, John Baker, signed, along with 627 of the resident freemen. Blackett and Ridley responded by declaring instructions to be inconsistent with their own commitment to a representative's "independency," but such a position jarred glaringly with the expectations of the instructors, who charged rhetorically, "Have they [Blackett and Ridley] any freedom, as our servants, to vote or determine contrary to the interest and instructions of Those who appoint them?"[77]

By October, the burgesses and residents were agitating for a petition to the Crown for the dissolution of Parliament in the "present alarming crisis." Handbills were distributed stressing the moral and political necessity of such an intervention; and although efforts were still made to enlist the local magistracy in the cause, White's attempt to read the prepared petition in Guild was obstructed by aldermen, who insisted that the Guild existed solely for the purpose of admitting freemen to the Corporation and not as a political forum. To emphasize his point, Sir Walter stood and blustered that he would "sooner have that right hand cut off, than sign such a petition"; the Great Patriot and his colleagues were hissed by the freemen as they left the Guildhall.[78] The efforts continued nonetheless, and meetings held in the Long Room of Forth House produced two petitions, one from the unenfranchised freeholders of the county of Newcastle and another from the burgesses and residents, both calling for dissolution of Parliament. These were presented at St. James's in early January 1770 by the chairs of the respective meetings, Thomas Delaval, Esq., and his brother, Sir Francis Blake Delaval, knight, both "outsiders" from the Corporation and supporters of opposition politics. Sir Francis, indeed, was a member of the SSBR and later the Constitution Society as well as being known widely for his festive and rakish lifestyle. The freemen's petition was signed by 900 men, 526 of whom were electors and 90 percent of whom were retailers and craftsmen.[79]

---

[77] *Chronicle,* April 29, 1769; *Freemen's Magazine, or Constitutional Repository* (Newcastle, 1774), 6; *Journal,* May 20, June 10, 1769. Given that the population of resident freemen was around 1,100 at this time, over half signed the instructions: *Courant,* May 20, 1769; *Freemen's Magazine,* 5.

[78] *Worcester Journal,* Oct. 12, 1769 (by this account, some of the handbills had the heading "No Petition, No Mayor, No Sheriff"); *Journal,* Oct. 7, 1769. *Freemen's Magazine,* 2, 41–2; *Newcastle Chronicle* (hereafter *Chronicle*), Oct. 14, 1769; [James Murray], *The Contest* (Newcastle, 1774), 23. In November 1770, Blackett stood in the Commons and rescinded his previous votes on the Middlesex election: Namier and Brooke, ii, 296.

[79] *Chronicle,* Oct. 21, 1769; *Journal,* Nov. 18, 1769; *Chronicle,* Nov. 18, 1769; PRO,

The citizens' assertion of their right to initiate political programs and direct their representatives, as well as the burgesses' attempt to coopt the Guild as the freemen's political forum, had all met with unremitting hostility and obstruction from the local magistracy; it was in this period that the phrase "a Sir Walter Blackett" was coined to refer to a duplicitous political turncoat.[80] Ironically, the magistrates' reaction to local political developments had the effect of enlarging radical concerns, centered in the first instance upon the issues raised by Wilkes and the Middlesex election, to include Corporation corruption and malfeasance. As a radical handbill distributed in September 1770 argued, the attempt of the Corporation to infringe upon "natural rights" by obstructing just and legal addresses to the king sprang from the same structural flaws that enabled it to subvert the chartered privilege of articulating grievances in Guild. The handbill went on to suggest a series of reforms that would make local government more accessible and accountable to the freemen. These included open account books (the writer pointed to the Infirmary as a model), the formation of a burgesses' committee to prevent encroachments on Corporation property, the administration of oaths against bribery to the twenty-four electors for Corporation office, and the enactment of stringent qualification for the office of chamberlain.[81]

The extra-institutional political culture of the town promoted the newly refocussed radical cause with enthusiasm. Despite the magistrates' having locked the belfries of the churches to prevent the bells from being rung, Wilkes's release from King's Bench prison in April 1770 was marked by extensive public rejoicing in taverns and inns, five different club celebrations and a performance of the tragedy *Cato.* One of the clubs, the Friends of Legal Liberty, began a subscription on Wilkes's behalf which was to be sent to the SSBR in London, payable at the town's four coffeehouses and at *Chronicle* printer Tho-

---

Home Office Papers, HO/55/2, Newcastle Burgesses to the King (1769); Knox, "Popular Politics and Provincial Radicalism," 237; George Rude, *Wilkes and Liberty* (Oxford, 1962), 129. In fact, a number of men signed both petitions: Knox, "Wilkism," 24n. Soon after this incident John White died, and the *Courant,* now in the hands of White's partner Thomas Saint, became firmly "ministerialist" in its attitudes and reporting.

[80] Thomas Bewick, *A Memoir,* ed. Iain Bain (Oxford, 1978), 53; *Songs from the Manuscript Collection of John Bell,* ed. I. Harker (Surtees Society, 196, 1983–4), 51–2.

[81] NRO, ZAN/M17/38, Society of Antiquaries MSS, Election papers, 1741–1800; Handbill, Sept. 29, 1770, *To the Free Burgesses of Newcastle.*

mas Slack's shop.[82] In the wake of the widespread show of support for
Wilkes, the burgesses and freeholders combined again to send a stridently worded remonstrance to the throne in 1770 which called for the
removal of the ministry. In the spring of the next year, William Smith,
surgeon, used the Guild to propose an address to Crosby and Oliver in
the Tower over the printers' case. ''Is it not alarming to Consider, that
now the Chief Magistrate of the city of London lies confined in the
Tower, for supporting the laws and Constitution?'' Smith shouted over
the objections of the magistrates. ''What London now suffers . . . Newcastle, and all the corporations of England, have reason to expect if the
Commons assembled in Parliament be suffered to proceed.'' An address
to Wilkes, Crosby and Oliver thanking them for their ''virtuous and
manly resistance'' to the current attempt of the House of Commons to
''supersede the law of the land and the rights of citizens'' was sent
soon thereafter, signed by the stewards of twenty-four of the town's
twenty-six active companies.[83]

The Town Moor dispute of 1772–3 strengthened the links between
Newcastle and metropolitan radicalism while imparting the former with
a greater sense of its own distinctiveness.[84] For the past eight years,
the Stewards Committee had been complaining to the magistracy about
encroachments on their rights, including the Common Council's cooption of revenues from the mines, quarries and enclosures and the local
gentry's erection of turnpikes over the moor. A petition of 1771 that a
portion of the Town Moor be enclosed and improved for the pasturage
of burgesses' animals was answered with the Common Council's *lease*
of a parcel of the moor to one Joshua Hopper, with the intention of
distributing the rents among the poor of the companies.[85] This action
was quickly interpreted by both the freemen and majority opinion as a

[82] *Courant,* April 21, 28, 1770; *Chronicle,* April 28, 1770; *Journal,* April 21, 28, 1770;
Sykes, *Local Records,* i, 271–2.
[83] *Journal,* May 12, 1770; April 13, 1771; *Chronicle,* May 12, 1770; for subscriptions
to defray the costs of petitioning and addressing see TWA, Company Records: 786/
2, Barber-Surgeons' Co. Minute Book, June 1, 1770; 938/2, Upholsterers', Stationers'
and Tinplate Workers' Minute Book, July 25, 1770; 151/6, Curriers' Fines and Accounts, June 29, 1770; for address to Crosby and Oliver see *Universal Magazine,*
April 1771, extracted in BL, John Bell Collection, LR 264b, fol. 49. Trinity House
sent a separate address to the London magistrates in May. Anti-administration demonstrations also marked the election of Wilkes and Bull as sheriffs in 1771: See
Courant, July 6, 1771.
[84] For the dispute see Lewis Namier, *The Structure of Politics at the Accession of George
III,* 2nd ed. (London, 1965), 95–9.
[85] *Journal,* May 11, 1771; *Proceedings of the Stewards . . . ;* TWA, Calendar of Common
Council Minutes, May 14, Sept. 30, Dec. 31, 1771; Jan. 20, 1772.

flagrant abrogation of freemen's rights. At a public meeting a committee of burgesses was elected to consider appropriate retaliatory action.
The committee, which included surgeons William Smith, Henry Gibson
and Nathaniel Bayles, the Hostman Alexander Adams, mariner Captain
Thomas Maude, bricklayer Thomas Maddison, and cordwainer Benjamin Brunton, plotted a course of action in conjunction with fellow
burgesses and residents and began to implement it the following May.
In true Wilkite style, the committee presided over a flagrant and organized trespass of the leased land, led by Gibson and Bayles, during
which hedges were burned down, fences torn and the cows of local
residents let in, destroying Hopper's corn and turnip crop. An irritated
and bewildered Hopper, at the Common Council's behest, brought an
action of trespass against the burgesses' committee in the Court of
Common Pleas in Westminster, and the case was set to be tried at the
assize of August 1773.[86]

Various clubs and companies quickly subscribed financial and moral
support for the forthcoming lawsuit. In July of 1772, radical freemen in
Newcastle formed the Constitutional Club of Durham, Newcastle and
Northumberland in order to integrate regional support for dissident politics and connect it with similar campaigns elsewhere in the country,
meeting quarterly in rotating locations and allowing admission by introduction. George Grieve, Alnwick freeman, part-time Newcastle resident
and SSBR member, was the first chair of the society, and Jasper Harrison, Newcastle attorney, its secretary; their letter to the SSBR written at
the first meeting declared that the raison d'etre of the Club was "to preserve the memory of the Middlesex election . . . to *mark* the conduct of
our representatives, and to resist . . . every attempt to violate the Rights
of Englishmen." Its timing was impeccable, for it drew national attention
to the Newcastle burgesses' plight and aided Grieve in procuring the
services of the radical recorder of London and Wilkes's lawyer, Serjeant
Glynn, to defend the freemen at the trial in August 1773.[87]

Glynn's forceful defense of the burgesses and adept examinations of
Newcastle aldermen forced the plaintiff, Hopper, into negotiating a deal

---

[86] TWA, 589/7, Common Council Act Book, Jan. 31, 1774 (summary of the case); for
similar Wilkite exploitations of the law see John Brewer, "The Wilkites and the
Law," in Brewer and John Styles, eds., *An Ungovernable People: The English and
Their Law in the Seventeenth and Eighteenth Centuries* (London, 1980), 128–71.

[87] *Journal,* July 4, 1772; *Chronicle,* July 3, 1773. Grieve's role in *founding* the club,
asserted in *The Biographical Dictionary of Modern British Radicals Since 1770,* 3
vols. (New York, 1978), i, 223, and repeated by Knox, "Wilkism," 31n, has been
greatly exaggerated.

which the burgesses' committee accepted and the court ordered to be drafted into a parliamentary bill at the Corporation's expense. In its final form, the bill conveyed the exclusive right of the burgesses and their widows to the Town Moor "forever" while providing for dual control of the pasturage by the burgesses and Common Council, with the former retaining veto power over potential leases and projected uses.[88] The acclamations which greeted this outcome were practically unbounded. Large parties of citizens decked with blue ribbons paraded the town with music, and toasted, cheered and acclaimed Serjeant Glynn in the streets and taverns. By October, the Wilkes's Head and Admiral Vernon inns in Fleshmarket were joined by a third tavern whose sign commemorated radical heroes, the Glynn's Head.[89] George Grieve and the Burgess Committee were equally acclaimed, the former presented with the freedom of at least nine companies, treated by a dozen more and publicly thanked in the newspapers.[90] And the "Glorious 10 August" became a radical holiday for the next several years, to commemorate the freemen's vindication of their rights and all participants' adherence to the principles of public-spirited patriotism, showing the nation that

> the honest and independent burgesses will all unite to oppose their known oppressors, and demonstrate to the world that neither noblemen nor baronets should ever influence them . . . they . . . are determined . . . to give an example to all other corporate towns, what the Newcastle burgesses will do to free themselves from the galling yoke of slavery they have so long suffered under: not only defending their personal rights, but steadily supporting independent elections, and every friend to the Glorious Cause of Liberty.[91]

As an episode in the local campaign waged by the freemen over their role and power in the Corporation, the Town Moor dispute destabilized

---

[88] *Chronicle* and *Courant,* Aug. 14, 1773. In fact, the magistrates attempted to subvert these intentions in their first draft of the bill by providing for moor rent to be administered as a charity by overseers of the poor and churchwardens, but the burgesses caught wind of it and successfully petitioned the parliamentary committee against this latest attempt at "oppression": TWA, Common Council Book, Jan. 6, May 13, 1774; *The Contest,* 24–9; *Journal,* June 11, 1774.

[89] *Chronicle,* Aug. 14, 21, Oct. 9, 1773. All three taverns were in Fleshmarket in 1778; see *Whitehead's Newcastle Directory* (Newcastle, 1778; repr. 1889), pp. 39–40.

[90] Grieve received the freedom of the Slaters, Smiths, Coopers, Bakers and Brewers, Masons, Barber Surgeons, Shipwrights, Millers, and Plumbers, Pewterers and Glaziers: *Chronicle,* Oct. 9, 1773; NRO, ZAN M17/52, Bakers and Brewers' Minutes and Orders, Sept. 2, Oct. 4, 1773; *Journal,* Nov. 27, 1773; *Chronicle,* Aug. 14, 1773.

[91] *Journal,* Aug. 6, 13, 1774.

the aldermen's control of the dynamics of civic politics. In the months preceding the trial, the attempt of burgesses to discuss the case in Guild was continually thwarted by the magistrates, and almost forced the disenfranchisement of Thomas White, who had "stopped," or challenged, the admission of thirty-four persons to their freedom in retaliation for mayoral interference in his pronouncements on the moor issue. As Matthew Ridley reminded Mayor J. E. Blackett, the power of the aldermanic and councilor bodies had to be exerted against the freemen's claims about their right to use the Guild for political discussion: "Unless you exert such an Authority . . . in a short time the whole Power will be transferred to the court of Mayor and Burgesses [i.e., Guild]." As a result, the barest vestige of popular participation in Corporation elections was eradicated in the October mayoral elections, when the magistrates refused to call upon electors who were members of or who supported the Burgess Committee for a vote.[92] Yet the magistrates' manifest bad faith throughout the moor dispute – which included hiring the burgesses' first lawyer away from them – and subsequent defeat at the hands of Glynn and the freemen gave the case national import and publicity, and portended the first contested parliamentary election in thirty-five years, creating widespread local enthusiasm for the promotion for "independent" candidates in 1774.[93]

The burgesses' campaign in the spring and summer of 1774 kept their cause in the public eye while deliberately integrating some of the various disparate communities constituting the political public within the town. For example, prosperous but disgruntled nonfree residents, excluded from the privileges of freedom while still paying its taxes, formed benefit societies in an effort to compensate for their relative deprivation.[94] The radical campaign strove to conscript them and other professional, middling and artisanal residents, regardless of legal status, into the regional and national radical effort to "purify" Parliament and circumvent executive corruption. Political clubs were particularly important in coordinating the activities of free and nonfree residents, dissenters and Anglicans, and even resident and nonresident freemen of

---

[92] TWA, Calendar of Common Council Minutes, April 19, 1773; 589/7, Act Book, April 22, 1773; NRO, Blackett MSS, ZBL 229/28, MR to JEB, May 8, 1773; *Chronicle,* Oct. 9, 1773. For details of the freemen's struggles in the Guild see Knox, "Wilkism," passim.

[93] See, e.g., *Norfolk Chronicle,* June 4, Sept. 10, 1774; *Journal,* Jan. 25, 1774.

[94] *Articles of the Falkirk Society, Begun May 15, 1749* (Newcastle, 1783); the name also suggests Scottish membership, which would reinforce their sense of exclusion from civic culture; dues were 5*s.* per quarter.

the town. One of these, the Lumber Troop, began a subscription for Mr. Miller, the printer of the *London Evening Post,* who was being prosecuted by Sandwich, and presided over the burning of "Jemmy Twitcher" in effigy in front of the Fleshmarket tavern; another, the Sydney Club, furthered radical political consciousness through weekly debates at local inns. Still others followed the lead of the Stewards Committee and the Constitutional Club in adopting a "test" for the candidates at the 1774 election which articulated demands for both a recognition of new forms of property and an easing of the conditions of small employers and wage-earners. Hence a pledge to promote parliamentary reform, the redistribution of seats from unpopulated to populous boroughs, and the enfranchisement of citizens like the Newcastle freeholders or residents of York – who had no votes anywhere, despite their being "equally independent, and chargeable with taxes like the rest of the kingdom" – was supplemented by demands for the reduction of regressive taxation on the necessities of life, "the people's bread, beer, soap, candles, leather."[95] Finally, various clubs and electoral associations and the newly formed "Committee for the Burgess's Candidates" undertook to canvass Newcastle freemen who resided in the inland towns and villages of Northumberland and Durham and the ports of Shields, Blyth, Sunderland, Wearmouth and Whitby. The numbers and sizes of the associations formed to support the radical cause in 1774 alone substantiate sympathetic writers' claims about the efficacy of such societies in producing advocates for "freedom and the constitution."[96]

When Blackett and Sir Matthew White Ridley (the senior Ridley had resigned in favor of his son) refused to subscribe to the test formulated by the Constitutional Club, the clubs, companies and stewards assembled to nominate the burgesses' candidates: Captain Constantine Phipps, MP for Lincoln, son of Lord Mulgrave and a nationally renowned Arctic explorer; and Thomas Delaval, Esq., established sponsor of Newcastle's dissident politics. Both men had made public pledges of their support for the principles of accountability and trusteeship in government and had supported radical causes from the Middlesex election and opposition to the Quebec bill to dissenters' most recent attempt at relief in 1772. While in London, the Burgess Committee arranged

---

[95] *Journal,* Feb. 19, April 21, March 19, June 11, 25, 1774; TWA, 1021/2, Goldsmiths' Company, May 31, 1774; *The Contest,* 30; NRO, ZAN M17/38, Election papers, handbill dated June 25, 1774.
[96] *Journal,* July 4, 16, 23, 1774.

for Phipps and Delaval, accompanied by Crosby, Sawbridge and Bull, to visit Newcastle freemen at the Hole-in-the-Wall Tavern in Fleet Street, and the candidates' canvass in Newcastle was attended by associations of citizens carrying green branches and wearing buff and green ribbons who congregated at the Surgeons' Hall to hear their new candidates' acceptance speeches.[97]

The clubs and associations were crucial to creating a sense of political community among radical supporters in the town and region, one which clearly differentiated itself within the larger community. The press played an equally large role in furthering radical causes and promoting the identification of Newcastle's citizens with national libertarian issues. In addition to the plethora of Wilkite or otherwise radical literature available for sale in the town, that veteran of opposition political journalism, Isaac Thompson, began publishing the *Literary Register,* which contained Junius's letters and other essays on colonial and political affairs.[98] Publications like Jean Paul Marat's *Chains of Slavery,* printed in Newcastle in the early summer of 1774, gave an international inflection to the issues at hand. Marat's emphasis on the necessity of spartan vigilance in public actions and his indictment of the whole panoply of public entertainments as but a hegemonic device that gave rulers "an ascendance over the minds of fellow citizens" struck a responsive chord in Newcastle's residents, dissenter and Anglican alike, who had witnessed the effects of patrician pageantry in their own town for decades.[99] In residence in Newcastle briefly in the spring of 1774, Marat had also prefixed an *Address to the Electors of Great Britain* to his work which reiterated the need for virtuous diligence in the face of potential horrors posed by parliamentary corruption and monarchical duplicity, and donated the book to several companies and the Lumber Troop; it was subsequently to be displayed outside the freemen's hustings at the election in October.[100]

Indigenous species of radical sermonizing and journalism may have had the most impact. The Reverend James Murray, Scottish Presbyterian minister of High Bridge meeting and indefatigable producer of

[97] *The Contest,* 30; *Journal,* June 11, July 16, 1774; [Constantine Phipps], *Letter from a Member of Parliament to One of His Constituents, on the Late Proceedings of the House of Commons in the Middlesex Elections* (London, 1769); *Chronicle,* Oct. 15, 1774.
[98] *Literary Register,* 1–2 (1769–70), passim; see also *Journal,* Feb. 17, 1770.
[99] *Chains of Slavery* (Newcastle, 1774), 6–40 and passim.
[100] P. M. Horsley, *Eighteenth Century Newcastle* (Newcastle, 1971), 207–8; TWA, 903/4, Housecarpenters' Co. Orders, Dec. 26, 1774.

radical propaganda with a sharp social edge, published *Sermons to Asses* in 1768 and *New Sermons to Asses* in 1771, which set the tone for much of the subsequent radical agitation with their vehement condemnation of passivity, fervent support for popular resistance and virulent attacks on elite self-interest, electoral venality and Church of England corruption. His uncompromising hostility to wealth and title and strictly nondeferential attitudes to those in authority earned him the respect and awe of many of his contemporaries; his concern for the poor, whom he saw as unmitigated victims of ruling-class aggression and avarice, made him a profound influence on Thomas Spence, who attended his weekly lectures on civil and religious liberty and became his devoted protégé.[101] In 1774, Murray began editing the acerbic *Freemen's Magazine,* which both reprinted pertinent news and letters on radical campaigns in other towns, such as London, York, Bristol and Worcester, and presented the historical context of current political issues in order to set before the northern counties "those Rights and Privileges, which have been secured to them, with much Trouble, and at the Expense of the Blood of their Ancestors."[102] In addition, his pamphlet *The Contest* ably incorporated Newcastle radicalism into a heroic narrative of the long and continuing struggle of the people against tyranny, of which the 1774 election would be the apotheosis, by chronicling "magisterial oppressions" since Sir Walter Blackett first ascended to power. Defining "Whig" and "Tory" in the terms familiar to some contemporary historians – Whigs were libertarians who opposed excessive executive power and taxation; Tories, divine-right despots who supported prerogative courts in church and state – Murray

---

[101] James Murray, *Sermons to Asses* (London, 1768), *New Sermons to Asses* (London, 1771), *An Alarm Without Cause* (Newcastle, 1780), *Eikon Basilike* (Newcastle, 1778), *The Fast: A Poem* (n.p., 1778) and, *Sermons for the General Fast Day* (London, 1781). For his weekly lectures and plan of land nationalization, which Spence would later adopt, see Dickinson, *Radical Politics in the North-East,* 7–8; Ashraf, *Life and Times of Thomas Spence,* 18–29; and Malcolm Chase, *The People's Farm: English Radical Agrarianism, 1775–1840* (Oxford, 1988), 42–4. See also Bradley, *English Radicalism,* 167–75.

[102] *Freemen's Magazine,* April–June 1774 passim. Murray's deployment of the radical rhetoric against "Jacobites and Tories" had a doubly heavy connotation in Newcastle, where residents remembered both the questionable loyalties of a portion of the local elite and the threats to local trade and life posed by the rebellions. It led the ingenuous Sir Edward Blackett to write a forceful letter to the *St. James's Chronicle* in 1769 protesting the town's loyalty to George III; unfortunately for the reputation of his colleagues in the Corporation, they chose this period to reerect the statue of Charles II in its former niche in front of the Exchange; it had been taken down 75 years earlier: NRO, ZBL 264/3 (2), EB to *Chronicle* (unsigned).

went on to describe the transmutation of the two parties that occurred in the early Hanoverian period when the Whigs replaced the Tories in office and became "tories" in principle themselves as a result of the inevitably corrupting impact of power. Blackett's popularity rested firmly upon his espousal of "whig" principles – "he openly made a merit of having in the first opposed the ministry in EVERY thing" – and his generous and conspicuous purse. His subsequent alliance with Ridley proved both the insincerity of both men's professed principles and the disregard which they had for their supporters, who had been attached to measures which they no longer adhered to. Such apostasy had proven conclusively that true Whiggism would continue to exist only outside Parliament unless the present election was successful.[103]

Thus, local propaganda and practices constructed a political community whose unity of interests was defined on the basis of both historical and contemporary alignments and issues. Though unabashed in deploying a self-legitimating reading of party history and labels, the narrative of politics transcended traditional party identities to coax and solicit a class of men who defined themselves in opposition to those who furthered or profited by the aggrandizement of power in the organs of the state. At the same time, it upheld notions of the "rights of citizens" that viewed those rights as residing not in property but in polity, not in land or even wealth but in vigilant activism in the public sphere on behalf of the public good. On the one hand, within the terms of the current campaign it was up to electors – a privileged category among "the people" – to lead the assault on overweening concentrations of power.[104] On the other, political subjectivity, like patriotism, was proffered as the product of specific practices – that is, of exhibiting "public-spiritedness," of acting *like* a citizen, and so was never particularly amenable to such containment.

In response to the wide-ranging radical campaign and the national attention it received, Blackett, Ridley and their supporters engaged in some strenuous politicking of their own. Although several of the companies refused their canvass or even forbade their admission into their halls, the 615 new freemen admitted to the Corporation two months before the election permitted themselves to be treated and cajoled by the magistrates in the traditional manner, and their propaganda dispar-

---

[103] *The Contest,* 19, 13–18, 12.
[104] In Newcastle and other corporate towns where freemen took their charters seriously, the notion of "rights" as an inheritable form of property inflected its use in particular contexts.

aged the "system of modern patriotism . . . introducing strangers and Aliens in the Room of Country Gentlemen."[105] The contrasts between the candidates' processions to the hustings on election day were noted in the local press: The magistrates' candidates, parading from Blackett's mansion in the middle of the town to the Guildhall, were accompanied by "a chain of great men . . . an association of power" all wearing red and purple cockades; Phipps and Delaval's procession, routed from the Barber-Surgeons' hall to Hume's tavern, contained hundreds of burgesses wearing green and buff badges, but not "one *lord,* one *baronet,* one *knight,* one *magistrate,* one *placeman* . . . or one *bishop*" among them.[106]

The radical candidates were decisively defeated by a margin of almost two to one, with 34 percent of the vote. But the magnitude of their defeat was not significantly greater than that of the Whigs in the last contested election in Newcastle, known as the "Great Contest," in 1741, when there were also higher rates of cross-voting and plumping.[107] Moreover, once residency rates are taken into account, the significance of the magisterial "landslide" is greatly qualified. Thomas Knox's detailed electoral analysis has shown that only 55 percent, or 1,191, of the voters were residents of Newcastle, and of these, *over half* voted for Phipps and Delavel; 40 percent of the vote from London and the ports also supported the burgesses' candidates. Hence 802 freemen voted for radical candidates, and the resident burgesses were correct in claiming that it was the county voters and other nonresident voters who swung the election in Blackett and Ridley's favor.[108]

At the same time, the social cleavages the election results have been purported to reveal do not, on close examination, appear particularly impressive. James Bradley's painstaking analysis of the vote in 1774 has shown that elite and professionals accounted for 1 percent of the radical vote, merchants 2 percent, retailers 33 percent, craftsmen and artisans 58 percent and laborers 6 percent; for the magistrates' candi-

[105] NRO, ZBL 229/58, MWR to JEB, June 3, 1774; for the admission of freemen see TWA, 596/2, MS Alphabetical List of Persons to be Made Freemen (n.d.); 596/26, [Jasper Harrison], List of the Freemen with Trades (1774); *A Summary of the Disputes* . . . (Newcastle, 1774), 23.

[106] *Summary of the Disputes,* 23; for Blackett and Ridley's street theater see *Journal,* July 9, Oct. 22, 1774.

[107] In 1774, there was 6% cross-voting and under 1% plumping; in 1741 the figures were 13% and 12% respectively. *The Burgesses' Poll at the Late Election of Members for Newcastle upon Tyne,* 2nd ed. (Newcastle, 1775); *The Poll at the Election for Members of Parliament at Newcastle upon Tyne* (Newcastle, 1741).

[108] Knox, "Provincial Radicalism," 237n; *Summary of the Disputes,* 24.

dates the proportions were 3, 15, 19, 53 and 9 percent respectively.[109]
Unsurprisingly, then, the radicals had nearly twice the proportion of
retailers, and the magistrates several times as many merchants, as their
respective opponents, but both shared a broad base of artisan and la-
borer support. And the small number of dissenters voting were divided
fairly equally between the two parties.[110]

What is more striking than the alleged commonalty of "objective"
socioeconomic rank of radical voters is their *relative* position within
local power structures. Hostile observers clearly discerned this bias in
the movement. One writer to the *Public Advertiser,* who professed to
be a freeman himself, observed:

> From the extent of Newcastle, and the trade of the inhabitants as
> general merchants, it happens that the middle set of men, attorneys,
> retail dealers, apothecaries, etc. (who in smaller corporations are gen-
> erally the little great men of the place) are here excluded. This bar
> to their ambition led some men to wish that the power and Manage-
> ment of all Public business should be taken out of the hands of the
> Mayor, Alderman and Common Council, and thrown into the hands
> of the body at large . . . hoping that they might thereby have some
> share in the administration.[111]

This characterization needs qualification but otherwise holds up.
Clearly craftsmen and artisans made up a considerable portion of the
grass-roots support for the radical movement in Newcastle; three of the
earliest activists in Newcastle radical politics were a glazier, a mason
and a carpenter, and it was in several of the building trades and craft
companies, particularly butchers and building tradesmen, that the freemen's candidates obtained the largest majorities. Some of these supporters were masters who in income and outlook were very much part
of the middling community; some were small masters who hired out
their own labor as well as that of their workers; others existed in still
more plebeian material circumstances but still retained the skills and
aspirations to respectability that attracted them to the "independence"
articulated in radical ideology and differentiated them, they believed,
from the mass of the laboring population. They were thus well posi-

[109] Bradley, *English Radicalism,* 272. Knox's figures also show 45% of resident craftsmen and 51% of resident tradesmen supporting the radical candidates: "Popular
Politics," 237.
[110] Knox, "Wilkism," 29n.
[111] Reprinted in *Chronicle,* July 3, 1773.

tioned to believe that greater access to the political process could help them maintain or restore autonomy to their lives.

However, middle-class participation and initiative were crucial to local dissident politics. Not only did over half the resident tradesmen vote for the radical candidates, but printers, publicans, innkeepers, booksellers, retailers and professionals kept the cause alive with their support. Indeed, the leaders of local radicalism tended to be, with the exceptions noted above, professional or semi-professional men involved in the creation and maintenance of the institutions of civic culture. George Grieve, friend of Wilkes and chair of the Constitutional Club, was honorary member of the Moor Committee, chaired the meeting to petition over the American war, and served as Newcastle's deputy to the Association movement. Equally ubiquitous, Nathaniel Bayles was swordbearer for the Corporation for over thirty years and a physician at the Infirmary, besides being the chairman of the burgesses' Town Moor committee. Alexander Adams, fitter, and Thomas Maude, master mariner, were trustees of the disabled seamen's charity and members of the Town Moor committee, and both were wealthy enough to subscribe to the fund to save the Newcastle Bank in 1772 and, along with the two radical candidates, to the building of the new Assembly Rooms.[112] Maude was also a promoter of the Crosby address, leading electioneer in 1774 and a participant in a disruption of the Guild which would be cited before King's Bench in 1775–6. William Smith, another surgeon at the Infirmary, was ubiquitous in radical causes through 1784. Jasper Harrison, attorney, was secretary of the Constitutional Club, ''cheque scrivener'' for the opposition in the election of 1774, and later chairman of the Protestant Association of Newcastle.

Combining professional, political and religious zeal were the group of nonconformists who were conspicuous figures in dissident politics. Dr. John Rotheram, Unitarian, physician, member of the Infirmary's House Committee and chairman of the Revolution Society, was later a prominent member of Newcastle's Protestant Association; Henry Gibson, apothecary and surgeon to the Infirmary and the public lunatic hospital and co-builder of the public baths in 1781, chaired the Friends of Legal Liberty, was a member of the Town Moor committee, promoter of the Association movement for parliamentary reform in 1779,

---

[112] *Journal,* Jan. 2, 1768; BL, Bell Collection, Subscribers to Save the Newcastle Bank, June 29, 1772; GPL, Cotesworth MSS, CJ6/11, List of Subscribers to the New Assembly Rooms (1774).

354 The sense of the people

and member of the Society for Constitutional Information in 1781.[113]
And Murray himself, though aggressively adopting a plebeian social
identity, was an articulate nonvoter who integrated the institutional and
extra-institutional aspects of the campaign with vigor. In many ways
Murray was a kindred spirit to James Burgh, another Scot whose tracts
on education and the plight of the poor placed him in the mainstream
of Scotland's "progressive" thinkers – but with a twist, for Murray's
strident opposition to clerical and aristocratic privilege and blistering
condemnations of the legal and political oppressions of England's ruling class were more audacious than Burgh's ponderous musings on the
delegatory principles underlying British representative institutions. Yet
for both Murray and Burgh, as for many other radical writers, social
and economic inequalities were rooted in and perpetuated by the political system: Despotism and tyranny produced and sanctified greed,
economic exploitation and immiseration of the poor, and radical political reform was the proffered solution.[114]

Hence the ideology and goals of the radical agitation transcended
religious as well as social differences, constructing a community of
interest among people of divergent material means who nonetheless
believed themselves to maintain sufficient independence to resist institutionalized power or restore it to a more pristine and responsive
condition, defining themselves against those who allegedly advanced
corruption and self-interest in the state. The rhetoric of the "leather
aprons" versus the "laced waistcoats" so often evoked in discus-
sions of the class dimensions of Newcastle radicalism must be seen
in light of this discursive strategy, one that sought to affront the sensibilities of local magisterial supporters who denigrated radicals as
"insolent" members of the "lower class of electors," impose ho-
mogeneity on the diverse forces involved in radical struggles, and
inflect the language of independence and patriotism with social as
well as political significance.[115] The language of politics continuously
constructed and negotiated notions of class, respectability and patri-

---

[113] TWA, 672/168–9, Infirmary Reports; *Courant,* Jan. 9, 1768; *Journal,* Nov. 3, 1770;
Nov. 9, 1771; Mackenzie, *Historical Account,* 527; *The Burgesses' Poll,* title page;
NRO, ZRI 25/11, Ridley MSS, Correspondence Concerning Newcastle Protestant
Association; *Courant,* June 25, 1763; *Journal,* Sept. 1, 1770; PRO, Treasury Solicitor
Papers (hereafter TS) 11/1133, Minutes of the SCI. Gibson also subscribed to the
bank fund in 1772.
[114] See Murray, *New Sermons to Asses,* 19–22, and *Sermons to Ministers of State* (Newcastle, 1780), 13–15. My comparison with Burgh is based on Carla Hay's interesting
reading of his work in "The Making of a Radical: The Case of James Burgh," *JBS,*
17 (1976), 90–117.
[115] Knox, "Wilkism," 31; Ashraf, *Thomas Spence,* 38.

otism on both sides, and the "classes" identified in radical discourse – for example, the magistrates, freemen and the unenfranchised, or aristocrats, "the people" and "the mob" – did not fit into neat, one-to-one correspondence but shaped perceptions and formations of the social categories themselves.

Charges of elite venality and self-interest should accordingly be understood in this ideological context, which privileged political position and practice over socioeconomic status per se. The magistrates' handling of Corporation funds had long spurred citizens' anger, for the money seemed to critics never to be applied to any useful public project. Instead it was spent on lavish feasts, ostensible "public amenities" which actually served the magistrates' needs, such as the roads over the Town Moor leading to their estates or the luxurious cultural arenas from which the majority of citizens were excluded. Hence, while the quays on the river decayed and the Tyne bridge lay in ruins after the flood of 1771, local elites preferred to subscribe large sums of money for the new Assembly Rooms rather than begin the rebuilding of a vital communications link which allowed humbler men to reach their place of employment every day.[116] Equally, their ostentatious, paternalistic style was seen to be a manifestation of their autocratic sensibilities, and the aldermen's tyrannical wielding of executive, legislative and judicial power was seen to perpetuate a range of oppressive structures, from an outmoded legal system which penalized the smaller creditor to the patrician custom of leaving stacks of unpaid bills at the establishments of local retailers and tradespeople.[117]

These unhappy proclivities seemed to be carried over into the conduct of Newcastle's representatives in Parliament, who snubbed and ridiculed the wishes of their constituents. Junius's "Advice to the Freemen of Newcastle" rehearsed the abuses of Ridley and Blackett in their dual roles as magistrates and representatives: They laughed at the freemen's instructions, made daring attempts on their natural rights and properties, and, with the "arbitrary domination of a feudal tyrant," attempted to tear the right of common out of their hands.[118] Not surprisingly, the freemen's attempts to recast the Guild as the burgesses' political forum for discussion of grievances and debate, being contin-

---

[116] *The Contest*, 6; NRO, ZAN M17/38, Election papers, handbill dated Sept. 29, 1770; *Freemen's Magazine*, 57–9; *Chronicle*, Aug. 13, 1774. Phipps and Delaval made a point of inspecting the quays down to Shields.

[117] *The Corporation: A Fragment* (Newcastle, 1774), 3, 5; *Freemen's Magazine*, 1, 61–5; *Journal*, Nov. 20, 1773; *Chronicle*, Dec. 22, 1770.

[118] *Freemen's Magazine*, 10; *The Contest*, 16.

ually obstructed by the magistrates, were ultimately failures,[119] for the self-perpetuating structure of local government made entrenched power within it virtually unassailable.[120] In such circumstances, the struggles over the Guild and the town's parliamentary representation demonstrated to a broad swath of residents, enfranchised and not, "the manifest tendency, from the Throne to the aldermen of Newcastle downwards, to suppress the SPIRIT OF ENQUIRY . . . in SUPPORT OF LIBERTY AND THE RIGHTS OF THE PEOPLE."[121]

Newcastle radicalism thus essentially offered a political critique of the current constellations of social and political power, one that condemned the networks of patronage, exclusivity and corruption in the local and national state and championed greater openness and accountability. At the same time, against the emasculating effects of magisterial domination, Newcastle radicalism upheld the masculinist model of patriotism that privileged the claims of white English free men over those of all contenders: aristocrats, foreigners, fops and gentlemen without the good of their country at heart. Hence the comparison posed in the radical press between Sir Walter Blackett and the explorer Captain Constantine Phipps: It was the difference

> Between the commander of a coach and six, and captain of a man of war.
> Between – the owner of a pack of dogs, and the leader of a crew of Brave British sailors.
> Between – a preserver of partridges, and persecutor of his neighbors; and a defender of his country, and friend to the liberty of the subject.
> Between – a killer of moor game, and a shooter of the French. Between – nothing, and something . . . [122]

---

[119] Residents did successfully press a writ of mandamus in King's Bench against the sheriff of Newcastle to resume the monthly sheriff's court for civil actions for debt under 40s.: *Freemen's Magazine*, 61–5; *Journal*, March 19, 1774.

[120] The constitutional issue came to a head in Oct. 1775, when Thomas Maude, Thomas White, Robert Michison and John Hewitson insisted upon their right to speak at will in the Guild and upon its coeval power with the Common Council. The magistrates brought an action of riot against them in King's Bench, and the court confirmed the power of the aldermen and Common Council against the freemen's claims: TWA, Calendar of Common Council Books, Oct. 1, 1775; PRO, KB 1/10, Michaelmas Term 1775 and Hilary Term 1776; *Chronicle*, Oct. 14, Nov. 25, 1775; Feb. 10, 1776. Ultimately the Stewards Committee was a more successful, if extra-legal, response to local oligarchy, capable of pressing the freemen's claims in the Corporation.

[121] *Journal*, Jan. 28, 1775.

[122] *The Contest*, 38.

III. EMPIRE, PROTESTANTISM AND THE PEOPLE

... it always appeared to me that a very great majority of the people were decidedly against the [American] War. – These writings and debatings which the War occasioned certainly served greatly to alter the notions and the opinions of the people respecting the purity of the British government and its representative system and this attempt at doing it away altogether in America seemed a prelude or forerunner to the same system of misrule ...

Thomas Bewick, *Memoir*[123]

In Newcastle, as in many other large towns, the impact of the colonial conflict had made itself felt long before war broke out. American grievances had been incorporated into pre-electoral propaganda in 1774, when "the past conduct of the House of Commons towards this country and its colonies" and the aid which local representatives had given "to the establishment of the Popish Religion in our Protestant dominions" were rehearsed as two of the central grievances which dutiful citizens were exhorted to redress at the polls.[124] When war was declared, the people of Newcastle heard it proclaimed in the streets "in silence." The Constitutional Club held frequent meetings to discuss the current critical situation of affairs, and an association against the war was formed in Newcastle in response to the London Association's circular letter urging people to unite in defense of British liberties. Another newly formed club, the Philosophical Society, debated the constitutionality of American resistance; by November the Society had decided that a republic was "productive of more real advantage to the governed, than ... a limited monarchy like our own."[125]

The outpouring of loyal addresses to the king galvanized the organization of a petition from the "Free Burgesses, Traders, and Inhabitants" of Newcastle against the war. The meeting, chaired by Grieve and Smith, was called in late October 1775 and served as a forum for the public debate on the war and the proper action to be taken in the face of government aggression. A petition was agreed upon as well as a set of instructions to Newcastle's representatives, and two letters of thanks voted to the Earl of Effingham and Lord Mayor Wilkes for their

---

[123] Pp. 93–4.
[124] NRO, ZAN M17/38, *To the Stewards and Wardens*, June 17, 1774; *Journal*, July 9, Oct. 8, 1774; *The Contest*, 18.
[125] Sykes, *Local Records*, i, 303; John Sainsbury, *Disaffected Patriots: London Supporters of Revolutionary America* (Montreal, 1987), 106–13; *LEP*, July 29 – Aug. 1, Aug. 5–7, 1775; *Journal*, Nov. 4, Dec. 9, 1775.

opposition to the ministry's actions.[126] The instructions advised Blackett and Ridley of their duty to listen to their constituents before going on to demand redress of American grievances and cessation of hostilities as well as the implementation of the parliamentary reform program contained in the 1774 electoral test. The petition to the Crown, left at Swarley's for signatures before being sent off, argued in more subdued language that American resistance was supported by both constitutional principles and the "rights of Humanity" and thus necessitated conciliatory measures on the part of the government.[127]

The magistrates, however, responded in kind. Blackett and Ridley not only refused to present the petition (Sir George Savile complied instead) but also acted with other aldermen and Anglican clergymen to organize a loyal address from the town. Purportedly signed by the "Merchants, Gentlemen, Traders and Inhabitants" of Newcastle, it proclaimed to the king their attachment to the principle of parliamentary sovereignty over the empire, and commended the current attempt to force "proper submission" from the colonists.[128] Yet the magistrates did not solicit widespread public support for their missive – indeed, their circumspection in composing and sending it off caused it to be dubbed the "Smuggled Address" by radical propagandists – and it was signed by only 169 persons. The anti-war petition, on the other hand, was signed by 1,135 residents, 54 percent of whom were electors and 86 percent drawn from the middling and artisanal community.[129] Members of the Town Moor committee and radical leaders like Murray and Rotheram, as well as two councilmen and an array of victuallers, printers, booksellers, engravers, schoolmasters, shopkeepers, tradesmen and craftsmen demonstrated their opposition to the war on commercial and libertarian grounds by signing the petition. Significantly, the mayor, Charles Atkinson, did not

---

[126] *Journal,* Oct. 21, 28, 1775.

[127] Ibid., Sept. 30, Nov. 4, 18, 1775; PRO, HO 55/28/19, Newcastle Burgesses Against the American War, 1775.

[128] PRO, HO 55/12/6, Merchants, Gentlemen, Traders and Inhabitants of the Town and County of Newcastle-upon-Tyne to the King, 1775.

[129] *The Newcastle Smuggled Address* [1775], handbill in BL, Bell Collection, i, fol. 81. The list of signers to the loyal address was topheavy with Corporation magistrates, clergymen and professionals: See PRO, HO 55/12/6; *Journal,* Dec. 2, 1775. Of the electors signing the petition, 85% would vote for the radicals' candidate at the 1777 by-election: John Phillips, "Popular Politics in Unreformed England," *JMH,* 52 (1980), 611. For the social structure of the petitioners see Bradley, *English Radicalism,* 374.

sign the address, a fact which, in conjunction with his conciliatory actions toward the freemen (allowing them to use the Guildhall for meetings), earned him the esteem of the radicals and the formal thanks of the burgesses at the end of his term of office.[130]

The informal political activities of the next several years indicate the extent of anti-war feeling in Newcastle. Elite propaganda efforts met with a rather discouraging response. In the fall of 1775, immediately after the burgesses had called a meeting to consider a petition, the magistrates had Thomas Saint print 1,000 copies of Wesley's *Calm Address* and distributed them gratis through the town. In answer, Saint and Wesley's effigies, labeled "Filmer, Hobbes, Ambition and Servility," were burned in Fleshmarket by the town hangman as crowds cried, "Thus may every traitor to his country perish."[131] The radical press was much more successful in mobilizing political opinion. Pro-American literature was as plentiful in Newcastle as in the capital, not least because Newcastle writers were prodigious contributors to it. The *Newcastle Weekly Magazine,* begun in 1776, reprinted anti-war essays and poems and extracts from an array of pamphlets, including Paine's *Common Sense.* It also included letters from Murray, currently visiting America, who railed against the immorality of the war and praised the high-spirited independence of the colonists, who had not been "reduced to a state of effeminacy by a course of extravagant luxury" as in England.[132] Once back in Newcastle, Murray emerged as the most voluminous and acerbic anti-war writer of the Northeast and reached a national audience with his relentless journalism. Besides his two-volume *Impartial History of the Present War with America,* which was published by subscription in 1778, he produced over a dozen pamphlets, sermons and poems which railed against the hypocrisy and devastation of the war and attacked the venality and delusion of those who supported it (here Wesley and the Anglican establishment came under special fire).[133] Other writers canvassed in the local press the legality of loyalist ad-

---

[130] *Chronicle,* Sept. 18, 1776. Innkeeper Martin Mordue, who supported the 1770 Wilkite petition, signed the pro-government address.

[131] *Journal,* Oct. 28, 1775.

[132] *Newcastle Weekly Magazine ... By a Society of Gentlemen* (Newcastle, 1776), 4–6, 117–20 and passim. The only extant copy is in the British Library.

[133] E.g., *An Old Fox Tarr'd and Feathered, Occasioned by What is Called Mr. John Wesley's Calm Address to Our American Colonies. By an Hanoverian* (London, 1775); *The Finishing Strokes to Mr. Wesley's Calm Address, to the People of England*

dresses, some even advocating a boycott of Manchester goods in retaliation for the sanguinary loyalism of the city; and anti-war tracts like Arthur Lee's *Appeal to the Justice and Interests of the People of Great Britain* and Price's *Observations on the Nature of Civil Liberty* were printed in Newcastle and sold individually or in quantities of 100.[134]

The enervation of street culture also reflects the division of local opinion into two unequal camps. Though royal anniversaries and guild days continued to be ostentatiously celebrated by loyalists with elaborate military spectacles and private entertainments, the British victory at Long Island in October 1776 was the first and only time that a victory over *American* forces was publicly celebrated in the town, and the last time that any public acknowledgment of the vicissitudes of the military was made until the defeat of the *French* at Pondicherry, India, in 1779.[135] Fast-days were treated with disgust by radical writers, who were wont to point out the high correlation between such fasts and British defeats. "Thus Lord North, despairing of subduing the Americans by bribery and force of arms, has recourse to *prayer*," Slack sneered in the *Chronicle;* " 'tis profanity indeed to invoke Heaven for the prosperity of injustice and cruelty."[136] Newcastle residents' refusal to join in the "rejoicings of their fellow subjects" seemed to reflect the general mood of pessimism the war had wrought. Though his judgment may have been colored by his own preoccupations, Bewick noted that it was in precisely this period, "when public matters cast a surly gloom over the character of the whole country," that a centuries-old strand of popular culture disappeared – the singing of ballads in the streets, by which the latter were "greatly enlivened, and many market day visitors, as well as the town's people, were often highly gratified." Of course, ballads could also serve as effective propagators of anti-government sentiment.[137]

(Newcastle, 1778); *The Fast: A Poem* (Newcastle, 1778); *An Impartial History of the Present War with America,* 2 vols. (Newcastle, 1778); *Sermons to Ministers of State: Dedicated to Lord North* (n.p., 1780). See also Welford, *Men of Mark,* iii, 218–19. Murray's *History* is based on accounts in the *Annual Register.*

[134] *Chronicle,* Sept. 16, 23, 30, Oct. 7, 1775; April 6, 1776. See also *LEP,* Oct. 7–10, 1775.

[135] See, e.g., *Courant,* Oct. 31, Sept. 26, 1778; *Chronicle,* March 20, 1779 (Pondicherry). Bells were rung from St. Nicholas's Church for the victory at Charleston in 1780, but there were no other public rejoicings; even Cornwallis's victory over the colonists in Sept. 1780 was not publicly observed.

[136] *Chronicle,* Aug. 21, 1779.

[137] *Chronicle,* Oct. 21, 1780; Bewick, *Memoir,* 41. Bewick blamed the magistrates for

In this context, the death of Sir Walter Blackett on February 21, 1777, resulted in a hotly contested by-election, during which local dissidents managed to wage a viable campaign that brought their candidate, Andrew Robinson Bowes, within ninety-one votes of defeating Blackett's heir and nephew, Sir John Trevelyan, who scraped by on the basis of the country vote. Such a feat would not have been possible without the swing of a large portion of formerly unconvinced citizens to the radical, or at least anti-war, camp – a group which included a number of merchants and professional men who had formerly supported the magistrates.[138] The pre-electoral propaganda exhorted electors to break the "CLOSET COMBINATION" of magisterial, aristocratic and clerical power which was attempting to force upon Newcastle a "hereditary representation." Parallels were drawn between the national and local situation: The animating principles of the North administration were the same as those of the despised Earl of Carlisle, to whom the representation of Morpeth was but a "septennial resource of some Thousands," and of the Newcastle magistrates, described in the radical literature as "a wretched set of Despots."[139] Significantly, Trevelyan declined the chance to be made alderman in Newcastle, seeing in acceptance of the office a serious threat to the success of his candidacy.[140]

The radicals' choice of the new husband of the Countess of Strathmore as their candidate was not as inconsistent with this anti-elitist ethos as may first appear, and in fact supported the principle of "measures, not men." Phipps, now Lord Mulgrave, had committed the gravest apostasy by swinging to the support of the North administration, and Bowes's opposition to the ministry and support of radical causes

the decline; and in fact the Common Council passed and printed an order forbidding singing clubs in public houses: BL, Bell Collection, i, fol. 128, Nov. 29, 1781. But see *Four Excellent New Songs* (Newcastle, 1776); they are loyalist and anti-American.

[138] Knox, "Popular Politics," 239–40, and "Wilkism in Newcastle," 33n. Bradley's occupational analysis of the elections of 1774, 1777 and 1780 shows that the war decreased retailer and increased artisanal support for radical politics: Retailers' percentage of the radical vote dropped from 33.1% to 28.2% in 1777 and then rose again slightly in 1780 to 28.8%; artisan support in the three elections was 58.3%, 60.2% and 61.7%: *English Radicalism,* 272. Significantly, men from these groups also provided a stable constituency for magisterial politics, providing the magistrates with 69–71% of their vote in these three elections.

[139] NRO, ZAN M16/Ab15, *Serious Reflections . . . : To the Worthy Independent Free Burgesses of Newcastle; Electioneering Journal,* Feb. 24, 28, March 4, 6, 1777; for a ferociously anti-aristocratic piece see *Canny Newcastle Yet: A Rare Election Song,* in Newcastle Central Library, Election Songs and Squibs.

[140] *Chronicle,* March 1, 1777.

were well known in the town. His speeches to the electors in Newcastle and at the Hole-in-the-Wall in London emphasized his hostility to the methods and manner of the current administration, his belief in the accountability of government, and his commitment to separating "the legislative and executive Authorities," the combination of which was considered by local radicals to be a central cause of the imperial crisis and a source of magisterial malfeasance.[141] The significance of the widespread local support for these principles (over half the resident voters and those from the ports and capital voted for Bowes) was not lost on them or the vanquished candidate. Bowes, "the 1068" who voted for him, Lord Effingham and Sir George Savile joined the pan-oply of heroes who were toasted by the Constitutional Club and various other societies who met on August 10 in 1777 and 1778 to commem-orate the burgesses' last victory over "arbitrary power," and a suc-cessful radical effort was confidently predicted for the next parliamentary election.[142]

In general, the American war directed attention more to the crisis in empire and national government than to elite occlusion in corporate affairs, and local political activities continued to focus on contributing to the anti-war campaign. In January 1778, for example, the "Friends of Humanity" in Newcastle was formed to contribute to the subscrip-tion for the relief of American prisoners started by pro-Americans in London.[143] Later that spring, continuing mismanagement of the war and the threat of French aid to the Americans portended ill for the preser-vation of the North American empire. In the midst of Corporation ef-forts to organize volunteers to protect the coastline, the burgesses called a general meeting to petition the Commons on the deepening national crisis. At the meeting, which was chaired by John Rotheram, speakers exhorted local citizens to unite with those of London, Norfolk and other towns and counties to press for an inquiry into the causes of current calamities, "whereby thirteen flourishing provinces have been lost, near thirty thousand of our fellow subjects slain and maimed, upwards of thirty-two millions of the public treasury squandered away, and an

---

[141] *Chronicle,* March 1, April 19, 1777; NRO, ZAN M16/Ab15, *To the Free and IN-DEPENDENT Burgesses of Newcastle; Chronicle,* Feb. 22, 1777. For hostility to Phipps, now Mulgrave, see *Journal,* Feb. 19, 1776.

[142] *Chronicle,* March 29, April 19, 1777. Bowes was fêted by 10 companies and given the freedom of 9. For club celebrations see ibid., May 3, Sept. 13, 1777; Aug. 16, 1778; *Journal,* Aug. 15, 1778.

[143] *Chronicle,* Jan. 17, Feb. 7, 1778. It was chaired by William Smith.

13. Admiral Augustus Keppel: Freedom Box (1779). Britannia and Neptune pay homage to Keppel as men-of-war stand guard. From the collection at the Laing Art Gallery, Newcastle upon Tyne. Photograph reproduced with permission of Tyne and Wear Museums.

enormous load of taxes daily increasing.''[144] The petition, which called for a "swift and honourable" reconciliation with America and the dismissal and prosecution of the king's ministers, was signed by 1,087 residents, some of them, according to the *Journal,* "gentlemen of consequence" who had formerly supported the administration.[145] The rapidly growing number of converts to peace thereafter was shown in the pointed demonstrations on behalf of Admiral Keppel throughout the Northeast in early 1779. Besides the illuminations and effigy-burnings of Palliser, Keppel was given the freedom of Trinity House and the thanks of the mayor. The gold box presented to Keppel was represen-

[144] TWA, Calendar of Common Council Books, Feb. 20, 1778; *Chronicle,* March 14, 21, 1778.
[145] *Journal,* March 28, 1778.

tative of local sensibilities (Plate 13): Crafted by local goldsmiths and beautifully engraved by Bewick and Ralph Beilby, it depicted Britannia, with cap and staff of liberty and shield on one side and Neptune on the other, bestowing upon Keppel the laurels of victory as merchant ships and men-of-war sail past in the background.[146]

The shifting political allegiances produced by the war were evinced in local movements for parliamentary reform. Since the war began, some of the younger aldermen, men whose political apprenticeship had been served during the early stages of the Wilkite agitation, such as Atkinson, Francis Forster, Jonathan Hedley and Hugh Hornby, had quietly joined the opposition or anti-war ranks. Indeed, Forster, who during his first mayoralty in 1769 had allied himself with his fellow magistrates against the Wilkite petition, emerged from his election to a term as mayor in 1779 a firm supporter of radical and anti-war politics.[147] Along with Bowes (currently high sheriff of Northumberland), company stewards, radical leaders and an assortment of local residents, they were involved in the organizational meeting called at the Guildhall to discuss joining in the petitioning effort for economic reform, which Forster chaired. The result was the election of a committee to correspond with other like-minded groups throughout the country and the drafting of a petition which demanded the adoption of the three-point economic reform plan. It was signed by 1,500 residents before being presented to the Commons by Savile and Grieve in March.[148] By late April, Parliament's dismissive attitude toward the reform petitions had led to the formation of an association to press for parliamentary reform, whereby electors required each candidate to pledge to support the reduction of places and pensions, triennial Parliaments, and a more equal representation through the addition of 100 additional county seats. The stewards of the companies obligingly promised to call their halls together in order to solicit the members' "optional subscription," and they were voted the thanks of the meeting along with Savile, Wyvill and Grieve, the last of whom had acted as Newcastle's deputy at the St. Alban's Tavern meeting in March.[149]

---

[146] *Chronicle,* Feb. 20, 27, 1770; *Courant,* 20 Feb. 1779. See TWA Calendar of Common Council Minutes, March 29, 1779, April 12, 1779. For the gold box see TWA, 659/451, Trinity House disbursements, i, March 1779.

[147] Hornby, Hedley and Atkinson may have signed the 1770 petition over the Middlesex election; see PRO, HO 55/5/2. *Chronicle,* Jan. 15, 1780.

[148] *Chronicle,* Jan. 22, 29, Feb. 5, 1780; *CJ,* 37 (1780), 747; *Chronicle,* March 11, 1780. Newcastle's lead was followed by Northumberland, where a similar petition, backed by the Duke of Portland and Lord Tankerville, was adopted at a county meeting.

[149] NRO, ZAN M16/Ab15, Handbill *To the Free Burgesses of Newcastle* [1780]; *Chron-*

The enthusiastic support of Newcastle radicals for Wyvill's "country" reforms may seem in one sense surprising. Yet if the Association platform did not go as far as Newcastle radicals would have liked, it represented the first stage of a viable reform program that possessed the socially prominent support necessary to get it a hearing at St. Stephen's. Equally significant, the idea of a reform of Parliament in response to the associated demands of the national citizenry was consistent with radical notions of the accountability of government to the governed and of the political worth of individuals. "If every elector in Britain, understood his own dignity," one local writer asserted, "he would never hesitate in uniting . . . to compel the representatives . . . to obtain a more equal representation of the people."[150]

The support for reform by a segment of the local magistracy, on the other hand, was stimulated largely by the desire, shared by elites in other parts of the country, to restore the luster to their tarnished leadership by supporting the purification of an obviously corrupted government. But it was also related to a refurbished ideology of authority which emerged as the Old Corps of magistrates died off. Blackett had died in 1777, Ridley in 1778; Partis and Surtees had retired. The remaining senior aldermen were men like Matthew Bell, a maverick in the 1750s but disinclined thereafter to involve himself in the day-to-day politics or concerns of his colleagues, and Edward Mosley and John Simpson, whose attempts to block the discussion of reform in the January Guild were overruled by the younger aldermen, some of whom may have had radical sympathies since 1770.[151] Sir Matthew White Ridley and J. E. Blackett thus remained the bulwarks of the Old Corps paternalistic style of politics in Newcastle, but even they were forced, by late 1780, to make some concessions to the freemen's cause. Hence, although local elites still retained a distinctive identity of interest, the terms and nature of that identity were changing, altered by the vicissitudes of a damaging colonial war and the challenges of dissident politics and signaled by a growing number of concessions to the ideology and goals of the radical agitation.

In the midst of these seismic political shifts, the Newcastle Protestant Association emerged as a force to be reckoned with, drawing in a range

---

icle, April 29, June 3, 10, 1780. See also *Leeds Mercury,* June 6, 1780. Newcastle was only one of four towns who sent deputies to discuss the plan of association in Feb. 1780: Ian Christie, *Wilkes, Wyvill and Reform* (London, 1970), 90n.

[150] *Chronicle,* June 10, 1780.

[151] PRO, HO 55/5/2.

of otherwise divergent political communities that made up the local political public. Long dismissed by historians as a product of the crude Catholophobic sensibilities of the English masses – the dichotomy Eugene Black sets up between the Association for parliamentary reform and the Protestant Association as the "children of light" versus the "children of darkness" is indicative – its complex political makeup belies such oversimplified equations.[152] In fact, the prejudices of the Protestant Association, however unsavory, were shared by men and women of all ranks and were inextricably bound up with arguments and fears about the nature of arbitrary power and its relationship to Catholicism that had been engraved in public consciousness for two centuries. Equally important, the radical Protestantism the Association articulated and upheld was a vehicle for a number of dispossessed or excluded communities in Newcastle and its environs to assert their status as members of the body politic.

Though influenced by the Protestant associations of London, Edinburgh and Glasgow, the Newcastle Association was an indigenous creature in both its nature and outlook. Under the guidance of James Murray, the local Association produced a monster petition to Parliament demanding the reinstatement of the penal laws against Catholics in order to "preserve the succession of the Illustrious House of Hanover . . . and to secure our civil and religious liberties" which was subsequently signed by 7,661 persons. In contrast to other locally generated petitions, it was the only one that Ridley would agree to present, though whether this was due to the evidence of massive constituency support, his agreement with its principles, or his concern to maintain his heritage as the champion of the Protestant interest is unclear.[153] Jasper Harrison appealed to the latter in his effort to persuade Ridley of the justness of the cause while also arguing for the "respectability" and "Benevolence" of the petition's supporters, who, he insisted, were two-thirds Anglican and one-third Scottish and English dissenters. In the event, far from being a sinister movement of the xenophobic lower classes, the Protestant Association in Newcastle had as "respectable" a backing as any political cause of the century.[154]

---

[152] Eugene Black, *The Association* (Cambridge, Mass., 1962), 152.
[153] *Chronicle,* Feb. 12, 19, 1780; Welford, *Men of Mark,* iii, 215; PRO, Treasury Solicitor Papers, TS 11/338, Copy of the Newcastle Protestant Association petition with signatures. For number of signers see *Chronicle,* March 18, 1780. The text of the petition was very similar to that used by the Protestant Association of the metropolis: See *CJ,* 37 (1780), 900; NRO, ZRI 25/11, Ridley MSS, printed copy of PA petition.
[154] NRO, ZRI 25/11, Harrison to Ridley, March 31, 1780; see also April 4, 1780. Of a

Why would the Protestant Association resound so strongly among the local community? To understand this it is necessary to see its various appeals. As a source of the national identity, Protestantism or its alter ego, anti-Catholicism, had demonstrated its ability to serve as the last resort of national bonding.[155] In a more immediate context, two Stuart invasions, the Quebec Act and war with the colonies, and two decades of radical politicking had enabled Catholic relief to be read as but the ministry's latest efforts to spread despotism and corruption through the empire. Thomas Slack's *Chronicle* had been reporting sympathetically on the London Protestant Association's efforts since January, pointing out the relationship between arbitrary power and an arbitrary religion: "Popery is best adapted for slavery, and protestantism for freedom; and is not the encouragement which popery at present meets, a proof that despotism is now aimed at?" From this perspective, the repeal of Catholic relief was of a piece with the string of libertarian issues agitated in the town since the early Wilkite period.[156] The political affiliations of the signatories attest to these radical links: Of a sample who could be positively identified as Newcastle voters, 47 percent voted for radical candidates in recent or forthcoming parliamentary elections, 33 percent split their votes and 19 percent voted for ministerial candidates.[157] Dr. Rotheram (who was chair), Jasper Harrison (secretary), Murray, Smith, Gibson, Hume, Brunton, Thomas Spence, printer Thomas Angus, Bewick, and the mayor, Francis Forster, were among those who supported both associations in the first half of 1780.

The Association and its goals could also appeal to the fears of "foreign" infiltration, paradoxically upholding persecution for the sake of "English" toleration and liberty, as British Protestantism had long undertaken to do. Denying a desire to persecute Catholics themselves, associators warned that the recent relief bill would enable Catholics to propagate their doctrines in mass-houses and schools and influence elections through their purchase of inheritable lands. James Murray's

---

sample of Newcastle voters who signed the petition, 47% were craftsmen and artisans, 16% retailers, 11% merchants and 26% gentry and professionals. See also George Rude, *Paris and London in the Eighteenth Century* (New York, 1970), 235–6, which also supports the "respectable" middling provenance of most of the London associators, if not the rioters.

[155] See Linda Colley, *Britons: Forging the Nation, 1707–1837* (New Haven, 1992).

[156] *Chronicle*, Feb. 12, 1780. The tavern where the magistrates put up their supporters was dubbed "Quebec Tavern" by radicals in 1777: *Election Journal*, Feb. 28, 1777.

[157] Sample of 212, 72 of whom were Newcastle voters; vote based on most recent vote in 1774 and 1780 elections.

Protestant Packet or British Monitor, a monthly devoted to combating
Catholic relief which based its arguments on English history, the current imperial crisis and seventeenth-century republican writings, also
made much of these connections while also drawing on the anti-luxury
arguments that so appealed to the "improving," rational sensibilities
of the middle classes.[158] Hence Catholicism, in 1780 still considered
by many British people to be a Continental religion of luxury, idolatry
and superstition, was seen as running counter to the spirit of improvement and the advance of knowledge in art, science and politics to which
English citizens believed themselves to adhere. In this respect, too, the
Newcastle Protestant Association shared with the parliamentary reform
movement some of the latter's beliefs about the causes of current corruption, including the conviction that government should be accountable to the governed. The petition itself stressed both the right of the
people to instruct Parliament and the duty of the Commons to gain the
"sense of the nation" before acting.[159]

Of course, a virulent anti-Catholicism was compatible with the entire
spectrum of political positions in England, and the Newcastle Association had many members who were emphatically not supporters of
dissident politics, including Wesley and his followers and probably half
of the English dissenters. But their reasons for opposing Catholic relief
were not that far removed from those of their more dissident colleagues.
As Wesley himself argued in a letter to the *Public Advertiser,* that the
Act of 1778 encouraged Catholics to preach, "raise seminaries, and to
make numerous converts day by day to their intolerant persecuting
principles" was evinced by the recent activities of several papists of
his acquaintance.[160] His misleadingly titled *Popery Calmly Considered*
may have represented no significant advance over the anti-popery literature issued by the government in 1745, but it did share certain
themes with the weekly anti-popery lectures obligingly provided by
Murray and Scottish Presbyterian ministers William Graham and John
Baillie.[161]

---

[158] *An Address to the Protestant Inhabitants of Newcastle* (1780); *The Protestant Packet or British Monitor,* 2 vols. (1780–1), Aug. 4, Aug. 18, Sept. 1, 1780.

[159] Black, *Association,* p. 131; NRO, ZRI 21/11, PA petition. The Protestant Association of Glasgow was much more strident, reminding George III that he "sways the Scepter merely on the Footing of His being a Protestant, and maintaining and defending the Protestant Religion, which he stands engaged to do by his Coronation Oath": *CJ,* 37 (1780), 724.

[160] Quoted in Black, *Association,* 157.

[161] *Chronicle,* Feb. 19, Mar. 18, 1780; Wesley, *Popery Calmly Considered* (Newcastle,

Drawing on religious, political and ethnic identities were the non-conformist and Scottish supporters of the Protestant Association. For them, the Association not only sparked their long-standing enmity to Catholicism but also articulated the common ground of their inclusion in the national and local political community. Local Methodists, for example, who had been castigated in the radical political culture of the town as "Tories" and "slaves," may have found in the Protestant Association a vehicle to express their own aspirations to political activism in a popular cause. Dissenters, largely excluded from formal politics, and local Scots, most of whom were also nonconformists, equally saw in the Association's anti-Catholic, radical Protestantism a basis of their own claim to full citizenship. The Scots in particular retained an "outsider" status in Newcastle as in the nation more generally, despite their infiltration of the army and empire. Local Wilkites had deferred little to the ethnic makeup of the local population in their support of the "rights of Englishmen" and denigration of "Scotch" and "Stuart" corruptions of the body politic, and anti-Wilkes demonstrations broke out around Newcastle as in Scotland in these years; as recently as 1777 the frequent exhortations to "ENGLISHMEN AND FREE-MEN" reminded them of their marginalized place in the local political culture.[162]

Prejudices about the Scottish "national" and political character also marred their public relations with English dissenters. Hence, in the aftermath of the campaign for relief from subscription to the Thirty-Nine Articles in 1772 – a petition which seven dissenting ministers in Newcastle, five of whom were Scots, had signed – Josiah Thompson saw fit to describe the "dissenting Interest" in Newcastle as follows:

> Almost all the Ministers coming from Scotland, and bringing with them the Prejudices of their Education and that invincible attachment to the Peculiarities of their own Country which so strongly marks the character of a North-Britain [*sic*], they have no one thing in

---

1780); William Graham, *False Prophets Unmasked* (Newcastle, 1780); John Baillie, *The Nature and Fatal Influence of Popery on Civil Society* (Newcastle, 1780). Other publications included *The Protestant Magazine,* which offered for 6*d.* per issue a history of popery "embellished with the Heads of the Reformers, and many lively Representations of the Pageantry, Idolatry and Cruelty of the Popish Church"; *A New Key to the Conclave or the Doctrines of the Councils of Latern, Constance and Trent: Made Plain to the Capacities of All Ranks of People, Shewing That Papists Cannot Keep Faith to Heretics . . .* (Newcastle, 1780); and Bishop Gibson's *The Danger and Mischief of Popery Set Forth* (Newcastle, 1780); written during the '45.

[162] *Chronicle,* April 9, June 4, 1768; *Literary Register,* passim; NRO, ZAN M16/Ab15, *Watch and Catch* [1777].

common with the English dissenters nor any Idea of those Principles
which alone give a Dignity and Importance to the Character.
Hence, whether as closet supporters of arbitrary power (as Wilkites
would have it) or as a species of Briton who could never attain English
standards of civilization (as Thompson suggested), Newcastle's Scottish
dissenters had few entrees into the political nation except through a
rabid anti-Catholicism and loyalty to Hanover that the Protestant Association upheld.[163] If Catholics were the "others" within and without
against whom the English national identity was partially defined and
valorized, anti-Catholicism allowed for a range of groups – Presbyterians, Methodists, Scots and others who were frequently marginalized
in the national community – to enact their own claim to citizenship by
defining who they were not. Their support of the Protestant Association
demonstrated their right to inclusion as part of "the people" whose
voice had to be recognized by Parliament.

The Newcastle Protestant Association, then, marked a convergence
of local political sentiments in a common cause, one that allowed its
participants to champion the Protestant component of the national identity and advance claims for recognition that other political, if equally
chauvinistic, communities did not permit. Perhaps because of the Protestant Association's widespread support and its members' commitment
to legitimate, "constitutional" remedies, local anti-Catholic violence
was at a minimum, although the magistrates did ask for extra troops
and intervened when a priest and his house were attacked.[164] And in
the aftermath of the London riots, while Saint railed in the *Courant*
against the treacherous, not to say treasonable, activities and implications of Newcastle committees and associations and blamed them
equally for inciting the Americans to rebel and for preventing their
reconciliation with the government, associators and reformers retaliated
by blaming the violence and "the people's" discontents on the ministry
and its war. Hence, far from splintering the radical movement locally,
the Protestant Association may have advanced the cause: The parliamentary election in September pitted Sir Matthew Ridley against two
radical candidates, Bowes and Thomas Delaval, and resulted in the
return of Ridley and Bowes.[165]

---

[163] Dr. Williams's Library, Thompson List, MS 38.6/4, fol. 59. For Wilkite anti-
Caledonianism see Chapter 4 and Colley, *Britons,* 112–13.
[164] Colin Haydon, "The Gordon Riots in the English Provinces," *Historical Research,*
63 (1990), 356–7.
[165] The strength of local dissidence was perceived to be formidable enough so that

The election itself was actually a more complex affair than in 1774 or even 1777, when political divisions accorded with the magisterial/freeman breach. In 1780, there were divisions within the community of middling electors between Delaval and Bowes (45 percent of the latter's vote resulted from plumpers), as there were among the elite, where an admittedly small minority helped Bowes on his way to victory (though only the zealous Mayor Forster voted for both radical candidates).[166] The atypicality of the election was demonstrated in the nominating meeting of the burgesses in August, when the three candidates gave speeches which sought to enumerate their respective qualifications. Although still refusing to subscribe to an electoral test, Ridley's expostulations on the duty of representatives and gratitude to the burgesses reflected his growing inclination to conciliate his constituents and his gradual progress to the Whig opposition in Parliament.[167] Delaval had championed the freemen's cause consistently since 1769, and at the meeting he subscribed to the electoral test and pledged support of both the three-point plan for parliamentary reform and reinstatement of Catholic disabilities. However, his personal differences with Bowes prevented the two from presenting a united front to the voters.[168] Bowes, on the other hand, was openly backed by Lord Ravensworth and the ministerialist Duke of Northumberland; he gave a speech (which was later reviewed by the burgesses at the Hole-in-the-Wall in London as one which "would have disgraced a Candidate to be Mayor of Garrat") stressing the extent of his considerable resources and his readiness to spend them in Newcastle, as well as his ability to use Court and aristocratic influence to serve the principles of independency.[169] Nevertheless, a better affront to the local elites' sensibilities could not have been created than the man, "Stoney" Bowes, himself. He was intensely disliked by the gentry of the town and

Trevelyan and other county elites declined to stand at this election: *Courant*, Feb. 5, 12, 19, March 14, 1780. By 1781, the Protestant Association was spent as a political force. A "Political Protestant Association" was formed in the area in response to Catholic relief efforts in the 1820s.

[166] See Knox, "Provincial Radicalism," 239–40.

[167] *Courant*, Aug. 5, 1780; NRO, ZAN M16/Ab15, Handbill *To the Burgesses and Residents* [1780]; Mackenzie, *Historical Account*, ii, 659. He had moved against the ministry's war policy in 1778, and in June of 1780 presented the Cumberland reform association's petition to the Commons.

[168] *Courant*, Aug. 5, 1780; *Chronicle*, Aug. 5, 1780. Delaval petitioned against Bowes for bribery, and the burgesses did so against Ridley for corruption: *CJ*, 37 (1780), Nov. 20.

[169] *Chronicle*, Sept. 2, Aug. 5, 1780; *Courant*, Aug. 5, 1780.

county like the Whites, Ridleys and Simpsons, and was universally considered to be an opportunistic and self-aggrandizing upstart, which in fact he was.[170] But, unlike Delaval, Bowes possessed an unassailable record in support of the rights and liberties of the subject against the "conspiracy of Nobles" in power and was a fervent supporter of the burgesses' right to participate in local government. Moreover, he believed in and later acted on constituency instructions, voting on motions to end the war and on commercial bills only after consulting with his electors.[171] It is thus fitting that he was returned with radical support; that he lost that support after becoming in 1783 a partisan of North, from whom he sought an Irish peerage; and that he was forced to decline a poll in 1784.[172]

The year 1780 was in many respects the high point of the radical campaign waged so energetically in Newcastle, for the political accommodation of local elites, in conjunction with national developments, ultimately undermined radical politics in the town. In 1782, Newcastle citizens were jubilant over the replacement of North by the Rockingham–Shelburne ministry in March, committed as they were to recognizing American independence and some (admittedly limited) measures of economic reform. This change in men and policies was considered by local radicals to be a victory for extra-parliamentary political opinion.[173] Perhaps more important, the redoubtable Sir Matthew Ridley voted in favor of Conway's motion to end the war, thus signaling his formal swing to the Rockinghamites. From this moment on, Ridley was the man of the hour, fêted and acclaimed by the freemen and residents. Unanimously elected as mayor the following autumn, he demonstrated his own willingness to accommodate the local radical cause by allowing freemen access to the Corporation records and papers relating to their properties and privileges. His popularity was such that, though he was a Foxite, it survived the nationwide repudiation of the coalition in 1784, in which Newcastle enthusiastically participated. Ridley and his running-mate, Charles Brandling, Esq., Northumberland landowner and a member of the county opposition, were returned without contest in the

---

[170] See the Ridleyite handbills in NRO, ZAN M16/Ab15 and ZRI 25/11. Matthew White particularly hated Bowes, and many of the local elite refused to go to his post-election ball in 1780. Bowes's later infamy was based on his abduction of his wife when she tried to divorce him. See Welford, *Men of Mark*, i, 380.

[171] *Chronicle*, Dec. 29, 1781; Jan. 26, 1782.

[172] Ibid., May 1, 8, 1784; British Library, Collection of Handbills etc. on Newcastle upon Tyne Elections, 1777 and 1784.

[173] *Chronicle*, March 23, April 13, 1782.

accompanying election after conceding the right of the burgesses to instruct their representatives – though on local, rather than national, issues.[174]

Radical politics was also attenuated by the death or removal of its former leaders and by fissures in its own ranks. By 1784, many of the activists of radical politics had died or moved away: James Murray died in 1782, Thomas Slack in early 1784; Thomas White was disenfranchised in 1781. Efforts to mobilize reform petitions in 1782 and 1783 were unsuccessful,[175] and remaining advocates were divided over the current thrust of parliamentary reform, expressing dissatisfaction with the "country gentlemen's" proposals that had been offered by Wyvill and were now being advocated by Pitt. From their perspective, it was the trading and manufacturing towns of Great Britain that needed to be given a larger share of the representation, not the counties. "No more independent class of men than merchants and manufacturers" existed, one writer averred, and they were much more knowledgeable in international commercial concerns than gentlemen of "entailed estates." Representation of the former should thus be the first concern.[176] Yet the petition for more equal representation, initiated and organized by the burgesses and residents in 1785 and calling for greater borough representation, was signed by only 738 "burgesses and inhabitants," half the number who had supported the reform movement in 1780.[177] Although soon to be revived by the international and national events of 1788–90, the broad-based radical agitation in Newcastle had, for the moment, fizzled out, drained by the psychological havoc which the American war had wrought, defused by the accommodation of the local elite, and appeased or discouraged by the reforming ministries.

Newcastle politics since the 1760s had posed significant challenges to gentry and oligarchic power in the town. Galvanizing populist, patriotic and Protestant identities among the citizenry and exploiting the arenas of the public sphere for dissident ends, local activists sustained a political, "class" critique of the status quo that contested the politics of deference. Intersecting with and informed by national agitations,

---

[174] Ibid., March 23, July 13, Aug. 3, 24, Sept. 7, 14, 28, Oct. 5, 19, Nov. 23, 1782; Oct. 18, 1783; Jan. 24, Feb. 14, 21, April 17, 1784.
[175] The middling inhabitants of Newcastle did associate to petition against the tax on receipts: ibid., June 14, 1783; Oct. 26, Sept. 28, 1782; Jan. 25, March 8, 1783.
[176] Ibid., April 15, May 17, 1783.
[177] Ibid., Feb. 26, Mar. 5, 26, 1785.

Newcastle radicalism constructed a political identity for its supporters that made it an imperative of citizenship to resist the iniquitous effects of "Lordly Combination[s] against Freedom," that is, of men in authority, from the king's ministers to Corporation magistrates, who exerted power inconsistent with the political and economic rights of the people. The patrician political culture which demanded deference as a prerequisite of political recognition, which considered independent burgess activity to be a species of "rebellion," or which proclaimed the incompetence of the people to judge the public good or standards of government prompted both derision and hostility from a significant portion of Newcastle's political public, whose members had proved their worth and status by their own contributions to local culture, improvement and prosperity.[178] Although radicalism's definitions of independence and patriotism created spaces that allowed for the acceptance and appreciation of aristocrats and gentlemen who behaved in appropriate public-spirited ways, these men had acted as individuals and patriots, however, not as part of the phalanx of patrician authority, distinguishing themselves by their adherence to useful public measures rather than by their social or political rank.

The politics of the war reinforced these definitions of citizenship and patriotism with a vengeance, and in doing so drew in a majority of middling and artisanal residents in the town. It was this constituency who engineered Bowes's near-victory and ultimate success in 1777 and 1780 respectively, who signed the anti-government petitions during the war, and who managed to sustain a remarkably coherent anti-war campaign in the town. They shared grievances with the colonists against the administration, felt themselves to be victims of corrupted governors and unenlightened policies, and resented a war that, waged in the name of imperial preservation, was unprofitable, unjust and patently designed to sever the imperial connection forever. Certainly the war disrupted credit and currency in the North as elsewhere in the nation, often with catastrophic results.[179] But more important than actual economic dislocation was the perception that the sources of the war and loss of

[178] Ibid., Aug. 5, 12, 1780; NRO, ZAN M16/Ab15, Handbill *To the Public Spirited Popular Class* [ca. 1780]; *Chronicle,* Aug. 12, Sept. 9, 1780; *A Protest Against the Petition of the Mayor and Burgesses of Newcastle. By the Newcastle House of Lords,* Feb. 6, 1780, in BL, Bell Collection, i, fol. 111.

[179] The profits of several local industries geared to the American trade were wiped out, e.g., glassmaking; banking suffered, and shipowners were hard hit by the loss of an inexpensive source of vessels: NRO, Carr-Ellison MSS, ZCE 11/3; Ashton and Sykes, *English Coal Industry,* 218.

colonies lay in the same overmighty concentrations of power in the state and locality which allowed government to pursue measures that were contrary to the sense of the people.

Of course, in Newcastle as elsewhere the American war divided the middling classes as dramatically as elites – divisions which the French wars would widen into chasms. Moreover, in this period we can witness the ways in which mid-Georgian radicalism could fall victim to its own "bourgeois" remedies and visions, particularly its increasing disdain for the traditional street theater of popular politics. Hence, in 1782 Rodney's victory over the French in the West Indies prompted jubilant public celebrations in Newcastle, complete with bell-ringing, bonfires and illuminations, of a sort which had not been seen in the town since the war began. Yet the public demonstrations provoked the radical printer Thomas Slack to insist crankily that though every English person should exult in the victory,

> the manner of displaying our sensations, would be much more to our credit, if instead of illuminating our houses (at the expense of the quiet of every private family) by raising tumults in the street, etc., the people raise a subscription in every town for the benefit of those widows and children, whose husbands and fathers have nobly lost their lives.[180]

Although undoubtedly satisfying some improving, patriotic sensibilities, the eschewal of crowd politics did nothing to broaden the base of radical support, and the politics of loyalism was quick to fill the gap.

[180] *Chronicle*, May 25, 1782.

8. *Clientage and its discontents: Norwich, 1715–1785*

> I advise, tomorrow, to parade,
> And form at once a glorious Cavalcade . . .
> As much I fear, no due Devotion they
> To our two Candidates would freely pay;
> It would be right by some small Bribe to bind
> The galling Fetters on each Wav'ring Mind;
> And for to make the Numbers still the more,
> Set ope' the *Workhouse,* nay the *Bridewell* Door:
> And from the Hospitals, without Reserve,
> All shall come forth, for they our Cause must serve.
> Thus by our shew strike Opposition down,
> Still let all see, that Place-men Rule the Town.
>
>

The N–RW–CH CAV—C–DE: A Satire
(Norwich, 1741)

Men who feel an honest warmth in whatever relates to their country's welfare are ever distinguished . . . [but] those who pursue party or self-interested motives, and who sacrifice the public good to venal purposes . . . never enjoy the attributes of Independence, *Freedom, Peace, Truth, Resolution, Goodness, Contentment, Philosophy, Oeconomy,* and *Taste,* virtues without which Fortune is a beggar.

Norfolk Chronicle, Sept. 14, 1782

The political culture of eighteenth-century Norwich has been seized upon by historians for exhibiting a number of divergent, if not entirely incompatible, phenomena: the ability of governmental and aristocratic patronage to tame and manage a large freeman borough, the determining role of economic interests in producing popular political loyalties,

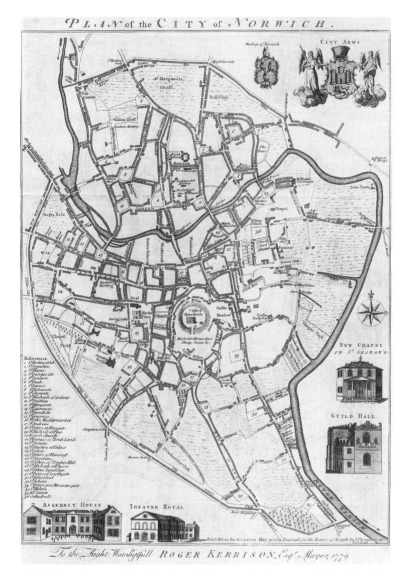

14. Eighteenth-century Norwich, from [J. Thompson], *History and Antiquities of the County of Norfolk*, vol. 10 (1781). Courtesy of Yale University Library.

the lack of "party" issues in "local" politics, and the emergence of modern, grass-roots "party" behavior, organization and mentality among provincial voters.[1] This chapter will provide an alternative, if no more disinterested, reading of Norwich politics that seeks to illiminate the complex ways in which patronage was accommodated and resisted, "trade" ideologically inflected and differentially defined, and political loyalties negotiated through competing notions of the nation and citizenship and participation in local processes of state.

I. COURT WHIGGERY AND THE POLITICS OF RESISTANCE

"The City for years hath been split into two factions or parties," William Arderon wrote of Norwich in 1750.[2] His observation was scarcely new. In 1681, Humphrey Prideaux, Dean of Norwich, decried the party violence which polarized his city's taverns, street culture and government, and the printer Henry Crossgrove echoed his lamentations thirty years later when he described Norwich as "distracted with Party Rage . . . Whig and Tory, High Church and Low Church, or to give it . . . in our Dialect . . . Croakers and Tackers make the two contending Parties."[3] Contemporaries' assessments of the strength of partisan divisions are corroborated by the number of parliamentary contests and by the much more frequent electoral struggles over local government. In the thirty-three aldermanic elections between 1717 and 1750, eighteen were contested, as were two or even three wards per year in the elections for councilmen; and the mayoral elections nearly always precipitated a protracted struggle at the polls.[4] The continuance of partisan conflict in early Hanoverian Norwich, therefore, is beyond dispute; how it endured despite the concerted efforts of the Whig regime to rout the Tory party in the city still requires assessment. Norwich was an anomaly in the age of the Whig ascendancy – an open constituency which

[1] Namier and Brooke, i, 342; Nicholas Rogers, *Whigs and Cities: Popular Politics in the Age of Walpole and Pitt* (Oxford, 1989), 304–42; B. D. Hayes, "Politics in Norfolk, 1750–1832" (Ph.D. diss., Cambridge University, 1958); John Phillips, *Electoral Behavior in Unreformed England* (Princeton, 1982).

[2] BL, Add. MS 27,966, Arderon Tracts, fol. 244.

[3] *Letters of Humphrey Prideaux, Dean of Norwich,* ed. E. M. Thompson (Camden Society, new ser., 15, 1875), 90; BL, Add. MS 5853, Strype MSS, fol. 107, Henry Crossgrove to Rev. Strype, Dec. 2, 1714.

[4] There were thus at least three and sometimes as many as six contested elections in Norwich almost every year in this period. Norwich Corporation politics are covered in detail in D. S. O'Sullivan, "Politics in Norwich, 1701–1835" (M.Phil. thesis, University of East Anglia, 1975).

boasted an energetic popular Whiggism, demonstrated in the streets and press as well as at the polls. What needs to be examined is the ability of local residents both to resist official Whiggism and to coopt it as a political program of their own.

Certainly, as Crossgrove's language suggests, the general issues which divided local opinion in the decade after the Hanoverian Succession were similar to those which had polarized the town and nation in the late Stuart period. Whigs and Tories had battled for control of the Corporation and parliamentary representation since the Exclusion Crisis, and although Tories dominated the Corporation, the parliamentary representation bounced back and forth between the two parties. By 1710, however, in the midst of the High Church fervor for Sacheverell, Tory Anglicanism emerged triumphant and seemingly unassailable from the fray, at the pinnacle of its local power and popularity. Tory success depended upon superior electoral organization, effective utilization of the lively out-of-doors political culture that centered in Norwich's taverns and coffeehouses – known haunts of Jacobite and republican radicalism – and its exploitation of a strident, xenophobic strand of High Church Anglicanism in a city where aliens and nonconformists were both numerous and visible.[5]

But the succession marked the beginning of the end to Tory fortunes in Norwich. Despite Coronation Day riots and the dominance of Tory loyalties amongst local elites, in 1715 the Whigs captured both parliamentary seats from their Tory incumbents after a riotous contest, to the surprise and dismay of many observers.[6] Local Whigs proceeded to engage in a flurry of activities designed to exploit their considerable advantages in order to expand their popular base in the town and capture the institutions of civic government. Norwich had direct and powerful ties with official Whiggism through the Walpole and Townshend families, both of whom maintained their seats in Norfolk, and despite Walpole's opportunistic forays into opposition in 1717–20, local Whigs could wave the beguiling wand of state patronage and economic protection in their efforts to win over the electorate throughout this period.[7]

[5] John Evans, *Seventeenth Century Norwich: Politics, Religion and Government 1620–1690* (Oxford, 1974); W. A. Speck, *Tory and Whig: The Struggle in the Constituencies* (London, 1970), 47–63; Prideaux, *Letters*, 156–62.

[6] *An Account of the Riots, Tumults, and Other Treasonable Practices, Since His Majesty's Accession to the Throne* (London, 1715), 8; Sedgwick, i, 291; BL, Add. MS 5853, fol. 107–107b, Henry Crossgrove to Rev. Strype, Feb. 10, 1715. Of the 155 elite voters, 102 voted for Tory candidates: Speck, *Tory and Whig*, Appendix b.

[7] Townshend became lord lieutenant of the county once its incumbent, the Duke of

The considerable power of the Church of England was also wielded on behalf of Whiggery's cause. The Norwich episcopacy had been, with one exception, stridently Low Church since the ejection of its nonjuring bishop, William Lloyd, in 1689; after the succession, in stark contrast to many other cathedral towns, the lower clergy were predominantly Whig as well. Successive bishops of Norwich refused licenses to any but impeccably Whig parish clergymen, and assiduously maintained a vigorous schedule of anniversary sermons in the cathedral and parish churches which the rising stars among the Whig clergy of East Anglia were appointed to preach, thus ensuring that on all important anniversaries the principles of early Hanoverian Whiggism would be trumpeted from three-quarters of Norwich pulpits.[8]

Adding significantly to the combined influence of miter and Crown was the support of the Protestant dissenters in Norwich. Their allegiance to the party which promised to banish schism Acts is almost a historical truism. Much more interesting than the fact of support was its operation, which strengthened the Whig interest among the textile trade and poorer freemen. The wealthy Presbyterian community was particularly well integrated within the Corporation. Benjamin Nuthall, John Spurrell, Robert Marsh, Peter Colombine and Philip Meadows all served as aldermen and mayors and took leading parts in running the charity schools and hospitals of the town. The Quaker Gurney family was also influential. John Gurney, known locally as the "Weavers' Friend" for his success in speaking against the importation of calicoes before the House of Lords in 1720, was a member of the Committee of Manufacturers, Waller Bacon's election agent in the 1734 Norwich parliamentary election, and a friend of Walpole's, from whom he declined an offer of a seat in Parliament in the 1730s.[9] As civic leaders,

---

Ormonde, was impeached in 1715, and one of Robert Walpole's lawyers, Robert Britiffe, replaced the Tory Richard Berney as MP from 1715 to 1734, when Walpole's brother Horatio took over: Sedgwick, i, 291.

[8] T. Turner, *List of Norfolk Benefices* (Norwich, 1843), 20–3; NNRO, PD 191/23/87, St. Benedict's Churchwarden Accounts and Vestry Resolutions, Jan. 28, 1730; *Norwich Gazette* (hereafter *Gazette*), Oct. 15, 1748; May 13, 1749; James Baldwin, *The Present Government the Ordinance of God: A Sermon Preached at the Cathedral Church of Norwich . . . 20 October 1718* (Norwich, 1718); Robert Butts, *A Sermon Preach'd . . . at the Cathedral Church of Norwich on Saturday, August 1, 1719* (Norwich, 1719); Matthew Postlewayt, *The Moral Impossibility of Protestant Subjects Preserving Their Religious or Civil Liberties Under Popish Princes . . . 5 November 1718* (Norwich, 1719).

[9] NNRO, Case 20, shelf d, Guardians of the Poor Minute Book, 1723–34, 1726, 1728; Cozens-Hardy and Kent, *Mayors*, 119–20; J. Chambers, *A General History of the County of Norfolk*, vol. 2 (Norwich, 1829), 1213; M. F. Lloyd-Prichard, "The Edu-

philanthropists and employers, these men possessed the good will of many of the more humble nonconformist weavers and dyers in Norwich, and were important bulwarks of the Whig regime in the city. They did much to chip away at Tory support within the industry, wooing rank-and-file dissenters and Church of England members alike with their vigorous support of their rights and livelihoods.[10]

The press, clubs and friendly societies equally bolstered popular Whiggism. William Chase, printer of the *Weekly Mercury or Protestant Packet* (continued in 1726 as the *Norwich Mercury*) and a councilman for Wymer ward, was the primary producer of printed propaganda for the Whigs, publishing pamphlets, broadsides, sermons and tracts in addition to the newspaper which championed the Whigs' defense of Englishmen's liberties, properties and religion against Tory–Jacobite plots to subvert them.[11] His efforts were supplemented by the clubs and societies which were formed specifically to solicit and solidify Whig support. A Whig Mughouse met at the Roebuck and Crown in the Tory parish of St. Swithin's, where its members did their best to duplicate the convivial and riotous activities of their brethren in the capital, "thrashing" Jacobite mobs for wearing white roses on guild or anniversary days. Another "loyal society" caballed at an inn in the predominantly Tory textile parish of St. Martin-at-Oak; any member who showed disrespect to the king or government was expelled. The Loyal Society of Worsted Weavers, formed in 1717 to commemorate George I's accession to the throne and comprising about sixty fairly prosperous master weavers, was primarily a benefit society, but its secondary function was resolutely political: Not only was the number of members to be limited to the age of the king, but all had to be "known . . . *Loyal Subjects of His Sacred Majesty King* GEORGE, *and His Protestant Successors*"; if a member voted Tory in any local or parliamentary election, or influenced any person outside the Society to do so, he would be thrown out. The additional requirements that all members be free-

cation of the Poor in Norfolk, 1700–1850," *NA*, 33 (1965), 323; J. B. Braithwaite, *Memoirs of J. J. Gurney* (Philadelphia, 1854), 14.

[10] See Nockold Thompson's annotated pollbook for the 1734/5 elections, in NRCL, which includes a list of Quaker voters. Thanks to Nick Rogers for giving me access to his copy.

[11] See BL, Add. MS 5853, fols. 108–9, C-G to HS, Aug. 15, 1715, for Crossgrove's animated complaints about Chase's paper and other publications. NRCL holds the extant copies of the *Weekly Mercury* and other printed ephemera published by Chase before the long run of the *Norwich Mercury* (hereafter *Mercury*) begins in 1726: See Colman Collection.

men and employers also suggest that the club functioned as a ward-level electoral device from which to plan strategy and organize votes.[12]

Whig initiatives also extended to less convivial realms. The Honourable Artillery Company, a city militia composed of Whig gentlemen and tradesmen, was formed under Townshend's commission in 1714.[13] Commanded by Captain William Hall and outfitted with splendid uniforms and arms, the members served both as a focus for Whig enthusiasm and as guerrillas for their party, becoming ubiquitous in Whig street theater and notorious for their propensity to use violence to suppress Tory effervescences. One observer described them as "Young men that marched up and down the streets armed with musquets and Bayonets to the great Disquiet of the Citizens of Norwich," and such an accounting put them in the most flattering of lights.[14] On Coronation Day in 1715, the Artillery Company forcibly impeded a search for Whig effigies in Mancroft ward ordered by the Tory mayor, and presided over the triumphant burning of figures of Mar and the Pretender in an enormous bonfire in the marketplace. The following spring, at the mayoral elections, the Company initiated some of the most serious riots of the century, in which dozens of Tory residents and several constables were seriously injured and the Riot Act invoked on five occasions. The Whig candidate Augustine Metcalfe carried the day, and the next morning an unrepentant city militia preceded the mayor-elect in the traditional procession to the cathedral.[15] The Tory magistrates' efforts to quell their violent activities were singularly unsuccessful. Mayor Peter Attesley managed to get successful indictments against two of the Artillerymen from a quarter-sessions jury for riot and assault during a Restoration Day celebration in 1715, but he was promptly reprimanded by the central government, and the indictments were overturned by the attorney general on Townshend's orders.[16]

All of these activities were designed to vanquish and demoralize Tory supporters in the town. And in fact, despite the retention of majority control of civic government, Tory leaders seemed stunned by the

[12] *Flying Post,* June 23–6, 1716; *Articles Agreed to by the Loyal Society, Held at Morse's Cellar in St. Martin's at Oak, Established in the Year 1717* (Norwich, n.d.); *Articles of Agreement, Made, Concluded and Agreed Upon, by the Loyal Society of Worsted Weavers in the City of Norwich* (Norwich, 1726), 3–11.

[13] BL, Add. MS 5853, fol. 107–107b, March 21, 1715; *Account of the Riots,* 8.

[14] PRO, SP 44/116, 337–9; BL, Add. MS 5853, fols. 107–108, March 21, July 18, 1715.

[15] NNRO, Mayor's Court Books, 1709–19, Oct. 19, 1715; NNRO, MS 217, Massey, *Acta Norvicensia,* 37, 60; *Gazette,* May 5, 1716; *Flying Post,* June 23–6, 1716.

[16] PRO, SP 44/116, 341.

Whig initiative, unable to rally with effective counter-tactics of their own. Yet extra-institutional Toryism remained strong, largely unscathed and even invigorated by the reversal of the party's fortunes. It was at this grass-roots level that the local Tory party, and especially its Jacobite wing, was able to offer resistance to the forces of official Whiggism and keep party spirits alive.[17] Indeed, the paranoia which prompted one of Townshend's spies to discern a plot among the "Pretender's party" to poison the minds of Norwich citizens through "Popish meetings, Popish Schools ... popish printers, etc." probably led him to exaggerate the pervasiveness of disaffection, but it was matched by the optimism of the Stuart agent who compiled the famous "Norfolk list" of 1721: He listed the names of twelve Norwich gentlemen and tradesmen who were ready to act on behalf of James III, including the former MPs for the town, five aldermen, two attorneys and a merchant. No less a luminary than Christopher Layer was a Norwich resident.[18] Moreover, the nonjuring congregation in Norwich survived the arrest of its leaders, a Mr. Cooper and the nonjuring Bishop of Norwich, Nathaniel Spinckes, in the autumn of 1716.[19] Jacobitism descended socially thereafter, disaffection centering, as Townshend's informer rightly noted, in the parishes of St. Giles and St. Stephen's and several others bordering on Mancroft ward, in both Wymer and Conisford. These parishes contained the highest number of Roman Catholics, and their residents were largely poor manufacturers, craftsmen and publicans; many of their taverns were well known throughout the city as Jacobite haunts.[20] It was, in the first instance, this largely plebeian and middling constituency that energized the out-of-doors Tory political culture in the decade after the succession, transmogrifying the sylvan

[17] This argument was first made in my doctoral dissertation, "The Rejection of Deference: Urban Political Culture in England, 1715–1785" (Yale University, 1985), chap. 7, and was subsequently adopted by Nicholas Rogers in "Popular Jacobitism in Provincial Context: Eighteenth Century Bristol and Norwich," in E. Cruickshanks and J. Black, eds., *The Jacobite Challenge* (Edinburgh, 1988), 123–41.

[18] PRO, SP 35/33/62, Norwich, Sept. 22, 1722; the list is printed in Paul Fritz, *The English Ministers and Jacobitism Between the Rebellions of 1715 and 1745* (Toronto, 1975), 143–6.

[19] G. M. Yould, "Two Nonjurors," *NA,* 35 (1973), 364–81; J. Overton, *The Nonjurors* (London, 1902), 467–96; *Gazette,* Sept. 29, Oct. 13, 1716.

[20] PRO, SP 35/33/62; NNRO, Dis 9, List of Popish Recusants, 1767; VSM 4, Register of Incumbents 1780; Case 13, shelf d, Papist estate returns 1745. Of those listed in the 1767 returns, 86% were poor manufacturers and craftsmen, 10.3% publicans and shopkeepers, and 2.8% gentlemen and gentlewomen.

rites of popular celebration into the emblems of dissent from Whig and
Hanoverian rule.

On the Pretender's birthday, June 10, disaffected inhabitants were
wont to wear white roses and gloves and to strew the streets of their
neighborhoods with sand and flowers, thus borrowing the "rebirth"
rituals of Guild Day to signal their hopes for a rather different kind of
political regeneration.[21] Restoration Day observances were similarly observed in the Tory parishes of St. Giles, St. Margaret's, St. John Timberhill and St. James's and the hamlet of Pockthorpe, where men,
women and children decorated the streets with flowers, sand, thyme
and sweet herbs, their doors with oak boughs and mayflower, and their
persons with gilded oak leaves.[22] Such demonstrations of Tory and
Jacobite loyalties were fitting taunts to Whig power, for the Whigs,
parading themselves as the Preservers of Monarchy, could seldom find
a pretence to suppress them. Hence in 1728 the newly elected Tory
mayor, Thomas Harwood, was bestowed with a garland of gilded white
roses by a crowd of enthusiastic women supporters on his inauguration
day, which happened to fall on June 10.[23] Of course, men and women
were taken up by the Whigs for the next decade for a range of "treasonable" offenses ranging from wearing horns and turnips at a public
review of the Artillery Company to the seditious remarks made by men
in their cups, such as the weaver who declared in a St. Paul's alehouse
that James Sheppard, an executed Norfolk rebel, "dyed as good a martyr as one of the Apostles," or Thomas Sherley of Wells, near Norwich,
who observed that "King George has no more Right to the Crown than
I have." But such treatment had the effect of making martyrs of those
prosecuted – Wells was sentenced to a public whipping across the
length of the town, but received only four lashes before he was rescued
by a sympathetic crowd – and the iceberg of popular Jacobitism proved
to melt very slowly over the century.[24]

[21] NNRO, Massey, 11; BL, Add. MS 5853, fol. 108; *Gazette,* June 16, 1716.
[22] *Gazette,* April 28, 1716; June 1, 1717; June 2, 1722; June 1, 1728; NNRO, Mayor's
   Court Book, May 28–9, 1716; Churchwarden Accounts, PD 26/73, St. Peter's Mancroft, 1701–50, and PD 191/23, St. Swithin's, 1608–1762.
[23] *Gazette,* June 8, 1728; NNRO, Massey, 15,; NNRO, PD 74/27, St. John Timberhill
   Churchwarden Accounts, 1717–18.
[24] *Gazette,* Aug. 4, 18, 1716; PRO, SP 44/79a, 233 (I thank Paul Monod for this reference); *Weekly Pacquet,* Oct. 13–20, 1716; *Gazette,* Aug. 4, 18, 1716; Jan. 19, 1717.
   See also NNRO, Case 12, shelf b (20), Informations and Examinations 1722–40, Aug.
   30, Sept. 1, 10, Oct. 8, 18, 1722. For the longevity of Jacobitism in Norfolk, see
   NNRO, Bradfer-Lawrence MSS, 4/10b, Molineux Correspondence, fol. 158, CM to
   P. Case, Oct. 13, 1770.

In the meantime, Jacobite sympathies could provide a check on as well as an occasion for dilating Whig power. Theater provided one such arena for their expression. At the performance by a local acting troupe in January 1716 of the farce about the rebel's defeat, *The Earl of Mar Marr'd,* the dramatic juncture at which the Pretender was proclaimed drew loud huzzas from the boxes and galleries, provoking Captain Hall and other members of the Artillery Company to stand and draw their swords, shouting, "Down with the Rebels!" For the rest of the evening, loud hisses swept the theater whenever George I was referred to in the play. It was scarcely surprising that the troupe's attempt to stage another comedy later that year was stopped by the authorities, though Henry Crossgrove feigned astonishment: Surely *Brazen-Faciano; or, The Profligate Puritan,* he declared, could not be "intended as a satyr upon any Person or Persons whatever (unless Dicko-Don-Quako is a Person) nor has it any the least Tendency to a Party Matter."[25]

Indeed, Crossgrove's Tory–Jacobite press also did its best to keep the cause alive. Councilman for Mancroft ward and the self-confessed enemy of Chase, Crossgrove was an avowed supporter of the Chevalier. "Norwich is not altogether *Germanized,*" he reported to Strype in 1715, adopting the phrase used by Francis Atterbury; "we have Persons here who are *real Englishmen* and can never cease to be so."[26] Relishing the supposedly enigmatic but very transparent political views put forth in his publications, especially his newspaper, *The Norwich Gazette,* or, as it was known locally, "The Royal Pacquet," he tested, and frequently crossed, the boundaries of permissible veneration for the exiled dynasty. To him, Charles I was the "Blessed Saint," and every January the *Gazette* reproduced a print of the royal martyr, accompanied by extracts from Clarendon describing his irreproachable virtue and the torment inflicted on him by his ungrateful "schismatical" people; the culpability of dissenters for this historic tragedy was always a major theme.[27] Restoration Day provided similar opportunities for innuendo and *double entendre*. Noting in 1717 that "many" people had

[25] *Gazette,* Jan. 21, Nov. 24, Dec. 7, 1716.
[26] BL, Add. MS 5853, fols. 108–9, HC to S, Aug. 15, 1715.
[27] See, e.g., *Gazette,* Jan. 30, 1725; Jan. 30, 1731. For some of his other Tory publications, including a new edition of last speeches of executed "loyal martyrs," a new installment version of Clarendon's *History of the Great Rebellion,* and reprints of Tory pamphlets see *Gazette,* March 3, 1716; Dec. 21, 1723; Jan. 25, 1718.

observed King George I's birthday the preceding Tuesday, he went on
to observe that

> Wednesday last being the Anniversaries of the Happy Royal Family,
> after a long and Miserable Rebellion and Usurpation of above 14
> Years, in which time this poor Kingdom labor'd under a most Ar-
> bitrary and Tyrannick Power of an Hypocritical Restless FACTION,
> who Revers'd the very Ordinances of both God and Man, setting up
> *Schism* and *Sacrilege* for *Sanctity* and *Salvation,* and *Treason* and
> *Murder* for *Law* and *Loyalty,* and all this (as they pretended) for
> *Christ and His Kingdom,* beginning every Act of their Villainy in
> the Name of the Lord, Cloaking their damnable Designs with an
> Hypocritical Pretence and Outside Shew of Devotion, I say, last
> Wednesday being the Anniversary of that Happy Restauration, on
> which *Religion* and *Liberty* returned with our BANISH'D KING,

it was observed with the utmost joy.[28] The influence and popularity of
his paper, as well as its content, made Crossgrove the object of Artillery
Company harassment and landed him in jail three times in this period.
But his incarceration, like the trials that followed it, had little effect
beyond making him a martyr in his own right, acquitted by sympathetic
county juries.[29]

Clearly, the extra-institutional political culture of the Whigs' opponents continued to flourish despite the latter's strenuous and harsh efforts to suppress it. Popular Jacobitism served among other things as
an effective code of resistance to newly established Whig power, sustaining an alternative political idiom whose rhetoric, rituals and symbols mimicked yet subverted the officially sanctioned loyalism of the
Whigs as the new party of church, king, liberty and peace, providing
the rich subtext on which the Whig reading of the blessings of the
current establishment constantly foundered. Upper-level Toryism in
Norwich, however, proved to be much less creative. As noted above,
Tory leaders in the Corporation reacted in a rather facile and defeatist
manner to the Whig offensive, despite their retention until 1720 of a
majority on the aldermanic bench. Their apparent lack of resolve led
to a series of political blunders, the most serious of which occurred
during the Tory aldermen's dispute with the Common Council in 1717–
18, when, in response to an unprecedented Whig majority in the lower
house, the Tory aldermen "elected" on their own the town clerk and

[28] *Gazette,* June 1, 1717; May 30, 1718; June 1, 1723; May 30, 1724.
[29] BL, Add. MS 5853, fols. 107–8, March 21, July 18, 1715; *Gazette,* June 14, Dec. 13,
1718.

clerk of the peace. The Whig councilmen promptly set up a populist cry against such a subversion of the "antient and undoubted Rights and Privileges of the Common Council," petitioned their MPs and initiated proceedings in King's Bench against Mayor Bubbin, with the predictable result that a writ was returned on June 21, 1717, ordering a new election for the corporate offices in question.[30]

Thereafter, the Whigs exploited their majority in the Council, pursuing measures designed to increase their electoral following, such as opening the Great Hospital of Norwich to poor dissenters.[31] More creatively, they introduced a new form of electoral corruption into Norwich, that of installing hundreds of new *prisoners* to vote in city elections. According to the information of a Tory alderman, who later prosecuted the Whig mayor and sheriffs for these practices in King's Bench, the procedure went as follows. Two days before an aldermanic or mayoral election, the Whig sheriffs went around the city and "arrested" any citizen who admitted to having even the most petty of debts. These prisoners were taken to the city jail and kept there until election day, at which time they would vote for the designated candidate and be allowed to return home. And because the jail straddled the boundary between Mancroft and Conisford wards, the bailiff would move all the prisoners to one side of the jail to vote in one ward, and then to the opposite side of the jail to vote in the other.[32] By such maneuvers, the Whigs captured control of the aldermanic bench in 1720. Predictably, despite the objections and petitions of freemen and Tory leaders alike, the right of prisoners to vote in local and parliamentary elections was confirmed by the Whig Corporation in 1722 and by Parliament in the Election Act of 1730.[33]

Toryism in Norwich was under siege, and its defenses seemed scarcely strong enough to withstand the assault. Yet remarkably, aided by the trade depression of 1718–20 and the South Sea Bubble fiasco of 1720–2, the High Church party was able to stage a comeback in the aldermanic elections of 1722, despite not putting forth parliamentary candidates that year, and to capture the mayoralty in May and an al-

[30] NNRO, Assembly Minute Books, April 16, May 20, 1717; *Gazette,* March 29, 1718; O'Sullivan, "Politics in Norwich," 67–72.
[31] NNRO, Assembly Minute Books, Dec. 23, 1718.
[32] PRO, KB 1/1 5 Geo., Easter 1719; *Gazette,* March 29, 1718; S. Webb and B. Webb, *English Local Government,* 2 vols. (Hamden, Conn., 1978), ii, 531n.
[33] *Gazette,* March 29, 1718; NNRO, Assembly Minute Book, Sept. 12, 1722; Francis Blomefield, *An Essay Towards a Topographical History of the County of Norfolk,* 11 vols. (London, 1805–10), iii, 445.

dermanic election and shrieval contest in August, despite recent revelations about the Layer plot.[34] Unnerved by this show of grass-roots support for the Tories, the Whigs responded by using pressure from the central government to overturn the shrieval election with a scrutiny, and the city's Whig MPs got a new Calico Act through Parliament in 1721.[35] Most important, the Whig assemblymen petitioned Parliament for an Election Act in January 1723, one which would force all resident adult males engaged in the worsted industry to take up their freedom. Such a law would, the petitioners argued, give the city "a supply of able magistrates," who were very scarce; at the same time, they requested that the financial requirements for the aldermen's sheriff be raised and that elections be regulated through the device of mayor-appointed clerks.[36] Naturally, the Act was obtained and went into effect the next year. The wager on Whiggery's strength among the worsted industry paid off: 400 weavers, dyers and others engaged in the wool trade immediately took up their freedom, and of those who can be traced in pollbooks, almost 70 percent voted Whig in 1734 and 1735.[37] More immediately, the Act successfully obviated the Tory threat, forestalling all contests but two between 1723 and 1727 and enabling the Whigs to capture two aldermanic seats from the Tories in Mancroft ward in 1724–5. The combination of high-level Tory defeatism, aggressive extra-parliamentary political tactics and state backing had given the Whigs a seemingly unassailable predominance in local and central government.

However, the formation of a coalition opposition in Parliament and the development of the anti-corruption critique of Court Whiggery without bolstered Norwich Toryism and its will to resist Whig power. The structures of both institutional and extra-institutional politics quickly took up Toryism's refurbished attack on Whig hegemony, transmuting the rhetoric of local Toryism into a more Hanoverian and ecumenical discourse that focussed on Walpolean corruption at all levels. The issues arising from the Whig ascendancy in local and national government thus revitalized and redefined political allegiances in Norwich.

---

[34] For the riots in 1719 and 1721 see NNRO, Massey, 32–5; Cozens-Hardy and Kent, *Mayors of Norwich,* 115. For elections: *Gazette,* May 5, Sept. 1, 1722.

[35] *Gazette,* May 5, 1722; Webb and Webb, *Local Government,* ii, 545–6; *Gazette,* Sept. 29, 1722.

[36] NNRO, Assembly Minute Books, Jan. 7, 1723; Blomefield, *Norfolk,* iii, 437–9.

[37] O'Sullivan, "Politics in Norwich," 92. Two Tory aldermen, Thomas Harwood and Edward Weld, were on the committee that prepared the petition to Parliament.

The adoption of a new strategy by local Tories was signaled quite clearly in the *Gazette* on Accession Day in 1726. Despite Crossgrove's ambivalence about *The Craftsman,* from the start he borrowed liberally from its pages and reprinted its provocative essays.[38] The joy of citizens throughout the city was attested to by bells, guns and loyal toasts to the king and the royal issue, Crossgrove reported, "which . . . gives audible Proof of the People's zeal for, and Allegiance to, the Illustrious Family . . . thro' [whose] . . . calm Government . . . the Commonalty have enjoy'd all Rights and Privileges due unto them, viz., free liberty of Conscience, a flourishing Trade, etc."[39] This summary of the fruits of Hanoverian rule was no doubt ironic, but it signaled acceptance of the opposition strategy to prosecute a loyal and bipartisan attack on Whig hegemony, an effort to which the resignification of the calendar was crucial. George II's accession and coronation the following year were observed with a lavish indulgence of traditional Tory festoons; in Crossgrove's own parish of St. Giles, green boughs, garlands and streamers adorned houses and shops, and comic dances were performed on a stage erected in the street; and Restoration Day was revamped to laud not only "the end to a devilish Usurpation" but also "the Glorious Day to which we owe the blessing of his present Majesty's happy Accession."[40]

Renewed Tory vitality was also demonstrated in the significant electoral recovery of 1727–9. The Tories succeeded in forcing a contest in the parliamentary election of 1727, putting up Richard Berney and Miles Branthwayte to stand against the current Whig members, Robert Britiffe and Waller Bacon. The latter set of candidates won with 56 percent of the vote, but the fact of opposition and the return of Berney to the Tory fold after a brief tryst with the Whigs (he had been made recorder of the city in the Whig interest) provided concrete evidence of the reemergent viability of the formerly discomfited party. The following spring, capturing Mancroft and Wymer wards in the councilor elections through the restoration of a more effective parish and ward organization, the Tories won a majority on the Council for the first

[38] J. B. Williams, "Henry Crossgrove, Jacobite Journalist and Printer," *Library,* 3rd ser., 5 (1914), 204–24, alleges that Crossgrove damned the opposition paper as "that vile republican paper" (218). But in fact the *Gazette* was quoting from Wye's letter about the role of the *Craftsman* in spreading "misrepresentations" about the excise bill: See *Gazette,* Jan. 13, 1733.
[39] *Gazette,* Aug. 6, 1726.
[40] Maypoles were erected throughout East Anglia on George II's coronation, despite its occurrence in October: ibid., June 24, July 1, July 8, Oct. 14, 21, 1727; June 1, 1728.

time since 1717, and then in May captured the mayoralty when Tory alderman Thomas Harwood beat Captain John Black of the Artillery Company.[41] Harwood's victory was observed with bell-ringing, guns and an impromptu parade, in which the new mayor was heaped with garlands and accompanied to his house by women who threw flowers in his path while a group of young men who carried a pole covered with old wigs called out, "Twelve Wiggs for a Penny."[42]

The Whig response to the reversal in Tory political fortunes was to boycott the Assembly for thirteen months between December 1728 and February 1730, an act which brought all local government and administration, except that which could be dealt with by committees, to a standstill.[43] The aldermen, including Mayor John Black, Timothy Balderstone, John Custance, John Harvey, Daniel Fromanteel and Philip Meadows, followed the boycott with a petition to Norwich MPs for a new Election Act – one ostensibly designed to keep local elections peaceful and free from corruption, but in fact intended to rout the opposition from the institutions of local government – which was obtained in the spring of 1730.[44] As the *Gazette* noted, the clear but unstated purpose of the Act was to circumscribe the economic and partisan dimensions of the electorate, depriving poorer freemen of their votes and depopularizing civic politics, and it fulfilled these dire predictions. Besides providing a more stringent qualification for freemen's voting – requiring twelve months of freedom for parliamentary elections and six months of residence in a ward for civic elections – it struck a double blow at popular political participation, reducing the number of councilors to be elected by the body of freemen to three per ward (these three coopted the ward's remaining quota), and, in imitation of Walpole's infamous Election Act for the City of London in 1725, giving the Court of Aldermen a veto over measures of the Council by requiring that the latter's resolutions be validated by a majority vote of aldermen. The Act did attack bribery by preventing the abuse of "mushroom freemen" before an election; but it did so by subjecting the most democratic wing of local government to aldermanic veto, circumscribing the civic electorate, and effectively disenfranchising poorer, more mo-

---

[41] O'Sullivan, "Politics in Norwich," 82–5; *Norwich Mercury* (hereafter *Mercury*), May 25, Sept. 1, 1727; *Gazette,* April 27, 1728. Parish committees like the Anglican charity school trustees, which included a number of Tory leaders, were used to plan strategy and mobilize votes.

[42] *Gazette,* June 8, 1728; *Mercury,* June 8, 1728.

[43] NNRO, Assembly Minutes, Dec. 3, 1728.

[44] Rogers, *Whigs and Cities,* 321; *Mercury,* March 8, 22, 1729.

bile voters (whose livelihoods depended upon the ability to move where employment arose) in the trades *other* than the textile industry (whose poorer voters had been forced to register as freemen by the 1723 Election Act), thus restricting the Tory electorate where the Whig electorate was not restricted.[45]

The immediate political consequences were alternatively predictable and unexpected. As hoped, the Act effectively disintegrated the Tory majority in Council. Although the Tories retained control of the sixteen seats for Mancroft, the Whigs soon held all forty-four seats in the other three wards.[46] Yet, interestingly, the Act worked to energize the opposition within Mancroft, stimulating the formation of organizational strategies – such as the use of conciliar nominees as whips to coopt other appropriate councilors and maintain contact with Tory leaders in other parishes – that made the ward an unassailable bastion of anti-Whiggism, immune from the encroachments of the predominant party for the first time.[47] More important, the debacle of 1730 encouraged the emergence of a more heterogeneous opposition to Court Whig power that would not be duplicated until the 1760s and 70s, whose sources and supports lay in a nexus of material, political and ideological developments. The improvement in communications and expansion of inland and coastal trade consolidated Norwich's leading position in the regional economy as a center of domestic trade, consumption and fashion; by the 1730s Norwich was the hub of an extensive distributive network of roads, canals and rivers that regularized channels of domestic trade.[48] Mancroft, with its spectacular markets and merchant houses, was the heart of this commercial retailing and distributive community, and opposition ideology which appealed to the "trading interest" had strong resonances within this sector of the local economy. "Trade" of course was an ideological construct in this period, and different conceptions of it in Norwich, as in other large provincial towns, mobilized very different political positions. The strong alliance between the Whigs and the worsted industry in Norwich after the Hanoverian Succession had been cemented by a definition of "trade" that

[45] For the Act, which gave Norwich a constitution providing for a bicameral legislature, see Blomefield, *Norfolk*, iii, 445–6; NNRO, Assembly Minute Books, May 5, 1731; Webb and Webb, *Local Government*, ii, 546–7; for its partisan consequences see Rogers, *Whigs and Cities*, 322–3.
[46] O'Sullivan, "Politics in Norwich," p. 49; *Mercury*, March 21, 1730.
[47] *Gazette*, March 10, 22, May 2, 1730; April 10, May 8, 1731; March 25, 1732.
[48] P. J. Corfield, "The Social and Economic History of Norwich, 1650–1850" (Ph.D. diss., University of London, 1976), 100–5.

focussed solely on the needs of the textile community. This identification was being challenged by domestic traders and retailers, who,
inspired by the patriot campaign at the center and provided with a
political language with which to identify and express their grievances,
began to demand that other commercial interests of the city be equally
recognized and advanced by Norwich MPs and Parliament. Accordingly the *Gazette* began to emphasize the serious threat which Walpolean high-level corruption posed to the "Liberties, Properties, Trade
and Navigation" of the whole kingdom and to support a more expansionist foreign policy.[49] In the process, Mancroft ward became the en-
gine of the vigorous campaign against the Walpolean regime, closely
associating itself with the patriot agitation of the county, metropolis
and nation. Even further, it conscripted some dissenters and opposition
Whigs in the city to join the cause; they recognized the political division of interest between the manufacturing and retail communities and
shared Tory hostility to the anti-libertarian measures of the Whig regime. Despite limited evidence, there are clear hints that this heterogeneous opposition first coalesced around the issue of the Election Act
in 1729, at which time Crossgrove commended the "whiggs" who
joined the Tories in opposing the odious bill. Thereafter, the bipartisan
composition of the opposition was frequently acknowledged in both the
Mercury and *Gazette;* in the former paper, in particular, the "Whigs
and Dissenters turned Tories" were common objects of Chase's scorn
and anger. Limited dissenting support for the opposition was also suggested by the vote in the 1734 and 1735 parliamentary elections.[50] Thus
the Tory-led opposition became a force to be reckoned with for the
next five years.[51]

The excise crisis provided both motive and opportunity for opposition supporters to test their political muscle. Tobacco merchants in Nor-

---

[49] See, e.g., *Gazette,* Jan. 6, 1733; April 13, 1734; Feb. 8, 1735.
[50] *Gazette,* March 22, 1729; *Mercury,* April 7, Sept. 8, 1733; *N–rw–ch C–v–c–de* (Norwich, 1741), 13–15; *An Alphabetical Draught of the Polls* (Norwich, 1735), which
shows the weaving and nonconformist parishes of St. James's and St. Paul's swinging
away from the Whigs in 1734–5, as well as a dozen individual dissenters (including
Quakers) in Mancroft, Northern and Wymer wards. For the *Craftsman*'s tentative and
admittedly underwhelming overtures to dissenters in this period see Aug. 25, Sept.
29, Oct. 6, 13, 1733, and April 3, 1736.
[51] Tory leaders included John Aldridge, ironmonger; Daniel Ganning, grocer; Bartholomew Harwood, silversmith; Timothy Money, upholsterer; James Elmy, worsted
weaver; Mark Addey, tailor; John Steward, merchant; and Crossgrove (all common
councilors for Mancroft); Thomas Alexander, hosier; Timothy Ganning, upholsterer;
William Varden, shopkeeper; and aldermen Edward Weld and Thomas Churchman.

wich sent instructions to town and county MPs directing them to oppose
the bill, and circular letters to other boroughs to mobilize forces of
resistance there; local celebrations, publications and artifacts kept the
causes of the campaign in the public eye. On the news of the bill's
withdrawal, festivities broke out in the taverns, inns and streets of the
parishes of Mancroft and several others in adjacent wards, and the
"Merchants and Tradesmen of Norwich" sent a letter of thanks to the
Norfolk Tory MP Sir Edmund Bacon for opposing the measure in Parliament.[52] Locally produced artifacts, including prints, silk handker-
chiefs and silk cloths "for Ladies Tea-Tables or Toilets" decorated
with the coats of arms of the "205 worthy Patriots" who voted against
the bill; a Bishop Blaize parade staged by a group of journeymen woolcombers carrying banners emblazoned "Liberty and Property"; and
favors imprinted with the likeness of the former Jacobite and now oppositionist lord mayor of London, John Barber, as well as boisterous
celebrations in St. Peter's Mancroft on the anniversary of the bill's
defeat commemorated the people's recent victory and rallied support
for the opposition cause.[53]

The Whigs responded with some strenuous politicking of their own.
The Whig press continued to identify the "national good" with promotion of the textile trade, a strategy made all the more urgent by the
industry's brief but harsh recession of 1734–5, when observers decried
the "ruinous condition" of many journeymen weavers. Walpole's protection of the industry, his commitment to maintaining peace abroad
and his attention to preserving religious liberty were all stressed – a
seductive triad which had been ingratiating itself among members of
the worsted industry since the succession.[54] To counter the inroads the
opposition made on the Whigs' constituency during the excise crisis,
Whig writers and canvassers invoked the Tories' less-than-tolerant past
with frequent allusions to the schism bill, and warned dissenters against
the wolves in sheep's clothing that their former adversaries were sure
to turn out to be.[55] The *Mercury* also denigrated the populist principles

---

[52] *LEP,* Jan. 4–6, 1733; *Gazette,* Jan. 13, March 31, April 7, 14, 21, May 25, 1733;
Craftsman, May 26, 1733.
[53] Artifacts: *Gazette,* Aug. 25, Sept. 22, Dec. 8, 1733; celebrations: ibid., April 13, 1734;
procession: ibid., Feb. 9, 1734.
[54] *Mercury,* Oct. 13, Nov. 10, 1733; May 4, 1734; *A Letter from a Weaver in Norwich*
(Norwich, 1734).
[55] *Mercury,* April 7, Sept. 8, Oct. 13, 1733. The paper frequently stressed the Catholic
and French connections of the putative "jacobites" in the opposition: See May 4,
1734; N. C. Hunt, *Two Early Political Associations* (London, 1966), 208–9.

espoused by the opposition as but another plot of the disloyal party to subvert the constitution. The opposition was colorfully if fancifully described as "*Jacobites, Malecontents* and *Republicans . . .* knit in one Body" to destroy the state, and opposition tactics and arguments were alleged to be undermining the constitutional balance by giving undue political weight to "the People" out-of-doors.[56] In perhaps the ultimate political affront, the Reverend Samuel Shuckford, in a January 30 sermon at the cathedral, quoted the royal martyr himself on the proper delimitations of popular participation:

> The true liberty of my Subjects consists not in sharing the Power of Government, but in living under such Laws as may give them the best Assurance of their lives, and propriety of their Goods . . . Having a share of the Government: that is nothing pertaining to them.[57]

However, the local Whigs' trump card remained government support, and in 1733 and 1734 it came in the form of Sir Robert Walpole himself. On his first visit, two months after the excise debacle, he was led into Norwich by a procession of local notables that included "near a Thousand Horse and a great Train of Coaches" to receive the freedom of the city, boxed in gold, in a public ceremony at the marketplace. The prime minister chose this occasion to inform the Norwich freemen of his plan to back the bill supported by local manufacturers to allow Irish wool into England duty-free, conflating the national and local interest by declaring that "the supporting the Woolen Manufacture, was what he had ever at Heart, and always esteem'd the true Interest of the Nation in general, and this City in particular." The following day his introduction of Horatio Walpole as prospective candidate produced cheers from the crowd who had gathered to see them. Walpole's next visit to Norwich was to vote, with much display and flourish, for the Whig candidates on election day; before polling, as Crossgrove noted with disgust, Sir Robert "condescended to take the Oath against *Bribery* and *Corruption*."[58]

The 1734 election was thus a crucial test of the viability of the coalition opposition in Norwich. It pitted two local men, Sir Edward Ward (who had formerly flirted with the Whigs) and Miles Branth-

---

[56] *Mercury,* Oct. 13, Nov. 10, 1733; Feb. 16, 23, March 9, May 4, June 1, 1734. See also Reed Browning, *Political and Constitutional Ideas of the Court Whigs* (Baton Rouge, 1982), 189–209.

[57] Samuel Shuckford, *A Sermon Preach'd at the Cathedral Church of Norwich on Wednesday, January 30, 1734* (Norwich, 1734).

[58] *The Quack Triumphant, or the N–r—ch Cavalcade* (London, 1733), 4; *Mercury,* July 14, 1733; NNRO, Assembly Minute Books, June 18, 1733; *Gazette,* May 18, 1734.

wayte, against the forces of official Whiggism, and after a vigorous contest during which the sheriffs allegedly engaged in illegal polling practices, the Whig candidates were returned by a very narrow majority. Some solace was provided for the local opposition when, a week later, the Country candidates Bacon and Wodehouse were victorious in the county election, despite Walpole's having spent £10,000 of his own money to prevent such an occurrence. Norwich citizens observed the victory with traditional sylvan festoons and a cheering accompaniment to the Norfolk freeholders, who rode out of town bedecked with gilt cockades.[59]

Nevertheless, the 1734 election cannot be written off as the assured defeat of an enervated party, for it exhibited a degree of polarization and partisanship among the electorate that had not been equaled before, nor would be again until 1784. First, the Whigs won by about 220 votes; among resident freemen, only 77 more persons voted Whig rather than Tory, in an election with 94 percent partisan voting, a percentage which compares extremely well with those of the post-1768 elections that historians have targeted as inaugurating "partisan" behavior among urban voters. In the 1735 by-election on Waller Bacon's death, in another large poll with a high turnout and 92 percent straight party voting, the Whigs won by 333 votes.[60] Secondly, the electoral showing of the opposition must also be considered in the context of a very high turnover rate among the electorate – calculated at 50 percent every five years – and the Election Acts which forced members of the textile trade to take up their freedom while excluding nontextile workers (who were likely to be Tory voters) from voting through residence requirements. Given that 53 percent of new admissions over this period belonged to the worsted industry, it can safely be assumed that the majority of new freemen were sympathetic to the Whigs; yet the opposition still retained the allegiance of just under one-half of the resident urban electorate in both 1734 and 1735.[61]

Further, the occupational and geographical breakdown of the poll in

---

[59] William Coxe, *Memoirs of the Life and Administration of Sir Robert Walpole,* vol. 1 (London, 1798), 456; *Gazette,* May 25, 18, 1734.

[60] *An Alphabetical Draught of the Polls for Members of Parliament for the City of Norwich, Taken May the 15th, 1734, and . . . Feb. the 19th, 1735* (Norwich, 1735). Phillips, *Electoral Behavior,* 216, calculates the rate of partisan voting in the elections of 1768, 1780 and 1784 at 89.1%, 87.4% and 98.3% respectively.

[61] The percentages on freemen's admissions are calculated from figures provided by Corfield, "Social and Economic History," 92–3; the figure for the rate of turnover is from Rogers, *Whigs and Cities,* 330.

1734 supports earlier contentions about the political divisions between the textile and retail trading communities.[62] Among resident merchants/ manufacturers, retailers and agriculturalists, the Tories maintained majorities (of 55, 69 and 65 percent respectively); among craftsmen and artisans, who accounted for two-thirds of Norwich voters in the first half of the eighteenth century and included the vast majority of men employed in the worsted trades, as well as among gentry and professionals, the Whigs predominated, capturing 56 and 63 percent of their votes respectively. Geographically, Tory support was concentrated in Mancroft and Conisford wards and in some adjacent retailing parishes like St. Andrew's and St. John Maddermarket.[63] Significantly, however, Tories also won majorities in some predominantly nonconformist and textile parishes in Wymer and Northern wards, such as St. Mary's Coslany, St. Martin at Oak, St. Paul's, St. James's, and St. Martin at Palace, which fact undermines the attempt to reduce political loyalties to either religion or occupation. Where Tory support was strikingly absent was in the traditional stronghold of the church, where of the sixty-one clergymen voting in 1734, forty chose the Whig candidates; even the parish churchwardens were divided between the two parties.[64] Predictably, state and corporate office-holders also voted Whig, and Whig loyalties also predominated among dissenters and outvoters, the latter reversing the trends in resident opposition support. Hence the election revealed the socially heterogeneous base of both parties, the almost invariable propensity of the majority of outvoters to poll for the Corporation-backed candidates, and the success of the Whig campaign to woo the worsted and dissenting communities with its promises of peace, prosperity and protection. The Tories lost further ground to their opponents in the 1735 by-election forced by Bacon's death. The former Tory and local merchant Thomas Vere ran in the Whig interest at the prompting of Horace Walpole and Mayor Philip Meadows, a dissenter and wealthy worsted manufacturer. Vere brought with him some of his formerly

---

[62] These assessments are based on my own analysis of the information contained in the 1734/5 pollbook, with supplemental ratebook figures. Nicholas Rogers has provided some important correctives to using pollbooks alone as guides to occupation and social status; see *Whigs and Cities,* 329; he kindly provided me with access to his copy of Nockold Thompson's annotated 1734/5 pollbook.

[63] Tories took majorities in Mancroft and Conisford of 58% and 54% respectively; the Whigs reversed these figures in Wymer and Northern wards, taking 54% and 59% of the vote.

[64] Compared with 15 and 21 for Whigs and Tories respectively in 1715: Speck, *Tory and Whig,* 119. NNRO, Parish Records: PD 165/81(s), St. Andrew's; PD 6/57(s), St. Clement's; PD 162/63, St. Peter's Parmentergate; PD 26/73, St. Peter's Mancroft.

Tory supporters, the Whig press engaged in the strenuous politicking it had the previous year, and Vere was returned, giving the Whigs a more substantial majority than in 1734.[65]

Why did the Tories lose ground? Given the extent of official Whig backing and influence in the town, the question should rather be how the forces of opposition managed to resist Whig power so effectively for so long. In both cases, the answer lies in the ideological divisions within the community as well as in the structural advantages and institutional controls instituted by Court Whiggery. The latter, of course, are the stuff of the mythology about "stability" and have been extensively documented in the historical literature. Indeed, in Norwich the Whigs' relentless institutional offensive inflicted lethal financial and psychological damage on Tory elites. Unlike their colleagues in the county, who had been able to foil the Walpolean electoral machine sufficiently to force a compromise in 1741, Tory leaders in the city were drained financially by the frequent political contests and were increasingly unwilling to challenge entrenched Whig power formally. Ward retired to his country seat following his loss in the 1734 election; Branthwayte, his finances decimated by two parliamentary contests, backed off from local political struggles and absorbed himself in his businesses and his Hethel estate. Thomas Vere, former Tory alderman, simply defected to the party of state patronage. As a result, the 1741 election was a disaster for the erstwhile Norwich opposition. The Tory leaders had approached Edward Bacon and Alderman William Clarke, both reputed opposition Whigs, to stand as their candidates; but Bacon consulted Horace Walpole on the matter, who arranged to have Bacon returned in the family interest at King's Lynn. Clarke was thus left to stand alone against the forces of official Whiggism, and after a poll of one day, in which 829 of the 2,450 voters who had turned out voted for the opposition candidate, Clarke quit the poll, convinced that his party could not maintain its cause.[66] The result was that until the 1760s Norwich lacked opposition elite leaders able and willing to stage a serious parliamentary challenge.

However, Whig ascendancy and Tory resistance were more than electoral strategies imposed upon an incognizant or compliant population; they were predicated upon contending identities and ideological constructions of patriotism, liberty and prosperity that shaped citizens'

---

[65] *Mercury,* Aug. 24, 1734; Jan. 4, 1735; Sedgwick, i, 291.
[66] Sedgwick, i, 426–7; *Gazette,* April 18, 1741; *Newcastle Courant,* May 2, 1741.

perceptions of material as well as political interests. The ways in which oppositionist patriotism constructed communities of interest have been well documented in this study. Its commercialist and libertarian rhetoric opposed the deleterious consequences of executive corruption on the domestic polity and England's position abroad, and sought greater accountability by government to "the people" as a check on such corruption. The Norwich version of this rhetoric placed particular emphasis on the Whig government's inequitable treatment of the middling trader. Before the 1735 by-election, Crossgrove asked how Norwich freemen could vote for the party that passed "Laws by which the Business of the greater Part of the fair Traders in every Kingdom is rendered very difficult, and to some almost impracticable ... Laws by which a great part of the Labour of the industrious artificers and workmen have been applied to maintain others in Idleness."[67] Given that Norwich citizens had firsthand knowledge of the ability of Whig patronage and power to disrupt the texture and tenor of local life, middling merchants and retailers as well as country gentlemen applauded the parliamentary opposition's campaign to preserve the rights of all English people "to reap the fruits of their honest industry" without fear of molestation. Patriot ideology drew in a particular sector of the local population in its campaign, allowing its supporters to legitimate their sectional interests and articulate their concerns for "trade" and independence through the universalizing mantle of the patriotic, public good.

Yet Whig ideology could also perform similar competitive work, justifying its domestic program and Eurocentric foreign policy in the language of patriotism and the national interest. Indeed, in addition to the outrageous fortunes of the Norwich woolen industry abroad that accrued from Walpolean policy and protection, the Whig emphasis on the defense of the Revolution and the Protestant succession, the glories of the British constitution and even the need to maintain appropriate "balance" by limiting the parameters of popular participation in the political process were all capable of mobilizing support from among the Norwich citizenry. First, by dwelling, often in salacious detail, upon the supposed tyrannical Jacobite sensibilities of their opponents, the Whigs were able to exploit the historical memories of High Church persecution of dissenters and confound any efforts of the opposition to mute them. Indeed, if patriot ideology attempted to deflect attention

---

[67] *Gazette,* Feb. 8, 1735.

from religious divisions by focussing on the issues of state power that were of concern to citizens of all denominations, Whig ideology did its best to keep sectarian wounds alive, focussing on Tories' historic mistreatment of nonconformity since Charles II's reign and their supposed current attachment to a Catholic Pretender. This propaganda was tailored to the most humble of voters: Before the 1734 election in Norwich, a "Dialogue between Dick and Tom, on Parliamenteering" was circulated which insisted that the only valid party distinction was between Whig and Jacobite, or "those that love King George and the REVOLUTION" and those "that [love] the *Pope* and *Pretender*."[68] This anti-Stuart, anti-Catholic rhetoric astutely played on Norwich dissenters' sensibilities; many had Huguenot forebears who had fled from persecution in Louis XIV's reign. Indeed, the government's otherwise empty promises to extend religious toleration were only given substance by the manipulation of these images of persecuting, intolerant Catholicism, for they reminded nonconformists of how benign Walpole's minimalist protection was by comparison.

Secondly, Whig ideology celebrated a loyalist patriotism that coaxed citizens to identify their interest with that of the state and ministry, a vertical definition of interest that was at once paternalistic and nationalistic, playing on the myth and vision of Britain's uniqueness as a beacon of liberty in the world. This construction made the essentially passive political subjectivity articulated since the succession crisis the heart of its patriotic imperative, encouraging all good subjects to support Whig governors to best protect their own and the nation's interest. "The Way to preserve our Liberties is, *Temperance, Publick Virtue and support of Government,*" the *Mercury* charged, not to engage in "faction and sedition." Of course, in the panoply of Whig heroes being championed in this period, Walpole himself was a luminary. "Great WALPOLE steady Atlas of our State, / Whose shoulders strongly bear a Nation's weight / Its present Glory and its future Fate" was how one versifier put it in the pre-electoral hubris of 1733–4. Such a view confirmed Whig leaders' self-image, but it also flattered the sensibilities of Norwich freemen: Since the Whigs' efforts to limit popular participation could only be justified by identifying "the people" of opposition ideology with the "mob," Norwich Whigs' status as a privileged, right-thinking group of electors was underscored by comparing them with the Tories' insensible multitude, who did not know the difference

[68] *Mercury,* May 4, 1734.

between slavery and freedom.[69] Whig ideology, then, constructed a coherent political identity of interest – those who supported the state, its
institutions and its leadership against foreign and domestic threats –
that helped shape the perceptions of material concerns. As much as
their creeping control of Corporation and ecclesiastical patronage and
solicitous cultivation of the worsted industry, the Whigs' construction
of an alternative idiom of patriotism was crucial to their success in
Norwich, rendering Whig power and Tory proscription comprehensible
to their supporters.

These contesting ideologies and visions were fought out in the period
between 1726 and 1741 in the streets and press as well as at the polls.
Yet the barrage of Acts and activities designed to obviate popular Toryism, circumscribe political participation and enervate opposition political culture never succeeded in their finite, if covert, goals. The Whigs
were never able to rout the opposition from the popularly elected organs
of local government – the Tories retained one-third to one-half of the
seats in Common Council – nor were they able to inhibit the vibrant
opposition political culture that flourished in the city's streets, taverns
and press. However, they did succeed in attenuating opposition within
institutional political channels, with results that were painfully on display in 1741.

The enervation of opposition in formal political institutions had a
number of effects on extra-institutional politics. The parliamentary defeats of 1734–5 exposed, first, the tentative nature of the coalition between Tories and dissident Whigs. Tories lost no time in blaming
dissenters for their resounding defeat in the by-election; and in response
to the perceived apostasy of their former allies, Tory writers and clergy
reverted to a virulent High Church rhetoric that was only strengthened
by dissenters' attempt to obtain repeal of the Test and Corporation Acts.
When that effort was defeated in the House of Commons in March of
1736 – an event about which the Whig press was screamingly silent –
Crossgrove reported "great Rejoycings" in Norwich, with illuminations and bell-ringing throughout the city.[70] For three years thereafter,
local opposition spokesmen were unabashed in their nonconformist-
baiting. The Reverend Robert Leeke delivered a sermon in the cathedral
and St. Andrew's parish church in 1738 on the martyrdom of Charles
I that emphasized all of the opposition's main themes – including the

---

[69] Ibid., Nov. 9, 1728; Nov. 10, 1733; June 1, 1734.
[70] *Gazette*, March 20, 1736.

people's right to resist illegitimate power and the illegality of both
"ship money" and excises – before reminding dissenters that, given
their forebears' role in fomenting the destruction of church and state
in the Stuart era, they should be meek, upright and above all silent in
the present, "instead of murmuring and complaining for want of more
favours."[71]

Such rhetoric subsided considerably in 1738–42, but its legacy hin-
dered the Tories' ability to expand their popular support and harness
political loyalties for the "patriotic" call for war with Spain. Despite
a hopeful Tory victory in an aldermanic contest in Colgate in 1739,
and a focus on Admiral Vernon's intrepid exploits and their possible
benefits for the textile and trading communities, both sides could appropriate the call for the expansion of trade.[72] Indeed, Norwich traders
and artisans were just as caught up in aspirations for British imperial
supremacy as those elsewhere, and they engaged in pro-Vernon effervescences: bought, sold and made Vernon artifacts, attended dramatic
enactments of the siege of Porto Bello and subscribed in advance for
the anniversary celebrations of his birthday and victories held at the
Admiral Vernon and Port Bello inns.[73]

But if Vernon's victories kept alive the smoldering anti-ministerial
grievances harbored by the town's domestic traders and importers, they
could also mobilize nationalist and pro-imperial sentiments of a more
loyalist kind. In the first instance, citizens hailed Vernon as a British
patriot whose valiant efforts on his country's behalf contrasted dramatically with the supineness and corruption of the ministry. "Brave
Admiral Vernon . . . the Downfall of Corruption, and a Parliament without a Place-Man or Pensioner" were toasts in Norwich after a flurry
of instructions demanding place and pension bills had been printed in
the newspapers.[74] Nonetheless, local Whigs, stimulated in part by the
awakened interest of worsted merchants in the Atlantic trade, attempted
to bask in the reflected glory of Vernon's achievements, pointing to

---

[71] Robert Leeke, *A Sermon Preached at the Cathedral Church, and St. Andrew's in Norwich, on Tuesday, Jan. 30, 1738* (Norwich, 1738).

[72] *Gazette,* Sept. 23, 1738; Feb. 24, 1739. For the steady growth in trade with the Americas since 1720 see Elizabeth Schumpeter, *English Overseas Trade Statistics, 1697–
1808* (Oxford, 1960), 26–8.

[73] *Gazette,* March 22, Nov. 15, 22, 29, 1740; May 23, 30, Nov. 14, 1741; NNRO,
Churchwarden Accounts: St. Andrew's, PD 165/81 (8), 1739–42; St. Clement's, PD
6/57 (s), 1740–1. Artifacts: *Gazette,* June 28, July 26, Nov. 22, 1740; March 21, May
23, 30, 1741; theater: *Gazette,* Jan. 3, 10, 1741; inns: BL, Add. MS 27,966, Arderon
Tracts, fol. 232.

[74] *Gazette,* Nov. 22, 29, 1740.

them as instances of superior ministerial vision. Chase made his own contributions to the pool of local Vernon artifacts and exalted the Norwich MPs as having "nothing more at heart than the Interest of Trade in general," and Whig aldermen and Artillery Company members presided as members of the newly formed Constitution Club over public festivities on Vernon's anniversaries.[75] The opposition press compared such tactics to those of the Court Whigs in London, who nominated Vernon for Parliament in an attempt to foil the patriot cause, and advised all "honest tradesmen" to vote for no one who was not on the Vintner Hall list in the forthcoming parliamentary election.[76] But the local Whigs' support of the war effort did go a significant way in confounding the dichotomy posed by opposition ideology between the (universalized) interests of "trade" and the (sectional) interests of the worsted industry which had allowed them to identify overseas trade as a specifically oppositionist cause. In contrast to most other towns, Norwich Whigs were successful in appropriating the patriotic and pro-imperial sentiments mobilized on behalf of Vernon in support of the ministry, thus strengthening their position among the freemen.

Hence, the Whigs' appropriation of patriotic imperialism, as well as Tory elites' financial and hence political demoralization, won the Whigs undisputed control of the town's parliamentary representation through the 1750s. Of course, resistance to the Whig ascendancy in Norwich did not collapse following the 1741 election, but its prospects were dimmed, and the patriots' apostasy of 1742 did little to revive them. Crossgrove reprinted the most savage attacks of the *London Evening Post* upon the opposition's one-time heroes, and the disillusionment and bitterness over 1742 were reflected in criticisms of Hanoverian foreign policy for the rest of the decade.[77] In the local context Norwich Toryism retreated into insularity after the 1741 campaign, a sort of moral collapse of the party that Crossgrove's death in September 1744 symbolized and the '45 completed. When news of the rebellion broke, Norwich's leading citizens joined other towns in organizing a loyalist association for defense, each member of which pledged to support and defend the king "with our Bodies, Lives and Estates." Tory and Whig,

---

[75] *Mercury,* March 22, May 17, 1740; May 23, 1741; NNRO, Case 18, shelf b, City Chamberlain's Accounts, Payments Without Orders, 1740–1, 1741–2; *Mercury,* May 9, 23, June 6, 1741.

[76] *Gazette,* May 9, 1741; *LEP,* May 23–6, 1741.

[77] Walpole's fall precipitated warm contests for councilors in Conisford and Mancroft, resulting in a reduction of the Whigs' majority in the Council to 4: *Mercury,* April 10, 1742; *Gazette,* Feb. 18, 25, Sept. 4, Oct. 9, 1742; Jan. 8, 1743.

churchman and dissenter joined this association, which included many aldermen, councilmen, attorneys, merchants and tradesmen as well as representatives from the various ranks of the worsted industry, and £10,000 was subscribed at the first meeting.[78]

Yet the memories of past Jacobite loyalties and the current ambiguous actions of some prominent Tory citizens enabled the Whigs to appropriate the patriotism of the moment as their own. Rumors of a conspiracy among Norwich Catholics to rise in favor of the Pretender and seize the city's arms, corroborated by the lord bishop, Thomas Gooch, and Mayor Simeon Waller, came to nothing, but their credibility was boosted by both the absence of some Tory councilmen from the association for defense and the refusal of the churchwardens of St. Peter's Mancroft, including three of the recalcitrant councilors, to allow the bells to be rung for Corporation purposes at parish expense. In fact, the churchwardens' decision was the product of a financial dispute with the Corporation over its payment of church rates on properties within the parish that had begun long before the '45; and there were many *Whig* councilmen who also refrained from subscribing to the association, indicating that it was probably financial rather than political scruples which inhibited potential associators.[79] But the "suspicious" behavior of Mancroft Tories was all that was needed to rile the Artillery Company into a renewed pitch of Whig authoritarianism, ready to suppress any sign of "treason" among the local population. In addition, Whig propagandists were wont to call on "all Denominations [to] unite as one Man in Defence of the very best Cause" while also pointedly reminding the dissenters of their own persecution, or that of their forebears, by papists in France.[80] The '45, in other words, allowed the Whigs to invoke older political identities and thus gain the upper hand in the contest for unconditional loyalty that was under way, and Whig confidence swelled with their success. The thanksgiving day for the suppression of the rebellion in October brought throngs of people into the marketplace in Mancroft, where an enormous triumphal arch was

[78] *Gazette,* Oct. 5, 1745; for the Loyalist Association see NNRO, Case 13, shelf d (2), Sept. 26, 1745.

[79] *Newcastle Journal,* Oct. 19, 1745; *Gazette,* Oct. 26, 1745. The councilors who did not sign included Tories Daniel Ganning, Mark Addey, Isaac Schuldham and James Elmy, all from Mancroft ward, and Whig councilors Charles Buckle and Hewitt Rand from Northern ward. For the dispute over bell-ringing see NNRO, PD 26/73 (s), St. Peter's Mancroft Churchwarden Accounts and Vestry Minutes, June 30, 1745; Jan. 12, March 31, 1746.

[80] *Mercury,* Oct. 12, 1745.

erected; it was inscribed "RELIGION, LIBERTY, VICTORY AND PEACE. To
the DELIVERER OF HIS COUNTRY" circling a pediment of the king's arms
and the "IMPERIAL crown." As Tory observers were well aware, both
the tone and content of the rejoicing were meant to imply that the
triumph of local Whiggery was part of the national "deliverance" being celebrated.[81]

The '45 thus gave the final blow to the campaign of resistance to
the Whig ascendancy in Norwich, one from which it would take a
decade to recover. In 1747, Court Whigs were able to compromise
Norwich's representation between two interests in their party, the Wal-
poles and the Hobarts, who were returned again uncontested in 1754.
Yet if local Toryism became less capacious and resilient, it is misleading to say it became an "enclave culture" resistant to "the onward
march of Whiggery."[82] Such a dichotomous characterization obscures
the resilience and immediacy of Tory–patriot ideology, the longevity
and force of its constructions of patriotism and the public good, and
its role in nurturing a politics of resistance to "illegitimate" constellations of power; it was no accident that the hybrid oppositionist and
anti-aristocratic campaign of the second half of the century would be
launched from Mancroft ward. In the event, both Whig and Tory politics of the period would have far-reaching political repercussions, nour-
ishing traditions of popular participation, strategies of mobilization and
organizational bases that would be used for diverse and contradictory
ends in the second half of the century.

II. PATRIOTISM AND INDEPENDENCY

[The] public spirit is not everywhere extinct . . . there still are some Patriot Sons
who, when the service of their Country calls, can break thro' the Ties of all
private connections [and] . . . brave Danger and Death in Defence of the Laws
and Liberties of their Native Land.

Norwich Mercury, Aug. 11, 1759

The 1750s were marked by a dilution of party conflict, the unification
of the local elite under the aegis of Pitt's ministry and the adoption of
a "patriotic" rhetoric by Norwich politicians, all of which succeeded
in revitalizing popular politics and an oppositionist perspective in Norwich. On the parliamentary level, the fruits of oligarchy were confirmed

---

[81] *Mercury,* Oct. 11, 1746; BL, Add. MS 27,966, fol. 68; *Gazette,* April 26, 1746.
[82] Rogers, "Popular Jacobitism," 136, and *Whigs and Cities,* 329–42.

when the removal of MPs John Hobart (son of the lord lieutenant of the county) and Horace Walpole to the upper house in 1756 allowed the return without contest of Edward Bacon, son of the former Norwich Whig MP who had negotiated with the opposition in 1741 but was currently recorder of Norwich in the Whig interest, and Harbord, cousin of Hobart and son of Whig landowner Sir William Harbord.[83] Civic politics also displayed a new quietism. Within the Corporation, the power bases of rival Whig and Tory interests had congealed and offices become more hereditary; in the wards, bipartisan nominating meetings and electoral deals spared the city many of the bloody and riotous contests of previous years.[84]

Of course, older partisan identities could still surface. The furor caused by the Calvinist Methodist James Wheatley's arrival in Norwich provoked a series of riots against him and his congregation in 1751–2 led by the Tory Hell-fire Club. The slogans orchestrating the rioters' assaults on the Methodist meeting-house – "Church and King! Down with the Meeting House" and even "Let us throw off George and Bring in Jemmy" – recalled long-standing political and dynastic disputes and popular enmity toward "dissenters."[85] Yet equally striking was the near-uniform hostility that the riots prompted from local elites. Dissenters were horrified by the "vulgar" appeal of the new sect that had provoked a mob attack on the Independent and Baptist meetings for the first time since Queen Anne's reign.[86] Among the magistracy, Whig and Tory displayed a high-level passive aggression – refusing to protect the preacher or his congregation from marauding crowds or indict anti-Methodist rioters – that was endorsed by the tradesmen and merchants who associated to help the magistrates "put a Stop to the Greatest of Enthusiasts called Methodists."[87] The riots and their after-

---

[83] Namier and Brooke, ii, 36–7, 579–80.

[84] NNRO, MS 453, History of Norwich, List of Aldermanic Elections, 1717–90; *Mercury,* May 3, 1755; Aug. 28, 1756. The Whigs remained dominant in the Court of Mayoralty and the Tories in the aldermanic and councilor seats for Mancroft; only 4 aldermanic elections were contested between 1751 and 1785.

[85] *A True and Particular Narrative of the Disturbances and Outrages That Have Been Committed in the City of Norwich, Since November to the Present Time* (London, 1752), 3–15, 27–8; John Walsh, "Methodism and the Mob in the Eighteenth Century," in G. J. Cuming and Derek Baker, eds., *Popular Belief and Practice* (Cambridge, 1972), 213–28.

[86] *Mercury,* May 30, June 18, Aug. 29, 1752; *Narrative,* 25–7.

[87] *Mercury,* Dec. 28, 1751; Feb. 8, March 28, Aug. 1, 8, 1752; *Narrative,* 20; Richard Hurd, *The Mischiefs of Enthusiasm and Bigotry: A Sermon Preach'd in the Cathedral Church of Norwich, at the Assizes, 29 July 1752* (London, 1752). Some anti-Methodist rioters were convicted in 1753: *Mercury,* Jan. 27, 1753.

math revealed the rapprochement being forged between the Whig and Tory elites in this period, a closing of the ranks of class and political power against threats to the status quo. At the same time, they were also suggestive of the wave of xenophobia that seized Norwich as well as other towns in the early 1750s, when hostility to the naturalization of foreign Protestants and Jews and to "foreign" influences and contagion in general was expressed and validated in petitions, street theater and the press.[88]

Ironically, the cracks in the Old Corps ranks caused by the Minorca crisis allowed this political concord to develop further when Newcastle's foreign policy disasters of the mid 1750s precipitated the swing of local public opinion and town and county leaders to the opposition camp. Leading the pack was George Townshend, Norfolk MP and direct descendant of Old Corps Whiggery, who organized anti-Newcastle and pro-Pitt forces in the county as well as in Parliament and was the force behind the barrage of addresses in 1756.[89] Despite the best efforts of Horace Walpole to the contrary, strongly worded addresses to the king were sent from both Norwich and Norfolk on the heels of the Minorca crisis, and anti-Byng demonstrations erupted in several neighboring villages.[90]

Subsequently, Pitt's patriotic war had widespread grass-roots support. The Norwich Common Council and citizens made their own contributions to the "rain of gold boxes" which showered on him and his colleague Henry Legge in 1757 praising the two men for their "Fidelity to His Majesty, and to their distress'd country . . . and their singular Zeal to extirpate that Corruption which has, to the dishonour of our Nation, been too avowedly and openly Patronized."[91] Although part of the local enthusiasm for Pitt and a vigorous war effort was rooted in expectation of material benefits, it was also clearly shaped by the patriotic hubris of the Great Commoner's administration. Fought to secure

---

[88] *Mercury*, March 9, 1751; Oct. 20, 27, 1753; June 1, 1754. Despite Horace Walpole's report that Norwich was "unaffected" by the agitation over the Jewish naturalization bill, there is evidence to the contrary: See, e.g., *Mercury*, Oct. 20, 27, 1753; June 1, 1754; A. M. Hyamson, "The Jew Bill of 1753," *Transactions of the Jewish Historical Society*, 6 (1908–10), 160–5. Francis Blomefield, *An Essay Towards a Topographical History of the Country of Norfolk*, 5 vols. (Fersfield and Norwich, 1741–5), ii, 18–20, 32–3, rehashed the myths about the murderous and avaricious practices of the Jews in Norwich in the eleventh and twelfth centuries.

[89] See BL, Add. MS 32,867, fols. 72–3.

[90] *Mercury*, May 29, Aug. 28, Sept. 11, 1756; BL, Add. MS 32,867, fols. 166–8, 262.

[91] NNRO, Assembly Minute Books, May 3, 1757; Paul Langford, "William Pitt and Public Opinion," *EHR*, 88 (1973), 54–80.

"Our Religion, Liberties and Properties from French Tyranny and Op-pression" at home and abroad,[92] the war simultaneously played on entrenched Whig fears of French power, Tory libertarianism and the well-established pro-imperial sensibilities in which both parties had a stake. France's status as a dangerous imperial rival threatening British properties at home and abroad was a menace which promoted consen-sus, and local citizens could rally together through anxiety and then elation over the spectacular British victories in America.[93]

Most rousing, perhaps, were the efforts to arm and train the Norfolk militia in 1757–9, deemed the most "constitutional and effective way" to defend the nation and coastline. Elite and middling groups of both parties, including the Whig aristocrats Lords Buckinghamshire, Anson and Walpole, Tory squires Sir Jacob Astley, Sir William Beauchamp Proctor and Sir Hanson Berney; the Norwich Corporation and Court of Guardians of the Poor; the elite Constitution Club; and the Anti-Gallican Society of tradesmen donated money to the cause, and about 1,000 more citizens volunteered their services for the Norfolk and Nor-wich Battalion, commanded by Townshend and the Tory gentleman Sir Armine Wodehouse.[94] The battalion's rigorous training and martial spirit were confirmed for local observers when it became the first county militia to march across England to Portsmouth in 1759, re-viewed en route and with great admiration by the king and the Prince of Wales. Townshend himself was sent to Canada, where he took com-mand at Quebec after General Wolfe's death. His eventual return to Norfolk was celebrated throughout the county, and he was given the freedom of Norwich for his service to his country.[95]

The heady blend of heroic militarism and masculinist patriotism be-ing espoused during the late 1750s not only displaced party loyalties but had the ironic effect of moving political discourse to the "left." The *Mercury* began reprinting the *London Evening Post*'s populist es-says on the nature of the English constitution and the necessity of both

---

[92] *Mercury*, Oct. 22, 1757. The East India Company at this time was establishing itself as the primary exporter of Norwich camblets to India and China.

[93] *Mercury*, Aug. 26, 1758; Aug. 11, Oct. 20, Dec. 1, 1759; NNRO, City Chamberlain Accounts, Case 18, shelf c, Payments by Orders, 1759–60; Assembly Book of Pro-ceedings, x, Case 6, shelf d, Aug. 30, 1758; Oct. 31, 1759. A pub called the King of Prussia opened in St. Stephen's Gate: *Mercury*, March 24, 1759.

[94] *Mercury*, April 3, 1756; July 16, Oct. 8, 1757; April 1, Oct. 28, Nov. 18, 1758; March 10, Aug. 11, 1759; R. W. Ketton-Cremer, *Norfolk Portraits* (London, 1945), 146–7, 152.

[95] *Mercury*, July 7, 28, Aug. 11, 1759; NNRO, Assembly Minute Book, x, Dec. 28, 1759.

accountability from government and vigilance on the part of the citizenry, and these principles were endorsed, albeit obliquely, by Norwich MPs. Harbord had declared his "independency" and commitment to a purified and accountable government in his election manifesto of 1756; his subsequent adherence to these principles won him the unflagging support and loyalty of Norwich voters for three decades. Bacon's advocacy of Pitt and the independent cause was more ostentatious, if shorter-lived: After being offered a place on the Board of Trade in 1759, Bacon made a show of first "consulting his constituents" in the Assembly and at a public meeting before accepting it, and the voters sealed their approval with his reelection in January 1760.[96]

Pitt's ministry and imperial wars, then, had unified the local elite; more than that, they had moved the city's Whig leaders to adopt a populist political rhetoric that could appeal to Whig and Tory citizens in the town. Indeed, patriot ideology of the 1750s neatly if temporarily reworked old stereotypes (for example, the ever-present danger of French tyranny and popery) to fit new contexts (imperial rivalry in America and the East) so that the English people at all levels could mobilize against the French threat to British culture, power and character at home and abroad. The unparalleled popularity of the Whig MPs Bacon and Harbord was such that when two Norwich aldermen contested their return at the 1761 general election, the magistrates received the most stinging defeat of the century.[97] But if their adoption of patriotic principles had given them a seemingly unassailable popularity with the freemen, it also awakened a renewed interest in and commitment to "independency" among some Norwich citizens, the political consequences of which were long-lived.

The breakup of political concord in Norwich began soon after Pitt's resignation, and was made evident on the thanksgiving day for the peace some time later. A group of councilors snubbed the city's official celebrations to dine separately at a tavern; their rather different set of political sentiments were indicated by toasts to the reduction of the national debt, the peers and commoners who opposed the late cider tax, and "the Patriots and Heroes of the Nation," Pitt and Wilkes.[98] This

---

[96] *Mercury,* Feb. 26, 1757; Dec. 15, 1759; *A Letter to the Independent Electors of the City and County of Norwich, from a Citizen* (Norwich, 1756); Namier and Brooke, ii, 236–7.

[97] Namier and Brooke, i, 342; *Mercury,* March 26, 1761.

[98] *Mercury,* May 7, 1763. The city's address of thanks to Pitt was passed in the Assembly only after heated debate: NNRO, Assembly Minute Books, Shelf 16, case d, 10, Feb. 24, 1762.

was the inception of the cause of "Independency" in Norwich, which, influenced by the Wilkite campaign in the metropolis and inflected through county and city political tensions, sought dissolution of the "overmighty" concentrates of power currently threatening the political process and the people's liberties at home and abroad. With a contingent of leaders in the Common Council and a broad base of support from among the citizens in Mancroft and Northern wards, the Norwich independents sought not only to sustain a viable political agitation for greater political accountability from the state but also to construct a definition of citizenship that vindicated the rights and political status of the middling traders and professionals against the power of undue influence and clientage.

The goals of "Independency" and the sensibilities upon which it was predicated were first revealed in the emergent division between elite and middling citizens in the institutions of local government, and were played out in the first seriously contested parliamentary election in thirty-four years. Councilors such as the brewer Benjamin Westall, the surgeon Elias Norgate, and the linen draper James Hudson voted to honor Lord Chief Justice Pratt for his decision on general warrants in 1764 against the wishes of the majority of aldermen, and sympathetic supporters met in their tavern clubs to toast all the "Friends of Liberty" who had voted against them in Parliament.[99] Soon thereafter, Harbord Harbord's votes against general warrants and for repeal of the Stamp Act won him the public thanks of the Common Council, but the former "patriot" Edward Bacon's votes for the ministry in both cases led angry independent councilors and freemen to mount an opposition to his reelection.[100] Accordingly, in the spring of 1767 they formed the Association against Electoral Venality and Corruption, with branches in the parishes to promote the preservation of "freedom and independency" in the forthcoming election. At the same time, dissident councilors challenged the aldermanic authority in the Assembly bestowed by the 1729 Election Act by asserting the right of the Common Council to inspect the Court of Mayoralty books at will, provoking the aldermen to prepare a legal case to protect their exclusivity.[101]

By the next November, the freemen had a candidate, Thomas Beevor – a Norfolk landowner, "Brother Buck," blood brother of Norwich

[99] *Mercury,* Feb. 25, 1764; *Gazette,* March 18, 1764.
[100] *Gazette,* March 10, 1764; *Mercury,* May 10, 1766.
[101] *Newcastle Journal,* May 9, 1767; NNRO, Case 16, shelf a, Mayoral Court Books, June 17, 1767.

15. *The Junction* (1768). Magisterial combinations of power attempt to circumvent the sense of the people in Norwich. Photograph reproduced with permission from the Norwich City Library.

brewer James Beevor, who pledged himself to oppose "all Attempts upon the *Liberty* of the *Subject* and every other UNCONSTITUTIONAL measure" at the nominating meeting at St. Andrew's Hall in November.[102] The response of John Gurney, Jeremiah Ives, Robert Harvey, Peter Colombine and other aldermen to this evidence of freemen's initiative was to pressure Harbord into renouncing the "independent" position he had taken thus far in the election to stand with his colleague, Edmund Bacon, thus provoking the independents to enlarge their campaign to attack this unwarranted "Junction" of the social and political power of Corporation elites. A formal protest at the aldermen's "conspiracy" to subvert the "people's right to choose" was signed by over 500 freemen, and subsequently a flood of literary and graphic propaganda publicized their case to the population at large. It was voters' chance to prove themselves "FREEMEN or SLAVES" in the forthcoming election, as one handbill put it, by "striv[ing] with your lives to procure a Free Parliament."[103] The cartoon entitled *The Junction* (Plate 15)

[102] *Mercury,* Nov. 14, 21, 1767.
[103] Ibid., Nov. 14, 1767; Jan. 9, 1768; NRCL, Colman 46D, *To the Electors of the City*

represented this division as the gulf between secular and ecclesiastical power on the one hand and the political legitimacy of "the people" on the other. It depicts a group of gentlemen and clergymen signing a parchment in a private room; one holds a paper inscribed "General Warrants," "Stamp Act" and "Beer"; another smirks, saying, "This Junction will silence Beevor's pretentions"; and Bacon carries a dwarfed Harbord under his arm. Through the window one could see a robust crowd of freemen crying, "Beevor Forever, No Junction."[104]

Although Harbord and Bacon won the election by a fairly comfortable majority, Beevor, consistent with the terms of his candidature, spent only £50 on the election and received votes from 45 percent of the resident electorate and almost 42 percent of all electors.[105] Mancroft, that old bastion of anti-Whiggism and continuing center of the town's retailers, traders and merchants, exhibited the largest measure of support for Beevor, followed by Northern ward, still dominated by the worsted industry, where the dissenting vote was split between him and the Corporation candidates. Not surprisingly, 825 of Beevor's 1,136 supporters had plumped for him, thus throwing away a vote rather than give it to either Corporation candidate.[106] The social contours of support for Beevor bore out his own assessment that "almost all the middle rank of tradesmen, the shopkeepers, and young men," along with "the inferior sort of people," were in his camp, for 45 percent of middling merchants and retailers and 43 percent of artisans and craftsmen polled for the independent candidate – men of middling means, concerns or aspirations who were attracted to the "independency" and autonomous political identity articulated in radical ideology. Among councilmen, 43 percent cast a vote for Beevor, with the majority coming from Mancroft and Northern wards. All the aldermen, on the other hand, voted for Harbord and Bacon, with the exception of

---

of Norwich [1768] and *To the Free and Independent Citizens and Electors of Norwich,* Nov. 28, 1767; *Mercury,* Nov. 14, 21, 28, 1767; Jan. 16, March 12, 1768. Norfolk was one of the few counties in 1768 that were fought entirely on the issue of general warrants: See *Remarks on a Letter to John Buxton Esq.* (London, 1768).

[104] NRCL, Colman 59A, *The Junction* [1768].

[105] Mancroft and Conisford gave Beevor the largest percentage of the vote, 55% and 48% respectively.

[106] NNRO, MS 4282, St. Mary's Baptist Church Book, 1691–1778, Membership List, Dec. 19, 1766; FC 19/1, Old Meeting (Congregational) Norwich Church Book, 1635–1839, Membership List, March 10, 1768; voting traced in *Poll for Members of Parliament* (Norwich, 1768). Members of Octagon Chapel voted largely for the Corporation candidates, with the exception of Elias Norgate, speaker of the Common Council, who voted for Beevor and Harbord.

Thomas Starling, mayor, and Bartholomew Harwood, both aldermen for Mancroft, and Nockold Thompson, Unitarian and former Court Whig activist.[107]

The election demonstrated a wide range of articulate and organized support for the independents' cause; even more important, it consolidated the bases for continuing activism centering on the nature and accountability of governing institutions. The "Free and Independent Citizens and Electors" of Norwich took seriously their mandate to canvass the actions of their representatives, issuing a set of instructions to the newly elected MPs on George III's accession day that delineated a twelve-point plan of parliamentary reform very similar in spirit and substance to that proposed by John Almon in his manifesto of January 1768. In addition to demands for place and pension bills, triennial Parliaments, and greater safeguards for the rights of electors and habeas corpus, the instructions urged representatives to work for a reduction in the power of the peerage by excluding eldest sons from sitting in the Commons, prohibiting Scottish peers from representing English boroughs, and inquiring into the "*Secret* Influence of that *Undermining Favourite,* by whose *Arbitrary Measures* and most *Pernicious Counsel* this once Happy and Flourishing Kingdom has been reduced from a State of *Power* and *Triumph* . . . into its present *Miserable* State of *Imbecility* and *Division,* of *Distress* and *Distraction.*"[108] Political societies and electoral clubs also focussed on keeping the causes of the independents' agitation in the public eye. Indeed, the number of radical dining clubs and tavern societies that existed in Norwich in this period was noted with wonder by part-time resident Sylas Neville, who attended a variety of them in the course of his visits to the city.[109] The Norwich Patriots, or Sons of Liberty, and the Free and Easy Society toasted "the glorious 1136" who voted for Beevor in 1768 and the "Independent Commons of the City of Norwich" at their meetings, thus shaping political memories of the election as a bold intervention on behalf of the peo-

---

[107] These figures are for single votes or pairings with Harbord: TB to Townshend, Dec. 7, 1767, quoted in Hayes, "Politics in Norfolk," 193; Phillips, *Electoral Behavior,* 267.

[108] *A Letter to John Day, Esq., Mayor of Norwich, Containing a Letter of Instructions to Harbord Harbord, Esq; and Edward Bacon, Esq . . . Oct. 25, 1768, Being the Day of His Majesty's Happy Accession to the Crown of* THESE REALMS (Norwich, 1768). Accession Day was used by radicals to underscore the contractual nature of the king's power; see Chapter 4. For Almon's reform manifesto see *Political Register,* 12 (1768), 224–5.

[109] Basil Cozens-Hardy, ed., *The Diary of Sylas Neville* (Oxford, 1950), 53–4, 331.

ple's liberties; the Sons of Liberty, who had organized many of the pre-electoral activities in 1768, also canvassed to maintain the parish associations against electoral venality and kept close ties with Wilkite groups in the metropolis.[110] Members of these and other clubs took their principles to the streets on Wilkite holidays, such as April 18, 1770, the day of Wilkes's release, when a number of woolcombers' and weavers' societies marched in procession through the city streets, their members wearing "caps of liberty" while guns were fired in the marketplace (courtesy of the Common Council), bells were rung in the various parishes, and "independent" citizens met in various taverns to drink to the day's event. "The low base-born mechanics," one sympathetic observer sarcastically remarked (alluding to Norfolk MP Thomas De Grey's recent indictment of the Wilkite petitioners), "the very scum of Britons, preserved . . . order and decency."[111]

Many of the dissident political clubs of Norwich were linked by membership and interest with the radical clubs of Norfolk. Free and Easy societies and lodges of Wilkite freemasons existed in a number of Norfolk towns; and the Sons of Liberty corresponded with the Star Club of King's Lynn, which supported the candidacy of Wilkes's friend Crisp Molineux for the city and of Sir Edward Astley for the county in the 1768 election. Though Molineux was not returned in that election, the Star Club and others like it played a pivotal role in procuring the successful return of Astley, who went on to become, with Sir George Savile, one of the leading opposition county MPs of the period.[112] Interestingly, Astley and Harbord became closely linked through their political positions and parliamentary conduct, frequently appearing on each other's behalf at public functions and elections.

At the same time, the election marked the emergence of a new and younger generation of leaders, partially based in the Common Council and including a number of dissenters, who would play an important part in the town's political life for the rest of the century. Surgeons

---

[110] *Norfolk Chronicle* (hereafter *Chronicle*), Sept. 2, Sept. 21, Nov. 25, 1769; *Mercury,* Jan. 2, 9, 1768.

[111] *Mercury,* April 21, 1770; *Chronicle,* April 21, 1770. See also NNRO, MS 487 i, Norfolk Assize Depositions, April 18, 1770. The Common Council also addressed Oliver and Crosby over the printer's case; Harbord delivered the message to them in the Tower: *Chronicle,* March 31, May 11, May 25, 1771.

[112] *Chronicle,* Aug. 5, Sept. 21, 1769; NNRO, Bradfer-Lawrence MSS, 4/10b, Molineux Letter Book, fols. 18–19, Jan. 15, 1768; Philodemos, *A Letter to the Gentlemen, Clergy, Freeholders, Free Burgesses and Other Electors of the County of Norfolk on the Subject of a Remonstrance to the Throne* (Norwich, 1770).

Elias Norgate and Robert Cooper; the merchants James Hudson, John
Corbauld, Reuben Deeve and William Cutting; and wool manufacturers
Thomas Troughton, William Powell, Abraham Robinson and William
Firth were among the independent contingent on the Common Council.
They helped to maintain vital links with the national agitation, involv-
ing themselves in a variety of civic initiatives and providing institutional leadership for the more broadly based radical politics in the
town.[113] In response to the loyalist address to the throne from the aldermen and "Principal Inhabitants" of Norwich in April 1769, which
expressed their approbation of administration actions during the late
riots in the capital, the independent councilors sent a letter of thanks
to Harbord for supporting the rights of citizens by voting to elect
Wilkes which was made available for citizens to sign in the Thatched
Tavern.[114] Some dissenters on the Council and off were also radicalized
by recent events, particularly their elders' recent role in organizing the
formal request for the "junction" between Harbord and Bacon.[115] Indeed, there is ample evidence of an earlier more middling version of
the radical dissenting culture for which Norwich would become famous
in the 1790s. Octagon Chapel in particular was an important source for
members of this community, staffed as it was with a succession of
ministers from Warrington Academy who brought with them the doctrines of materialism and necessity in religion and republicanism in
politics, but both Baptist and Independent congregations also contributed their share.[116] Meeting in taverns and coffeehouses, chapel and
church, these men and women influenced the larger political community through the arenas and institutions of urban culture. Neville, for
example, who was connected with Commonwealth radicalism through
his friendships with Caleb Fleming and Thomas Hollis, frequently discussed religious and political topics in taverns and teahouses with Uni-

[113] Norgate, speaker of the Common Council before becoming an alderman in 1779,
served on several hospital committees and was active in promoting civic medical
amenities; Crowe, councilman and surgeon, alderman in 1772 and at age 24 the
youngest mayor ever elected in the city, was a prominent supporter of the Norfolk
and Norwich Hospital and, with Philip Meadows Martineau (a friend and, again, a
surgeon), founded the public library in 1784: Basil Cozens-Hardy and Ernest A. Kent,
The Mayors of Norwich (Norwich, 1938), 139; NNRO, Assembly Minute Books,
Sept. 21, 1765; MS 453, History of Norwich; Neville MSS, MC7/414–18, passim.
[114] *Mercury,* April 15, 29, May 6, 1769.
[115] Ibid., Nov. 14, 1767.
[116] H. McLachlan, *The Unitarian Movement in the Religious Life of England* (London,
1934), 89–90; NNRO, Octagon Records; St. Mary's Baptist; Old Meeting, Norwich
(Congregational).

tarians like the divines Hoyle and Enfield, the Taylors, Elias Norgate and
Phillip Meadows Martineau, all of Octagon Chapel.[117] Norgate and Martineau were particularly aggressive *agents provocateurs* in the out-of-
doors political culture of Norwich, in the early 1770s forming, for
example, a ''calves'-head'' debating club, for the ostensible purpose of
deliberating whether or not a prime minister was more harmful to English constitutional liberty than royal power.[118] Others became involved in
the Feathers Tavern petition of 1772 (four Norwich ministers signed it)
or produced radical propaganda in favor of petitions and the people's
rights for local and London newspapers; Neville himself wrote letters
and tracts for the radical press in London to accommodate the ardent
campaigns of the indefatigable Fleming.[119] Hence, Norwich dissenters
were both close to the main currents of radical nonconformist thought and
participants in the indigenous varieties of dissidence, illustrating again
the connections of the provincial city with the national political scene.

Above all, perhaps, the events of the late 1760s and early 1770s
consolidated the ideological constructions of Norwich Independency
that would give the cause legitimacy and lasting relevance for a substantial cross-section of citizens. In the historical narrative constructed
by propaganda, addresses, instructions and protests, the 1729 City Election Act, the ''junction'' of economic and political power in the hands
of a small group of elites that had been growing since the middle
decades of the century, and the insidious belief of the aristocracy that
they were entitled to manage local and national political life were all
made to bear the explanatory weight of the current political crisis and
to justify the people's past and current attempts to reassert their liberties
and rights. In doing so, of course, this critique participated in the predominant radical view of the aristocracy as monopolists of land, rotten
boroughs and sinecures, prompting Norwich independents to agree that
the exclusion of peers from the ''popular'' organs of state was necessary to root out corruption and restore public virtue and patriotism.
Aristocrats and other men in power needed to be reminded that they
were but ''machines erected and set up for the public safety and emol-

[117] NNRO, Neville MSS MC7/349, letters 1–5 (1770–2);/747, letters 1–2 (1767, 1777);
/414–17, misc. letters and papers, passim; Neville, *Diary,* 53–4.
[118] NRCL, Colman 46D, *To E——B——,* Norwich, April 10, 1766; *Chronicle,* Feb. 6,
1773.
[119] Congregationalist ministers Samuel Newton and Robert Forsaith and Baptist ministers
Samuel Fischer and Henry Finch signed the petition: Dr. Williams's Library, MS
38.6, Thompson's List, 56. *Chronicle,* Aug. 5, Oct. 29, Nov. 11, Dec. 6, 1769; Neville
MS MC7/349, letter 4, CF to SN, Jan. 3, 1771.

ument," one Norwich writer declared, and that "thousands of their countrymen have equal, or perhaps greater qualifications for their office."[120] But local dissidents were especially articulate in their indictments of the concentration of great wealth and power and the resulting uncontrolled operation of clientage as engines of political and social corruption. Significantly, the problem was frequently articulated through a series of dichotomies: land and industrial manufacturing versus trade and commerce (first adumbrated in 1738–42), great wealth versus small, or the "Landed" versus the "Mercantile Interest," as the writers of the public letter to Bacon put it in 1765.[121] The devastating consequences of the predominance of land and wealth were, by this account, embodied in the current political crisis:

> The large manufacturer, availing himself of these tools of corruption, has . . . the command of (perhaps) one hundred votes, when an Elector, of as much worth and consequence (not in the Manufactory) has but his own single voice in the service of his country . . . Thus the man of property, who scruples to grow rich at the expense of the public treasure, and the nation's morals, [and] cannot use the same corrupt means is cheated of his vote: the little elector is brib'd, or bully'd out of his; the conscientious is persecuted, and the public interest is betray'd.[122]

Thus, only men of sufficient but middling means – "the man of property, who scruples to grow rich at the expense of the public" – could be truly independent, retaining and generating political virtue among their peers, their so-called betters and the "lower class of electors." The attributes of Independency were articulated through the axes of class as well as gender, working to distinguish middle-class and artisanal males as patriotic citizens, in contrast to those below as well as above: the "lower class of electors" as well as the "grandees."

Not surprisingly, Norwich independents continued their efforts to "mark the conduct" of their representatives up to the 1774 election. Both Harbord and the erstwhile Bacon received the Council's formal thanks for voting for the continuation of Grenville's Election Act; and Astley's leading role in the local and national radical political community was acknowledged by the Council's honorary grant to him of the freedom of the city. Perhaps as a result of Bacon's apparent vote against parliamentary corruption and certainly because of Harbord's

[120] *Letter to John Day,* passim; *Chronicle,* March 24, 1769.
[121] NRCL, Colman 46D, *To E——B——* April 10, 1766.
[122] Ibid., *To the Electors of the City of Norwich.*

public espousals of "revolution principles" and unassailable record in the causes of Independency, the radicals did not attempt to put forth a candidate at the 1774 general election, although they did urge local electors to require a pledge from the candidates to support parliamentary reform, and Harbord and Bacon were returned unopposed.[123] The independents' initiatives had made it clear to local elites and county aristocrats that the impact of "influence" could be challenged and even attenuated. In both cases, the practices and expectations of Independency had succeeded in setting the terms of political support.

III. REVOLUTION, REFORM AND THE PEOPLE

We plainly declare ourselves unwilling to commit any more of our National Glory to Attaint, and the Persons of more of our Countrymen to Foreign Hardships and Perils . . . that they shall, by the same Errors, be exposed to the same Calamities and Disgraces which many of those have fallen into who have already been sent forth. Without wise Counsel at Home we cannot have Empire or Reputation Abroad.

Petition of the citizens of Norwich and Norfolk
against the American war, 1778

The perspective forged by the imperatives and diagnoses of Independency influenced local perceptions of the looming imperial crisis. In Norwich, as in most commercial centers in Britain, empire had a hold on citizens that was largely psychological, providing a "frontier" which enhanced aspirations and sometimes profits but always inspired a nationalist ardor to which questions of economic interest could seem irrelevant. Accordingly, when in January 1775, some months before war was declared, a group of merchants, manufacturers and tradesmen met to consider a petition to Parliament against government policy in the colonies strictly on "commercial" grounds, protests were made on two levels. The aldermen and wealthy manufacturers objected to the petition on the basis of the "insignificant" amount of Norwich trade with America, not exceeding £40,000 to £50,000 per year, which, according to them, made such an intervention indefensible, and withdrew with the intention of launching a counter-petition. A second group of

---

[123] *Mercury,* May 25, 1771; May 7, 1774; for Harbord's express support of the delegatory theory of representation see ibid., May 13, 1769. For the excessive optimism of historians and eighteenth-century aristocrats alike about the impact of patrician influence see Phillips, *Electoral Behavior,* 267; for its limitations in large boroughs see Frank O'Gorman, *Voters, Patrons and Parties* (Oxford, 1989).

tradesmen and merchants argued, however, that commercial considerations only placed the colonial situation in too "partial and contracted"
a light: "When a body of people, subjects of the British empire, have
been condemned and punished without examination . . . when the constitutional privilege of trial by jury has been subverted and persons
supposed guilty of criminal offenses are to be brought from America
to England to undergo tedious processes in law," then "the friends of
freedom" in England must express their apprehension over measures
threatening to the constitution.[124] The petition was sent in its original
form, but the meeting had clearly drawn the domestic battle lines which
would remain in place for the next decade.

Once war had broken out, the opposition to it became strident, reflecting in part the ties of kith and kin that East Anglian residents had
long maintained with New England colonists, as well as the more immediate impact of ideological divisions upon perceptions of the crisis.[125] Local writers described the consequences of the war in lurid
colors. "Our empire is split asunder!" one opponent to the war cried;
"the ties which united us are *dissolved in brothers' blood* – and we
can never again be the same people!" Equally vivid language was used
to attack the short-sightedness and impracticality of the old mercantilist
system in general and the war effort in particular.[126] Other anti-war
propaganda deliberately aimed to counter the nationalist appeal being
made in support of the war, particularly after European entry seemed
certain. *Peace with America, or Ruin to England,* an address directed
to the "Husbandmen, Manufacturers, Seamen and Day Labourers of
England," delineated the ways in which war against "our American
brethren" differed morally and politically from the wars for national
preeminence over France and Spain, before examining, in painstaking
detail, America's crucial importance to the whole British empire.
"North America is our grand concern," the writer concluded.[127] On all
counts, imperial ruin, followed by the total annihilation of British constitutional liberty, was predicted as the ultimate end of the measures of
the ministry.

---

[124] *Chronicle,* Jan. 21, 1775.
[125] David Fischer, *Albion's Seed: Four British Folkways in America* (Oxford, 1989), 10–
50, 195–200; Linda Colley, *Britons: Forging the Nation, 1707–1837* (New Haven,
1992), 138–9.
[126] *Chronicle,* Sept. 6, 1776; Jan. 24, 1778; see also June 8, 1776; Jan. 17, 24, March
7, July 18, 1778.
[127] Ibid., March 7, 1778.

The loyalist constituency in Norwich, which increased in size and intensity with the threats of attack on the East Anglian coast, fought back with measures of its own. Its leadership and motivations, as well as those of its opponents, were revealed in the subscription and petitioning movements of 1778. Early in the year Townshend organized a county meeting to rally the friends of government by raising a subscription to aid the war effort. Held at the Maid's Head Inn in Norwich and chaired by North supporter Sir John Wodehouse, the meeting was attended by the Norwich aldermen and other city and county notables, including the Hon. Henry Hobart, the Earl of Buckinghamshire's brother.[128] However, the smooth resolution of the business at hand was disrupted by the intervention of a group of vocal anti-war activists, who objected to the subscription as "dangerous, unconstitutional and calculated only to obtain an apparent sanction of the county of Norfolk to the measures of the Administration." In the ensuing debate, William Windham of Felbrigg made his public political debut by giving a forceful anti-war speech that won for him the subsequent acclaim and support of the Norwich independents. Vindicating the colonists as a "much-injured people" who had shed their blood "in the Common Cause of Empire," he went on to list the imperial, financial, practical, commercial and political catastrophes wrought by the current attempts to vanquish them, concluding that most men of "property, judgement and independency" must demonstrate their enmity to ministers who had "given the most glaring proofs of incapacity and temerity, and afforded the strongest presumption of being inimical to the constitution of the kingdom." His speech was seconded by Thomas Coke, member for Norfolk since his father's death in 1776, before they and a handful of others adjourned to the White Swan in Mancroft to draw up a protest against the subscription for their own supporters to sign.[129]

The county meeting had laid bare the divisions among local elites; it also stimulated the articulation of polarized opinion in the larger political community. The *Chronicle* was filled with angry letters from citizens who railed against "the minions of the Nobility, Gentry and Clergy . . . who are disposed to contribute still farther to the *desolation* of America and the *depopulation* of their *own* Country"; and Wind-

---

[128] This and the following account, unless otherwise noted, is taken from the *Chronicle*, Jan. 31, 1778.

[129] R. W. Ketton-Cremer, *The Early Life and Diaries of William Windham* (London, 1930), 187–8.

ham's speech was reproduced as a handbill.[130] Nonetheless, within one
month, a subscription of £6,599. 11s. 6d. had been raised from 173
individuals – a fitting testimony to the wealth and status of the contributors. Seven Norwich aldermen, including Roger Kerrison, Sir Thomas Churchman, John Gay and Benjamin Day; other bankers and
merchant-manufacturers like the Iveses, Pattesons and Colombines; at
least a dozen Anglican clergymen; assorted county gentry; and Thomas
Beevor himself were among the men who donated to the support of
British troops in America. Crouse noted the association of wealth and
power which supported the pursuit of "bloodthirsty" measures, jux-
taposing the 152 "placemen, pensioners, subalterns, Roman Catholics,
Scotsmen, clergy, yeomen and other plebeians" and 12 men in the
"Trading Interest" who had contributed to the subscription with the
body of independent citizens who had not.[131] And there was substance
to Crouse's satirical parallel, for by early February radical and anti-war
forces had mobilized a monster petition against the American war
which was signed by 5,400 citizens of Norwich and Norfolk.[132] The
petition echoed opposition objections to the loyalist subscriptions of
1745 and anticipated those of the Society for Constitutional Information
in 1782 by questioning the dubious constitutional legality of the current
practice of "Persons of great Power and Rank" raising money and
men for the king's service by means of voluntary contributions. It then
declared the signatories' unwillingness to support the American war
with men or money, and demanded the dismissal of North, an immediate end to the war and an inquiry into its "true grounds and conduct."[133]

These animosities were also expressed in Corporation politics. Although only seven Norwich aldermen had contributed to the subscription, others displayed their support of the government by heading
loyalist celebrations on royal anniversary and victory days or by voting,
as a block, to send congratulatory or commiserating addresses to the
king. A small but significant group of aldermen, including Harbord,
James Crowe and Mayor Nathaniel Roe, supported the independents in
their opposition to the war.[134] In the Common Council, pro- and anti-

---

[130] *Chronicle*, March 14, March 21, April 4, June 6, 1778; *The Speech of the Rt. Hon.
   William Windham* (Norwich, [1778]), in NRCL, Colman 60A, Misc. Broadsides and
   Handbills.
[131] *Chronicle*, Feb. 21, 28, 1778.
[132] Ibid., Feb. 7, 1778; *Annual Register*, 21 (1778), 130–1.
[133] *CJ*, 36 (1776–8), 710–11; PRO, Treasury Solicitor Papers, TS 11/1133, fol. 111.
[134] *Chronicle*, June 6, 1778; June 5, 1779; June 10, 1780; June 9, 1781 (all king's

war forces were more evenly matched. Following the furor raised over the subscription and petition, the two houses of local government tussled over the granting of the city's freedom to General Cornwallis for his "military character" and "constitutional zeal." Passed by a two-thirds majority in the Court of Mayoralty, the grant finally passed the Council by four votes, but only because – according to Crouse, who was a councilman for Mancroft – the members of the lower house had been deceived by the aldermen into thinking that Cornwallis's representation of the state of affairs in America had prompted the ministry to give up the war effort and seek reconciliation. In retaliation and to demonstrate its true loyalties, the Council voted Admiral Keppel the freedom of the city the following February for his support of the "Dignity and Superiority of the British Flag," over the objections of the magistrates.[135] Support for the anti-war petition was also bolstered from the pulpit and in the streets, where firebrands like the Baptist minister Rees David denounced the government's "hypocritical fasts" in support of "arbitrary principles," and no victories over the colonists were ever publicly celebrated.[136]

As rhetoric on both sides suggests, the political battles fought over the war continued and intensified longer-standing struggles in Norwich over the nature and distribution of power in the state, local and central, and carried over into the politics of reform. "Nothing is more talked of here at present than an Association of this county and City," a Norwich correspondent wrote in late 1779. And indeed, a county meeting was called at the Norwich Shire House to consider a pro-reform petition and was attended by prominent politicians of the city and county.[137] The meeting provided an opportunity for loyalist aldermen to get back at their opponents and colleagues who had disrupted their meeting the year before: Bacon, Wodehouse and Kerrison called the meeting "unconstitutional and dangerous" and the petition inconsistent with "the just and necessary power of the representatives of the people," and left the Shire House to raise a formal protest against the petition.[138] Nevertheless, a petition for economic reform was adopted

birthday); May 27, June 3, 1780 (victories); NNRO, Assembly Book of Proceedings, ii (1774–80), Feb. 24, 1778.

[135] NNRO, Assembly Book of Proceedings, Feb. 24, 1778; Feb. 24, 1779; *Chronicle*, Feb. 28, 1779; Feb. 5, 1780.

[136] *Chronicle*, March 31, 1781; May 25, 1782; R. David, *The Hypocritical Fast, with Its Design and Consequences* (Norwich, 1780).

[137] *York Courant*, Jan. 18, 1780; NNRO, MC 50/36/2/3, Folkes MS, Folkes to High Sheriff [Jan. 1780].

[138] *Chronicle*, Feb. 5, 1780; *Mercury*, Feb. 5, 1780; Hayes, "Politics in Norfolk," 202–

on the Yorkshire model, demanding retrenchment in the spending of
public funds, abolition of sinecures and "unmerited" pensions, and
reduction in the emoluments of offices, all in order to shrink that "great
and unconstitutional influence of the Crown" which currently threatened the people's liberties and constitution. A committee of correspondence was then formed which included Harbord, Astley, Fellowes,
Molineux, Townshend and Norwich aldermen Addey and Crowe.[139]

The aldermen's opposition to the petition had done nothing to improve their public relations with the freemen. Crouse printed a score
of letters and essays which denounced the assumptions that "associations [of public-spirited citizens] may tend to create *anarchy* and *confusion*" and that parliamentary representatives were not accountable to
the larger body of English people.[140] The Norwich magistracy showed
their support for such discredited sentiments when they brought forward
a ministerial candidate for Parliament later that year, Alderman John
Thurlow, brother of the lord chancellor, thus dropping the popular anti-
war, pro-reform Sir Harbord Harbord. Although Harbord accommodated them by withdrawing his candidacy, the independents would have
none of it and nominated Harbord and William Windham, currently
abroad, as their candidates. "The present moment is perhaps one of the
most critical that occurred in the history of this country," Crouse announced; "the existence of this once great and powerful Empire depends upon the present conduct of the People."[141] Election propaganda
echoed this warning, lambasting the "Family Compact" of the rich,
intermarried merchant-manufacturers and aldermen who were attempting to force the city's representation on the freemen by obstructing the
electoral process with influence and corruption. "DARE TO BE FREE IN
THE WORST OF TIMES," one handbill challenged; "convince these
Mighty Men, this arbitrary Cabal, that you are not the Dupes they take
you for."[142] Bacon's record as a Norwich representative was unflatter-

3. The protest was ultimately signed by almost 100 county gentry, clergy and aldermen.
[139] *Chronicle,* Feb. 26, 1780; Hayes, "Politics of Norfolk," 203.
[140] *Chronicle,* Feb. 12, 19, 26, 1780.
[141] Ibid., Sept. 9, Sept. 16, 1780; *A Narrative of the Proceedings at the Contested Election for Two Members to Represent the City and County of Norwich in Parliament*
(Norwich, 1780); *Chronicle,* Sept. 9, 1780.
[142] NRCL, Colman 46D, *To the Electors of the City and County of Norwich, from an
Associator* [1780] and *To the Inhabitants of the City of Norwich* [1780]. See also *To
the Independent Citizens and Freeholders of the City and County of Norwich* [1780].
Kerrison, who as treasurer of the guardians of the poor and private banker had a vast
influence, was nicknamed "Roger Cash" by the independents in 1780.

ingly summarized. He had supported "all violent, arbitrary, and UN-CONSTITUTIONAL measures of the government" from general warrants to the present ruinous war, thus furthering despotic principles in government and religion at home and abroad. In contrast, Harbord had supported every measure, in and out of Parliament, that bolstered the causes of liberty and public honor. The contrasts posed by Thurlow and Windham were made equally straightforward: One man stood for ministerial corruption, freemen's subservience to the overmighty magistracy and national slavery; the other, for a free Parliament, imperial preservation and Independency.[143] In both cases, the connections between national and local authority and corruption and virtue were made abundantly clear.

Pro-ministerial propaganda took up a rather different set of issues to construct an equally coherent political community, one that adhered to a revitalized hostility to dissenters and thus repudiated the imperialist, missionary evangelism that dissenters and Anglicans had shared at the end of the last war. Casting dissenters once more as the ultimate subversives in Britain and America, government supporters chose, significantly, colonialist language to belittle and marginalize nonconformists' support of American rights and to demonstrate their dangerous otherness in the domestic and imperial polity. Echoing the Bishop of Bristol's recent declaration that dissenters were "worse than Hottentots" in their principles, Harbord and Windham's supporters were described as "A *motley tribe of various hue . . . Dissenters, Churchmen, Thou and Thee . . .* The Pope's Tiara, Cardinal's Hat." The newly forged unity of the local dissenting community in Norwich against governmental measures was grist to the mill, and voters were called upon to defeat "the DUPLICITY of the QUAKERS and the CANT OF THE PRESBYTERIANS" by electing Bacon and Thurlow.[144]

The election returned Harbord at the top of the poll, with Windham and Thurlow coming within 130 and 96 votes respectively of beating Bacon, who came in second. Independents were jubilant at what they considered to be a stunning stand for the peoples' liberties against elite encroachment, and orchestrated a victory celebration in which Harbord

[143] NRCL, Colman 46D, *A Few Queries Relative to the Parliamentary Conduct of Mr. B***** [1780]; *Questions for the Inhabitants of Norwich to Propose to Themselves at This Important Crisis* [1780]; *Narrative*, 18–21; *Liberty!* (n.d., [1780]); *To the Worthy Freemen and Freeholders of the City of Norwich* [1780].
[144] Keith Feiling, *The Second Tory Party 1714–1832* (London, 1938), 138; *To the Independent Gentlemen, Clergy, Freemen, and Freeholders of the City of Norwich* (Norwich, 1780); *The Congress of Religion*, in *Narrative*, 1–32.

was chaired by an enormous crowd and toasts were made to the "spirit which has now prevail'd," the reduction of the influence of the Crown, peace with America and "Success to Mr. Windham on the first vacancy."[145] Although the proportion of support for the independent candidates in Mancroft and Northern wards had fallen off since 1768, it had grown significantly in the other two wards, so that Harbord and Windham together captured 50 percent or more of the vote in all four in an election with 81 percent turnout.[146] Bacon's return and Thurlow's majority were achieved through the nonresident vote, which swung in their favor. In eighteen parishes – three in Conisford, two in Mancroft, six in Northern and seven in Wymer – a majority of the electors voted for one or both of the independent candidates.[147] Moreover, middling support for the independent candidates was strong: Between half and two-thirds of the middling freemen in Norwich voted for Independency in 1780.[148]

However, the social configuration of ideological politics remained complex, consistent with the predominant interpretation of these struggles as ones of the people's rights, the nature of representation and the consequences of state corruption at home and abroad. Norwich confounds the pattern suggested in some other towns during the American war of a socioeconomic basis to government–opposition splits.[149] The Norwich Corporation was split to a degree unparalleled since 1734. Minor officers, of course, from bailiff to surveyor of lights (windows), voted overwhelmingly for the magisterial candidates, as did clergymen, who were less divided in favor of the government candidates than in 1768. Among the aldermen, five voted for independent candidates, and three more split their votes between the two parties; among the councilors, a smaller percentage in Mancroft and Northern voted for independent candidates than in 1768, and a larger percentage in the other

---

[145] *The Poll for the Members of Parliament for the City and County of Norwich* (Norwich, 1780); *Chronicle,* Sept. 16, 1780.
[146] Harbord and Windham took 57% of the Mancroft vote, 54% of Northern, 51% of Wymer and 50% of Conisford.
[147] O'Gorman, *Voters, Patrons and Parties,* 184. The parishes were: Conisford – St. Etheldred, St. John Sepulchre, All Saints'; Mancroft – St. Stephen and St. Peter's Mancroft; Wymer – St. Benedict, St. Swithin, St. Andrew, St. Michael at Plea, St. Martin at Palace, St. Helen, and Heigham; Northern – St. Michael Coslany, St. Mary, St. Martin at Oak, St. Augustine, St. Clement, St. Saviour.
[148] Phillips, *Electoral Behavior,* 279.
[149] James Bradley has argued for such divisions in Newcastle, Bristol, Great Yarmouth and Liverpool: *Religion, Revolution and English Radicalism* (Cambridge, 1990). For my disagreements with Bradley's interpretation of Newcastle politics see Chapter 7.

two wards. Of the local elite as a whole, however, 45 percent voted for an independent candidate, a proportion twice as high as in 1768. And the 1780 election saw the appearance of Norwich dissenters as a united political interest for the first time since the early Hanoverian era.[150] Besides Norgate, Windham's election agent in 1782–4, prominent dissenters in the radical campaign included William Foster, attorney; William Unthank; Edward Rigby, surgeon; William Wilkins; the Taylors and the Martineaus; and even the Barnards and the Gurneys, who had supported the Corporation candidates in 1768 but whose swing to the opposition political camp inaugurated by the 1780 election endured.

The 1780 election exemplified how divisions over the war produced socially diverse but ideologically coherent groupings while also demonstrating the strong attraction of Norwich middling sorts to opposition politics. Of course, as elsewhere, the self-ascribed group of "independent citizens" included individuals from widely divergent economic and social standing, from professionals, merchants and substantial retailers to small shopkeepers and artisans, and over half of the independent vote came from craftsmen, artisans and laborers – a group which also provided 68 percent of the administration candidates' vote. Only the middling sorts, comprising about one-quarter of the electorate, consistently returned a majority or near-majority of their votes to opposition candidates and provided the backbone of radical politics and the anti-war effort in 1780.[151] As independent leader and Windham agent Elias Norgate noted, the extent of the Corporation interest lay largely with "a few opulent Individuals, whose weight as Manufacturers is counterbalanced by many very respectable in Business" who supported the independent cause, including "the weight of the manufacturing influence, in Numbers and collectively in Importance; a considerable majority of all ranks of Tradesmen, together with a warm attachment of the inferior classes of Freemen."[152]

---

[150] In Mancroft, 75% of councilors voted for at least one Independent candidate but only 38% for both; in Northern, Conisford and Wymer, between 42% and 45% voted for at least one. Aldermen John Addey, Elias Norgate, John Gay (who had also contributed to the subscription for augmenting the king's troops), Thomas Rogers and Nathaniel Roe voted for both independent candidates. For the dissenting vote see Phillips, *Electoral Behavior,* 300–1.

[151] *Chronicle,* Sept. 17, 1776; Phillips, *Electoral Behavior,* 277, 267. Significantly, the proportion of middling sorts supporting independent and radical candidates dropped below 50% (to 40%) for the first time in 1796.

[152] BL, Add. MS 37, 908, fol. 7, Windham Papers, EN to WW, Feb. 19, 1782.

The independents acted quickly to capitalize upon their success in the 1780 election by forming the Independent Association to secure Windham's election at the next vacancy. The Independent Club, or "Free Blues," as it became known, dedicated to the propagation of "*Freedom, Peace, Truth, Resolution . . . Economy and Taste,*" employed strategies and tactics that were scarcely new; but they were exceptionally effective in the highly polarized political atmosphere of Norwich in the early 1780s, allowing the club to take a leading role in corporate and parliamentary politics for the next decade. Besides sponsoring anniversary meetings to commemorate "the glorious 11 September" at inns in all the wards, the club revitalized ward and parish organization in order to contest mayoral and councilor elections, successfully capturing Mancroft ward for its party in 1782 and retaining it until 1789.[153] Most important, the Independents continued to ground their campaigns on the issues raised by the American war and reform. The parliamentary support for Conway's motion to end the war in the spring of 1782, and still more the dismissal of North and instatement of Rockingham, were acclaimed as victories for "the Independent Interest." On the former occasion, the bells of St. Peter Mancroft were rung all day; and on the latter, residents of Surrey Street hung out an enormous transparency inscribed "THANKS TO HIS MAJESTY FOR THE LATE CHANGE IN MINISTERS," the Independent Club held a public meeting to promote a formal thanks to the king from the general body of citizens, and a group of women proposed forming a "patriotic association in defence of their liberties" and addressing the queen on the occasion.[154] As Crouse perceptively noted, much of the public joy displayed stemmed from participants' belief that the new ministers would both end the war and restore "the constitutional rights of the people to equal representation and frequent elections . . . from an inattention to which, all the calamities, the losses, and disgraces which this country has sustained . . . may be ascribed."[155]

---

[153] *Chronicle,* Sept. 14, 1782; July 19, Sept. 13, 1783; Sept. 17, 1785; NNRO, Assembly Minute Books, 1782–9 passim.; NRCL, Colman 3E, *To the Worthy Freemen of Norwich* (Norwich, 1782); *Chronicle,* April 12, May 3, June 2, 1783. The use of anniversary meetings and electoral clubs was imitated by Hobart in his contests with Beevor in 1786–7: *Chronicle,* Sept. 22, 1787.

[154] *Chronicle,* March 9, 1782; NNRO, Assembly Minute Books, April 20, 1782; *Chronicle,* June 8, April 27, May 4, 1782. Both houses of Assembly drew up formal thanks to the king for the change in ministers: NNRO, Assembly Minute Books, April 28, 1782.

[155] *Chronicle,* March 9, 1782.

Yet if North's fall and the end of the war it seemed to augur produced a collective sigh of relief in the nation, they also produced conflicting expectations as to the ultimate consequences of North's
dismissal, and kept political animosities alive. For many members of
the Norwich and Norfolk elite, the new ministry only marked the end
of a politically embarrassing war which had undermined their local
status and authority, and they expected to return to the pre-war status
quo. Their alleged knee-jerk loyalism and hypocrisy shown at a Norfolk
county meeting chaired by former ministerialist Hobart to thank the
king for his change in ministers so irked the Norwich Independents that
efforts were made to raise a protest against it, denying that the assemblage represented the sentiments of the county. "The present ministry
will always be the toast of some folks," one observer sneered,
"whether Lord Rockingham . . . or Lord Beezelbub, be the head of
it."[156] The reforming ministries of Rockingham and Shelburne had the
effect, ironically, of damping down enthusiasm among sectors of the
public in Norwich, as elsewhere, for any further change in the institutions of state. Country gentlemen and civic elites in particular who
had once supported reform retrenched their positions, convinced that
Shelburne's economic reforms had addressed the main causes of corruption and that North's dismissal against the wishes of the king had
proven that the power of the Crown was not as great as had been feared
or that continuing restructuring in the crushing climate of imperial loss
and heavy taxation could be disastrous. Among Norwich Independents
pro-reform sentiment remained strong, and in the autumn of 1782 a
group of sympathetic aldermen and councilors attempted to enlist Norwich in the association for parliamentary reform. But they were blocked
by their colleagues in both houses, a debacle repeated the next spring
when the aldermen suppressed the summons for the upper and lower
houses to meet to consider the Yorkshire proposals, so that too few
members arrived to constitute an Assembly. Although measures to cur-
tail the "dominion of Lords and powerful men" continued to be demanded by Norwich Independents after the defeat of the 1783 reform
initiative, their only solace was to commission a portrait of Harbord to
hang in St. Andrew's Hall in honor of his vote for parliamentary reform
that spring.[157]

---

[156] Ibid., May 4, May 11, 1782.
[157] *Chronicle,* Nov. 23, 1782; June 14, 1783; Jan. 17, 1784; Christopher Wyvill, *Political
Papers,* 4 vols. (London, 1795), iv, 257; Ian Christie, *Wilkes, Wyvill and Reform*
(London, 1970), 170.

The sense of the people

The coalition and Pitt's ministry muddied the waters further while also revealing the diverse range of forces that the anti-war agitation had contained. Consistent with the situation in the county, where the strength of anti-coalition opinion had forced the sitting MP and Foxite Thomas Coke to decline a poll, pro-Pitt sentiments were very visible in Norwich in early 1784. In the Assembly, a formerly pro-North group of aldermen – Harvey, Patteson and Marks – organized an address to the king thanking him for dismissing the "powerful and violent Confederacy of Men" recently at the head of the state, and three months later granted the freedom of the city to Pitt. These actions were representative of a broader cross-segment of community opinion: Many were hostile to the coalition for political and material reasons, such as its attempt to "subvert" the power and influence of the main exporter of Norwich camblets in India and the Far East, the East India Company.[158] However, some Norwich Independents were ardent Foxites (including some dissenters, although many were alienated by the coalition), and they led a large group of citizens who were alarmed by the alacrity with which elites in Norwich and throughout the country "licked the boots of prerogative" in the present circumstances.[159]

Hence, despite the setbacks to the reform movement nationally and locally, issues concerning the proper distribution of power in the state remained important in the 1784 parliamentary election in Norwich. Harbord's popularity was as strong as ever among his constituents (helped in this regard by his absence on the vote over the East India bill), so that he had the support of both parties; the election thus settled down between Windham, a Foxite, whose candidacy the Independents had kept alive through propaganda and public spectacle since 1780, and Hobart, a Pittite, former North supporter and the Earl of Buckinghamshire's brother. Windham's standing among the Norwich voters as an anti-war candidate helped obscure the facts of his former appointment as lord lieutenant of Ireland under the coalition (from which he had quickly resigned) and his lack of enthusiasm for, if not outright opposition to, parliamentary reform; it also helped him weather the crisis brought on by an impolitic pre-electoral speech at the White Swan in which he declared his own *"dispassionate judgement"* to be the "SOLE AND FIXED RULE" of his parliamentary conduct. The Norwich Independents had in fact been sending Windham periodic reviews of

---

[158] NNRO, Assembly Minute Books, Jan. 21, May 3, 1784; *Chronicle,* Feb. 7, 1784, *To the Electors of Great Britain;* John Cannon, *The Fox–North Coalition: Crisis of the Constitution, 1782–4* (Cambridge, 1970).

[159] *Chronicle,* Jan. 31, Feb. 7, 1784.

his political behavior throughout the early 1780s, which Windham took care to answer without ever admitting an obligation on his part to follow constituent instructions. His ill-advised assertion at the White Swan, in a climate in which the nature of representation was a topic of sustained and widespread interest, was a gift to Hobart's campaign. Hobart himself proclaimed his commitment to obey constituency instructions, and his supporters produced an ingenious parody of *Coriolanus,* with Windham as the protagonist and Norgate as Menemius, as well as more prosaic propaganda in which Windham was portrayed as the tool of Fox and Dissent.[160]

The Independents, however, drew upon the standing antipathy to aristocratic power, important in Norwich radical politics since the 1760s, to attack Hobart as a hypocrite, courtier, aristocrat and fop; his past treacherous support of North and the American war were held up as proof of his overriding commitment to support the power of the peerage and his "Lordly family" at the expense of "the Majority of the People." They also pointed out that if deference to majority constituent opinion was inviolable, Harbord could not have opposed the American war. This was obviously the most successful appeal, for Windham beat Hobart in the closest-fought election since 1734, with an 85 percent turnout and only 1.7 percent split voting, the lowest percentage of the century. Harbord, who was unable to canvass because of ill health, received votes from 90 percent of the electorate; Windham received 51 percent and Hobart 48 percent.[161]

The 1784 election was thus fought over established concerns in Norwich politics, continuing alliances that were first forged in the Wilkite agitation and endured through the American war. From the perspective of the Norwich Independents, political divisions were reducible to the conflict of interest between the "majority of the People" and the "Monopolists and Plunderers" who seemed to be in charge of the British state.[162] In this context, Norwich's relations with the Younger Pitt were very telling. Pitt, whose moral probity, commitment to a "re-

---

[160] NRCL, Colman 3E, *To the Electors of Norwich* [1782]; *Chronicle,* Sept. 13, 1783; *The Election Magazine* (Norwich, 1784), 4; Cecelia Baring, ed., *The Diary of William Windham* (London, 1866), 109; Phillips, *Electoral Behavior,* 149; *Election Magazine,* 7–9, 15, 23–6. Windham did in fact adhere to the indisputable right of MPs to act according to their own judgment; see BL, Add. MS 37,908, fols. 7, 15–17, 27–30.

[161] *Election Magazine,* 38–43, 46; *The Poll for Members of Parliament for the City of Norwich, Taken the 5th Day of April, 1784* (Norwich, 1784). Within the wards, Mancroft and Northern returned 56.7 and 51.9 percent of their votes to Harbord and Windham, compared with 50.2 and 48.6 percent in Conisford and Wymer. Figures on split voting from Phillips, *Electoral Behavior,* 216.

[162] *Chronicle,* Sept. 18, 1784.

spectable'' level of reform, sympathy for dissent and yet due regard
for established institutions and property rights made him the champion
of an improbably large number of interests, disappointed various supporters in multitudinous ways. In Norwich, the Independents were suspicious if not hostile to this opponent of Fox who was also the friend
of reform, whereas "Court" supporters like Hobart were wont to sing
his praises. Moreover, middling retailers and tradesmen in Norwich
were quickly roused to an intense dislike of Pitt by his series of commercial measures of 1783–5, and organized and demonstrated against
them. The "Merchants, Bankers and Traders" of Norwich sent instructions to their MPs to obtain a repeal of the receipt tax in November
1783; the "Shopkeepers of Norwich" did likewise with regard to the
shop tax in 1785; and manufacturers petitioned against Pitt's Irish commercial propositions the same year. On the day on which the shop tax
of 1785 went into effect, the retailers of Norwich draped their shops
in black mourning crepe and staged a mock funeral for "the Death of
Commerce" which ended with Pitt's effigy being hung and burnt on
Castle Hill, "amidst the groans and hisses of the oppressed
thousands."[163] It was not until the French wars that these groups accommodated themselves to his ministry.

Yet it was also under Pitt's administration that Norwich citizens (and
indeed, those in other towns in Norfolk) produced their only petition
for parliamentary reform since 1780.[164] Pitt's reform proposals for abol-
ishing thirty-six rotten boroughs, redistributing their representation
among the metropolis, the counties and unrepresented towns, and opening up closed boroughs to greater popular control may have alienated
his radical supporters by their inadequacy but seemed to the Norwich
citizens assembled at Guildhall to tackle the central problem of nonaccountability in the state. As James Hudson and the Reverend Mr.
Morgan put it in their speeches before the crowd, these measures could
restore Parliament to its original principles, the deviations from which
had been proven in the House's inability

> upon many occasions, to speak the sense of its Constituents, and to
> pursue the interests of the People, especially in supporting the Min-
> ister of the day in carrying on the late unnatural and ruinous war,
> which has entailed upon us, and it is feared, our posterity, irreme-
> diable evils.

[163] Ibid., Nov. 15, 1783; May 28, July 9, 1785.
[164] Petitions in favor of Pitt's plan for parliamentary reform were also sent from Great
Yarmouth and King's Lynn: Cannon, *Parliamentary Reform,* 92.

The petition was read and copies of it left to be signed "by freemen and other inhabitants" at Johnson's and Tuck's coffeehouses. Though it implicitly endorsed the entire Pittite program, the petition explicitly demanded only the restoration of triennial Parliaments and a "more equal representation of the people" – a surprising, yet curiously appropriate "old Tory" position for Norwich's radical Whigs to take.[165] But it did little to resolve the issues of accountability that the Independent cause had raised and that would continue to be canvassed in the next two decades. In the meantime, the reformist impulses of the Norwich middle classes would be vented in such worthy undertakings as the Society for Universal Good Will, devoted to aiding "Scots, natives of Ireland, and other foreigners," and the Society for the Abolition of the Slave Trade.[166]

Hence, bolstered by traditions of civic participation and new and more complex forms of political organization and leadership, Norwich radicalism differed in focus and substance from that of Newcastle, where decades of political exclusion had played a major part in igniting the flame of dissident politics. Norwich's quasi-democratic institutions of local government, the official representation given to Norwich dissidence in the Assembly and Court of Mayoralty, as well as elite leadership and recognition, worked to sustain a wide-ranging oppositionist campaign in the people's name to render established institutions more accountable to the governed. In so doing, of course, they bestowed those institutions with a legitimacy that would ultimately work against their more radical reform. If the overmighty men in power locally and nationally could be circumvented by the interventions of the people in institutional and extra-institutional politics, then the accountability of the House of Commons could be assured, and more fundamental democratic restructuring would be unnecessary. Such a position was somewhat to the "right" of the artisanal radicalism of the 1790s for which Norwich would shortly be renowned; but it helps restore the historical

[165] NNRO, MC 7/758, Neville papers, handbill, March 8, 1785; *Chronicle,* March 5, 12, 1785. The vagueness in wording was also part of the reformers' strategy to draw in the greatest support; see *A Second Address to the People, from the Committee of Association* (York, 1781).
[166] *An Account of the Scots Society in Norwich, 1775–84* (Norwich, 1784); *A List of the Society for the Abolition of the Slave Trade* (London, 1788); women were members of both societies. For Norwich politics after 1785: Albert Goodwin, *The Friends of Liberty: English Democratic Movement in the Age of the French Revolution* (Cambridge, Mass., 1979); C. B. Jewson, *The Jacobin City* (Glasgow, 1975). Much work remains to be done on women Jacobins of the 1790s.

specificity of political dissidence in the first three decades of George III's reign. Arguably, Norwich radicalism, grounded upon the city's open if increasingly outmoded political structures, provided a sterling example of the way the traditions of eighteenth-century English populism could work among the middling classes to privilege resistance over proportional representation, the people's right to call their governors to account, and their viable, protected role in the political process as "virtual" or actual electors over their proportional, one-to-one vote. Hence membership in the SCI was thin locally before 1789, and support for its radical goals of universal manhood suffrage and annual Parliaments underwhelming. Major Cartwright's criticisms of the assumptions of moderate reformers – "the electors are *not* the People," he asserted; "they are nothing more than a faint shadow of the People" – lacked resonance and urgency in Norwich, where most of the current generation of radical activists believed that the two were close enough not to warrant further inquiry into their relationship. On the other hand, the ideological constructions of Independency endorsed extra-legal qualifications for citizenship – for example, habits of mind and political practices that sought to procure freedom from the restraints of "great men's" clientage in social and political as well as economic terms – that also enabled a wider range of artisanal and middle-class subjects, men and women, to enact or imagine their own claims to political status.[167]

The politics of Independency of Norwich thus meshed with and contributed to the national radical campaign in discourse and practice. Despite their differences, the spirit and substance of the radical agitations in Norwich and Newcastle shared a conceptualization of the status quo that damned the politics of the overmighty and the corruption of the nation's representative institutions which prevented them from attending to the wishes and sensibilities of independent citizens. "Local" or provincial agitations like these (of which the Association movement must be considered as one) in the end constructed the various "national" campaigns to create alternative political communities and notions of political subjectivity that fit uneasily with or straightforwardly contradicted those encoded in the political culture of oligarchy and deference. In both Newcastle and Norwich, the middling and artisanal classes seized the political initiative in the name of the people in order

---

[167] As is clear from Jewson, *Jacobin City,* and the correspondence of Anne Plumptre in NNRO, MS 4262.

to stake their own claims in national affairs. The strategies, concerns, remedies and heterogeneous personnel of these movements provided a lasting legacy for demotic politicians in future decades.

Finally, the distinct yet ultimately inextricable nature of local and national politics was demonstrated during the American war, when both the war and the reactions it galvanized at home deepened and enriched the current political critique in ways that had a profound impact on domestic sensibilities. The logic of opposition to the war led, inexorably, to an opposition to the government which perpetuated it, and corroborated the radical view that the British government could not represent the will of the people. These views were not "determined" by or even necessarily related to economic dislocation or hardship.[168] Rather, the most devastating perception was that the war for the colonies had the same consequences as political measures at home, impoverishing the poor, punishing the weak or different, and aggrandizing the corrupt, dependent and avaricious. Unlike the wars with France a decade later, when people of property and many without rallied in support of the government, political divisions during the American war were too virulent to be salved by the fictions of national, social and cultural unities. In this sense, the war was more than a divisive issue in local and national politics for a decade: It produced and legitimated categories of inclusion and exclusion, belonging and otherness that would impact popular politics for the next half-century.

---

[168] Economic recovery in Norwich after 1785 was quick, and local merchants enriched themselves on privateering and prizes taken from the French as much as merchants elsewhere. See NNRO, Neville Papers, MC 7/417, Phillip Martineau to N., March 30, 1779.

Conclusions: The people, the state and the subject

I pretend not to prophetic intuition, but, from public appearances,
Great Britain seems hastening to a revolution or a dissolution.
                              Indignatus, *Norfolk Chronicle,* July 18, 1778

A foolish or effeminate Prince, surrounded by a venal Senate, to
whom the very name of virtue is either unknown or odious, was
not born to retain dominions acquired by republican wisdom, and
republican valour: nor could a People, which had lost all pretensions to govern itself, long expect to rule over others.
                              SCI, *The Second Address to the Public* (1782)

Almost a century has now revolved since the memorable era of the
Revolution . . . Since that period Britain has acquired a new political existence, and held a bolder career in arts and arms. From the accession of Queen Anne to the commencement of the American war,
she was the first power in Europe, and the prime mover in the political system. Seated on a small island, hardly to be distinguished in
the map of the world, she spread over the four continents, held the
balance among the nations, and gave law to the globe.
   Everything human, however, has its period: Nations, like mortal
men, advance only to decline; dismembered empire and diminished
glory mark a Crisis in the constitution; and, if the volume of our
frame be not closed, we have read the most brilliant pages of our
history.
               "The English Constitution," *Newcastle Chronicle,*
                                            Aug. 19, 1786

As these quotations suggest, in the second and third decades of George
III's reign English people found themselves in a peculiar position –

peculiar because current experience seemed to contradict the goals and results of half a century of successful wars against their European rivals for empire and glory. In 1778 and as late as 1786, the England that had orchestrated British imperial ascendancy seemed to be in danger of a precipitous collapse, its martial spirit sapped and the components of the national identity, the people's relationship to the state, and the nation's role in the world unintentionally reconfigured. However brief in duration, it was a moment that gave many English people pause, forcing them to confront their history and future, a moment intimated by Edward Gibbon's magisterial jeremiad on Roman decline and evoked most recently, if less resonantly, by Alan Bennett's dramatic Tory panegyric to George III.[1]

Yet prior to this crossroads, the national becoming had been no less fraught, if somewhat less palpable, and the politics of "the people," frequently if not invariably oppositionist, played no small role in negotiating and defining its import and implications. It "is quite wrong," Linda Colley has recently averred, to assert that "it was only through oppositional activity that men and women outside the governing elite advanced their claims to recognition."[2] Whether this is an empirical or moral admonishment is unclear, but in either case it was in fact oppositionist politics and patriotism that first formulated and retailed across a broad social spectrum the notions of political subjectivity and rights that justified extra-parliamentary participation in the political process and accordingly were appropriated by both radical and loyalist political cultures in the later decades of the century. The resilience and vibrancy of the politics which claimed to be animated by "the sense of the people" have been documented in this study. Josiah Tucker, quoted at the beginning of this book, underestimated its participants' resourcefulness and aspirations when he said the people "have nothing to fear, and very little to hope from the Great," for, particularly as the century progressed, increasing numbers of citizens became conscious of their political importance and claimed the right to regulate their superiors' political behavior. Initially, the vehicle for this increased public involvement was party. In the first half of the century, partisan and dynastic disputes kept the people politically engaged, and this engagement was legitimated by disgruntled and excluded elites' deliberate appeals to the people for help back into office. The Tory–patriot op-

---

[1] Edward Gibbon, *The Decline and Fall of the Roman Empire* (London, 1776–88); Alan Bennett, *The Madness of George III* (London, 1992).
[2] *Britons: Forging the Nation, 1707–1837* (New Haven, 1992), 372.

position of the 1730s and 1740s simultaneously exploited and expanded the political nation, ultimately galvanizing a national agitation that could exert effective pressure on those within doors. In the second half of the century, long after Tory proscription had ended, the causes and rhetoric of radical politics continued to extend and enmesh the popular and the political in ways that contested and resisted elite hegemony while also mapping out the terrain and audiences for elite authoritarian appropriations of radical strategies and techniques. Throughout the period, the forms and expansion of the state and empire fostered and renewed an anti-corruption critique of authority that identified the social, moral and national ills with the distribution and exercise of political power. By conceptualizing the state as an arena where a variety of groups contended and illegitimate interests could hold sway, this critique valorized the people outside the state as the final arbiters of the legitimacy and effectiveness of power within it.

The extra-parliamentary political culture of the eighteenth century was not necessarily urban, but it was primarily so. Indeed, it was the larger provincial centers that, in conjunction with the capital, served as engines of the anti-Walpolean campaign and radical agitation under George III. Besides evincing an enduring electoral vitality, towns maintained resources and arenas which stimulated political consciousness and facilitated the emergence of a self-generating extra-parliamentary politics. In Newcastle and Norwich, as in other towns across the country, the arenas of provincial urban culture, from news rooms, libraries and coffeehouses to civic charities and the press, provided some of the crucial cultural bases from which men and women situated between the great and the poor could claim or aspire to "independence" in political and social, as well as economic, terms. Provincial urban culture imbricated the national contexts of prosperity and imperial expansion with local change and contestation, multiply constituting and signifying the "national" in the process. Above all, urban political culture supported the sites and practices which enabled "the people" to transform themselves into citizens through their actions in the public sphere, despite the strengths of clientage, oligarchy, and gender and class inequalities.

The ideologies and practices of extra-parliamentary politics could also work to delimit the political nation. The exigencies and traumas of war and empire that forged the nation-state itself authorized masculinist definitions of patriotism and the national character that, at different moments, excluded or subordinated a range of "others" within the national and imperial polity: women, effeminates, aristocrats;

Catholics, Dissenters, Jews; Scots, ''Indians,'' Africans; slaves and the
''rabble.'' The ideological strategies that defined relations with the state
in terms of sexual, class or racial difference thus privileged the claims
of some white middling or upper-class men to political power, and
although they did not prevent other groups from identifying with the
imperatives of citizenship, they did devalue or obscure the latter's contributions to national affairs and naturalized their continuing exclusion
from formal politics.

Of course, as Michael Taussig has recently argued, the ''discovery''
that race, gender and nation are social constructions is not an end in
itself but only a means to begin answering the question ''If life is
constructed, how come it appears so immutable?''[3] The short answer
is that it did not always, at least not invariably. For the language and
strategies of oppositionist and radical patriotism challenged the seemingly ineffable structures and imperatives of patrician hegemony by
defining the patriot through position and practice rather than birth,
through merit and discipline rather than entitlement. Oppositionist ideologies endorsed extra-legal qualifications for citizenship – attributes
of mind and taste (''public-spiritedness,'' disinterest), activism in the
public good, freedom from the restraints of patrician clientage in cultural, political and economic realms – that, if still partially predicated
upon the hierarchies of property and gender, also enabled a wider range
of individuals to enact or imagine their own claims to political subjectivity. Indeed, the anti-aristocratic critique developed by radical journalists, polemicists and clergymen in the 1770s and 1780s was
appropriated by Mary Wollstonecraft, who deployed its language and
images of sexual difference to lambaste social and political artifice and
the gender order itself – all ''hereditary distinctions'' of birth that she
found abhorrent, degrading and in need of extirpation. Seeing in the
''masculine'' as then conceived much to admire and in the ''feminine''
too little, and recognizing both as cultural constructions that were not
anchored to biological bodies, Wollstonecraft recommended that men
and women, the effeminate and feminized alike, become more
''manly,'' austere, forceful, disciplined and self-directed in order to
forge the virtuous polity that would vindicate their rights.[4] Despite its

---

[3] *Mimesis and Alterity: A Particular History of the Senses* (New York, 1993), xvi.
[4] See *A Vindication of the Rights of Women,* ed. Miriam Brody Kramnick (New York,
1985), passim and esp. 186–92, 256–8. I am aware, of course, of Wollstonecraft's
concomitant essentialism with regard to ''nature'' and motherhood, but too little is
made of her more liberatory play with political and gender categories in the text.

shifts and mutations through the axes of class, nationality and gender, it is important to recognize in the political critique proffered by eighteenth-century patriots the rudimentary construction of a nonessentialist subject, defining the self in terms of qualities of mind, performance and position rather than biology, "nature," or innate characteristics.

Finally, national as well as supra-national bonding, and domestic as well as imperial relations, are all family romances, in that they are all a working out of desire and prohibition, authority and subordination, inequalities and hierarchies. This study has emphasized the immense importance of empire to domestic political sensibilities and consciousness in the processes of nation- and state-building. The patriotic opposition under Walpole, for whom success was inextricably tied to demands for war with Spain and colonial acquisition, actively cultivated nascent imperialistic sensibilities, defining English identity not only in terms of birthrights, liberties and constitutional traditions, but also of English expansion in the world. This identification of "patriotism" with empire, so useful in mobilizing political support from among the middling and commercial classes, was strengthened by Pitt in the late 1750s and still exploited by the Wilkite radicals in the 1760s and early 1770s. The American war brought an abrupt end to this perquisite of political dissidence, if not to its inflection of extra-parliamentary politics as a whole. The colonial crisis was perceived by many to be part of a larger political problem, one that stemmed from the corruption and nonaccountability of the British state; it caused many citizens to question the much-vaunted excellence of British political institutions themselves. The American conflict thus had lasting repercussions, the effects of which would linger long after wartime battles and antagonisms had been forgotten. Indeed, the vehemence of British reaction to Revolutionary France was calibrated to no small degree by the dismay, shock and denial produced by the war for America and imperial dismemberment, when the former colonists' repudiation of British parliamentary institutions and identities led English people ultimately to assert and defend with an unparalleled aggressiveness their superiority and excellence over all contenders. In the meantime, however, English men and women in the 1780s looked back on the preceding century with an injured and nostalgic pride, mesmerized by the essential unity which empire seemed to have imparted to past national experience, yet convinced that the zenith of British glory had already been passed. "If the volume of our frame be not closed," the Newcastle writer noted, "we have read the most brilliant pages of our history."

Of course, the nature of empire would soon be redefined, and imperial aspirations rekindled, in the brighter and more complacent light of nineteenth-century experience. The British state itself was acquiring a new respectability from 1782 onwards – that is, after the fall of North and the eventual ascent to power of the young William Pitt – that segued neatly into a more authoritarian and disciplinary attitude toward its subjects at home and overseas. As the 1790s progressed, the state began to be seen not as a corrupt structure operating for the benefit of the "Court" and its minions but as a necessary force for stability and order in dangerous times, and a proper place for the employment of gentlemen, if not scholars. Not coincidentally, as the state became more "respectable" (a process not unrelated to its increasing representation by the king, a figure whose value as symbol for the state and cynosure for national sentiment grew as his powers declined),[5] the status and acknowledgment of "the people" outside its networks underwent continuing contestations and transformations. The Court Whig view of the state as the locus of a sovereignty from which there could be no appeal was gaining ground among a number of social groups who formerly had insisted that the people were the ultimate arbiters of political power, and the "sense of the people" was becoming contested by "public opinion" or the "middle class" as the tribunal outside the state to which authority must be held to some degree accountable.[6] These shifts registered more than the gradual yielding of the categories of Enlightenment universalism to High Victorian particularism and scienticism; they also exhibited a shift in the alignment of forces for stability and property at all levels on behalf of the state and the establishment. Nevertheless, for a broad swath of the less contented, from Chartists to suffragettes, the English people's right to resist and cashier their governors and to advance their claims for full citizenship by acting like political subjects would continue to be embraced for a century and more to come. Latter-day dissidents clearly owed more to the "sense of the people" in the Hanoverian decades than they, or their historians, are willing to let on.

[5] Colley, *Britons*, 195–236.
[6] See, e.g., Dror Wahrman, "Virtual Representation: Parliamentary Reporting and the Languages of Class in the 1790s," *P & P*, no. 130 (1992), 111–12; Patrick Joyce, *Visions of the People: Industrial England and the Question of Class 1848–1914* (Cambridge, 1991).

Appendix: Women's occupations in four urban directories, ca. 1768–1783

I. PROFESSIONAL

Appraisers and Auctioneers	2	Midwives	2

II. MERCHANTS/MANUFACTURERS

Brewer	6	Brokers	2
Brandy and Wine Merchant	1	Corn and Coal	1
Butter and Cheese Merchants	2	Hop Merchant	1
Glass Warehouse	1	Linendrapers	16
Smallware Manufacturer	1	Woolendrapers	2

III. RETAILERS

Bakers	6	Boarding Schools	14
Butchers	8	Boarding Houses	3
Barber and Peruke Maker	1	Chandler	1
Cheesemonger	1	China Dealers	2
Clockmaker	1	Confectioners	8
Coachmaker	1	Dealer by Commission	1
Druggist	1	Flour Shops	2
Fruit Dealer	1	Glovers	2
Grocers and Tea	19	Haberdashers	2
Hackney Horse Keeper	1	Hucksters	9
Hardware and Toy Shops	7	Mantua Makers	9
Inn and Tavernkeepers	55	Palls and Cloaks	43
Milliners	43	Pawnbrokers	3
Pastry Schools	3	Potseller	1
Perfume Dealers	3	Shopkeepers	6
Robemaker	1	Spirit Dealers	2
Silversmith	1	Tallow Chandler	1
Tailors	4	Writer	1
Tobacconists	2		

IV. CRAFTS/ARTISANS

Anchorsmith	1	Blacksmith	1
Blackworker	1	Braziers	2
Bricklayer	1	Brickmaker	1
Callenderers	4	Chairmaker	1
Clothpresser	1	Cook	1
Cooper	1	Corkcutter	1
Duffelmaker	1	Dyers	4
Hatters	4	Hosiers	6
Hotpressers	2	Leather Cutters	2
Patten and Trunk Maker	1	Plumbers and Glaziers	4
Saddler	1	Shagmaker	1
Shoemaker	1	Tinner	1
Throwsterers	5	Weaver	1
Woolcomber	1		

V. AGRICULTURAL

Cowkeeper	1	Gardener	1
Farmers	2		

Sources: Whitehead's Newcastle Directory (Newcastle, 1778; repr. 1889); *Norwich Directory or Gentlemen's and Tradesmen's Assistant* (Norwich, 1783); *Manchester Directory for the Year 1772* (London, 1772); *Liverpool's First Directory* (Liverpool, 1766; repr. 1907).

Select bibliography of primary sources

I. MANUSCRIPTS

Avon Reference Library

Calcott MS
Society for the Reformation of Manners
Gough Somerset MS

British Museum

Additional Manuscripts:
Arderon (27,966)
Bowes (40,478)
Egmont (47,096)
Newcastle (32,686, 32,703–4, 32,867)
Joseph Richmond (27,420)
Strype (5,853)
Windham (37,873, 37,908)

Gateshead Central Library

Cotesworth MSS
Ellison MSS

Huntington Library

Elizabeth Robinson Montagu MSS
Pulteney MSS
Townshend MSS

Liverpool Library and Record Office

Holt-Gregson MSS

Norfolk and Norwich Record Office

Bradfer-Lawrence MSS, Crisp Molineux Letter Book
Gurney MSS
MS History of Norwich
Ketton-Cremer MSS
Mackerell's History of Norwich
Massey, Acta Norvicensia
Neville MSS
Transactions of the Fraternity of the United Friars

Norwich City Records

Assembly Books of Proceedings
Assembly Minute Books
City Chamberlain Accounts
Guardians of the Poor Minute Books
Mayor's Court Books
Norfolk Assize Depositions
Norfolk and Norwich Hospital Minutes and Orders
Papists' Returns, 1717, 1743–45
St. George's Company, Wastebook
William Clarke's notes on St. George's Company
Ratebooks, 1733–5, 1773–5

Clerical, Episcopal and Nonconformist Records

Churchwardens' Accounts

St. Andrew's
St. Benedict's
St. Clement's
St. George's Colgate
St. George's Tombland
St. John Timberhill
St. Michael at Plea
St. Margaret's Mancroft
St. Peter's Mancroft
St. Peter Parmentergate

Visitation Records

Registers of Incumbents
Visitation Books
Visitation Processes
Visitation Returns
Register of Meeting Houses
List of Popish Recusants

Nonconformist Meeting Houses

Octagon Chapel, Church trusts, Building accounts, Misc. records
St. Clement's Colgate (Baptist), Church Book
St. Mary's (Baptist), Church Books
St. Mary's Congregational (Independent), Church Books

Northumberland Record Office

Allgood (Nunwick) MSS
Blackett (Maften) MSS
Carr-Ellison (Hedgeley) MSS
Delavel MSS
Ridley (Blagdon) MSS

Society of Antiquaries MSS

Election ephemera, 1741–87
Bakers and Brewers' Company Records
Northumberland Quarter Sessions, Papers and Orders, 1710–16
Churchwardens' Accounts: St. Nicholas's Parish, St. Andrew's Parish

Visitation Books

Archedeacon Sharp, 1723
Bishop Chandler, 1736
Unspecified, 1774

Tyne and Wear Archives

Armourers, Feltmakers and Curriers' Company, Order and Minute Books,
    Stewards' Correspondence
Bewick Papers, Cash and Work Books
Maude-Ogden MSS
Hanover Square Chapel Minute Books
Barber-Surgeons' Company, Minute and Order Books
Bricklayers' Company, Account and Minute Books

Butchers' Company, Minutes and Disbursements
Carpenters' Company, Accounts
Coopers' Company, Minute and Account Books
Cordwainers' Company, Order and Cash Books
Goldsmiths' Company, Minute and Account Books
Hostmen's Company, Minute and Account Books, Register of Members
Joiners' Company, Order Book
Merchant Adventurers' Company, Journals and Account Books
Sailmakers' Company, Minute Book
Skinners and Glovers' Company, Order and Account Books
Trinity House, Journals and Account Books
Upholsterers, Tinplate Workers and Stationers, Minute Book

Newcastle Corporation Records

All Saints Vestry Minutes
City Chamberlains' Accounts
Common Council Act Books
Common Council Minute Books
Calendar of Common Council Minute Books
Mayoral Court Books
Newcastle Dispensary, Annual Reports
Royal Victoria Infirmary, Annual Reports and House Committee Books
Misc. Petitions, etc. (394/10–29)
Misc. Freemen's Records (596/7–26)
Misc. Corporation Notes (109/1–3)
Quarter Session Minute Books
St. John's Vestry Minutes
Ratebooks
Land Tax Books

Public Record Office

Assize Court Records, Northeastern Circuit (Assi 45/2–4)
Home Office, Petitions (HO 55/2–28)
King's Bench Court, Affadavits (KB 1/5–11)
State Papers, Domestic (SP 35, 44)
Treasury Solicitors' Papers (TS 11/388, 961, 1133)

SPCK Library

Letterbooks of Society for the Reformation of Manners

Dr. Williams's Library

Evans MS
Thompson's List

Worcester City Record Office

Audit of City Accounts
Chamber Order Books

II. NEWSPAPERS AND PERIODICALS

Periodicals

Annual Register
The Freeholder
Freeholder's Magazine
Gentleman's Magazine
Lancashire Magazine, or the Manchester Museum
London Magazine
Monthly Review
Newcastle General Magazine
Newcastle Literary Register
Newcastle Weekly Magazine
Political Controversy, or Weekly Magazine
Political Register
The Political State of Great Britain
Protestant Packet, or British Monitor
Scots Magazine
Universal Magazine
Universal Spectator

London Newspapers

The Champion
The Craftsman
Daily Courant
Daily Gazetteer
Evening Post
Examiner
Flying Post
Fog's Weekly Journal
General Evening Post
London Evening Post
Middlesex Journal
Mist's Weekly Journal
Monitor
Parliamentary Spy
Post-Boy
Post Man
Public Advertiser

Read's Weekly Journal
Robin's Last Shift
St. James's Evening Post
The Shift Shift'd
Shift's Last Shift
Weekly Journal, or British Gazeteer
Weekly Journal, or Saturday's Post
Weekly Pacquet
The Whisperer

Provincial Papers

Chester Courant
Bristol Gazette and Public Advertiser
Bristol Post-Boy
Bristol Postman
Cumberland Pacquet; or, Ware's Whitehaven Advertiser
Felix Farley's Bristol Journal
Gloucester Journal
Leeds Mercury
Liverpool General Advertiser
Manchester Mercury
Newcastle Chronicle
Newcastle Courant
Newcastle Journal
Newcastle Weekly Intelligencer
Norfolk Chronicle, or Norwich Gazette
Norwich Gazette
Norwich Mercury
Salisbury Journal
Worcester Postman
York Courant

III. PAMPHLET AND SERMON COLLECTIONS

Avon Reference Library
Beinecke Library, Yale University
British Library
Guildhall Library, London
Houghton Library, Harvard University
Huntington Library
Institute of Historical Research, University of London
Liverpool Library and Record Office
Manchester Central Library
Newcastle Central Library
Norwich City Library

York City Library
Dr. Williams's Library

IV. DIRECTORY AND POLLBOOK COLLECTIONS

Institute of Historical Research, University of London
Newcastle Central Library
Norwich City Library
Widener Library, Harvard University

Index

Club of 27, 64
clubs and societies, 31, 34, 47, 54–
  73, 91–2, 146, 191–2, 210, 214,
  230; nonpolitical, 61–3, 190–1;
  oppositionist, 63–70, 163, 160–6;
  pro-American, 240; Wilkite, 69,
  210, 214–15, 217; *see also*
  Newcastle; Norwich
Cobbett, William, 237
Cocoa Tree, 64
Coercive Acts, 239
coffeehouses, 30, 32, 47, 145, 290,
  305, 325, 342, 414, 431, 437; *see
  also* urban culture
Coke, Sarah, 48
Coke, Thomas, 419, 428
Colchester, 88, 239
Colley, Linda, 4, 174, 436
Colombine, Peter, 380, 410, 420
Constitution Club (of Norwich), 64,
  149, 402
Constitutional Club of Newcastle,
  Northumberland and Durham, 69–
  70, 344–5, 347
Constitutional Society (of London),
  221, 240
Cook, Capt. James, 275
Cornwall, 260
Cotesworth, William, 291, 319–21
Coventry, 99, 128, 151, 177, 229,
  239, 243, 296
Cowper, Mary, first Countess
  Cowper, 99
Craftsman, The, 27, 123, 127, 130,
  132, 134, 325, 389
Crisis, The (1714), 100
Crisis, The (1775–6), 242–3
Crosby, Brass, 219, 266, 348
Crossgrove, Henry, 114, 378–9,
  385–6, 392, 398, 400, 402
Crouse, John, 420–2, 426
Crowe, James, 422
Crowe, Rev. William, 246, 278
Cruger, Henry, 247
Cumberland, 249
Cumberland, Duke of, *see* William
  Augustus, Duke of Cumberland
Curwen, Samuel, 257

customs, popular: and print culture,
  33; and political culture, 21–2,
  106–7, 111, 125–6, 231–4, 360
Cycle Club, 64

Daily Gazetteer, 182
Dalrymple, Sir John, 241
Dalton, Isaac, 113
Darlington, 189
Dartford, 196
Dartmouth, 159
David, Rees, 246, 421
Day, Thomas, 260, 262, 273
*Declaration of Those Rights of the
  Commonalty of Great-Britain*, 261
Declaratory Act, 248, 253
Delaval, Sir Francis Blake, 341
Delaval, Thomas, 341, 347–8, 351–
  2, 370–2
Denby, 151
Derwentwater, James Radcliffe, third
  Earl of, 33, 321–2
Devizes, 230
Devonshire, Georgiana Cavendish,
  fifth Duchess of, 51
dissenters, political role of, 97–8,
  107–8, 121–2, 270–1; *see also*
  Newcastle; Norwich
Dodd, Anne, 48
Dorchester, 88
Dover, 229
Durham, 216, 232, 347

Earl of Mar Marr'd, 95, 385
East India Bill, 428
Edinburgh, 141, 151, 167, 366
effeminacy, 71–3, 94–5, 185–205,
  219–21
Effingham, Thomas Howard, Earl of,
  248, 256, 357, 362
elections, parliamentary, 9, 36, 85,
  98–9, 106, 121, 150–1, 177, 228–
  30, 240–1, 265, 268; *see also*
  Newcastle; Norwich.
elections, civic, 150, 240–1; *see also*
  Newcastle; Norwich
electoral oaths and pledges, 133,
  228, 230, 327, 336, 342, 347

Past and Present Publications

General Editor: PAUL SLACK, *Exeter College, Oxford*

Family and Inheritance: Rural Society in Western Europe 1200–1800, edited by Jack Goody, Joan Thirsk and E. P. Thompson*
French Society and the Revolution, edited by Douglas Johnson
Peasants, Knights and Heretics: Studies in Medieval English Social History, edited by R. H. Hilton*
Town in Societies: Essays in Economic History and Historical Sociology, edited by Philip Abrams and E. A. Wrigley*
Desolation of a City: Coventry and the Urban Crisis of the Late Middle Ages, Charles Phythian-Adams
Puritanism and Theatre: Thomas Middleton and Opposition Drama under the Early Stuarts, Margot Heinemann*
Lords and Peasants in a Changing Society: The Estates of the Bishopric of Worcester 680–1540, Christopher Dyer
Life, Marriage and Death in a Medieval Parish: Economy, Society and Demography in Halesowen 1270–1400, Zvi Razi
Biology, Medicine and Society 1840–1940, edited by Charles Webster
The Invention of Tradition, edited by Eric Hobsbawm and Terence Ranger*
Industrialization before Industrialization: Rural Industry and the Genesis of Capitalism, Peter Kriedte, Hans Medick and Jürgen Schlumbohm*
The Republic in the Village: The People of the Var from the French Revolution to the Second Republic, Maurice Agulhon†
Social Relations and Ideas: Essays in Honour of R. H. Hilton, edited by T. H. Aston, P. R. Coss, Christopher Dyer and Joan Thirsk
A Medieval Society: The West Midlands at the End of the Thirteenth Century, R. H. Hilton
Winstanley: 'The Law of Freedom' and Other Writings, edited by Christopher Hill
Crime in Seventeenth-Century England: A County Study, J. A. Sharpe†
The Crisis of Feudalism: Economy and Society in Eastern Normandy c. 1300–1500, Guy Bois†
The Development of the Family and Marriage in Europe, Jack Goody*
Disputes and Settlements: Law and Human Relations in the West, edited by John Bossy
Rebellion, Popular Protest and the Social Order in Early Modern England, edited by Paul Slack
Studies on Byzantine Literature of the Eleventh and Twelfth Centuries, Alexander Kazhdan in collaboration with Simon Franklin†
The English Rising of 1381, edited by R. H. Hilton and T. H. Aston*
Praise and Paradox: Merchants and Craftsmen in Elizabethan Popular Literature, Laura Caroline Stevenson

The Castilian Crisis of the Seventeenth Century: New Perspectives on the Economic and Social History of Seventeenth-Century Spain, edited by I. A. A. Thompson and Bartolomé Yun Casalilla

* Published also as a paperback
† Co-published with the Maison des Sciences de L'Homme, Paris